GOVERNMENT AND THE MARKETPLACE

· · · · · · · · · · · · · · · · · · · ·

SECOND EDITION

· · · · · · · · · · · · · · · · · · · ·

GOVERNMENT AND THE MARKETPLACE

· ·

SECOND EDITION

Peter Asch
Rutgers University

Rosalind S. Seneca
Drew University

The Dryden Press
Chicago New York San Francisco Philadelphia
Montreal Toronto London Sydney Tokyo

· · · · · · · · · · · · · · · · · ·

Acquisitions Editor: Elizabeth Widdicombe
Project Editor: Teresa Chartos
Design Director: Jeanne Calabrese
Production Manager: Kathy Harsch
Permissions Editor: Doris Milligan
Director of Editing, Design, and Production: Jane Perkins

Text and Cover Designer: Nina Lisowski
Cover Photographer: Peter Peric´
Copy Editor: Siobhan Granner
Text Type: Palatino Roman

Library of Congress Cataloging-in-Publication Data

Asch, Peter.
    Government and the marketplace.

    Includes bibliographies and index.
    1. Industry and state—United States. 2. Trade regula-
tion—United States. I. Seneca, Rosalind.
II. Title.
HD36 16.U47A82   1989   338.973   88-7147
ISBN 0-03-021662-1

Printed in the United States of America
890-038-987654321
Copyright© 1989, 1985 by The Dryden Press, a division of
Holt, Rinehart and Winston, Inc.

Address orders:
The Dryden Press
Orlando, FL 32887

Address editorial correspondence:
One Salt Creek Lane
Hinsdale, IL 60521

The Dryden Press
Holt, Rinehart and Winston
Saunders College Publishing

For Rita and Joe

The Dryden Press Series in Economics

Asch and Seneca
Government and the Marketplace,
Second Edition

Breit and Elzinga
The Antitrust Casebook: Milestones in Economic Regulation, *Second Edition*

Breit and Ransom
The Academic Scribblers,
Revised Edition

Campbell, Campbell, and Dolan
Money, Banking, and Monetary Policy

Dolan and Lindsey
Economics, *Fifth Edition*

Dolan and Lindsey
Macroeconomics, *Fifth Edition*

Dolan and Lindsey
Microeconomics, *Fifth Edition*

Eckert and Leftwich
The Price System and Resource Allocation, *Tenth Edition*

Fort and Lowinger
Applications and Exercises in Intermediate Microeconomics

Gardner
Comparative Economic Systems

Hyman
Public Finance: A Contemporary Application of Theory to Policy,
Second Edition

Johnson and Roberts
Money and Banking: A Market-Oriented Approach,
Third Edition

Kaufman
The Economics of Labor Markets and Labor Relations, *Second Edition*

Kidwell and Peterson
Financial Institutions, Markets, and Money, *Third Edition*

Landsburg
Price Theory and Applications

Link, Miller, and Bergman
Econograph II: Interactive Software for Principles of Economics

Nicholson
Intermediate Microeconomics and Its Application, *Fourth Edition*

Nicholson
Microeconomic Theory: Basic Principles and Extensions,
Fourth Edition

Pappas and Hirschey
Fundamentals of Managerial Economics,
Third Edition

Pappas and Hirschey
Managerial Economics,
Fifth Edition

Puth
American Economic History,
Second Edition

Rukstad
Macroeconomic Decision Making in the World Economy: Text and Cases,
Second Edition

Welch and Welch
Economics: Theory and Practice,
Third Edition

Yarbrough and Yarbrough
The World Economy: Trade and Finance

PREFACE

This book is concerned with government activity in the marketplace. As such, it is suitable for use in upper-level undergraduate, economics, and business school courses that deal with topics usually called "government and business," "public policies toward business," or "government regulation of business."

Observers of American economics and politics frequently pose some pointed questions about the role of government in what is largely a private enterprise system. For example, if we truly believe in the market, why is public intervention so extensive? Do our government programs generally follow reasonable patterns, providing improvements in social and economic welfare? Or is the picture more ominous—one of government encroachment into the arena of private decision, to the detriment of efficiency and freedom?

Our approach to such questions is consistently to emphasize the economic analysis of public policy—both the motivations for and the effects of government action. Some background in economics is therefore necessary. At a minimum, a course in the principles of microeconomics is required. Familiarity with intermediate microeconomics, although not essential, is also helpful. Although the discussions of theoretical topics are largely self-contained, we also attempt to make accessible to students a number of recent analytical developments that carry important implications for public decision making. Our view is that one need not be an economic theorist to grasp and appreciate relevant concepts, but the stronger one's background, the easier the assimilation process is likely to be.

There have been many developments in government policy toward industry since the first edition of this book was written. In particular, the movement to deregulate transportation and telecommunications has significantly altered the structure of these industries as well as the public policies that affect them. The energy industry now appears workably competitive and is no longer subject to such extensive regulation; and new policy issues have arisen in the areas of antitrust and in consumer and worker protection.

There have also been changes on the theoretical front. Our understanding of natural monopoly, the strategic behavior of oligopolists, and markets for information has increased. Concepts of fairness and justice in economic policy have come to the fore.

CHANGES IN THIS EDITION

The developments we have noted above are reflected in this edition. We have introduced a separate chapter on the telecommunications industry and expanded our coverage of transportation. The chapter on energy has been dropped. Our discussion of consumer protection issues has been revised and expanded, and we have added a section on worker protection. We have introduced new discussions of justice and placed greater emphasis on efficiency–equity tradeoffs in our consideration of policy issues.

We have tried throughout this edition to provide clear discussions of theoretical topics, supported by additional real-world examples. The policy sections have been updated to include what are in some instances important new developments. Many diagrams have been redrawn for greater clarity, and we have added captions so that readers may work through a diagram without the need to refer back to a separate section in the text. We have also tried to respond to a very large number of helpful specific suggestions that we have received from readers of the first edition.

This edition is accompanied by a new *Instructor's Manual* that focuses on important aspects of each chapter and provides answers to the Discussion Questions.

ORGANIZATION

We have organized the text as follows:

- Part I sets forth the basic issues, including much of the relevant theory underlying government intervention in the marketplace.

- Part II deals with government policies that encourage competition and reliance on the market—the antitrust laws and related enforcement programs.

- Part III, labeled "old-style" regulation, discusses policies in which government substitutes its own decisions for those of the market, at least to a degree. This includes the regulation of industries traditionally defined as public utilities.

- Part IV, labeled "new-wave" regulation, focuses on some forms of public control that represent a relatively recent expansion of government's role. This expansion, especially in the areas of environmental and consumer protection, is in part a response to economic analyses of problems posed by public goods, externalities, and inefficiencies in information markets.

ALTERNATIVE COURSE OUTLINE

This book is organized in such a way that the relevant theory is systematically developed first (Part I) and then applied in the discussion of three major policy areas (Parts II, III, and IV). The advantage of this approach is that it allows us to apply the full range of tools developed in Part I to each policy area and issue.

Some instructors, however, may prefer that theory and policy chapters be intermingled. Others may find that the book contains more material than can be comfortably covered, particularly in courses that run only one-quarter of an academic year. In either case, the following alternative organization of chapters may prove useful.

Introduction to the Issues
Chapter 1   A General Overview
Chapter 2   The Virtues of the Marketplace
Chapter 6   Corporate Responsibility: An Answer to Market Failure? (This is a floating chapter and may be inserted at any point.)

Antitrust: Theory and Policy
Chapter 8   The Realm of Antitrust
Chapter 3   Market Failure: Monopoly
Chapter 4   Market Failure: Oligopoly
Chapter 9   The Structure of Industry: Measurement Problems and Evidence
Chapter 10   Antitrust and Market Power
Chapter 11   Antitrust and Market Behavior
Chapter 12   The Effects of Antitrust: Does It Accomplish Anything?

Public Utilities Regulation: Theory and Policy
Chapter 13   Regulation: Rationale and Basic Principles
Chapter 14   Regulatory Responses to the Basic Problem
Chapter 15   Dynamic Efficiency, Optimal Investment, and Regulatory Incentives
Chapter 16   Regulatory Dilemmas: The Case of Electricity
Chapter 17   Regulation and Public Policy Paradoxes: Transportation
Chapter 18   Regulation and Public Policy Paradoxes: Telecommunications
Chapter 19   General Assessments

New-Wave Regulation: Theory and Policy
Chapter 20   Why New-Wave?
Chapter 5   Market Failure: Public Goods, Externalities, and Information Problems
Chapter 21   Consumer and Worker Protection
Chapter 22   The Environment

Acknowledgments

In preparing this book, we have received a great deal of help and encouragement from our colleagues. We are especially grateful to Almarin Phillips (University of Pennsylvania) and Bruce Seaman (Georgia State University) who gave us generous and incisive comments at all stages of the original manuscript. Numerous helpful suggestions for the first edition were also provided by James Albrecht (Columbia University), John Allison (University of Texas), Ralph Bradburd (Williams College), Lawrence DeBrock (University of Illinois), John Fizel (University of Wisconsin-Eau Claire), Devra Golbe (Hunter College), Larry Herman (Kenyon College), Joseph Hughes (Rutgers University), Harvey Levin (Hofstra University), David Levy (Federal Trade Commission), Matityahu Marcus (Rutgers University), Jack Morgan (University of North Carolina at Wilmington), Jon Nelson (Pennsylvania State University), Cordelia Reimers (Hunter College), George Sweeney (Vanderbilt University), and William Vickrey (Columbia University). Lydia Schafhauser gave us helpful research assistance.

A number of instructors who have used the text in class were kind enough to send us detailed comments and suggestions that we have used in preparing the second edition. These include Louis H. Henry (Old Dominion University), Patrick Kelso (West Texas State University), Stan Long (University of Pittsburgh-Johnstown), Mark McBride (Miami University), and Patricia Pando (Houston Baptist University). The revised manuscript has been read by Paul Graeser (Northern Illinois University), Dennis Ray (University of Wisconsin-Madison), Stephen Walters (Loyola College of Maryland), and Anthony Marino (University of Southern California), all of whom have provided generous and useful criticisms and suggestions. Many helpful comments have also been received from our students and those of other instructors. Needless to say, we bear the sole responsibility for any errors or confusions that may remain.

At the Dryden Press we have benefited from outstanding editorial and professional assistance and encouragement. We are especially indebted to Liz Widdicombe, Stephanie Pawlak, Teresa Chartos, Siobhan Granner, Doris Milligan, Cate Rzasa, and Judy Sarwark, all of whom have guided the book through various stages of development, revision, and production.

This edition of the book now resides in computer disk files, which should greatly facilitate future revisions. We express deep thanks to Andra Velsor for the major, and often frustrating, effort to bring this about.

Finally, we must thank our families for their encouragement and forebearance. For both of us, this is, of course, the greatest debt of all.

Peter Asch
Rosalind S. Seneca
October 1988

About the Authors

Peter Asch, Ph.D. (Princeton) is a Professor of Economics at Rutgers University in New Brunswick, New Jersey. He previously served as an economist at the Antitrust Division of the Department of Justice and as a consultant to public and private agencies on issues of public safety and antitrust policy. Professor Asch is the author of *Industrial Organization and Antitrust Policy* (Wiley, 1983), *Racetrack Betting: The Professors' Guide to Strategies*, with Richard E. Quandt (Auburn House, 1986), and *Consumer Safety Regulation: Putting a Price on Life and Limb*, (Oxford University Press, 1988). Professor Asch is a frequent contributor to professional journals; his articles focus on safety regulation, industrial organization and antitrust policy, and issues of market efficiency. He currently teaches graduate and undergraduate courses in economics and public policy.

Rosalind S. Seneca, Ph.D. (University of Pennsylvania) is a Professor of Economics at Drew University in Madison, New Jersey. She previously served on the faculties of Columbia University and Hunter College of the City University of New York. She is a regular participant in the Knight-Bagehot Fellowship Program at the Columbia Graduate School of Journalism. Professor Seneca has written several articles on aspects of economics policy and currently teaches courses in industrial organization and government regulation of industry.

CONTENTS

PART ONE

. . . .

The Basic Issues

CHAPTER 1

. . . .

A GENERAL OVERVIEW

INTRODUCTION

This book is concerned with three major areas of government activity in the American marketplace:

1. Policies that encourage competition and reliance on the market, primarily the antitrust laws;

2. Policies by which the government supersedes the competitive process and substitutes its own decisions to some degree, encompassing industries traditionally defined as public utilities (e.g., electricity, transportation, and communications) and subjected to direct regulation;

3. Newer types of regulation that represent an expansion of government's role, including such areas as consumer protection and the environment.

Although these areas cover a substantial amount of territory, they are far from exhaustive. We do not discuss a number of special cases of government intervention, such as capital and insurance markets, health care and research, or education; and policies such as monetary and fiscal controls that affect the marketplace indirectly (although importantly), are similarly ignored. These omissions reflect the unhappily universal need to economize.

There has always been controversy about the role of government in a private enterprise economy. That government has some legitimate role to play in the economic life of a nation such as the United States will not be denied by any sensible person. Whether we should have public economic policies is thus not a serious question. We must rather ask whether the policies we have adopted are, in both nature and degree, desirable. Unfortunately, there is no consensus here. Some persons want government to do less, others more. Individuals may rail against high taxes and big government, yet insist on the maintenance or expansion of a particular public program from which they benefit.

The question of what constitutes good government, thus has no precise, objective answer. This book, however, is written in the belief that the issue can be approached in consistent and sensible ways, even if—ultimately—we must agree to disagree.

At the outset, it is important to recognize the historical and social circumstances which have resulted in the body of laws which regulate industry.[1] For example, the Great Depression in the 1930s—a time of high unemployment, falling prices and wages, and poverty for large numbers of people—resulted in a wave of regulation in the transportation, energy, communications, agricultural, and financial industries. These laws, many of which were designed to keep prices from falling further and to protect the financial viability of the regulated firms, were passed in a time of economic distress, but continued to be applied after the return of prosperity, during and following World War II—in economic circumstances that were entirely different. In the decades following World War II, technological and economic changes stimulated the growth of competition in regulated industries and led to a re-evaluation of the appropriate role of government regulation. The recent thrust toward deregulation reflects these changes.

The influence of economists on regulatory policy has increased significantly in the last two decades.[2] Their contribution has been to articulate the theoretical issues involved, to provide empirical studies of these issues, and, ultimately, to advocate particular policies both from the academic arena and as policymakers themselves. Their success is reflected particularly in the reduction of government's role in regulating transportation and communications, but it can also be seen, for example, in recent changes in the basic air and water pollution control laws passed in the early 1970s. Given the continued influence of economists on regulatory policy, the issues discussed in this book are of particular current importance.

Throughout this book, we use economic theory to analyze economic policy. This requires that we distinguish between positive economics—the systematic description of real-world economic relationships—and normative economics—the evaluation of the economic state of the world. Description involves the complicated task of economic measurement; evaluation requires that we specify our economic (and social) goals so that we can assess economic performance and determine those circumstances in which government action is appropriate. For example, we may describe the automobile industry as an oligopoly, make observations about the prices, quantities, and quality of automobiles produced, and study the investment, advertising, and distribution policies of the major firms. However, we can only evaluate the industry's performance if we specify the criteria by which it is to be judged good or bad.

---

[1]See Thomas K. McGraw, ed., *Regulation in Perspective: Historical Essays* (Cambridge, Mass.: Harvard University Press, 1981); and Thomas K. McGraw, *Prophets of Regulation* (Cambridge, Mass.: Harvard University Press, 1984).

[2]See Paul L. Joskow and Roger G. Noll, "Regulation in Theory and Practice: An Overview," *Studies in Public Regulation,* ed. Gary Fromm (Cambridge, Mass.: MIT Press, 1983); and Martha Derthick and Paul J. Quirk, *The Politics of Deregulation* (Washington, D.C.: Brookings, 1985).

Thus we can say that automobile prices are too high and quantity and quality too low only if we know how to define the correct prices, quantities, and qualities.

We devote substantial space, particularly in Chapters 2, 3, and 5, to setting out the evaluative criteria, namely efficiency and equity, by which we can assess what we mean by good performance. We also recognize, particularly in the subsequent parts of the book, that while some instances of government intervention may advance the public interest (by correcting market failures and improving efficiency), other examples of intervention may reflect attempts to redistribute income from some groups to other groups, with unfavorable efficiency consequences. Just as markets may fail to produce a desirable result in all situations, so government institutions may also fail. Therefore, when we recommend new policies, we must understand both market and government institutions and base our analyses and recommendations on a realistic recognition of the limitations of each.

The vast scope of current government policies unquestionably creates huge costs and benefits for society. Diatribes against big government are, implicitly, a claim that the costs outweigh the benefits, at least at the margin. Serious efforts to compare the two sides, however, encounter enormous difficulties. Certain policy effects—most notably the saving of lives, the losing of lives, and the changing of the quality of life for better or worse—are widely regarded as immeasurable. Do those who insist that dollar valuations of some benefits and costs are absurd have a serious point? And if so, does this cut the legs out from under the effort to pose many issues in an economic context? Even for those policies that may have economically measurable consequences, the success of government intervention may depend as much on the perceptions of whether or not the policy is fair as on whether it promotes the efficient allocation of resources, and neither fairness nor efficiency can be unambiguously defined.

These are some of the critical issues that this book addresses. We attempt to provide a consistent and coherent approach to questions rather than clear-cut answers, which often do not exist. We devote equal attention to the theoretical underpinnings of policy and to the policy itself. This is an especially challenging task in areas such as consumer protection, where existing theory is limited, and where ethical and social issues seem to dominate orthodox economic concerns. There is also much new theoretical work to evaluate in the traditional areas of regulation.

In Part I we develop the framework that we use to evaluate government policy in the three major areas: antitrust, old-style regulation, and new-wave regulation, discussed in Parts II, III and IV, respectively. In Chapter 2 we assess the virtues of the marketplace and introduce the important concepts of allocative efficiency and equity. In Chapters 3, 4, and 5 we examine the main causes of market failure—monopoly and the existence of public goods, externalities, and information problems. It is the analysis of such market failures that provides a rationale for government intervention. In Chapter 6 we consider one alternative sometimes suggested as a substitute for government intervention in the presence of market failure—corporate responsibility.

The remainder of this chapter is devoted to an introductory assessment of the government's role in the U.S. economy. First we discuss some basic economic functions of government in all modern developed economies. Next we consider the constitutional legitimacy of government in the economy and discuss briefly its legal history. In the final section, we describe the nature and scope of government in the U.S. economy and examine some measures of the size of its activity.

SOME BASIC ECONOMIC FUNCTIONS OF GOVERNMENT

Questions about the origin and legitimacy of government have been a focus of study for centuries and are still of basic importance to modern societies. Wars and revolutions are the most violent manifestations of the fact that individuals differ intensely in their views about the proper nature of their own and foreign governments. Less dramatic conflicts are often resolved through legislative and constitutional changes. Even the routine day-to-day workings of modern governments often reflect a process of decision making that continually redefines the appropriate role of public action in society.

Many variations in the economic and political organization of nations exist. These variations range from the centrally planned economies of the USSR and some Eastern European countries to the mixed economies of the United States and Western Europe, that support both free enterprise and government sectors. This is not the place for a lengthy discussion about theories of the state. However, some basic functions of government are necessary for the success of any modern economy, including control of the judicial and law enforcement systems and the monetary system.[3]

In a private enterprise economy, the ownership and exchange of property—including all production and consumption activities—occur within a complex system of property rights. Such rights define the limits of property ownership and exchange. For example, one may grow roses on one's own land but not use the land as a dump for toxic wastes; one may own a car but not use it to drive across a neighbor's yard; one may sell one's land or car to someone else, or refuse to do so.

Both the ownership and exchange of property, including the purchase and sale of productive inputs and outputs, typically involve agreements or contracts between individuals. The general characteristics of contracts, and the problems associated with making and enforcing them, thus become key determinants of the institutions that evolve in any society.[4]

---

[3]We could lengthen this list to include, for example, defense and the education of children. One could also note, as we do below, that individuals can and sometimes do resolve conflicts outside the public legal system. Indeed, it becomes quickly apparent that even these basic functions of government are subject to dispute.

[4]One classic work on property rights is Richard A. Posner, *Economic Analysis of Law* (Boston: Little, Brown, 3d ed., 1986), especially Chapters 2 and 3. Posner suggests that for a system of property rights to generate an efficient allocation of resources it must have three characteristics—universality (all resources should be owned, or ownable, by someone); exclusivity (the owner can exclude others from benefits derived from the property); and transferability (the resources can be traded from less to more productive uses). In later chapters we discuss issues of market failure

Consider a simple transaction—buying a loaf of bread. When you enter a supermarket, it is the store that owns the loaf of bread and offers to sell it at a specified price. If you are willing to pay that amount of money in a legally acceptable form—legal tender, such as cash, but not necessarily a personal check or credit card—you can acquire rights to that loaf.

As an American consumer, you no doubt assume that the bread you buy is a safe and wholesome substance. If you find that it contains a foreign object, you may demand compensation from the supermarket. Should the store refuse, you may appeal to an outside arbiter—a court of law—to resolve the conflict. By similar token, the supermarket may use the judicial system to enforce its rights. If you pay for your bread with a counterfeit bill, and refuse to make good when the store manager objects, you may find yourself in court. We use the courts to resolve disputes concerning the rights of contract-making individuals. However, court decisions can influence subsequent decisions in other conflicts—a potential benefit to society that is successfully exploited only when such precedents are incorporated into the general body of law. This is achieved when the government administers the courts.[5]

The need for government control of the monetary system is also directly related to the problem of enforcing contracts made in monetary terms. In a rare advocacy of government monopoly rather than competitive individual suppliers, Milton Friedman put the problem in these terms:

> What is involved is essentially the enforcement of contracts, if the failure of an issuer (of money) to fulfill his promise is in good faith, or the prevention of fraud, essentially of counterfeiting, if it is not....Moreover, the pervasive character of the monetary nexus means that the failure of an issuer to fulfill his promises to pay has important effects on persons other than the issuer or those who entered into a contract with him in the first instance or those who held his promises. One failure triggers others and may give rise to widespread effects.[6]

The existence of pervasive third-party or external effects of individual contract-making leads to the identification of a role for government to monitor and, in some cases, alter the nature of contracts. The existence of external effects as a prime cause of the failure of markets to generate an efficient allocation of resources is discussed in detail in Chapter 5. We suggest here that contract making itself, regardless of particular circumstances, involves such substantial externalities (or spillovers) that a government is needed to make and enforce the laws governing such activity.

---

at some length. Such issues can usually be couched in terms of adequate or inadequate contract making. As we note below, one of the government's basic functions is to preserve the whole system of rights within which contracts can be made.

[5]It has been observed that the provision of judicial services has sometimes preceded the formation of the state, and that private court systems have been and are still viable. Submitting disputes to a clergyman is an old practice among some groups, and there is at least one television show ("People's Court") in which people agree to abide by the decision of a private "judge" in a television studio. For a general discussion see W. M. Landes and R. A. Posner, "Adjudication as a Private Good," *Journal of Legal Studies* 8 (March 1979): 235–284; and comments by A. Denzau, P. D. Carrington, and G. C. Hazard, Jr. in the same issue.

[6]M. Friedman, *A Program for Monetary Stability* (New York: Fordham University Press, 1961), Chapters 1 and 6.

Such basic government functions as control of the monetary system and the organization of the judicial system are not generally in dispute. We consider the wide range of government policies about which there is substantially more controversy later in this chapter. Let us first consider briefly the constitutional legitimacy of government regulation at both federal and state levels.

THE LEGAL HISTORY AND STATUS OF GOVERNMENT CONTROL OF INDUSTRY

Three questions are pertinent here: First, where does the power to intervene in the private sector lie? Second, how specific is the law about the legitimate role of government as a regulator of industry? Third, what in particular does the law say about the characteristics of public utilities?[7]

Article 10 of the Constitution states: "The powers not delegated to the United States by the Constitution, nor prohibited by it to the States, are reserved to the States respectively, or to the people." Specific clauses in the Constitution give the federal government, through acts of Congress, various economic powers, such as the power to "regulate commerce among the several states," to collect taxes, to pay debts, to provide for defense, and to control navigation. The interpretation of the extent of these powers and questions of conflict between federal, state, and individual rights are decided through the process of judicial review with the U. S. Supreme Court as the ultimate arbiter.

The growth of the regulatory powers of the federal government is authorized by the so-called elastic clause (Article 1, Section 8) of the Constitution, which gives Congress the power "to make all Laws which shall be necessary and proper for carrying into Execution the foregoing Powers, and all other Powers vested by this Constitution in the government of the United States, or in any Department or Office thereof."[8]

The broad interpretation of this clause by Congress and the courts has allowed the federal government to expand its powers over time. Thus the Constitution has proven a flexible document allowing changing public perceptions of the role of government to be reflected in the passage of new laws.[9] For example, the growth of interstate commerce meant that more and more economic activity within a state tended to spill over into the broader interstate economy. This made it increasingly difficult for individual states to pass regulatory laws that could be shown to affect only the intrastate economy. The

---

[7]The main sources for the discussion are: M. T. Farris and R. J. Sampson, *Public Utilities, Regulation, Management and Ownership* (Boston: Houghton-Mifflin, 1973), Chapters 1–4; P. J. Garfield and F. Lovejoy, *Public Utility Economics* (Englewood Cliffs, N.J.: Prentice Hall, 1964), Chapter 1; C. F. Phillips, Jr., *The Economics of Regulation* (Homewood, Ill.: R. D. Irwin, 1969), Chapter 3; and Alfred E. Kahn, *The Economics of Regulation*, vol. 1 (New York: Wiley, 1970), Chapter 1.

[8]See Farris and Sampson, *Public Utilities*, 38.

[9]One of the objectives of this book is to evaluate the extent to which the scope and nature of government regulation of the private sector have changed in recent years. Most of our analysis is in economic terms. The elastic clause quoted above has meant that changes in economic policy have not been significantly restricted for constitutional and legal reasons.

elastic clause then allowed the federal government to regulate economic activity within states on the grounds that interstate commerce was also involved. However, the expansion of government power, whether federal or state, has not gone unchallenged as a brief summary of the development of the specific legal rationale for government regulation shows.

Among many legal decisions, two can be singled out as the most important: *Munn v. Illinois*[10] and *Nebbia v. New York*.[11] In 1870 the Constitution of Illinois designated grain elevators as public warehouses, and in 1871 the Illinois legislature passed a law which prescribed maximum rates for grain storage facilities. Munn and Scott, elevator owners, charged higher rates than the statute permitted. They were found guilty in state courts and appealed to the Supreme Court on the grounds that state regulation had forced them to charge lower prices than they would have freely set, thereby reducing the value of their property and depriving them of it "without due process of law."[12] The Supreme Court upheld the lower court decision, declaring that when private property is "affected with a public interest, it ceases to be *juris privati* only," and can therefore be subject to government regulation. The failure of the Court to identify precisely under what circumstances private property was "affected with a public interest" was forcefully noted in the dissenting opinion by Justice Field:

> If this be sound law . . . all property and all business in the State are held at the mercy of a majority of its legislature. . . .
>
> The public is interested in the manufacture of cotton, woolen, and silken fabrics, in the construction of machinery, in the printing and publication of books and periodicals, and in the making of utensils of every variety, useful and ornamental; indeed there is hardly an enterprise or business engaging the attention and labor of any considerable portion of the community, in which the public has not an interest. . . .
>
> The legislation in question is nothing less than a bold assertion of absolute power by the State to control at its discretion the property and business of the citizen, and fix the compensation he shall receive. . . . The decision of the court in this case gives unrestrained license to legislative will.

In cases that followed *Munn v. Illinois*, government regulatory power was extended to banks, insurance companies and insurance agents,[13] as well as to industries such as natural gas, electricity, water, and transportation, which had traditionally been accepted as subject to government control. Government power to regulate was denied for such industries as food, clothing, fuels, employment agencies, and gasoline service stations. But the lack of a definition of public interest led to half a century of legal argument concerning which industries were or were not subject to regulation under the law.

[10]94 U.S. 113 (1877)

[11]291 U.S. 502 (1934)

[12]Contrary to the Fourteenth Amendment to the Constitution.

[13]See Kahn, *Economics of Regulation*, Vol. 1, p. 3, for a detailed list of these cases.

An economist, having failed to find any simple economic definition of natural monopoly,[14] might well read with sympathy the arguments of those judges who resisted the expansion of government regulation on public interest grounds and who viewed attempts to classify industries in this way as futile.[15] Indeed, in *Nebbia* the Supreme Court finally rejected the public interest argument. In upholding the right of the Milk Control Board established by the State of New York to control prices, the Court declared:

> It is clear that there is no closed class or category of businesses affected with a public interest, and the function of courts in the application of the Fifth and Fourteenth Amendments is to determine in each case whether circumstances vindicate the challenged regulation as a reasonable exertion of governmental authority or condemn it as arbitrary or discriminatory.... The phrase "affected with a public interest" can, in the nature of things, mean no more than that an industry, for adequate reason, is subject to control for the public good.... There can be no doubt that on proper occasion and by appropriate measures the state may regulate a business in any of its aspects, including the prices to be charged for the products or commodities it sells.
>
> So far as the requirement of due process is concerned, and in the absence of other constitutional restriction, a state is forced to adopt whatever economic policy may reasonably be deemed to promote public welfare, and to enforce that policy by legislation adapted to its purpose. The courts are without authority either to declare such policy, or, when it is declared by the legislature, to override it. If the laws passed are seen to have a reasonable relation to a proper legislative purpose, and are neither arbitrary nor discriminatory, the requirements of due process are satisfied, and judicial determination to that effect renders a court *functus officio*.

Thus, the emphasis shifted from the public interest justification of regulation to the argument that the police powers of the states (which they retain under the Tenth Amendment, to protect the health, safety, morals, and general welfare of their citizens) enable them to regulate virtually any business if there is a demand for such legislation.[16]

---

[14]See Chapters 3 and 12 for a detailed exposition of the definition of natural monopoly.

[15]This issue is essentially the same as the problem of determining the extent and nature of externalities (discussed in Chapter 5). Virtually any production or consumption activity undertaken by an individual or firm will affect others in ways that are not fully taken into account by a corresponding market transaction. The larger the external costs and benefits of an economic activity the greater the resulting misallocation of the unregulated market and the stronger the rationale for government regulation. As noted, the classification of externalities for policy purposes is difficult and it is not surprising that, given the economic complexity of the problem, a useful classification has not been forthcoming from the courts.

[16]Some recent literature reexamines this justification for government intervention in the economy. See for example, Thomas R. Haggard, "Government Regulation of the Employment Relationship," and Norman Carlin, "Substantive Due Process: A Doctrine for Regulatory Control," in Tibor R. Machan and M. Bruce Johnson, eds., *Rights and Regulation* (Cambridge, Mass.: Ballinger Publishing Company, 1983); Antonin Scalia, "On the Merits of the Frying Pan," *Regulation* 9 (January/February 1985); and the reply to Scalia by Richard A. Epstein, "The Active Virtues," in the same issue. One argument runs as follows: protection of individual rights against the state is guaranteed in both the Fifth and Fourteenth Amendments to the Constitution (these state that no person shall be deprived of life, liberty, and property without due process of law), and should include protection against both arbitrary actions of the executive branch and misguided laws passed by Congress. The judiciary has the obligation not only to ensure that government

Note, however, that while the public interest rationale for regulation was rejected by appealing to the power of the states to implement their laws (providing they are not arbitrary or discriminatory), conflicts between federal and state authorities are resolved in favor of the federal government whenever it is judged to have constitutional power.[17]

In spite of the *Nebbia* decision, the concept of a "public utility" has retained its place in the law. In a 1943 case arising from a law exempting public utilities from government price controls, Justice Vinson identified four essential elements of the public utility concept:

> If a business is (1) affected with a public interest, and (2) bears an intimate connection with the process of transportation and distribution, and (3) is under an obligation to afford its facilities to the public generally upon demand, at fair and non-discriminatory rates, and (4) enjoys, in a large measure an independence and freedom from business competition brought about either (a) by its acquisition of monopoly status, or (b) by the grant of a franchise or certificate from the State placing it in this position, it is . . . a public utility.[18]

This statement confuses the conditions for government regulation (such as natural monopoly) with the results of regulation, for example, the obligation to provide service on demand at reasonable prices. But Justice Vinson did draw attention to the fact that public utility status carries with it both rights and obligations. Government regulation may give advantages to an industry by preventing the entry of other firms, but it also may obligate regulated firms to serve the public "generally upon demand"—a requirement that assigns them the status of *common carrier*. The evolution of the law thus permitted any type of regulation deemed reasonable, and gave special attention to public utilities by defining (albeit unclearly) the rights of and obligations to the public of certain key industries.

Part III discusses the theoretical problems associated with the regulation of prices and profits and shows the forms that regulation has taken in specific industries.

(executive and congressional action) is undertaken following appropriate procedures ("procedural due process"), but also that laws passed by Congress are overturned on "substantive" grounds, that is, if they infringe on the rights of citizens ("substantive due process"). Since the 1930s government regulation of economic affairs has resulted in a whittling away of individual rights; a reduction in the scope of government intervention would therefore be a step backwards towards the original constitutional intention. In this argument, the overexpansion of government has resulted from the failure of the judiciary to fulfill its appropriate role as protector of the Constitution. Thus, for example, the widespread adoption of minimum wage laws during the 1930s (which previously had been struck down by the courts) can be viewed as a failure of the courts to protect the rights of individuals to work for a lower wage if they so choose. Hence, the abolition of such laws would be a move towards economic freedom for the individual rather than reverse.

[17]For example, in the famous Shreveport case (*Houston East and West Texas Railway Co. v. United States*, 234 U. S. 342 (1914), Congress was allowed to regulate intrastate commerce where the absence of such regulation would be discriminatory and burdensome on interstate commerce. However, decisions in *Cooley v. Board of Wardens of the Port of Philadelphia*, 53 U. S. 298 (1851) and *County of Mobile v. Kimball*, 102 U.S. 691 (1880) did identify circumstances under which the states had the power to regulate specifically local problems.

[18]*Davies Warehouse Co. v. Brown*, 137 F. 2d 201, 212–213 (1943).

THE NATURE AND SCOPE OF GOVERNMENT IN THE U.S. ECONOMY

One of the most important issues in modern political debate is the size of government and its effect on our lives. A common complaint is that government has grown so large that it threatens to strangle the free enterprise system to which we owe our prosperity; it restricts our individual freedom to use our talents as we wish and to reap our just rewards. Many differing views about the appropriate role of government in a free enterprise economy vie for supremacy. But there is little disagreement about the basic premise—that government has grown steadily larger over the last century and that its scope and impact on the economy have continuously broadened.

In the final section of this chapter we examine alternative ways of measuring the size and impact of government. Since government is such a complex institution, it is important to begin with a brief description of its characteristics, particularly those that affect economic policy.[19]

The separation of the three branches of government—legislative, executive, and judicial—is based in the Constitution. The checks and balances through which the separation is enforced provide a government in which lines of authority are, by design, crossed. The clear-cut theory that the legislative branch makes the laws, the executive administers and enforces them, and the judiciary acts as interpreter and judge, is a highly simplified model of what are in reality very complicated rules.

There is much interaction among policymakers in government, and between policymakers and the individuals and institutions whom the policies affect. The final form of a policy, usually an act of Congress, is the result of this interaction; its enforcement generates another round of interaction that may carry it so far from original intentions that another round of policymaking arises to get things back on track. This means that government economic policy is constantly evolving and it is often difficult to identify cause-and-effect relationships. Has antitrust policy in fact preserved competitiveness? Has government price and profit regulation in electricity improved efficiency in that industry? Have the environmental protection laws improved the quality of the environment? Such questions may not have clear-cut answers.

There are three specific areas of economic policy with which we are concerned: antitrust laws, old-style regulation, and new-wave regulation.

The Antitrust Laws

These laws were passed by Congress to maintain and foster competition in the private sector. Widespread belief in the need for such laws had grown rapidly following the Civil War. Under common law, which the United States inherited from Great Britain, contracts to engage in anticompetitive conduct (such as

---

[19]For a detailed account see C. Wilcox and W. G. Shepherd, *Public Policies Toward Business*, 5th ed. (Homewood, Ill.: Richard D. Irwin, Inc., 1979), Part I, Chapters 1–4. See also B. M. Mitnick, *The Political Economy of Regulation* (New York: Columbia University Press, 1980).

price-fixing agreements) were not legally enforceable; but government took no active role to prevent such arrangements from occurring. During the latter half of the nineteenth century, a number of state antitrust laws were enacted in order to fill the gap. These were widely regarded as ineffective, and in 1890 the Sherman Act brought the federal government into the picture as a major force.

The main burden of public enforcement of these laws lies with the Justice Department and the Federal Trade Commission—two agencies that are not always in agreement about the nature of their tasks. The courts, and particularly the Supreme Court, have substantially influenced the evolution and impact of the antitrust laws in their interpretation of specific cases. The nature and effects of antitrust policy, are discussed in Part II.

Old-Style Regulation

Our second area of interest is government regulation of specific industries such as electricity, transportation, and communications, (some of which are called public utilities). Regulation of these industries occurred early in their development (hence the term *old-style* regulation) and has been carried out in a peculiarly American way. In most cases the industry remains privately owned, but government undertakes to regulate—that is, monitor and, in many cases, mandate—the setting of prices, the profits that can be earned, and the number and quality of services provided. Often, the regulated firm (or firms if the industry is not a monopoly) is legally protected against competitive entry by new firms. While the legal basis for such detailed government intervention in the private market springs from an act of the legislative branch, the activity of regulation—identifying and enforcing the rules for specific cases—is often carried out by a commission. For example, the Interstate Commerce Commission regulates railroads, trucks, and water carriers; the Federal Communications Commission regulates interstate commerce related to telephone and other telecommunications services (see Table 1.5). At the federal level, commission members are appointed by the President for their expertise in public policy and their knowledge of the particular industry that the commission regulates. They are responsible to Congress for carrying out the regulatory laws. However, they often carve out areas of authority independent of all branches of government, which, in the short run at least, are hard to challenge. Appeal through the courts for those dissatisfied with commission policy is always available, but may be costly. At the state level of regulation—for example, in electricity and natural gas—the regulatory commissions vary in size and constitution. In some states commissioners are elected rather than appointed; their constitutional authority ultimately affects the type of policies which they carry out. A state regulatory commission which consists of elected members may be much more responsive to consumer protests against higher rates than to the urging of the utilities to promote profitability.

In general, the way in which commissions are selected, and the daily interaction between a regulating commission and the regulated industry, often serve to forge a common purpose between the two groups. This may imply that the interests of the industry are upheld at the cost of the broader public interest, which becomes the victim of such an alliance. Thus, while the rationale for regulation by commissions is to serve the public interest, the evolution of the regulatory process often produces very different consequences.

Many studies have investigated the relationship between regulating commissions and regulated industries, the causes and effects of their relationship, and the rationale for seeking change.[20] The economic issues associated with the rationale for regulation will be discussed in Part III.

New-Wave Regulation

The third type of government intervention also involves a direct government impact on the decision-making processes of privately owned firms. It comprises a series of government attempts to mitigate the undesirable social consequences of private decisions, both within the firm and on the environment. New-wave regulation typically applies to the relevant activities of many firms scattered throughout the economy whereas old-style regulation applies to firms within a specific industry. For example, Congress established the Occupational Safety and Health Administration (OSHA) in 1970 to ensure safe working conditions for workers in all industries and the Equal Employment Opportunity Commission to protect workers against racial and sexual discrimination by employers (among other things). The Clean Air Acts, in contrast, are designed to protect the external environment against the pollution created by industrial activity. The Food and Drug Administration protects the public against dangerous drugs, foods, and cosmetics (refer to Table 1.5).

Some people argue that the regulations imposed by new government commissions affect the internal management decisions of firms and substantially increase their costs; the benefits of such regulations are diffused among the population and are either unknown or, if measurable, substantially less than the costs.[21] By contrast, the major impact of old-style regulation is on firms and consumers in a specific industry who are more likely to directly perceive the gains or losses they experience. Certainly, the difference in incidence and distribution of benefits and costs between old- and new-style regulation creates variations in the way the regulatory structure works and, ultimately, affects the course of change in regulated industries.

---

[20]See B. M. Mitnick, *Political Economy of Regulation*. Mitnick uses a detailed framework to analyze theories of regulation, and suggests that the evolution of the independent commissions differs so much between industries that a uniform theory of regulatory origin may not be tenable. See also M. Bernstein, *Regulating Business by Independent Commission* (Princeton, N.J.: Princeton University Press, 1955); G. Stigler, "The Theory of Economic Regulation," in *The Bell Journal of Economics and Management Science*, 2 (Spring 1971): 3; and P. W. MacAvoy, *The Regulated Industries and the Economy* (New York: W. W. Norton and Company, 1979) for a chronological introduction to this literature.

[21]See W. Lilley III and J. C. Miller III, "The New Social Regulation," *The Public Interest* No. 47 (Spring 1977): 49–61; and M. L. Weidenbaum, *Business, Government and the Public*, 3d ed. (Englewood Cliffs, N.J.: Prentice-Hall, 1986).

Levels of Regulation: Federal, State, and Local

No general principle exists that determines how regulatory tasks are shared by federal, state, and local governments. Regulation by individual states has often preceded federal controls and state commissions exert authority in both traditional and new areas of public control. Regulation of telephones, electric power, gas, and railroads, for example, evolved at the state level. State commissions have the power to regulate prices, issue licenses, and monitor service in these industries.[22] Other areas of state regulation embrace the management of natural resources, water rights, and environmental pollution, as well as public health and safety (including regulations against smoking in public places), licensing automobile drivers, and, more recently, administering such income transfer programs as unemployment and disability payments.

The growth of interstate commerce has meant that individual state economies have become more closely linked, and require greater policy coordination that the federal government might be expected to provide. To some extent, conflicts between state and federal regulatory authorities are inevitable. While voters in different states may feel differently about how business activity should be regulated, the federal government, elected by the nation as a whole, may ultimately prevail in enforcing a uniform policy. The resulting conflict is sometimes portrayed as a local/state/federal jurisdictional dispute.

In light of this summary of the policy process, let us now return to our original question: What is the size and scope of government?

Some Measures of Government Size

We can quickly see that the issue posed above is itself restrictive. The reason for asking about the size of government is to be able to say something about the impact of the government on the economy. After all, almost every industry's development has been shaped to some degree by decades of government involvement and might have been entirely different under different government policy. Crude measures of government quantity cannot tell us about the complex nature of policy or the ways in which it has influenced industry development over time. The numbers provide a series of snapshots rather than a moving picture. Bearing this in mind, let us look at several possible measures of government size.

Total Government Expenditures Total expenditure is the broadest measure of government activity and includes transfer payments—the way by which most income redistributions are effected. The first three rows of Table 1.1 show that government expenditure in current dollars increased by 183 percent over the decade 1970–1980, and by almost 66 percent between 1980 and 1986. For each period, the increases in federal expenditures are relatively larger than state and

[22]See C. Wilcox and W. G. Shepherd, *Public Policies toward Business*, 334–338 and Table 13-4 for a description of state commissions and list of budget expenditures for 1972–1973.

Table 1.1   Total Government Expenditures

	1970	1975	1980	1985	1986	Percent Change 1970–1980	Percent Change 1980–1986
Total government expenditures (billions of current dollars)	338.0	586.9	957.6	1500.7	1588.5	183.3	65.9
Federal government expenditures (billions of current dollars)	205.1	357.1	602.1	984.9	1030.8	193.6	71.2
State and local government exp. (billions of current dollars)	132.9	229.8	355.5	515.8	557.7	167.5	56.9
Total government exp. (billions of $1972)*	386.3	455.3	506.1	581.7	601.7	31.0	18.9
Fed. government exp. (billions of $1972)	237.4	280.1	325.1	398.3	413.8	36.9	27.3
State and local government exp. (billions of $1972)	150.5	177.2	185.6	194.5	202.9	23.3	9.3
Total government exp. in $1972 as percent of constant $ GNP	35.9	37.9	34.3	33.6	33.9		
Fed. exp. in $1972 as percent of constant $ GNP	22.1	23.3	22.0	23.0	23.3		
State and local exp. in $1972 as percent of constant $ GNP	14.0	14.7	12.6	11.2	11.4		

*To deflate the government figures, we used the national income accounts implicit price deflator for government purchases of goods and services. Federal, state, and local expenditures were deflated by the price deflator for federal purchases of goods and services and state and local purchases respectively.

Source: *Survey of Current Business*, U.S. Department of Commerce.

local increases (rows 2 and 3). However, when these values are expressed in *constant* (1972) dollars to remove the effect of price inflation over time (rows 4–6 in Table 1.1), the increase is much less dramatic, although still significant.

Federal government expenditures rose by about 37 percent in real terms during the 1970s, and by more than 27 percent between 1980 and 1986. Note that the increase in real state and local expenditure, which was somewhat less than the increase in real federal spending in the 1970s, declined significantly between 1980 and 1986.

This picture of rapid government expansion over the last 15 years, however, changes further when constant dollar government expenditure is expressed as a percentage of constant dollar GNP (rows 7–9). This ratio has actually fallen over the entire period for total government expenditure and for state and local government expenditure, with the federal component remaining essentially the same during the 1970s and rising only very slightly between 1980 and 1986.

Table 1.2 Government Purchases of Goods and Services

	1970	1975	1980	1985	1986	Percent Change 1970–1980	Percent Change 1980–1986
All government purchases of goods and services (billions of current dollars)	218.9	338.4	537.8	815.4	864.5	145.7	60.7
Federal government purchases of goods and services	95.6	123.1	197.0	354.1	366.6	106.1	86.1
State and local government purchases of goods and services	123.2	215.4	340.8	461.3	497.6	176.6	46.1
Constant $ government purchases as percent of constant $ GNP	23.3	21.8	19.3	20.1	20.3		
Constant $ federal government purchases as percent of constant $ GNP	10.3	8.0	7.2	9.0	9.0		
Constant $ state and local government purchases as percent of constant $ GNP	13.0	13.8	12.1	11.1	11.3		

Source: *Survey of Current Business*, U.S. Department of Commerce.

Government Purchases of Goods and Services

The same mixed picture emerges if we measure government size by its contribution to gross national product—that is, by government purchases of goods and services (Table 1.2). The undeflated figures show very large increases for both 1970 to 1980 and 1980 to 1986. The increases in state and local purchases are large relative to the increase in federal government purchases during the 1970s, and are significantly smaller during the 1980s. By contrast, when constant dollar purchases of goods and services are expressed as a proportion of constant dollar GNP, we observe that for all three measures the ratio has declined slightly over the entire period. But note that for total government and federal government purchases, the entire decline occurred during the years 1970 to 1980 with subsequent small rises, whereas the decline in the state and local ratio continued throughout the period 1970 to 1986. In other words, this measure of relative government size shows declines for the decade before the Reagan administration and rises during the administration—contrary to much popular wisdom.

Government Employment

In Table 1.3 we see that the number of people employed by government rose by about 30 percent between 1970 and 1980, and hardly at all between 1980 and 1986 (row 1), with state and local employment registering substantially larger increases than federal government employment over the entire period (rows 2

Table 1.3 Government Employment

	1970	1975	1980	1985	1986	Percent Change 1970–1980	Percent Change 1980–1986
Total government employment (including armed services) (thousands)	12,535	14,720	16,241	15,803	16,415	29.6	1.1
Federal government employment	2,705	2,748	2,866	2,739	2,875	6.0	.3
State and local government employment	9,830	11,973	13,375	13,064	13,540	36.1	1.2
Government employ-ment as percent of total labor force	14.6	15.5	14.9	14.0	14.0		
Federal government employment as percent of total labor force	3.1	3.0	2.6	2.4	2.5		
State and local govern-ment employment as percent of total labor force	11.4	12.6	12.3	11.6	11.5		

Source: *Survey of Current Business,* U. S. Department of Commerce.

and 3). However, the proportion of the total labor force employed by govern-ment at all levels (row 4) changed very little between 1970 and 1986, and the proportion employed by the federal government has fallen over the period (row 5).

These figures do not conform entirely to the popular perception of an ever-growing government; nor do they suggest that President Reagan can claim extensive credit for curbing the size of government. The record of the last decade and a half has been one of government growth in absolute size, but of some stability in size relative to the economy, with perceptible declines during the last half of the 1970s. The declines represent, in part, the winding down of government activity following the Vietnam War and also perhaps the success-ful efforts of policymakers to curb government spending and taxation in response to national demands. Such efforts have succeeded in preventing significant growth in government size during the 1980s but not in achieving further declines. Recall, however, that such crude measures of government size cannot reflect precisely the complex impact of policymaking on the private sector; at most they convey some idea of the total value of resources used in the government sector.

Changes in the Structure of Government Spending

A more detailed picture emerges when we look at finer breakdowns of govern-ment spending. Table 1.4 shows the share of government outlays by function for the years 1971, 1981, 1985, and 1987. The biggest items are income and social security payments (row 12), national defense (row 1), interest (row 17),

Table 1.4 Budget Outlays by Function:
Percentages of Total Budget Outlays

	1971	1981	1985	1987 (estimated)	Change 1971–1981	Change 1981–1987
1. National defense	35.9	24.3	26.7	27.8	↓	↑
2. International affairs	1.9	1.7	1.7	1.4	↓	↓
3. General science, space technology	2.0	1.0	.9	.9	↓	↓
4. Energy	.5	1.6	.6	.4	↑	↓
5. National resources and environment	1.9	2.1	1.4	1.4	↑	↓
6. Agriculture	2.0	.9	2.7	3.1	↓	↑
7. Commerce and housing credit	1.1	.6	.4	.9	↓	↑
8. Transportation	3.8	3.6	2.7	2.7	↓	↓
9. Community and regional development	1.4	1.4	.8	.6	=	↓
10. Education, training, employment and social services	4.7	4.7	3.1	2.9	=	↓
11. Health and medicare	7.0	10.0	10.5	11.0	↑	↑
12. Income and social security	26.2	34.3	33.5	32.8	↑	↓
13. Veterans benefits and services	4.6	3.5	2.8	2.6	↓	↓
14. Administration of justice	.6	.7	.7	.8	↑	↑
15. General government	1.0	.7	.5	.7	↓	=
16. General purpose fiscal assistance	.3	1.0	.7	.2	↑	↓
17. Interest	9.3	12.6	13.7	13.5	↑	↑
18. Undistributed off-setting receipts	-4.0	-4.6	-3.5	-3.7		
Total budget	100.0	100.0	100.0	100.0		

Source: *The Budget of the United States* for various fiscal years. Note that the percentage total in each column is only approximately 100 percent because of rounding.

and health and medicare (row 11). In 1971 national defense comprised 35.9 percent of total budget outlays and was by far the largest item. By 1981 its share had dropped to 24.3 percent and top place had been taken by income and social security payments (including unemployment compensation, and the like), which had risen from 26.2 percent in 1971 to 34.3 percent in 1981. Indeed, over the decade of the 1970s there was a clear shift in priorities away from defense and towards other social goals with income and social security payments and health and medicare showing rises in their budget shares, and education and community and regional development holding constant. In addition, the budget shares going to energy and natural resources and the environment show significant increases during the 1970s. The picture changes somewhat during the 1980s. The share of defense rose between 1981 and 1987, but still remained substantially below its 1971 level at the end of the Vietnam War. While the share of health and medicare payments continued to rise in the 1980s, the share of income and social security payments fell, and the shares of education, community and regional development, the environment, and energy fell dramatically to below their 1971 shares. Interest payments continued to rise, reflecting the growing burden of the federal budget deficit.

These budget shares tell us something about government spending priorities in different areas of the economy. They do not, however, tell us about the impact of that spending in the specific industries affected by government. For example, row 5 in Table 1.4 shows that in 1987, 1.4 percent of government outlays were in the area of natural resources and environment, down from 1.9 percent in 1971 and 2.1 percent in 1981. Some of this money supported the Environmental Protection Agency which, among its other activities, monitors and regulates the pollution output of firms; some money was spent on government research projects for pollution control; some was spent maintaining national parks; and so on. Although one might be interested in how patterns of spending have changed in all these areas, this book is concerned with government regulation in the private sector, which is not specifically identified in the breakdown of shares in Table 1.4.

More detail about the regulatory activities of government is seen in Table 1.5, which shows the regulatory costs of selected federal agencies. The "new" agencies listed in the table are those that pursue new-wave regulation of the firm's internal or external environment which is not specific to a particular industry. The costs of the regulatory activity of these selected agencies (expressed here in current dollars) have grown significantly over the years 1975 to 1980, with the Equal Employment Opportunity Commission showing the most dramatic growth. From 1980 to 1987 the rate of growth of costs increased for the Environmental Protection Agency and declined for the other new agencies listed, with the Consumer Product Safety Commission showing an actual decline in costs. Note that the growth in total federal budget expenditures was 69 percent from 1975 to 1980, and 71 percent from 1980 to 1986 (calculated from Table 1.1). The record for the old agencies, those concerned with the regulation of public utilities and whose efforts are concentrated in specific industries, also shows rapid growth in regulatory costs for the period 1975 to 1980. The Federal Energy Regulatory Commission shows the most rapid growth in this category. During the period 1980 to 1987 the Civil Aeronautics Board was abolished and the regulatory costs of the Interstate Commerce Commission declined, reflecting its diminished role in the regulation of trucking and railroads. However, the costs of the other agencies listed continued to increase. Note also that the size of the dollar outlays of the new agencies are much bigger on the whole than for the old.

Even if we conclude from Table 1.5 that government expenditures for the regulating agencies have grown rapidly over the last 15 years and assume that larger expenditures indicate more regulation by these agencies, we still have no measure of how this additional regulation has affected individual industries. Indeed, one of the most difficult questions we address is how to assess both qualitatively and quantitatively the impact of government on private firms. How does government policy affect the firm's decision-making process, the quality and price of its products, its investment, and its profits? And, ultimately, what costs and benefits have been generated by the present regulatory policies? How much could society gain by changing them?

Table 1.5   Regulatory Costs of a Selection of Federal Agencies[a]
(fiscal years, millions of dollars)

	1970	1975	1980	1985	1987 (estimated)	Percent Change 1975–1980	Percent Change 1980–1987
New Agencies (fiscal years, millions of dollars							
Consumer Product Safety Commission	—	37	43	36	35	16.2	-18.6
Environmental Protection Agency	205	794	1,360	1,928	2,682	71.3	97.2
Equal Employment Opportunity Commission	13	55	124	163	170	125.5	37.1
Occupational Safety and Health Administration	—	97	191	220	229	96.9	19.9
National Highway Traffic Safety Administration	32	104	136	114	138	30.8	1.5
Old Agencies							
Interstate Commerce Commission	27	47	78	50	47	66.0	-39.7
Civil Aeronautics Board[*]	11	18	29	5	—	61.1	—
Federal Communications Commission	25	47	76	96	103	61.7	35.5
Federal Energy Regulatory Commission[**]	18	33	68	98	103	106.1	51.5
Securities and Exchange Commission	22	45	72	105	115	60.0	59.7

[*]Abolished in 1984.

[**]1970 and 1975 data are for the Federal Power Commission.

[a]Selection of agencies is based on the framework presented in M. L. Weidenbaum, *Business, Government and the Public,* Chapter 2, which shows the spheres of influence of the new agencies compared with the old agencies.

Source: Paul N. Tramontozzi with Kenneth W. Chilton, *U.S. Regulatory Agencies under Reagan 1980–1988,* Center for the Study of American Business, Washington University, OP. 64, May 1987.

In the following chapters we provide a framework for evaluating the impact of government policy on the economy by looking first at the outcome of a perfectly competitive system with no government (Chapter 2), followed by a look at the conditions under which the market fails and possible areas for government intervention (Chapters 3–5).

SUMMARY

We presented an overview of the development of government regulation and observed that there are divergent attitudes about the appropriate role of government in a free-enterprise economy. Two basic functions of government are seldom disputed, however: enforcement of laws and control of the monetary system. We considered the constitutional legitimacy of government intervention in the nation's economic life. Antitrust policy, old-style regulation, and new-wave regulation comprise the major policy categories. Finally, we looked at different measures of government size and their limitations for inferring the government's impact on the economy.

CONCLUSION

While the *Nebbia* decision removed much of the confusion surrounding the legitimacy of government intervention in the private sector mainly by removing constitutional barriers, intervention can still take place only if it is in the public interest. The interpretation of this term continues to spread confusion when government power to regulate the market is challenged.

Moreover, the economic rationale for regulation is not as clear-cut as it might at first appear. The purpose of this book is to present systematically the economic rationale for government intervention and to explain the many difficulties with the theoretical approach. Actual policies will be evaluated using both theoretical findings as a benchmark for comparison and knowledge of alternative types of government and market institutions to assess the desirability of different policies.

Discussion Questions

1.   Does the three-way classification of government regulation—antitrust policy, old-style regulation, and new-wave regulation—leave out any significant industrial policy areas? What might they be?

2.   Describe and evaluate the different measures of government size. Are such measures useful for assessing the impact of government on the economy?

3.   Is the term "public interest" a useful concept when it is used to define the limits of government intervention in the economy? Are there any constitutional limits to such intervention?

4.   What economic and political factors explain the changing structure of thegovernment budget in the post-World War II period?

Selected Readings

Asch, P., *Industrial Organization and Antitrust Policy*, Rev. ed. New York: John Wiley and Sons, 1983. *A comprehensive approach to antitrust policy with theoretical underpinnings.*

Kahn, A. E., *The Economics of Regulation*. New York: John Wiley and Sons, 1970. *An advanced approach to both the theory and practice of regulation; comprehensive and an excellent reference.*

MacAvoy, P. W., *The Regulated Industries and the Economy*. New York: W. W. Norton and Company, 1979. *An empirically well-documented and detailed analysis of the effects of both old- and new-style government regulation on industrial performance over the last two decades.*

McCraw, T. K., *Prophets of Regulation*. Cambridge, Mass.: Harvard University Press, 1984. *Fascinating biographies of four famous regulators (Charles Adams, Louis Brandeis, James Landis, and Alfred Kahn), the historical and social circumstances of their lives, and their influence on regulatory policy.*

Mitnick, B. M., *The Political Economy of Regulation*.   New York: Columbia University Press, 1980. *An interesting interdisciplinary analysis of the basic processes and organizational forms of regulatory institutions.*

Weidenbaum, M. L., *Business, Government and the Public*, 3d ed. Englewood Cliffs, N. J.: Prentice-Hall, 1986. *An original assessment of the impact of the new government regulation on the functioning of business organizations.*

Wilcox, C. and W. G. Shepherd, *Public Policies toward Business*, 5th ed. Homewood, Ill.: Richard D. Irwin, 1979. *A comprehensive treatment of government regulation of industry, including excellent accounts of regulatory institutions and procedures.*

CHAPTER 2

· · · · · · · · · · · · · · · · · · · ·

THE VIRTUES OF THE MARKETPLACE

Although government plays a substantial role in the U.S. economy, most economic decisions have been and are now made in private markets. What shall be produced, how it shall be done, and who shall receive the fruits of the productive processes are largely determined by individual consumers and business managers—not by public agency officials. The characterization of the American economy as a "private enterprise" system is thus accurate, although subject to qualification. The underlying idea is that consumers and managers should be free ordinarily to determine their own economic decisions without government interference.

In this chapter we shall examine the argument for letting the market make society's important economic decisions, and hence for the nonintervention of government in the free market system. We shall also take note of some qualifications, suggesting that markets do not in all circumstances function well. Before examining these matters, we must first recognize explicitly that the relevant issues here concern what is or is not desirable. This is the realm of normative or welfare economics, raising the general question, "What constitutes a good society?" Rather than providing a complete framework for answering this question, we confine ourselves to introducing the important concepts of efficiency and equity, the major criteria used by economists in evaluating economic performance.

ALLOCATIVE EFFICIENCY

The traditional economic rationale for the free market is that it allocates scarce resources in the best possible way. It will be useful to begin by examining this contention carefully.

Figure 2.1 Demand and Supply

The market tends toward equilibrium at point E. At lower out levels such as Q*, inventories would be depleted and producers would expand production; at higher levels such as Q', inventories would accumulate and producers would cut output.

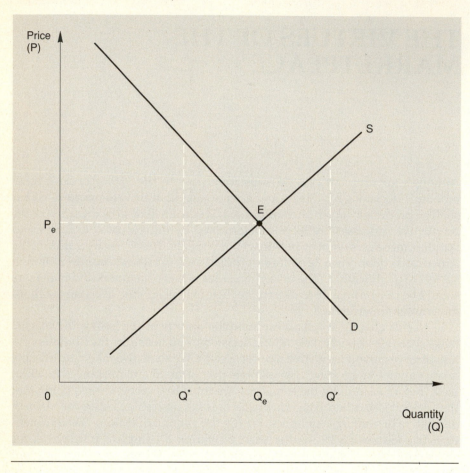

The Intuitive Argument

The intuitive argument is straightforward. Consider the basic supply-and-demand diagram of Figure 2.1. Demand curve D slopes downward, showing that consumers buy more of a product at lower prices.[1] The upward-sloping supply curve S states that more is produced and offered to the market at higher

---

[1]The reasons for this slope are termed the *substitution* and *income* effects. (1) When the price of a product falls, it becomes cheaper *relative* to other things, and consumers will tend to *substitute* the cheaper item–the substitution effect. (2) For a given money income, a fall in the price of a product will cause a rise in consumer purchasing power, thus a rise in the consumption of all normal goods—the income effect.

prices. The reasons for this slope are plausible, although somewhat less obvious than those on the demand side.[2]

As students learn quickly, the market will tend toward equilibrium at point E. Price P_e and quantity Q_e will be established and will persist until supply or demand conditions change. Were price to exceed P_e, there would be an excess supply of the product in question. Inventories would accumulate and suppliers would tend to reduce output and cut price, moving the market back toward E. However, if price were below P_e, the market would be faced with excess demand. Inventories would fall, shortages might appear, and suppliers would respond by increasing their outputs and raising price—again, taking the market back toward point E.

The question at this point becomes not "What happens?" but "What is so good about it?" Why is the market equilibrium—point E—so desirable? In what sense are price P_e and output Q_e the best possible combination?

To suggest an answer, we must reinterpret the D and S curves. Demand may be viewed as a measure of the *value* consumers attach to market outputs. In Figure 2.1, for example, Q_e units of output are demanded (can be sold) at price P_e. It is reasonable to observe that this price—let us say $2—reflects the value or benefit consumers attach to this output at the margin. Someone is willing to pay $2 for the marginal (last) unit of output. Thus, that unit is *worth* at least $2.[3] As the negative slope of D indicates, marginal value falls as quantity rises. Or, in reverse, the scarcer an item the higher its value. Demand price is at any point a statement of what consumers are willing to pay for something, that is, how highly they value it. And it is for this reason that economists sometimes refer to a demand curve as a marginal benefits (or marginal value) function.

Similarly, the supply curve may be interpreted as a measure of the cost of any level of output. It is what society gives up in terms of resources to obtain that output. This view of supply requires a brief explanation. Consider the firm's short-run marginal cost curve, MC, in Figure 2.2. It shows that the cost of producing, say, the Q_nth unit of output is $1. Higher output levels push the cost of each additional (marginal) unit above $1, while the marginal cost of units less than Q_n is below $1.

Suppose we now specify that the supplying firm can sell any amount of its product at a price of $1 per unit. How much will it supply? If the company is interested in profits, the answer is obvious. All units that cost less than $1 to produce are profitable and will be supplied. Units that cost more than $1 are unprofitable since they return only $1 when sold; these will not be produced.

Note that it is the *marginal* cost and *marginal* revenue of output that are critical to the profit-seeking firm. The firm's management must ask whether

---

[2]The neophyte's common explanation—that supply slopes upward because producers like higher prices—is essentially irrelevant. The slope depends upon a reasonable (but not inevitably correct) assumption about the behavior of *costs* as production increases. A supply curve should be thought of as a type of cost curve.

[3]This is merely a statement of the basic economic proposition that the value of a product or service is defined by what people will pay for it.

Figure 2.2 Marginal Cost and Supply

At a price of $1, a profit-seeking firm will supply all units of output that cost less than $1 (MC < $1) to produce. It will therefore supply Q_n units.

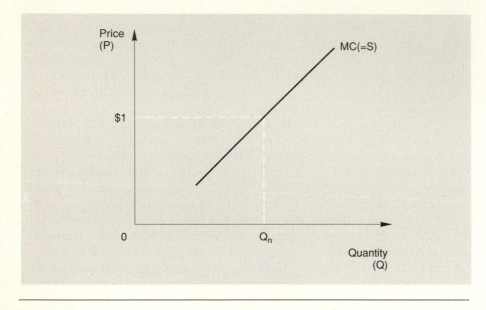

one more (or one less) unit of output will improve or worsen the profit picture. Without an answer, the best possible profit cannot be earned, except as a matter of sheer good luck.

Diagramatically, the profit-maximizing firm will supply precisely Q_n units in Figure 2.2. To supply less would be to forego profits on some units. To supply more would mean that some units are sold at a loss. But this means that MC *is the firm's supply curve*—specify the price and MC indicates the most profitable quantity to supply.[4] Or, to return to our original point, the supply curve measures the cost (at the margin) of any output quantity. This is true for each firm and for the market as a whole.[5]

Notice the implication of the argument to this point. If in Figure 2.1 output is Q^*, we can easily see that economic welfare is not at a maximum. Additional units could be produced at a marginal cost (supply price) that is lower than the marginal value (demand price) consumers place on those units. An increase in output would therefore yield a *net benefit* to society, and this is precisely what the market will provide as it moves toward equilibrium E.

---

[4]It should be noted that this is a short-run definition. The derivation of the long-run supply curve is more complicated, particularly for the market as a whole (see below).

[5]The market (short-run) supply curve is the horizontal summation of each firm's S or MC curve. The market will supply at any price the sum of what each firm will supply at that price.

Conversely, at Q' economic welfare would be increased by reducing output (units between Q_e and Q' are being produced at marginal costs greater than the marginal benefits consumers see in them). Once again, the market will do the job as suppliers cut back toward E.

The market thus achieves the remarkable result of balancing the marginal costs and benefits of production (or other activities). Where costs are relatively high, activity contracts; where low, activity expands. In either case, society gains. This type of balance, which (as we shall soon see) occurs in perfect competition, is sometimes referred to as *marginal cost pricing*, or $P = MC$. Activities are pursued to the point at which their market price, a reflection of marginal benefit, is just equated with the marginal cost of the resources used up by the activity.

Perfect Competition

The intuitive argument above assumes implicitly some characteristics of markets that must now be made explicit. These conditions define perfect competition:

1.   Many small firms, such that no one firm can have a perceptible impact on total market supply;

2.   A homogeneous, or perfectly substitutable, product;[6]

3.   Easy entry and exit of firms; and

4.   Perfectly informed buyers and sellers.

If these conditions hold, the demand curve facing any firm will appear virtually horizontal, as d in Figure 2.3. This curve reflects the individual company's impotence as one of many sellers of a homogeneous product. It can sell at the market price P_m, but should it try to raise its price the slightest bit higher, it will sell nothing. Buyers will simply turn to other sellers of the same commodity. By similar token, the company can sell any amount it produces at price P_m—for it is, by assumption, so small that its output has no noticeable impact on market supply or price.

The competitive firm thus has no pricing decision to make. Price is dictated by market supply and demand. The firm must decide only how much to sell at the market price.[7] If the company's marginal cost function is MC in Figure 2.4, it will supply precisely q_e (this is exactly the result we have just seen in relation to Figure 2.2). At any lower quantity, the company is foregoing profitable sales; but output above q_e would mean that some unprofitable units are being sold (profits can therefore be raised by eliminating those units). Output q_e is thus the *profit-maximizing* level.

---

[6]This is a very strong assumption. It means that consumers regard the offerings of all sellers as identical in all relevant respects, and thus have no preference for any seller over any other. This is a stronger statement than that the rivals' products are physically alike or identical.

[7]A company could of course sell at a price below the market level, but if it cares about profits it would have no reason to do so.

Figure 2.3 The Competitive Firm's Demand Curve

Horizontal demand curve d shows that the competitive firm has no power to affect price. If it raises its price the slightest bit above the market level P_m, it will sell nothing.

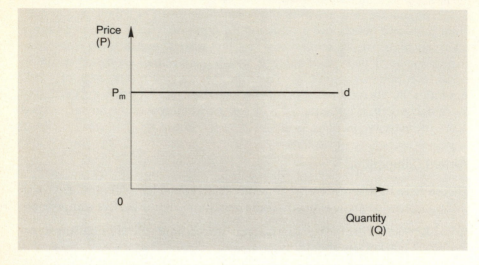

Figure 2.4 Profit Maximization for the Competitive Firm

The competitive firm maximizes profits by producing output q_e. At this point it supplies only those units it can sell at a price (P_m) higher than their marginal cost (MC).

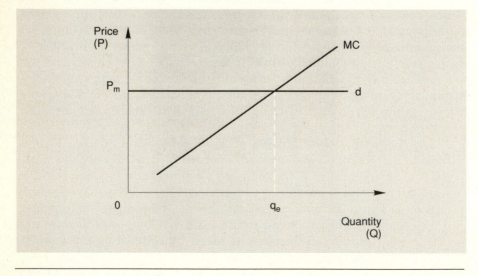

Although q_e is a profit-maximizing output, we cannot tell from Figure 2.4 whether the firm actually earns a net profit (profit maximizing simply means that it does as well as possible). To see whether the company makes a profit, we

Figure 2.5 Competitive Firm Equilibrium: The Long-Run Zero-Profit Case

In the long-run, the competitive firm continues to maximize profits, but its long-run average costs (LRAC) now equal the market price (P_e). The firm thus earns a zero profit.

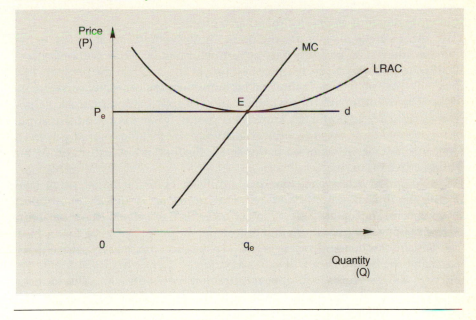

must compare *total revenue* with *total cost*. Profit is total revenue (TR) minus total cost (TC). In Figure 2.4, total revenue is implied by the demand curve (it is PQ, the rectangle under any specified price–quantity point); but total cost cannot be inferred (the MC curve ignores the possibility of fixed costs).

In the short-run, the firm might enjoy profits or suffer losses, but the long-run expectation in a perfectly competitive market is that profits will tend toward zero. This condition is depicted in Figure 2.5. The profit-maxmizing price coincides not only with marginal cost (MC), but also with long-run average cost (LRAC) as well. Thus average revenue per unit and average cost per unit are equal. Profit (TR – TC) is zero.

Why should this be the case? Free entry and exit are the key. If net profits exist in the short run (that is, if P > AC), profit-seeking firms will be drawn into the market, market supply will expand, and price will be forced down to the level of cost. If net losses exist (P < AC), some firms will be forced to exit, supply will contract, and price will be forced up until all costs are covered. Thus, if there are no barriers to entry or exit, the long-run tendency of the market is to eliminate profits or losses—that is, to move to a zero-profit (or zero-loss) position.

It is important to bear in mind that this *zero-profit* condition has a very specific meaning in economics: it is zero profits in *excess* of a normal profit or rate of return. The companies in question no doubt earn some profits in the sense in which an accountant or the Internal Revenue Service uses the term. But these profits are not "pure" or "economic" or "excess." They are just sufficient to pay the firm's owners (stockholders) the return they require to keep their money in the company. In accounting terms a profit exists, but in economic terms this return is necessary to the company's operation, and is therefore regarded as a cost rather than a profit.

An example may clarify the point. Suppose that investors can earn 8 percent interest on perfectly safe government bonds. They will not choose instead to invest in Alpha Corporation unless Alpha offers the prospect of *at least* an 8 percent return—actually a bit more since the company carries some risk. This return, paid *via* dividends and/or appreciation of stock values, comes from a fund popularly known as "profits." But it is a fund that Alpha *must earn and pay* in order to attract the investment that the company needs to continue as a viable business. In this sense, the fund is not really a profit, but rather a cost of survival.[8]

We can now derive the long-run supply curve for the industry. In Figure 2.6(b), the industry supply and demand curves are S_1 and D_1, equilibrium market price and quantity are P_1 and Q_1 (point E_1). At price P_1, the typical firm is just making a normal profit and producing output q_1 in Figure 2.6(a). Now suppose market demand increases to D_2. In the short run, market price will rise to P_2 and the typical firm will expand output to q_2 (moving up along its MC curve). Excess profits will appear, attracting new entrants. The industry supply curve will thus shift outwards (to S_2) and the final result will be that price again will fall to equality with average cost. In this example, at P_1, the profits will be competed away. The new equilibrium is at E_2, where S_2 and D_2 intersect. The long-run industry supply curve shows how much output the industry will produce at each price after the effect of entry has been taken into account. It goes through points E_1 and E_2 and, in this example, is a horizontal line, reflecting *constant costs*. Whether this is the usual case, or whether the new P = AC level is higher or lower than the initial level is uncertain. If the entry of new firms tends to push up the production costs of all firms, perhaps by bidding up input prices, the new price and cost level will be higher—the industry will exhibit increasing average costs and the long-run industry supply curve will slope upwards. In Figure 2.6(b), the assumption is that this does not occur. Notice that if new entries were actually to decrease costs for all firms, the long-run industry supply curve would slope downwards.

One further observation: whether companies actually behave as profit maximizers is a question that has long interested economists. In a perfectly competitive market, however, the firm has no choice. It *must* maximize profits in order to survive the long term (notice that in Figure 2.5, only one point (E) enables the firm to cover all costs, including compensation of investors; this is the profit maximizing combination of price and quantity). Indeed, this will tend to be the case in any market characterized by free entry.

We can thus see that the working of the unimpeded market achieves the

---

[8]See Chapter 15 for further discussion of this point.

Figure 2.6 Long-Run Supply Curve

Panel (a) shows that at price P_1 the competitive firm supplies q_1, earning zero profits. When demand increases from D_1 to D_2 in panel (b), raising price to P_2, the firm temporarily earns higher profits. But new entry shifts the market supply curve from S_1 to S_2, and price falls back to P_2. The market is now supplying a larger output (Q_2 instead of Q_1) at the old price—thus its long-run supply curve (LR supply) is horizontal.

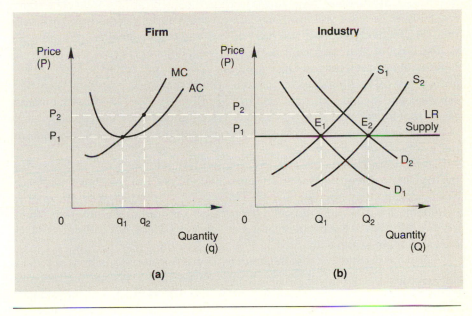

extraordinary result of allocating society's resources correctly, that is, it chooses optimal production points—under certain, competitive conditions. What is likely to happen in other circumstances, where elements of monopoly exist, is the subject of Chapter 3.

Henceforth, we refer to the best possible allocation of resources achieved by competitive markets as allocative efficiency or *Pareto optimality*. A more rigorous exposition of this concept is presented in Appendix 2A.

THE MEANING OF SOCIAL CHOICE: EFFICIENCY VERSUS EQUITY

As we have seen, a central argument for allowing the free market to make our economizing decisions is that it will use scarce resources as efficiently as possible. Society, however, cares also about other things—for example, equity, fairness, or justice. What sort of a job should we expect markets to do in this important area?

Human Rationality

The market may be thought of as a mechanism for translating the interests of rational human beings into social decisions. Indeed, if people were not rational, we might wonder about the virtue of a market mechanism that efficiently carries out their desires. Buyers and sellers freely express their individual preferences and decide, in the aggregate, where our resources will be used.

Even at this very basic level, however, complications arise. The word rational can have several meanings. One, which underlies modern microeconomics, is what Herbert Simon has called *substantive rationality*.[9] This implies that an individual must have a clear objective or choice criterion, that is, a well-defined set of preferences. Once a rational person has identified her preferences, she will then proceed to make choices so that these preferences are best satisfied under certain constraints to which all consumers are subject: income, prices that must be paid for goods and services, and quality and characteristics of available commodities. Analyses of consumer behavior ordinarily assume these constraints to be given.

One immediately obvious problem with this view of rationality is that the information required for utility-maximizing behavior may be unavailable. The consumer may not be able to find out enough, or the appropriate amount of information may be too great for the person to assimilate. In either case there exists a solution to the problem of maximizing behavior, but individuals lack the capacity to achieve it.

Sen has pointed out that the standard definition of rationality is not much more than a statement that people choose consistently.[10] As such, it omits such motivations as commitment and loyalty which may influence an individual's choice as much as the pursuit of personal satisfaction. Further, it turns out, there is a good deal of evidence that suggests that people do not make decisions with much consistency. This evidence raises fundamental questions about the desirability of market outcomes, which are determined largely by individual choice. It also points to very specific issues concerning the need for protection of consumers and workers, which we consider in detail later (Chapter 21).

More troubling issues remain. Consider the following phenomenon suggested by Schelling.[11] When an individual buys and smokes a package of cigarettes, we may infer that such behavior reveals a preference for smoking cigarettes. However, at the same time, this same person may pay a large sum of money to attend a smoking clinic, hoping to change his buying and smoking behavior. What is his true preference? Is this person a rational consumer?

---

[9]Herbert Simon, "From Substantive to Procedural Rationality," in F. Hahn and M. Hollis, eds., *Philosophy and Economic Theory* (New York: Oxford University Press, 1979).

[10]A. Sen, "Rational Fools: A Critique of the Behavioural Foundations of Economic Theory," *Philosophy and Public Affairs* 6 (1977): 317–344.

[11]T. Schelling, "The Intimate Contest for Self-Command," *The Public Interest* 60 (Summer 1980): 94–118.

Consider, in a somewhat similar vein, the "sour grapes" phenomenon explored by Elster.[12] Seeing that he cannot reach the grapes, the fox declares, "They are sour, I don't want them after all." Equivalently, a woman might say, on perceiving that a multitude of economic and social constraints will prevent her from becoming a professional baseball player or a neurosurgeon, "I don't want to do that, I would rather become a librarian." When the individual's perception is that certain constraints prevent her from attaining particular jobs or goods, her evaluation of the desirability of those jobs and goods may change. Which are her true preferences? What is her rational pursuit of an occupation?

One way around such questions is simply to define rationality in terms of the process of choice rather than its outcome. Simon calls this *procedural rationality*, stating: "Behavior is procedurally rational when it is the outcome of appropriate deliberation."[13] Individuals may be unclear about their preferences and subject to a variety of motivations. The future is uncertain, and the results of one's actions cannot, in general, be predicted with total confidence. Under the circumstances, the best one can do is to adopt a sensible procedure for identifying and following preferences. One may still make mistakes, yet do as well as possible given both informational and economic limitations.

We see, then, that even the rudimentary notion of a rational person pursuing self-interests in the marketplace is subject to some difficulty. Yet when we look at society as a whole, the problem of choice becomes vastly more complicated.

Introducing Equity or Justice

Social as opposed to individual choice involves comparing and ranking different economic states of the world for a group— the community or the whole society. At a very simplified level, consider Roz, who likes eggs, and Joe, who likes cereal. To maximize Roz's welfare, we would simply devote more resources to the production of eggs; to maximize Joe's welfare, we need only produce more cereal. But how would we maximize the welfare of the community consisting of Joe and Roz? Indeed what do we mean by the welfare of this community and how should we decide what serves it best?

Consider another case: would social welfare improve if we were to adopt a negative income tax that raises the incomes of the poor while lowering those of the rich? Would it improve if we were to abolish all income taxes, allowing the fortunate to keep all their income (and perhaps giving them an incentive to earn more), while the unfortunate would likely do without the benefit of tax-financed public welfare programs? An answer to such questions requires some notion of equity or justice.

---

[12]Jon Elster, "Sour Grapes—Utilitarianism and the Genesis of Wants," in Amartya Sen and Bernard Williams, eds., *Utilitarianism and Beyond* (Cambridge, England: Cambridge University Press, 1982), pp. 219–238.

[13]Simon, "From Substantive to Procedural Rationality," 68.

One approach is to suggest that what is good for society—the social good—can be defined by somehow combining or aggregating individual preferences. The nineteeth century thinkers known as Utilitarians suggested that the satisfaction individuals derive from the consumption of goods can be measured and added together to provide a measure of social welfare.[14] Social welfare is maximized when this sum is the greatest.

Consider two important implications of this approach: first, if one hundred dollars is worth more, in terms of the satisfaction it provides, to a poor person than to a rich person, then social welfare will rise if that sum of money is in fact transferred. More generally, redistributions of income from high to low income groups will increase social welfare. However, a second implication of the Utilitarian approach is that an economic policy which increases the satisfaction of a rich person *by more* than it decreases the satisfaction of a poor person is also desirable. In both cases social welfare rises; but in the first case the distribution of income has become more equal, while in the second case inequality has very likely increased. The point is that when the social good is defined as the sum of individual satisfactions, the distribution of welfare among the members of society is in itself of no significance. Yet we are discussing equity or fairness, which (as most people define it) is precisely a distribution issue.

Modern attempts to construct a social ranking of alternative economic states from individual preference rankings, that is, a social welfare function, confronted a different problem. The Nobel Prize-winning insight by Kenneth Arrow[15] was the *impossibility theorem* in which he proved that under certain mild conditions it is impossible to derive a social welfare function from individual preference rankings.[16]

When weight is given to what individuals in a society want, conflict seems inevitable. In the political arena we have democratic institutions that attempt to reconcile these conflicts. In the economic realm, the market system attempts the reconciliation by coordinating the buying and employment decisions of individuals. We now see, however, that even at the most basic level, the outcome of choices based on individual preferences cannot be unambiguously evaluated.

Rights   Another approach to the problem of defining economic justice is to shift the focus toward a consideration of individuals' rights rather than toward their relative standard of living. Two opposing views can be contrasted here. Robert Nozick believes that individuals have broad rights to their own bodies, to the fruits of their honest labors, and also to pass on these fruits in the form of

---

[14]See John Stuart Mill, *Utilitarianism* (London: Collins, 1861). See also Sen and Williams, *Utilitarianism and Beyond.*

[15]Kenneth J. Arrow, *Social Choice and Individual Values*, 2d ed. (New York: Wiley, 1963).

[16]The difficulty, although very basic, is not easily described in intuitive terms. See Amartya Sen, *Collective Choice and Social Welfare* (San Francisco: Holden Day, 1970) for a complete account of the problems associated with the development of consistent criteria of social choice based on individual preferences.

bequests to their heirs.[17] Government has only minimal powers to abridge these rights. When rights conflict, reconciliation can be achieved through contracts between individuals and through the voluntary formation of groups. In Nozick's world, the free market system, untrammeled by government interference, is the best protector of individual rights.

John Rawls, in contrast, suggests that individuals' rights can only be defined in the context of their relationship to others within society.[18] He argues that the distribution of income is not only basic to the definition of a just society, but also that improving the welfare of the worst-off group in society is paramount. Whereas Nozick would tolerate a rather unequal distribution of income if it were the product of voluntary and honest individual effort and exchange, Rawls would prescribe an institutional structure that continued to redistribute income from the rich to the poor as long as that redistribution raised the incomes of the poorest group. The unregulated market could not be expected to achieve this redistribution; Rawls therefore sees the need for substantial government intervention in the market system.

Both views take into account the idea that allowing people to keep the fruits of their labor gives them an incentive to use their resources and talents wisely, but Rawls would sacrifice a great deal more of the total product of society in order to improve the welfare of the poor.

Both these visions of society are justified by appealing to certain basic ideas about human beings and their morality. Rawls, for example, bases his view of a just society on the idea that it would be chosen by moral individuals behind a "veil of ignorance"—people who have no idea where they would wind up in the distribution of welfare.

In the real world of economic policy-making, ideas of justice may be rougher. William Vickrey observes:

> Injustice appears to be felt whenever legitimate expectations are disappointed through the intervention, actual or imagined, of a human agency. Disappointments perceived as the result of natural forces, 'acts of God,' or even the workings of an impersonal marketplace are less likely to be thought of as injustices . . . . A practical consequence of this is that if a legislator or public official wishes to rectify what on some overall principle is characterized as an injustice by a measure that appears to be to the disadvantage of some and the advantage of others, the result is likely to be felt as an injustice by the disadvantaged and reacted to much more vigorously by them than it is acclaimed by the benefitted. Justice as the fulfillment of legitimate expectations is likely to prove an extremely conservative principle.[19]

In later chapters we shall observe that the distributional consequences of proposed changes in regulatory policy may indeed influence the success of the policy—as much or more than its potential for increasing efficiency.

---

[17]Robert Nozick, *Anarchy, State and Utopia* (New York: Basic Books, 1974).

[18]John Rawls, *A Theory of Justice* (Cambridge, Mass.: Harvard University Press, 1971).

[19]William Vickrey, "Justice, Economics and Jurisprudence," *Social Research* 46 (Summer 1979): 274.

We turn now to some further qualifications of the idea that unconstrained markets invariably deliver good economic performance.

Some Qualifications

The allocative efficiency case for the competitive market is logically unassailable. The implications of this argument for social decision making, however, must be treated cautiously, and we have already noted the first reason for caution. Markets may be efficient, but people care also about fairness. The market, if it functions well, may satisfy the marginal Pareto conditions (refer to Appendix 2A), but the particular results that emerge will depend also on the distribution of income and wealth (that is, spending power) in society.

The values that we place on things via the market are defined not only by our individual preferences, but also by our ability to pay for them. If lovers of Mozart opera recordings have high incomes with which to express their demands, the market is likely to deem them important—that is, profitable—and to supply the recordings at some appropriate price. If Mozart lovers are paupers, however, the market is unlikely to provide the recordings no matter how strongly their passions run. However, *both* outcomes may be Pareto optimal—they simply result from different distributions of the ability to pay for something.[20]

The Pareto criterion has little to say about this issue. One may, then, be aware of the virtues of Pareto efficiency, yet also believe that income and wealth are distributed incorrectly (unfairly). Two questions are then worth posing, without immediate answers: (1) Can an ethically correct distribution of spending power be agreed upon by society? (2) If the correct distribution *cannot* be defined or achieved, what is the importance of achieving Pareto-efficient outcomes?

These questions raise policy issues that we consider further below. For the present, let us consider a few more qualifications to the the idea of market optimality.

The Impossibility of Perfect Competition   Introductory economics students are fond of pointing out that the competitive model, to which we pay so much attention, is unrealistic as a description of actual markets. They are of course correct. In very few areas do we see swarms of tiny competitors, a truly homogeneous product, unrestricted entry, and perfectly informed buyers and sellers (some agricultural markets such as wheat and corn are the closest approximation). There are, moreover, some general reasons for this absence.

1.   *Economies of large scale* operation frequently make the small (competitive-sized) firm impractical; it could not and would not survive in a contest with larger, lower-cost rivals.

---

[20]It is thus apparent that there exist *numerous* Pareto optima, at least one for every conceivable distribution of income! This is one reason why some observers believe that the Pareto optimality of a market system is not an especially strong recommendation. Such optimality is consistent with distributions that any or all of us might regard as terribly unfair.

2.   Incentives to *differentiate* even physically similar products are often strong. A seller may do better if customers believe his goods are distinctive rather than the same as everyone else's. (Consider aspirin, beer, cigarettes, and cola drinks: rival brands of each are very much alike, yet producers devote large resources to convincing consumers that their particular offerings are better—apparently with some success.)

3.   *Entry* into markets is frequently difficult, either because of such natural barriers as scale economies or artificial ones (the need for a license; the tying up of technical know-how via patent or closely guarded trade secret; or perhaps advertising itself).

4.   *Information* as a rule is costly, and is thus likely to be imperfect. The implications are varied: new competitors may not enter a market simply because they are unaware that the particular market is profitable. Consumers may be subject to exploitation because they suffer some ignorance about the goods they buy.

5.   *Transaction costs* are the costs firms incur after they have entered the market. Searching for information, bargaining with customers and suppliers, and drawing up contracts are examples of transaction costs. The costs of contracting may be substantial if parties to a transaction are uncertain about each other's honesty or reliability or about contingencies that may occur during the period of the agreement. Such costs may be less for established firms than for new firms, and they may enhance the imperfections of markets.

Whereas there is no natural law against the existence of competitive markets, the necessary conditions occur together only by coincidence and not very often. The relevant question thus becomes: Given that perfect competition is the ideal allocator of resources, how *important* is this in an imperfect world? What is the significance of an ideal that is seldom, if ever, attained?

Externalities   The argument for competitive efficiency presupposes that there is no divergence between private and social valuations. The marginal utilities (or benefits) that consumers see coincide with society's benefits, and producers' marginal costs are identical to those of society. However, divergences—which are usually called *externalities*—are quite common.

The classic case involves environmental pollution because pollution costs that are important to society may fall largely outside the market. Suppose, for example, that a chemical company dumps its untreated wastes into a river, thereby contaminating the water supply for downstream users. These users—communities, fishermen, and swimmers—suffer real costs. But because they are not, for the most part, participants in chemical market transactions, the harm they suffer is unlikely to be reflected in chemical prices or output levels. Real social costs are created by the pollution that accompanies chemical production, but the market does not take notice.

Clearly, even a perfect market will not do a very good job of allocating resources here—both chemicals and water pollution will be overproduced, meaning that the marginal costs of output are not justified by marginal benefits. We are therefore likely to impose public limits on the polluting activity rather than simply accepting the market's judgment.

INTERNAL ("X") EFFICIENCY

A distinctive virtue of properly functioning markets is that they force firms to be internally efficient in a number of ways. Such *X efficiency* amounts to a rather strict cost-minimization condition.[21]

Suppose that a company can pursue its activities in either a more or less efficient way. Standard economic theory assumes that the more efficient route will always be chosen——and it surely will *if* the firm in question is under strong competitive pressure. As we have seen, the best long-run outcome for such companies is just to cover all costs (including a normal profit). Any failure to minimize costs will jeopardize the firm's future.

One might ask why a competitive market is needed to induce this sort of efficiency. Would not the managers of any organization choose less costly rather than more costly ways to operate, just as a matter of good business practice? Frequently, of course, the answer is yes. Few executives are likely to pursue inefficiency deliberately. They do not ask themselves, "How can I waste some company resources today?"

The issue is more subtle, however. Running a truly efficient corporation means more than avoiding flagrant waste. One must continually search out more effective ways to do things; plan and invest in knowledge of new techniques; and make hard decisions to cut out well-established traditions. The tight ship has few frills, yet frills, such as job perquisites, are enjoyable.

The optimally efficient firm of the microtheory textbook might not be the most pleasant place to work. Even here, however, some slack is likely to exist. Perfect efficiency is never attainable, if only because the condition would be a costly one to monitor and supervise.[22] Even corporate management is likely to enjoy a little fun and relaxation on the job!

The notion that companies with a monopoly power cushion—those that are not forced to high levels of efficiency just to survive—will choose to follow some relatively inefficient procedures, is not absurd. The cost of these X inefficiencies, while they are difficult to measure, are potentially significant and provide a further qualification to arguments for the efficiency of the market.

NONECONOMIC VIRTUES OF THE MARKETPLACE

Efficiency arguments for the market, such as those described above, are plainly economic in nature. It may be, however, that an equally or more important social rationale for the market system can be made on noneconomic

---

[21]The term "X efficiency" was coined and developed by H. Leibenstein, "Allocative Efficiency v. 'X-Efficiency,'" *American Economic Review* 56 (June 1966).

[22]Another way of viewing the problem of inefficiency within corporations is in terms of the principal–agent framework. We reserve this discussion until Chapter 15.

grounds. Before examining some suggestions to this effect, however, we need to look a bit further at the distinction between economic and noneconomic considerations. The line of demarcation is fuzzy and different people may find it in different places.

The Impersonality of the Market   This may be cited as a noneconomic virtue. The point is not that we value impersonal organizations for their own sake (in fact, we tend to complain about them), but rather that such a market can base its rewards and penalties only on individual performance. It is in that sense an objective, unbiased evaluator; there is no room for pernicious discrimination.

Objectivity, however, has its costs. A perfectly functioning market will pay people precisely according to the value of what they contribute. But what then becomes of the handicapped or those whose particular skills do not happen to be highly valued or those who simply have no skills? In these instances the market will be harsh, and anyone with the faintest egalitarian leanings is unlikely to be satisfied with its dispensations. As noted, there is no reason to expect that the income distribution generated by even a perfect market will be subjectively regarded as fair by most people.

The Democracy of the Marketplace   An important noneconomic virtue that many see in the market is its consistency with the democratic ideal. This characterization assumes that strictly competitive conditions hold. The competitive model describes a market in which there is zero concentration or perfect equality of economic power. No individual or small group can perceptibly affect prices or output quantities. It is participants in the aggregate rather than special interest or subgroups that make economizing decisions.

To restate the point, everyone is part of every decision, therefore no one exerts undue influence. The market is a bit like a political election in which all citizens have the right to cast votes (thus common references to the dollar votes of consumers). As we have noted, however, there is one weakness in this analogy. Because the distribution of buying power across society is unequal, some consumers have more votes than others. The perfect market will be perfectly sensitive to consumer desires—this is the essence of its efficiency. But in the United States and virtually every other economy, some citizen consumers will be in a better position than others to define those desires.

It is for this reason that the idea of the "market as democracy" cannot be pushed to an extreme. If one believes that the one-person-one-vote principle is essential to democratic decision making, then even the freely competitive market falls a bit short. If, on the other hand, one regards the distributional status quo as ethically correct or acceptable, then the market may well appear to be the best possible mechanism for reaching economic decisions.[23]

---

[23]In the United States, the status quo is determined both by market rewards and numerous government policies that modify the pattern of those rewards. Whether the policies have significantly or adequately reduced the inequalities that the market generates is a controversial question.

Process versus Results As we have pointed out, noneconomic arguments for the market may be based on a regard for the competitive decision process, as distinct from the particular results which emerge from that process. What is important, in other words, is not so much what we decide but how we decide it. Competition is thus not to be defined in terms of performance (or result) patterns—price at marginal cost, and so on—but simply as the mechanism that happens to yield these results.

While this may be a plausible characterization of the noneconomic viewpoint, it does not necessarily imply conflict with the economic position. Indeed, one could argue that the distinction between the two may be smaller than it appears at first glance. An economist examining a properly functioning market will note that decisions are inherently correct ones. The economic value of any activity is defined by the willingness of consumers to pay for it. A market that reflects this willingness accurately must therefore make wise choices. It is our preferences that define economic wisdom.

The means and ends of competitive markets are thus closely linked. So much so, in fact, that to term them noneconomic and economic, respectively, may appear to draw a somewhat artificial distinction. This point should not yet be pushed to an extreme, however; the distinction between means and ends may be clearer in imperfect market settings.

The Market and Human Happiness A somewhat different question that some people have addressed is whether market optimization and human happiness coincide, or even have much to do with each other. Market advocates contend that economic efficiency creates greater welfare or well-being (the terms are notoriously difficult to define). Sometimes the contention is modified as follows: efficiency permits possible welfare gains, without a corresponding possibility of losses. The underlying argument is plausible. Greater output may not assure happiness, but it is likely to increase our comfort and pleasure somewhat. Therefore, it may help and won't hurt.[24]

While plausible, however, such arguments may be challenged. The grounds for challenge are numerous, so we shall take note of only a few of the main possibilities.[25]

1. Happiness may be largely a function of one's relative position in society. If so, then absolute increases in income (more real output per person) will, by themselves, provide little satisfaction.[26]

---

[24]Or in simpler terms: You can't buy happiness, but if you're going to be miserable, it's best to have money.

[25]For an interesting book on this and related topics, see: T. Scitovsky, *The Joyless Economy* (New York: Oxford University Press, 1976).

[26]This may be one reason why the proportion of people describing themselves as happy holds constant over long periods in which significant income gains occur. See R.A. Easterlin, "Does Economic Growth Improve the Human Lot?" P.A. David and M.W. Reder, eds., *Nations and Households in Economic Growth: Essays in Honor of Moses Abramovitz* (New York: Academic Press, 1974).

2.   In a similar vein, our striving to get ahead—to improve our relative position—may take an emotional toll, contributing to dissatisfaction and unhappiness. At least one prominent psychiatrist has stated that competitiveness (the provider of so many economic goods) is the source of his profession (the provider of patients). This may be good for psychiatrists, but not so good for the occupants of their couches!

3.   Happiness may depend to an important extent on the interest and satisfaction of one's work. Yet there is no particular reason to think that job satisfaction rises with increasingly efficient production methods. The reverse may be true instead. If so, the efficiency gains that supply us with greater consumption opportunities may simultaneously reduce our work-related enjoyments. On balance, at least some of us may be worse off.

4.   Our focus on materialistic well-being—personal income, profit, and loss— may have seduced us into ignoring other important and satisfying values. Don't we all know of worthwhile activities that could not survive in the market? Religious and cultural organizations are obvious examples. Most people surely believe that churches, museums, and orchestras are worthwhile institutions. Yet the continued existence of such organizations rests heavily on public subsidies and would likely fail a market test in many cases.

SUMMARY

The economic virtues of the marketplace are strong indeed. Free markets organize literally millions of activities in a relatively efficient manner. Under the strict conditions of perfect competition, we could even expect to achieve optimal efficiency in the Pareto sense of the term. Furthermore, markets have some important noneconomic characteristics that are highly appealing in a democratic society. Is there also a negative side to the market system? Of course, as we shall see in the next three chapters.

CONCLUSION

We have seen that a strong case can be made for the market as a reconciler of private and social interests. It takes the selfish motives of individual buyers and sellers and channels them into socially optimal economic decisions.[27] The force of the case is impressive. It may be advanced in pure economic terms (efficiency of resource allocation) or as the basis of a sociopolitical (democracy) or ethical (reward based on contribution) position. One may not be fully persuaded by these arguments; even in a determinedly capitalistic society,

---

[27]Some people find it surprising, perhaps even distressing, that society's well-being in a market economy depends upon individual greed. The word "greed," however, is heavily loaded with negative connotations. One might instead point out that markets facilitate an enlightened self-interest, such that one can pursue one's own goals only by doing socially valuable work.

antimarket voices are heard. But the arguments possess logical consistency. If one is to reject the market, it must be on other grounds.

Several important questions and qualifications to the case for the market exist. Two already noted are:

1. The desirability of the market presupposes that it functions perfectly, or at least tolerably. Yet imperfection is the real-world rule. (Significant elements of monopoly and externalities alone characterize the large majority of American markets.) What, then, is the importance of the proof that perfect markets behave perfectly?

2. Even the perfect functioning of markets, in efficiency terms, does not preclude gross unfairness.

We can easily observe that all market-oriented economies are characterized by substantial government intervention.[28] This implies that some problems are not amenable to market solution, and, more specifically, that points 1 and 2 are quantitatively important.

It is undoubtedly true that allowing most economic decisions to be determined by market forces will leave society with serious human problems to be resolved. The market fails to solve these problems, and may at times exacerbate them. But alternative, nonmarket solutions are seldom obvious. Where market results are unsatisfactory, we can and will act to modify them. Any suggestion that we ought to replace the market to a substantial degree, however, deserves a cautious response seasoned with some healthy skepticism.

Discussion Questions

1. "The most basic virtue of the market is that, under certain circumstances, it translates the self-interest of many individuals into economizing decisions that are socially desirable." Explain why you agree or disagree.

2. A profit-maximizing firm must always focus on the margin, that is, the costs and revenues of the next unit (or the last unit) produced. Why is this so?

3. "Economic analysis shows that perfect competition produces Pareto optimal results. Since perfect competition seldom exists in the real world, this demonstration is of limited importance." Do you agree?

4. Most people would agree that even perfectly efficient markets would not assure human happiness. Is this because happiness has nothing to do with efficiency? Is it because efficient markets have side effects that may make people unhappy? Can you suggest some other reasons?

---

[28]Japan and West Germany are widely regarded in the United States as outstanding examples of efficient and progressive economic systems. Both these nations have government sectors that are proportionately much larger than our own.

5.   "The desirable results of markets depend upon rational behavior by large numbers of individuals. If many people are not rational then the argument for the market is weakened." Do you consider this to be a reasonable statement?

Selected Readings

Bator, F. M. "The Simple Analytics of Welfare Maximization." *American Economic Review* 47 (March 1957). *A detailed but straightforward discussion of the properties of market outcomes; now a standard analysis.*

Friedman, M. *Capitalism and Freedom.* Chicago: University of Chicago Press, 1962. *A collection of Friedman's essays containing some staunch defenses of market virtues.*

Okun, A. *Equality and Efficiency: The Big Trade-Off.* Washington, D.C.: Brookings Institution, 1975. *An eloquent discussion of the virtues and the limitations of markets.*

Scitovsky, T. *The Joyless Economy.* New York: Oxford University Press, 1976. *Are market outcomes satisfying even if they are efficient? Interesting discussions by a noted economist.*

APPENDIX 2A
The Optimality of Perfect Competition

In this appendix we demonstrate that a system of perfectly competitive markets will automatically satisfy the marginal conditions for a Pareto optimum, a fundamental concept in welfare economics.

Consider first the meaning of an improvement in society's well-being. This is potentially a complicated matter that we will discuss shortly, but let us begin with Pareto's definition: an improvement is any change that helps some member(s) of society and harms no one. At least superficially, this is a noncontroversial definition. When some people are better off and no one is worse off, the welfare of the group as a whole—society—has improved.[a]

The Pareto *optimum* may then be defined as that state of affairs in which no further (Pareto) improvements are possible—a situation such that the welfare of some member(s) of society can be improved *only by harming* the welfare of some other member(s). All the costless improvements—those that hurt no one—have already been made.[b]

With this definition in mind, consider an extremely simple economy containing:

- Two utility-maximizing consumers, A and B.
- Two products or outputs, X and Y.
- Two factor inputs i and j, both useful in producing each of the outputs and both fixed in supply.

It can now be shown that a Pareto optimal use of resources will exist if three specific conditions are satisfied.

The first condition of Pareto optimality (Equation 2A.1) identifies the appropriate allocation of goods X and Y between consumers A and B.

$$\frac{MU_{XA}}{MU_{YA}} = \frac{MU_{XB}}{MU_{YB}} \tag{2A.1}$$

where MU_{XA} is defined as the marginal utility of good X to consumer A (that is, the addition to A's utility from the consumption of one additional unit of X), and so forth.

---

[a]The criterion may seem reasonable, but it should not be taken as an objective or scientific statement. The Pareto notion of a social welfare improvement does rest on a value judgment, as we shall see.

[b]This description suggests that the Pareto optimum is nothing more or less than a particular kind of *efficiency* condition—one in which all changes that imply some benefit and no cost have already occurred.

This condition states that the marginal utility ratios or *marginal rates of substitution* (MRS) are the same for both consumers.[c] Were this not the case, either consumer (or both) could gain with neither suffering harm by voluntary trading of goods.

Consider a numerical example in which the ratios are unequal:

$$\frac{MU_{XA}}{MU_{YA}} = \frac{10}{10} \quad and \quad \frac{MU_{XB}}{MU_{YB}} = \frac{20}{5}.$$

Suppose now that consumer A trades one unit of good X to Consumer B; B in turn pays A two units of good Y. Consumer A is better off than before—he has lost 10 utiles (hypothetical units of utility) by getting rid of A, but has increased utility by 20 utiles from the (two units of) Y received in return. On balance A's total utility has gone up by 10. Consumer B, however, is also better off than before: she has given up two units of Y, which she valued at 10 utiles, but received one unit of X, with a value of 20 utiles. Her total utility also has gone up by 10.

We may thus conclude that if the equality does not hold, welfare-improving exchanges are possible and a Pareto optimum cannot exist. Equality of the MRS is the condition for Pareto-optimal distribution of goods among consumers.

The second condition of Pareto optimality (Equation 2A.2) identifies the appropriate division of resources i and j between goods X and Y.

$$\frac{MP_{iY}}{MP_{iX}} = \frac{MP_{jY}}{MP_{jX}} \quad or, equivalently, \qquad\qquad \textbf{(2A.2a)}$$

$$\frac{MP_{iX}}{MP_{jX}} = \frac{MP_{iY}}{MP_{jY}} \qquad\qquad \textbf{(2A.2b)}$$

where MP_{iX} is the marginal product of input i in the production of good X (that is, the addition to the total product of X produced when one additional unit of input is added), and so forth.

Equation 2A.2a states that the marginal product ratios or *marginal rates of transformation* (MRT) for each input in its alternative productive uses are equal. If they are not, the production of one or both goods could be increased (with no reduction in the other) by trading inputs—that is, switching some of each into its more productive use.

It may help to think in terms of the same sort of numerical example we have seen for Equation 2A.1. Using any arbitrary set of numbers, it is easy to show that if the MRTs are unequal, inputs may be switched so that one or both outputs increases and neither declines. (Simply switch each input toward the use in which it is relatively more efficient.)

---

[c]The condition would apply similarly to many goods and many consumers.

The third condition of Pareto optimality (Equation 2A.3) identifies the appropriate amount of goods X and Y that should be produced according to their relative costs and the relative preference of consumers A and B.

$$\frac{MU_X}{MU_Y} = \frac{MC_X}{MC_Y} \quad \text{or, equivalently,} \qquad \text{(2A.3a)}$$

$$\frac{MU_X}{MC_X} = \frac{MU_Y}{MC_Y} \qquad \text{(2A.3b)}$$

where MU_X is the marginal utility of good X (to any consumer), MC_X is the marginal cost of X, and so forth.

Equation 2A.3a states that the MRS (consumers' marginal utility valuations of the two goods) must equal the marginal cost ratio of the goods (which is also the MRT).

Equation 2A.3b states that the utility-to-cost ratio must the same at the margin for each good produced. If the ratios were unequal, society would be better off producing more of the good that yields a high utility to the last dollar and less of the other (low-ratio) good. The former provides larger benefits relative to costs at the margin and is thus a better buy. But if society's welfare can be increased in such unambiguous fashion, a Pareto optimum does not exist. Optimality in the output levels of goods X and Y occurs only where the ratios are equal, where no free improvements are available.

When all three conditions hold, our simple economy is at a Pareto optimum. No change in the distribution of goods among consumers, the allocation of inputs to productive uses, or the amounts of goods produced can help one of our consumers without simultaneously hurting the welfare of the other. Moreover, the Pareto conditions will automatically occur if each market in the economy is strictly competitive. The demonstration is quite simple.

Recall the first condition for a Pareto optimum, Equation 2A.1. The marginal utility ratios (MRSs) of goods X and Y are the same for consumers A and B. (Were they not, the consumers could undertake mutually beneficial trades.)

We know that utility-maximizing consumers must equate MU_X/P_X with MU_Y/P_Y.[d] In competitive markets, however, every consumer faces the same prices for all goods. Each consumer therefore equates her MRS (MU ratio) to *the same price ratio*. Thus, the MRSs of both (all consumers) are equated with each other. That is:

$$\frac{MU_{XA}}{MU_{YA}} = \frac{P_X}{P_Y} = \frac{MU_{XB}}{MU_{YB}}.$$

The demonstration that competitive markets satisfy the second Pareto condition (Equation 2A.2) is almost as simple. To survive in such markets, as we have noted, firms must act as profit maximizers. But profit maximization

[d]Anyone who does not know this should immediately consult an introductory economics text. Look under "utility maximization" or "demand utility."

requires that producers hire each input they use to the point at which that input's price[e] just equals the value of its marginal product (that is, its marginal revenue product).[f] In competitive markets, this value is simply the price of the product times the input's marginal product. Thus:

$$P_i = \text{value of } MP_i = (MP_{iX})(P_X) = (MP_{iY})(P_Y), \text{ and}$$

$$P_j = \text{value of } MP_j = (MP_{jX})(P_X) = (MP_{jY})(P_Y).$$

Dividing the top equation by the bottom equation, we have:

$$\frac{MP_{iX}}{MP_{jX}} = \frac{MP_{iY}}{MP_{jY}}.$$

Competitive markets therefore satisfy the second Pareto condition (expressed as Equation 2A.2b).

The third condition (Equation 2A.3) states that the MU/MC ratio is the same for both (all) goods produced. We have already noted that utility-maximizing consumers act so that:

$$\frac{MU_X}{MU_Y} = \frac{P_X}{P_Y}.$$

But we also know that in perfect competition price equals marginal cost. That is,

$$P_X = MC_X \text{ and } P_Y = MC_Y, \text{ which implies}$$

$$\frac{P_X}{P_Y} = \frac{MC_X}{MC_Y}.$$

Consumers thus equate their MRS (MU ratio) with the price ratio of the goods X and Y. But in competitive markets, the marginal cost ratio for producers is equal to the same price ratio. (In fact, the marginal cost of each good is precisely equal to its price.) Thus MRT (= price ratio) = MRS, and competitive markets fulfill the third condition.

We therefore conclude that a system of perfectly competitive markets implies Pareto optimality. This is not necessarily a stronger conclusion than that suggested by our earlier intuitive arguments in this chapter, but the demonstration is a somewhat more careful one.

---

[e]We assume competitive markets for inputs i and j ensuring that producers of X and Y cannot influence input prices.

[f]This is a fundamental point in basic microeconomics. The price of an input is its incremental cost to the firm, while the value of its marginal product (its marginal revenue product) measures its incremental revenue or benefit to the firm. If these two values are not equal, the firm can increase its profits by changing the amount of the input it employs: if the input costs less than it adds to company revenues than to costs, the firm should expand its use. The argument is analogous to the somewhat more general point that profit maximization requires equality of marginal cost and marginal revenue.

CHAPTER 3

· · · · · · · · · · · · · · · · · ·

MARKET FAILURE: MONOPOLY

Even a cursory glance at the industrial structure of the U. S. economy reveals that perfect competition is virtually nonexistent. Many American industries, particularly in manufacturing, are dominated by a few large firms (see Table 9.4 in Chapter 9). However, the overall structure of industry is quite varied, ranging from relatively atomistic industries such as dresses and furniture to highly concentrated ones such as automobiles, detergents, and transformers. The idea that dominance by one firm in an industry is undesirable, often creating an important issue on the political agenda, has a long history. In 1776 Adam Smith wrote:

> Since the establishment of the English East India Company . . . the other inhabitants of England, over and above being excluded from the trade, must have paid in the price of the East India goods which they have consumed, not only for all the extraordinary profits which the company may have made upon those goods in consequence of their monopoly, but for all the extraordinary waste which the fraud and abuse, inseparable from the management of the affair of so great a company must necessarily have occasioned.[1]

Modern U. S. antitrust policy originated with the passage of the Sherman Act of 1890 which declared in Section 2 that "every person who shall monopolize, or attempt to monopolize, or combine or conspire with any other person or persons to monopolize any part of the trade or commerce . . . shall be guilty of a misdemeanor. . . . "[2]

One recent view of the problem of monopoly is that of Walter Adams:

> The competitive market is not . . . a gift of nature. It is a social artifact that must be nurtured by the constant vigilance of public authority. It must be shielded from private subversion—that is, collusion, predation, exclusion

---

[1] Adam Smith, *The Wealth of Nations* (New York: Random House, 1937): 596.

[2] 26 Stat. 209 (1890). This is the original wording. Criminal violators of the Sherman Act today are guilty of a felony.

and concentration—and also from government subversion–that is, the public storm shelters built to protect special interests from the so-called Schumpeterian gales of creative destruction.[3]

Whether or not monopoly power is an example of market failure depends on one's view of its causes and consequences. Some see it as the direct result of the misuse of government power. Others see it as the natural and inevitable result of the competitive process. The appropriate role for government may then be to curb monopoly rather than to create it.

In this chapter we provide a framework within which these issues can be evaluated. The first section begins with a simple definition of monopoly power and identifies some major problems with the definition. Next we evaluate industry performance under monopoly using the social welfare concept developed in Chapter 2.

MONOPOLY POWER DEFINED

The definitional task seems straightforward enough: a monopoly exists when there is only one firm in an industry, it produces a product for which there are no close substitutes, and entry barriers are sufficiently high that no new firms can enter to take advantage of high profits. If we add the familiar assumption that the firm is a profit maximizer with a known cost structure, we can determine the firm's price, output, and profits.

Suppose there is a monopolist in the steel industry. Since there is only one firm, the demand curve facing the firm, D in Figure 3.1, is identical to the industry demand curve for steel and is downward sloping; MR is the corresponding marginal revenue curve. (Recall from micro theory that the slope of the MR curve is twice as steep as the slope of D, which is also the average revenue curve.) In the short run, capital is fixed; SAC and SMC are the single firm's short-run average and marginal cost curves, respectively, for steel production. The firm maximizes its profits by producing a level of output such that marginal revenue and marginal cost are equal. Thus it produces Q_m units and charges price P_m. Excess profit per unit is equal to the distance KL, and total excess profits earned on Q_m units are equal to the area P_mKLJ.[4]

In Figure 3.1 the price-output position P_m, Q_m also happens to be (by construction) the long-run profit-maximizing position for the firm since the amount of capital which generated the short-run average cost curve SAC is also the optimal (cost-minimizing) amount. (LAC and LMC are the long-run average and marginal cost curves, respectively.) The short- and long-run average cost curves are tangent at point L and the firm could not produce output Q_m at lower cost. Note that long-run average costs would fall if the firm were to expand output, but since it is already maximizing profits at Q_m it has no

---

[3]Quoted in B. Bock, "No-Fault Monopoly: A Debate within a Debate," *Across the Board*, 16 (November 1979): 56.

[4]To see this, note that Q_m units are sold at price $OP_m = Q_m$K. The average cost of producing Q_m units is Q_mL. Therefore, the excess of price over average cost is KL = excess profit per unit. Total excess profits are therefore equal to KL multiplied by Q_m units, or the rectangle P_mKLJ.

Figure 3.1   Monopoly Determination of Price and Quantity

The monopolist chooses output so as to maximize profits where SMC=MR at Q_m, and charges the maximum price the consumers will pay for that output, P_m. The long-run equilibrium output for the firm is also Q_m because LMC is also equal to MR at Q_m.

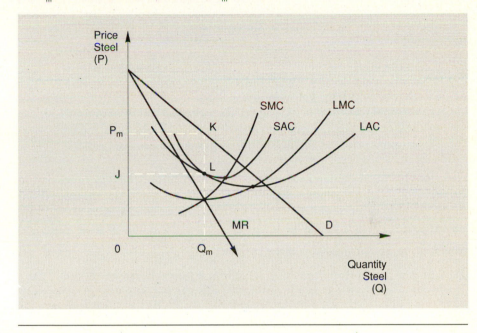

incentive to do so. Since there is, by definition, no possibility of entry by new firms in response to excess profits earned by the monopolist, these profits persist indefinitely.

Like the concept of perfect competition, monopoly can be viewed as a polar case, a type of industrial organization that is well-defined in theory. It serves as a pedagogic device which can be contrasted with the perfectly competitive model and used as a basis for general evaluative statements. However, as soon as we turn to the real world and attempt to identify industries that are pure monopolies or have monopolistic characteristics, two closely related problems emerge: defining the industry product and entry barriers.

Industry Definition

The problem of product, and hence of industry, definition can be better understood if we first introduce the important concept of the elasticity of demand.

Elasticity of Demand   Recall the basic economic idea that the quantity demanded of a good by consumers depends inversely on the price charged. Thus, if tastes, incomes, and the prices of other goods are held constant, a fall in the price of butter will result in more butter being demanded by buyers. The elasticity of a demand curve measures the extent to which quantity demanded will respond when the price changes. More specifically it is the ratio of the percentage change in quantity demanded to a given percentage price change which generates the change in quantity. Thus:

$$e = -\frac{\Delta Q}{Q} \Big/ \frac{\Delta P}{P} = -\frac{\Delta Q}{\Delta P} \cdot \frac{P}{Q}$$

where

ΔQ = change in quantity demanded;
ΔP = change in price;
Q = original quantity (or average of the original and final quantities); and
P = original price (or average of the original and final prices).

Note that for most demand curves elasticity is different at every point on the curve.[5] For example, along a straight-line demand curve the inverse of the slope, $\Delta Q/\Delta P$, is the same at every point, but the price–quantity ratio, P/Q, changes as price falls (quantity rises and P/Q falls). Thus, as price falls, the elasticity of demand (which is the product $\frac{\Delta Q}{\Delta P} \cdot \frac{P}{Q}$) also falls. Indeed, all straight-line demand curves have an elastic portion (at the top of the curve, that is, when the price is high), a unitary elastic point (at the midpoint of the curve), and an inelastic portion (at the bottom of the curve, that is, when the price is low). Therefore, when we refer to the elasticity of a demand curve this is not strictly correct since demand curves have differing elasticities along their length. We should qualify our statement and refer to the elasticity "at the prevailing price," or "at the profit-maximizing price." However, this qualification is often omitted, with the understanding that we are confining our discussion to the relevant portions of the demand curve.

Note also that there is an important relationship between the value of the elasticity of demand and the extent to which the value of total sales or revenue changes when price rises or falls. If demand is elastic (elasticity greater than one), a fall in price will cause total revenue to rise, since the rise in quantity more than offsets the price fall which generated it. If demand is inelastic (elasticity less than one), a price fall will reduce total revenue. For unitary elastic demand (elasticity equal to one), total revenue remains unchanged when the price changes.

Product Definition   Consider now the definition of an industry as the collection of firms that produce the same or similar products. The elasticity of the industry demand curve—the responsiveness of quantity demanded to a change in the product price—will be determined mainly by the nature and prices of

---

[5]However, a demand curve with the shape of a rectangular hyperbola (for which price times quantity equals a constant) has an elasticity of one at every point.

Figure 3.2   The Elasticity of the Demand Curve Depends on Substitutes

When pens are not a good substitute for pencils, the demand for pencils will not fall much when their price rises—a movement from R_1 to R_2 along demand curve D_1. When pens are a good substitute for pencils, the demand for pencils will fall more when the price rises. Hence, the demand curve for pencils will be more elastic —a movement from R_1 to R_3 along demand curve D_2.

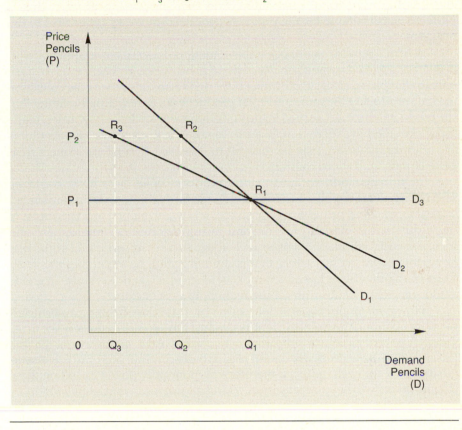

available substitutes.[6] For example, suppose that pens and pencils are viewed by consumers as close substitutes for fulfilling the objective of writing a letter. The industry demand curve for pencils is given by D_1 in Figure 3.2. Now if the price of pencils rises from P_1 to P_2, some consumers will substitute the now cheaper pens, and the quantity of pencils demanded will fall from Q_1 to Q_2. There is a movement up and backwards along the demand curve for pencils, from R_1 to R_2 in the figure. With still more consumers recognizing greater substitutability between pencils and pens, a rise in the price of pencils from P_1 to P_2 will cause the quantity demanded of pencils to fall more, from Q_1 to Q_3, as

[6]Other factors—for example, whether the item is important (housing) or unimportant (tooth-picks) in one's budget, or whether one has a strong desire or "need" for it—will also affect its price elasticity of demand.

more buyers shift to the now cheaper pens. In other words, the demand curve for pencils becomes more elastic, D_2 in the figure, and the movement is from R_1 to R_3 along D_2. If consumers consider that pencils and pens are perfect substitutes, the demand curve for pencils will be perfectly elastic (horizontal) at the original price, P_1, D_3 in the figure. This is, of course, the shape of the demand curve facing a perfectly competitive firm that produces a product that is perfectly substitutable for the products produced by every other firm in the industry.

A firm's power to raise price above marginal cost (its monopoly power) is inversely related to the elasticity of its demand curve, and hence, as we have seen, to the presence of substitutes.[7] If we define an industry as the collection of firms producing the same or similar products, we are essentially saying that the products of firms classified in the same industry are close substitutes, while those classified in different industries are not substitutes. Which substitutes are relevant, however, may be difficult to observe. If most consumers treat pencils, pens, and even typewriters as close substitutes, it is sensible to classify them in the same industry, and a single producer of all these items could be said to have a monopoly of writing implements. If a new writing implement (for example, word processing equipment) is now developed by a firm outside the industry, the elasticity of demand facing the original monopolist will increase, and its monopoly power will erode. In a sense, one could argue that any firm producing a product that is differentiated, however slightly, from those of all other firms has a monopoly of its product, and that since all goods are to some extent substitutes, pure monopoly cannot exist.[8]

However, for purposes of data collection, data classification, and empirical investigation, it is useful to identify product groups and to classify the firms supplying those products as belonging to one industry. To the extent that the classification draws industry boundaries so that not all appropriate substitutes are included for each industry, measures of monopoly power based on these classifications will be subject to error.[9] This does not mean that some monopoly

---

[7]If the firm's demand curve is expressed as p = f(q), and the elasticity of demand as

$$e \ = \ \frac{-dq}{dp} \ . \ \frac{p}{q}$$

then total revenue equals p.q and marginal revenue (MR) equals p (1 - 1/e). In equilibrium marginal revenue equals marginal cost (MC). Therefore, p (1 - 1/e) = MC and p = MC/ (1 -1/e)). Therefore, p and e are inversely related.

[8]If only one firm had the right to produce insulin (without which diabetic consumers would die) then the extent to which the monopolist could raise price without losing any sales volume at all would be limited only by consumers' incomes. This is an extreme example of pure monopoly.

[9]The *Standard Industrial Classification Manual* (1972, Executive Office of the President, Office of Management and Budget) lists the following distinct four-digit industries:

   3572 Typewriters,

   3951 Pens and Mechanical Pencils,

   3952 Lead Pencils, Crayons, and Artists' Materials.

This suggests that, at least for government classification purposes, substitutability in consumption is not the only relevant consideration in defining the product market. See Chapter 9, footnote 19, for a discussion of the limitations of the Standard Industrial Classification (SIC).

does not exist, but simply that it may be hard to observe and measure, and therefore that testing hypotheses about the economic effects of monopoly power is likely to prove difficult.

Notice, finally, that there is usually a geographical component in the definition of a market. For example, milk is much the same all over the country. Yet, for New Jersey residents, milk produced in Miami is not generally a viable substitute for milk produced in New Jersey because of its perishable nature and the cost of transportation. In this case, market boundaries may be as much the result of the relative costs and pricing policies of firms in different locations as of the inherent characteristics of the product.

Barriers To Entry

A second important problem in the definition of monopoly arises when we consider entry barriers. A perfectly competitive market system requires that resources be fully mobile between alternative uses. Thus, for example, an increase in demand for fish will raise prices and profits in the fishing industry and provide an incentive to firms from other, now relatively less profitable, industries to transfer resources to fishing. As we saw in Chapter 2, this shift of resources will allow the increased demand to be met with supply expansion greater than currently existing fishing firms can provide and will result in prices and profits falling once again.[10] Thus, industry expansion and contraction occurs in response to shifts in consumer demand. Of course, excess profits can also arise from changes on the cost side. A technological innovation that lowers the costs of existing firms will also raise their profits above normal. If resources are mobile, entry will occur, insuring that industry price falls to the new, lower level of minimum average cost.

An impediment to the flow of resources into an industry is called a barrier to entry; barriers to exit impede the flow of resources out of an industry. Both concepts are important for determining whether a firm truly possesses monopoly power. How best to define entry barriers and their significance for industry structure, monopoly in particular, has been the source of some controversy.[11] The role of exit barriers has recently received attention as well.

Legal Barriers   Entry into certain industries is forbidden or controlled by the government. For example, it is illegal to set up a radio station or carry first-class mail without a government license. Such entry regulations usually apply to the so-called public utilities, in which the government sanctions and preserves a monopoly market structure and regulates prices and profits. The historic, legal, and economic rationale for such regulation will be discussed at greater length in Chapter 13.

---

[10]Note that the final level of industry price and output will be determined by the shape of the long-run average cost curve for the industry. Only in the presence of constant costs will the price after entry be the same as the price that prevailed before the demand shift which induced the entry.

[11]See J. V. Koch, *Industrial Organization and Prices* (Englewood Cliffs, N.J.: Prentice-Hall, 1974), Chapters 5 and 6, for an excellent discussion.

Entry into certain occupations is controlled by government. For example, it is illegal to practice as a brain surgeon or a barber, trade on the commodities exchange, or oversee a firm's financial records without a government license or certificate. The supply of inputs to the industry—whether monopolistic or competitive—is thus limited by government policy. This is somewhat different from restricting entry into the industry which uses these inputs, providing all firms are free to compete for these scarce resources.[12]

Patents, which we also discuss below, are exclusive government-granted rights to a method of production or a product and are also a type of legal barrier to entry.

Economic Barriers   We use the term economic barriers to entry to encompass various circumstances that permit a monopolist to pursue policies—for example, pricing, product differentiation, advertising, and innovation—that successfully prevent the entry of new firms into the industry. There are two major categories: absolute cost advantages and scale economy advantages. Within the scale economy category we encounter the important concept of natural monopoly.

Absolute Cost Advantages   In the simplest case, shown in Figure 3.3, the monopolist's long-run average cost curve lies everywhere below the long-run average cost curve of the prospective entrant. (For simplicity, we have assumed constant costs, but this is not essential to the argument.) If the monopolist chooses any price below P_1, entry of a higher-cost firm is blocked at all output levels. Any price above P_2 will yield greater than normal profits for the monopolist, though not necessarily maximum profits.[13]

Absolute cost advantages can be traced to the exclusive ownership of inputs by incumbent firms. To take an extreme case, suppose a firm has the exclusive right to a certain crucial input without which production cannot take place. That firm will enjoy a monopoly of production. Patents are the prime example of this kind of barrier. Exclusive ownership of a mine or land with unique characteristics also falls into this category.

Note that a firm that, for example, owns the only diamond mine in the world also has the right to sell it. The price it sets is determined by the present value of the firm's stream of expected future profits. The buyer of the mine, therefore, would have to pay this high price to the selling monopolist, and, in the absence of unforeseen increases in demand or decreases in costs, all excess profits from the diamond business earned by the buyer would be eliminated.

---

[12]A key question here is what are the various political, economic, and social forces that cause individuals and groups to use government to establish laws that create entry barriers. Some answers to this question are offered in different parts of this book. For example, in this chapter, on page 75, we discuss the theory of rent-seeking, and in Chapter 15, on page 343, we discuss "capture" theories of regulation. In other places we refer to the origins of particular regulations, and the circumstances in which they were passed into law.

[13]The strategy of setting a price so as to prevent the entry of higher-cost firms is called stay-out or limit pricing. We will pursue the ramifications of this strategy at greater length in Chapter 4.

Figure 3.3   Absolute Cost Barrier to Entry

The long-run average cost of the established firm lies below the long-run average cost of the entrant because the established firm has exclusive ownership of particularly efficient inputs to which the entrant does not have access. If these inputs could be accurately measured and priced, the two cost curves would coincide.

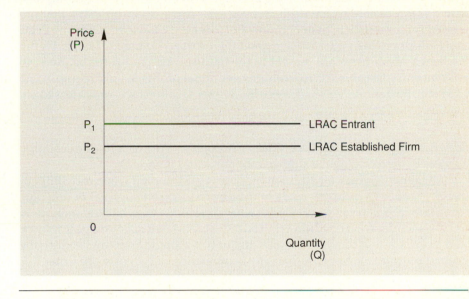

This phenomenon is called capitalization of rents and means that monopoly profits appear as excess profits only to the initial owner of the firm.[14] Once the firm changes hands, these profits enter the selling price and become a cost to the buying firm which, while still a monopoly, does not earn a monopoly return.[15]

This example has more general implications for the existence of absolute cost advantages. If all factors were measurable and replicable, and if market participants had perfect information, then any scarce, economically efficient factor of production would command a price and all firms would be on an equal footing to bid for the factor. This means that all firms would face the same cost curves; absolute cost differences would not exist. In practice, of course, there are many characteristics of the production activity and internal organization of firms which may not be measured or even perceived by firms without experience of producing the product. These characteristics are, in a sense, exclusively owned inputs. They may not be duplicated at all, or may be duplicated imperfectly. Technologically advanced, rapidly changing indus-

---

[14]See D. Dewey, *Microeconomics: The Analysis of Prices and Markets* (New York: Oxford University Press, 1975), 173-186, for a clear and detailed discussion of this point.

[15]Of course, if buyer and seller have been wrong in their estimation of future profits, then excess profits (or losses) may be earned by the buyer in the future.

tries are more prone to develop such absolute cost advantages since the existing firms innovate, take out patents, and target new markets at a fast rate, thereby creating informational gaps between themselves and potential entrants.[16]

Notice, however, that it is not necessarily true that an industry in which potential entrants face an absolute cost disadvantage will support only one firm. It is possible to have 10, or even 100, firms in an industry that are relatively more efficient than entrants. But for entry to be barred, existing firms must adopt pricing policies that exploit their cost advantage. Thus, in Figure 3.3, when many firms are present in the industry, keeping price below P_1 to prevent entry, but above P_2 to assure supernormal profits, would require some kind of collusion. As we shall argue in Chapter 4, collusion is much less likely if many firms are involved.[17]

Scale Economy Barriers: The Case of Natural Monopoly   We explain scale economy barriers by introducing the strange case of natural monopoly. [18]

In general terms, a natural monopoly is said to exist when the competitive process in an industry leads to the dominance and survival of only one firm. Two questions arise: (1) Under what conditions does natural monopoly exist? (2) Under what conditions is it sustainable? A natural monopoly may be said to exist in a particular market if and only if a single firm can produce the desired output at lower cost than any combination of two or more firms.[19] A natural monopoly is said to be sustainable if it is not profitable for rival firms to enter and provide viable competition.[20] Both existence and sustainability depend on the shape (characteristics) of the cost curves facing all producers rather than on absolute cost differences between firms. There is also a normative issue involved, namely that when natural monopoly is present, the appropriate government policy may be to designate that firm as a public utility. Government then regulates the firm's prices and profits to prevent it from exploiting its monopoly position at the expense of consumers.

The conditions for the existence and sustainability of natural monopoly, and the normative issue of appropriate governmental response will be dis-

---

[16]The personal computer industry may be an anomaly!

[17]It is possible, in perfect competition, for firms to have differences in average costs. Then the industry will be in equilibrium where price equals the average cost of the marginal (highest cost) firm, and the intramarginal (lower cost) firms will be earning economic rents. However, if, over time, the hidden efficient factors are priced and their rents capitalized, all firms will end up with identical cost curves. Our definition of barriers to entry leading to monopoly rests on the argument that the hidden factors which give rise to lower costs are not priced and that cost differences will persist creating the opportunity for stay-out pricing.

[18]It must be noted immediately that much recent theoretical and empirical work has revealed that the concept of natural monopoly and its relationship to economies of scale is complicated. (See William W. Sharkey, *The Theory of Natural Monopoly* [Cambridge, England: Cambridge University Press, 1982], for a complete exposition of the issues.) In this chapter we make only a brief foray into the difficult territory. In Chapter 13 we offer a more systematic introduction to the issues.

[19]Sharkey, *Theory of Natural Monopoly*, 54.

[20]Ibid.

Figure 3.4 Scale Economies as a Barrier to Entry

The established Firm A chooses its profit-maximizing output where LMC=MR at Q_1, and sets price at P_1.

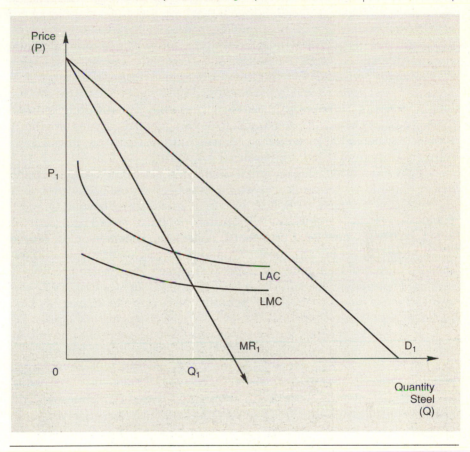

cussed systematically in Chapter 13. Since our task in this chapter is to explain how economies of scale can be a barrier to entry, we will not concern ourselves too much with unravelling the complexities of precise conditions. Rather we present a particular example to illustrate the relevant ideas.

Consider a firm that produces a single product, electricity (measured in kilowatt-hours). Both its long-run average cost curve, LAC, and its long-run marginal cost curve, LMC (which lies below LAC), in Figure 3.4, are declining over the relevant output range (that is, for output levels which lie to the left of the industry demand curve). The reasons for the decline may be loosely referred to as economies of scale, but, as we shall see, will almost always be the result of some significant indivisibility in the production process.

Assume first that Firm A is alone in the industry; it is a monopoly. The industry and Firm A's demand curves coincide at D_1 in Figure 3.4. The firm maximizes profits and produces where $MR_1 = LMC$, at output Q_1 and price P_1.

Now suppose a second firm, B, is waiting in the wings to enter the industry if it can make greater than normal profits by doing so. We assume that B faces exactly the same cost curves as A: LAC and LMC in Figure 3.4. Thus A has no absolute cost advantage over B. Suppose that Firm B assumes that Firm A will continue to produce Q_1 units of output regardless of what B does.[21] In order to sell additional units, Firm B must reduce price below P_1 and move along the residual demand curve, D_2 (the portion of A's demand curve which lies below P_1) shown in Figure 3.5.[22] Firm B's marginal revenue curve is therefore MR_2 in Figure 3.5, and its profit-maximizing output is Q_2; B's price is P_2. If the product is homogeneous, A is now also forced to sell output Q_1 at price P_2; total industry ouput is $Q_1 + Q_2$ which, by construction, lies on demand curve D_1 at point V. Firm A may not be happy with this outcome, since B's entry has forced down industry price from P_1 to P_2 and reduced A's profits.

Had A produced a higher output in the first place (and charged a lower price), B's residual demand curve would have been shifted backwards, making entry less profitable for B. If A were to increase output beyond Q_3 and to lower price below P_3 (see Figure 3.7), B's demand curve would necessarily lie below D_3. There would be no price that B could charge to make a profit. Indeed, A could simply set out to produce Q_3 and charge P_3 (or just below it) and thereby prevent B from entering in the first place. Thus A can preserve its monopoly position in the industry by charging a stay-out (or limit) price of P_3 and still make excess profits of RS per unit. Note also that P_3 exceeds LMC by RT.

In Figure 3.8, B's entry is prevented even if A charges a profit-maximizing price of P_1, since any price charged by B below P_1 (along residual demand curve D_2) will fail to cover long-run average costs; only one firm will survive, again creating a monopoly situation.

This definition of a barrier to entry due to scale economies depends crucially on the assumption that B makes about A's behavior on learning of B's attempt to enter. If B continues to assume that A will maintain its output, then even if A fails to charge the entry-limiting price and B enters, A may actually expand output sufficiently fast so that B's profits will be eliminated. There is an alternative, however: A may merge or form a cartel with B and both firms will presumably pursue an entry-limiting price to prevent any further entry.

[21]This assumption is known as the Sylos postulate (see Chapter 4). A detailed discussion of the implications of this assumption can be found in F. M. Scherer, *Industrial Market Structure and Economic Performance*, 2d ed.(Chicago: Rand McNally, 1980), 244.

[22]Construction of the residual demand curve is described as follows (see Figure 3.6). Firm A initially confronts demand curve D_1, and sells output Q_1 at price P_1. The residual demand curve is obtained by subtracting Q_1 from every output point on D_1, since at every price B can sell the market demand less the Q_1 units which A is supplying. Graphically we simply shift D_1 back toward the vertical axis by distance OQ_1 (a parallel shift). The residual demand curve is thus D_2. Notice that it originates at P_1 (at this price, no additional or residual output is demanded). Were A to sell ouput Q_3, B's residual demand curve, obtained in precisely the same way would be D_3. Here Q_3 units of output (horizontal distance OQ_3) would be subtracted from D_1 at every point. The residual demand curve envisioned by Firm B thus depends directly upon the output (and price) choice made by A.

Figure 3.5 Scale Economy Barriers to Entry: The View of the Entrant

With industry output (shown in Figure 3.4) at D_1, and Firm A producing output Q_1, Firm B's residual demand curve is D_2. B will maximize profits by producing where MR_2 = LMC, that is, Q_2 units of output. B's best price is now P_2. Total industry output will now be A's output plus B's output, that is, $Q_1 + Q_2$. This output can only be sold at B's price P_2. Note that price P_2 lies below A's original price P_1.

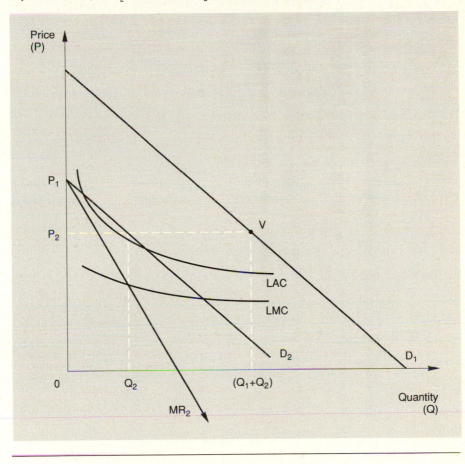

We thus see that a situation in which only one firm will survive the competitive process may depend not just on cost, but also on demand and the behavioral interactions between established firms and potential entrants.

Note that in our original example we assumed that all firms face identical cost curves. This is a strong assumption, especially if the technology of production requires large and complex equipment. Yet Harold Demsetz has argued, precisely on the basis of this assumption, that the presence of decreasing costs per se is no barrier to a competitive result.[23] He argues that as long as

---

[23]H. Demsetz, "Why Regulate Utilities?" *Journal of Law and Economics*, 11 (April 1968): 55–65.

Figure 3.6 The Residual Demand Curve

With industry demand at D_1, potential entrant Firm B assumes that established firm A will continue to produce Q_1 units of output. At price P_1 the market will only absorb Q_1 units, and there is no demand for B's output. If price falls below P_1, then Firm B can supply the market demand minus the Q_1 units which Firm A is continually supplying. Thus B's demand curve is curve D_1 minus Q_1 units, or D_2. When B assumes that A will continue to produce Q_3 output units, then B's demand curve shifts back to D_3. Note that B's residual demand curve will originate on the price axis at that price at which all A's output is just absorbed by the market.

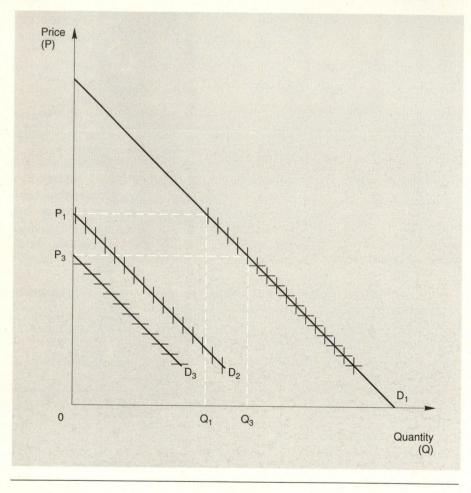

a customer is in a position to make a new contract each year for the supply of a product, there is no reason to accept the established firm's offer if it is not the best. It may not be the best if both established firms and entrants face the same cost curves, that is, there is no absolute cost advantage for incumbents. As long as there are many supply offers from potential producers, the actual supplier may differ each year. The final price will not be a monopoly price but a

Figure 3.7 Scale Economy Barriers to Entry: The Stay-Out Price

If Firm A chooses to produce Q_3 units of output and sell them at price P_3, then Firm B's residual demand curve, D_3, will lie just below LAC and there is no output at which B can enter and make a profit. P_3 is therefore the stay-out price.

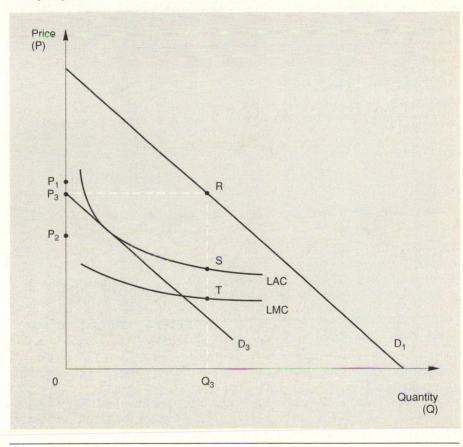

competitive one, achieved by competition among potential producers to be the sole supplier for the coming year.

A detailed consideration of the transaction costs involved in making contracts suggests that Demsetz's view of the power of potential entry is overly optimistic.[24] Once a firm is established in an industry, it may have many opportunities to renew contracts with buyers which new firms do not have, apart from technological advantages it enjoys as a result of past production

---

[24]See especially, O. E. Williamson, *Markets and Hierarchies: Analysis and Antitrust Implications* (New York: The Free Press, 1975).

Figure 3.8 Scale Economy Barriers to Entry with Relatively Low Demand

With industry demand at D_1, Firm A selects output Q_1 (where $MR_1 = LMC$) and charges price P_1. At this price, B's residual demand curve lies everywhere below LAC, and B will not enter.

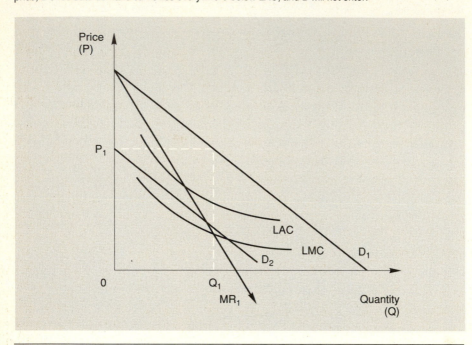

experience.[25] However, Demsetz's point that a competitive price could result from a natural monopoly is not at odds with our conclusion that the final price and output combination in an industry characterized by substantially decreasing average costs depends on cost, demand, and behavioral conditions that are likely to vary widely from case to case.

Barriers to Exit

For publicly regulated firms, barriers to exit frequently take the form of a government requirement that these firms must provide goods or services to all customers whether or not it is profitable to do so. For example, the U.S. Postal Service must provide mail service to all those who request it. (Recall our

---

[25]Williamson's emphasis on the complexity of making contracts mirrors the idea that it is the nonreplicability and nonmeasurability of factors of production which create absolute cost advantages for the established firm. Since production cannot take place without contracts with input suppliers and customers, the opportunity of the established firm to make more favorable contracts than a potential entrant may be sufficient to deter entry even if the technological cost structure facing both firms is identical. In this case, the nonreplicability of contracts is the source of entry barriers, and Demsetz's fundamental assumption that incumbents have no absolute cost advantage is disputed.

discussion of the legal history of government regulation in Chapter 1.) Firms charged with the obligation to provide service to all are called common carriers. In return for assuming such duties, government protects their monopoly status. Thus, legal barriers to exit are often accompanied by legal barriers to entry.[26]

For unregulated firms, a short-run barrier to exit exists when the firm has invested funds in fixed capital that cannot easily be liquidated. As long as price exceeds average variable costs (that is, as long as revenues more than cover running costs), the losses from an unprofitable business will be reduced by continued operation rather than by immediate shutdown. In the long run, of course, all unprofitable, unregulated businesses will close as creditors become impatient.

The existence of short-run impediments to exit because of sunk costs paradoxically has implications for entry barriers.[27] Recall our original example of scale economy barriers in which the established firm is A and the potential entrant is B. If Firm B recognizes that its entry will force down industry price and threaten the profits of both firms, it may be more reluctant to enter. This is especially true if entry involves investment in fixed capital that cannot easily be recovered. If, on the other hand, Firm B expects a rapid sale of its equipment should it be necessary to recoup its fixed costs, and believes that industry price will fall only after a lag, then it may enter in order to earn excess profits for a short time. Thus B's entry is more likely if B perceives no barriers to exit should entry turn out to be unprofitable.

In conclusion, recall our original definition: A monopoly exists when there is one firm in an industry, producing a product for which there are no close substitutes, and where barriers to entry are high. Over time, monopoly power may be reduced by the production of substitutes that increase the elasticity of the industry demand curve and by the dissemination of information that increases the opportunity for potential entrants to replicate or purchase exclusively owned factors of production.

However, controversy arises over the importance of barriers to entry for the perpetuation of monopoly. There are several schools of thought. One, following Stigler, maintains that the only true barriers to entry are legal barriers.[28] Absolute cost barriers result from the failure of the price system to reflect

---

[26]The necessity for legal barriers to entry to protect the monopoly status of common carriers is part of the dispute about the deregulation of industries such as transportation and communications. Some argue, for example, that in the absence of government-enforced barriers to exit, deregulation of trucking or telephones will mean that small rural communities will not receive service because they have relatively low demand and are costly to serve. Profit-maximizing firms would exit from these routes unless forced by law to remain. To protect the monopoly status and revenue earning capacity of these firms on their more profitable routes, legal entry barriers are needed. (See D. Dewey, "Neglected Issues in Collective Rate-Making," *Third DANA/ATA/ Foundation Academic Symposium* (Stanford University, December 8–9, 1981).

[27]See W. J. Baumol, J. C. Panzar, and R. D. Willig, *Contestable Markets and the Theory of Industrial Structure* (New York: Harcourt Brace Jovanovich, 1982).

[28]G. J. Stigler, *The Organization of Industry* (Homewood, Ill.: Richard D. Irwin, 1968).

hidden (or unmeasurable) factors of production.[29] Scale economy advantages, which permit the established firm to produce at a higher output and sell at a lower price, may have the effect of excluding potential entrants. However, as long as both the established and entering firms face the same cost curves, the fact that the established firm is in a position to exclude the entrant does not reflect a barrier but rather the working of the competitive process.

Another school of thought, following Bain, argues that since legal barriers, absolute cost advantages, and economies of scale in fact result in the exclusion of new firms, they are all true barriers to entry.[30]

The disagreement between these two schools of thought is basically one of definition, though it may well imply divergent views about the importance of entry barriers. The Bain view implies a rather wider role for government intervention (if one believes that barriers require intervention) since entry barriers, and hence monopoly power, will be found more often under this definition than under the Stigler definition. At the same time, one might accept the Bain definition yet argue that some of what it includes as barriers are socially harmless, or at least not worth correcting.

A more recent view of the mobility of resources, and barriers to mobility, emerges from the work of Williamson and others on transactions costs.[31] As we described in Chapter 1, every market transaction involves an implicit or explicit contract between the transactors. The contracts may be simple or complicated depending on circumstances, but all impose costs, small or large, on the transactors. Firms can be viewed as institutions which economize on transactions costs by taking transactions out of the marketplace and organizing production within another type of institutional (often hierarchical) setting. Thus, for example, a firm which produces automobiles may either purchase tires from a tire-producing firm, or it may make the tires itself. If it purchases from another firm, it must draw up a contract with the tire producer for delivery of a certain quantity of tires at a certain time. If it produces the tires itself, it must plan its production schedule in its own tire division. The costs of each type of contract may be different. In any case, the firm must then make contracts with buyers of automobiles to sell the finished product. The network of contracts which each firm needs in order to carry out a competitive business may take time and energy to set in place. There may be substantial cost advantages for an established firm that has been able to build up a network of goodwill with suppliers and customers, thus reducing transactions costs. A new entrant may not have immediate access to this network, even though the entrant's production costs are the same or lower than the established firm's. Thus the sum of transactions and production costs may often be higher for a

---

[29]An extreme argument may be made that, if markets work properly, all hidden factors will always be priced, all firms will always face the same cost curves, and absolute cost advantages will never exist. The measurement problems of verifying these kinds of arguments are enormous.

[30]J. S. Bain, *Barriers to New Competition* (Cambridge, Mass.: Harvard University Press, 1965).

[31] See Oliver E. Williamson, *The Economic Institutions of Capitalism* (New York: The Free Press, 1985).

new entrant and a barrier to entry is the result. (Williamson investigates the circumstances bearing on the ease of entry.) The prescriptions for appropriate government policy depend also on the specific firm and industry characteristics at issue.

We now turn to the basic case for government intervention in the presence of monopoly.

MONOPOLY: GOOD OR BAD?

Evaluations of economic policy require a clear understanding of social goals. In this section we present the traditional static case against monopoly as a form of market organization, drawing on the ideas developed in Chapter 2. We then introduce an important complication to the argument—the theory of the second best. Finally we consider some dynamic issues.

The Static Case against Monopoly

Efficiency   We saw in Chapter 2 that perfect competition yields a Pareto optimal allocation of resources such that any reshuffling of inputs among competing uses, products among consumers, or change in the relative quantities of products produced, cannot make anyone better off without making another person worse off. More specifically, we developed the conditions necessary for a Pareto optimal allocation of resources and showed how a perfectly competitive system would satisfy these conditions. Since a monopolist sets prices higher than the perfectly competitive price and produces a lower output, the overall allocation of resources is different from the competitive allocation and hence from the Pareto optimal allocation. One therefore suspects that society will be less well off under monopoly.

To pursue this suspicion, we introduce a simple partial equilibrium framework to which we can refer in later chapters.[32] Consider a single industry, steel, which is perfectly competitive. In Figure 3.9, D is the industry demand curve. S is the industry supply curve (horizontal, implying constant marginal and average costs).[33] The competitive price, P_c, is determined where supply equals demand, at output Q_c—point B in Figure 3.9.

To show that the competitive price is also the social welfare maximizing price, let us define the net social benefit (welfare) generated by the production of steel as:

---

[32]In partial equilibrium analysis, we consider one market at a time. We assume that Pareto optimality conditions are satisfied elsewhere in the economy and that all demand and supply curves in every other market remain constant. General equilibrium analysis allows us to consider the interaction between all markets in the economy and is, of course, a great deal more complicated. Our partial equilibrium welfare approach is based on the classic article by O. E. Williamson, "Peak-Load Pricing and Optimal Capacity under Indivisibility Constraints," *American Economic Review* 56 (1966): 810–827.

[33]Constant costs for the industry do not imply that marginal or average costs for constituent firms are horizontal (recall Chapter 2). Were that the case in a perfectly competitive market, the size of the firm would be indeterminate.

Figure 3.9 Monopoly and Perfect Competition Compared

The competitive price and output combination is P_c, Q_c. The monopoly price and output are P_m, Q_m. Net welfare under competition is area P_cFB, and under monopoly is area P_cFAC. The net welfare loss due to monopoly is the difference between these two areas, namely triangle ABC.

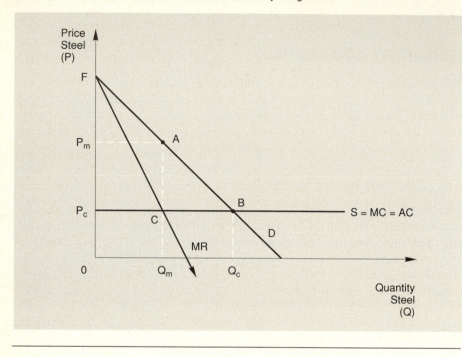

$$W = TR + CS - (TC - R)$$

where W is net social welfare, TR is total revenue, CS is consumers' surplus, TC is total cost, and R is intramarginal rent.

Total revenue (TR) is the price of the product, P, multiplied by the number of units sold, Q. Whether or not a fall or rise in price, which generates a rise or fall in the quantity sold, increases or decreases total revenue depends on the elasticity of the demand curve at that point.[34]

Consumers' surplus (CS) is a measure of the amount by which the total benefit accruing to consumers from the consumption of any amount of a product exceeds the amount they actually pay. In Figure 3.9, suppose the quantity bought by consumers is Q_m. The price which induces consumers to buy the last unit of Q_m is P_m—this is called the reservation price. However, when nothing is produced, the price which induces consumers to buy the first unit of steel is just below OF. This means that consumers' willingness to pay for the first unit of Q_m is a great deal higher than their willingness to pay for the last

---

[34]See p. 54.

unit. Indeed, the price must fall from OF if consumers are to increase their purchases along demand curve D. This reflects the diminishing value which consumers put on marginal units as the quantity they buy increases. If we sum over all units the willingness to pay for each marginal unit, we can identify the total willingness to pay for Q_m units as equal to the area $OFAQ_m$. Since, for Q_m units, consumers only pay P_m per unit—so that their total expenditure on Q_m units is equal to area OP_mAQ_m—the purchase of Q_m units at P_m generates a consumer's surplus equal to area P_mFA. Consumers' surplus is then defined as the excess of consumers' total willingness to pay for a given quantity over what consumers actually do pay, that is, over total revenue. It is a monetary measure of the net benefit which consumers derive from the purchase and consumption of a product.[35]

Total cost (TC) is the cost of all factors of production, reflecting the full social cost of production activity. (In Figure 3.9 the total cost of producing Q_m units of output equals the area OP_cCQ_m.) If, in the process of production, the firm imposes external costs on society (for example, in the form of noxious waste discharges), then the total private cost to the firm will diverge from the social costs of its activity. Since we are engaged in creating a measure of net social welfare, the total cost measure should include full social cost. Alternatively, we can assume the absence of external costs, in which case, total and private costs will coincide.

In a perfectly competitive system, if the supply curve for a commodity is upward sloping, and the market price and quantity are P_1 and Q_1 respectively in Figure 3.10, then the shaded area between the price line and the supply curve is a measure of intramarginal rent (R). It is the sum of payments to all factors of production before the last (to the intramarginal factors) beyond that necessary to keep them in the industry. These rents disappear when the supply curve is completely elastic. Therefore, to the extent that factors are in scarce supply, intramarginal rents are a measure of surplus earned by the suppliers of factors.

Assume for simplicity that factors of production are available in perfectly elastic supply, and therefore that intramarginal rent, R, is zero. Thus, our measure of social welfare, W, equals $(TR + CS) - TC$. We can now view it as the excess of the total value to the consumer from consuming the product ($TR + CS$ equals the entire area under the demand curve) over the total cost to society (borne by producers) of producing the commodity.[36] When we write W as $CS + (TR - TC)$, we see that it equals the sum of consumer's surplus plus excess profits earned by producers. The use of this measure of welfare therefore involves adding welfare across different groups. It implies, for example, that if some policy change causes consumer's surplus to increase and excess profit

---

[35]Extensive literature is devoted to assessing the theoretical and empirical legitimacy of the concept of consumer's surplus. For a critical approach and introduction to the literature, see P. Asch and R. S. Seneca, "The Demand Curve and Welfare Change: A Reconsideration," *Journal of Post Keynesian Economics* 11 (Spring 1980): 392–404.

[36]In mathematical terms: $TR + CS = \int P.dQ$.

Figure 3.10 Intramarginal Rent

Each point on the upward sloping supply curve S represents the price which must be paid to induce the firm to produce each corresponding output. When output Q_1 is produced, each output unit commands a price of P_1. The difference between this price and the price which would in fact have induced production is called intramarginal rent, and is represented by the shaded area.

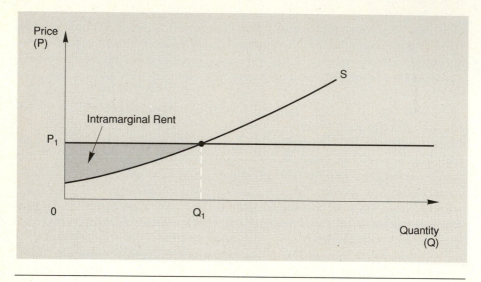

to decrease by a smaller amount, then social welfare increases on balance even though producers are made worse off by the change.[37]

The ethical underpinnings of this approach are controversial.[38] One rationale, noted by Williamson, is that the theoretical apparatus of partial welfare economics allows us "to derive benchmark relations, if nothing else, and as there is no well-specified alternative (the claim that our assumptions are not obviously satisifed needs to be articulated before it becomes useful), we will proceed on this basis."[39]

Our objective is to find that level of output which maximizes W, and the corresponding price. In Figure 3.9 this occurs where price (P_c) equals industry

[37]We develop the W measure as a means of comparing the allocative efficiency of two different states of the world, but it is immediately obvious that W involves distributional considerations which are supposed to be avoided in discussions of efficiency. One unconvincing way out is to assert that as long as the gainers from a policy change can compensate the losers, then welfare has increased. However, as long as the compensation is not actually paid, the distributional question remains.

[38]See I. M. D. Little, *A Critique of Welfare Economics*, 2d ed. (London: Oxford University Press, 1957).

[39]Williamson, "Peak-Load Pricing," 811. See also Paul L. Joskow and Roger C. Noll, "Regulation in Theory and Practice: An Overview," in Gary Fromm, ed., *Studies in Public Regulation* (Cambridge, Mass.: MIT Press, 1983) for a full discussion of benchmarks for comparison in regulated industries.

marginal cost at output Q_c.[40] At Q_c net welfare, W_c, is given by:

$$W_c = OP_cBQ_c + P_cFB - OP_cBQ_c = P_cFB.$$

$$\text{(TR)} \qquad \text{(CS)} \qquad \text{(TC)}$$

No other uniform price will yield as large a welfare area.

Now consider the same industry organized as a monopoly. We make the major assumption that neither the demand nor cost structure of the industry is changed from that obtained under perfect competition. The monopolist's demand curve is D, the same industry demand curve as before. Its marginal cost curve is horizontal and identical to the competitive supply curve at S = MC. The profit-maximizing price and output for the monopolist occur where marginal revenue (MR in Figure 3.9) equals marginal cost, at Q_mP_m.[41] Excess profits, defined as TR – TC, are now earned and equal to the area P_cP_mAC. Net social welfare is now:

$$W_m = OP_mAQ_m + P_mFA - OP_cCQ_m = P_cFAC$$

$$\text{(TR)} \qquad \text{(CS)} \qquad \text{(TC)}$$

This area is less than $W_c = P_cFB$, by triangle ABC. The effect of the monopoly has been to raise price above marginal cost and to reduce output from Q_c to Q_m. Resources valued at Q_mCBQ_c are thereby released to be reabsorbed elsewhere in the economy (in less valuable uses). The area ABC represents a net loss of consumer's surplus or willingness to pay, commonly referred to as the deadweight loss triangle. It is the satisfaction that consumers forego by not receiving Q_mQ_c units of steel. It is also a monetary measure of the lost utility, and hence of the Pareto inefficiency, induced by monopoly pricing.

Both intuitively and diagrammatically it is obvious that a monopolist will charge higher prices than a competitive market, other things being equal, and will produce less. This is clearly undesirable for consumers as a general rule; however, it is desirable for monopolistic sellers, whose profits swell.

What our analysis has demonstrated is that monopoly is socially costly in the following sense: it invariably hurts consumers more—by a larger dollar amount—than it helps sellers, and thus generates a net social loss. This par-

---

[40]Differentiating we have:

$$\frac{dW}{dQ} = \frac{d(TR + CS)}{dQ} - \frac{dTC}{dQ} = 0.$$

Now $\frac{d(TR+CS)}{dQ}$ is the first derivative of total value with respect to quantity; this is marginal value or price in this context. $\frac{dTC}{dQ}$ is the first derivative of total cost with respect to quantity and is equal to marginal cost. Thus we have

$$\frac{d(TR + CS)}{dQ} = \frac{dTC}{dQ} \text{ or } P = MC.$$

[41]Note that we are assuming that a single uniform price is to be charged, that is, each output unit is sold at the same price. Other pricing systems may also be adopted (first-degree price discrimination, for example) that will yield the efficient output. We discuss price discrimination at the end of this chapter and in Chapter 11; and other types of pricing in Chapter 14.

ticular analysis is diagrammatically straightforward, but it is unfortunately not so clear intuitively. Consider a slightly different route to the same point.

Referring to the Pareto optimality conditions in Chapter 2, we saw that Condition 3 was automatically achieved under perfect competition:[42]

$$\frac{MU_x}{MU_y} = \frac{MC_x}{MC_y}$$

This condition means that the relative value that consumers put on the marginal units of X and Y is just equal to their relative marginal costs.

Suppose now that Industry X is a monopoly. In Industry X, $P_x > MC_x$ and for the two-industry (X and Y) economy

$$\frac{P_x}{P_y} > \frac{MC_x}{MC_y}$$

Since consumers are still maximizing utility we have:

$$\frac{MU_x}{MU_y} = \frac{P_x}{P_y} > \frac{MC_x}{MC_y}$$

In other words, quantities of X and Y are consumed such that the satisfaction enjoyed by consumers for the last unit of X (relative to the satisfaction gained from the last unit of Y) is greater than the relative marginal cost of X compared with Y. Good X is being produced in a quantity that is too small in the sense that at least some could be made better off and no one worse off if more X and less Y were produced. Thus, once again, we conclude that the effect of a monopoly is to reduce allocative efficiency by holding industry output below its optimal level.

We now consider the effect of uniform monopoly pricing on equity, and then discuss losses due to rent-seeking behavior.

Equity In Figure 3.9 we saw that price is higher and output lower under monopoly, $P_m Q_m$, than under competition, $P_c Q_c$. Furthermore, under competition excess profits are zero, and consumer's surplus generated by the sale of Q_c units at price P_c, is equal to $P_c FB$.

Under monopoly, excess profits are $P_c P_m AC$ (= (TR–TC)) and consumer's surplus is equal to triangle $P_m FA$ yielding a total net social benefit for the production of Q_m units equal to $P_c FAC$.

---

[42]Recall that this occurred because consumers and producers are utility and profit maximizers and face the same set of prices. Thus we have

$$\frac{MU_x}{MU_y} = \frac{P_x}{P_y} = \frac{MC_x}{MC_y}$$

Under competition the area P_cP_mAC is part of the consumer's surplus triangle P_cFB. The change in industrial organization from competition to monopoly, therefore, involves a redistribution of income from the consumers to producers of steel.[43] Whether or not such a redistribution is desirable depends on judgments about the merits and/or needs of the gainers (steel producers) and losers (steel consumers). This is not a strictly economic issue.

Consider, for example, the unlikely case in which the steel firm which earned monopoly profits was entirely owned by widows and orphans with no alternative income sources, while consumers of steel belonged to the wealthiest group in society. The monopoly profits of the firm would then cause a redistribution of income from wealthy consumers to poor producers. A society that viewed the existing distribution of income as unfair might regard such a redistribution as desirable. The more likely case, however, is that owners of the monopoly firm are already better off than the consumers, and the redistributive effect of the monopoly away from consumers toward the owners of the firm is more likely to be regressive.[44] In any case we need a coherent theory of justice to evaluate the desirability of the redistribution.

The Social Cost of Rent-seeking Behavior   A different measure of the loss due to monopoly has been offered by Richard Posner who has suggested that the efficiency loss due to monopoly is much larger than area ABC in Figure 3.9.[45] Posner focused on the area of excess profits earned by the monopolist, area P_mACP_c. He argued that much or all of these monopoly profits are used by the firm's owners to acquire and maintain their monopoly position, through lobbying and other activities designed to achieve favorable treatment by government. This converts what we have called the redistributive transfer (from consumers to producers) into a type of social waste. The entire profits area, P_mACP_c, should then be added to the welfare loss triangle to yield a much higher efficiency loss than the area ABC. However, it may not be appropriate to attribute the entire profits area P_mACP_c to rent-seeking waste. The monopolist need only push its marginal expenditure to the point of equality with the marginal benefits of that expenditure (using some measure of political effectiveness). That expenditure may well be less than the amount of the entire profits area.

[43]The term "producers of steel" means all those groups who earn income from steel-producing activity—including stockholders, managers, workers, and input suppliers. However, the division of excess profits in steel among these groups may vary, depending, for example, on the elasticity of supply of different factors. If skilled workers or particular inputs are in scarce supply, they may command higher prices than inputs which are abundant. (Recall, however, that a constant supply (MC) curve for the industry already assumes perfectly elastic factor supplies.)

[44]W. S. Comanor and R. H. Smiley, "Monopoly and the Distribution of Wealth," *Quarterly Journal of Economics* 89 (May 1975): 177–194, have provided a rare empirical attempt to estimate the effect of monopoly on the distribution of wealth and have concluded that it is strongly regressive.

[45] R.A. Posner, "The Social Costs of Monopoly and Regulation," *Journal of Political Economy* 83 (August 1975): 807–827.

The Theory of the Second Best [46]

The apparently neat conclusion that the effect of a monopoly is to reduce allocative efficiency is unfortunately not as useful for policy as it might first appear.

The second best theory argues that when the economy is a mixture of competitive and noncompetitive markets, a change in the status of one market yields no generally predictable implication. Suppose that the steel industry is monopolistic and the cotton textile industry is competitive. Too little steel (and too much cotton) are produced. Moreover, outputs in a variety of industries related to steel will be too low. Fewer cars, for example, will be produced because steel is underproduced and overpriced. Similarly, there will be less demand for automobile workers, for tires and tubes, and for rubber and other materials used in the production of tires. In contrast, production of steel substitutes will be encouraged by the steel monopoly, and may be overproduced, as are cotton textiles and its complements. There is, in other words, a myriad of allocative distortions.

Given this situation, suppose we ask: Is it worthwhile to encourage more competition in the production of a different product, say alcoholic beverages, which happens to be a partial monopoly? The strict answer provided by the theory of second best is: *a priori*, we cannot tell. To introduce more competition in alcoholic beverages will set off another series of changes—more production in alcohol and some related markets, less production in others. Will allocative welfare overall be better once these changes work themselves out? Who knows?

Since public policy toward competition is usually piecemeal, affecting just one or a few industries at a time, the question raised by second best arguments is a pertinent one.[47] At times it is even important.[48] However, second best should not be interpreted to mean that all policies affecting the competitive status of any market have completely unknown and unpredictable implications. The lesson of second best theory is rather that the implications may be quite involved and need to be defined.

---

[46]See the classic article by R. G. Lipsey and K. Lancaster, "The General Theory of Second Best," *Review of Economic Studies* 24 (October 1956): 11–32.

[47]There is a large body of literature about second-best theory and its implications for policy. One clear and accessible summary, which also contains ample references, can be found in "Reflections of an Applied Welfare Economist," Presidential Address presented at the Annual Meeting of the Association of Environmental and Resource Economists, September 6, 1980, Denver, Colorado, by J. V. Krutilla, published in *The Journal of Environmental Economics and Management* 8 (1981): 1–10.

[48]An example is the case of the polluting monopolist. Both monopoly and external (pollution) costs are likely to be socially harmful, and an ideal public policy would deal optimally with both problems. In the absence of an optimal policy toward pollution, however, the "best" policy toward monopoly is less clear; and vice versa. Despite this, the Department of Justice (which deals with monopoly) and the Environmental Protection Agency (which treats pollution problems) show no sign of coordinating their policy efforts. For a discussion of the issues, see Chapter 22.

Figure 3.11   First-Degree Price Discrimination

With demand at D and marginal revenue MR, a profit-maximizing monopolist will charge uniform price P_m, sell output Q_m, and earn profits equal to P_mBCF. With perfect price discrimination, the monopolist produces Q_D, and earns profits equal to JAGH.

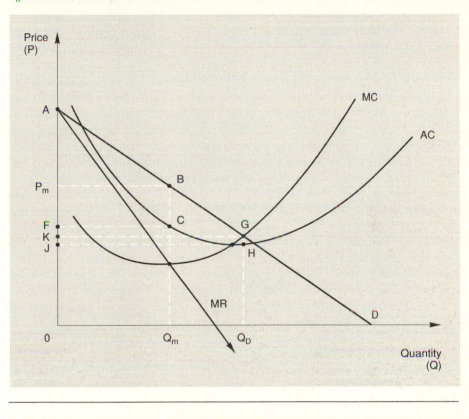

We now consider a different form of monopoly pricing which has implications for both efficiency and equity—price discrimination.

Price Discrimination   To this point, we have argued that a profit-maximizing monopoly firm will charge a price higher than marginal cost, which generates allocative efficiency losses. However, monopoly power often permits a firm to pursue a different kind of policy—price discrimination. Price discrimination occurs when the price-to-marginal-cost ratio for a commodity differs for different customers or groups of customers. It can persist only if the groups are separated and arbitrage is impossible. This is often the case for the services produced by regulated firms, for example, electricity, telephone calls, toll bridges. Price discrimination will often enable the monopolist to earn more profits than would be possible under a uniform pricing system. Conceivably, one may regard this result as inequitable, yet it may be accompanied by an improvement in efficiency.

To understand these points, consider first the extreme case of price discrimination known as perfect or first-degree discrimination.[49] In Figure 3.11, D is the demand curve for a service and MR is the marginal revenue curve; the average and marginal cost curves are AC and MC, as shown. The profit-maximizing monopolist who can charge only a uniform price will produce where MR = MC, at Q_m, and will charge price P_m, earning excess profits of P_mBCF. (The consumer's surplus generated by the $P_m Q_m$ combination is P_mAB and net welfare is FABC.) Now consider a situation in which each consumer buys only one unit of the commodity and the monopolist knows the maximum willingness-to-pay of each consumer for that one unit. Rank the consumers by their maximum willingness to pay, so that any point on demand curve D shows the maximum willingness to pay for the last unit by the marginal customer. (This is simply another way of looking at the conventional demand curve.) The monopolist, knowing each consumer's maximum willingness to pay, charges each consumer that maximum price. The marginal revenue curve will then coincide with the demand curve. The profit-maximizing output, where the maximum willingness-to-pay for the last consumer equals marginal cost, is now Q_D. Note that Q_D is a higher output than Q_m. It is in fact equal to the competitive output level, which occurs where the demand curve intersects the marginal cost curve.[50] Total revenue is now the total area under the demand curve, OAGQ$_D$; total cost is OJHQ$_D$. Profits are equal to the difference between total revenue and total cost, that is, JAGH. Thus the monopolist has extracted the full consumer's surplus from every consumer.

However, Q_D is also the output for which P = MC. Now the uniform price that maximizes net welfare is OK, yielding a net welfare equal to JAGH. If the government were to regulate the monopolist's price at marginal cost, the same output would result as is produced with perfect price discrimination. The difference would lie in the distribution of gains. The perfectly discriminating monopolist takes the whole area JAGH, whereas under marginal cost pricing, consumers take AGK of that area, and only KGHJ remains for the firm.

The fact that the output under perfect price discrimination is identical to the welfare-maximizing output—albeit with a different distribution of gains—makes it difficult to argue that price discrimination is invariably undesirable. Indeed, there are cases wherein price discrimination makes it possible for a

---

[49]Most microtheory texts have discussions of price discrimination. A particularly full discussion is in S. T. Call and W. T. Holahan, *Microeconomics* (Belmont, Calif.: Wadsworth Publishing Company, 1980): 292–302.

[50]The comparison between the output of the discriminating monopolist and the perfectly competitive industry's output is a short-run comparison in which the short-run MC curve of the monopolist can be directly compared with the industry supply under competition. In the long run, the competitive supply curve is considerably more complicated (recall Chapter 2, p. 32) as is the comparison.

monopolist to stay in business when uniform pricing would not, and when it is in society's interest to have the monopoly service produced. (We consider this possibility further in Chapter 14.)

It is not clear, however, that one would seriously propose perfect price discrimination as a regulatory solution to the problem of natural monopoly. It would surely be perceived by many as inequitable even if its effect on the existing income distribution were not regressive. Moreover, in practice, it is unlikely that any firm could identify the maximum willingness-to-pay of individual consumers. It might, however, be able to approximate by dividing them into groups. This is sometimes called second-degree discrimination. Alternatively, the firm might, for each commodity and each consumer, charge a higher unit price for a small number of units, reducing unit price as the size of purchases grows. Such *volume* or *quantity* discounts plainly induce consumers to buy larger amounts of the monopolist's goods. Note, however, that a consumer cannot be forced to buy the marginal unit if her maximum willingness-to-pay does not exceed the actual price by at least a small amount.

In Chapter 11 we discuss third-degree price discrimination, and in Chapter 14 continue the discussion of first-degree price discrimination as a regulatory policy.

The Dynamic Effects of Monopoly

The dynamic effects of monopoly power on efficiency over time cannot, even in theory, be separated from equity issues. For if the effect of monopoly is to increase economic growth over time, then the economic well-being of people in all income groups may be improved even while rich stockholders of powerful firms gain relative to poor consumers.

To evaluate such a possibility would require a more careful look at the theory of social choice. We turn here to a more detailed discussion of the dynamic effects of monopoly in industrial organization.

When we discuss economic growth in terms of the economy as a whole, we often start by listing the main factors that shift a society's production possibility curve outward: technical progress, growth in the labor force, and capital investment. New investment means giving up consumption today in order to make capital goods that can be used to produce more (consumption and capital) goods in the future. In a free enterprise system, growth-generating circumstances work through individual firms. Firms will undertake cost-reduction investment and develop new products if they have access to the necessary information, technology, and capital, and if they believe that these activities will be profitable.

The question now at issue is not what causes firms to innovate, but more specifically, whether the market structure within which the firm operates will affect its propensity to innovate; and, if so, how. The answer is important. So far the main case against monopoly is that industry output at any moment is below the optimal (and, *ceteris paribus*, below the competitive market) level. But if a monopoly market structure generates lower costs over time, then the

Figure 3.12 The Dynamic Benefits from Monopoly

With marginal costs MC_1 the competitive price is P_c, where MC_1 intersects the industry demand curve D. If the industry is dominated by a rapidly innovating monopolist who discovers cost curve MC_2, the monopoly output wil be Q_m where MR = MC_2, and the monopoly price will be P_m, lower than P_c.

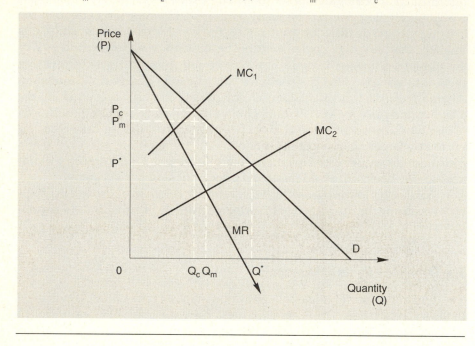

dynamic gains from monopoly may eventually outweigh the static efficiency losses.[51]

In Figure 3.12, industry marginal cost under competition is MC_1, industry demand is D, and the competitive price and output are P_c and Q_c. If the marginal cost under monopoly is much lower, at MC_2, because of the monopolist's vigorous innovation, then the monopoly price will be lower at P_m and output higher at Q_m than under competition. Of course, the socially efficient price-output combination with marginal costs at MC_2 is at P^*Q^*, but this is really an irrelevant comparison point since, the argument goes, MC_2 would not have been achieved in the absence of monopoly.

Since the concepts of perfect competition and monopoly are essentially static in character, theoretical arguments about which type of market structure

---

[51]In one example, Scherer calculates: "If a monopolistic economy starting from a 10 percent static allocation disadvantage could grow at the rate of 3.5 percent per annum, it could overtake the competitive system in 20 years." Scherer, *Industrial Market Structure*, 22. Note also that adding up net gains over time raises an issue of intergenerational equity. If future gains from monopoly outweigh today's losses, we can impute a net gain to monopoly; but we must be willing to say that gains enjoyed by future generations are sufficiently important to outweigh the costs suffered by the present-day members of society.

provides the most favorable dynamic environment tend to be varied and imprecise. We suggested in Chapter 2 that competition may be necessary to provide the stimulus to inventive efforts. Yet, some qualifications arise. The small zero-profit firm may lack the financial resources with which to pursue an ambitious research and development (R&D) program. Yet it is precisely the ambitious program that is most likely to yield important results. Moreover, if innovations are rapidly copied by rivals, then the innovator's reward is eaten away, and the incentive to progress is dampened.[52]

It is for these reasons that many observers believe inventive activity will flourish more in (partially) monopolistic rather than competitive circumstances.[53] Larger, more powerful companies with both the resources and the incentives, may do the better job. Presumably, however, the monopolist's position must not be too strong. If there are no threatening rivals, the incentive to develop new products and processes may again diminish.

Since theoretical expectations are not precise, the issue of technical efficiency has received much recent attention from empirical investigators. If we cannot decide in principal what is going to happen, we must resort to the facts. Without attempting to review the voluminous literature, a few pertinent points about the evidence may be noted.[54]

1.   Measuring inventive activity is no easy task. Two common measures— R&D spending and patents—have rather serious deficiencies.

2.   Larger firms spend more on R&D than smaller firms, but do not seem generally to spend proportionately more.

3.   There is some evidence that industries of moderate concentration are more active researchers, especially where some threat of entry by new rivals is present; but the case is not an overwhelming one.[55]

4.   Patterns of inventive effort and output seem to be highly idiosyncratic to specific industries, and thus tend to defy easy generalization.

SUMMARY

In this chapter we have defined a monopoly as an industry which consists of only one firm, producing a product for which there are no close substitutes, and where barriers to entry exist to protect the established firm's power. We

---

[52]Notice that significant innovation by a single competitor may be inconsistent with the assumptions of a strictly competitive market. How, for example, could one firm introduce a distinctly "new" product in a market of homogeneous products?

[53]The idea that most invention and innovation will occur in imperfect markets has long been associated with J. A. Schumpeter, *Capitalism, Socialism, and Democracy*, 3d ed. (New York: Harper, 1950).

[54]For good surveys, see J. M. Vernon, *Market Structure and Industrial Performance: A Review of Statistical Findings* (Boston: Allyn and Bacon, 1972); M. Kamien and N. Schwartz, "Market Structure and Innovation: A Survey," *Journal of Economic Literature*, 13 (March 1975).

[55]Concentration of a market is most frequently measured by the combined market share of the four largest firms (called the four-firm concentration ratio). See Chapter 9.

have identified a number of theoretical and measurement difficulties associated with this definition.

We have identified three kinds of social loss that can be attributed to monopoly:

1.   Efficiency losses, incurred when monopoly prices exceed the marginal costs of production. This means that the commitment of resources to producing the monopolist's output is too small, and consumers will be offered less at higher prices than under competition.

2.   Equity losses, incurred because monopoly redistributes income from consumers (who pay higher prices for the product) to producers (who earn excess profits). These profits are protected over the long run by barriers to entry.

3.   Rent-seeking losses, incurred when producers use the excess profits they can earn under monopoly conditions through lobbying and other expenditures necessary to acquire and maintain their monopoly position.Finally, we suggested that there may be some dynamic benefits from a monopoly market structure if a firm that is to some extent protected from entry has an incentive to undertake more investment and innovation.

CONCLUSION

Our definition of monopoly has emerged as less clear-cut than its polar opposite, perfect competition. Whereas the theoretical construct is useful, identification of real-world monopoly is complicated both by definitional ambiguity and by measurement problems. Furthermore, the welfare implications of monopoly are difficult to assess for a variety of reasons, including theoretical imprecision (especially on the dynamic side) and the aforementioned problems of definition and measurement.

We shall return to these practical issues in Chapter 9 by examining the structure of U.S. industry and the extensive efforts of investigators to subject hypotheses about industry structure and behavior to empirical tests. We now turn to a consideration of markets that present even greater conceptual problems than those encountered to this point: oligopolies, or markets dominated by a few firms.

Discussion Questions

1.   Why is it necessary to consider barriers to entry and barriers to exit as separate categories?

2.   Evaluate Demsetz's argument that the presence of decreasing costs is not necessarily a barrier to competition.

3.   "The existence of monopoly depends on the existence of well-defined industries. As industries become more diverse, monopoly will disappear." Discuss.

4. Does the theory of the second best mean that we must reject the definition of efficiency presented in this chapter, and so reject all attempts to evaluate the relative efficiency of a monopoly market structure?

5. Should economists take stands on issues of equity, or should they confine themselves to identifying and assessing considerations of efficiency alone? Is there a clear-cut distinction between efficiency and equity?

Selected Readings

Comanor, W. S. and R. H. Smiley, "Monopoly and the Distribution of Wealth," *Quarterly Journal of Economics* 89 (May 1975): 177–194. *A rare empirical estimation of the effect of monopoly on the distribution of wealth.*

Dewey, D., *Monopoly in Economics and Law*. Chicago: Rand McNally, 1966. *An interesting approach, also emphasizing the origins of antimonopoly law.*

Hicks, J. R., "Annual Survey of Economc Theory: The Theory of Monopoly," *Econometrica* 3 (January 1935): 1–20. *A survey of the various strands of the early development of monopoly theory.*

Lipsey, R. G. and K. Lancaster, "The General Theory of the Second Best," *Review of Economic Studies* 24 (October 1956): 11–32. *The original exposition of this important theory.*

Posner, R. A., "The Social Cost of Monopoly and Regulation," *Journal of Political Economy* 83 (August 1975): 807–827. *An examination of the costs of activities designed to capture and maintain monopoly rents—an important contribution to the new literature on rent-seeking.*

Robinson, J., *The Economics of Imperfect Competition*. London: Macmillan, 1933. *The foundation for much of the modern work on the theory of monopoly, monopolistic competition, and price discrimination.*

CHAPTER 4

. . . .

MARKET FAILURE: OLIGOPOLY

Once we move away from the polar market structures of perfect competition and monopoly, we enter the real world of industries that have varying combinations of competitive and monopolistic characteristics. The term imperfect competition is sometimes used to describe any market structure that lies between perfect competition and monopoly. However, economists usually split these intermediate cases into two structural categories—monopolistic competition and oligopoly. Monopolistic competition (which lies towards the competitive end of the spectrum) refers to industries that consist of many (small) firms producing a differentiated product. Oligopoly (closer to the monopoly end), refers to industries dominated by a few large firms producing either a homogeneous or differentiated product. Although both industrial types are represented in the U.S. economy, in this chapter we focus on oligopoly: identifying the ways in which it differs from pure monopoly and the possible need for government intervention.

Industries such as cigarettes, steel, aluminum, and breakfast cereals all have oligopolistic market structures. Typically, they show little hard price competition. Rather, price leadership is common: one firm sets price, the others follow. Although apparent price uniformity is one result, unpublished price discounting to individual buyers is common, as is heavy advertising and the development of differentiated products, especially in consumer goods industries. However, while the general structural characteristics of oligopolistic industries produce some predictable patterns of behavior, the actual price, advertising, and investment policies chosen under a given set of circumstances vary widely and are hard to predict.

The central difficulty in oligopoly analysis lies in the uncertain environment within which firms make decisions. We have not yet examined the impact of uncertainty on firm behavior in detail, partly because it is a complex issue that would require lengthy discussion beyond the purpose of this book. The models of perfect competition and monopoly are sufficiently revealing to allow us to preserve the simplicity of the discussion by introducing uncertainty only in a peripheral way.

An oligopolist's position within the industry is such that, as one of only a few large firms, its decisions about price, output, investment, and product type will have a large impact on rivals. They know the identity of the decision maker and, being relatively large themselves, are in a position to react. Rational oligopolists realize that their decisions, are likely to cause their competitors to respond, but the nature and extent of the response are seldom known with certainty. The ultimate outcome of an oligopolistic market is therefore uncertain.

In oligopoly, we must analyze not simply the reaction of one firm to uncertainty, but rather the whole process of interaction between firms in which every action creates new conditions for rivals, who in turn take (unforeseeable) actions that create further uncertainty.

THE MUTUAL INTERDEPENDENCE PROBLEM ANALYZED

One appropriate starting point for analyzing oligopoly is the Cournot duopoly model.[1] Suppose that there are only two firms in the industry (Cournot's example involved two owners of adjacent mineral springs), each producing a homogeneous product for which marginal cost may for simplicity be assumed to be zero. Both firms seek to maximize their profits. The market demand curve is known to both sellers and is linear, DB in Figure 4.1. Two crucial assumptions concern the behavior and interaction of the sellers. First, each seller is assumed to be an output adjustor, viewing the decision variable as output rather than price. (As we shall see, the behavior of price in the Cournot model is somewhat fuzzy.) Second, each seller assumes that the output of the rival is fixed and will not respond to any choice the original seller may make.[2]

Suppose Seller A initially occupies this market as a monopolist—facing demand curve DB in Figure 4.1; the corresponding marginal revenue curve is DA. Seller A will produce that output which maximizes profits (assuming zero marginal cost). This occurs where marginal revenue is also zero at OA.[3] Now assume Seller B enters the market and chooses a profit-maximizing output based on the assumption that A's output is fixed at OA. The remaining demand left to B is the section JB of the market demand curve for which JH is the corresponding marginal revenue curve (AH = 1/2 AB). Given zero marginal cost, Seller B will now produce AH units of output. The total industry output

[1]This model was formulated by the French economist Augustin Cournot in 1838. See A. Cournot, *Researches into the Mathematical Principles of the Theory of Wealth* (Paris: 1838).

[2]This assumption (sometimes referred to as the Cournot assumption) is essentially equivalent to the Sylos postulate in subsequent literature; see Chapter 3, page 62.

[3]Recall from basic microtheory that when the demand curve is a straight line, the corresponding marginal revenue curve bisects the distance from the origin to the point where the demand curve meets the abscissa; thus OA = 1/2 OB.

Figure 4.1   The Cournot Duopoly Model

Industry demand is DB. Seller A enters and mazimizes profit by producing OA (monopoly output). This leaves demand segment JB for Seller B, who enters and produces profit-maximizing output AH. The sellers adjust their outputs until Cournot equilibrium OG is achieved, with each firm producing OF.

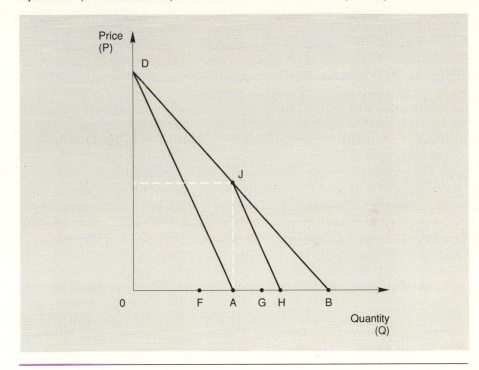

is now OA (produced by Seller A) plus AH (produced by Seller B). However, further adjustments will occur under the behavioral assumptions of the model. Seller A now assumes that B's output will remain equal to AH, that is, that B will continue to produce one-quarter of the total demand at zero price, which is OB. A's optimal output will now be one-half of the remaining demand, (1/2 (OB – AH)), less than A's original output (OA = 1/2 OB). Seller A will, therefore, reduce output. But this reduction will in turn cause B to reassess her position and increase output, since B now assumes that A's new output will remain fixed. The end result of these adjustments will be a total output of OG (equal to 2/3 OB) with each firm producing one-half OG (equal to 1/3 OB; that is, OF equals FG).[4]

[4]A's output will be OB (1 - 1/2 - 1/8 - 1/32 . . . .) = 1/3 OB; B's output will be OB (1/4 + 1/16 + 1/64+ . . . .)=1/3 OB.

Note first that output OG lies between the monopoly output OA, and the competitive or efficient output OB, that would maximize net welfare.[5] Moreover, OG is an equilibrium position such that, once it has been reached, there will be no tendency for either firm to continue further adjustments. This is an important result for two reasons: first, most theories of the firm (and industry) are expressed in terms of equilibrium output and price configurations. These equilibria are then used as benchmark positions for normative evaluations of firm and industry performance. Thus, for example, in Chapter 2, we discussed the final output choices of competitive firms that result in price equal to marginal cost. We did not consider in detail the process by which these choices are made or what happens if firms are temporarily out of equilibrium. The Cournot model demonstrates that oligopoly may produce comparable equilibria. In this case the result is that net social welfare with two firms is higher than that produced by a monopoly, but not as high as that of a purely competitive market.

The second significant aspect of the Cournot model is that it demonstrates the extent to which specific behavioral assumptions determine the market outcome. The assumption that each seller believes the rival firm's output to be fixed, regardless of what the original seller does, means that the initial seller, A, willingly reduces output (that is, concedes market share) as B enters, and continues to do so until an equilibrium is reached. Neither A nor B learn that each is, in fact, adjusting to the other's behavior, even though both do so repeatedly. Were both sellers to recognize explicitly their mutual interdependence, the outcome would be very different, though not necessarily predictable. The fact that the model fails to make explicit how prices are set also serves to emphasize the difficulty of developing a satisfactory model of oligopolistic industries.[6]

In general, behavioral assumptions about oligopolistic interaction affect the shape of firms' perceived demand curves. An example is shown in Figures 4.2(a) and 4.2(b). D_1 is the industry demand curve for steel. Assume that there are only two steel-producing firms, A and B. At the current price P_1, industry quantity demanded is Q_1, of which Firm A produces one-third, Q_{A_1}, and Firm B produces two-thirds, Q_{B_1}, ($Q_1 = Q_{A_1} + Q_{B_1}$); Firm A is at point A_1, and Firm B is at point B_1 in Figure 4.2(a). If both firms reduce their price to P_2, the total quantity demanded will increase to Q_2. Once again, Firm A will produce one-third (Q_{A_2}) and Firm B two-thirds (Q_{B_2}) of this amount ($Q_2 = Q_{A_2} + Q_{B_2}$). Firm A

---

[5]At OB, the price or marginal value of the last unit equals zero and is thus equal to marginal cost. Since both total revenue and total cost are zero, net social welfare equals triangle ODB and consists entirely of consumer's surplus. The model does not pursue the question of how the competitive firm would remain viable at zero price.

[6]A clear, mathematical exposition of the Cournot model and its relationship to other oligopoly models is found in Michael Waterson, *The Economic Theory of Industry* (Cambridge, England: Cambridge University Press, 1984), Chapters 2, 3, and 4. For lucid mathematical discussion of a range of topics in imperfectly competitive markets, see James M. Henderson and Richard E. Quandt, *Microeconomics Theory*, 3d ed., (New York: McGraw-Hill, 1980).

Figure 4.2 Demand Curves for Oligopoly

(a.) Industry demand is D_1. At price P_1, quantity Q_1, is demanded. Firm A produces one-third (Q_{A_1}), and Firm B two-thirds (Q_{B_2}) of Q_1. When price falls to P_2 demand quantity rises to Q_2, and both firms maintain their respective market shares. A's constant shares demand curve is D_A, and B's is D_B.

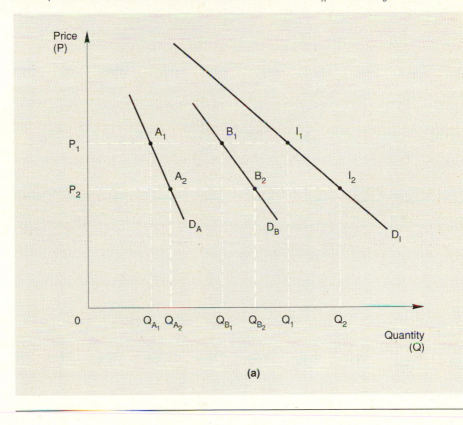

(a)

is now at point A_2, and Firm B is at B_2. The firm demand curves D_A and D_B trace out the quantities which each can sell at each price under the assumption that both charge the same price.[7]

Now suppose that Firm A reduces its price unilaterally to P_2. If the product sold by both firms is truly homogeneous, a price reduction by Firm A would cause all buyers to shift to A so that A's demand quantity would expand

---

[7]F. M. Scherer, *Industrial Market Structure and Economic Performance*, 2d ed. (Chicago: Rand McNally, 1980). Scherer refers to curves D_A and D_B as "constant shares" curves because they imply that, with every simultaneous price change, each firm maintains a constant share of the market—in our case, Firm A one-third and Firm B two-thirds. We have made the strong assumption that both firms charge the same price. If the firms produce a differentiated product, then a firm's constant shares demand curve can be drawn under the assumption that price differentials between firms remain constant.

(b.) Firm A unilaterally reduces its price from P_1 to P_2. If the product is homogeneous, Firm A captures the entire industry demand quantity Q^* at price P_2; A's demand curve is D_A'. If products are differentiated, A's demand curve is D_A'' for unilateral price cuts.

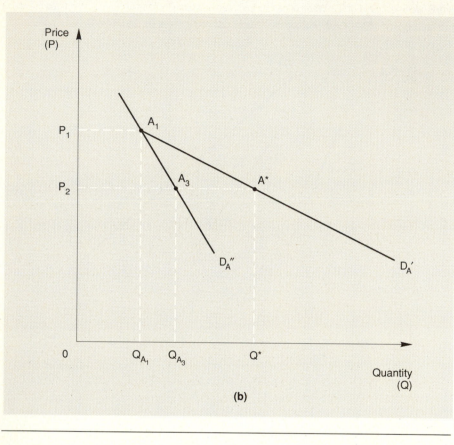

(b)

to Q^* to point A^* (along D_A' in Figure 4.2(b)), i.e., A would sell the entire industry demand at P_2, and B would sell nothing.[8] Firm B would not likely accept this and might match or undercut A's price. A price war, if it ensued, would be most destructive for both firms. One cannot predict, without making more specific assumptions about the cost structures and behavior patterns of both firms, what the final price and market shares would be.

In particular, one cannot predict the extent to which Firm A will anticipate Firm B's response before A initiates a price change. For a price war to persist, each firm must assume that its own price cut will be the final move in

___

[8]Demand curve D_A' in Figure 4.2(b) is drawn under the assumption that both firms set the same price at P_1 but that for all prices below P_1, Firm A is reducing price while firm B keeps its price at P_1. If Firm A were to set a price below firm B at all prices, then A would capture the whole market at every price and A's demand curve would be the same as D_1 in figure 4.2(a).

the game. If, instead, it is systematically undercut by its competitor and continues to play the price-cutting game anyway, this either implies an element of naiveté´ (each firm continues to expect that its own price cut will be final, despite the fact that its rival always retaliates) or a calculation that it can withstand the profit losses associated with a price war longer than its competitor and will eventually emerge as the sole surviving firm.[9]

When products are differentiated in oligopoly, a price cut by one firm may not affect the demand for its competitor's product quite so dramatically. In this situation, when Firm A cuts price from P_1, with Firm B holding its price at P_1, A expands its market share at the expense of B, but does not capture the whole market. In Figure 4.2(b), D''_A, represents A's demand curve, assuming that B keeps price at P_1. Thus when Firm A cuts its price to P_2, its sales go to Q_{A_3} (point A_3 on D''_A). Clearly, the lower the substitutability between rival oligopolists' products, the less damage each stands to sustain from a price war. Indeed, rather than cutting prices, an investment project that is designed to increase the firm's product differentiation (real or perceived) may be a more productive and ultimately less costly way for an oligopolist to maintain or increase its market share.[10] The threat of a price war, however, always lurks in the background as a possibility that firms will rationally seek to avoid.

One model which attempts to explain the avoidance of price wars is the kinked demand curve.[11] In Figure 4.3, an oligopoly firm is currently producing output Q_1 and charging price P_1. The firm assumes that if it were to lower price below P_1, all its rivals will follow suit. The firm would therefore move down its constant shares demand curve, AD. The additional output which it would sell at lower prices is a result of the expansion of industry demand as all firms lower price, not a result of increased market share. On the other hand, the firm believes that if it raises price above P_1, none of its rivals will follow, and it would lose market shares as it moved back along the more elastic demand curve Bd. Thus the firm views its demand curve as BJD, with a kink at the current price–output point, J. The marginal revenue curve which corresponds to this demand curve is the discontinuous curve BKLM (with the discontinuity between K and L). Suppose the marginal cost curve intersects the marginal revenue curve between K and L. Then the profit-maximizing price-output

[9]This discussion of price-cutting is presented as an illustration of oligopolists' demand curves. It is not an approach which can be used to analyze real-world price wars because it does not take costs into account. The issue of predatory pricing, which occurs when a firm cuts price below its own or its competitor's average variable or marginal cost, and the likelihood, importance, and significance for policymaking of this strategy, has given rise to a large body of literature. For a discussion of the issues, see Chapter 11.

[10]Product differentiation is also a recognized method for deterring entry into the industry. See R. Schmalensee, "Entry Deterrence in the Ready-to-Eat Breakfast Cereal Industry," *Bell Journal of Economics* 9 (Autumn 1978): 305–327.

[11]R. Hall and C. J. Hitch, "Price Theory and Business Behavior," in T. Wilson and P. W. S. Andrews, eds., *Oxford Studies in the Price Mechanism* (Oxford: Clarendon Press, 1951); and P. M. Sweezy, "Demand under Conditions of Oligopoly," *Journal of Political Economy* 47 (1939): 568–573.

Figure 4.3 The Kinked Demand Curve Model of Oligopoly

The oligopolist's initial output is Q_1 at price P_1. If it lowers price, and competitors follow suit, the relevant demand curve is JD. If it raises price, and competitors do not, the demand curve is JB. The kinked demand curve is BJD. The marginal revenue curve is BKLM—discontinuous between K and L. If MC intersects MR anywhere between K and L, then P_1, Q_1 will remain the profit-maximizing price–output combination.

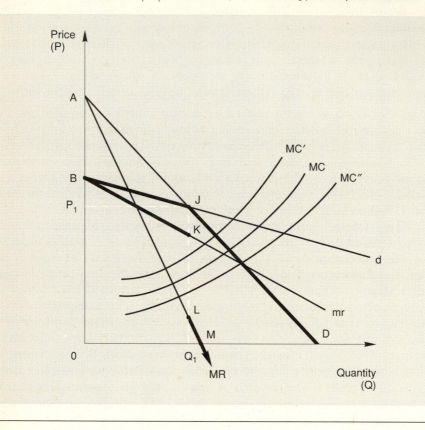

---

combination (where $MR = MC$) is P_1Q_1. Even if marginal cost shifts up to MC', or down to MC'', the firm's profit-maximizing position remains unchanged. In other words the firm's profit-maximizing price will be the same within some range of cost conditions.

The kinked demand curve was introduced in the 1930s to explain apparent price rigidities in oligopolistic industries.[12] Although the model has intuitive appeal, its empirical contribution to analysis has been long debated. Are

---

[12]A modern version of this model in game-theoretic terms is found in Waterson, *Economic Theory of Industry*, 31.

oligopoly prices more rigid than those in other industries?[13] Perhaps, but a clear answer is not as clear as one might expect, in part because the prices of actual transactions (as opposed to published list prices) can prove difficult to observe.

Notice that the kinked demand model does not explain how the initial price–output combination P_1Q_1 was established. The model simply shows that once set, price will tend to persist; under the assumptions attributed to firms, neither price raises nor price cuts look very appealing. These assumptions are essentially pessimistic. Clearly if the firm lowered its price and no one followed, the firm could increase its market share substantially (along demand curve Bd). On the other hand, if it raised price, and everyone followed, profits for all firms might rise. To assume the opposite in both cases is therefore to assume the worst, and maintaining price at its current level avoids the risk of substantial losses resulting from any change in price. In fact, as we have noted, many oligopolistic industries are characterized by price leadership, a pattern that does not follow the assumptions of the kinked demand model, but rather assumes that rivals will follow the leader's initiatives in any direction.

The possibility that greater profits can be earned if all firms raise price simultaneously leads us to consider another way in which oligopolistic firms can attempt to avoid the instability which their mutual interdependence fosters—collusion.

COLLUSION

Collusion is an agreement among rivals not to compete but rather to fix industry price at some mutually acceptable level. When it enters a price-fixing agreement with its competitors, a firm relinquishes its independence to make its own price and output decisions. Instead it accepts and adheres to the group-determined policy. No firm would be likely to tolerate such a large curtailment of its power if it did not anticipate substantial gains from doing so.

Assume that an industry consists of two firms producing an identical product and that high barriers to entry exist. If both firms also have identical costs,[14] the price that maximizes profits for the group of two (thus, for the industry) is the monopoly price. In Figure 4.4, D_A is the constant shares demand curve for each firm drawn under the assumption that both firms always set an identical price. D_I is the industry demand curve and is equal to the horizontal sum of the two firms' demand curves. MC_A is the marginal cost curve for each firm and MC_I is the horizontal sum of the two identical marginal cost curves.

If the firms set prices together, they effectively become a monopolist. Their profit-maximizing price–output combination occurs at P^*Q_I, where the

---

[13]For an excellent review, see F. M. Scherer, *Industrial Market Structure*, 164–168.

[14]This is an heroic assumption. Relaxing it leads to questions about the stability of collusive agreements. See p. 95.

Figure 4.4 Collusion

The industry demand curve is D_I, with marginal revenue MR_I. Assuming two identical firms, D_I is horizontally twice the size of either firm's demand curve D_A. Industry marginal cost, MC_I, is twice each firm's marginal cost MC_A. If they collude, the firms will choose the price–output combination that maximizes industry profits: P^*Q_I where $MR_I = MC_I$.

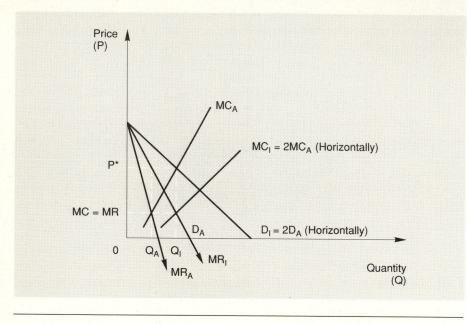

marginal revenue curve for the industry, MR_I (identical to D_A in Figure 4.4), equals MC_I. In this simple case the total output and profits of the industry are divided equally between the two firms.[15] At P^*Q_I, each firm receives half the industry excess profits, higher than the normal profits that would be earned under competition.

The potential gains from collusion are clear and yet it can be argued that, even in the absence of legal prohibitions, price fixing is not always the most profitable route for firms to take. There are two major difficulties associated with collusion: the first concerns the process by which the collusive agreement is reached and the likelihood of its being maintained; the second concerns the problem of entry and its effect on the stability of the agreement.

---

[15]To see this consider demand curve D_A in Figure 4.4. This is the demand curve for Firm A drawn under the assumption that Firms A and B always sell at the same (collusive) price. Then MR_A is A's marginal revenue curve, and A's individual profit-maximizing output is found where MR_A equals MC_A, at Q_A, half of the industry output. In other words, if two firms with identical costs agree to charge the same price, their share of industry output and profits will be exactly half.

The Collusion Process: Problems in Reaching
and Maintaining Agreements

An agreement among firms to fix prices above the competitive level also involves output restriction. In our example above, the output limitation for each firm is the same because of the assumption of identical costs. But if costs differ substantially between firms, the industry profit-maximizing allocation of output between firms equates the marginal costs of all firms. This implies a smaller output (and smaller profit) for high-cost firms than for low-cost firms.[16] Firms that stand to receive a low share of the collusive profits might be less willing to enter the agreement in the first place, since the effect of doing so is to freeze their shares at relatively low levels. However, without the participation of all firms, the fixed price may not stick.

Even if an agreement could be reached about the price and output shares of all firms, there are strong incentives for individual firms to cheat by increasing output and selling the additional units at secretly discounted prices. Of course, if the price-cutting is discovered by the other firms in the group they may well retaliate, thus destroying the collusive agreement. The fact that mutual cooperation yields higher profits for all does not remove the incentive for firms to cheat.

A prime case in point is the familiar prisoner's dilemma, which has intrigued observers of collusive behavior for many years. Price-cutting (cheating) appears to each firm to be a profitable strategy regardless of what others may do; yet if all cheat, prices are eroded, profits fall, and all firms are worse off than they would have been had they stuck to the collusive agreement.

In Figure 4.5(a), $D_{collusive}$ is the demand curve facing the individual firm, drawn on the assumption that all other firms charge the same price, here $P_{collusive}$. Note that this price and the resulting quantity sold, $Q_{collusive}$, yield the firm a profit-maximizing (monopoly) position at $E_{collusive}$. The firm, however, has a more tempting alternative. If all others remain faithful to the agreement by charging $P_{collusive}$, the firm may cut its price to $P_{cheating}$ and expand its sales along demand curve $d_{cheating}$. This demand curve is drawn on the assumption that all other firms charge $P_{collusive}$, while the firm in question does as it likes. It is not surprising that cheating pays. For while other firms adhere to a relatively high price, the cheater can expand sales very substantially by undercutting a bit. (This is simply to observe that the cheating demand curve $d_{cheating}$ is more elastic than the collusive demand curve $D_{collusive}$.)

Suppose, however, that the firm assumes that others will cheat rather than sticking to the agreed price. Figure 4.5(b) shows that if all others go to price $P_{cheating}$ while the firm in question remains at $P_{collusive}$, its sales will disappear! $D_{collusive}$ is no longer relevant—the agreement has broken down—and

---

[16]For the group as a whole to produce efficiently, the total costs of production for the group must be minimized; the marginal costs of production must be equal for all firms. The equal marginal cost condition will only be met when relatively low-cost firms produce most of the total output and high-cost firms keep their production (and marginal costs) small.

Figure 4.5 Prisoner's Dilemma

$D_{collusive}$ is the demand curve facing a firm assuming that all other firms charge the same price. $P_{collusive}$/$Q_{collusive}$ is the price–output combination of a firm adhering to a collusive agreement. If the firm cheats on the agreement, and secretly cuts its price to $P_{cheating}$, its sales and profits will expand as it moves along demand curve $d_{cheating}$.

If all other firms cheat and charge price $P_{cheating}$, while our colluder continues to charge $P_{collusive}$, sales will fall to zero as the sole remaining colluder is forced backwards along $d_{cheating}$.

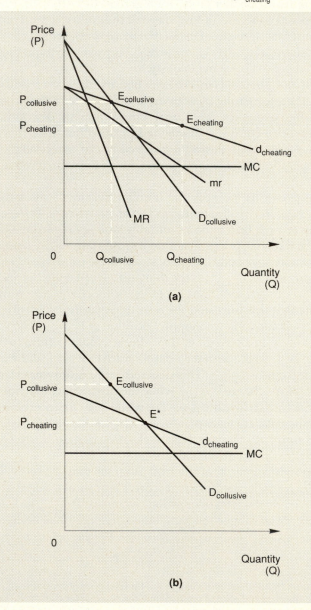

sales are described by $d_{cheating}$. This is, to be sure, an extreme case, but the underlying point is generally valid: if all others cheat, the firm cannot afford to be faithful to the higher collusive price. Thus the colluder's (or prisoner's) dilemma: individually, each firm is better off cheating than sticking to the agreed price, regardless of whether it believes others will do the same; but if all cheat, all are ultimately worse off. Cheating in these circumstances is termed a *dominant strategy*—it appears to yield better results regardless of what rivals may do.

Collusive agreements are designed to reduce the essential uncertainty that faces all oligopolists, but in fact this uncertainty may well remain even after the price-fixing agreement has been reached. It is reflected in the ever-present incentive to cheat.

There has been much controversy concerning the likelihood and viability of collusive agreements among oligopolists. The heart of the issue is whether oligopolistic industries behave sufficiently like monopolies to be treated as such for public policy purposes. If oligopolistic firms routinely succeed in collusion to raise price close to monopoly levels, it can be argued that antitrust policy should be vigorously pursued even against firms whose market position does not amount to monopoly. On the other hand, if collusion between oligopolists is unlikely, or if agreements are ineffective (in other words, if competition is strong among rival oligopolists), then antitrust policy has a more limited role.

In a 1964 study, Stigler examined the conditions under which collusive agreements are likely to be maintained.[17] He suggested that agreements are more likely to stick if secret price-cutting is easily detected by the other members of the cartel. If collusion is illegal, it may be difficult for the cartel to monitor its members' prices directly. However, if a cheater is selling more than would be the case under cartel rules, this may suggest to the others that there is secret price-cutting. Stigler relates the likelihood of detection to such industry variables as the Herfindahl concentration index (see Chapter 9). The lower the concentration, the more likely it is that secret price-cutting will go undetected. The temporal pattern of buying is also pertinent: the less frequently buyers enter the market, the less likely they are to perceive, take advantage of, and report secret price-cutting. This is also the case for the number and size distribution of both buyers and sellers (large buyers may be needed to take advantage of small price cuts).

Williamson suggests that the difficulties involved in reaching agreement in the first place may be so great as to make collusion an uncommon phenomenon.[18] When competing firms produce a variety of differentiated products, making and enforcing an agreement will involve the detailed specification of many prices and output levels. In other words, the transactions costs of the agreement are high. Moreover, the uncertainty of future cost and demand will

[17]G. J. Stigler, "A Theory of Oligopoly," *Journal of Political Economy* 72 (February 1964): 44–61.

[18]O. E. Williamson, *Markets and Hierarchies: Analysis and Antitrust Implications* (New York: The Free Press, 1975); 234–247.

make profit-sharing agreements difficult to achieve. If collusion is illegal, any agreement would have to be achieved secretly or through tacit means (without direct negotiation). Williamson suggests that this may be a virtually impossible task. Yet even if he is correct, price-fixing, when it does occur, may well reduce economic welfare. In Chapter 11, we discuss government policy toward collusion and see how some of the implications presented here have been dealt with in the law.

The Effect of Entry

Thus far we have assumed that the number of firms in the industry, and hence the number of potential colluders, is given. Once we introduce the possibility of entry into the model we see that the established firms in an oligopoly must broaden their perspective beyond the industry boundaries and consider the effect of their price and output decisions on potential entrants.

In Chapter 3, we saw that a monopolist could successfully prevent entry through stay-out or limit pricing. In oligopoly, the strategy of pricing to deter entry is complicated by the fact that there are several firms in the industry. Only if all firms simultaneously set a price below the average costs of potential entrants will entry be deterred, but this implies collusion by the established firms. Analyses of the effect of the entry threat on the pricing strategy of oligopolistic firms usually consider two different types of industry structure:

1. Industries in which there is a dominant firm or a dominant (colluding) group and many small "fringe" firms. Entry and exit take place among the fringe firms, so that the amount of additional output which any entrant adds to industry output is relatively small.

2. Industries in which there is a dominant firm or dominant (colluding) group and the entry threat comes from one or a few large firms with the capacity to enter at high-output levels.

In the first case, the insignificance of the output of fringe firms means that for all intents and purposes, these small companies are price-takers—they take the price of the dominant firm or group as given and ignore the extent to which their output affects the market. In the second case, the entering firm can depress industry price significantly by adding a large amount to current output levels; this possibility is recognized by both the entrant and the established firms. Let us examine each case in turn.

Case 1. Entry Threat from Small Fringe Firms   In Figure 4.6(a) the demand curve facing the dominant group is D_1 and its corresponding marginal revenue curve MR_1.[19] Marginal and average costs of the dominant group are constant (the line

---

[19]We will not spell out too closely the assumptions under which D_1 is drawn. It could be the industry demand curve if there are, at the start, no fringe firms in the industry. If there are already fringe firms in the industry, then D_1 could be itself a residual curve of the kind we describe below.

Figure 4.6 Entry by Small Fringe Firms

(a.) The demand curve of the dominant group is D_I, with corresponding marginal revenue curve MR_I. Marginal and average costs are constant at level P_c. In the absence of an entry threat, the dominant group will choose the profit-maximizing price–output combination $P_m Q_m$, where $MR_I = MC$.

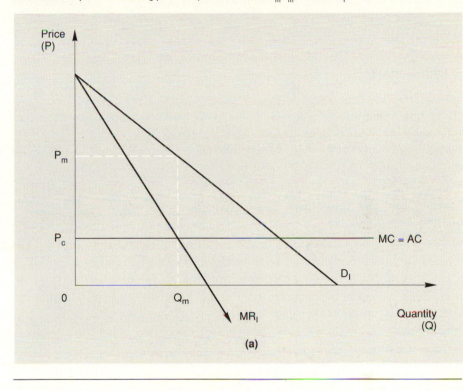

(a)

$MC = AC$ at level OP_c). In the absence of any entry threat, the profit-maximizing group would presumably set the monopoly price P_m and produce Q_m where MR_I equals MC. Now consider the possibility of entry by small firms, each of which sees that its potential addition to industry output is so small as to have a negligible effect on industry price. These fringe firms view themselves as perfect competitors facing a horizontal demand curve at the going price. However, in this case the price is set not by supply and demand, but by the dominant group.

We assume further that the marginal costs of the potential entrants are higher than the costs of the dominant group. Since the firms are price-takers, their marginal cost curve is their supply curve, as it is in the case of purely competitive firms. This supply curve is given by S_e in Figure 4.6(b). If the dominant group sets price P_m, fringe firms will enter the industry and supply an additional Q_s. Total industry output will now be $Q_m + Q_s$, far greater than consumer demand Q_m, at that price. There will be surplus output of Q_s, and downward pressure on industry price. If the dominant group anticipates this

(b.) S_e shows the amount fringe firms will supply for each price set by the dominant group. If the dominant group allows fringe firms to supply what they wish at each price, the residual demand curve for the dominant group is D_r, found by subtracting horizontally the S_e curve from the D_l curve.

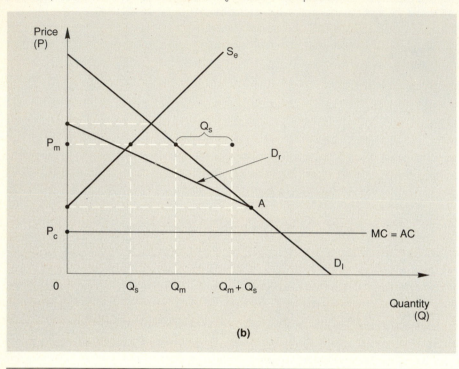

(b)

sequence of events, a different strategy from straight monopoly pricing is clearly required. One benevolent strategy is that the dominant group allows the entrants to supply all they like at the going price. The demand curve which remains to the dominant group is then D_r in Figure 4.6(b). This curve is derived by subtracting horizontally the curve S_e from the original dominant group demand curve, D_l (recall Chapter 3). The corresponding marginal revenue curve, shown in Figure 4.6(c), is then MR_r and the profit-maximizing price–output combination for the dominant group is $P'Q'$ where MR_r equals MC. At price P' the fringe firms will supply Q'_s and the total industry output is $Q'_s + Q' = Q_T$. The market is cleared at price P'. Note that by conceding part of its market share to the entrants, the dominant firm has been forced to reduce its price from P_m to P'. Thus the competitive threat from entrants has achieved what one would expect—erosion of the monopoly price.

This solution implies that the dominant firm will tolerate some entry. If it wishes to prevent entry entirely, it could increase its own output to Q_L, in Figure 4.6(d), forcing industry price down to P_L and making it completely unprofitable for potential entrants to supply anything at all. P_L is therefore the limit price.

(c.) The dominant group's demand curve is D_r, and the marginal revenue curve is MR_r. Q' (where MR_r = MC) is the profit-maximizing output for the group. At the associated price P', fringe firms supply Q', and total industry output is Q_T.

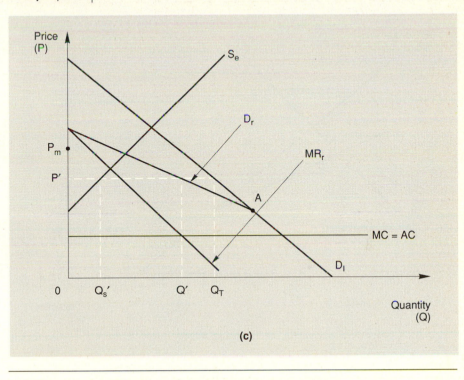

(c)

Indeed, in this model, the dominant group can effectively regulate the amount of entry by its choice of price. The closer is price to P_m, the greater the amount of entry; the lower the price, the less the entry.[20] Note that the limit price, P_L, still lies above the dominant group's average cost curve and allows it per unit excess profits of AB. But P_L is substantially lower than the monopoly price (P_m) and not much above the competitive level, P_c. Therefore, while the limit pricing strategy may achieve the goal of preserving the established group's dominance, it also may result in near-competitive prices. The threat of competition from potential competitors, it appears, may be as effective in keeping prices low and output high as competition from existing competitors.

[20]The model presented here is essentially static. Recently, models have been developed which attempt to take into account rates of entry and to trace changing market shares over time. See the seminal article by D. W. Gaskins, Jr., "Dynamic Limit Pricing: Optimal Pricing under Threat of Entry," *Journal of Economic Theory* 3 (September 1971): 306–322.

(d.) To prevent fringe firms from entering the market, the dominant group will set price at P_L; unit profits will be AB. P_L is the stay-out or limit price. By comparison, $P_c Q_c$ would be the price–output combination under competition.

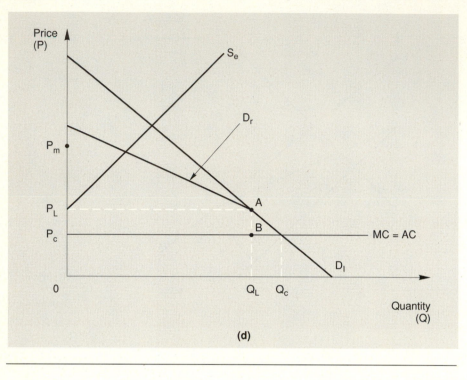

(d)

Case 2. The Threat of Large-Scale Entry

Consider the situation in which the dominant group is faced with the threat of entry from a firm capable of producing a sufficiently large output to affect industry price significantly. Now the pricing strategy of the dominant group must surely be influenced by its expectations of the potential entrant's behavior. Similarly, in making a bid for entry, the entrant must take into account the reaction of the established group to its threat. All the complexities of price and output strategy (resulting from mutual dependence between established oligopolists) which we have described above also pertain to the established group and the large potential competitor.

It is now useful to view the situation from the standpoint of the entrant rather than the dominant group. Assume first that the entrant has no absolute cost disadvantage. Its average cost of producing each level of output is identical to that of the established group, given by AC in Figure 4.7. D_I is the industry (dominant group) demand curve. The position of the prospective entrant's demand curve depends, as usual in the oligopoly setting, upon what assumptions are made about the reaction of the dominant group to prices and outputs set by the entrant. Assume that the dominant group maintains its

Figure 4.7 Large-Scale Entry

Industry demand is D_I. If the dominant group sets price P_1 it sells Q_1 units of output. Assuming established firms keep output at Q_1, and entrant will face demand curve D_e. Price P_L set by established firms would shift D_e back sufficiently to D_L, depriving entering firms of profit. P_L is the stay-out price.

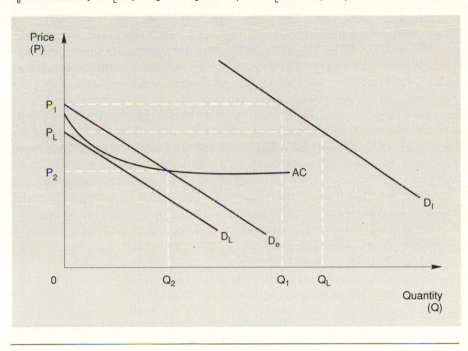

output regardless of the entrant's behavior. This assumption is called the Sylos postulate.[21] Thus if, for example, the established group sets price P_1 and produces Q_1, the entering firm's output will be an addition to Q_1, and will only be sold at prices below P_1. Therefore the demand curve facing the entrant will be that part of D_I which lies below P_1 and is shown horizontally displaced so that it originates at P_1 on the price axis, D_e in Figure 4.7. In this case the entrant can profitably enter at any level of output between zero and Q_2 at prices between P_1 and P_2. It is most likely that, as the entrant is selling at a price below P_1, the established group's price will be pulled down also. Indeed, if the product is homogeneous across all firms and if the market is not segmented, the established firms must reduce their price to equal the lower price of the entrant if they are to sell anything at all. The extent to which the entrant has

[21]It was first suggested by P. Sylos-Labini, *Oligopoly and Technical Progress* (Cambridge, Mass.: Harvard University Press, 1962). It is very similar to the basic assumption underlying the Cournot duopoly model. See also, F. Modigliani, "New Developments on the Oligopoly Front," *Journal of Political Economy* 66 (June 1958): 215-232; and D. Needham, "Entry Barriers and Non-Price Aspects of Firms' Behavior," *Journal of Industrial Economics* 25 (September 1976): 29–43.

power to lower industry price depends partly on the shape of its average cost curve, which determines at what output scale it can achieve minimum average costs. The entrant's power to lower price also depends on the elasticity of industry demand, which determines the extent to which industry price must fall to absorb the entrant's additional output.

Under the Sylos postulate the limit price is P_L. At no price below P_L can the entrant cover its average costs; its demand curve D_L lies everywhere below AC. But now the limitations of the Sylos postulate become evident. If the established firms set price P_L and entry occurs anyway, then industry price will be forced below P_L to a level which is unprofitable for all firms (recall that the cost curves for all firms are assumed to be identical). Now the established firms have the choice of accepting the entrant into the dominant (collusive) group, which implies output and profit reductions for the established firms, or attempting to drive the entrant out again by vigorous price-cutting.[22] But as we have seen, price wars are perceived as mutually destructive and will most likely be replaced by some kind of cooperation which must include the entrant. Therefore, whether the entrant risks entry depends on its perception of the probable reaction of the established firms. The established firms' strategy in the face of actual (or even potential) entry will depend on their perceptions of the entering firm's ability to withstand a price war, as well as on the objective market conditions of cost and demand.

One could argue that the established firm has an interest in making the entrant believe that its price and quantity will be maintained. But if it fails to convince the entrant, price maintenance does not look rational—which is something a clever entrant will see in advance! Thus, the established firm may look for a more convincing strategy.[23]

The basic point is that the Sylos postulate allows us to define an outcome, a solution to the problem of how oligopolies set prices. Without it, we are back at the beginning with no systematic way of analyzing the industry; yet the postulate remains unconvincing.

GAME THEORY AND OLIGOPOLY

Many of the models we have discussed in this chapter can be reformulated in terms of game theory.[24] Game theory seeks to define rational strategies for players who enter a game—a situation of conflict—against rivals whose behavior is uncontrollable and perhaps unpredictable. Oligopoly plainly fits this description.

Although we shall not pursue game-theoretic models in detail, the broad outlines of this influential branch of analysis are worth noting. Suppose that

---

[22]See Scherer, *Industrial Market Structure*, 246–248, for a lengthier discussion of this point and a neat analogy to the nuclear arms race.

[23]See A. Dixit, "Recent Developments in Oligopoly Theory," *American Economic Review* 72 (May 1982): 12–17, for a review of the literature on strategic entry barriers.

[24]The theory of games was introduced by John von Neumann and Oskar Morgenstern, *The Theory of Games and Economic Behavior* (Princeton, N.J.: Princeton University Press, 1944).

one has a choice of several strategies, and faces a single rival who has a similar array of choices. In some circumstances, the theory recommends an exceedingly conservative approach known as a minimax or maximin strategy. Assume that whatever you do, your rival will react so as to inflict on you the worst possible outcome. You should therefore choose the course of action that leaves you as well off as possible *after* this retaliation occurs. In effect, you must go for the best among a poor set of alternatives.

In other circumstances, game theory suggests that the rational player must do everything possible to prevent his opponent from predicting what he will do. How can this be accomplished? Game theory recommends that the choice of action be randomized—one might, for example, decide what to do by flipping a coin. The brilliant rival might always outguess the player in question, but cannot outguess a coin toss—at least not more than half the time on average! This randomized approach to choice is known as a mixed strategy.

Game theory has had enormous impact on the direction of market analyses in economics, yet the general consensus is that it has not been successful in answering the question, "How do oligopolies behave?" There are at least two reasons for this failure.

First, the approaches suggested by the theory—the minimax/maximin and the mixed strategy—do not appear to be realistic descriptions of business behavior. Most business managers are unlikely to follow the extremely pessimistic prescriptions of the minimax, or, on the other hand, to decide corporate policy by flipping coins. In fairness, however, this observation does not challenge the validity of game theory, which is intended to define the nature of rational strategy rather than to describe what managements actually may do.

The second reason why game theory has not been able to resolve basic questions about oligopoly is, in a sense, more serious. The theory has great difficulty dealing with complex situations. For example: game theory may provide precise recommendations for optimal strategies where (1) there are only two players or rivals; and (2) the game is of a constant-sum nature—that is, the rivals are fighting over a total payoff whose size is fixed. An example of such two-person constant-sum games is duopolists competing for shares of a market of given size. When these simplifying assumptions are dropped—so that there are more than two rivals and/or the total payoff is variable—it frequently proves impossible to define determinate solutions.[25]

These difficulties are not, of course, confined to the theory of games, which has provided important insights to the analysis of oligopolistic situations.[26]

[25]This is precisely what happens in prisoner's dilemma cases such as those we described above. Although there are only two rivals, the total payoff varies (profits are higher if all collude than if all cheat). Even in this relatively simple situation, neither game theory nor any other analytical approach can predict what will happen.

[26]For a superb but moderately technical exposition of game theory, see R. Duncan Luce and Howard Raiffa, *Games and Decisions* (New York: Wiley, 1958). Readers interested in enjoyable nontechnical discussions should see J. D. Williams, *The Compleat Strategist* (New York: McGraw-Hill, 1954); and Morton Davis, *The Art of Decision-Making* (New York: Springer-Verlag, 1986).

SUMMARY

In this chapter we have wended our way through the complicated world of oligopolists—firms that are large relative to the industry and whose large competitors are likely to react to any changes in price and output that the firm initiates. If the oligopolist is a rational decision maker, it will take the reaction of rivals into account before decisions are made.

We considered various models that characterize the interaction between an oligopoly firm and its rivals. The Cournot model resulted in a market outcome between the competitive and monopoly positions. The kinked demand curve model offered an explanation for the stability of prices in oligopolistic industries. We then focused on the likelihood that oligopolists will collude and considered some of the conditions which might foster or hinder such behavior. Finally, we considered the impact of potential entry on the behavior of established firms.

CONCLUSION

The analysis of oligopolistic market structures is more complicated than that of pure monopoly because of the mutual dependence between firms. In addition, the problems of industry definition, identification of entry barriers, and assessment of the threat of entry also exist for oligopoly as for pure monopoly. From a normative standpoint, one can argue that in a short-run static framework with high barriers to entry, colluding oligopolists will behave much like a pure monopolist and set a price which will generate the same allocative efficiency losses as those associated with pure monopoly. Since it is difficult to imagine that collusive conduct will produce countervailing social benefits with any frequency, most economists would agree that society has an interest in preventing such behavior.[27]

As we have seen, however, effective collusion is not the inevitable outcome of oligopoly. Price competition among established firms may break out, and the effect of both actual and potential entry is likely to push industry price below the monopoly level. Where price and output finally come to rest will depend not only upon industry cost and demand conditions, but also upon the process of interfirm rivalry within the industry.

The difficulties of oligopoly analysis mean that clear-cut rules for government policy are not completely obvious. There is a case for preventing collusive behavior, but, as we shall see in Chapter 11, the identification of collusion for policy purposes presents significant problems. Generally, we might wish to promote industrial structures in oligopoly that will encourage competitive tendencies while retarding the prospects for collusive activity. Some suggestions of this sort have been advanced and have at times been taken seriously by

---

[27]Some observers disagree. For an interesting discussion, see D. Dewey, "Information, Entry, and Welfare: The Case for Collusion," *American Economic Review* 69 (September 1979): 587–594.

the courts. But, as we shall see in later discussions, attempts to secure desirable patterns of behavior via policies that affect market structure confront impos-ing—sometimes disastrous—pitfalls.

Discussion Questions

1.   "The behavioral assumptions underlying the Cournot model are so unrealistic as to render the model useless as a tool for analyzing oligopo-lies." Discuss.

2.   Is there likely to be a significant difference in industry performance between industries consisting of only one dominant firm and industries dominated by two or three large firms?

3.   Some economists argue that the widespread use of stay-out pricing means that monopolistic and oligopolistic market structures can no longer be viewed as potentially important policy targets. In other words, with stay-out pricing, monopoly doesn't matter. Discuss this view.

4.   Oliver Williamson suggests that the difficulties of reaching collusive agreement may be great. What are these difficulties and in which indus-tries might they be the greatest?

Selected Readings

Fellner, William. *Competition among the Few*. New York: Knopf, 1949. *The oligopoly problem introduced*.

Gaskins, D. W. "Dynamic Limit Pricing: Optimal Pricing under Threat of Entry," *Journal of Economic Theory* 3 (September 1971): 306-322. *A seminal article in the theory of limit pricing-advanced*.

Modigliani, F. "New Developments on the Oligopoly Front," *Journal of Political Economy* 66 (June 1958): 215-232. *A classic survey, still current*.

Schelling, Thomas. *The Strategy of Conflict*. Cambridge, Mass.: Harvard University Press, 1960. *A sophisticated analysis of the dynamics of rivalry*.

Stigler, George J. "A Theory of Oligopoly," *Journal of Political Economy* (February 1964): 44-61. *A much-quoted study that points up the theoretical significance of the Herfindahl index*.

Sylos-Labini, P. *Oligopoly and Technical Progress*. Cambridge, Mass.: Harvard University Press, 1962. *The famous book which introduced the Sylos postulate*.

Williamson, O. E. *Markets and Hierarchies*. New York: The Free Press, 1975, 234-247. *An interesting critique of current theories of oligopoly and a new approach*.

CHAPTER 5

· · · · · · · · · · · · · · · · · · · ·

MARKET FAILURE: PUBLIC GOODS, EXTERNALITIES, AND INFORMATION PROBLEMS

Certain types of goods and services are commonly provided by government, for example, national defense, police protection, fire protection, education (primary and secondary), highways, bridges, and tunnels.[1] Why should this be? What is it about these particular kinds of commodities that calls for public provision? The answers are found largely in the concepts of public goods and externalities, two closely related properties which suggest that the private market may fail to function efficiently.

PUBLIC GOODS

A public good—sometimes referred to as a social or collective good—is essentially nonmarketable in its purest form and thus presents a very clear case for government supply. Such commodities have two main characteristics:

- *Nonrivalrous consumption* (or joint supply). Consumption of the good by any individual, A, does not impede consumption by any other individual, B. By similar token, if the good is supplied to any person, A, it can also be supplied to others at little or no additional cost.
- *Nonexcludability*. The benefits of the public good cannot be (easily) confined to certain individuals within the community, that is, if the good is provided to any individual, it is difficult or impossible to exclude all other individuals from enjoying its benefits as well.

Pure public goods possess both these characteristics in extreme form. Commonly cited examples (which are not numerous) are national defense and lighthouses. Many goods, however, may possess only one of these characteristics, or both to a less extreme degree, so that the dividing line between a

---

[1]Some of these goods, such as education and police protection, are also provided privately in certain instances.

purely private and a purely public good is blurred. This in turn complicates the rationale for government provision.

Roads, theaters, and parks are examples of goods characterized by non-rivalrous consumption, but only up to a certain capacity level. If a theater has 300 seats, then up to 300 people can use it simultaneously. The 301st person, however, can use the theater only if one of the original 300 gives up a seat. Beyond the capacity level, then, the theater becomes a private good character-ized by rivalry in consumption. The congestion problem of roads and parks, and also of electricity and telephone supply, similarly occurs when the joint supply characteristic of these goods disappears in the presence of a capacity constraint.[2]

Oil is a good that is not in joint supply. It occurs as a stock or pool beneath the earth's crust. Many wells can be drilled into a common oil pool, and the more oil removed from one well, the less remains to be removed from the others. However (in the absence of government), it may be very difficult—costly—to exclude individuals from drilling, especially if the oil pool extends over a large area.[3]

Rationale for Collective Provision

Both nonrivalrous consumption and nonexcludability imply that markets cannot supply the good in question efficiently. If we were to rely on the market to provide public goods, then the outcomes would lack the usual virtues of market activity.

The reasons for such market failure are easily seen in the pure public goods case of national defense. Let us suppose that the United States is defended in part by a mobile fleet of submarines armed with nuclear warheads (which is in fact the case). The purpose of the fleet is deterrence. Should an adversary attack, all or most of the submarines are expected to survive and to then inflict tremendous damage on the aggressor.

The service provided by the nuclear submarines plainly possesses the public goods characteristics noted above. Consumption is nonrivalrous: the protection that I receive in no way diminishes the protection that others receive from the fleet; once protection is provided to any one of us, all others may enjoy

---

[2]Such goods may or may not have exclusion difficulties. Tollbooths, for example, may be installed on turnpikes with few entrances and exits, but are not feasible on most other road systems because of the numerous possibilities for access. Theaters and parks may have gates, and electricity and telephone service utilize metering devices which may be switched on and off to monitor use.

[3]Note that exclusion problems arise only in the production of oil. They do not arise at the consumption end, and oil is therefore a purely private good in consumption. Another example of a good with a similar combination of characteristics is the fisheries. Too many fishermen will deplete the size of the fish stock. In the long run a lower catch for all fishermen will result. Thus, one fisherman's catch from the common fish stock will reduce his fellow fisherman's expected catch by a given small amount. However, many fishermen may fish simultaneously and effective exclusion is costly. See R. Turvey, "Optimization and Sub-optimization in Fishery Regulation," *American Economic Review* 54 (March 1964): 64–76.

it at zero additional cost. Furthermore, the service is nonexcludable. Once national defense is supplied, there is no way to withhold its benefits from any person or group within the country.

It is this last characteristic that provides the most potent and obvious source of market failure.[4] It is possible to sell a good in the marketplace only if those who do not pay for it do not receive its benefits. This is why we cannot have companies offering national defense policies or contracts.[5] If I decide not to buy such a policy, the defense supplier has no way to deny me the protection of the nuclear fleet.

Public goods thus give rise to what is usually termed a free-rider problem. Since I will receive the benefits of the defense system whether or not I pay for it, my incentive to pay is at best limited and perhaps nonexistent.[6] I may well prefer to let others pay and take a free ride on their beneficence. But all others have exactly the same incentive. If we leave the job of defense to the market, then it simply may not be done.

Although nonexcludability is the fundamental cause of market failure in public goods, it is not the only difficulty. Consider one other peculiarity. Public goods are in a sense consumed in equal amount by all individuals. (I am protected by our nuclear fleet just as much as you are.) Yet we are likely to *value* the good differently; hawks may believe that defense is worth more than doves do. To see the complication that arises here, recall the Pareto efficiency condition from Chapter 2: the marginal rate of substitution (MRS) or marginal utility ratio, between goods X and Y must be the same for all consumers. We observed earlier that the competitive market assures such efficiency by offering goods X and Y to all consumers at the same prices. Since utility-maximizing consumers A and B each equate their MRS (marginal utility ratio) to the same price ratio, the MRS of each is the same. That is

$$\frac{MU_{XA}}{MU_{YA}} = \frac{P_X}{P_Y} = \frac{MU_{XB}}{MU_{YB}}$$

Moreover, since the marginal cost of each good (MC_x, MC_Y) equals its competitive market price, it follows that

$$\frac{MU_X}{MU_Y} = \frac{P_X}{P_Y} = \frac{MC_X}{MC_Y}$$

Suppose now, however, that whereas X is an ordinary private good, Y is our public good, national defense. Consumers A and B value Y differently, both

---

[4]For a useful and more detailed discussion, see J. G. Head, *Public Goods and Public Welfare* (Durham, N.J.: Duke University Press, 1974), especially Chapter 3.

[5]Notice, however, that this does not preclude markets in defense weaponry. A gun or a bomb is marketable even though national defense protection is not.

[6]I may of course be an upright citizen who insists on paying my fair share of program costs. But no manager of a defense system could reasonably rely on such motivation in a large enough number of people to fund the system.

Figure 5.1 Private and Public Goods Compared

(a.) Market demand for a private good is the sum of the quantity that each consumer demands at each price. If A and B are the only consumers, market demand (D_{a+b}) is thus the horizontal summation of A's demand (D_a) and B's demand (D_b). The market output will be nine units, and market price $10, where S and D_{a+b} intersect.

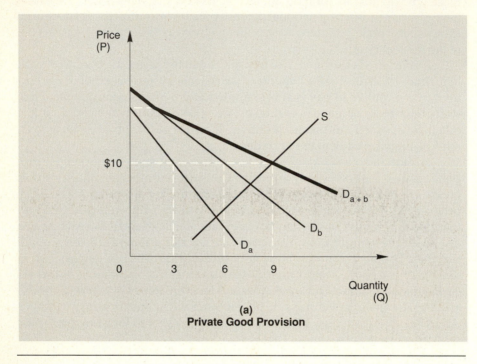

(a)
Private Good Provision

absolutely and relative to X. Yet becaue Y is public, each must consume the same amount of it. Pareto efficiency presupposes that all consumers maximize utility ($MU_X/MU_Y = P_X/P_Y$). But this condition can now be met only by charging different consumers different prices to reflect the variation in their marginal valuations of Y. Or, to turn the point around, the Pareto efficiency condition is no longer quite the same as it was in the private goods case.

This point may not be intuitively obvious, so we shall examine it in a more familiar way using the supply and demand diagrams of Figure 5.1. Figure 5.1(a) shows the demand for a private good by consumers A (D_a) and B (D_b). If A and B are the only consumers, market demand (D_{a+b}) is obtained by horizontally summing D_a and D_b. That is, the quantity demanded by the market at any price is simply the sum of Consumer A's demand quantity and Consumer B's demand quantity at that price. In Figure 5.1(a), a price of $10 is determined by market demand and supply, S. Consumer A demands three units and Consumer B demands six, thus market demand at P = $10 is nine units. Each consumer has adjusted consumption of the good so that its price equals the consumer's marginal valuation of it.

(b.) Market demand for a public good is the sum of the value that each consumer places on any specified quantity of that good. If A and B are the only consumers, market demand (D_{a+b}) is the vertical summation of A's demand (D_a) and B's demand (D_b). The efficient output occurs at Q^*, where S and D_{a+b} intersect.

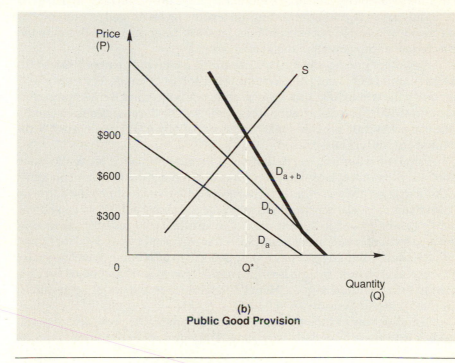

(b)
Public Good Provision

   In the case of a public good as shown in Figure 5.1(b), we assume the same two consumers. Market demand for this good, however, is quite different than for the private good. We cannot derive it by adding up the quantities that each consumer will demand at a given price. Recall that every individual consumes an equal amount of a public good. If amount Q^* of national defense is supplied, each consumer must consume Q^*. The relevant question thus becomes: What is the community's valuation of any given output level? Graphically, the market—really the community—demand curve, (D_{a+b}), is now the vertical summation of D_a and D_b. In Figure 5.1(b), market supply, S, and demand, D_{a+b}, determine output Q^*. Consumer A values Q^* at $300 while B thinks it is worth $600, thus the aggregate marginal valuation that consumers A and B place on Q^* is $900. Each point on D_{a+b} tells us this valuation for a different level of output in our two-person community.
   Notice the difficulty that now exists. The amount $900 represents the sum of A's and B's willingness to pay for the marginal unit of defense when output is Q^*. The marginal cost of defense is also $900 at that output level. Therefore Q^* appears to be the socially efficient output. However, the question

is now what price to charge each consumer.[7] One plausible pricing scheme would be to charge each consumer her marginal valuation—$300 for A and $600 for B. This would ensure that the distribution of benefits between the two consumers was not significantly different after the provision of Q* than before. (Demand curves D_a and D_b reflect initial income levels as well as preferences, and consumers would not express a demand for the good unless this demand reflected an improvement in their satisfaction.)[8]

Any other pricing scheme that generated a total payment of $900 for the marginal unit of Q* would also ensure provision of Q* units. For example, B could pay the whole $900 and A pay nothing, or both A and B could pay equal amounts ($450). The distributional outcome will be different for each combination of prices, but, provided that the prices paid by A and B sum to $900, the optimal output will be achieved.

Recall now our original definition of Pareto optimality: No reallocation of resources can take place so as to improve the welfare of at least one consumer without making another worse off. In Figure 5.1(b) we identified the output at which marginal social benefit equals marginal social cost as Q*, but also showed that Q* can be priced in such a way as to substantially redistribute income between two consumers. For example, if B were forced to pay $900 for Q* and his individual willingness to pay is only $600, then he is being overcharged for Q*; whereas A, whose marginal willingness to pay is $300 and whose price is zero, is being undercharged. Hence Q*, while it is the social optimum, is optimal for no single individual.

Another way of looking at the complications in the provision of public goods is in terms of marginal cost pricing. The joint supply condition, as noted, means that once the good is provided to anyone, others may also be supplied at zero or very low cost. Recall, however, the welfare virtues of marginal cost pricing, P = MC. If additional consumers can be provided with a public good at zero marginal cost, then the correct price for such people to pay is, in an economic welfare sense, zero! At this point, however, the viability of the market is again in grave doubt. In Chapters 13 and 14, we discuss in more detail the fundamental dilemma of pricing public goods at marginal cost when the resulting revenues are insufficient to cover the total cost of provision.

It is worth noting that none of these difficulties arises in the case of private goods. If I consume an apple pie, you cannot consume that pie. Furthermore, neither of us can eat the pie unless we pay for it. The benefits of pie consumption are confined to those who are willing and able to pay, and the pie is therefore a marketable or private good.

---

[7]Since a public good such as national defense is not marketable, price may be viewed not as an ordinary market price, but rather as a sum that government must obtain—probably via taxation—to finance the program.

[8]The pricing scheme suggested here is known as the Lindahl solution. See E. Lindahl, *Die Gerechtigkeit der Besteuerung* (Lund, 1919). For a recent survey, analysis, and bibliography of Lindahl's work and subsequent critiques see J .G. Head, *Public Goods and Public Welfare*, Chapter 6. See also M. McGuire and H. Aaron, "Efficiency and Equity in the Optimal Supply of a Public Good," *Review of Economics and Statistics*, 51 (February 1969): 31–39.

The general inefficiency of the market as a public goods supplier may be emphasized with a simple example. Suppose that there are five neighboring farmers, each of whose crops would benefit from a rainfall. Each farmer calculates that the value of his crops would increase by $500 if there were a good rain. The social value of the rain, ignoring other possible effects, is therefore the sum of the private values, $2,500.

Suppose also that there is a cloud-seeding company that can with some probability of failure (assumed for simplicity to be zero) produce the needed rainfall. If the rainfall is forthcoming, it will rain over the entire five-farm area; smaller areas cannot be served. The price that the company charges for a cloud seeding and subsequent rain is $1,500.

The inefficiency of the private market should already be evident. No individual farmer will contract for a rainfall. The cost of doing so ($1,500) exceeds the benefit ($500) that each would receive in return. Yet the full social benefits of the rain ($2,500) exceed its costs ($1,500). From a social standpoint the rainfall is worthwhile and should be produced. Yet, because of the public goods nature of the service (it is nonexcludable and presents a free-rider problem), the private market will not get the job done.[9]

What is the solution? Some sort of collective action may help. If the farmers were to form a cooperative association, each contributing $300, the rainfall could be purchased and every farmer would enjoy a net benefit worth $200. Alternatively, the collective arrangement could be governmental. A public body could tax each farmer $300 and contract for the rainfall with precisely the same result. It is for reasons such as these that government is usually regarded as a necessary agent if public goods are to be supplied in adequate quantity. This is not to imply that a governmental solution will always be ideal. As we have seen, the definition of an optimal public goods supply is problematic, and even with a clear definition, governments may make poor choices. The unregulated private market, however, offers little hope of reasonable solutions to problems of this kind.

How significant is this sort of difficulty? There are, as we noted at the outset, relatively few pure public goods—cases in which providing a commodity to one person makes it impossible to withhold it from all others. In some important areas, however, exclusion is technically possible but costly. Suppose, for example, one were to establish a private police force to protect only

---

[9]Even if the benefit of rain to each farmer were to exceed its cost, the free-rider problem would not vanish. Each farmer might reason: It may be worthwhile for me to pay the cloud seeder, yet if I do, everyone else will enjoy a free ride on my rain. Better I should wait until someone else breaks down and hires the cloud seeder. Then I can enjoy the free ride! Mancur Olson, in *The Logic of Collective Action* (Cambridge, Mass.: Harvard University Press, 1971), relates the way individuals make this kind of calculation to the size of the group that will benefit from public goods provision. He suggests that for small groups, provision is more likely than for large groups for two reasons: (1) the benefits to one individual may exceed his costs, making it worth his while to provide it for all; and (2) the costs of organizing a small number of people are lower than for large numbers. Thus for example, if only five farmers benefit from the cloud-seeding opeation, a group is more likely to form than if the benefits are distributed among 500 or 5,000 farmers.

those who pay for the service. If a member of this force were to see a crime in progress, she would need to determine whether the apparent victim is a paid-up subscriber before taking action! This scenario is a bit far-fetched—although private guard services akin to police forces do exist—but the nature of the difficulty is clear. To exclude noncontributors from receipt of the service is possible, but may prove extremely inconvenient in at least some instances.

Consider the somewhat less far-fetched example of a local road system. Excluding noncontributors from using the system is clearly possible (this is exactly what we do with turnpikes, and some bridges and tunnels). But imagine the cost of making every street and highway a toll road! Numerous tollbooths would have to be constructed and personnel hired. Significant waiting costs might be imposed on drivers. Such a system is possible, but local governments are not likely to regard it as practical.

Optimal Provision

While even the strongest free market advocate will concede the existence of some public goods that require collective, usually governmental, provision, we have seen that the problem of deciding the amount that should be supplied is generally not simple. For private goods we can in principle identify the relative quantities that will yield a Pareto optimal or socially efficient allocation of resources. However, for public goods the efficiency and equity criteria for determining optimal supply cannot be separated.

How much in the way of national defense, police protection, road building and maintenance, etc., should we have? Are there any guides for the public program manager? These questions have elicited some rather pessimistic conclusions from economists. Richard A. Musgrave, for example, has noted that:

1. Since no one can be excluded from the benefits of a public good, no one has an incentive to reveal true preferences about them.[10] Yet the government must determine these preferences before it can decide how to satisfy them efficiently. A way must therefore be found to induce people to reveal their preferences.

2. Even if it is assumed that the true preferences of all members of society are known, "there is no single most efficient solution to the satisfaction of social wants or to the problem of supplying services that are consumed in equal amounts by all . . . a more specific welfare function is needed to secure an optimal solution."[11]

---

[10]This problem is pervasive and may give people an incentive either to overstate or understate their true preferences. Suppose, for example, the state plans to run a highway through my house and asks me what compensation I require. I might well respond by saying: "My house is priceless! Even $10 million would not be sufficient compensation!"

[11]R. A. Musgrave, *The Theory of Public Finance* (New York: McGraw-Hill, 1959), 10, 84ff. 134.

Although not all analysts reach quite such a gloomy conclusion, it is apparent that definition of an optimal supply of a public good presents very formidable difficulties.[12] The primary complication arises because any quantity decision regarding a public good—in itself a resource allocation decision—cannot really be disentangled from considerations of equity. What seems efficient, therefore, will not necessarily appear to be fair.

Suppose that we seek to determine the socially appropriate amount of national defense, a pure public good that everyone consumes in identical amounts once a production decision is made. Citizens have widely varying preferences about defense. At one extreme are those who believe that all military spending is immoral and/or futile. At the other extreme are those who view U.S. military superiority as society's most urgent need. Given these divergent preferences, and the impossibility of a market-type solution, what is the most efficient decision with respect to the level of national defense? Indeed, what does most efficient mean?

The nature of the problem is quite clear. The efficient level of an activity is ordinarily defined as that which equates costs and benefits at the margin. As we have seen, however, this condition is not readily satisfied in the public goods area. Our earlier examples show the problem as one of pricing: the correct solution might involve charging a different price to each member of society. We may now turn the coin and look at the problem in quantity terms. Since everyone must consume the same amount of national defense, any output decision will impose burdens on some. To spend heavily on defense will insult and frighten the doves; yet to spend less will chagrin the hawks. Any conceivable choice will imply some distribution of satisfactions and dissatisfactions across all members of society. Thus the determination of an output level is closely tied up with the equity issue.

One may respond correctly that output decisions in private markets also have equity consequences. While true, however, the linkage is much weaker. If I do not like a private market decision, I can usually make some adjustment. But individual adjustments are not really possible in the case of public goods. I can decide how much bread or ice cream I will purchase, but I cannot avoid buying a specified quantity of nuclear submarine protection once government decides I will have it. The flexibility of the market is lost, and undesirable choices are inevitably imposed on some consumers.[13]

All this is not to suggest that decisions concerning national defense or other public goods cannot be made. We make them continually, usually

[12]See, for example, Head, *Public Goods and Public Welfare*, Chapter 4.

[13]There is a further complexity. In models that define the optimal supply of public goods, it is assumed that not only may consumers differ in their relative valuations of a particular public good, but that they can put a value on them in the same way as for private goods. As we have noted elsewhere (P. Asch and R. S. Seneca, "The Demand Curve and Welfare Change: A Reconsideration," *Journal of Post Keynesian Economics* 2 (Spring 1980)), since consumers do not buy national defense in incremental units in the same way as they do tea, it may not make sense to ask them to put a value on the marginal unit of defense. Thus, the behavioral assumptions underlying demand curves for public goods are tenuous.

through the political process. The point is rather that a decision to supply any amount of a public good carries extensive welfare implications for society. It is thus no mere quantity decision, but a decision about the distribution of people's welfare.   Under the circumstances, a best possible decision about defense spending is not definable on pure efficiency grounds.   Any decision yields welfare consequences that can be assessed only with reference to notions of equity and justice.

EXTERNALITIES

External costs and benefits, sometimes termed spillover effects, are another characteristic of some economic activities that may argue for public intervention in the marketplace.   The implication of these effects is less severe than the public goods case, because externalities usually imply limited market inefficiency rather than a full-scale breakdown.   The inefficiency, moreover, may be reduced or eliminated by modifying market incentives rather than abandoning the market entirely.

Definitional Issues

An external cost or benefit is one that falls outside the market, affecting third parties (who might be termed innocent bystanders)—persons who are not directly involved in the activity that generates the externality. It is, in the words of Baumol and Oates, "an unintended side effect."[14] The classic, and by far the most important, case is that of environmental pollution.

Consider the chemical manufacturer who produces sulfur dioxide (SO_2) along with chemicals. The SO_2 is likely to create real economic costs: outdoor building surfaces deteriorate more quickly and therefore require more frequent painting and maintenance; the health of some people will be affected adversely over time; and the atmosphere will become less pleasant, an effect that may reduce residential property values in the surrounding area. It is unlikely, however, that the bulk of these costs will be felt by either the manufacturer or the manufacturer's customers (who may be quite distant from the production facility). Much of the burden is likely to fall instead on residents of nearby communities who are not parties to the (manufacturing) activity that generates the problem.

The important point of this example is that neither the producer of chemicals nor his customers will have a clear incentive to limit the pollution implied by their transactions. Although pollution costs are real, others bear them. Thus a portion of these pollution costs—perhaps the lion's share—is likely to be ignored. The result is that too much pollution, along with the chemicals, is produced—too much in the sense that it is more than society would choose if its full costs were taken into account.

---

[14]W. J. Baumol and W. E. Oates, *Economics, Environmental Policy and the Quality of Life* (Englewood Cliffs, N.J.: Prentice-Hall, 1979), 75.

Figure 5.2   Market Output and Socially Desirable Output in the Presence of External Costs

Market demand curve D and supply curve S_m determine equilibrium output Q_m. The hypothetical supply curve reflecting external as well as private costs of production is S_s, which would imply an optimal output Q_o.

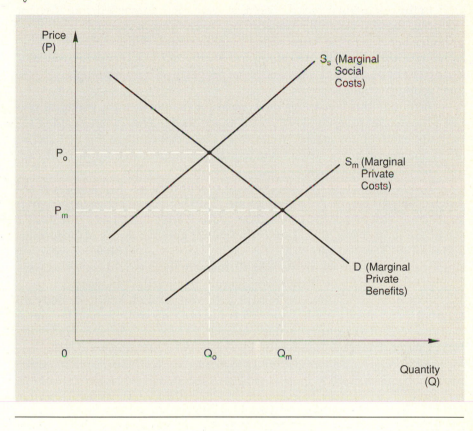

This last point is critical, for it suggests that the free market is likely to fail as the servant of society. Whereas the market may accurately reflect the private costs and benefits of chemical production, it cannot take account of externalities. In Figure 5.2, for example, D is the market demand for chemical products and S_m is market supply, reflecting the private costs of manufacturing chemicals and distributing them to customers. Recall that these curves measure the marginal benefits and marginal costs, respectively, of various output levels. Market output in Figure 5.2 will tend toward Q_m.

S_s represents the full social cost of supplying the chemicals—private manufacturing and distribution expenses plus the external costs of pollution. The socially appropriate level of production is therefore Q_o, at which point full costs and benefits are equated at the margin. The problem is now graphically evident: market output, Q_m, exceeds the social optimum, Q_o. By ignoring a portion of the cost of chemical production, the market has overproduced both chemicals and pollution.[15] By the same token, it has also underpriced chemicals and pollution, at P_m. The price for which the marginal benefit to consumers of the last unit of chemicals is just equal to the marginal social cost of chemicals, including the external cost, is P_o, higher than P_m. Thus the market generates a price for chemicals which is too low.

In the case of an external benefit, the situation is reversed. Suppose, for example, that by tastefully landscaping its campus, a research laboratory provides benefits to the surrounding neighborhood. The neighborhood becomes aesthetically more appealing, and nearby residents enjoy this amenity, as do passers-by and bird watchers. Local property owners are delighted to see their property values increase.

Although this scenario is more pleasing than that of the chemical polluter, the market is again likely to fail. Since the benefits of landscaping are partially external, the market understates the social value of this activity. In effect, the research laboratory is inadequately compensated for its landscaping, and the activity is therefore likely to be undersupplied.

It is worth noting that the problem of externalities is qualitatively not much different than that of public goods. The distinction between the two is largely one of degree. Most externalities can be viewed as representing a mild public goods problem. Recall our earlier public goods example of the farmers and rainfall. The difficulty there was really one of external benefits: were any single farmer to contract for the rainfall, his neighbors would benefit as well. The benefits of rain would spill over (literally!) onto adjacent farms.

Similarly, a pollution abatement program, undertaken to remedy an external cost, is itself a public good. We could not very well clean up the air for everyone except Mr. Jones who has refused to pay for the abatement program. In the case of water pollution, we might conceivably clean up a pond and refuse Jones admission to its shores without payment. Yet even here the public goods problem persists; whereas Jones could be excluded, the cost of doing so may be excessive.

Property Rights and the Coase Theorem

Economists now recognize that many externalities problems may usefully be viewed as an absence of well-delineated and enforced property rights. Such rights, in the words of Werner Z. Hirsch, refer to:

> Legal relationships . . . between a property owner and another person. One

---

[15]Externalities frequently involve both a private good (here chemicals) and a public good (actually a public "bad" in the case of pollution). The solution to the problem may be to create a new public good (a pollution abatement program). In the immediate example, a tolerable or efficient level of pollution might be achieved simply by reducing the output of chemicals or by "unbundling" chemicals and pollution, that is, adopting a less-polluting technology of chemical production. In either event, some reduction in chemical production is probable.

has a property right when one is able to compel another legally to do or not to do a given act.[16]

A landowner, for example, may prevent someone from dumping toxic chemicals on his land. An automobile owner may prevent others from using her car or charge them a fee for doing so. Property rights in these instances are clearly defined. When this is not the case, difficulties arise. As Seneca and Taussig put it:

> Externalities may be explained as the consequence either of an incomplete set of property rights or by the inability or unwillingness of the state to enforce public or private property rights.[17]

Or, to restate the point slightly, an externality implies conflicts whose resolution requires a comprehensive and enforced system of property rights assignments.

Air and water pollution are examples of problem areas. Ownership of clean air and clean water does not exist in the same sense that it does for land or automobiles. Property rights are obviously difficult to establish for such nonstationary substances. If you dump trash on my front lawn, I can act to stop you. But if you spew smoke into the air miles from my home and the pollutants are wafted into my living room, my recourse is less clear. I simply do not have an established property right to prevent your pollution—at least not until and unless a court grants it to me. It is the law as interpreted by the courts that assigns the distribution of property rights among individuals and enterprises.

This brings us to an important question. What is the socially correct response to problems created by externalities or inadequate property rights? Can an appropriate policy be defined? In addressing this issue, it is necessary once again to distinguish between equity and efficiency considerations. It may be possible to devise an efficient policy—one that leads to a reasonable quantitative limitation, say, on polluting activities—that is nevertheless regarded by most of us as patently unfair. Alternatively, we might pursue policies that are, by general consensus, fair, yet leave us with too much or too little pollution from a resource allocation standpoint.

The issues are complicated, and it may help to look at an example. Let us suppose that the chemical company referred to above pollutes the air heavily. This so enrages residents of the immediate neighborhood that they form a Community Protective Association (CPA) to fight the polluter. The association hires a lawyer and sues the company for polluting the community's atmosphere. In the ensuing trial, the association contends that local residents have the right to enjoy clean air. The company responds that it has the right to discharge its wastes into the atmosphere and that the resulting pollution of the area, while unfortunate, is not illegal. The ultimate decision of the court therefore involves the appropriate assignment of property rights.

At this point several considerations are pertinent. The equity question is straightforward (even though it may not be objectively answerable): Who

---

[16]W. Z. Hirsch, *Law and Economics* (New York: Academic Press, 1979), 8.

[17]J. J. Seneca and M. K. Taussig, *Environmental Economics*, 3d ed. (Englewood Cliffs, N.J.: Prentice-Hall, 1984), 59.

should bear the major cost of the externality? If the court rules in favor of the company, the CPA is without much further recourse. There is no way to force the company to limit its pollution, except perhaps to mount a publicity campaign or to lobby for new pollution control laws. Area residents in the meantime will continue to pay for the pollution by incurring increased maintenance expenses, seeing property values decline, and perhaps experiencing health problems. Alternatively, a decision in favor of the CPA places the main burden on the chemical manufacturer. The company will likely be required to purchase and install pollution control equipment and perhaps to cut back on its manufacturing activities as well. These changes will tend to increase costs and prices to consumers and probably reduce revenues, thereby lowering profits.[18] Each of us may believe that one or the other decision, and the resulting distribution of the burden, is more fair, but our beliefs are of course quite subjective.

The Coase Theorem   Consider now the efficiency or resource allocation question: Regardless of who pays, should the pollution continue or cease? (For simplicity, let us assume that these are the only possibilities; smaller changes in pollution levels are ruled out.) In a seminal article, Ronald Coase offered the following theorem:

> If the contesting parties can freely negotiate a dispute arising from a property rights conflict, they will arrive at the efficient solution—i.e., the solution that directs resources to their most highly valued uses. Furthermore, this solution will be reached regardless of a court's assignment of property rights. [19]

In terms of our example, this theorem says that if the chemical producer and the CPA are free to negotiate with each other (that is, if the transactions costs of negotiation are negligible), the court's decision about legal liability will have *no effect on whether the pollution continues or stops.*

This remarkable conclusion may be illustrated with the aid of some arbitrarily chosen numbers. Suppose that:

- The chemical company values its ability to pollute the air at $10,000 (that is, if it were forced to stop polluting, its profits would fall by this amount).
- Association members place a value of $15,000 on the abatement of the company's pollution (this represents the sum of their pollution costs).

We may now predict that whatever the court says, the pollution will stop. If the court rules in favor of the CPA, the company must legally end its polluting activities and (assuming effective enforcement) that is the end of the story. But suppose that the court finds that the company has a right to continue polluting. At this point the CPA will negotiate with the company, offering to pay it

---

[18]The ultimate effect on the chemical firm will depend partly on the structure of the industry within which it competes.

[19]R. Coase, "The Problem of Social Cost," *Journal of Law and Economics* 3 (October 1960): 1–44. For a thorough critique of the Coase theorem see S. Wellisz, "On External Diseconomies and the Government-Assisted Invisible Hand," *Economica* 31 (November 1964): 345–362.

something more than $10,000 (but less than $15,000) to stop its pollution. Suppose the association were to offer $13,000 (there may be some haggling and we cannot predict exactly what the settlement price will be). At $13,000, the company receives $3,000 more than it costs to end the pollution—a profitable bargain. It also makes sense for the CPA to agree to this settlement. Their members must pay only $13,000 to obtain a result that they value at $15,000. This scenario illustrates the workings of the Coase theorem in a particular situation. (A more general demonstration of the theorem is given in the appendix to this chapter.) In a purely allocative sense, the court's decision is irrelevant. The pollution is going to stop.

The assumption of negligible transactions costs, however, is crucial to this conclusion. In many circumstances, of course, such costs will be important and perhaps even prohibitive.[20] This is why, in the real world, environmental externality disputes are so frequently resolved by courts or legislatures rather than by private negotiations. The most dramatic implication of the Coase theorem has somewhat limited applicability. The theorem nevertheless generates some extremely important implications.

One of these implications is that where negotiation is impossible—too costly to occur—legal rules that impose liability for externalities exclusively on one party or the other may be highly inefficient. In one classic example, a railroad runs through farmland, emitting sparks that damage crops planted next to the tracks. A law holding the railroad responsible for all damages will not discourage farmers from planting crops right up to trackside. A law holding the farmers responsible will not encourage the railroad to find ways of limiting its sparks. The most efficient solution would likely involve some effort by both sides, and it cannot be reached by a legal rule that assigns full liability to one side or the other.[21]

A further implication of Coase's analysis concerns the equity effects of externalities solutions. In our pollution example, the court's decision will not affect the allocative outcome, but will clearly have a major impact on who bears the burden of the final result. We have already noted that the question "Who should pay?" must be answered subjectively. Many people are likely to suggest that the chemical manufacturer should bear the primary cost. After all, it has created the pollution and might thus be considered to blame for the problem.

As Coase argues, however, there is a sense in which such an answer oversimplifies matters. In fact, the question of who is to blame may not be meaningful. Externalities problems are mutual or reciprocal. Suppose that I produce smoke that you inhale. It is true that if I did not produce the smoke,

---

[20]For example, suppose that a million people are affected by the pollution. Some are unaware of it, others are aware but unwilling to contribute to a collective association (they would rather free ride), and those willing to contribute place varying values on the CPA. The chances are that the association will not be formed and that negotiations will not occur.

[21]American courts increasingly recognize that in some circumstances it is appropriate for litigating parties to share liability. In such cases, they are applying rules (such as *comparative negligence*) that assign a portion of the financial responsibility for damages to each side.

there would be no problem. But it is also true that if you did not inhale it, there would be no problem! In a sense, then, we are both responsible for the difficulty. Remove either one of our actions and the problem disappears![22]

Some voters will no doubt be unpersuaded by this argument, believing that the polluter bears more ethical responsibility than the victims. This is a perfectly acceptable value judgment, but even those who believe it strongly should not lose sight of Coase's important observation. Externalities are reciprocal in nature, whatever one's ethical point of view. All conceivable resolutions are costly, and in most instances the costs will be shared by the creator and the sufferer alike.[23] Equity considerations are of course important, and the distribution of these costs usually will respond to the type of solution adopted.[24] But it may be unwise to allow the search for fairness to obscure entirely the efficiency question: what is the least costly method of resolving the problem?

This is not a trivial question. Suppose that in our pollution example, the chemical company could eliminate its emissions by spending $50,000, but local residents could have eliminated the effects of the pollution at a cost $40,000 (perhaps by air conditioning their homes and painting them with a pollution-resistant compound). Requiring the company to solve the problem may satisfy one's sense of fairness, but only at the price of $10,000 in wasted resources. There is no a priori reason to think that those affected by externalities will as a general rule be able to resolve things more cheaply than those who create them. But single-minded pursuit of fair solutions that ignores this possibility will likely incur substantial costs in certain cases.[25]

Marginal Cases

The public goods and externalities examples that we have discussed are all plainly severe. They create sizable problems and require some public response. This is not always the case, however. In some instances an external affect may be clearly present but minor. The question then is whether the magnitude of the externality justifies the cost of government intervention. In

[22]It is clear from this example that the externality problem is closely bound up with location. If you smoke and I can walk away without any cost to me, then the problem disappears, as it does if you smoke but do not mind walking away from me. But if neither of us can move without incurring a cost, then the reciprocal nature of the problem arises. Zoning laws to define boundaries of residential and industrial areas have arisen partly in response to the externality implications of location.

[23]Even if legal liability is placed on the chemical manufacturer, the cost increases that result are likely to push up the price of chemicals and other products that contain chemicals. Consumers of all such products, some of whom are pollution sufferers, therefore bear part of the cost of the resolution.

[24]One complication is that some victims of the externality may not be alive at the same time the polluter is. For example, acid rain may damage forests for future generations. In such cases, victims will be underrepresented in negotiations over how much to pay to stop the pollution.

[25]Notice that the equity problems that may be implied by efficient solutions are themselves amenable to modification. Government could, for example, place the burden on pollution sufferers to protect themselves, but then subsidize the costs of doing so.

still other circumstances there may be disagreement about whether an externality exists. It is in these gray areas that policy choices are especially controversial.

Consider the issue of automobile safety. If I drive a car without brakes or a horn—or if I am not qualified to drive, it is you who may be hurt. The argument for laws that require brakes, horns, and licensing tests is therefore quite apparent. The issue is less clear, however, when we look at such safety devices as collapsible steering columns or seat belts. There are still some spillover effects, if only because reductions in traffic injuries and fatalities will lower insurance costs for all drivers, including those not involved in accidents. Yet some people believe that these safety requirements are an unwarranted intrusion on private choice. Although drivers who choose not to buy and wear a seat belt, may be imposing an external cost on society, they themselves bear the major risk of their own decision.

Another debatable area of public intervention is support for higher education. The case for public subsidy at the primary and secondary levels is strong.[26] I will benefit in many ways from the presence of a literate, educated population: wiser political decisions are likely to be made, greater competence and inventiveness in the economy will raise my standard of living, and so on.[27] These effects are not only important but plainly external—beyond the direct benefits that I receive by purchasing my own education or that of my children. As a taxpayer I am therefore willing to turn over some of my income to local government (usually in the form of property taxes) for educational purposes. The argument, as before, is that if we were to rely solely on the private demand for education, ignoring the external benefits, the market would underallocate resources to this activity.

In the case of college and university education, however, the picture is less clear-cut. The question is not whether higher education is worthwhile, but only whether the market will provide a socially adequate amount of it. The benefits of higher education, while substantial, may be largely private. They accrue directly to educated individuals, taking such forms as higher incomes and more interesting careers. Some external benefits no doubt exist, but their magnitude is difficult to estimate. College graduates often make important contributions to society, and some indexes of national economic well-being are correlated with educational levels. But do these observations reflect externalities sufficient to justify heavy public subsidies? Aid to education is not only widespread, but expensive as well. Consider government funded scholarship and loan programs, state and locally financed colleges and universities, federal and state research grants to private and public institutions.

The most appropriate public policy is hard to specify for two reasons. First, cause-and-effect relationships are unclear. Would the graduate who

---

[26]The argument that government should subsidize education, however, does not necessarily imply that it should run the school systems. Public subsidies to privately operated activities are feasible, and suggestions for educational voucher systems would do just that.

[27]It is, moreover, likely that the competent and inventive people will not fully capture the rewards for their skills in the marketplace.

makes a major contribution to society have done so even without college training? Equally important, would he have purchased that education had there been smaller public subsidies to offset its cost (that is, had the price been higher)? Do nations prosper because they have strong educational systems? Or do prosperous nations choose to devote more resources to education? The role of higher education is surely important, but quantitative estimates of its external effects are elusive.

Other examples could be discussed, but the point should now be clear. The existence of an externality is not alone sufficient justification for government to act. It must also be concluded that the spillover is of a magnitude that makes public action worthwhile. It is on this latter point that many of our most vigorous policy debates center.

INFORMATION PROBLEMS

Information is critical to virtually all economic decisions. A production manager cannot very well choose an output target without knowing production costs, which in turn require knowledge about the availability, quality, and prices of factor inputs. Marketing managers considering new product introductions need to know whether sufficient demand exists to justify a positive decision. Consumers need information in order to make sensible choices: what goods are available, who sells at what prices, and how the qualities of alternatives may vary.

Problems of inadequate information, or the absence of efficient markets in information, are therefore potentially serious. Notice, however, that adequate information is not perfect or complete any more than an adequate environment is perfectly free of pollution. Information, like other commodities, is costly to produce. An efficient level is simply one that balances those costs against the benefits of the activity.[28]

Nevertheless, there are a number of circumstances under which markets in information will be not only imperfect but inefficient, and in which the inefficiency is sufficiently important to warrant public action.

Public Goods Aspects

There are instances in which information looks very much like a public good. Consider a classic example: the production and dissemination of information about the safety of a new drug. This information will consist of data about the side effects of the drug, gathered from experimental and perhaps clinical trials. These data will possess two characteristics familiar from our discussion above:

1.   *Nonrivalrous consumption.* My use of the drug safety data does nothing to diminish anyone else's ability to use it.

---

[28]For a very important analysis, see George J. Stigler, "The Economics of Information," *Journal of Political Economy* 69 (June 1961): 213–225.

2. *Nonexcludability.* It would be difficult or impossible to confine use of the safety information to those willing to purchase it. The reason is at least twofold: information has a tendency to leak, especially where this does not diminish the welfare of the source; and society would not ethically condone withholding the information, from those unable to pay for it.[29]

Information about the safety (or risks) of a new drug is thus squarely in the public goods arena. This is a key reason for public regulation of drug safety in all advanced societies. We may disagree about the desirability of particular regulatory policies—in fact, a source of continuing controversy—but few people would seriously suggest that we leave drug safety decisions purely to the private market.

A somewhat less clear-cut example involves the production of information about consumer products generally. Such information is a valuable commodity for which consumers are willing to pay, and there are some private suppliers, for example, Consumers Union, specialized books, magazines and guides, investment advisory services, medical diagnosticians, and the like. Public goods problems nevertheless intrude.

Consumers Union, for example, cannot easily prevent nonsubscribers from learning about and making use of its product evaluations in *Consumer Reports*. Subscribers tell others or lend them copies of the magazine. Libraries make copies available to their members. When a report is especially newsworthy, it will be reported to wide audiences via the mass media. Consumers Union itself manages to survive as a nonprofit organization, but it is reasonable to surmise that such problems of excludability discourage many prospective suppliers from entering information markets. Once again, the essential difficulty is of a public goods nature.

Other Problems

Information markets may be inefficient for a number of other reasons having to do with the costliness of producing and supplying information. Brief reflection will suggest that the costs of obtaining adequate information in consumption markets vary widely. Buying a pair of socks is easy; inspecting the product will convey a reasonably accurate notion of its quality. (Here Phillip Nelson refers to the good as a *search product*—one whose characteristics can be largely assessed prior to purchase.)[30] Buying an automobile or a computer is another story entirely. Relatively few consumers can make a confident quality judgment of such products by inspecting the items. They are termed *experience products*, suggesting that the consumer must actually purchase and use them in order to evaluate their major qualities.

As a rule, we expect that good information will be more costly (that is,

---

[29]For an interesting discussion of the principle of gossip, see K. Greenawalt and E. Noam, "Confidentiality Claims of Business Organizations," in H. Goldschmid, ed., *Business Disclosure: Government's Need to Know* (New York: McGraw-Hill, 1979), 378–412.

[30]Phillip Nelson, "Advertising as Information," *Journal of Political Economy*, 82 (July–August 1974).

more difficult) to obtain in more complex product markets. There are actually two separate problems in these cases. First, consumers may not be able to obtain *enough* information in a quantitative sense, often because its public goods characteristics discourage information producers, as in our example above. Alternatively, the problem may be that whereas a large amount of information is available, most consumers are unable to understand it. Few of us, for example, are well-equipped to interpret and act on technical reports of drug safety experiments. These two types of problems show up in various specific forms and may carry different policy implications. Consider a few examples.

Product Hazard Information   In practice, most information about product hazards is not traded in explicit markets, but is provided by manufacturers themselves. (The reason is largely the public goods problem.) This raises an obvious incentives question: Will suppliers tell consumers enough about the dangers of their goods? A widely accepted answer appears to be no. As Cornell, Noll, and Weingast put the point:

> A private market economy provides too little information about hazards. A firm has no incentive to advertise the potential dangers of its own products, especially when its competitors do not.[31]

The issue is actually less straightforward than it may appear at first glance. Clearly, manufacturers will not enjoy telling consumers that their products may injure or even kill them! Nevertheless, some important reasons for disclosure of dangers exist. Serious hazards do not remain forever invisible to consumers. Furthermore, injured consumers can and do sue manufacturers, sometimes winning substantial damages awards. Under the circumstances, manufacturers may choose to advertise product risks, as unpleasant as the task may be. There remains, however, the possibility that hazards will be inadequately publicized.

Informational Asymmetries   Asymmetries in information (rather than generalized underproduction) may impede efficiency and, in extreme circumstances, threaten the existence of viable markets. Perhaps the best known example, analyzed by Akerlof, concerns the market for used cars.[32] Such cars may be of acceptable quality or they may be "lemons." The difficulty is that, whereas most buyers have little ability to distinguish, sellers usually have a very good idea of the category to which their offerings belong. Thus, the asymmetry.

Akerlof shows that where the imbalance is complete, a market in used cars cannot function. Since buyers cannot distinguish good cars from lemons, one price will prevail (ceteris paribus). But if a car sells at the same price

[31]N. W. Cornell, R. G. Noll, and B. Weingast, "Safety Regulation," in H. Owen and C. W. Schultze, eds., *Setting National Priorities: The Next Ten Years* (Washington, D.C.: Brookings Institution, 1976), 465.

[32]G. A. Akerlof, "The Market for Lemons: Asymmetrical Information and Market Behavior," *Quarterly Journal of Economics* 84 (August 1970): 488–500.

whether it is good or bad, sellers will be motivated to offer only bad cars. Lemons will take over the market, and the market may then collapse.

Why has this not occurred? The obvious answer is that private market arrangements have been devised that lessen the problem. Buyers often insist that a mechanic inspect a car before an agreement is reached.   Sellers may provide some protection (and information as well) by offering guarantees. Buying a used car nevertheless remains a risky transaction in many cases.

Processing Problems   Informational deficiencies, as noted, may arise in two distinct ways. Information may be inadequately supplied, as in the public goods examples described above; or individuals may lack the ability to interpret and make use of available information even though it exists in sufficient quantity. The latter circumstance is often referred to as a problem of information processing.

The importance of processing problems varies widely across markets. Most consumers, for example, have little trouble dealing with the information conveyed by the cooking instructions on food packages. (There are of course exceptions, for example, young children and functional illiterates.) Difficulties are more widespread where the information is more complex, for example, instructions for assembling some children's toys. In extreme cases, certain information is understandable only to experts, for example, data about the technical qualities of audio equipment.

Despite the potential importance of information-processing problems, exploration of the consequences has been limited for two reasons. First, the problems themselves are difficult to identify except in extreme circumstances. Do consumers understand thoroughly the information provided about such products as automobiles, lawnmowers, vitamin pills, or stereo receivers? Do they make good use of such information? It may prove quite difficult to tell. Second, even the existence of a clear processing problem may not carry obvious public policy implications. Where information itself is undersupplied, the policy prescription is apparent: encourage or require more of it. But where processing is the rub, what are we to do? To supply more information that consumers do not understand will be futile. One might suggest that better— more easily interpreted—information be encouraged or required. The suggestion is worthwhile (if self-evident) in some cases. Frequently, however, it amounts to well-intentioned but rather fuzzy advice.

THE ROLE OF GOVERNMENT

We have seen that severe externalities and public goods imply market failure and a consequent argument for government intervention. In extreme cases such as national defense, the intervention is unavoidable. The breakdown of the market is so complete that if the activity in question is to occur at all, government must supply it.

In less extreme circumstances—a moderately polluting industry or an industry in which information is undersupplied—the market outcome is merely inefficient. There may be room for improvement via public policy, but it is not necessary that government actually take over and organize the affected activity. Numerous policy options are likely to exist. Unfortunately, but not surprising, it is easier to identify reasons for public intervention than to specify what the best type of intervention would be. There may be a social consensus that government should do something about a particular problem, but little agreement as to what or how much should be done.

Pure Public Goods

Although the case for public action is clearest for such pure goods as national defense, this is also an area in which definition of an optimal policy is very difficult. The market will not provide a service that society regards as vital. Government must therefore enter, but enter to do what?[33] What is the correct amount of national defense? How should it be financed? These points are so fundamental that they differ little from some broader questions raised much earlier: What do we mean by social welfare? How can we determine whether one public action is socially superior to another?

We have seen that such questions do not have simple answers. It would take a rash person indeed to state with any assurance that he knows either the socially correct level of defense spending or the best tax system to finance it. We each have our opinion, but our opinions differ, and that is precisely the problem.[34]

One may in fact argue that definition of the optimal defense policy in any precise manner is beyond the realm of practicality. Rather, we might usefully concentrate on finding a socially acceptable process for making defense policy choices. If we are satisfied that the decision mechanism is reasonable, then (as argued in Chapter 2) we may be willing to accept the outcome that emerges from that procedure. The chosen menu of defense goods and services, and the system to finance it, are satisfactory not because each of us agrees that the particular configuration is precisely what we would have chosen, but rather because we agree that the means of choosing the configuration was reasonable.

What is the reasonable decision process? The one we employ is a political mechanism driven by a democratic voting system. One may not care much for the present administration's national defense policies, and some may actively seek to change them. But in a basic way, most of us accept such policies as the

---

[33]As we have frequently noted, government is not the only form of collective action. Many voluntary organizations provide a variety of collective goods. The free-rider problem for them is more severe than for government because such organizations, while they may impose dues, lack the power to tax.

[34]The Nobel Prize–winning insight by Kenneth J. Arrow, in *Social Choice and Individual Values*, 2d ed. (New York: Wiley, 1963) was an "impossibility theorem" in which he proved that under certain mild conditions it is impossible to derive a social welfare function from individual preference rankings. This finding led to a torrent of literature examining its implications. See Y. Ng, *Welfare Economics: Introduction and Development of Basic Concepts* (New York: Wiley, 1980) for a review.

product of a decision process that we see as superior to alternative processes. Since this book is concerned mainly with the government's impact on the private sector, we do not discuss extensively governmental provision of pure public goods. However, in Part III, where we consider traditional areas of public regulation, the process of public decision making is addressed in some detail.

Less Severe Externalities

When an activity generates an important externality, the market result is an inefficient level of both the activity and the external effect. Where chemical production creates external pollution costs, the market overproduces both chemicals and pollution. The general direction of an appropriate public policy is thus evident: both chemical and pollution outputs should be reduced.[35]

Such an effect can be obtained in different ways. One possibility is simply to pass laws that prohibit all pollution and impose severe penalties on violators. While this may be a superficially appealing policy, it is seldom practical. Attainment of a zero pollution level is likely to be either technically impossible or extravagantly expensive.

A second alternative is to establish a regulatory agency such as the Environmental Protection Agency, with authority to define permissible pollution limits and rules. This approach is widely utilized and may well have produced significant environmental improvements. There are, however, some important potential weaknesses in the use of regulation as a device to resolve externalities conflicts. These are discussed further in Chapter 22.

A third approach, favored by many economists, would retain market incentives to the greatest degree possible.[36] Rather than mandating a specific result—for example, a given level of air pollution—this approach attempts to bring home to all market participants the true social costs and benefits of their actions. Taxes on activities that generate external costs and subsidies to those that create external benefits would be the typical policy tools employed. These problems will be explored further in Chapter 22.

Merit Goods

There is a further area of public intervention in the market, usually called merit goods or wants, that we have not yet discussed explicitly. Clearly, much government activity cannot be rationalized as a response to externalities or public goods problems. Examples are subsidies for such items as school lunches and housing and heavy excise taxes on alcohol and tobacco (which might be termed "merit bads"). Musgrave has described these as goods "considered so meritorious that their satisfaction is provided for through the

[35]Were the externality a benefit rather than a cost, the appropriate policy would increase outputs.

[36]For an informative discussion of the general virtues of retaining market incentives, see C. L. Schultze, *The Public Use of Private Interest* (Washington, D.C.: Brookings Institution, 1977).

public budget, over and above what is provided for through the market."[37]

Merit goods, then, can be and are supplied in markets and may not create obvious externalities. Yet we choose to intervene publicly in their provision. What are the reasons for doing so? As Musgrave points out, the distinction between merit goods and public goods is not always firm. We may for example, provide free health care to the poor as a matter of merit, but health care has some aspects of a public good (you have a definite interest in my freedom from tuberculosis). The issue reaches farther, however, so let us depart from such fuzzy definitional cases.

Some examples of merit goods, such as the school lunch program, involve a distribution motive. We subsidize lunches at least partly because students from impoverished families could not otherwise afford good quality food. Since food quality is important, (meritorious), we do not want a youngster's ability to enjoy it to be fully dependent on her family's income. One may question the efficiency of the particular program we have established—would it not be better to subsidize the needy students directly, while withholding the subsidy from the more affluent?[38] But few will argue with its objectives.

The most controversial instances of merit goods intervention involve an apparent rejection of consumer sovereignty that we usually take as a given in welfare analysis. Consider high taxes on liquor or our earlier example of a seat belt requirement for cars. Do these policies not reflect a plain and simple refusal to accept the verdict of free markets? Some of us may feel that alcohol consumption is unwise or even immoral. We are not prepared to outlaw it (the lessons of Prohibition are remembered) but are quite happy to penalize and perhaps discourage it a bit. By similar token, we may believe that equipping all cars with seat belts is the proper thing to do—so much so that we remove the choice from the market, legislating the result instead. Both policies have similar effects: changes in output (and price) levels from those that consumers would have determined for themselves.

Inadequate Information

Government responds in various ways to problems of inadequate market information. At times, the policy is completely straightforward: since information is lacking, we require more of it. This is the justification for a large number of product labeling requirements, most of which have been adopted during the last 30 years.

Frequently, however, we respond to inadequate information with stronger measures, for example, product safety standards in foods, drugs, cosmetics,

---

[37]R. A. Musgrave, *Theory of Public Finance*, 13.

[38]This is a fair question that raises issues beyond the scope of the immediate discussion. For example, what is the correct distribution of income? And (once we define the correct distribution) are in kind or cash transfers the better means to attain it?

and motor vehicles. The arguments for these policies (which are discussed in more detail in Chapter 21) tend to be more controversial. It may be that otherwise adequate information is difficult for many consumers to understand (or process). Some individuals may not be capable of evaluating risks rationally and therefore need protection from themselves. At times, the rationale for intervention comes close to paternalism (although this is seldom admitted): we know what is best for you. Where this element appears, continuing controversy is virtually guaranteed.

SUMMARY

In this chapter we have described the main ways in which markets may fail to function efficiently. Public goods and externalities are the classic, traditional cases. Information problems have received increasing attention from economic analysts and are regarded as highly important. Each of these circumstances implies that the usual virtue of market efficiency is absent.

It is obvious that whenever the market fails in a serious way, we will be reluctant to rely on it to solve our economizing problems. The case for most government intervention is tied directly to these major market failures.

CONCLUSION

There are clear cases of market failure that argue for collective intervention. While the cases for intervention may be strong, however, government programs designed to mitigate market failure provoke extensive, perhaps increasing, debate. Why is this so?

The Pervasiveness of Externalities

External costs and benefits arise in all societies but are likely to be of particular importance in an economy such as that of the modern United States. One reason is industrialization, which gives rise to a complex set of pollution problems. The very techniques of production create externalities that might be largely absent in a less developed, more agrarian setting.

Urbanization and expanding population exacerbate the difficulty. How a family disposes of its garbage, or whether its members quarrel noisily would matter little to others in a frontier society. One's nearest neighbors might be miles away. In a densely populated city, however, many acts become visible, audible, and frequently bothersome to others. The spillovers multiply quickly.

It also may be that our concern with certain activities, notably those that degrade the environment, rises with our level of economic well-being. Pollution is sometimes termed a rich nation's problem, one that people struggling just to survive will ignore.

These factors suggest that externalities will be relatively common and may be viewed with increasingly serious concern in a society such as ours. As concern rises, so do demands for government action to resolve conflicts.[39] The growth of certain kinds of public activity in recent years may well be related to a proliferation of perceived externalities problems.

One might in fact question whether in our modern society there remain many purely private acts. If individual utilities are interdependent (such as when my well-being depends not only on my own material goods but on how well or poorly you are doing), then virtually all actions create spillovers. Spillovers thus defined, however, carry us beyond the practical limits of public policy. We cannot sensibly invoke government every time someone lifts a finger on the ground that finger lifting is annoying to others. Where to draw the line between private and external effects of activities, however, is a source of disagreement that is not likely to disappear soon.[40]

Equity and Efficiency Again

The entanglement of equity and efficiency in externalities problems is, as noted, severe. It is at times possible to define, with tolerable imprecision, the efficient resolution of an externality, such as the appropriate limitation on a polluting process. But the policy that will achieve this result is likely to impose a series of benefits and costs on different groups, some of them quite indirect and unintended.

Consider the relatively simple example of mandatory pollution control equipment for new cars, a program that has been in effect in the United States for some years. If we confine our attention to health effects, the major beneficiaries of this program are those people who would have become ill or whose existing illness would have been aggravated in the absence of the control devices. (Notice that these individuals may not be identifiable. We may have estimates of how many are affected, but not who they are.) Major burdens are borne by purchasers of new cars (the devices are costly and will tend to push up prices) and by the owners and employees of auto manufacturing companies, whose profits are reduced somewhat by the program.

If the effects ended here, the equity issue already would be complex. In fact, however, other groups also will be affected. All those involved in the production and sale of goods complementary with cars will suffer from a policy that, by increasing production costs, reduces automobile output. Similarly, those in competing areas—other modes of transportation—will be helped.

Will the overall result be fair? Fairness is, of course, a matter of individual judgment, but the pattern of costs and benefits implied by this program is a least partially haphazard. The worker in the radio plant that supplies automobile manufacturers is hardly to blame for pollution. Yet the policy designed to curb pollution could conceivably cost him his job. It is highly probable that

---

[39]As do private efforts, frequently of a legal nature.

[40]Perhaps the most controversial area includes such things as prostitution, pornography, gambling, and the use of certain drugs. Sometimes termed victimless crimes, these are activities that excite considerable indignation but may not imply clear external effects.

examples of inequity in any program that responds to externalities will not be difficult to find.[41]

The Costs of Public Policy

Public action to deal with social needs is not a free good. Agencies must be established and administrative costs may be high. Furthermore, as business executives are fond of pointing out, the agencies frequently impose costs on those they regulate. This is in fact part of their job. The polluter who is forced to reduce pollution, for example, will suffer real economic losses as a result.

Some observers contend that when all costs are examined, government can be seen frequently to come up with solutions for our ills that are worse than the original problems. Intervention is, to be sure, costly. There is no guarantee that public agencies, acting even with the best intentions, will be completely fair or completely efficient. We cannot rule out the possibility that the cure will be worse than the disease. This possibility is sometimes termed government failure. Consider the following example. In the late 1960s a government agency (the Food and Drug Administration) banned artifical sweeteners containing cyclamates because laboratory experiments showed that it caused cancer in animals. The ban contributed to sharply increased consumption of saccharin, which until the early 1980s was the only low-calorie sugar substitute left on the market. Further experiments showed that saccharin was probably a stronger carcinogen than cyclamates, which in retrospect appear quite safe. The government's ban on cyclamates—intended to reduce cancer risks for consumers—may therefore have increased that risk. Was the Food and Drug Administration inept or malicious? Certainly not. The point is simply that a public agency, like private individuals, can make mistakes.

Where the private market fails, however, chances for improvement exist. These chances become more abundant as the failure becomes more serious. It is at times popular to observe that government is the problem rather than the solution. Yet in the wide-ranging area of market failure, it is not government that creates the motivating difficulty.

The issues raised in this chapter will be discussed at greater length in Part III, where we focus on the problems of pricing for public utilities, and more generally, on the problem of direct regulation of industry by the government. Externalities, information, and associated problems of market failure are discussed in particular in Chapters 21 and 22.

Discussion Questions

1.   What we term public goods are usually services (such as national defense and police protection), whereas tangible products (such as bars of steel

---

[41]Even without government intervention, the ordinary working of the market may have capricious effects. For example, any increase or decrease in the demand for a product, will produce costs and benefits for individuals who are in no way responsible for the change.

and kegs of beer) are ordinarily traded in private markets with relatively little governmental regulation. Why should this distinction exist?

2.   This chapter has reviewed some important examples of market failure that provide arguments for government intervention. Some people, however, believe that government intervenes too much, that government is the problem, not the solution. What would such people say about the problems posed by public goods, externalities, and informational inefficiencies? Can a strong case against public intervention be made where these problems exist?

3.   "Virtually everything an individual or business does affects other people. In a sense, then, externalities are universal, but we would not want universal governmental regulation of individual or business activity." Do you agree? Is the definition of externalities implicit in this statement a reasonable one?

4.   Is there a clear market failure justification for the following government programs:

   a. Health warnings on cigarette packages?

   b. Non-smoking regulations in movie theaters?

   c. Speed limits on highways?

   d. Anti-gambling laws?

Selected Readings

Baumol, W. J., and Oates, W. E. *Economics, Environmental Policy, and the Quality of Life.* Englewood Cliffs, N.J.: Prentice-Hall, 1979. *A discussion of recent developments in environmental quality and environmental protection policy.*

Coase, R. "The Problem of Social Cost," *Journal of Law and Economics* 3 (October 1960): 1-44. *An important and widely cited analysis of externalities problems.*

Head, J. G. *Public Goods and Public Welfare.* Durham, N. C.: Duke University Press, 1974. A *thorough discussion of public goods and the policy issues they pose.*

Seneca, J. J. and Taussig, M. K. *Environmental Economics,* 3d ed. Englewood Cliffs, N.J.: Prentice-Hall, 1984. *A lucid general text on the economics of environmental problems.*

APPENDIX 5A
The Coase Theorem

A somewhat more general view of the Coase theorem is shown in Figure 5A.1. Company A engages in a productive but polluting activity. The marginal benefits that A obtains from this activity are represented by MB_A. The marginal costs imposed on B (the surrounding community) after B has made all possible adjustments, are given by MC_B. Total benefits and total costs for any given activity level are then equal to the areas under the marginal benefit and marginal cost curves, respectively.

If left to its own devices, A would pursue the activity to level OR, at which point A's marginal benefits are zero and total benefits are at a maximum (e + f + g). At OR, however, B incurs total costs equal to f + g + h. Net social welfare (W = benefit - cost) is:

$$W = e + f + g - (f + g + h)$$

or:

$$W = e - h$$

The optimal activity level for society is at OS, where net benefit is maximized (W = e + f - f = e > (e - h)).

The question at this point is whether the market will reach the optimum point OS without governmental intervention. Here the Coase theorem argues as follows:

1. Suppose that A is not liable for damages imposed on B. B is willing to pay as much as g + h to induce A to reduce the activity level from OR to OS. But A will accept anything more than g to initiate such a reduction. If A and B can bargain freely, they will agree to some payment (greater than g but less than g + h) under which the polluting activity is limited to OS.

2. Suppose that A is liable for damages imposed on B. If A were to pursue the polluting activity to OR, it would then be compelled to pay B an amount equal to f + g + h. A's net benefit at OR is thus reduced to:

$$e + f + g - (f + g + h)$$

or:

$$e - h$$

Figure 5A .1 The Coase Theorem: Marginal Benefits and Marginal
Costs of a Polluting Activity

In this diagram, A is a polluter and B is a pollution victim. MB_A shows the marginal benefits that A obtains
at various levels of polluting activity. MC_B measures B's marginal pollution costs at the various activity
levels. Areas under MB_A (e, f, g) reflect the total benefits derived by A at different activity levels. Areas under
MC_B (f, g, h) reflect the total costs suffered by B at different activity levels. A's optimal activity level, at OS,
is reached through bargaining.

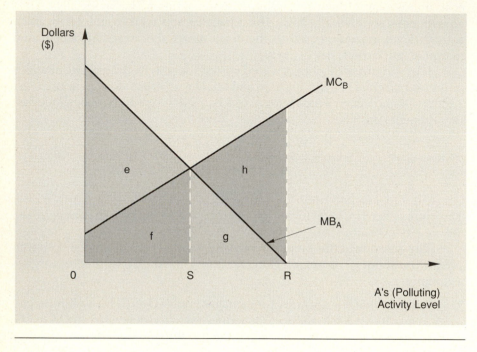

But at OS, A's net benefit (after paying damages of amount f) is (e + f) - f
= e > (e - h). A is therefore better off at OS than at OR, and will "voluntar-
ily" restrict his polluting activity accordingly.[a]

This is a somewhat more general depiction of the Coase theorem. A and B will
reach the socially desired activity level regardless of which party bears legal
liability for the external cost of pollution. Once again, however, this result
assumes that bargaining between the concerned parties is not only feasible but
costless.

[a]Also note that when A is liable for damages, MC_B becomes A's marginal cost curve. Therefore,
A's choice of output level OS maximizes A's net benefit from pollution. It does so because at OS,
marginal benefit equals marginal cost.

CHAPTER 6

· · · · · · · · · · · · · · · ·

CORPORATE RESPONSIBILITY: AN ANSWER TO MARKET FAILURE?

The social responsibility of American business has been widely discussed for several decades. Although the subject is an amorphous one, there are several reasons for examining it briefly.

1. As we have observed in the preceding three chapters, there are many ways in which markets may fail to act optimally. The possibilities for failure assume, however, that business firms behave as simple maximizers of their own self-interest. If corporations really act responsibly—whatever that may mean—then our concerns may be eased. Perhaps business conscience and statesmanship can save us from at least the worst effects of market failure.

2. By very similar token, responsible behavior on the part of our major corporations might reduce the need for governmental intervention. Self-regulation, in other words, could replace public regulation, at least to some degree.

The very idea that socially responsible behavior by business is desirable raises again the issue of morality and the marketplace. Do we in fact believe that markets produce unethical, or irresponsible, results with some frequency? Is this the motivation underlying arguments for business statesmanship? And, if so, is the conscience of corporation executives a sufficient substitute for either the discipline of efficient markets or the constraints of governmental policy?

WHAT IS SOCIAL RESPONSIBILITY?

As we have observed in some detail, the firm of standard neoclassical theory behaves rationally and acts in its own interest. The underlying rationale of the marketplace does not merely tolerate such selfish motivation, but requires it. For it is precisely the pursuit of profits by private managers that leads to socially desirable outcomes.

If one believed that markets function perfectly at all times, there would be little room for the notion of responsibility as something distinct from normal business behavior. Profit maximization in perfect markets implies the social good, and we could not therefore want our corporations to do otherwise. Moreover, business managers themselves would have little discretion. The market would force them to act with maximum efficiency because deviators could not survive long.[1]

The notion of socially responsible business behavior must therefore be tied to imperfections in markets, and specifically to those imperfections that imply some leeway or discretion for the firm. The company's managers must be free to choose responsible courses of action, which means that responsibility presupposes some degree of market power. As a practical matter this should not bother us—because concentrated power is a common condition. We do not encounter the truly impotent competitor very often. Having said that power is prerequisite to responsibility, however, we must confront the problem of defining the latter.

Some discussions of social responsibility are couched in very general terms. We may be told, for example, that the responsible business executive is one who takes account of the conflicting interests of different groups within society and attempts to balance their claims; who is concerned with the welfare of society and human betterment; or who pursues "those lines of action that are desirable in terms of the objectives and values of our society."[2] The trouble with such descriptions is that they are vague. Business managers are extremely plausible, and no doubt sincere, in explaining why virtually any policy that they adopt is in the social interest.[3] Moreover, what is good for General Motors may very well be good for America much of the time. If we did not believe that, we would presumably move to abandon the market system.

A number of writers have attempted to provide somewhat more specific notions of business responsibility. Clark C. Abt, for example, observes on the basis of his experience, widespread agreement among managers that responsible behavior includes such things as:

- Obeying major laws;
- Honest and truthful dealings with customers, employees, and other enterprises;
- Humane treatment of employees;
- Attempting to provide a fair return on investment to stockholders; and
- Providing equal employment opportunities for entry-level jobs only.

---

[1] Recall that the competitive firm has virtually no latitude in its behavior, because profit maximization is the sole route to long-term survival. There can thus be no real issue of managerial motivation in such a market.

[2] H. R. Bowen, *Social Responsibilities of the Businessman* (New York: Harper & Row, 1953), 6.

[3] This observation is not confined to business people. Don't we all believe that the things we do are socially useful—or at the very least, not harmful?

Abt further reports majority agreement on the following:

- Obeying all laws, including those weakly enforced;
- Restricting pollution and unsafe practices and products;
- Complete truthfulness in advertising;
- Modest contributions to local charities; and
- Providing equal employment opportunities at all job levels.[4]

Among the forms of behavior that, according to Abt, only a minority of management would include under the social responsibility heading are improved social justice; and active efforts to achieve equal employment opportunities, to reduce pollution, and to improve the quality of life of employees, consumers, and local residents.

Abt's listings are instructive in suggesting where business managers themselves may believe responsibility lies. It is apparent, however, that these examples of responsible action remain rather nonspecific. What is humane, honest, truthful, fair, and even equal tends to be very much in the eye of the beholder. Moreover, it is not clear that the socially responsible behavior of Abt's managers in all cases requires a true exercise of responsibility. To obey a major law, for example, is socially desirable. If, however, violation is likely to trigger serious penalties (including unwanted publicity), then the policy of obedience does not represent a discretionary decision to advance the social welfare. It is simply a pattern of behavior that society, in its own interest, imposes on the firm.[5]

Where, then, does the concept of social responsibility apply? In broad terms, the answer must be: in circumstances such that the interest of the firm and that of society diverge and where society has taken no prior action to remedy the divergence. Responsible behavior must at this point involve some sacrifice by the firm, the choice of society's interest at the expense of its own. This is not to suggest that the high-minded manager must commit corporate suicide to demonstrate a loyalty to the social good. Henry G. Manne puts the point succinctly:

> Corporate social responsibility must begin with the idea that the expenditure or activity be one for which the marginal returns to the corporation are less than the returns available from some alternative expenditure. That is not to say that the company must in absolute terms lose money but simply that it makes less money than would otherwise be the case.[6]

Absent some loss of potential profit or revenue, responsibility has no real content. It is merely our old friend, private optimization, perhaps exercised over the long run, with some public relations effort tacked on. George A.

---

[4]C. C. Abt, *The Social Audit for Management* (AMACOM, 1977), 8 ff.

[5]Keith Davis appropriately defines social responsibility as "a firm's acceptance of a social obligation *beyond the requirements of the law.*" (Italics added.) See K. Davis, "The Case For and Against Business Assumption of Social Responsibilities," *Academy of Management Journal* 16 (June 1973): 312–322.

[6]H. G. Manne and H .C. Wallich, *The Modern Corporation and Social Responsibility* (Washington, D.C.: American Enterprise Institute, 1972), 4.

Steiner and John F. Steiner point out that, as commonly defined, socially responsible actions may increase short-run profits, increase long-run profits, or have no clear impact on profits. In common usage, then, the term may be vague to the point of having no meaning.[7] Some writers appear to regard social responsibility as a form of enlightened self-interest, but the distinction between enlightened self-interest and some variety of constrained profit maximization is not obvious and very likely nonexistent.

In more specific terms, we may refer to some common and familiar situations in which the market fails to enforce a coincidence of private and social welfare. These include:

1.   *Monopoly* As we have seen, the profit-seeking monopolist produces too little. Socially responsible behavior might thus be presumed to require some increase in output (and decrease in price).[8]

2.   *Significant externalities* Recall the case of the company that may produce cheaply in private terms while creating substantial pollution, or limit its pollution, but incur higher private costs. In the absence of public penalties for polluting, the profit-maximizing solution is likely to involve too much pollution. Socially responsible behavior therefore implies some voluntary restriction, higher costs, and reduced profits.

There are, then, two important areas in which private and social interests diverge. These are not the only possible instances, but extensions of the list become more controversial. Consider, for example:

3.   *Discrimination*   Labor market discrimination, based especially on race and sex, is an unfortunate but undeniable part of our economic history. It has led some people to suggest that we should not merely end discrimination, as the law already requires, but also provide some positive aid for members of those groups that were most pervasively victimized in the past. If such assistance, usually categorized as affirmative action, is considered socially desirable, then companies may again find themselves in conflict with society. Profit maximization requires that firms hire the most efficient workers. An affirmative action approach suggests that companies should go out of their way to hire workers who have suffered from discrimination, even where some sacrifice of efficiency might be implied.[9]

---

[7]G. A. Steiner and J. F. Steiner, *Business, Government & Society: A Managerial Perspective*, 3d ed. (New York: Random House, 1980), Chapter 13.

[8]Thus the suggestion of Martin Bronfenbrenner that in order to behave responsibly toward consumers, firms must set product prices and specifications as if they were perfect competitors. See M. Bronfenbrenner, "The Consumer," in James W. McKie, ed., *Social Responsibility and the Business Predicament* (Washington, D.C.: Brookings Institution, 1974), 169–190.

[9]Advocates of affirmative action sometimes contend that it is not costly for employers. It is doubtful that this contention is consistently accurate. Where is it true, however, compliance with affirmative action no longer requires a clear exercise of social responsibility as we have defined it.

Affirmative action programs are, of course, highly controversial. Although the need to assist victims of past discrimination can hardly be doubted, some people regard affirmative action as a euphemism for reverse discrimination and reverse discrimination as a social evil. The nature of responsible behavior with respect to past discrimination is thus a matter of disagreement.

4.   *Product and occupational safety* If one believes, as do consumer advocates such as Ralph Nader, that markets consistently undersupply safety—that is, expose consumers and workers to too much risk—then there is once again a conflict between private and social interests and room for responsible action.[10] The quantity of safety that maximizes company profits is too small socially. Socially responsible behavior therefore involves the production of additional safety with some attendant sacrifice of profits.

There is, however, a substantial question about the premise of the argument that markets as a rule produce too little safety, and extensive legislation creating safety requirements exists in some areas (see Chapter 21). Whether socially responsible business behavior implies the voluntary devotion of additional resources to product and job safety is therefore debatable.

ARE AMERICAN CORPORATIONS SOCIALLY RESPONSIBLE?

Whether social responsibility is widely practiced is an unanswerable question in the sense that evidence of an objective nature may be impossible to obtain. Anecdotes abound and examples of both responsible and appallingly irresponsible behavior may be cited.[11]

Many corporations support worthy charities, at times anonymously. Yet the tobacco industry's trade association mounts publicity campaigns to convince people that smoking is not dangerous to health; asbestos companies for years did little to protect their unknowing employees from medically established hazards; and the Ford Motor Company at one point decided to save a relatively small amount of money by placing its Pinto gasoline tanks in a position highly vulnerable to puncture and explosion. Such examples by themselves are of little use; the issue cannot be addressed by referring to the actions of isolated companies here and there.

A large amount of survey data dealing with the social performance of business has been gathered. Such information covers a large number of companies and will conceivably permit some interesting observations. We may see, for example, that many corporation executives believe it is socially important to recruit disadvantaged persons in the labor force, but not to provide remedial training or counseling for employees who need it. All such

---

[10]See R. Nader, M. Green, and E. J. Seligman, *Taming the Corporate Giant* (New York: W. W. Norton, 1976).

[11]For some examples of the latter, see R. Heilbroner, et al., *In the Name of Profit* (Garden City, N.Y.: Doubleday, 1972).

data, however, is fatally flawed for our purposes. What these surveys do in effect is to ask business managers: Are you socially responsible? The answer is invariably a resounding "Yes!" But this is not a particularly useful piece of information.

What can be said, then, about the social responsibility of American businesses? At one end of the spectrum, it is clear that many—perhaps most—business executives pay attention to issues beyond profit and loss. Indeed, there is no reason to doubt their sincerity when they claim to care deeply about the course of society. But to know that managers care is to say nothing about whether or how corporate policies respond to notions of the social good. This is the fundamental problem.

The question of whether corporations in general act responsibly can be approached with reference to the traditional economic assumption of profit-maximizing behavior. Is there reason to believe that firms do not as a rule attempt to maximize profits? (If so, then responsible behavior becomes a plausible, although not inevitable, alternative.) The evidence on profit maximization like that on social responsibility itself is partially spongy and anecdotal, but there is some hard information as well.

There can be little doubt that the executives of large corporations wield some discretionary power, except perhaps in intensely competitive or exceptionally depressed industries. Corporate owners (stockholders) simply cannot exert very fine control over the day-to-day operations of their companies. Managers are accordingly free to depart from strict maximizing policies.[12] At the same time, however, there is now broad suspicion—supported by a substantial body of evidence—that they cannot and do not depart very far.

Executive compensation is frequently tied (via bonuses, stock options, and the like) to company profit performance, although profits are not the sole determinant of managerial income.[13] It also appears that the ability of corporate leaders to hold onto their jobs is directly related to profitability.[14] Indeed, some observers attribute the recent productivity problems of the U.S. economy in part to a preoccupation by managers with short-term profits. In this view, our business decision makers are so concerned with immediate payoffs that they may ignore the critical long-term investments whose rewards (partly in the form of productivity improvement) would not be forthcoming for several years.

Definitive statements are not possible, and conditions will of course vary among firms. But it seems probable that any manager who deliberately eases

[12]There is also such substantial uncertainty in business decision making that the strict maximizing policies may be difficult to identify.

[13]For one among many interesting empirical studies, see R. T. Masson, "Executive Motivations, Earnings, and Consequent Equity Performances," *Journal of Political Economy* 79 (November/December 1971): 1278–1292. A good survey of managerial motivation issues is provided by L. E. Preston, "Corporation and Society: The Search for a Paradigm," *Journal of Economic Literature* 13 (June 1975): 434–453.

[14]See M. Crain, T. Deaton, and R. Tollison, "On the Survival of Corporate Executives," *Southern Economic Journal* (January 1977): 1372–1375.

up on the pursuit of profits—whether for social responsibility or other reasons—is taking a risk. It is difficult to believe that many such persons could or would ignore the interests of their stockholders in any substantial way over a prolonged period of time. This does not mean that companies act irresponsibly. Most managers surely have notions of what is ethical and may pursue profits or revenues subject to the constraint that they do not act in socially unacceptable ways. Any claim, however, that executives push profits into the background in order to advance the greater good of society must be viewed skeptically. Absent systematic evidence, this simply is not a compelling contention.

IS SOCIAL RESPONSIBILITY DESIRABLE?

It may seem odd to question the desirability of responsible behavior. Does it not go almost without saying that our captains of industry should consider social objectives when they make decisions that affect us all? Who could want our fate to be determined by narrow-minded individuals whose sole concern is with the bottom line?

In point of fact, the issue is not so simple. Consider first the widely cited statement of Milton Friedman:

> Few trends could so thoroughly undermine the very foundations of our free society as the acceptance by corporate officials of a social responsibility other than to make as much money for their stockholders as possible. This is a fundamentally subversive doctrine. If businessmen do have a social responsibility other than making maximum profits for stockholder, how are they to know what it is?[15]

Friedman is a well-known conservative, but any liberals among us would be foolish to dismiss his argument for that reason. Ben W. Lewis, an economist with a much different viewpoint, has expressed a remarkably similar position:

> The weakness of corporate conscience . . . is that it has nothing to do with economizing. Its presence may assure us that the men who make the decisions will be well-intentioned and good, but it tells neither them nor us anything about the shape of goodness; it tells no one what society wants done and, hence, what to do.[16]

The point that Friedman and Lewis make is an important one that may be illustrated with a hypothetical example. Let us suppose that Alpha Chemical Company has a major decision to make. It can continue to dump its untreated wastes into a river—an act that kills fish, hinders recreation, and forces downstream communities to build water treatment plants in order to use the river as a source of drinking water.[17]

Alternatively, it can introduce a new technology that eliminates water pollution entirely. This will eliminate pollution costs for other users of the river, but will raise the company's production costs, thereby cutting its profits

---

[15]M. Friedman, *Capitalism and Freedom* (Chicago: University of Chicago Press, 1962), 133.

[16]Ben W. Lewis, "Economics by Admonition," *American Economic Review*, 50 (May 1959): 384–398.

[17]It is assumed that no laws exist to interfere with this course of action.

and raising chemical prices for its customers. Finally, Alpha could compromise, cutting back but not eliminating its pollution of the river. What should the company do? What is the responsible course of action?

It is likely that many people would regard the socially responsible solution as obvious: Alpha Company should adopt the new technology and stop imposing external costs on users of the river. This might be regarded as very responsible behavior while the compromise solution is moderately responsible. Consider, however, the complexity of the issue as shown in Figure 6.1 Q_1 represents Alpha's current (high pollution) output, which is lower than the competitive level Q_c.[18] The socially efficient output, determined by a balancing of social costs and benefits at the margin is Q^*. If Alpha continues its present (irresponsible) behavior, Q_1 persists. Very responsible behavior will put us at Q_3 while the moderately responsible compromise leads to Q_2. Notice that as Figure 6.1 is drawn, neither complete nor partial responsibility gets us to the socially efficient point. It looks as though moderate responsibility will be slightly better than continued irresponsibility, but very responsible behavior is the worst. Moreover, the figure could plausibly be redrawn so that any effort to be responsible would worsen social welfare!

One may object that Figure 6.1 loads the argument against social responsibility, and in a way it does. There are undoubtedly situations in which the obviously responsible course of action leads to a welfare improvement. On occasion, we might even get within reach of an optimal solution. But the broader lesson holds in all cases: the desire to act responsibly does not assure that forthcoming action will be socially good, much less as good as possible. In an allocative welfare sense, it may improve or worsen things.

One may, of course, counter this point with the familiar argument that allocative welfare is not everything. True enough. We may wish to consider distributional equity, but is the equity situation clear? A reduction of Alpha Company's profits will hurt the interest of some groups—Alpha's stockholders, employees (including managers), and customers (including the customers of the companies that buy from Alpha). It will help other groups—fishermen, swimmers, boaters, and the residents of communities that use the river as a drinking source. One might decide after careful examination that such a transfer of welfare is desirable. Then again, one might not. Most likely, different people will disagree on the merits.

This raises a further, perhaps even more compelling, objection to relying on Alpha Company's sense of responsibility. Pollution is a serious social problem, and it is society's problem. Do we wish to rely on the discretion of a particular corporate executive to decide the proper amount of pollution for all of us? Many persons, the authors of this book included, would say no, regardless of how well-meaning that executive might be. The costs of pollution

[18]Since Alpha has discretion, the company is a (full or partial) monopolist. When an activity creates external costs, it may be socially preferable that the activity occur under monopolistic rather than competitive market conditions. Monopoly tends to restrict the overproduction that would otherwise result. This point is discussed more fully in Chapter 22.

Figure 6.1 Alternative Outputs of a Polluting Chemical Manufacturer

Q_1 = Company output under current technology with no consideration of social responsibility
Q^* = Socially appropriate output (takes account of pollution externality)
Q_2 = Company's moderately responsible output (reduces but does not eliminate pollution)
Q_3 = Company's very responsible output (under costly new technology which eliminates external pollution
          costs)
Q_c = Output if chemical market were purely competitive

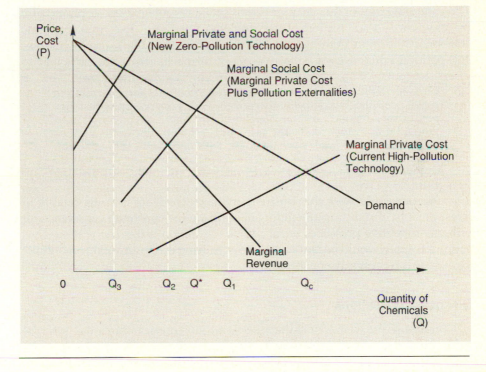

are not fully escapable, but there are choices to be made. No individual can decide what these choices shall be, least of all an individual who is not accountable to the public for her decisions.

A final possibility may be noted. Perhaps one opposes pollution on ethical grounds, believing that it is simply wrong for any person or company to impose external costs on innocent bystanders.[19] Such an individual must argue either for the complete elimination of polluting activities (a clear absurdity in many instances) or for some form of compensation to its victims. Yet even if one is committed to this position, it would make little sense to rely on social responsibility to bring it about.

---

[19]The logic of this position has little to recommend it. For a strong criticism, see H. Demsetz, "Social Responsibility in the Enterprise Economy," *International Institute for Economic Research, Reprint Paper 10*, April 1979.

As we have seen, the free market will not impose strict controls on polluting activities. Indeed, the problem of devising a policy of appropriate controls is formidable no matter who is to do it. Yet the case for putting this task in the hands of a group accountable to society—a governmental body—is a very strong one.

CONCLUSION

The essential point of this chapter is that social responsibility—economizing by conscience—is a symptom of our problems, not a cure. To rely on corporate statesmanship is to demonstrate clearly that neither the forces of market competition nor our own collective decision mechanisms are sufficient to direct the course of our economic future. In Lewis's eloquent words:

> Certainly, if those who direct our corporate concentrates are to be free from regulation either by competition or government, I can only hope that they will be conscientious, responsible and kindly...and I am prepared to be grateful if this proves to be the case. But, I shall be uneasy and a little ashamed...to be living my economic life within the limits set by the gracious bounty of the precious few. If we are to have rulers, let them be men of good will; but above all, let us join in choosing our rulers—and in ruling them.[20]

No one could wish that business managers will act unconscionably or irresponsibly. But the argument for substituting the corporate conscience for either competitive pressures or for public regulation is less than persuasive. Indeed, to do so would be tantamount to admitting the failure of our economic system as it is presently constituted.

Discussion Questions

1. Suppose we wish to test the assertion that American business is on the whole more socially responsible today than it was 20 or 30 years ago. How could we proceed? What information should we gather and examine? Do you think we are likely to find a reasonably clear conclusion?

2. "As a consumer, I hope that the companies whose products I buy are socially responsible." "As an investor, I would not want to put my money into socially responsible corporations." Are these sensible statements? Is there any inconsistency between them?

3. The Ford Motor Company has been sued successfully by a number of consumers, following explosions in Ford Pintos. The gas tank in some Pinto models was positioned so as to be highly vulnerable to puncture and explosion in rear-end collisions—a problem that company officials were apparently aware of at the time the models were designed and built. Is this an example of corporate irresponsibility? Should we undertake

[20]Ben W. Lewis, "Economics by Admonition," 395.

new government policies to avoid this sort of problem? If so, what kinds of policies would be appropriate?

Selected Readings

Lewis, B. W. "Economics by Admonition," *American Economic Review* 50 (May 1959): 384-398. *A strong argument against the assumption of social responsibilities by business.*

McKie, J. W., ed. *Social Responsibility and the Business Predicament.* Washington, D.C.: Brookings Institution, 1974. *A selection of readings about the social obligations of business managers.*

Nader, Ralph, et al. *Taming the Corporate Giant.* New York: W.W. Norton, 1976. *Some arguments about the need for corporate responsibility.*

Preston, L. E. "Corporation and Society: The Search for a Paradigm." *Journal of Economic Literature* 13 (June 1975): 434–453. *A survey of the literature dealing with topics such as managerial motivation.*

CHAPTER 7

. . . .

SUMMARY OF THE ISSUES

We have seen a number of basic reasons why the U.S. economy relies primarily on private market decisions but also accords an important role to government as an intervenor or modifier of those decisions. Viewed in broad terms, this mixture of private and public activity is appropriate. Markets are a very effective economizer of society's resources and will do a uniquely effective (optimal) job when unimpeded by imperfections. In some instances, however, various imperfections may cause markets to fail. Even an efficiently functioning market may at times produce results that most of us would consider unfair.

Where the market failure or inequity is believed to be serious, collective intervention to correct the problem—usually via government—may be in order. Yet the decision to intervene is not always simple or easy. It requires that we answer such questions as:

- When does a particular market fail to a serious degree?
- What is fair, and when is a market outcome so unfair as to be intolerable?
- If we agree that a market is performing poorly, is there good reason to expect that government can do better? If so, what kind of intervention will produce improvement?

These questions are basic to sensible decisions about public policy. The answers, however, are not always clear-cut. In fact, there is often substantial disagreement among people examining the same evidence.

WHAT IS SIGNIFICANT MARKET FAILURE ?

The Benefit–Cost Comparison

In the chapters above we have discussed some potentially fundamental sources of market failure: monopoly or oligopoly acting in monopolistic fashion, public goods and externalities, and information deficiencies that are sometimes a public goods problem. When any of these difficulties is severe, society,

151

acting through its political representatives, may reach a consensus that public correction is in order. There is, for example, broad acceptance of the need for government policies in such areas as national defense, highway construction, airplane safety, and environmental protection.

When market failure is less obviously severe, however, the decision to intervene (or to leave the market alone) may be highly controversial. Policies with respect to education, consumer and worker protection, transportation, broadcasting, abortion, prostitution, and so on fall within this category. Thus, we do not observe a simple dichotomy between market failure and success. Rather, success–failure is a continuum. Reasonable people may disagree about where on the continuum a particular market falls and at what point, or degree of failure, government intervention is justified.

Although no one is about to resolve these disagreements in a fully objective way, it is useful to consider what the sources of conflict may be. Take the very specific example of government policies designed to discourage deceptive and misleading advertising (discussed in detail in Chapter 21). This effort is pursued primarily by the Federal Trade Commission (FTC) and has historically been a relatively small program in budgetary terms.

Virtually everyone would agree that deceptive and misleading advertising is an undesirable activity. Who, after all, is going to defend purposeful misinformation? Yet the public program to combat deception is controversial, and some intelligent observers argue that we would be better off without it. Where does the disagreement between supporters and critics lie?

Advocates of FTC policies might rest their arguments on obvious ethical grounds: the deliberate dissemination of false or otherwise misleading information is simply wrong, and cannot be justified by other gains. An individual may justify a white lie by contending, for example, that it may be necessary to avoid hurting someone's feelings. No such rationale is open to the advertiser who tries to convince consumers that its product has virtues that it does not in fact possess. The latter action, many believe, is inconsistent with the behavior of a decent society. Such a society, therefore, should not tolerate it and the FTC program is accordingly justified.

Critics of the policy are likely to argue in rather different terms. One argument is that deception is undesirable, but there are some strong market incentives against it. The problem may therefore not be a serious one in many markets, and where it is serious, consumers have recourse through the legal system.

Another argument contends that FTC policies to discourage deceptive advertising may be quite expensive in an opportunity cost sense. They detract from the ability of the commission to do other things that critics of this program consider more valuable. The thrust of this position is that whereas action to deter false advertising may produce some good results, the program is likely to cost more than it is worth; that is, it would fail a cost-benefit test. This reasoning suggests that deception should be treated as an economic rather than a moral issue. It is undesirable, but does not fall beyond the pale of socially acceptable conduct. "Puffing" (that is, an exaggerated advertising claim) is not equivalent to murder.

We shall not attempt to decide in the immediate instance who may be right or wrong. But the notion that public policies ought to be subjected to cost-benefit comparison deserves some attention. On the surface, this is not a very provocative suggestion. Who would seriously argue that we should pursue public programs *without* considering the prospective gains and losses? Why should we undertake efforts that cost us more than the benefits they yield?[1]

Perhaps surprisingly, some people do object to the use of cost–benefit tests in deciding on public projects. A common argument is that certain kinds of results cannot and should not carry a price tag—some things are not quantifiable in dollar terms.[2]

A frequently cited example is human life. Suppose that a highway safety program that costs $1 million per year will save three lives per year. (Obviously such a prediction is subject to error, but let us accept it as reliable for the sake of simplicity.) The benefits of the safety program are otherwise negligible. Should the program be undertaken? An answer requires in effect that we decide whether it is *worth* $1 million dollars to save three lives annually. "But," some may object, "this is heartless! Who but a bloodless economist or actuary would even think of placing a price tag on people's lives?!"

In fact, no one wants to place price tags on lives. Few sensible people believe that it can be done. Yet some assessment of costs and benefits is necessary for reasonable policy decisions. No one really argues that we should adopt programs without looking at what they will cost and what they are likely to yield. Furthermore, this need for information does not disappear simply because saving lives happens to be the main benefit of a particular program.

Indeed, deciding whether a given lifesaving effect is or is not worth a particular expenditure of resources is at times an unavoidable task.[3] To protest that we cannot put a dollar value on a human life will not get around the problem. At best, it will lead us to act on the basis of arbitrary assumption rather than more careful examination. At worst, it could lead to absurd results.[4]

We have strayed a bit from the initial question: What is a significant market failure? The benefit–cost test provides a potentially useful answer: A

---

[1]No individual acting rationally does something unless it is worthwhile. One interpretation of worthwhile is simply that the benefits of the action outweigh (or justify) its costs.

[2]See, for example, Steven Kelman, "Cost–Benefit Analysis: An Ethical Critique," *Regulation*, 5 (January/February 1981): 33–40.

[3]For an excellent discussion of relevant issues, see T. T. Schelling, "The Life You Save May Be Your Own," in S. B. Chase, Jr., ed., *Problems in Public Expenditure Analysis* (Washington, D.C.: Brookings Institution, 1968).

[4]Suppose we accept the assertion (no doubt correct in certain circumstances) that human life is *infinitely* valuable, thus beyond any price tag. If taken as a basis for public policy, this statement implies that we must devote all available resources to lifesaving activity because nothing else could provide remotely comparable benefits. We would be forced to abandon programs that support education (except perhaps medical education), recreation, and cultural activities (museums and rock concerts may be nice, but they don't save lives). We would also have to cease such activities as automobile driving, which costs many thousands of lives every year. The point of these examples is not to argue that human life is of little value. Surely it is valuable, and all of us might well judge that the lives of those close to us are of infinite worth. Rather, as these examples suggest, the belief that life is infinitely valuable cannot serve as a useful basis for policy choices.

failure is significant and is therefore a candidate for corrective policy if that policy can be undertaken in a way that yields benefits greater than its costs. We will not decide to invoke public policy every time we see a favorable benefit–cost comparison, if only because we lack the resources to do all worthwhile things. Moreover, measurement difficulties will often limit the confidence we have in the comparisons that we are able to draw. In principle, however, the benefit–cost test is a useful starting point.

ARE MARKETS FAIR?

As we have duly noted, the question "What is fair?" has no truly objective answer. Fairness is in the eye of the beholder and if two or more beholders disagree, there is no obvious principle that will determine who is correct. A number of pertinent observations about markets and fairness are nevertheless possible.

If by fairness we refer to economic results such as the distribution of income and wealth, the argument for the market is not especially strong. Suppose, for example, that we have a market system that yields Pareto optimal results (that is, a purely competitive system). This tells us only that to improve someone's welfare we must make someone else worse off. It says nothing about how well or how poorly anyone does at the optimum. Further, it is perfectly consistent with a society in which some live in abundance while others starve—a situation that many of us would regard as flagrantly unfair.

By somewhat the same token, a competitive market system implies that everyone will be paid according to *marginal productivity*—the value of what he or she produces. Some people are, for a variety of reasons, unproductive. Do we believe it is fair that such people be paid so little that they cannot survive? We hope not!

If by fairness, however, we refer to opportunity rather than outcome, the case for the market is stronger. There is a sense in which a competitive system accords everyone the same chance for success and failure. No one in such a system possesses disproportionate clout. Competitive firms cannot discriminate on the basis of, say, race or sex because it is too costly to do so.[5] It is precisely the impersonality of the competitive market that implies that rewards will be based solely on performance.

In practice, of course, we operate far from the ideal. Some sellers and buyers do count more than others. They are bigger in the sense that they have more to spend. Market discrimination is a sad but undeniable aspect of our history. A variety of antidiscrimination laws has been in effect for some years, yet income differentials between whites and blacks and between men and women suggest that past problems are not yet close to resolution.

---

[5]The market, however, will not necessarily act to correct discrimination that occurs elsewhere. For example, labor markets give preference to more highly qualified job applicants even if the access to such qualifications is discriminatory.

Can government intervene to make markets fairer? If we define fairness as equal opportunity, the answer is yes. (Antidiscrimination laws have effects even though past patterns of discrimination do not disappear quickly.) If by fairness we mean results, the answer is less clear. The first problem is that we are unlikely to agree on what pattern of results is fair. Some argue for policies that would diminish income and wealth inequalities sharply.[6] Others respond that such policies inevitably dampen incentives, thereby reducing the size of the economic pie in which we all share. As a practical matter, we may reach some compromises. We adopt a network of welfare and other income-transfer programs that ease poverty for many, but do not dramatically alter the distribution of income and wealth.

Many agree that the equity–efficiency conflict, which we have observed in a number of contexts, is potentially serious. Efforts to be fair by their very nature modify the market system of rewards and punishments. If, for example, we assure people a decent standard of living (whatever that may mean) *regardless* of their contribution to society's output, might we not take the edge off the desire to contribute?

Such questions generate intense controversy, in part because the possible answers are strongly influenced by one's view of human nature and by one's current or expected position in society. The controversy suggests that policies designed to make markets fairer may be based largely on what we have termed noneconomic considerations. In addition, they may be subject to rapid change.[7]

A LOOK FORWARD AND BACK

The essential virtue of the marketplace is that it channels self-interest to the public good. Each of us, seeking our own reward, must contribute to the commonweal, for it is precisely (and only) such contribution that the market rewards. Self-interest, if not actually enlightened, is put to good use.

Government intervention in markets is in most instances tied directly to the market failures we have discussed earlier. In the case of antitrust policy, the subject of Part II of this book, the purpose of intervention is to promote competition. The virtues of the marketplace presuppose a competitive environment, yet there is no reason to believe that competition will automatically flourish throughout the economy. The prevention of monopoly and monopolistic practices thus offers a rationale for collective efforts to keep markets workably (if not perfectly) competitive.

What we term old-style regulation, covered in Part III, applies largely to public utility industries. Here the argument for government intervention is again tied to the absence of competitive vigor, but with a difference. Public utility–type industries have characteristics that suggest that competition may

---

[6]See, for a strong egalitarian argument, J. Rawls, *A Theory of Justice* (Cambridge, Mass.: Harvard University Press, 1971).

[7]For a lucid discussion of pertinent issues, see A. M. Okun, *Equality and Efficiency: The Big Trade-Off* (Washington, D.C.: Brookings Institution, 1975).

not be fully workable. (They are in some cases termed natural monopolies.) In these instances, government usually permits full or partial monopoly, but then moves to control the performance of the affected markets.

New-wave regulation, which we consider in Part IV, consists mainly of protections—for consumers and workers, and of environmental quality. The rationale for this type of intervention is varied. Environmental concerns arise primarily from externalities associated with pollution. Programs to protect consumers and workers may also be tied to externalities in some instances. The more common argument, however, is that inadequate information makes it difficult or impossible for many people to protect themselves adequately, especially where physical safety is at issue.

In thinking about these varied policies, it may be helpful to keep one general point in mind. The use of public action to modify the performance of a market economy is a perpetual balancing act. We may push ahead here, believing that a firmer correction of the market is needed, but pull back there, sensing that our intervention has become overly intrusive. The issues are often complex and the judgments difficult. It is precisely for these reasons that simplistic solutions or rules of thumb should be resisted.[8]

Many people are happy to tell us that markets are invariably good, and that government intervention is the problem, not the solution. Others will be equally glad to assert the reverse, that it is government that must save us from the exploitations of invariably imperfect (perhaps even malevolent) markets. Both groups are worth listening to, but their positions should be assessed with care and skepticism. Both are subject to the old saw, "Often wrong but never in doubt."

Discussion Question

1.   It is sometimes claimed that government should undertake certain policies without regard to their costs and benefits. For example, something should be done because it is the right or ethical course of action even though its costs might outweigh its benefits. Do you agree? Do you think most economists would agree? What about philosophers?

---

[8]For classic discussions of problems in democratic government decision making, see James M. Buchanan and Gordon Tullock, *The Calculus of Consent* (Ann Arbor, Mich. University of Michigan Press, 1962); and Anthony Downs, *An Economic Theory of Democracy* (New York: Harper and Row, 1967).

PART TWO

· ·

Antitrust Policy

· ·

CHAPTER 8

· · · · · · · · · · · · · · · · · · ·

THE REALM OF ANTITRUST

This part of the book focuses on antitrust policies, an area of government intervention that tends to rely heavily on the functioning of the market rather than on replacing it with other forms of decision making. It is important to bear in mind that economic arguments for the marketplace presuppose effective competition. There is no compelling reason to expect the powerful monopolist to behave in a socially useful fashion, unless perhaps one has strong faith in corporate vision and statemanship or simply believes that any private decision is necessarily good.

Antitrust is frequently described as that set of arrangements—laws, enforcement agencies, courts—that seeks to encourage and protect competition in those segments of the economy where competition is feasible. It is a largely prohibitory body of rules of the game, spelling out what business managers may not do in their search for profits or other objectives. While this sort of description of antitrust is acceptable, it is also highly simplified and tends to submerge some important problems.

Encouraging competition, for example, has no specific meaning until the term itself is defined. Yet it is abundantly clear that the meaning of competition, the ways in which it should be measured, and the effects of many public actions upon it are subjects of much disagreement. The disagreements are in part technical. Economists looking at a given body of theory and evidence may draw different conclusions about the likely effects, for example, of breaking large firms into a group of more numerous, smaller rivals. In significant part, however, the disagreements are based on distinctive views of the world. Competition is a word that many, especially in the United States, attach to desirable forms of market structure and behavior. What is termed competitive thus becomes partly a matter of what one regards as desirable.

It is also an oversimplification to divide the economy conceptually into segments within which competition is feasible or infeasible. Such categories may make some sense at the extremes (for example, wheat farming and electricity production) but many gradations lie in between. The pertinent policy question is not usually: Can competition work? But rather, can the degree of competition that exists be improved by public intervention?

WHY A PUBLIC ANTITRUST POLICY?

Although the evils of monopoly are widely understood, it is worth beginning with our standard query: Why is there a need for public intervention (in this case, a government effort to limit monopoly)? Why not leave solution of the problem to the market itself or, alternatively, to purely private actions within the existing legal system?

This question is not frequently raised. Even Milton Friedman, an economist with a strong preference for private resolution of most problems, cites without discussion "monopoly and similar . . . imperfections" as justification for government action.[1]

Posner advances the argument a bit by noting that a monopolistic agreement such as price-fixing injures "others, consumers who are not party to the contract," and points out that simple refusal by the courts to enforce such agreements is not an adequate remedy.[2]

Elzinga and Breit have argued that the elimination of monopoly (something roughly akin to modern antitrust policy) is a "public good in the purest sense . . . both indivisible and nonexcludable."[3] There is a classic free-rider problem: once monopoly is eliminated, all consumers of affected products benefit. But because there is no easy way to withhold the benefits from those who fail to pay for the removal of monopoly, no one will have incentives as an individual to support such an effort.

As we have seen, monopoly implies a net social burden under some circumstances. That is, the costs it creates for consumers (in higher prices and smaller outputs) exceed the gains (profits) that accrue to sellers. It follows that society is better off without monopoly, but the free-rider problem, among other things, helps to explain why a socially beneficial activity will not be undertaken privately. That government has a legitimate role to play in supporting competitive markets is widely (perhaps universally) agreed. Just what that role should be, in concept and practice, however, is a subject of continuing controversy.

DEFINING COMPETITION

As noted, it is necessary to define competition in order to specify the content of policies toward competition. It is surprisingly difficult, however, to formulate a definition that most observers of government–market relationships would

---

[1]M. Friedman, *Capitalism and Freedom* (Chicago: University of Chicago Press, 1962), 28.

[2]R. A. Posner, *Economic Analysis of Law* (Boston: Little, Brown and Company, 1972), 114–115.

[3]K.G. Elzinga and W. Breit, *The Antitrust Penalties* (New Haven, Conn.: Yale University Press, 1976), 4ff.

agree to. The points of contention, moreover, are not mere quibbles. The disagreements about the nature of the competitive state are fundamental ones.

Economic Approaches

Traditionally, economic approaches to competition have been identified with an emphasis on conditions of market structure such as concentration, the condition of entry, and the nature of products sold (the usual distinction is between homogeneous and differentiated goods).[4] The importance of structure is clearly visible in the purely competitive model: it is the large number of small competitors, freedom of entry, and homogeneity of products together that determine all facets of market behavior. Behavior, in other words, flows from a precisely defined set of structural conditions.

Emphasis on market structure suggests that competition is, in effect, a type of environment, specifically, one in which no individual or small group has the power to dictate the terms under which goods will be offered to the market. Such absence of power or control not only implies a uniquely efficient use of resources, but also is often regarded as consistent with the principles of a democratic society.

Two difficulties with the structural approach to competition deserve mention. First, its theoretical clarity is lost once the polar cases of pure competition and pure monopoly are abandoned. In oligopoly markets, for example, it may prove difficult to predict whether or how small structural changes would affect the condition of competition. The second problem is that while market structure is indeed a *policy variable*, amenable to change (for example, via judicial manipulation), pursuit of perfectly competitive structures is in most instances an inappropriate goal. There are many markets in which technically efficient production is incompatible with small firm size.[5] Moreover, to the extent that society is concerned with product and process innovation over time, the definition of optimal market structure becomes more difficult.

Market Performance

Alternatively, competition may be defined by market performance criteria—such observable magnitudes as prices, output levels, and profit rates. To approach the term in this way is to suggest that what matters is market results rather than the environment. Mark S. Massell, for example, has said:

---

[4]This is not to suggest full agreement within the economics profession, however. A substantial number of modern economists argue that structure has been overemphasized.

[5]The distinction between technical production efficiency and the efficiency of society's resource allocation is worth repeating. Technical efficiency refers to the minimization of production costs, given that output decisions have been made. Allocative efficiency refers to output or production decisions and requires roughly that we use our resources in those activities that we value most highly.

Conceptually, the ultimate judgment about the effectiveness of competition in a market should be its performance. How competitive are the prices, the production, the innovations, the consumer choices?[6]

Although many economists might agree with Massell, performance-based definitions of competition also encounter difficulties in an antitrust context. First, it is not clear that performance is directly amenable to public regulation in a private market setting. For an agency or court to impose for example, a profit limitation on a given group of firms would smack of the more severe controls that we see in the publicly regulated industries. Such a dictate largely abandons the private enterprise premise that the market should work its will.

Additionally, there is often no clear benchmark against which to judge observed performance patterns. We know, for example, that in perfect competition, price will be forced into equality with marginal cost. Depart from the strict competitive conditions and the equality vanishes. But there is little *a priori* basis on which to characterize any observed degree of price-cost discrepancy as either competitive or monopolistic.

Finally, some important measurement problems arise. This is especially troublesome where data are available mainly at the firm level and firms are diversified—a pattern typically found in large American corporations. Our analytical arguments generally apply to the relatively narrow product market or line of commerce.[7] To know the overall profitability of a firm that operates in a dozen markets may not help us to assess the degree of competition within any one of them.

Conduct

Perhaps the most popular notion of competition, especially within the business and legal worlds, is tied to the nature of decisions made by the firm and market. The essence of competition in this sense is active rivalry—an independent struggle to acquire customers.[8] It is neither an environment nor a result, but a process.

The antithesis of competition thus defined (that is, monopoly) is some restraint on rivalry, such as coordinated, concerted, or collusive behavior. It is the avoidance of the competitive battle, however achieved. The legal test is sometimes drawn quite narrowly: an acceptable competitive state may simply

---

[6]M. S. Massell, *Competition and Monopoly* (Washington, D.C.: Brookings Institution, 1962), 221.

[7]Narrower line-of-business data are now gathered by the Federal Trade Commission for many large corporations. As this bank of information grows, finer performance examination will become easier.

[8]Scherer refers to "an independent striving for patronage by the various sellers in a market." F. M. Scherer, *Industrial Market Structure and Economic Performance*, 2d ed. (Chicago: Rand McNally, 1980), 10. Brooks notes that competition "in its ordinary business sense means that rival companies. . . attempt to divert trade from each other." R. C. Brooks, "Businessmen's Concepts of INJURY to Competition," *California Management Review* 3 (Summer 1961).

be one in which no identifiable restrictive or exclusionary practices occur.[9] How the existence and extent of such practices should be discerned becomes a central policy issue, which will be discussed in some detail below. Suffice it to say here that the available, direct measures of market conduct may be quite inadequate as a basis for assessing competition.

Broader Notions

Some writers argue that competition is most usefully defined without specifically prescribed links to structure, conduct, or performance. Robert Bork, for example, contends that competition is "any state of affairs in which consumer welfare cannot be increased by judicial decree."[10] Jesse Markham has argued, in a similar vein, that a market is "workably competitive" when "there is no clearly indicated change that can be effected through public policy measures that would result in greater social gains than social losses."[11]

Where does this variety of suggestions leave us? It is apparent that experts disagree about the nature of competition. The alternative definitions are not necessarily inconsistent with one another. A competitive market structure, for example, should produce competitive conduct and performance. But once we leave the pure extremes of competition and monopoly, the structure–conduct–performance linkages are greatly weakened. (A particular size distribution of firms, for example, might lead either to fierce rivalry or to collusion.) The multiplicity of definitions suggests that policymakers should be looking at, and relying on, widely divergent criteria.

It is worth repeating that the main distinctions may be ideological. Persons concerned with the democratic quality of decisions—that is, who participates in the process rather than what result emerges—may well stress a structural approach. Those who stress efficiency in production and innovation are more likely to look to performance, while those who believe a good, hard fight is what matters will emphasize conduct. These categories, however, should not be regarded as rigid or exclusive. Some will argue that effective competition must embrace all three.

A useful perspective was offered by Ben Lewis some time ago:

> Results alone throw no light on the really significant question: have these results been compelled by the system—by competition—or do they represent simply the dispensations of managements which, with a wide latitude

---

[9]The terms restriction and exclusion have particular legal meanings. Quite obviously, restriction and exclusion in some sense always accompany market activity. If, for example, a manufacturer of soups contracts to buy his onions and mushrooms from a particular supplier, other suppliers are excluded from that transaction, which represents a particular portion of the market.

[10]R. H. Bork, *The Antitrust Paradox* (New York: Basic Books, 1978), 51.

[11]J. W. Markham, "An Alternative Approach to the Concept of Workable Competition," *American Economic Review* 40 (June 1950): 361.

of policy choices at their disposal, happen at the moment to be benevolent or "smart"? This points up the real issue.[12]

THE ANTITRUST LAWS

The development of modern antitrust in the United States is tied to the rapid expansion and industrialization that followed the Civil War. A trust, strictly speaking, is a legal device.[13] But during the latter nineteenth century, the word was broadly and pejoratively applied to large, powerful, ofttimes abusive industrial enterprises. As Sherman puts it: "Trust stood for monopoly, and in America this is the period that gave monopoly its bad name."[14]

The response to such widely shared sentiment was a brief, generally unsuccessful experience with state antitrust laws, followed in 1890 and again in 1914 by the adoption of the major federal antitrust statutes.

The Sherman Act (1890)

Section 1. Every contract, combination in the form of trust or otherwise, or conspiracy, in restraint of trade or commerce among the several States, or with foreign nations, is hereby declared to be illegal.

Section 2. Every person who shall monopolize, or attempt to monopolize, or combine or conspire with any other person or persons, to monopolize any part of the trade or commerce among the several States, or with foreign nations, shall be deemed guilty of a misdemeanor . . . [Section 2 was amended in 1975 to elevate the status of offenses from misdemeanor to felony.]

The Clayton Act (1914)

Section 2. That it shall be unlawful for any person engaged in commerce . . . to discriminate in price between different purchasers of commodities . . . where the effect of such discrimination may be to substantially lessen competition or tend to create a monopoly in any line of commerce: provided, that nothing herein contained shall prevent discrimination in price between purchasers of commodities on account of differences in the grade, quality, or quantity of the commodity sold, or that makes only due allowance for differences in the cost of selling or transportation, or discrimination in price in the same or different communities made in good faith to meet competition. [Section 2 was amended to prohibit various specific practices by the Robinson-Patman Act of 1936.]

Section 3. That it shall be unlawful for any person engaged in commerce . . . to lease or make a sale or contract for sale on the condition, agreement, or understanding that the lessee or purchaser thereof shall not use or deal in

---

[12]B. W. Lewis, "The Effectiveness of the Federal Antitrust Laws: A Symposium," D. M. Keezer, ed., *American Economic Review* 39 (June 1949): 706–707.

[13]It is a fiduciary arrangement under which one or more persons (trustees) administers property for the benefit of another or others (beneficiaries). Combinations of firms often used this device to manage their interests jointly.

[14]R. Sherman, *Antitrust Policies and Issues* (New York: Addison-Wesley, 1978), 32.

the goods ... of a competitor or competitors of the lessor or seller, where the effect ... may be to substantially lessen competition or tend to create a monopoly in any line of commerce.

Section 4. That any person who shall be injured in his business or property by reason of anything forbidden in the antitrust laws may sue ... and shall recover threefold the damages by him sustained.

Section 7. That no corporation... shall ... acquire ... the whole or any part of the stock or share capital of another corporation ... where the effect of such acquisition may be to substantially lessen competition between [the two] ... or to restrain ... commerce or tend to create a monopoly in any line of commerce. [Section 7 was amended in 1950 to prohibit corporate acquisition of stock or assets "where in any line of commerce in any section of the country, the effect ... may be substantially to lessen competition, or to tend to create a monopoly."]

The Federal Trade Commission Act (1914)

Section 5. That unfair methods of competition in commerce are hereby declared unlawful. [Section 5 was amended in 1938 by the Wheeler-Lea Act to prohibit "unfair or deceptive acts or practices ... "]

It could not have been clear in 1890 just how the Sherman Act would change the substance of the existing law of monopoly. Terms such as *restraint of trade* and *to monopolize* carried some meaning under common law, but were far from precise. The new law did, of course, establish a public policy rather than leaving matters entirely in the hands of private litigants. But in so doing, it provided neither potent remedy for violations, nor new funds for the Department of Justice, the agency charged with enforcing the law.[15]

The Clayton Act took aim at a number of specific practices that were not being handled consistently under the Sherman Act. It has had important impact, although it must be noted that the original merger restriction (Section 7) had little effect prior to the Celler-Kefauver Act of 1950, amending Section 7. On the other hand, the private treble-damage provision (Section 4) has proved something of a sleeping giant, exerting considerable influence in recent years.

The Federal Trade Commission Act established the Commission and provided it with broad, though rather vague, authority under Section 5. The FTC has functioned in significant part as a consumer protection agency (discussed in Chapter 21), but does overlap with the Justice Department in a number of antitrust areas.

CONCLUSION

This section of the book is organized as follows. Chapter 9 explores the existing structure of American industry and some of the important observed relationships between industry structure, conduct, and performance. These discussions set forth the empirical basis for much of our modern antitrust policy.

---

[15]See R. Sherman, *Antitrust Policies*, Chapter 3.

Chapters 10 and 11 examine our public treatment of the two major policy areas: market power and market behavior. In each chapter, development of legal doctrine is traced and subjected to economic analysis and (frequently) criticism. Chapter 12 discusses the overall effectiveness of antitrust policies, a matter of significant disagreement among economists, lawyers, and other policy officials.

Discussion Question

1.   The antitrust laws are designed to promote competition, but competition is a difficult term to define. Which of the various definitions discussed in this chapter makes the most sense to you? Which is closest to the meaning of the term outside the realm of economics and business?

CHAPTER 9

· · · · · · · · · · · · · · · · · ·

THE STRUCTURE OF INDUSTRY: MEASUREMENT PROBLEMS AND EVIDENCE [1]

The phenomenon of monopoly power, discussed in Chapters 3 and 4, influences firm and industry performance in important ways. In turning to antitrust policy—one of the major responses to monopoly power in the real world—a number of essentially empirical questions come to the fore. What is the structure of American industry and how monopolistic or competitive does it seem to be? Can the degree of monopoly be confidently inferred from structural information? Which measures are most appropriate to such a task? Perhaps most important, what do our observations of structure–conduct–performance relationships suggest for a sensible public policy?

First we describe the structure of the economy as a whole. Next we discuss some general problems associated with measuring monopoly power and introduce the structure–conduct–performance paradigm for analyzing industrial organization. We consider some practical difficulties that arise when we attempt to measure industry structure, conduct, and performance. Next we examine the econometric approach to identifying empirically the relationships between industry structure and industry performance. Finally, we assess what light (and how much!) has been shed on our knowledge of industrial organization by the empirical literature and what guidelines it suggests for policy-making.

---

[1] There are many excellent discussions of these topics. The best initial source is F. M. Scherer, *Industrial Market Structure and Economic Performance*, 2d ed. (Chicago: Rand McNally, 1980). The size and comprehensiveness of this book is an indication that the structure and performance of American industry is a complex topic. In this chapter, we confine ourselves to raising basic points that will be useful for our discussions in later chapters.

THE STRUCTURE OF THE ECONOMY

Consider first the economy as a whole. Which industries are the most important? Which firms? Has there been much change in the relative importance of industries and firms over time? In Table 9.1 the relative importance of the major industrial sectors is measured by the percentage of national income originating in each.[2] By far the largest sector in 1965 was manufacturing, generating 30.5 percent of national income. Second was wholesale and retail trade with 15.0 percent, and next the government and services sectors. Two decades later, in 1985, manufacturing was still the most important, but its share had dropped to 21.0 percent. Wholesale and retail trade had retained their share, but had been overtaken by the services sector, which now had 18 percent. The finance, insurance, and real estate sector had continued to grow, but still had not overtaken the government sector, which had grown to 14.7 percent.

It is interesting to compare the sectors whose shares have declined with those whose shares have increased over the period 1965 to 1985. Agriculture, manufacturing, and transportation have all declined in relative importance, while mining and construction, communication, electric and gas, wholesale and retail trade, finance, insurance and real estate, services, government, and the rest-of-the-world sectors all show increased shares, mostly taken from the large decline in the share of manufacturing. Note the continuing small share of the communication sector. The share of the government sector rose between 1965 and 1975, but has since declined.

Changes in sector sizes result (among many other things) from changes in technology, shifts in population, changes in demand, and the influence of foreign trade. These changes in turn affect productivity, overall prices, and living standards. The relative decline of the agricultural and manufacturing sectors and the rise in size of the government and service sectors have sometimes been blamed for the erosion in average productivity in the American economy during most of the last decade and a half (only very recently reversed).[3] In fact, the sources of productivity decline are complicated.[4] Changing sector sizes should not be used to explain all our economic ills, but should be viewed as a record of what is happening.

We turn now to the size and relative importance of firms in the economy as a whole. (It bears repeating that, by contrast, monopoly power refers to the relative importance of firms within a specific industry.) Concern about the absolute size of U.S. corporations is not new. The question of the desirability of

---

[2]Share of national income is only one way of measuring relative sector sizes. A broader picture would also include relative sector shares in gross national product and in total employment.

[3]For a more detailed description of changes in the manufacturing sector since 1955, and a more optimistic assessment of its current state, see Michael F. Bryan, "Is Manufacturing Disappearing?" *Economic Commentary* (Federal Reserve Bank of Cleveland, July 15, 1985).

[4]See E. F. Denison, *Accounting for Slower Economic Growth: The United States in the 1970's* (Washington, D.C.: Brookings Institution, 1979), for a full analysis of this problem.

Table 9.1 Percent of National Income Originating in Different Industrial Sectors

Sector	1965	1970	1975	1980	1985
Agriculture, forestry, and fisheries	3.8	3.2	3.6	2.8	2.4
Mining and construction	6.2	6.3	6.4	6.7	6.6
Manufacturing	30.5	27.1	25.1	24.2	21.0
Durable goods	18.8	16.1	14.8	14.4	12.6
Nondurable goods	11.7	11.0	10.3	9.9	8.4
Transportation	4.1	3.7	3.6	3.7	3.4
Communication	2.0	2.1	2.1	2.2	2.1
Electric, gas, and sanitary services	2.1	1.8	1.9	2.0	2.5
Wholesale and retail trade	15.0	15.2	15.8	14.6	15.2
Finance, insurance, and real estate	10.9	11.3	11.1	13.4	12.9
Services	11.3	12.9	13.4	14.3	18.0
Government and government enterprises	13.5	15.9	16.2	14.1	14.7
Rest of the world	0.8	0.6	0.9	2.1	1.2
Totals*	100	100	100	100	100

*Totals sum only approximately to 100 because of rounding.

Source: *Survey of Current Business*, United States Department of Commerce.

mergers, for example, can be viewed not only as a problem of monopoly power (the power of a firm to dominate its own industry) but also as a problem of broader economic and political power—the ability of a firm to influence the course of economic development and government policy within the whole economy.

Two issues are involved here: (1) Has the relative importance of large firms been increasing over time, such that the economy is becoming dominated by fewer and larger firms? (2) If so, does this matter? For example, is there a relationship between size and political power? Are such relationships changing over time?

The first task is to decide on a measure of firm size. A firm is an institution which buys inputs, produces and sells outputs, and in the process generates income. One can therefore measure the size of the firm by examining the quantity or value of its inputs, the quantity or value of its final outputs, or the amount of income it generates. Which measure one chooses will depend both on the purpose for which the information is needed and on the availability of data. Thus, if one is interested in the structure of the labor market, firm size might be measured by the number of its employees, an input measure. If one is interested in a firm's monopoly power within its industry, then final sales may be a more appropriate measure of size. It is not immediately evident which index of firm size is best for studies that relate the firm to the economy as a whole. Clearly, a firm's income-generating power embodies the net result of its production activities. Perhaps the best measure of this magnitude is *value added*, defined as value of final sales minus purchases of goods and services from outside the firm, or the value the firm adds during the production process to the intermediate products and raw materials it buys. Value added is equal to the firm's expenditures on wages, rent, and interest, with profit the residual

Table 9.2 Share of Total Value Added by Manufacturing Accounted For by the 50, 100, 150, and 200 Largest Manufacturing Companies*

Company Rank Group	1947	1954	1963	1972	1982
Largest 50 companies	17	23	25	25	24
Largest 100 companies	23	30	33	33	33
Largest 150 companies	27	34	37	39	39
Largest 200 companies	30	37	41	43	43

*Percent of value added by manufacturing.

Source: U. S. Bureau of the Census, "Concentration Ratios in Manufacturing," Table 1, *1982 Census of Manufacturers*.

item. Unfortunately, value-added data are not as readily available as data on assets, employment, and sales.[5]

The relative importance of firms in the economy is usually summarized by an aggregate concentration index, which describes the share of national size or activity accounted for by the largest firms. For a clear picture, it is useful to divide the economy into major sectors and to consider the relative importance of large firms in each of these. Much attention has been paid to concentration in manufacturing (although by 1985, manufacturing generated only 21 percent of national income). However, it should be stressed again that the share of the largest firms in the total activity of the whole economy or in an economic sector such as manufacturing does not measure monopoly power. Such power refers to a firm's ability to raise price above cost and is determined by its position in the industry. Table 9.2 shows the share of value added accounted for by the 50, 100, 150, and 200 largest manufacturing companies. Thus, in the first row (first column) we see that in 1947 the share of value added in manufacturing accounted for by the largest 50 companies was 17 percent. That share rose to 25 percent in 1963 and remained quite stable through 1982. The share of the largest 100 companies rose from 23 percent in 1947 to 33 percent in 1963 and remained at 33 percent for the next two decades. The share of the largest 150 and 200 companies rose very slightly between 1963 and 1972, and has remained constant since then. Thus, one cannot infer from the table that there has been any significant increase in the aggregate concentration of the manufacturing sector in recent years.

Table 9.3 fills out the picture of concentration changes by tracing the changing shares of the same companies over time. To read this table, look at the

[5]Note that if there are substantial differences between industries with respect to the type and size distribution of firms, then each size measure will inevitably involve some bias. For example, if we measure firm size by number of employees, labor-intensive firms will appear relatively large and capital-intensive firms relatively small. If we measure firm size by final sales, then vertically integrated firms will be underestimated in size compared with firms producing at only the final level. By contrast, the value-added measure weights vertically integrated firms relatively heavily compared with those producing only at the final stage.

Table 9.3 Share of Total Value Added by Manufacturing Accounted for by the 50 and 100 Largest Identical Manufacturing Companies[*]

Year of Company Ranking and Company Rank Group	1947	1954	1963	1972	1982
1982					
Largest 50 companies	12	18	21	23	24
Largest 100 companies	15	23	27	30	33
1972					
Largest 50 companies	12	19	22	25	21
Largest 100 companies	17	25	29	33	30
1963					
Largest 50 companies	15	22	25	21	19
Largest 100 companies	21	29	33	29	28
1954					
Largest 50 companies	16	23	24	20	17
Largest 100 companies	21	30	31	27	26
1947					
Largest 50 companies	17	21	21	17	15
Largest 100 companies	23	27	28	24	21

[*]Percent of value added by manufacturing.

Source: "Concentration Ratios in Manufacturing," Table 2.

first row and last column. The largest 50 companies in 1982 (where size is measured by share of value added in the manufacturing sector) had a joint share of 24 percent. (This is exactly the same as the figure at the top of the last column in Table 9.2.) Moving back along the first row to the fourth column, we see that those 50 companies that were largest in 1982 (and had 24 percent in that year) accounted for 23 percent of value added in manufacturing in 1972, 21 percent in 1963, 18 percent in 1954, and 12 percent in 1947. Moving down to the last two rows, first column, we see that the 50 companies that had the largest share of value added in 1947 had 17 percent in that year. (This figure also appears in Table 9.2, row 1, column 1.) The share of these same companies increased to 21 percent in 1954 and 1963, declined to 17 percent in 1972, and to 15 percent in 1982. Reading Tables 9.2 and 9.3 together suggests that while aggregate concentration may have been rising between 1947 and 1963, there has been quite a bit of turnover among the firms at the top. One could also argue that there was substantial stability over the 30-year period—particularly since the 50 companies that were largest in 1947 had not lost shares by 1972.[6]

[6]It is impossible to characterize turnover rates as fast or slow, or good or bad, without specifying some systematic criteria.

Table 9.4 Aggregate Concentration Ratios Based on Largest 50 Firms in Various Nonmanufacturing Sectors

	1960	1965	1967	1970	1975	1977
Banking						
Percent share of assets	39.1	39.4	—	34.3	35.7	35.5
Percent share of deposits	38.5	38.4	—	32.2	33.5	31.9
Life Insurance						
Percent share of assets	87.7	85.5	84.4	82.9	80.3	79.1
Percent share of insurance in force	83.1	77.4	75.5	73.5	70.9	71.0
Electric and Gas Utilities						
Percent share of assets	—	—	58.1	60.3	60.4	59.8
Percent share of net income after taxes	—	—	54.0	54.6	52.9	53.4
Retail Trade						
Percent share of sales revenues	16.3	17.2	18.8	19.8	21.0	20.5
Percent share of employment	—	17.1	18.4	21.4	21.0	20.1
Transportation						
Percent share of sales revenue	53.2	55.5	59.7	58.1	66.0	—
Percent share of employment	—	—	35.0	35.3	37.2	35.0

Source: From L. J. White, "What Has Been Happening to Aggregate Concentration in the United States?" *Journal of Industrial Economics* 29 (March 1981): 227, Table II.

In 1981 Lawrence J. White calculated aggregate concentration ratios for some major nonmanufacturing sectors.[7] These are presented in Table 9.4. For electric and gas utilities, retail trade, and transportation aggregate concentration increased up to the mid-1970s and has since shown slight declines. Concentration in the banking and life insurance sectors declined over the whole period, with only banking showing a slight increase in the early 1970s.

White also provided aggregate concentration data for the entire private sector and concluded that "the data indicate that aggregate concentration in the private sector in the 1970s apparently has not increased and probably has diminished slightly."[8]

Tables 9.1 through 9.4 describe the relative size of the various sectors of the economy and the importance—that is, relative size—of the largest firms within each sector. The data show that the number of companies accounting for a major share of corporate activity and wealth in most areas is relatively small. It would not be surprising to find that these large firms exert some

[7]L. J. White, "What Has Been Happening to Aggregate Concentration in the United States?" *Journal of Industrial Economics* 29 (March 1981): 223-230.

[8]White, "What Has Been Happening," 229.

influence on the functioning of the economy, perhaps via political means that affect the formulation of government policies.[9]

The numbers in these tables, however, do not address the phenomenon of monopoly power within any industry.[10] Such power—the ability to control price or other terms of supply—presents distinctive measurement problems. It is to this issue that we now turn.

MEASURING MONOPOLY POWER: THE STRUCTURE–CONDUCT–PERFORMANCE PARADIGM

In Chapter 2, we emphasized the distinction between the objectives of social choice and the mechanism by which the objectives are pursued. If the major social objectives are efficiency and equity, then to the extent that these goals are fulfilled we can say that the performance of the social system is good. If the social system employs the free market mechanism, and more specifically perfect competition, then we might argue that the economic performance of society will be good because perfect competition yields a Pareto optimal allocation of resources. Of course, the end results of perfect competition will not necessarily be equitable. This immediately alerts us to the possibility that since economic performance has so many dimensions, an economic system (such as competition) that gives good performance in one area (for example, efficiency) may yield bad performance in another (say, equity, or technical progress).[11]

Consider specific industries within the economic system. Can we transfer our ideas about the fulfillment of social objectives (in terms of good or bad social performance) directly to individual industries? The theory of the second best suggests that the answer is no and that satisfying the Pareto optimality conditions in one industry or sector alone, when they cannot be satisfied in all

[9]See L. M. Salamon and J. J. Siegfried, "Economic Power and Political Influence: The Impact of Industry Structure on Public Policy," *American Political Science Review* 67 (September 1977): 1026–1043, for an empirical study of this point. See also R. S. Seneca and D. E. Haight, "The Concept of Power: Antitrust as an Illustration," *Antitrust Bulletin* 23 (Summer 1978), for a more general discussion of the meaning of power and the interaction of firms, industries, and government in economic policymaking.

[10]Until recently aggregate concentration, such as that seen above, was presumed to carry virtually no implication for the structure of specific industries within the aggregate. High concentration at a national level could be consistent with intense competition in specific industries. R. Clarke and S. W. Davis have established that a formal relationship does exist between the two concepts. They show that "the level of aggregate concentration is proportional to a weighted sum of concentration in individual markets." R. Clarke and S. W. Davis, "Aggregate Concentration, Market Concentration and Diversification," *Economic Journal* 93 (March 1983): 182-1920. See also M. S. Silver, "On the Measurement of Changes in Aggregate Concentration, Market Concentration and Diversification," *The Journal of Industrial Economics* 33 (March 1985): 349-352.

[11]In Chapters 2 and 3, we argued that the competitive system might simultaneously satisfy the efficiency and equity criteria of society. While conflict between performance goals may often occur, it is not inevitable.

industries simultaneously, will not necessarily improve social welfare. This means, for example, that setting price equal to marginal cost in one industry when prices are not equal to marginal cost everywhere else is not necessarily appropriate.

Whether industry performance can be unambiguously described in equity terms is also not clear, since equity is a concept that applies to society as a whole. So, while we may identify the gains and losses from the operations of a single industry, it may prove difficult to make a statement about the net social effect.

Despite these difficulties, good industry performance is usually defined in the same way as good social performance. The general equilibrium concepts which apply to society as a whole are carried over without much modification into the partial equilibrium framework of the individual industry. Thus, for example, we proceed under the assumption that perfect competition within a single industry will yield an efficient allocation of resources and (as we have seen in Chapter 3) that pure monopoly will produce an inefficient allocation. In imperfect markets, however, both the efficiency and equity results may be theoretically indeterminate.

It is therefore logical to turn to empirical studies in an attempt to identify the actual determinants of good economic performance that theory has failed to reveal. Most empirical work in industrial organization is based on the structure–conduct–performance paradigm. The framework is that of a single industry. (The problem of industry definition, discussed in Chapter 3, thus arises immediately.) The paradigm implies causality: industry structure determines conduct and conduct in turn determines performance (see Figure 9.1). As we shall see, most empirical studies presuppose these causal links and most criticisms of the paradigm suggest that the causal direction may, in some circumstances, go the other way.

An industry's structure—its relatively stable organizational characteristics—refers to the number and size distribution of firms, the nature of its production technology, the shape of industry cost and demand curves, and the extent of product differentiation among firms. Entry conditions are usually included as structural characteristics. Thus the notion of industry structure implies a set of economic conditions which are, at least in the short run, given. The conditions act as constraints on firm behavior or conduct.

Firm conduct includes all the firm's policies that reflect both its goals and the ways in which it perceives and interacts with rivals. Thus the price and output decisions of the firm, its choice of investment rate, its choice of product differentiation, and even its advertising, marketing, and innovation decisions may all be included as elements of its conduct.

It is immediately apparent that the line between structure and conduct is not fully clear. Since a firm's choices today (about price, investment, advertising, and so on) determine its product characteristics and market share (that is, its structural position) tomorrow, it is not always apparent which things we should classify as constraints on a firm's behavior and which are simply manifestations of its choices.

Figure 9.1   The Structure–Conduct–Performance Paradigm

The causal direction, shown by the double arrows, is from structure to conduct to performance. The single arrows show the feedback effects in the other direction.

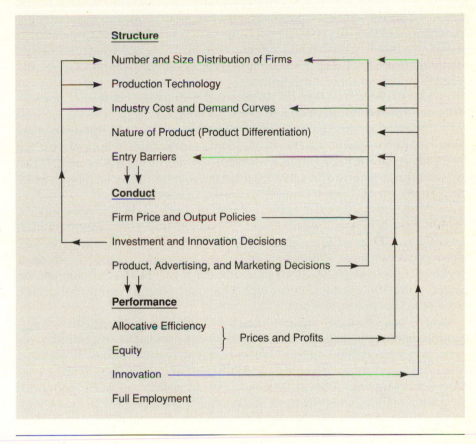

The usual line of argument is to say that structure affects conduct. For example, under perfect competition, the structural constraints are severe. The individual firm has no leeway whatever to pursue any goal other than profit maximization and has no rational option but to sell at the going market price. But if industry structure allows firms any market power at all, for example, if there are only a few firms or if products are differentiated, then each firm can (within limits) choose its price, output, and rate of investment. Its conduct becomes an important determinant of its ultimate performance.[12]

[12]Some will argue that the connection between commonly observed structural measures and firm leeway is very weak and that it can be misleading to infer the latter from the former. See, for example, F. M. Fisher, "Diagnosing Monopoly," *Quarterly Review of Economics and Business* 19 (Summer 1979): 7–33.

The implications that arise when we consider the reverse line of argument—that conduct determines structure— may be viewed in terms of entry. Entry conditions are usually regarded as structural. But we know that entry may be discouraged by pricing strategies on the part of established firms—a form of conduct. Since the possibility of a successful limit-pricing strategy is determined by industry concentration, the basic cost structure of firms, and the difference between established and entering firms' costs, perhaps we would do better to confine the term structure to these underlying characteristics. But even this does not solve the definitional problem, since the cost of production itself is influenced by firms' decisions about technology, the nature of products, and innovation, all of which are part of conduct.

One way out is to emphasize the short-run versus long-run distinction. Entry may occur and be affected by the firm's own policies in the long run, but in the short run entry conditions are fixed. Thus, we can include as structure all those constraints on the firm that are fixed in the short run, even though in the long run many of these are subject to the firm's control.

 Structure and conduct are similarly intertwined on the demand side. Firm demand curves, as we have seen, depend on the firm's perception of its position within the industry and on the likely reaction of its rivals to the price and product changes it initiates. In the case of perfect competition, these feedback effects are (rationally) ignored by the firm.[13] In all other markets the shape of the firm's demand curve will depend on structure and on behavioral assumptions—that is, conduct.

The terms structure and conduct, though they may be hard to disentangle from a definitional standpoint, are both positive concepts. By contrast, the term performance has both positive and normative dimensions. As we have suggested, performance implies the fulfillment of ultimate social objectives. Suppose we extend the list of social goals to innovation and full employment (in addition to allocative efficiency and equity).[14] There are now two problems. First, as we have seen, the objectives may conflict. For example, high monopoly profits, which are inefficient and inequitable, may lead to greater investment and innovation, and hence to cost savings, lower prices, and higher living standards in the long run.

Second, measures of such broadly defined social objectives are hard to devise. We must often refer to imperfect proxies such as price levels and profits, which can be good or bad depending on how they have been generated. High profits are good for some groups and bad for others. So are high prices. As we have seen, a firm with monopoly power can set a price above

---

[13]See J. R. Robinson, "What Is Perfect Competition?" *Quarterly Journal of Economics* (November 1934); reprinted in W. Breit and H. M. Hochman, *Readings in Microeconomics* (New York: Holt, Rinehart and Winston, 1968). Robinson presents a fuller discussion of the meaning of the horizontal demand curve.

[14]These objectives are often used in economics texts as most appropriate for the U.S. economy. It can be argued that, except perhaps for equity, they are themselves not ultimate objectives but proxies for the broader goals of individual happiness, social harmony, and so on, which one could enumerate and discuss at greater length.

marginal cost and may make greater-than-normal profits over time. This is good for the owners of the firm but bad for consumers. Furthermore, monopoly pricing, quite apart from the equity issue, leads to allocative inefficiency.

If, on the other hand, high profits are caused by an outward shift in demand, then a competitive industry in which firms price at marginal cost may experience above-normal profits in the short run. These profits will attract entry by new firms, thus eliminating the excess profits. In this case, the existence of high short-run profits is a crucial signal that induces the competitive market to respond to changing demand conditions.

These two complexities—the conflict of objectives and the confusion between the objective and its measure—lead, as we shall see, to some basic disagreements about the meaning of the results of empirical studies and their relevance to policy-making.

Definitional problems aside, the structure-conduct-performance paradigm identifies the traditional argument of causal effect in the economics of industrial organization. Market structure determines firm conduct, which in turn determines firm and industry performance. While feedback effects from performance and conduct to structure are not denied, the emphasis is on the "structure determines performance" approach, with conduct the facilitating link.[15]

PRACTICAL PROBLEMS OF MEASUREMENT

Empirical tests of the links between industry structure, conduct, and performance require that measures be devised for each concept. The literature on measurement is extensive.[16] We will not attempt a full review, but rather will identify some of the most commonly used measures in each category and take note of their characteristics.

Structure

The number and size distribution of firms in an industry, often summarized in a concentration index, is a basic structural index of competitiveness. Two measures that attempt to combine information about the number and size

[15]Not all economists subscribe to the structure–conduct–performance paradigm. For a comprehensive critique, see W. D. Reekie, *Industry, Prices and Markets* (New York: John Wiley and Sons, 1979).

[16]In fact, it is so large as to be unwieldy. Good summaries will be found in Scherer, *Industrial Market Structure*, 267–296; L. W. Weiss, "The Concentration-Profits Relationship and Antitrust," in H. J. Goldschmid, H. M. Mann, and J. F. Weston, eds., *Industrial Concentration: The New Learning* (Boston: Little, Brown and Co., 1974), 184-233; J. M. Vernon, *Market Structure and Industrial Performance: A Review of Statistical Findings* (Boston: Allyn and Bacon, 1972); B. Curry and K. D. George, "Industrial Concentration: A Survey," *The Journal of Industrial Economics* 31 (March 1983); and L. W. Weiss, "Concentration and Price—A Progress Report," in Robert L. Wills, Julie A. Caswell, and John D. Culberton, eds., *Issues after a Century of Federal Competition Policy* (Lexington, Mass.: D. C. Heath, 1987), 317–332.

distribution of firms are the four-firm concentration ratio and the Herfindahl (Hirschman) index, sometimes called the H index.

Four-Firm Concentration Ratio   This measures the combined size of the four largest firms in an industry, expressed as a ratio to total industry size. If final sales is used as the measure of size, then the four-firm concentration ratio is simply the percentage of total industry sales held by the four largest firms— their joint market share. In monopoly, the four-firm concentration ratio is 100 percent (the single largest firm having all the sales). In a competitive industry, the four-firm ratio will diminish as the number of firms and the equality of their size distribution increases.[17]

Since the four-firm concentration ratio is often used almost inter-changeably with the term *industry concentration* and also as an immediate indicator of changes in industry structure, it is important to bear in mind the following points. There is nothing particularly sacred about the number four—it is, in fact, arbitrary.[18] Industries that have the same four-firm ratio may have very different two-firm or eight-firm ratios. In other words, the four-firm ratio does not reveal the size distribution of firms within the top four, nor does it measure the relative importance of smaller firms outside the top four. (A concentration curve that traces the values of the one-firm, two-firm, three-firm, etc. ratios would give this information but cannot easily be used in statistical work because it is not a single number.) However, a change in the four-firm ratio tends to reflect only significant changes in industry structure, a desirable characteristic (it is insensitive to the entry or exit of minor firms). All other things being equal, the higher the four-firm ratio, the stronger is the presumption of concentrated market power.

Some examples of four-firm concentration for different industries are shown in Table 9.5. For industry definitions we have taken the five-digit (major product group) classification of the Standard Industrial Classification (SIC) of the federal government.[19] This classification will frequently be much too

---

[17]If there are N equal-sized firms in the industy, the four-firm concentration ratio will be $\frac{4}{N}$, a number that decreases as N increases.

[18]The four-firm basis of the concentration ratio has no grounding in theory—it is a creature of the Census data gathering convention. J. E. Kwoka, Jr., has demonstrated that the choice of concentration ratio may make a significant difference when used in statistical studies to predict profitability, and that the two-firm ratio, rather than the four-firm ratio may be a better choice. J. E. Kwoka, Jr., "Does the Choice of Concentration Measure Really Matter?" *Journal of Industrial Economics* 29 (June 1981): 445–453.

[19]The SIC code is a system of industry definitions of differing breadth. Thus, for example, the two-digit SIC number 20 refers to the major industry group "food and kindred products." The three-digit number 201 refers to the industry group "meat products." The four-digit number 2011 refers to the product group or industry "meat packing (slaughtering) plant." The five-digit number 20111 refers to the product class "fresh beef," and the seven-digit number 20111-12 refers to the product "whole carcass beef." These definitions are often determined more by the problems faced by government data collectors than by the economic considerations of substitutability in production and consumption outlined in Chapter 3. See F. M. Scherer, *Industrial Market Structure*, 59-64, for a good discussion of the limitations of SIC data.

Table 9.5 Share of Value of Shipments of Each Class of Product Accounted for by the Four Largest Companies: Selected Industries

Industry SIC Code	Title	1958	1963	1972	1977	1982
20210	Creamery butter	11	8	37	30	29
1086	Bottled and canned soft drinks	11	11	14	14	15
20992	Chips (potato, corn, etc.)	35	41	49	52	(D)
21110	Cigarettes	80	(D)	84	88	90
2251	Women's hosiery (except socks)	—	34	34	50	59
26211	Newsprint	62	57	49	47	49
26471	Sanitary napkins and tampons	97	(D)	91	97	98
28133	Carbon dioxide	80	78	75	75	63
28442	Perfumes, toilet water, and colognes	34	44	48	54	41
32710	Concrete block and brick	3	5	5	4	9
36122	Power and distribution transformers	80	76	67	70	72
37241	Aircraft engines for military aircraft	—	97	96	(D)	(D)

Source: "Concentration Ratios in Manufacturing," *1982 Census of Manufacturers*, Table 6. (D) indicates number withheld to avoid revealing figures for the individual companies.

narrow (include too few substitute products in an industry). Since firms tend to specialize, concentration ratios tend to be higher for narrowly defined industries than for more broadly defined industries. Nevertheless, the range of concentration levels for those industries shown in Table 9.5 is very wide and is a good indication of the variety of industrial structures that make up our economy.

The Herfindahl Index [20] This index also attempts to capture the number and size distribution of firms in a single measure. It is defined as:

$$H = \sum_{i=1}^{N} \left(\frac{q_i}{Q_i}\right)^2$$

where

q_i = the size of an individual firm.

Q_i = the size of the industry (therefore $Q_i = \sum_{i=1}^{N} q_i$).

N = the number of firms in the industry.

The Herfindahl (or H) index, then, is the sum of squares of the market shares of all firms in the industry. Since each firm's market share is squared before it enters the sum, the index attaches very small weight to the shares of small firms, ensuring that unimportant changes at the industry's fringe do not

[20]Cited in G. Rosenbluth, "Measures of Concentration," in *Business Concentration and Price Policy* (Princeton, N.J.: Princeton University Press, 1955), 57–100.

significantly change the value of the index. The upper value of this index is one (a pure monopoly). Its lower value is $1/N$, reached when all firms are of the same size and decreasing as N increases.[21]

Because it combines two different kinds of information—the number of firms and their market share—the Herfindahl index can yield strange rankings of industries which differ significantly in these respects. For example, the value of H for an industry, I, consisting of four equal-sized firms is:

$$H = \sum_{i=1}^{4} (.25)^2 = .25$$

This is rather low on the scale of 0 to 1. (Note that the four-firm concentration ratio for this industry is 100 percent, the highest value.) The value of H for another industry, II, consisting of one firm with 50 percent of the market and 50 small firms, each with 1 percent, is $(.50)^2 + 50(.01)^2 = .255$. (The four-firm ratio in this case is 53 percent.) Industries I and II have very different structures, but approximately the same H value. (Note that the four-firm ratio for Industry II is approximately half that for Industry I, even though Industry II's largest firm is much larger than any of the firms in Industry I. This is an example of the fact that the four-firm concentration measure obscures the distribution of market share among the largest firms.) In spite of its weakness, the Herfindahl index is often preferred to the four-firm concentration ratio because it is better able to indicate the relative importance of dominant firms.[22]

It is important to bear in mind that indexes of concentration do not directly measure the competitiveness of industries. A highly concentrated industry could be intensely competitive; an industry of low concentration might lack competitive vigor. Concentration is a fundamental structural characteristic of an industry and, according to the structure–conduct–performance paradigm, may have an effect on the conduct and performance of firms in that industry. Concentration is often used to characterize competitiveness, but, as we have suggested, competition is essentially an adjacent phenomenon. It cannot at the same time be defined by an industry's structure and be used to define it.

---

[21]Thus the H value for an industry with N equal-sized firms is:

$$N \left(\frac{1}{N}\right)^2 = \frac{1}{N}$$

[22]The Herfindahl (Hirschman) index is perhaps the only concentration index with a solid basis in microtheory. See G. J. Stigler, "A Theory of Oligopoly," *Journal of Political Economy* (February 1964): 44-61. Theoretically and empirically Stigler relates the Herfindahl index to the likelihood that collusive agreements among oligopolistic firms will be undermined by secret price-cutting. Thus, according to Stigler, the funny rankings are correct theoretically even if they are intuitively surprising. The lack of a clear intuitive interpretation is the major limitation of the Herfindahl index, at least for policy purposes. Nevertheless, it is used by the Department of Justice to determine guidelines for mergers that could be challenged. See P. Asch, *Industrial Organization and Antitrust Policy*, rev. ed. (New York: John Wiley and Sons, 1983), 292 n. 81.

Conduct

The behavior of firms (with respect to prices, output, quality of products, innovation, and so on) cannot by its nature be measured as a single number or index. Firms are constrained in their actions by the market structure in which they operate. But if they have any market power at all, firms have the option to set various prices and to respond in different ways to their rivals. Indeed, behavior is intrinsically a dynamic concept, implying both an initial act of choice and a following sequence of choices as firms interact with each other.

Studies of firm behavior are of two kinds: case studies that examine the history, development, and current policy of individual firms; and general theories of behavior. General theories attempt to take into account the complexities of modern firm organization, while at the same time drawing conclusions which may hold in a variety of circumstances. In a classic article, Fritz Machlup distinguished between marginal, behavioral, and managerial theories of the firm.[23] The familiar marginal theory views the firm as having a single goal—profit maximization—and all the necessary information about costs and demand to pursue this goal. Changes in either cost or demand will alter the marginal trade-offs facing the firm and result, virtually automatically, in changes in prices and output. Behavioral theories, such as that developed by Cyert and March, attempt to explain in detail the process by which firms make decisions and to examine the extent to which the external environment affects the decision-making process.[24] Managerial theories of the firm concentrate on the goals of the firm's managers.[25] They view managers as utility maximizers, suggest plausible utility functions, and examine the effects of different utility functions on the ultimate decisions of firms.

While each approach may add to our understanding of firm behavior, the immediate question is whether any of these approaches lends itself to empirical measurement. For the marginalist theory, the question of measurement is practically moot. Given cost, demand, and the goal of profit maximization, there is only one performance outcome (price, output, investment rate, and so on) for each set of cost and demand curves. Behavior, being assumed, need not be measured. Behavioral theories lend themselves to econometric modeling (Cyert and March provide a mathematical formulation of their model and offer a specific test, using data from a large retail department store). Managerial theories can also be tested econometrically, using data for individual firms.[26]

---

[23]F. Machlup, "Theories of the Firm: Marginal, Behavioral, Managerial," *American Economic Review* 57 (March 1967): 1–33.

[24]R. M. Cyert and J. G. March, *A Behavioral Theory of the Firm* (Englewood Cliffs, N.J.: Prentice-Hall, 1963).

[25]See for example O. E. Williamson, *Economics of Discretionary Behavior: Managerial Objectives in a Theory of the Firm* (Englewood Cliffs, N.J.: Prentice-Hall, 1964).

[26]The field of managerial economics deals with modern approaches to understanding firm behavior. See J. L. Pappas and M. Hirschey, *Managerial Economics*, 5th ed. (Hinsdale, Ill.: The Dryden Press, 1987), for a comprehensive introduction. See O. E. Williamson, "The Modern Corporation: Origins, Evolution, Attributes," *Journal of Economic Literature* 19 (December 1981): 1537–1568, for an excellent survey.

The conclusions of such models may be varied—that firms pursue different goals, or they pursue similar goals differently, or they maximize utility yet have different utility functions. Nevertheless the focus for society and the policymaker still remains the idea of industry competition—its benefits and drawbacks. Since generally valid observations about firm decision-making processes may not be possible, another approach is to infer firm behavior from the market structure within which the firm operates and the performance results of that behavior that we can observe (price and output levels, rates of investment). In other words, since the identification and measurement of firm conduct does not generate systematic or simple results, one route is to ignore it and concentrate on testing the relationship between structure and performance.

Structure will tell us something about the likelihood of different forms of conduct. For example, in a market consisting of many small firms, all selling a slightly differentiated product, where entry is easy (for example, restaurants), collusion is quite unlikely because of organizational difficulties. Therefore, the observed price structure, a measure of the performance of the industry, will probably not have resulted from collusive tactics.

While there is no direct index of the decision-making process, there are two measures that tell us something about the firm's options. These are measures of market power—the elasticity of the firm's demand and the cross-elasticity of demand—reflecting the firm's ability to raise price above marginal cost. One could classify such measures as structural, but in theory at least, they go beyond structure to the extent that they embody the firm's perceptions of its rivals' reactions (and these are behavioral characteristics).

Elasticity of Demand   Recall from Chapter 3 that the elasticity of an industry's demand curve is the ratio of the percentage change in industry quantity demanded to the given percentage price change which generates the change in quantity. The main determinants of industry elasticity of demand are the nature and prices of available substitutes that determine the strength of the substitution effect of a price change and the size of the income effect. The more narrowly defined is the industry, the higher its elasticity of demand is likely to be.

The elasticity of a single firm's demand curve depends both on the elasticity of the industry demand at prevailing price levels and on the firm's position within the industry. A perfectly competitive firm has no power at all to set price. Its demand curve is therefore horizontal at the going price and its elasticity of demand is infinitely large. In Figure 9.2(a), D is the industry demand curve, S is the industry supply curve, and P is the competitive market price. Figure 9.2(b) shows the perfectly competitive firm's demand curve, horizontal at price P. The pure monopolist has a demand curve which is identical to the industry demand curve. The elasticity of the monopolist's demand curve, at each price, is therefore the same as the industry elasticity. For all other market structures the firm's elasticity of demand depends both on the market structure and on the firm's behavior, based on the way it perceives the reactions of other firms.

Figure 9.2   Demand Elasticities Compared
(a.)   Under competition, price is set by supply and demand.
(b.)   The perfectly competitive firm faces a completely elastic demand curve—horizontal at the going price.
(c.)   An imperfectly competitive firm that produces a differentiated product faces demand curve d_2, drawn under the assumption that price changes will not be followed by competitors. The less elastic demand curve d_1 is the constant shares curve.

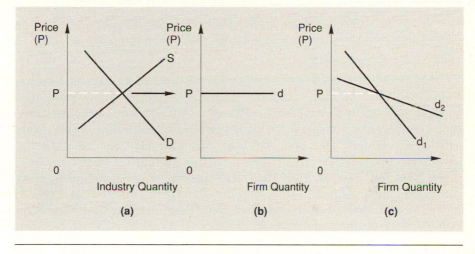

In Figure 9.2(c) two demand curves are shown for an imperfectly competitive firm. Demand curve d_1 shows the amounts Firm A can sell if all firms charge the same price; d_2 represents the quantity Firm A can sell at every price if all other firms hold their prices constant at P. At price P, the elasticity of demand for curve d_2 is greater than for curve d_1. This is to be expected. If all other firms keep their prices constant while Firm A reduces its price, the substitution effect will be large as Firm A gains market share at the expense of the other firms. But along the constant shares curve, d_1, the inter-firm substitution effect is eliminated and the increase in quantity that results from a price fall comes from inter-industry substitution and the income effect only.

The profit-maximizing price of an imperfectly competitive firm is inversely related to the elasticity of demand.[27] This price will be higher the lower the elasticity, and the firm's power to raise price above marginal cost correspondingly higher. Industry demand curves and their corresponding elasticities can be estimated using econometric techniques.[28] However, firm demand curves are essentially unobservable because of their dependence on the firm's perceptions of its market position and rivals' likely responses to its own

[27]Recall Chapter 3, p.56.

[28]See for example J. Dean, "Estimating the Price Elasticity of Demand," and "The Price Elasticity of Demand for Automobiles," both in E. Mansfield, ed., *Managerial Economics and Operations Research*, 4th ed. (New York: W. W. Norton and Company, 1980), 101-123.

decisions. Elasticity is thus a most appropriate theoretical proxy for a firm's market power, but is not often useful in providing a practical measure.

Cross-Elasticity of Demand   This is a measure of substitutability between two products. It is defined as the ratio of the percentage change in the quantity demanded of good x to the percentage change in the price of another good y (or vice versa), That is:

$$e_{xy} = \frac{\Delta Q_x}{Q_x} \bigg/ \frac{\Delta P_y}{P_y} = \frac{\Delta Q_x}{\Delta P_y} \cdot \frac{P_y}{Q_x}$$

If x and y are substitutes, a rise in the price of y will cause consumers to switch their expenditure towards a cheaper substitute x, so that the quantity of x demanded will rise. In this case e_{xy} will be positive. The greater the substitutability between the two goods, the higher the absolute value of e_{xy}. Two goods with high cross-elasticities of demand should presumably be classified in the same market. When they are not, the market demand curve for each good will tend to be highly elastic, since the substitution effect of a price rise of one good will then be high. A firm's cross-elasticity, like the firm's elasticity of demand, is difficult to measure and is unlikely to qualify significantly the information embedded in measures of elasticity.[29]

Performance

Allocative Efficiency   The measurement of industry performance as defined in terms of ultimate social objectives poses enormous problems. Efficiency, equity, and progress are all complex concepts which cannot easily be summarized in a single index. One important exception, however, is reflected in the work of Arnold C. Harberger and the series of studies which followed it.[30]

In Chapter 3, we discussed the static case against monopoly and developed a partial equilibrium framework that allowed normative comparisons between the two polar types of industrial organization—monopoly and per-

[29]We would be unlikely to conclude on the basis of elasticity that a company has substantial power, and then change our minds when we see the cross-elasticities. High cross-elasticities mean that the firm is severely constrained, but this will show up in the measure of elasticity as well. In terms of Figure 9.2(c), high cross-elasticities imply a big difference in the slopes of d_1 and d_2. Suppose the firm thinks rivals will match a price rise. If they do not and if cross-elasticities are high, this implies that the firm has made a big error. But the error could be discussed without reference to cross-elasticity simply as a mistake in management's assumption about rival response, that is, about the shape, and hence the elasticity, of the firm's own demand curve.

[30]A. C. Harberger, "Monopoly and Resource Allocation," *American Economic Review* 44 (May 1954): 77-87. For a review and critique of Harberger's original article and subsequent studies, see S. C. Littlechild, "Misleading Calculations of the Social Costs of Monopoly Power," *Economic Journal* 91 (June 1981): 348-363.

Figure 9.3   Monopoly Welfare Loss Measured

The competitive price is P$_c$, the monopoly price is P$_m$. The area of welfare loss due to monopoly pricing is equal to triangle ABC.

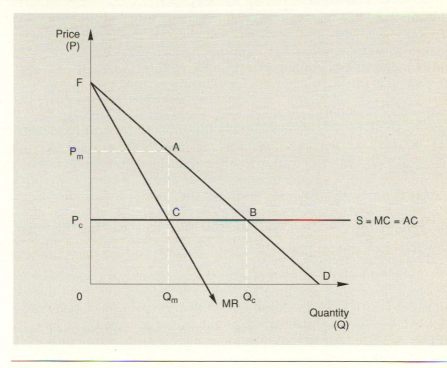

fect competition. Figure 3.6 (reproduced as Figure 9.3) identified the demand and cost curves for a single industry and compared the competitive price, P$_c$ (= MC), with the monopoly price, P$_m$ (substantially higher than MC). The net welfare, or allocative efficiency loss associated with monopoly price, P$_m$, as opposed to competitive price, P$_c$, is triangle ABC. Recall that we made a series of stringent assumptions about demand and cost to arrive at this conclusion. In particular we assumed constant average costs (hence MC = AC at every output level). In industries that have imperfectly competitive structures, the prices of firms will likely be higher than marginal cost, but not as high as the pure monopoly price. How high the price is will depend on the extent of price competition between firms, whether or not collusive agreements can be maintained, and the ease of entry into the industry. But to the extent that price lies anywhere above marginal cost, allocative efficiency losses will occur. In principle, they can be measured by triangle ABC.

Harberger's important contribution was to provide an empirical estimate of the size of triangle ABC for each industry in the manufacturing sector and to sum these welfare losses to equal the total cost of imperfectly competitive market structures in manufacturing.[31] He concluded that the total welfare loss associated with monopolistic market structures was $59 million dollars per year—less than one-tenth of 1 percent of national income.

This small sum was surprising and suggested that the social resources marshalled over the years to enforce antitrust policy might have been better used elsewhere. Subsequent studies have modified Harberger's methodology and arrived at larger welfare loss estimates.[32] Much could be said about the approach and specific assumptions of these studies, but we shall confine ourselves to two basic points. First, the difficulties arising from the stringent assumptions associated with the theoretical derivation of the welfare loss triangle carry over to the empirical model. The benchmark for comparison is the competitive price; welfare losses result from industry prices above this level. However, as we know from the theory of second best, when all prices cannot equal marginal cost, a price close to marginal cost in any given industry will not necessarily be better than one farther away. In other words, each individual deadweight triangle measures the welfare loss from a single monopoly *if* perfect competition exists everywhere else. If monopoly exists elsewhere, the individual triangles do not measure the welfare loss. Therefore, summing up partial equilibrium welfare losses across industries to arrive at an overall total loss figure is not valid.

Second, there is the problem of using observed profits as a benchmark for measuring distortions produced by monopoly pricing. We have already emphasized that high profits do not necessarily spring from monopoly power. While it is true that consistently high profits cannot be earned in an industry without significant barriers to entry, competitive industries may earn short-run excess profits as a result either of outward shifts in demand or cost-saving technological changes. These excess profits are presumably desirable in that they serve to attract resources into the industry.[33] Harberger's assumption of

---

[31]He obtained an expression for the welfare loss triangle whose area is measured as half the base times the height. He rearranged terms to obtain an expression in terms of total industry sales, the elasticity of demand, and the relative price distortion due to monopoly:

$$\text{Triangle ABC} = 1/2(PQ)ek^2$$

where

$$P \cdot Q = \text{total industry sales.}$$
$$e = \text{elasticity of demand.}$$
$$k = \frac{P_m - P_c}{P_m} = \frac{\Delta P}{P} = \text{relative price distortion.}$$

Using industry data for the years 1924 to 1928 Harberger assumed an elasticity of demand of one. He estimated the relative price distortion by examining the divergence of actual profits for each industry from the average rate of profit for all manufacturing industry. PQ, as noted, was measured by total industry sales.

[32]A study by K. Cowling and D. C. Mueller, "The Social Costs of Monopoly Power," *Economic Journal* 88 (December 1978): 727–748, produced a figure for net welfare loss of 13 percent of gross corporate product. This study was the focus of Littlechild's critique. See also the reply to Littlechild by Cowling and Mueller in *Economic Journal* 91 (September 1981): 721–725.

[33]Harberger proceeded as though average profit equals normal profit, although the observed average may contain some monopoly reward. If it does, then the monopoly distortions are understated.

constant average costs allows him to equate P-AC (profit per unit) with P-MC (the monopoly price distortion). If, in the short run, this assumption does not hold, P-AC may be positive even if prices are equal to marginal cost. Simply observing profits does not allow us to decide what these profits reflect.

In a recent study, Masson and Shaanon develop an empirical model of oligopoly to estimate welfare losses in industries that are neither perfectly competitive nor pure monopolies. They conclude that "the size of the deadweight triangle averages 2.9 percent of value of shipments for a sample of 37 industries."[34] They also shift the benchmark of comparison and estimate the potential welfare losses that would be incurred if pure monopoly pricing were practised in each industry, that is, if firms in each industry were to maximize joint profits with no threat of entry. They estimate that the welfare losses under monopoly would be 11.6 percent. The difference between actual losses (2.9 percent) and estimated monopoly losses (11.6 percent) is 8.7 percent. They attribute 4.9 percent to the benefits of potential competition (that is, to the threat of entry from firms outside the industry) and 3.8 percent to actual competition. The advantage of choosing monopoly prices as an alternative comparison point is that it gives a different perspective on the actual welfare loss estimate. Whereas 2.9 percent is higher than Harberger's original 1 percent estimate, it is a great deal lower than the 11.6 percent of pure monopoly. Viewed in this way, one might conclude that actual deadweight losses attributable to imperfect competition are not as important relatively as they may at first appear.

Apart from the way Harberger estimated the welfare loss triangle, more fundamental objections to his approach have been raised. Harvey Leibenstein suggested that, contrary to the accepted assumption of economic theory, monopolistic firms do not minimize costs.[35] Thus, their cost curves lie above the competitive cost curves and resources are squandered. He used the term X-efficiency to describe the various determinants of productivity improvement over time in firms that have not apparently altered their inputs. He further suggested that such efficiency would be exploited by firms subject to competitive pressure, but not by firms protected from it. The potential gains to society from X-efficiency (shifting down the cost curves of monopolists) could be much larger than the potential gains in allocative efficiency from lower prices and higher outputs.

As we noted in Chapter 3, Richard Posner also suggested that Harberger had measured the wrong area.[36] He focused on the area of excess profits, $P_m ACP_c$ in Figure 9.3, and argued that much or all of these monopoly profits are used by firms' owners to acquire and maintain their monopoly positions.

[34]Robert T. Masson and Joseph Shaanan, "Social Costs of Oligopoly and the Value of Competition," *Economic Journal* 94 (September 1984): 520–535.

[35]H. Leibenstein, "Allocative Efficiency versus `X-Efficiency,'" *American Economic Review* 56 (June 1966): 392-415.

[36]R. A. Posner, "The Social Costs of Monopoly and Regulation," *Journal of Political Economy* 83 (August 1975): 807–827.

This converts what we have called the redistributive transfer (from consumers to producers) into a type of net social waste. The profits area, P_mACP_c, should then be added to the welfare loss triangle to yield a much higher efficiency loss than triangle ABC. Masson and Shaanan provide a variety of measures of welfare losses which include these rent-seeking losses.[37] These range in magnitude from 4 percent to 41 percent of the value of shipments, significantly higher than most estimates of the size of the welfare loss triangle alone.

The Lerner Index   AC in triangle ABC (Figure 9.3) shows the extent to which monopoly price lies above marginal cost. In 1934, Abba Lerner proposed a monopoly power index defined as (P-MC)/P, the excess of price over marginal cost, expressed as a percentage of price.[38] For a perfectly competitive firm the value of this index would be zero, since P = MC. For a (profit-maximizing) pure monopolist, for whom marginal cost equals marginal revenue, the index equals the inverse of the elasticity of demand, 1/e, and will be higher the lower the elasticity.[39] Presumably low values of the Lerner index indicate less social welfare loss due to monopoly than higher values. Note that the index does not itself measure welfare loss, but rather the divergence of price from marginal cost, which occurs only in the presence of monopoly power. As long as one does not substitute P-AC (per unit excess profit) as a proxy for P-MC in the index, any empirical test should yield an accurate measure of the monopoly price distortion.[40] Unfortunately, marginal cost data for firms and industries are difficult, if not impossible, to find.[41] Proxies must be used and accuracy may be lost.

Profits   As we have seen, high profits in an industry may reflect a variety of circumstances and do not necessarily indicate the presence of monopoly power. Nevertheless, profits are used in numerous empirical studies as a general measure of firm and industry performance. Attempts have been made to measure excess profits by subtracting a normal profit component from published profit figures.[42] However, published profit figures are subject to impor-

---

[37]Masson and Shaanan, "Social Costs of Oligopoly," 532.

[38]A. P. Lerner, "The Concept of Monopoly and the Measurement of Monopoly Power," *Review of Economic Studies* 1 (June 1934): 157–175.

[39]L = (P - MC)/P. For a profit-maximizing monopolist in equilibrium, MC = MR. Recall that MR = P(1 - 1/e) where e is the elasticity of demand and equals -(dQ/dP)(P/Q). Therefore L = (P - MR)/P = (P-P(1 -1/e))/P = 1 -(1 -(1/e)) = 1/e.

[40]See, for a relevant discussion, W. M. Landes and R. A. Posner, "Market Power in Antitrust Cases," *Harvard Law Review* 94 (March 1981): 937–996.

[41]Since most firms do not collect marginal cost data, marginal costs must be estimated econometrically from cost functions.

[42]The Bain index of monopoly is R - C - D - iV, where R is the total receipts, C is current costs, D is depreciation, V is the value of owners' investment, and i is the rate of return this investment could earn in its next best alternative use. iV is therefore a measure of the normal rate of return, R - C -

tant accounting distortions.[43] For example, assets may be valued in sharply different ways (at historical or at reproduction cost), and wages and salaries often contain elements of rent. Thus, when profits are estimated as the rate of return on equity after taxes, $\dfrac{\Pi - T}{E}$, the profit and equity figures may exhibit substantial noise. Bias may result from the tendency of all firms to report profits close to the mean, that is, highly profitable firms tend to understate their profitability while less profitable firms overstate theirs. If this occurs with much frequency, the true variation in the numbers is obscured.

Expenditures on advertising and research and development pose further problems for profit measurement. These items are usually treated as current expenses. Yet both advertising and R&D have long-term effects that suggest they might be more appropriately considered as investments. To do so, however, would likely alter somewhat the measured profitability of most companies, especially those with heavy advertising and R&D programs.

These deficiencies in profit data clearly suggest the need for caution in empirical studies that employ them. It is clear that the true picture of corporate profitability is subject to some distortion in the figures reported by firms. There is, however, one saving grace. Many of the important inaccuracies in profit data are of an essentially random nature. They do not systematically bias the results that we are likely to observe between profit rates and other structure or performance measures. While this does not reduce the significance of the measurement difficulty, the problem of random noise in empirical relationships is not totally unmanageable.

STRUCTURE–PERFORMANCE MODELS: EMPIRICAL STUDIES

Most empirical studies of industrial organization in the United States have been undertaken within the framework of the structure–conduct–performance paradigm. Since the observation and measurement of conduct is so difficult, many observers omit it and attempt to establish a direct empirical relationship between the structure of industries and their performance. The usual estimation technique is linear regression, a method of estimating a statistical relationship between a single dependent variable (variable to be explained) and one or more explanatory variables.[44]

D measures accounting profit, and the difference between the two [(R - C -D) - iV] is excess profit. [See J. S. Bain, "The Profit Rate as a Measure of Monopoly Power," *Quarterly Journal of Economics* 60 (February 1951): 271–292.]

[43]For a full account see L. W. Weiss, "The Concentration-Profits Relationship and Antitrust," in Goldschmid, Mann, and Weston, eds., *Industrial Concentration*, 16.

[44]For two good introductions to the field of econometrics and linear regression in particular, see H. J. Cassidy, *Using Econometrics: A Beginner's Guide* (Reston, Va.: Reston Publishing Company (Prentice-Hall, 1981) and P. Kennedy, *A Guide to Econometrics* (Cambridge, Mass: MIT Press, 1980).

Regression: An Example[45]

The Basic Approach Suppose we hypothesize that, in general, firms' profit rates are higher, the higher their market shares. We can express this relationship mathematically as

$$\Pi_i = \alpha + \beta MS_i \tag{9.1}$$

where

Π_i = the ith firm's profit rate (rate of return on equity).
MS_i = the ith firm's market share, measured as percent.
α = the value of Π_i when MS_i is zero. [46]
β = the rate at which Π_i changes as MS_i changes.

Suppose we have a sample of 100 firms. We know each firm's profit rate and market share. These data are typically cross-sectional—the variables are observed at a single time (or each variable is expressed as an average value over a given time period). If the data are plotted on a graph, they might form the pattern shown in Figure 9.4. Here, each numbered dot shows the profit rate and market share observation of one firm in the sample. The line drawn through the dots is the sample regression line described by the equation:

$$\hat{\Pi}_i = \hat{\alpha} + \hat{\beta} MS_i \tag{9.2}$$

where

$\hat{\alpha}$ = estimated value of the parameter α.
$\hat{\beta}$ = estimated value of the parameter β.
$\hat{\Pi}$ = estimated value of profits, given $\hat{\alpha}$ and $\hat{\beta}$ for each value of MS.

The sample regression line has two main characteristics. First it is the line that best fits the observations.[47] Second, it is the line that best represents the true relationship (if such exists—remember it has only been hypothesized) between profits and market share. Suppose we find that the estimated parameters have the following values: $\hat{\alpha} = 5; \hat{\beta} = .25$.
The sample regression function is:

$$\hat{\Pi} = 5 + .25 \ MS. \tag{9.3}$$

---

[45]This example is drawn from the work of W. G. Shepherd, *The Economics of Industrial Organization* (Englewood Cliffs, N.J.: Prentice-Hall, 1972), 261-277.

[46]This does not make much sense as it stands since a firm which has zero market share would presumably not be producing any output and would not earn a profit. We could modify the interpretation and let α be the profit rate for a firm with a very small market share—that is, the profit rate for a perfectly competitive firm. In general, however, intercept terms are not considered very important, in part because they lack a meaningful interpretation. The slope value, β, is the most important parameter.

[47]The best fitting line is the line that minimizes the sum of squares of the vertical distances of the dots from the line.

Figure 9.4 A Sample Regression Function—Profits against Market Share
Each observation represents the profit rate and market share of each firm in the sample. The sample regression line is the best estimate of the true relationship between market share and profits, where the profit rate is the dependent and market share the explanatory variable.

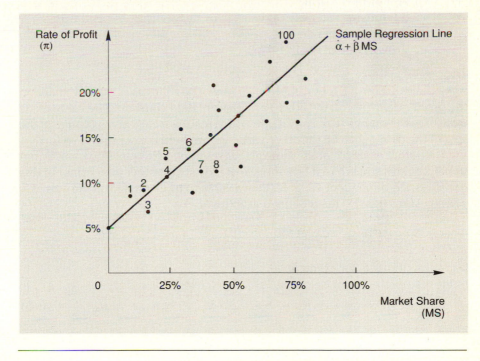

This would mean that an increase in a firm's market share of one percentage point (say from 15 percent to 16 percent, or from 25 percent to 26 percent) would lead on the average to an increase in the firm's profit rate of .25. Or, more generally, that each 10 percent of added market share adds about 2.5 percent to the profit rate.[48]

Multiple Regression   Of course, most economic relationships cannot be explained in such simple terms. There are many different factors which affect profits, not all of them related to market structure. We can take these other variables into account by estimating, for example, a multiple regression function, such as:

$$\hat{\Pi}_i = \hat{\alpha} + \hat{\beta}_1 MS_i + \hat{\beta}_2 S_i + \hat{\beta}_3 A_i + \hat{\beta}_4 E_1 \tag{9.4}$$

[48]Shepherd maintains that this relationship is so stable that it can be used as a rule of thumb. Shepherd, *Economics of Industrial Organization*, 270.

where

$\hat{\Pi}_i$ = estimated profit rate, say, on capital investment.
MS_i = market share of the ith firm.
S_i = size of the ith firm.
A_i = advertising intensity of the ith firm (advertising expenditure as a percent of sales).
E_i = growth rate of the ith firm.
$\hat{\alpha}$ = estimate value of $\hat{\Pi}$ when all other variables are zero.

Now the value of $\hat{\beta}_1$, for example, measures the changes in market share on the profit rate, when all the other variables are held constant. The value of $\hat{\beta}_2$ measures the change in the profit rate which results from a given change in the size of the firm, when all the other variables are held constant; and so forth.

Another example of the multiple regression technique is given in Equation 9.5 below, and is based on a sample of industries rather than firms. In this equation, the dependent variable (the variable to be explained) is the industry price-cost margin.[49] This is defined as follows:

$$PCM = \frac{\text{Value added - Payroll}}{\text{Value of shipments}} = \frac{\text{Price - Cost}}{\text{Price}}$$

So we might have, for example,

$$P\hat{C}M_i = \hat{a} + \hat{b}_1 K_i + \hat{b}_2 C_i + \hat{b}_3 S_i + \hat{b}_4 A_i + \hat{b}_5 R_i \qquad \textbf{(9.5)}$$

---

[49]Shepherd, *Economics of Industrial Organization*, 273. As Shepherd points out, PCM should ideally be a measure of the relative gap between price and marginal cost. Since marginal cost data are not readily available, a measure of the relative divergence between price and average variable cost is used. The measure $\frac{\text{Value added - Payroll}}{\text{Value of shipments}}$ can be broken down as follows: Value of shipments can be viewed as total sales equal to total revenue equal to $P \bullet Q$. Value added equals value of shipments minus variable costs excluding labor costs. Therefore,

$$\text{Value added - Payroll} = \text{Total revenue - Total variable costs}$$
$$= PQ - TVC$$

Now we have

$$\frac{\text{Value added - Payroll}}{\text{Value of shipments}} = \frac{PQ - TVC}{PQ}$$

Dividing numerator and denominator by Q we have $\frac{P - AVC}{P}$ where AVC (Average Variable Cost) $= \frac{TVC}{Q}$. Shepherd stresses appropriately that this is an industry measure. However, it is not an average of firm profit rates since these are measured as the excess of revenue over cost expressed as a ratio of assets or equity.

where:

$\hat{\text{PCM}}_i$ = estimated price-cost margin of the ith industry (a ratio).

K_i = capital intensity of the ith industry (measured by a capital/output ratio).

C_i = concentration of the ith industry (measured by the four-firm concentration ratio).

S_i = size of the ith industry (measured by the log of assets).

A_i = advertising intensity of the ith industry (measured by the ratio of advertising expenditure to sales).

R_i = revenue growth of the ith industry.

As before, $\hat{a}$ is the value of $\hat{\text{PCM}}$, when all other variables are zero; $\hat{b}_1$ measures the extent to which the price-cost margin increases for any given change in capital intensity, all other variables being held constant; and so on.

In one study,[50] Shepherd estimates the parameters of Equation 9.5 as;

$$\hat{\text{PCM}}_i = 9.045 + .011K_i + .089C_i + 1.051S_i + .017A_i + 2.723R_i.$$

Thus an increase in industry concentration of one percentage point is associated with a rise in the price–cost margin of .089. An increase in concentration of ten percentage points will cause an increase in the price–cost margin of about .9 (nearly 1 percent). But a given increase in advertising will have a much smaller effect on the price–cost margin: if advertising intensity increases by 10, the price-cost margin will only increase by $(.017) \times 10 = .17$, less than one-fifth the response of PCM to changes in concentration.

Problems of Interpretation

Reliability   The interpretation of estimated regressions such as those above involves a number of interrelated problems. First is the question of the reliability of the individual estimators and of the sample regression function as a whole.[51] Recall Equations 9.1 and 9.2. Equation 9.2, $\hat{\Pi} = \hat{\alpha} + \hat{\beta} \text{ MS}$, is the best-fitting regression line drawn through sample data points showing the market share and profitability of firms in the sample. Had another sample been drawn from the population, the observed sample data points would have been different. The values of $\hat{\alpha}$ and $\hat{\beta}$ which define the best-fitting sample regression function would also have been different. Since we have only one

[50]W. G. Shepherd, "Elements of Market Structure: An Inter-Industry Analysis," *Southern Economic Journal* 38 (April 1972): 531-537.

[51]See D. Gujarati, *Basic Econometrics*, 2nd ed.(New York: McGraw-Hill, 1988), Chapters 3 and 7, for a detailed account of the assumptions underlying the classical linear regression model and of the Gauss-Markov theorem which identifies the properties of estimators derived under these assumptions.

sample, we cannot directly observe any other estimated values of $\hat{\alpha}$ and $\hat{\beta}$ than the ones we have. Therefore we cannot directly observe the extent to which $\hat{\alpha}$ and $\hat{\beta}$ vary depending on the sample chosen. But it is possible to estimate the distribution, mean, and variance of these parameters from the sample data and arrive at conclusions about their reliability. One such procedure is called estimating confidence intervals. If the relationship between MS and Π is a precisely estimated one, then our confidence intervals will show that $\hat{\alpha}$ and $\hat{\beta}$ will not vary much no matter which sample is chosen.

Interdependence of Variables   Another important problem in regression analysis is interdependence.[52] In order for our estimated regression coefficients to be reliable, the explanatory variables should be independent of each other. In other words, each should have an independent effect on the dependent variable. However, it is often the case that the explanatory variables which are appropriate for explaining a given dependent variable are, by their nature, interdependent. This creates immediate statistical difficulties. Indeed, the whole field of econometric theory has developed partly in response to the statistical estimation problems raised by interdependent variables. The interdependence phenomenon creates problems in the economic interpretation of estimated relationships, particularly in identifying the causal direction of the relationship.

For an example, recall Equation 9.5:

$$P\hat{C}M_i = \hat{a} + \hat{b}_1 K_i + \hat{b}_2 C_i + \hat{b}_3 S_i + \hat{b}_4 A_i + \hat{b}_5 R_i \qquad \textbf{(9.5)}$$

This equation is interpreted to mean that an industry's capital intensity, concentration ratio, absolute size, advertising intensity, and revenue growth all have an independent effect on the price–cost margin, (the size of each effect being measured by the parameters $\hat{b}_1$ to $\hat{b}_5$. The causal direction is that the five explanatory variables determine price–cost margins. However, many more complicated interpretations can be offered. For example, both high capital intensity and high advertising intensity may act as barriers to entry into the industry. High barriers lead to high profits, or at least to the maintenance of excess profits over a period of time. But high barriers may also affect the industry's concentration ratio since new entry cannot occur to take advantage of excess profits, and current concentration levels will tend to be maintained. Furthermore, to the extent that established firms have sufficient market power (reflected in the concentration ratio) to conduct a limit-pricing strategy, the profit rate may be held down by established firms in order to forestall entry. This effect will be greater when the other barriers to entry (advertising and capital intensity) are lower. Thus, limit-pricing (which keeps price–cost mar-

---

[52]This problem is ultimately also a sampling problem.

gins low) may preserve high concentration ratios in the absence of other effective entry barriers. As a result, relatively high concentration levels may be associated with relatively low price–cost margins.[53]

What the estimated regression will tell us is the net effect of all these interactions. Whether this net effect is meaningful depends partly on the soundness of the sampling and estimation techniques, and partly on the economic strength of the interaction effects.

SUMMARY

In this chapter we first examined the structure of the economy as a whole by looking at the changing shares of national income coming from different economic sectors. We looked at measures of aggregate concentration, that is, of the importance of firms in the economy as a whole. We then turned to the measurement of monopoly power—the power of firms within industries—and described the structure-conduct-performance paradigm. We introduced two measures of industry structure (the four-firm concentration ratio and the Herfindahl index) and two measures of conduct (the elasticity of demand and the cross-elasticity of demand), discussing the strengths and drawbacks of each measure. For measures of performance we discussed the welfare loss triangle (first measured by Harberger), the Lerner index, and the use of profits as a proxy for monopoly power. We then turned to empirical estimates of the relationship between structure and performance and described the technique of linear regression. Finally we discussed some of the difficulties of regression for estimating economic relationships of the kind that interest us here.

CONCLUSION

Measurement of the relationships among structure, conduct, and performance provides us with extremely useful kinds of information. It may suggest, for example, whether apparently monopolistic structures are associated with the sort of resource misallocation that traditional economic theory predicts. Or whether such structures appear to reflect economies of scale or strong inventive performance. There are, however, some limitations to the lessons that can be drawn from observed relationships and it is important to recognize these as well.

---

[53]In a study by David Levy, "Specifying the Dynamics of Industry Concentration," *Journal of Industrial Economics* 34 (September 1985): 55-68, the direction of causality is explicitly reversed, and concentration becomes the dependent variable. A model is developed for identifying the determinants of concentration, some of which (barriers to entry, for example) also appear together with concentration as explanatory variables in the studies in which profits are the dependent variable. See also Richard E. Caves and Michael E. Porter, "The Dynamics of Changing Seller Concentration," *Journal of Industrial Economics* 29 (September 1980): 3–15.

Profit Rates and Structure

As we have suggested above, it is possible to obtain reasonably good statistical explanations of the variation in profitability that exists among firms and industries. At the firm level, for example, market share, growth, and advertising intensity are usually found to be important (and positive) determinants of the profit rate. Concentration also is significant in the majority of studies that examine it, but its effect is considerably weaker than market share.

As interesting as this information is, however, it is subject to a qualification that arises quite frequently in the social sciences: observed relationships (correlations) among variables may reveal relatively little about cause and effect. Yet some notion of cause and effect will usually be necessary if clear policy implications are to be drawn.

The relationship between profit rates and structural variables such as shares, concentration, or entry barriers is a prime case in point. There is widespread (although not universal) agreement about the nature of what can be observed but sharp and continuing controversy about what the observed relationships may mean. Does the statistical association between profit rates and concentration (or shares), for example, reflect monopolistic misallocation or the efficiency of large firms? Do high profits result from high prices or from low costs? Or is it some combination of the two? These are questions that cannot be answered simply by referring to the regression equations we have discussed above because what is observed is consistent with both causal alternatives. Plainly, however, our view of what public policy ought to do about concentrated industries (or dominant firms) depends heavily upon which chain of cause and effect is most accurate.

A number of economists have tried to distinguish empirically between the alternatives. Important studies by Harold Demsetz and Sam Peltzman reach a similar conclusion: concentration is likely the result of efficiency, and the higher profit rates that accompany higher concentration are thus a payment for superior performance.[54]

Although the findings of Demsetz and Peltzman are provocative, many economists do not regard them as definitive.[55] Causation remains elusive to some degree even under the bright light of empirical ingenuity. Furthermore, the dichotomy implied by our initial question—does the concentration–profits relationship reflect misallocation or efficiency—is likely to be something of an

---

[54]H. Demsetz, "Industry Structure, Market Rivalry, and Public Policy," *Journal of Law and Economics* 16 (April 1973); and S. Peltzman, "The Gains and Losses from Industrial Concentration," *Journal of Law and Economics* 20 (October 1977): 229–263.

[55]See R. S. Bond and W. Greenberg, "Industry Structure, Market Rivalry, and Public Policy: A Comment," *Journal of Law and Economics* 19 (April 1976): 201–204; and F. M. Scherer, "The Causes and Consequences of Rising Industrial Concentration," *Journal of Law and Economics* 22 (April 1979): 191-208. See also L. W. Weiss, "Concentration and Price," for a discussion of the relationship between changes in concentration and changes in prices.

oversimplification. Other causal factors almost surely influence patterns of concentration and profits, perhaps quite substantially.[56]

Profit Rates and Advertising

Observed relationships between profitability and measures of advertising raise very similar questions of interpretation. Is the strong positive association of profits and advertising intensity a sign that heavy advertising raises entry barriers, thereby permitting established firms to earn monopoly profits? Some observers believe so, but alternative explanations are not hard to find. It may be, for example, that profitable firms and industries choose to invest in advertising, thus reversing the causal argument completely. Perhaps advertising, a type of informational service, is simply a valuable activity that earns an appropriately healthy reward in the marketplace. Or the observed statistical relationship might be spurious, possibly the result of deficient accounting practices by firms.[57]

The list of empirical relationships whose proper interpretation is subject to debate could be lengthened considerably. The point, however, would in most instances be the same. Cause and effect can be difficult to determine, especially in areas where underlying theories of events are weak or ambiguous. Disagreements of interpretation may persist less because different individuals examine different facts than because they bring divergent prior beliefs and expectations to the study of problems.

Discussion Questions

1. What is the difference between aggregate concentration and market concentration? What implications does each concept have for government policy?

2. Tables 9.2 and 9.3 give data describing how concentration in manufacturing has changed over time. How might one evaluate these changes?

3. Provide a critique of the structure–conduct–performance paradigm as an approach to the understanding of industrial organization.

4. Take any three measurable industry variables such as concentration, profitability, and advertising. Use one as the dependent variable and the other two as explanatory variables. Tell a convincing story to justify the estimation of such a regression and predict what your results would be. Do this for all three variables in turn. Does this exercise tell us anything about empirical studies in industrial organization?

---

[56]For a discussion of some possibilities, see O. E. Williamson, "Dominant Firms and the Monopoly Problem," *Harvard Law Review* 85 (June 1972).

[57]An argument to this effect is made by H. Bloch, "Advertising and Profitability: A Reappraisal," *Journal of Political Economy* (March/April 1974): 267-286.

Selected Readings

Demsetz, H. "Industry Structure, Market Rivalry and Public Policy." *Journal of Law and Economics* 16 (April 1973). *A much quoted argument that concentration results from efficiency.*

Fisher, F. M. and J. J. McGowan, "On the Misuse of Accounting Rates of Return to Infer Monopoly Profits." *American Economic Review* 73 (March 1983): 82-97. *A recent critique of the measurement of one of the key variables used in empirical investigations of industrial organization and profits.*

Goldschmid, H. J., H. M. Mann, and J. F. Weston. *Industrial Concentration: The New Learning.* Boston: Little Brown and Company, 1974. *This volume contains many excellent papers on different aspects of industrial organization and public policy. See in particular L. W. Weiss, "The Concentration-Profits Relationship and Antitrust," 184-233.*

Harberger, A. C. "Monopoly and Resource Allocation." *American Economic Review* 44 (May 1954): 77-87. *The original study measuring the total efficiency losses from monopoly.*

Kwoka, J. E., Jr. "Does the Choice of Concentration Measure Really Matter?" *Journal of Industrial Economics* 29 (June 1981): 445-453. *A clear, succinct article suggesting that the appropriate choice of concentration measure is important and is not the four-firm concentration ratio.*

Reekie, W. D. *Industrial Prices and Markets.* New York: John Wiley and Sons, 1979. *An interesting critique of the structure-conduct-performance paradigm.*

Scherer, F. M. *Industrial Market Structure and Economic Performance*, 2d ed. Chicago: Rand McNally, 1980. *The major treatise on the subject, containing comprehensive references to the literature as of 1980.*

CHAPTER 10

· · · · · · · · · · · · · · · · · ·

ANTITRUST AND MARKET POWER

We turn now to legal interpretations of the antitrust laws and the economic plausibility of legal doctrine. Any categorization of antitrust—such as the power-versus-behavior dichotomy—is bound to be somewhat arbitrary and artificial. Issues overlap one another. The existence of market power and its use can be extremely difficult to separate.[1]

Underneath such ambiguity, however, the distinction raises one of the most significant issues in modern antitrust policy: should power in itself ever be cause for public concern, or should we move only against actions (behavior) that may create or abuse existing power? Although a fully objective answer to this question is not possible, the question itself deserves careful attention.[2]

In this chapter, we consider two major areas of antitrust enforcement that impinge directly upon market power: monopolizing and mergers. (The latter may contribute to power but, as a rule, stop far short of legal monopoly.) We turn then to an economic analysis of these enforcement programs and to some final policy observations.

MONOPOLIZING

Legal Status

Section 2 of the Sherman Act makes it illegal to "monopolize or attempt to monopolize." This might seem to mean that a company holding monopoly power or control of a market violates the law. In fact, American courts have never explicitly said this in cases brought under Sections 1 and 2, although they may have approached such a position on occasion.

---

[1]Judge Learned Hand, in the *Alcoa* decision of 1945, described the distinction between the existence and exercise of monopoly power *as "purely formal."*

[2]For a relevant discussion, see R. S. Seneca and D. E. Haight, "The Concept of Power: Antitrust as an Illustration," *Antitrust Bulletin* 23 (Summer 1978): 339–369.

The Standard Oil Decision   An early major test of the Sherman Act came in 1911 with the Supreme Court's decision in *Standard Oil Co. of New Jersey v. U.S.*[3] Standard, a holding company, dominated the domestic petroleum refining industry with about 90 percent of national refining capacity. The Supreme Court accepted at the outset the contention that the company's dominance had been achieved by unsavory means. These included preferential (and secret) rebates from the railroads, predatory price cutting, and other unfair practices that drove rivals from the market.[4] At stake in this case was not only Standard's status under the Sherman Act, but, more broadly, the criteria on which an overwhelmingly powerful firm would be judged.

The government urged a strict test: Section 1 of the Sherman Act bars *every* combination in restraint of trade. Standard Oil was such a combination and should be found in violation with little further argument or qualification. The Supreme Court, while finding against the company, rejected this urging. Chief Justice White wrote for the Court that it is the nature—not the simple fact—of the restraint that determines its legality, and that *"the rule of reason* becomes the guide."[5] Standard Oil violated Sections 1 and 2 not by virtue of its size or (clearly monopolistic) market position, but rather because of the unreasonable or undue character of its restraints.

On what basis is reasonableness to be judged? The Supreme Court stressed the company's intent as evidenced by its acts. Standard's massive presence created "the prima facie presumption of intent and purpose to maintain dominancy . . . not as a result of normal methods of industrial development, but by new means . . . ." And this presumption was "made conclusive" by the predatory conduct in which the firm engaged. Power alone might thus engender suspicion, even strong suspicion; but a company's intent could be inferred only from its observed behavior.

The government had unquestionably won a major battle: effective application of the Sherman Act to a powerful trust. Standard Oil was judged guilty and dissolved. The antitrust law was not only alive but potent. This decision, however, obfuscated the issue for many years to come. The legal fate of the dominant firm would apparently depend henceforth upon its reasonableness, the normality of its rise to power. The Supreme Court had claimed the power to distinguish between natural and unnatural firm growth or, as Bork put it, between "'good' trusts and 'bad' trusts."[6] But the basis of this distinction was not fully clear and has never become so.

---

[3]221 U.S. 1 (1911).

[4]For an argument that Standard did not use predatory practices to achieve its position, see J. S. McGee, "Predatory Price Cutting: The Standard Oil (NJ) Case," *Journal of Law and Economics* 1 (October 1958): 137–169.

[5]221 U.S. 1 (1911). Italics added.

[6]R. H. Bork, *The Antitrust Paradox* (New York: Basic Books, 1978), 34.

Developments between the Wars   In *U.S. v. United States Steel Corp.*, we see what is presumably an example of the reasonable, and therefore legal, combination.[7] U.S. Steel, a holding company, had controlled over 50 percent of domestic steel production early in the twentieth century, but its share had fallen to about 40 percent by the time the government brought a Sherman Act suit charging restraint of trade and monopolization.

At the initial trial, the district court dismissed all charges against the company. Two of the four judges on the court argued that U.S. Steel's growth was a natural response to economies of large-scale operation and that no illegal intent to monopolize could be discerned in its history. The other two claimed that the company had been formed with an intent to monopolize but that the effort had failed.

The dismissal was upheld by the Supreme Court, which concurred largely with the latter view. Whatever wrongful purpose may have existed "could not be executed; whatever there was of evil effect was discontinued before this suit was brought." None of the "brutalities" that Standard Oil had directed against its rivals were to be found here. Indeed, no competing firms claimed that U.S. Steel had tried to drive them from the market. In the absence of abhorrent behavior, said the court, "[W]e must adhere to the law, and the law does not make mere size an offense. It . . . requires overt acts."

This opinion, while broadly consistent with *Standard Oil*, did not clarify the rule of reason. Size by itself does not violate the Sherman Act. An intent to monopolize or restrain trade must also be demonstrated.[8]   Yet the Supreme Court did not deny that the company had intended to monopolize. Rather, it concluded that the intent had failed to create a monopoly and had not led to the brutalizing of rival firms.

Between 1920 and 1945 there was effectively no development of anti-monopoly policy. This hiatus ended abruptly with Judge Learned Hand's decision in *U.S. v. Aluminum Co. of America.*[9]   Alcoa had been for several decades the sole domestic producer of virgin (or primary) aluminum. The company's position had originally rested on patent rights to aluminum production processes at the turn of the century, but had persisted beyond the life of these patents into the 1930s. In 1937, the government sued, charging that Alcoa had monopolized the virgin aluminum ingot market.

Judge Hand identified two critical questions: (1) Did the company hold a monopoly of this market? (2) If so, had it monopolized within the meaning of Section 2? The first question raised some subsidiary issues of market definition. Was secondary aluminum (scrap that is used in the same processes as

[7]251 U.S. 417 (1920).

[8]The courts have long held that monopolistic intent is inferable from a company's general pattern of behavior, and have not required a separate showing of "specific intent" to achieve a wrongful result apart from the means employed.

[9]148 F.2d 416 (2d Cir. 1945). Because four of the nine Supreme Court justices disqualified themselves, the Court lacked a quorum to hear this case. Accordingly, it gave the Court of Appeals for the Second Circuit the authority to render a final judgment.

primary) a part of the market? Should that portion of Alcoa's output retained for its own fabrication plants be counted in its market share? After disposing of these issues, Judge Hand ruled that the company's market share was over 90 percent, clearly a monopoly.[10]

Was this monopoly unlawful, that is, had the company monopolized? At this point, Judge Hand departed quite dramatically from the tradition of *Standard Oil* and *U.S. Steel,* stating:

> [F]rom the very outset, the courts have at least kept in reserve the possibility that the origin of a monopoly may be critical in determing its legality . . . . This notion has usually been expressed by saying that size does not determine guilt; that there must be some "exclusion" of competitors; that the growth must be something else than "natural" or "normal"; that there must be a "wrongful intent," or some other specific intent; or that some "unduly" coercive means must be used . . . .
>
> [Alcoa] insists that it never excluded competitors; but we can think of no more effective exclusion than progressively to embrace each new opportunity as it opened, and to face every newcomer with new capacity already geared into a great organization. . . . Only in case we interpret "exclusion" as limited to maneuvers not honestly industrial, but actuated solely by a desire to prevent competition, can such a course as Alcoa's. . . be deemed not "exclusionary." So to limit it would in our judgment emasculate the Act; would permit just such consolidations as it was designed to prevent . . . .
>
> In order to fall within Section 2, the monopolist must have both the power to monopolize and the intent to monopolize. To read the passage as demanding any "specific" intent, makes nonsense of it, for no monopolist monopolizes unconscious of what he is doing . . . . Alcoa meant to keep, and did keep, that complete and exclusive hold upon the ingot market . . . . That was to "monopolize" that market, however innocently it otherwise proceeded.[11]

Alcoa, a dominant firm in its market, had thus violated the law without demonstrating specific intent; indeed, the company may have proceeded innocently. In Judge Hand's opinion, it is only necessary that it proceeded deliberately to achieve and maintain its position. Only if the firm were the passive beneficiary of monopoly, only if monopoly were thrust upon it, would Section 2 not apply. Judge Hand's opinion is based on a distinctive view of the Sherman Act:

> Congress did not condone "good trusts" and condemn "bad" ones; it forbade all. Moreover, in so doing, it was not necessarily actuated by economic motives alone.[12]

Alcoa does not quite state that the purpose of the law is to limit economic power in itself. The possibility that a powerful firm—a monopolist—will not

---

[10]The market definition problem is of considerable interest, although it is not our primary concern at this point. Any legal test that relates to a company's degree of power or dominance in a market presupposes that such dominance is measurable. In the immediate case, Alcoa's market share could have been calculated to be 33 percent, 64 percent, or 90 percent; and the court's conclusion on this point was critical to the outcome of the case.

[11]The passage referred to in the final paragraph is from an early Supreme Court decision, *Swift and Co. v. U.S.*, 196 U. S. 375 (1905).

[12]148 F.2d 416   (2d Cir. 1945).

violate the Sherman Act is left open. But the possibility is remote, requiring a showing that monopoly was achieved unconsciously.

The Alcoa decision generated controversy that persists to this day. It raised the most fundamental policy issue—how to deal with the well-behaved monopolist—and reached a conclusion that seemed to break sharply with precedent. It is therefore especially ironic that the decision produced no remedy of consequence. Judge Hand deferred the government's request for dissolution of Alcoa pending post-war developments in the aluminum industry. At the end of World War II, government sale of its own aluminum plants altered industry structure as Reynolds Metals and Kaiser Aluminum entered. In 1950 the government again requested dissolution, but a district court ruled that any break-up of Alcoa's facilities or staff would, by weakening the company, threaten the competitive balance of the industry.[13]

After World War II In *U.S. v. United Shoe Machinery,* Judge Charles Wyzanski was presented with circumstances in some ways similar to those surrounding Alcoa.[14] United Shoe dominated the market in machines used to manufacture shoes with a sales share estimated at 75 to 85 percent. Its position, attacked by the government under Section 2, was based on the company's own machinery innovations developed earlier in the century. In fact, United Shoe had been acquitted of Sherman Act charges in 1918 on the grounds that its acknowledged monopoly position was based in legal patents.[15]

Judge Wyzanski termed the shoe manufacturing industry highly competitive, and United's own behavior in the shoe industry "free from any taint of . . . wrong-doing." Yet, he noted, the company had employed a system of leasing its machines that created obstacles for rival machinery suppliers. Lessees faced contracts running for 10 years and carrying the requirement that a United machine must be used to full capacity as long as there was work to be performed. Replacement of one United machine by another was offered at particularly favorable terms, and repair services were provided without separate charge.

The effect of these provisions, Judge Wyzanski concluded, was to restrict competition in shoe machinery. United's market strength was thus "not attributable solely to defendant's ability, economies of scale, research, natural advantages, and adaptation to inevitable economic laws." The firm's dominance rested in some part on deliberate acts, even though these acts, taken alone, represented legitimate and normal business practice. This was sufficient basis for Judge Wyzanski to find Section 2 violations.

The judge's conclusion seems clearly based on his belief that United's practices raised barriers to entry into the shoe machinery market and suppressed a second-hand market in machinery that could have limited the

---

[13]91 F. Supp. 333 (1950). Alcoa's market share in 1948 had fallen to 51 percent, with Reynolds holding 31 percent and Kaiser 18 percent.

[14]110 F. Supp. 295 (1953).

[15]*U.S. v. United Shoe Machinery Co. of New Jersey,* 247 U.S. 32 (1918).

company's power. In a sense, then, the *United Shoe* decision does not go quite as far as *Alcoa* in attacking power as such. Judge Wyzanski took pains to tie illegality to the defendant's behavior. Yet the behavioral standard is most stringent, suggesting that any dominant firm charged under Section 2 would find it exceptionally difficult to argue successfully the legality of its position. The remedy, however, was limited. The government's request for dissolution was considered unrealistic and denied. United Shoe was instead directed to open up its leasing provisions and to encourage sales as well as leasing of its machines.

The period following 1953 has seen relatively slow development of monopoly law.[16] In *U.S. v. Grinnell Corp.* the Supreme Court observed that a Sherman Act Section 2 offense has two elements: (1) "possession of monopoly power" and (2) "the willful acquisition or maintenance of that power."[17] But because the defendant's power was achieved "in large part by unlawful and exclusionary practices," the issue of the good trust—prominent in *Alcoa* and *United Shoe*—never arose.

Recent Developments   Three major monopoly cases brought by the government in recent years have produced one important result but little legal precedent. In 1969 the Department of Justice charged International Business Machines Corporation with Section 2 violations, alleging that the company held roughly a 70 percent share of relevant computer markets and that it practiced persistent discrimination.[18] In 1982, after 13 years of voluminous discovery and trial proceedings, the government dropped the case, stating that it lacked merit. One might be tempted to ascribe this result to a pro-business attitude on the part of the Reagan administration, but the computer industry had undergone substantial changes in the intervening years. IBM, still a strong force in U.S. computer markets, was subject to significant competition both internationally and in some domestic product lines.

In 1974 the Department of Justice sued the American Telephone and Telegraph Company, seeking to break off both Western Electric (AT&T's equipment manufacturing branch) and its Long Lines Department.[19] Under a settlement reached by the government and the company in 1982, AT&T was divested of its 22 operating subsidiaries accounting for almost two-thirds of its assets. The company retained its other operating divisions and was permitted to enter unregulated communications and data processing markets.

---

[16]The duPont cellophane case, *U.S. v. E. I. duPont de Nemours and Co.*, 351 U.S. 377 (1956) is noteworthy for its treatment of market definition issues, but is unrelated to the cases under discussion.

[17]384 U.S. 563 (1966).

[18]*U.S. v. International Business Machines Corp.*, 69 Civ. 200 (S.D.N.Y.). The company's alleged market shares—for example, 67 percent of installed general-purpose digital computers—were somewhat lower than those of Alcoa and United Shoe. The government's suit focused to an important degree on exclusionary practices that it claimed IBM had pursued.

[19]*U.S. v. American Telegraph & Telephone Co.*, Civil Action No. 74-1698.

The competitive effects of the AT&T settlement are not yet fully clear and provide a source of continuing interest and controversy. (We consider these effects in greater detail in Chapter 18.) The operating subsidiaries, which supply mainly local telephone service, have generally prospered in their regulated markets—more so than many had expected. AT&T itself has encountered substantial difficulties in adjusting to its new role as an unregulated competitor. (Its experience in computer markets, for example, has been quite dismal to date.) From the standpoint of consumers, the effects of divestiture have been mixed. Long-distance telephone rates have declined substantially and the available variety of equipment choices has expanded. Local service, however, has become somewhat more expensive (in an irregular geographic pattern) and complaints about service quality seem to have multiplied. Whatever the final verdict, the AT&T settlement represents the most significant restructuring of a major American corporation in many years. Remarkably, the government succeeded in breaking up a company whose record of innovation and service quality in telecommunications was exceptional—an outcome that some economists regard as the antitrust equivalent of shooting oneself in the foot.

The FTC brought suit in 1972 against four major breakfast cereal manufacturers (Kellogg, General Foods, General Mills, and Quaker Oats), citing a shared monopoly supported by various practices designed to stabilize the market and to preclude entry.[20] The case was unusual in its attack on a monopolistic group, in its contention that long-standing marketing techniques had created pervasive barriers to new competition, and in its proposed remedies, which included some divestiture and trademark licensing. Early in 1982, however, the commission dropped the case, following an adverse decision by an administrative law judge and strong criticism from within the Reagan administration.

Economic Assessment

Monopoly case law as it has evolved under the Sherman Act provokes varied interpretation. The courts, while applying stringent behavioral codes to firms that dominate particular markets, have never made the possession of monopoly power illegal. Some observers, probably including a large number of business managers, see the law as an effort to punish mere size even in the absence of wrongful intent—an attack on the very efficiency of the successful competitor.

Although isolated legal statements may invite such a view, this does not seem a plausible position in light of precedent and past results. Even the strongest statements by the courts—in *Alcoa* and *United Shoe*—produced minor effects. The power of our largest corporations has been disturbed only twice in our recent history: the Standard Oil break-up of 1911 and (arguably) the AT&T

---

[20]*Kellogg Co., et al.*, Docket 8883 (April 27, 1972).

settlement of 1982. Realistically, major firms are not threatened in any substantial way under existing Sherman Act precedent.

MERGERS
Legal Status

Firms may grow internally or by merger—that is, by acquiring others. The motivations for merging thus include the motivations for growth itself. A firm's management may see large size as efficient either because true economies or pecuniary economies of size are available.[21] They may wish to build empires or to diversify activities across a wide range of markets, thereby reducing company exposure to risk. Merger may prove more attractive than internal expansion for at least two reasons: it is often much faster, and it avoids the need to compete for market position with others—the position is simply purchased.[22]

The last point suggests not only why mergers have been a popular method of growing, but also why antitrust attention has focused on them. It is obvious that the acquisition of one firm by another—especially if the two are rivals—may hold anticompetitive implications. As noted earlier, there was little in the way of public antimerger policy prior to 1950. The original Section 7 of the Clayton Act proscribed only stock acquisitions, and its language seemed confined to cases in which competition between the merging partners would be reduced.

These limitations were so important that few Section 7 cases were prosecuted. Indeed, most merger activity could be challenged only under the stricter tests of the Sherman Act. It was, in fact, the government's failure to win a major Section 1 merger case that stimulated enactment of the Celler-Kefauver Act amending Section 7 in 1950.[23]

The new Section 7 extended the prohibition of anticompetitive mergers to asset acquisitions and to mergers in which competition between the partners might be unaffected. This meant that not only horizontal acquisitions (between competitors) but also vertical (between firms in a customer–supplier relationship) and conglomerate (all other) mergers were within reach of the law.

Horizontal Mergers   Legal precedent with respect to horizontal mergers was established rather quickly. In 1958 a district court held that Bethlehem Steel's

---

[21]A pecuniary economy implies that larger outputs can be produced more cheaply even though there may be no real saving of resources involved. For example, if my company is large, it can bargain for a better price from materials suppliers. The company's production costs are thus reduced, but there may be no true efficiency in any broader sense.

[22]These attractions suggest that acquiring firms should be willing to pay a premium, some amount above the apparent market value of the acquired partner. For some evidence on the size of such premiums, see Peter O. Steiner, *Mergers: Motives, Effects and Policies* (Ann Arbor, Mich.: University of Michigan Press, 1974).

[23]*U.S. v. Columbia Steel Co.*, 334 U.S. 495 (1948).

acquisition of Youngstown Sheet and Tube would violate amended Section 7.[24] The decision relied heavily on the following arguments:

1.   A merger between the second (Bethlehem) and sixth (Youngstown) largest firms in the steel industry would eliminate a significant competitor.

2.   It would further increase concentration in an already concentrated market.

3.   It would set a precedent under which further concentration-increasing mergers might be encouraged.

The court rejected the argument that a merged Bethlehem-Youngstown company would be better able to compete with U.S. Steel, still the nation's leading manufacturer.

The district court's emphasis on company shares and market concentration as evidence of anticompetitive effects in a merger was endorsed by the Supreme Court four years later in *Brown Shoe Co. v. U.S.*[25] This case involved the acquisition by Brown, the nation's fourth leading manufacturer and a minor retailer, of G. R. Kinney, the largest family-style retail chain and twelfth largest manufacturer. Although the decision turned mainly on vertical arguments (to be discussed later), the Court considered horizontal effects as well. Brown and Kinney together would hold no more than a 5 percent retail share nationally, but their market shares within certain cities would have been substantially higher.

Said Chief Justice Warren:

> The market share which companies may control . . . is one of the most important factors to be considered when determining the probable effects of the combination. . . [on competition] . . . . In an industry as fragmented as shoe retailing, the control of substantial shares of the trade in a city may have important effects on competition.

The government had sustained its burden of proof, and the merger violated Section 7.

The Supreme Court took a broadly similar position in *U.S. v. Philadelphia National Bank.*[26] It held that the merger of the second and third largest commercial banks in the Philadelphia area—Philadelphia National Bank (PNB) and Girard Trust—would abridge the statute. Section 7, the Court claimed, reflected a congressional intention "to arrest anticompetitive tendencies in their 'incipiency.'" To permit a merger resulting in a firm "controlling an undue percentage share" of the market would run counter to this intent. PNB and Girard would jointly have held about 36 percent of area deposits, a level that the Court regarded as presumptively anticompetitive.

It was now clear that strict structural tests of lessened competition were being applied. The government could prove a probable lessening by showing

---

[24]*U.S. v. Bethlehem Steel Corp.*, 168 F. Supp. 576 (S.D.N.Y., 1958).

[25]370 U.S. 294 (1962).

[26]374 U.S. 321 (1963).

that a merger would increase market shares and concentration, and decrease the number of competitors, in a relevant market. Such a showing, moreover, was decisive; it could not be outweighed by other evidence that the merger in question would carry "social or economic . . . credits."

Two cases decided by the Supreme Court in 1964 posed somewhat novel issues for horizontal merger standards. *U.S. v. Continental Can Co.* challenged the acquisition of the third largest producer of glass containers (Hazel-Atlas) by the second largest producer of metal containers (Continental).[27] Although the companies competed with one another in a few areas, their primary activities were not in the same market. In finding the merger illegal, the Court did examine concentration and market shares in a combined market comprised of metal and glass containers, but it did not tie its decision solely to these data. Justice White rather noted that "judgment under Section 7 is not to be made by any single qualitative or quantitative test." Continental and Hazel-Atlas were becoming increasingly competitive, said the Court, and the law deals with "probable and imminent" as well as with existing competition. The merger was thus denied in part because it reduced the potential for future competition between the firms.

The significance of potential competition was further emphasized in *U.S. v. Penn-Olin Chemical Co.*[28] Pennsalt and Olin-Mathieson had jointly formed Penn-Olin to enter the southeastern section of the country as a producer of sodium chlorate. A district court had dismissed Section 7 charges, arguing that since both firms were unlikely to enter the southeastern market on their own, the joint venture did not imply a probable lessening of potential competition between them.

The Supreme Court concluded that this test was inappropriate; that is, that potential competition need not presuppose a high probability of entry by both. One firm might have entered while "the other remained at the edge of the market," exerting a beneficial competitive threat. Elimination of such a threat— even if actual competition between the companies never materialized—could be construed as a lessening of potential competition.[29] The case was remanded (returned to the lower court) for reconsideration under a less restrictive standard.[30]

A 1966 Supreme Court decision, *U.S. v. Von's Grocery Co.*, suggested to some observers that the government could win virtually any horizontal merger

[27]378 U.S. 441 (1964).

[28]378 U.S. 158 (1964).

[29]This notion of potential competition was reinforced by the Court in *U.S. v. Falstaff Brewing Corp.*, 410 U.S. 526 (1973). Falstaff, a national brewer that did not operate in New England, sought to enter the New England market by acquiring Narragansett. A district court dismissed the case on the grounds that since Falstaff had no intention of entering New England on its own, no potential competition between the firms could be affected. The Supreme Court again held that the wrong test had been applied. Potential competition does not require a conclusion that the potential competitor will enter, or plans to enter, the relevant market. The mere fact that a threat of entry is posed by the outsider is significant even though it may never occur.

[30]The lower court again approved the venture in a decision upheld by the Supreme Court on a tie vote. *U.S. v. Penn-Olin*, 389 U.S. 308 (1967).

case it cared to prosecute.[31]   The acquisition by Von's of Shopping Bag Food Stores yielded the emergent firm a 7.5 percent share of retail grocery sales in the Los Angeles market. Citing a decline in the number of market competitors and a trend toward supermarket chains, Justice Black found the merger illegal. It presented, he wrote, "exactly the threatening trend toward concentration which Congress wanted to halt."

That the Court had erected imposing structural barriers to horizontal merger could not be seriously questioned. The competition that Congress meant to protect was defined—at least for Section 7 purposes—as large numbers of relatively small rivals. It was this atomistic environment that the Court was determined to maintain insofar as possible, apparently at any cost. Justice Stewart, in a sharp dissent in *Von's*, complained that the decision created a "startling per se rule . . . contrary to the language of Section 7, contrary to the legislative history of the 1950 amendment, and contrary to economic reality."

Vertical Mergers   The government also moved actively, albeit less frequently, against vertical mergers under the new law.[32] *Brown Shoe*, discussed above in a horizontal context, was decided largely on vertical grounds: how would competition be affected if a major shoe manufacturer acquired a prominent retail shoe chain? The Supreme Court tied its conclusions to the notion of vertical foreclosure. When a supplier acquires a customer (or vice versa), it is possible to preclude competing suppliers (customers) from that customer's (supplier's) segment of the market.

The Brown Shoe Case   In this case, Brown Shoe, a manufacturer, acquired G. R. Kinney, a retail chain outlet. By the company's own admission, Kinney stores would have carried only Brown shoes after the merger was implemented. Thus other manufacturers might have been foreclosed from selling through a significant distribution channel. Brown Shoe argued that the competitive vigor of the industry would not be significantly affected by the merger. The percentage of the market that would be foreclosed was in fact quite small. The Court, however, observed that no merger between a shoe manufacturer and retailer "could involve a larger potential market foreclosure," and stated:

> [T]he trend toward vertical integration in the shoe industry, when combined with Brown's avowed policy of forcing its own shoes upon its retail subsidiaries, may foreclose competition from a substantial share of the markets . . . .

Further, said the Court:

> [We recognize] . . . Congress' desire to promote competition through the protection of viable, small, locally owned business. Congress appreciated

[31]384 U.S. 270 (1966).

[32]In *U.S. v. E. I. duPont de Nemours and Co., et al.*, 353 U.S. 586 (1957), the Supreme Court held that duPont's partial stock acquisition of General Motors was illegal under the original Section 7. The merger reduced competition, said the Court, by effectively foreclosing other manufacturers of automotive finishes from GM's segment of the market. The decision represents a rare and atypically effective use of the older provision.

that occasional higher cost and prices might result from the maintenance of fragmented industries. . . .

The *Brown Shoe* decision has been widely criticized by economists for the reasoning embodied in the last passage. While the Court claimed to value competition, its purpose was to protect "small, locally owned businesses." Moreover, a merger that posed any threat to such businesses could not be legally saved by other benefits. The most important potential benefit— increased efficiency in the emergent firm—could in fact condemn the merger precisely because it might pose a threat to smaller, less efficient rivals!

Economic Assessment In economic terms, the Court's implicit idea of competition has been myopic and confused. Disagreements about the effects of vertical mergers are common, but the possibility that they will create efficiencies cannot logically be precluded.[33] It is, of course, true that the economic model of pure competition implies an atomistic or fragmented market structure. But to argue that the achievement of efficiencies must be anticompetitive if it forecloses the less efficient is to turn on its head the rationale of the market.

Competition is, in essence, a process that forces maximal efficiency and tolerates nothing less. The idea that competition can somehow be enhanced by protecting less efficient competitors is therefore contradictory. One might argue that there is some social value in maintaining small companies even where they are inefficient relative to larger enterprise. But competition simply is not a component of such value.

Conglomerate Mergers   The government also has enjoyed some success in attacking conglomerate mergers under Section 7. *Pure conglomerates*, in which there is no economic relationship between merging firms, are unusual; but a more substantial number that do not quite fit the horizontal or vertical mode (despite some relationship between the companies) are usually placed in this category. One common form is *market extension*, a merger in which the acquiring firm expands its markets—either in product or geographic terms—into new but adjacent areas.

In *Federal Trade Commission v. Procter & Gamble Co.* the Supreme Court ruled on the first major product-extension merger to arise under amended Section 7.[34] Procter, a huge manufacturer of household items including soaps and detergents, acquired Clorox, the nation's leading producer of liquid bleach. The products of the two firms were complementary rather than competitive and utilized similar retail distribution systems. This case presented the Court with a somewhat new situation. The tests of lessened competition developed

---

[33]For an illustration of these disagreements, see R. H. Bork, "Vertical Integration and Competitive Processes," and W. F. Mueller, "Public Policy toward Vertical Mergers," both in J. F. Weston and S. Peltzman, eds., *Public Policy toward Mergers* (Pacific Palisades, Calif.: Goodyear Publishing Company, 1969). For an important, substantially broader, discussion of vertical integration, see B. Klein, R. G. Crawford, and A. A. Alchian, "Vertical Integration, Appropriable Rents, and the Competitive Contracting Process," *Journal of Law and Economics* 21 (October 1978): 297-326.

[34]386 U.S. 568 (1967).

earlier—concentration in horizontal cases, foreclosure in vertical cases—could not be applied. Indeed, the distinctive feature of the conglomerate merger is that no direct structural changes occur in affected markets.

In upholding the FTC's view that the merger violated Section 7, Justice Douglas argued rather that: (1) the presence of Procter—not only a large manufacturer, but also the nation's leading advertiser—in the bleach market would discourage both entry of new rivals and aggressive competition by existing firms; and (2) potential competition between Procter and Clorox would be eliminated. The latter argument harks back to *Penn-Olin* and *Falstaff*. Procter had considered entering the bleach market on its own. To do so by purchasing Clorox would have eliminated in advance its prime rival in that market. The objective probability that Procter would have entered *de novo* may have been low. But, as we have seen, the Supreme Court was prepared to give heavy weight to a competitive threat even where the threatening company had shown no inclination to do more than ponder while remaining on the edge of the market.

The Court stated further, in language reminiscent of *Brown Shoe*, that although "some mergers which lessen competition also result in economies," such economies "cannot be used as a defense." There was, however, no strong argument that this merger would have produced genuine technical efficiencies. It was rather advertising economies of a primarily pecuniary nature that seemed most probable.

The importance of potential competition in market extension acquisitions was reiterated in an FTC opinion, *The Bendix Corp., et al.*, in 1970.[35] Bendix, a diversified manufacturer with a position in automotive parts, agreed to acquire Fram Corporation, a producer of various filters and the third largest firm in the aftermarket for passenger car filter replacement parts. The commission found that Bendix was committed to enter the passenger car replacement market, either by "a toe-hold acquisition of a small firm" or "a market leader like Fram."[36] In finding the merger illegal, the commission further stated:

> While the industry was in need of a more beneficial acquisition . . . Bendix effected a merger with Fram—thus eliminating the competition, which clearly would have been substantial, that Fram and other industry members would have had to meet if Bendix had made, and expanded, a toe-hold acquisition of a small firm.

Recent Developments   The government's remarkable record of success under Section 7 ended in 1974 with three Supreme Court decisions that suggest changes in merger policy.

U. S. v. General Dynamics Corp. involved the merger of two major coal producers, United Electric Coal and Freeman Coal Mining (the latter a subsidi-

---

[35]Docket No. 8739, 77 FTC 731 (1970).

[36]Readers may observe an asymmetry in the legal treatment of a potential competitor's intentions. When the firm's own studies or statements suggest some desire to enter the new market, this seems to weigh heavily against the merger in question. If, however, the potential entrant has shown no apparent interest in entering *de novo*, that fact is accorded no weight whatever.

ary of Material Services, which was in turn controlled by General Dynamics).[37] The government argued, as it had in previous horizontal cases, that the merger would increase shares and concentration in markets already showing a sharp decline in the number of competing sellers.

The Court, however, observed that almost all of the acquired firm's (United Electric) coal reserves were tied up under long-term contracts, the basis for most sales in the coal industry. Since the company had virtually no uncommitted reserves, said the Court, its competitive significance was minimal:

> United Electric was a far less significant factor in the coal market than the Government contended . . . . [Although the company had produced] relatively large amounts of coal, its current and future power to compete for subsequent long-term contracts was severely limited by its scarce uncommitted resources . . . .

The government's market share and concentration statistics, based on already committed reserves, were accurate but irrelevant, and the Section 7 test of substantially lessened competition had not been met.

Shortly thereafter, the Supreme Court rejected Section 7 challenges to two commercial bank mergers. In *U.S. v. Marine Bancorporation, Inc.* the National Bank of Commerce (NBC), a Seattle subsidiary of Marine, acquired the Washington Trust Company in Spokane.[38] The government argued that potential competition would be eliminated by the merger. The Court, however, pointed out that state banking laws in Washington precluded most entry routes for NBC into Spokane. Since the argument that entry could occur in the absence of the merger was "unpersuasive," neither the potential competition line of reasoning nor the government's market share showing proved an anticompetitive effect.

In *U.S. v. Connecticut National Bank et al.* the government claimed that Connecticut National's acquisition of First New Haven National Bank would eliminate potential competition between the two.[39] The Supreme Court remanded, finding that the district court had erred in delineating both the product and geographic markets relevant to the case. Commercial and savings banks, said the Court, are separate lines of commerce that should not have been placed together despite some competitive overlap. The relevant geographic market was the local area of the acquired bank rather than the state of Connecticut as a whole. Indeed, observed the Court, were the entire state the relevant market, the banks would have to be treated as direct rather than potential competitors.

[37]415 U.S. 486 (1974).
[38]418 U.S. 602 (1974).
[39]418 U.S. 656 (1974).

Economic Assessment

By the late 1960s, formidable legal obstacles to merger had been established by the courts. Horizontal acquisitions by leading firms seemed illegal, virtually on a *per se* basis, and any merger showing a projected increase in concentration and market shares was highly vulnerable. Vertical acquisitions were in jeopardy wherever a significant foreclosure was a plausible result. The doctrine on conglomerates—including market extension mergers—was less well developed (and perhaps more ad hoc). The courts, however, were not hospitable to such mergers where both partners held strong market positions and where the acquiring firm might have been expected to enter *de novo* in the absence of merger.

Did the 1974 cases herald a new era of antitrust merger policy, in which the Supreme Court is more sympathetic to the claims of defendants? Blair and Heggestad have argued cogently that although these decisions reflect a more sophisticated treatment, the Court has not changed direction.[40] In neither of the banking decisions, for example, was the importance of potential competition denied; rather the Court insisted that such potential must be shown persuasively to exist. If Blair and Heggestad are correct, merger precedent remains intact. It is clear, however, that the government must exercise care in its definition of relevant markets and its contention that firms that do not now compete may compete in the future. This in itself marks a departure from the precedent of the 1960s.

The recent emphasis of antitrust courts on potential competition focuses attention on the condition of entry. In specific cases, one might suspect that the potential for competition between firms depends upon the probabilities that either will enter the other's market. At times (for example, the *Penn-Olin* decisions) the courts pay attention to such probabilities, but more frequently they do not.

Do the courts practice bad economics when they fail to consider the issue? Not necessarily, for two reasons. First, the estimation of actual entry probabilities is no easy task. In many instances, it probably cannot be accomplished with much confidence, and judges (to say nothing of juries) are ill-equipped for the effort. Second, some courts have suggested that the role of potential competition is more closely tied to perceived than to actual probabilities of entry. What is important in this view, is not so much the objective likelihood of entry by a potential competitor; rather, it is the subjective estimate of this likelihood made by the other firm's management. Clearly, the measurement of subjective managerial beliefs about the threat of entry is no job for the courts. It may even be beyond the competence of most economists!

---

[40] R. D. Blair and A. A. Heggestad, "Some Remarks on Recent Merger Decisions," *Industrial Organization Review* 5 (1977): 109–114.

Merger Guidelines and Treatment

The standards imposed by the courts in merger cases in a sense tell only part of the policy story. The courts can apply standards only to those mergers that are challenged, usually by the federal government. The question then becomes: What mergers will the government oppose? In 1968 and again in 1982, the Department of Justice issued detailed guidelines that address precisely this question.

The 1982 guidelines with respect to horizontal mergers focus on two structural elements: the effect of the merger on market concentration, as measured by the HHI (Herfindahl-Hirschman Index); and on the condition of entry. As a general rule, the Antitrust Division will not oppose a merger unless it produces an HHI greater than 1,000 in a relevant market—the rough equivalent of a market of 10 equal-sized firms.[41] Even in more concentrated markets, however, a merger is unlikely to be challenged if it raises the HHI value by much less than 100 points. (A merger of firms with market shares of 10 percent and 5 percent, or firms with 25 percent and 2 percent, would increase the HHI by precisely 100 points.)[42] Furthermore, mergers probably will not be challenged regardless of their effects on concentration as long as entry into the market is easy.

Eleanor Fox, in an interesting survey, concludes that "the 1982 Guidelines virtually rule out challenge to most mergers."[43] Among the mergers that would not have been challenged under the current rules are Brown Shoe, Continental Can, and Von's grocery. Clearly, the criteria followed by the enforcement agencies are bound to have a profound effect on the nature and impact of all antitrust policies—perhaps more so than anything the courts may say.

Has the federal government taken a much more permissive attitude toward corporate mergers recently as the guidelines may suggest? Although this question has no simple answer, some relevant data appear in Table 10.1 What we see most generally is that there has been no obvious upturn in the *number* of merger announcements during the 1980s, but that a dramatic rise in the *dollar value* of the announced mergers has occurred. This type of information, on its own, proves nothing. It is consistent, however, with the possibility (which some view with pleasure and others with alarm) that the government's antimerger policy is now lenient, and thus permits relatively large acquisitions to occur.

---

[41]The HHI as the Department of Justice calculates it, differs slightly from our earlier description of the Herfindahl index, in that the department ignores the decimal point in squaring firms' market shares. The HHI ranges from a value of about zero (many infinitessimally small firms) to 10,000 (a single firm with market share of 100 percent; squaring the share and ignoring the decimal yields 10,000). The Department of Justice considers any market with HHI less than 1,000 to be unconcentrated, while those above 1,800 are highly concentrated. Between these values, the concentration level is of possible concern.

[42]$10^2 + 5^2 = 125$; $15^2 = 225$. Difference = 100. $25^2 + 2^2 = 629$; $27^2 = 729$. Difference = 100.

[43]"The New Merger Guidelines—A Blueprint for Microeconomic Analysis," *Antitrust Bulletin* 27 (Fall 1982): 519–591.

Table 10.1   Recent Merger Trends in the United States

Year	Net Merger and Acquisition Announcements	Total Value (millions of dollars)	Base*
1975	2,297	11,796	848
1980	1,889	44,346	890
1981	2,395	82,618	1,126
1982	2,346	53,755	930
1983	2,533	73,081	1,077
1984	2,543	122,224	1,084
1985	3,001	179,768	1,320

*Number of mergers and acquisitions upon which total value is based.
Source: W. T. Grimm Co., *Mergerstat Review*, 1985.

TREATMENT OF MARKET POWER

Economic Analysis

It may be observed that our public treatment of market power under the antitrust laws follows two distinctive routes. *Established* positions are only occasionally challenged and rarely touched in any direct way under the Sherman Act. Efforts to attain *new* positions of power via merger, however, have been vigorously resisted under the Clayton Act. In combination, these policies may seem to protect the status quo. Old power is left largely alone while new challengers are suppressed.[44]

There is, however, a plausible economic argument for this sort of dichotomy. When firms grow large by internal means, they must as a rule compete with others for their position. There is, accordingly, some presumption that such firms are efficient—that they have achieved their size because, in one way or another, they have done a better job than rivals of serving the market. This is, of course, not a certainty, but it may be regarded as a reasonable presumption in the absence of contrary evidence.

In the case of growth by merger, however, the situation is different. Mergers may increase efficiency, especially where firms are initially suboptimal in size or degree of integration. But such growth is not usually subjected to a market test. When one firm acquires another, it may increase its market power, but the increase does not represent the result of competition. The efficiency presumption is therefore weaker, and it may make good sense to respond to this sort of growth with greater skepticism, as reflected in stricter policy standards.

Whatever path policy follows, however, it is certain to provoke controversy because of a stubborn underlying fact: large size in a corporation may at once reflect both efficiency and concentrated power. Yet we are likely as a

[44]This is an oversimplification. If the new challenger grows by means other than merger, it will not be subjected to more stringent legal scrutiny than established powers.

society to seek the former and distrust the latter.[45] The standard diagrammatic analysis is shown in Figure 10.1 in which the market confronts a demand curve, D, and a (marginal and average) cost curve, C.[46] If one thinks of the market as initially competitive, price and output levels will tend toward p, q. Suppose then that firms in the market combine. There may be two effects: (1) efficiencies are achieved that shift the cost function down to C' but (2) market power is concentrated sufficiently to permit restriction of output. The net result then might be a move from p, q to p', q'.

Measurement   How is this change to be evaluated? The measurement problem is one that we have encountered before (see Chapter 3, p. 69). Consumer welfare has been reduced because higher prices are charged for fewer units. The reduction is conventionally measured by the deadweight loss triangle, W.[47] On the other hand, real resources are saved. There is thus a loss in allocative efficiency but a gain in productive efficiency.[48] Whereas the production of output level q' would have cost Oq'Xp initially, it now costs Oq'YU, a saving represented by the rectangle, Z.

Is this change, on balance, desirable? The answer plainly depends on the relative size of the beneficial and costly components, but some new problems now arise:

1.   The measurement of areas W and Z is unlikely to be straightforward. Even if it were technically manageable, few if any courts would be equipped to deal with the problem.

2.   The simple diagrammatic argument ignores values other than allocative and productive efficiency. (Or, alternatively, it fails to define the weights that society may wish to attach to these good and bad effects.) Perhaps the degree of power attained when firms combine implies a redistribution of income or political influence that might alter our judgment about the desirability of the change.

The point is not that this type of analysis is either incorrect or unhelpful, but simply that it is unlikely to produce clear policy prescriptions.

Although precise measurement presents problems, we have noted (in Chapter 9) the existence of substantial economic concentration in the United States. Quite a few industries, especially within the manufacturing sector,

---

[45] In other words, size may carry costs and benefits. This can hardly surprise any student of economics.

[46] See O. E. Williamson, "Economies as an Antitrust Defense: The Welfare Trade-offs," *American Economic Review* 58 (March 1968): 18–36.

[47] Use of this triangle as a welfare measure, however, rests on some precarious assumptions. See P. Asch and R. S. Seneca, "The Demand Curve and Welfare Change: A Reconsideration," *Journal of Post Keynesian Economics* 2 (Spring 1980).

[48] The loss of allocative efficiency, moreover, is substantial in the sense that, despite more efficient production, consumers appear worse off.

Figure 10.1 Welfare Costs versus Efficiency Gains

In an initially competitive market, D is demand and C is (marginal and average) cost. The market will locate at p, q. If firms in the market undertake an efficient (cost–reducing) merger, C falls to C'; but the firms now have market power and locate at (p', q'). The change to a more efficient market with concentrated power has two effects: cost savings (rectangle Z) and deadweight, or misallocation, loss (triangle W).

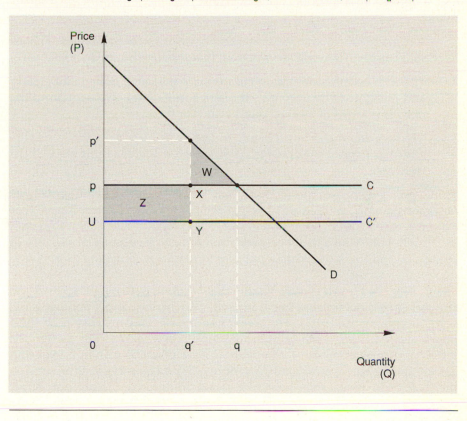

appear dominated by a few firms.[49] At an aggregate level, the 200 largest manufacturing corporations control well over 50 percent of all corporate assets and about 40 percent of value added.[50] Should this picture cause us concern? Perhaps, but recall two qualifications. First, although aggregate concentration is high, it apparently has not increased—and may have decreased somewhat—

[49]Carl Kaysen and Donald F. Turner, for example, found that in 1954 about 59 percent of manufacturing sales originated in structurally defined oligopolies (that is, industries whose structure suggests dominance by a few). These estimates, moreover, were based on broad market definitions that probably understated true concentration levels. C. Kaysen and D. F. Turner, *Antitrust Policy* (Cambridge, Mass.: Harvard University Press, 1959).

[50]A variety of estimates is cited in J. M. Blair, *Economic Concentration* (New York: Harcourt, Brace Jovanovich, 1972), Chapter 4.

in recent years. Second, no index of concentration (regardless of how carefully it is constructed) measures competitiveness directly.

Sources of Power: Nature, Competition, Luck How society wishes to deal with concentrated economic power must depend in significant degree upon how and why such power arises. Consider three possibilities within a particular market:

1. A firm grows to dominate its market because of scale economies. That is, size-based efficiency is so important that smaller entities do not survive.

2. The firm becomes dominant because it is managed more competently and farsightedly than rivals. It offers a more attractive bargain to the market in terms of product quality and/or price.

3. The firm dominates by accident. Although not especially farsighted, its offerings happen to appeal to consumers—it is in the right place at the right time.

Public policy responses are likely to vary widely. The first case represents natural monopoly, justified and perhaps dictated by real economic forces. (For a more detailed discussion, see Chapter 13.) Society may well decide to permit such monopoly, which could be prevented only by a substantial sacrifice of resources, and also to regulate it in order to reduce or eliminate its ability to exploit the market.

The second case is sometimes described as competitive superiority.[51] The firm has grown not because size is in itself efficient, but simply because it has won the competitive battle. The position of such a company may pose some problems. After all, resource misallocation is undesirable even though the moving force is an effective competitor. As a practical matter, however, a society such as ours is most unlikely to tamper with a market position based on merit. To do so would, at the very least, raise a troublesome incentive question: How can we expect firms to strive for maximum efficiency and success if too much success is penalized?

In the third instance—that of accidental success or luck—the issue becomes more complicated. Since the firm's power was not clearly deserved, society might be reluctant to tolerate it. Yet a problem remains: we are not in the habit of removing power (or property) acquired by luck, or even of attempting to determine whether luck was in fact responsible for a strong market position. Short of a Standard Oil situation, in which a company's dominance is seen to be the result of unacceptable behavior, there is unlikely to be a consensus to deconcentrate markets—that is, to roll back existing firm power.

---

[51]This term is taken from an interesting paper by Harold Demsetz, "Industry Structure, Market Rivalry, and Public Policy," *Journal of Law and Economics* 16 (April 1973).

Assessment

An important part of the policy problem posed by market power is empirical rather than ethical. We may not be able to ascertain why a dominant firm has become dominant. There are no easy tests to distinguish merit from luck. Even if society were prepared in principle to restrict unearned power, we would be unsure of how to identify it. This uncertainty may well explain why existing concentrations of power have not been challenged more widely under the Sherman Act.

Strong faith in the market—sometimes referred to as a Chicago School approach—suggests that where power is concentrated, one should presume that it is efficiency-justified unless persuasive evidence argues otherwise.[52] When carried to the extreme, this position becomes tautological. If the market invariably dictates the most efficient size distribution of firms, then any degree of concentration we observe, even where it implies overwhelming market power, must be justified by its efficiency. The existence of size and power becomes the evidence of its own desirability. In less extreme forms, this argument does not preclude a finding that concentrated power is unjustified by economic forces. But it places a heavy burden of proof on anyone who seeks to make such a showing.

Our public treatment of established market power may be termed highly conservative. We will not disturb economic concentration without compelling reasons, in part because we cannot be certain of the consequences. Our policies toward mergers may be interpreted in a similarly conservative light. Some years ago Richard B. Heflebower noted such a rationale for early court decisions denying mergers under the new Section 7.[53] Whether an acquisition will actually reduce competition may not ordinarily be predicted with certainty because both theory and evidence tend to be inconclusive. The prudent (and conservative) course is therefore to err in the least damaging direction. Prohibiting a beneficial merger is such an error. While it may defer the achievement of efficiencies, it does not preclude it, and the policy itself is easily reversible if it is found to be misguided. To permit harmful mergers, on the other hand, may impose more serious long-term costs that are not readily reversed when the error is discovered.

Are our public policies toward economic power sensible? Any answer will, of course, provoke disagreement, but the underlying basis of the disagreement should be clearly recognized. Those who favor minimal government intervention commonly state their position in terms of market virtue. Concentrated power arises because, in all likelihood, it is economically efficient. If by chance it should occur accidentally, it cannot persist without a sound market

---

[52]J. S. McGee, for example, states: "In the absence of artifical strictures, there is a strong presumption that the existing structure of industry is the efficient structure." See J. S. McGee, "Efficiency and Economies of Size," in H. J. Goldschmid, H. M. Mann, and J. F. Weston, eds., *Industrial Concentration: The New Learning* (Boston: Little, Brown and Company, 1974).

[53]R. B. Heflebower, "Corporate Mergers: Policy and Economic Analysis," *Quarterly Journal of Economics* 77 (November 1963).

justification. To turn the point around, inefficient concentrations are bound to break down as more efficient market alternatives appear.

People who believe that government should do more to limit economic power often make either or both of the following points:

1.   The virtues of the market presuppose competition in some structural sense that precludes concentrated power. Concentrated markets therefore cannot possess the usual virtues, and arguments along such lines are pointless.

2.   Although market concentration may in certain cases be compatible with competition (in a nonstructural sense), it is more likely to evolve as the result of some form of market failure.[54]

Both positions imply, for slightly different reasons, that the expectation that markets will produce desirable results is not usually valid where concentration is high.

This sort of disagreement sounds economic because it is couched in economic terms. The conflict, however, may involve broader social values. Ms. Smith, for example, might have technical efficiency as a top priority—that is, a belief that we should minimize the resource cost of our output. That productive efficiency could imply a substantial concentration of the power to make economic decisions is simply not a concern. Mr. Jones on the other hand, could desire that economic decisions be made democratically in the sense that no one participant or small group in the market can dictate or control them. That such dispersal of power may imply inefficiency of production in some areas, with a consequent sacrifice of resources, is to Jones a small price to pay in order to maintain wide participation in the market.

Economic analysis is unlikely to settle this kind of disagreement, because Smith and Jones have different objectives. (It may, however, help to define their conflict clearly.) In practice, the disagreement may yet be reconcilable. Smith may concede that beyond some point, small efficiency gains are not worth the costs of additional concentrations of power, while Jones might admit that any degree of inefficiency, no matter how extreme, in order to maintain atomistic markets is not tolerable.

PROPOSED REFORMS

Proposals for antitrust reform are about as old as antitrust itself. In the realm of market power, a number of rather familiar suggestions were included in the late Senator Philip Hart's Industrial Reorganization Act, which we discuss in more detail in Chapter 12. This legislative proposal would have made the possession of monopoly power illegal.

---

[54]See O. E. Williamson, "Dominant Firms and the Monopoly Problem: Market Failure Considerations," *Harvard Law Review* 85 (June 1972): 1512–1531.

The Hart bill echoed the sentiments of others who advocate a government challenge to power itself as opposed to power with abuse or intent.[55] Such proposals, although introduced with some frequency, have made little headway in Congress. As we have seen, any law that would make the existence of monopoly power illegal and would require its dissolution as a remedy, would represent an extreme change in the public policies pursued under American antitrust. Although this type of reform has generated a good deal of discussion, prospects of enactment must be regarded as remote.

Proposals to place absolute size limits on merging companies have also been advanced recently. Under one suggestion, no firm with $2 billion or more in sales or assets could make any acquisition. No firm with $100 million or more could enter into a merger creating a firm with $2 billion or more or absorb a company with a 20 percent or larger share of a $100 million or larger market. Such proposals are aimed mainly at conglomerate acquisitions; it is improbable that any horizontal or vertical merger of such magnitudes could survive existing Clayton Act standards.

SUMMARY

In this chapter, we have surveyed antitrust policy responses to market power. Very few firms have been broken up under the monopolization provisions of the Sherman Act. Indeed, there have not been many attempts made to do so. Mergers, especially those between rivals, have been treated more stringently by the courts. In recent years, however, there has been some relaxation of legal standards. The courts have been more willing to conclude that mergers may not be anticompetitive even where they increase market concentration. The U.S. Department of Justice has followed guidelines that permit many sizable acquisitions to proceed without challenge. Is this a good policy? As we have explained, there is no simple answer to this question. Rather, we point out the complexities in searching for an answer.

CONCLUSION

The basic question of what we mean by competition and monopoly has not been resolved by antitrust. The courts have been quite consistent in associating high market shares and concentration with monopoly power. But while the association makes some sense, it is not inevitably accurate. A firm's dominant market share may be transitory, as in the case of the innovator whose business will be eroded as soon as rivals succeed in copying him. Alternatively, the share may be dependent on the firm's ability to continue to offer a better product or price than its rivals. If the high share is thus precarious (even though persistent), it is not clear that monopoly is the proper description while the firm operates under serious competitive pressure. Where the firm's free-

[55]See, for example, H. Simons, *Economic Policy for a Free Society* (Chicago: University of Chicago Press, 1948); and Kaysen and Turner, *Antitrust Policy*.

dom to act is closely constrained, even an impressive market share does not necessarily imply that it has much power.

A final difficulty in connecting market share with monopoly is the need to define the market. It is generally true that concentration of specified firms' shares gets higher as the market is defined more narrowly. Many firms could be said to have a monopoly of their own product (the Coca-Cola Company produces all Coca-Cola), but decreasing shares of markets that encompass progressively more substitutes (all cola drinks; all sodas; sodas and other beverages). However, defining the market correctly, or even specifying what correct means, is often a real problem. It is therefore conceivable that, in some instances, the appearance of a monopoly share results from a too-narrow drawing of market boundaries. We turn next to antitrust policy toward market behavior—the uses and possible abuses of market power as opposed to its mere existence.

Discussion Questions

1. "Some economists contend that a company holding a monopoly in a market must have monopolized that market. The courts have never agreed, however, ruling that monopoly is necessary but not sufficient to prove that monopolizing has occurred." Explain your agreement or disagreement.

2. Suppose that a company holds 100 percent of a major market because it produces a better product than would-be rivals are able to produce. How would a court be likely to react if the company is charged with monopolizing this market? How should the court react?

3. "The emphasis of American courts on intent in monopolization cases is unfortunate. Intent, after all, is a state of mind. The courts have thus forced themselves to become mind readers—something that few judges are equipped to do." Is this an accurate observation? Is it an important one?

4. Antitrust merger cases sometimes are dominated by arguments over market definition. In such instances, the merging firms typically argue for a broad definition of relevant markets, while the government proposes narrower definitions. Why is this the typical pattern?

5. In 1984 a leading petroleum producer, Texaco, proposed to acquire a smaller but significant rival, Getty. What do the court decisions discussed in this chapter suggest about the legal prospects of such a merger?

Selected Readings

Keyes, L. S. "The Shoe Machinery Case and the Problem of the Good Trust." *Quarterly Journal of Economics* 68 (May 1954): 287-304. *Lucid discussion of public policy toward the well-behaved monopolist.*

Manne, H. G. "Mergers and the Market for Corporate Control." *Journal of Political Economy* 73 (April 1965): 110-120. *An important analysis of mergers as a check on managerial behavior.*

McGee, J. S. "Predatory Price Cutting: The Standard Oil (N.J.) Case." *Journal of Law and Economics* 1 (October 1958): 137-169. *Classic analysis of Standard Oil's behavior and the role of predatory pricing in monopoly.*

Mason, Edward S. "Monopoly in Law and Economics." *Yale Law Journal* 47 (November 1937): 34-49. *A still-pertinent discussion of the ways in which economists and lawyers define competition and monopoly.*

Steiner, Peter O. *Mergers: Motives, Effects, Policies.* Ann Arbor, Mich.: University of Michigan Press, 1975. *Clear, thorough analyses of a broad range of issues in corporate mergers.*

Williamson, Oliver E. "Economies as an Antitrust Defense: The Welfare Tradeoffs." *American Economic Review.* 58 (March 1968); and "Economies as an Antitrust Defense Revisited." *University of Pennsylvania Law Review.* 125 (April 1977): 699-736. *Basic welfare analysis of mergers and other activities that may create monopoly power.*

CHAPTER 11

· ·

ANTITRUST AND MARKET BEHAVIOR

We turn now to public antitrust treatment of market behavior. As noted, it is somewhat artificial to distinguish between policies toward power and policies toward behavior because the two are quite intimately linked. Indeed, where firms are powerless—in strictly competitive markets—their behavior is predetermined. Only one course of action is consistent with long-run survival. The existence of power implies that firms have discretion to behave differently—although not without regard to market forces, as some naive statements have it.

There is nevertheless considerable basis in law for treating market behavior as a separate policy category. The Sherman Act speaks of conspiracy and the act of monopolizing; the Clayton Act refers to price discrimination and exclusive dealing; the Federal Trade Commission Act proscribes unfair or deceptive acts. All these are elements of behavior. While they may require power—the purely competitive firm, for example, could not discriminate—power does not necessarily imply that the practices will occur. The courts, moreover, have devoted considerable effort to defining the conditions under which a wide variety of behavioral patterns is or is not permissible.

In approaching each area of behavior—collusion, price discrimination, vertical restraints, predatory pricing—we shall first consider the development of legal precedent and then proceed to ask whether the rules in question have a consistent economic rationale.

COLLUSION

Section 1 of the Sherman Act, which makes "every contract, combination . . . or conspiracy, in restraint of trade" illegal, has been employed by the government to combat collusive corporate behavior—most frequently price-fixing or market-dividing agreements. The rationale for some public policy against collusion is straightforward and even obvious.

As we have seen in Chapter 4, many behavioral possibilities exist in oligopoly, including forms of rivalry that most business managers would regard as ruinous or cutthroat. Collusion—essentially an agreement among rivals not to compete—is thus a clear temptation. It may avoid much unpleasantness and, if executed perfectly, might even enable a group of competing firms to act as if they were a single monopolist (that is, as maximizers of their joint profits). Society's interest in preventing such behavior is apparent. Effective collusion will yield the same distortions as monopoly: prices that are too high, outputs that are too low, and probable impacts on the distributions of income and wealth. On the other hand, it is difficult to imagine that collusive conduct will produce countervailing social benefits with any frequency. While possible justifications cannot logically be ruled out, arguments in favor of collusion tend to be unimpressive from a social standpoint.[1]

Despite the apparent clarity of this situation, there is a fundamental difficulty in devising public policies toward collusion. How is collusion to be defined? The problem is at once conceptual (what do we mean by the word collusion?) and practical (what kinds of evidence will constitute proof of its existence?).

Consider the following illustration. Firms Alpha and Beta are dominant rivals in the market for organic fertilizer. The fertilizers produced by both companies are physically identical and most customers will buy from the one that offers the lower price. The possibilities for mutually harmful price competition are clear. If Alpha and Beta go at each other aggressively, price may be bid down so far that little or no profit remains for each. If on the other hand, the companies can somehow avoid such aggression, they will be able to maintain a higher, more profitable price—perhaps one in the neighborhood of the monopoly level, as in Figure 11.1.

Plainly, the firms' mutual interest is in the latter course, but how can they achieve it? Consider two scenarios:

1. The sales managers of Alpha and Beta meet and agree to charge no less than the current price, $100 per ton of fertilizer.

2. Without any communication between company representatives, Alpha and Beta naturally and rationally stick to the $100 price. Each may be tempted to cut price and attract customers away from the other. But both refrain, recognizing that any short-term gains are likely to be outweighed by later losses as the rival retaliates and price warfare occurs.[2]

---

[1]Some observers disagree. See, for an interesting discussion, Donald Dewey, "Information, Entry, and Welfare: The Case for Collusion," *American Economic Review* 69 (September 1979): 587–594.

[2]Alpha is likely to reason as follows: "Since Beta is charging $100, we would do better to charge $90 or $95. The trouble is that if we do that, they won't stay at $100. They will either match us— in which case we've gained nothing—or, even worse, they might undercut us. Either way, it does not pay us to go below the current ($100) price." If Beta reasons the same way, however, neither will budge from the $100 price—at least not downward!

Figure 11.1 Collusion

In this highly simplified diagram, Firms Alpha and Beta confront identical demand curves, D, and identical constant cost functions. It is in the best interest of each to maintain price as close to the monopoly point as possible, while consumers—and society as a whole—will benefit more as the price approaches the competitive level. It should be noted that, in this diagram, D represents the demand curve of either firm, drawn on the assumption that both firms charge the same price. Under different pricing assumptions, the position and shape of the curve could be substantially altered. (Refer to Chapter 4.)

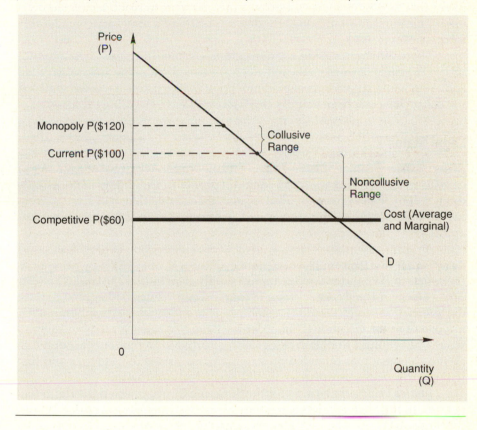

Have the companies in these two scenarios colluded to fix price? In the first case the answer is surely yes. Alpha and Beta have overtly agreed not to compete, but to maintain a price above the competitive level.

The answer in the second scenario is less obvious. The companies have not communicated, and one might therefore argue that no agreement has in fact occurred. The important point, however, is that without overtly agreeing to anything, they have still reached the collusive result—the same price that would have been set had they openly conspired. They have tacitly agreed, but whether this amounts to legally defined collusion is an open question.

This example is very much oversimplified. In many markets it is unlikely that agreement on price (or other terms of supply) will be easy. Independent firms have strong conflicting interests. Each would like to take away the others' customers even though mutual cooperation may be preferable to unrestrained rivalry. Under many circumstances, firms will be sorely tempted to cheat even after agreeing to a fixed price. This is the familiar prisoner's dilemma, discussed in detail in Chapter 4.

Cheating is not the only problem that a prospective collusive group must resolve. Members of the group may have sharply conflicting preferences (for example, more efficient firms will tend to prefer relatively low prices). It is likely that any agreement will prove more difficult to reach tacitly than via open communication, although the degree of difficulty may vary considerably from market to market.[3]

These difficulties aside, the definitional problem remains. It is unavoidable. A policy toward collusion must be based on some notion of what collusion is and what kinds of evidence point to its existence. As we shall see, the courts have not been entirely clear or consistent in treating these issues.

Legal Status

In early cases arising under Section 1 of the Sherman Act, proof of collusive or conspiratorial conduct was not a common problem. Defendant firms usually did not deny their agreements, but argued instead that they had acted reasonably and thus legally. They proceeded, in effect, as if a *rule of reason* would be applied.

Rejecting a Rule of Reason The first hints that this was not to happen came from the courts in 1897 and was made unmistakably clear in 1927. In *United States v. Trans-Missouri Freight Association*, 18 railroad companies had agreed to form the association which would (1) establish rates and rules for members and (2) impose fines for violations.[4] In order to change its rates, a member railroad would be required to obtain association approval. Defendants argued that their agreement was intended only to maintain reasonable charges and that without it, ruinous competition would pervade the industry.

Justice Peckham, writing for the Supreme Court, rejected the claim that because each firm individually has the right to charge reasonable prices, it may enter agreements with rivals to do the same:

> What one company may do in the way of charging reasonable rates is radically different from entering into a combination with competing roads to keep up the rates to that point. If there be any competition the extent of the charge for service will be seriously affected. . . . Competition will itself bring charges down to what may be reasonable, while in the case of an agreement to keep prices up, competition is allowed no play. . . .

The position that the simple fact of an agreement—not the legitimacy of its terms—is what matters was reinforced in *Addyston Pipe and Steel Co. v.*

---

[3]For example, in markets characterized by differentiated products, rapidly shifting demands, and larger numbers of firms, tacit cooperation will be more difficult simply because the mutually desirable price is less obvious.

[4]166 U.S. 290 (1897).

United States.[5] Six cast-iron pipe manufacturers had agreed to divide their markets into geographic territories, within each of which prices were fixed. The companies maintained that the price established for each territory was reasonable. In a circuit court opinion, Judge Taft (later President Taft) found that while the prices charged were not reasonable:

> We do not think the issue an important one, because . . . [there is no] question of reasonableness open to the courts. . . . [The tendency of the agreement] was to give defendants the power to charge unreasonable prices, had they chosen to do so.[6]

The Supreme Court cited this statement approvingly in upholding Judge Taft's decision.

The illegality of collusive agreements, regardless of their terms or market effect, was asserted categorically by the Supreme Court in *United States v. Trenton Potteries Co.*[7] Twenty-three corporations and twenty individuals had combined via Trenton Potteries "to fix and maintain uniform prices" for sanitary pottery. In the group's initial trial, the judge had instructed the jury that it could find a violation without considering whether the prices fixed had been reasonable. It did so, but the appeals court reversed this decision, holding that the judge's instruction was improper—that is, that the reasonableness of fixed prices was essential to the determination of a violation of law.

The Supreme Court upheld the trial court, thus restoring the jury verdict. Said Justice Stone:

> The aim and result of every price-fixing agreement, if effective, is the elimination of one form of competition. . . . Agreements which create such potential power may well be held to be in themselves unreasonable or unlawful restraints, without the necessity of minute inquiry whether a particular price is reasonable or unreasonable. . . .

The issue was thus clearly settled. Price-fixing agreements are illegal *per se.* Neither the circumstances surrounding the agreement nor its actual impact on price is pertinent. There is no rule of reason here. This position has been followed by American courts with almost no deviation to the present time.[8]

Implied Conspiracy   The problem of defining that collusion or conspiracy to which a per se prohibition applies has taken on more significance as defendants (not surprisingly) have become less willing to admit such conduct. Rather than claiming "we colluded in a reasonable way," the more common defense has become "we had no agreement."

[5]175 U.S. 211 (1899).

[6]*United States v. Addyston Pipe and Steel Co.,* 85 F. 271 (6th Cir. 1898).

[7]273 U.S. 392 (1927).

[8]The only significant exception was *United States v. Appalachian Coals, Inc.,* 288 U.S. 344 (1933). Here the Supreme Court found that formation of a joint selling agent by 137 coal manufacturers did not violate Section 1, in part because it would not have significant impact on the market. Under a per se rule, this should have made no difference.

In *Interstate Circuit, Inc. v. United States,* the Supreme Court declared a doctrine of implied conspiracy.[9] Eight motion picture distributors in Texas acceded to identical demands by Interstate Circuit, a first-run movie theater chain. In a letter sent to each distributor, Interstate insisted that subsequent (second-run) showings of its films be limited to theaters charging at least 25 cents (!) admission and that the films not be shown on double bills. The distributors, each of whom knew that others were receiving an identical letter, complied with Interstate's demands.

Although there was no direct evidence that the distributors had explicitly agreed with one another to comply, the Supreme Court found a Section 1 violation. Said the Court:

> It taxes credulity to believe that the several distributors would . . . have accepted and put into operation with substantial unanimity such far reaching changes in their business methods without some understanding that all were to join, and we reject as beyond the range of probability that it was the result of mere chance . . . .

American Tobacco Co. v. United States reinforced the notion that conspiracy may be implied circumstantially, absent direct evidence of an agreement.[10] In finding the "Big Three" tobacco manufacturers (American, Liggett and Myers, and R. J. Reynolds) guilty of numerous Sherman Act violations, the Supreme Court viewed a long history of detailed parallel behavior by the three—behavior that seemed clearly aimed at driving out producers of economy-brand cigarettes who had entered the market in the early 1930s. When the economy brands appeared, the Big Three adopted identical pricing patterns that at one point appeared to fall below cost. They avoided competition with each other in tobacco auction markets, but did enter auctions for lower economy-grade tobaccos, an act that had the effect of bidding up tobacco costs for the economy producers. There was no direct evidence of an agreement among the three companies, but Justice Burton, writing for the Supreme Court, said:

> No formal agreement is necessary to constitute an unlawful conspiracy.
> Often crimes are a matter of inference deduced from . . . [a defendant's] acts.

Conscious Parallelism   Several other cases involving similar inferences produced, by the late 1940s, an apparently strong doctrine of conscious parallelism.[11] That is, companies acting identically, each in full knowledge of what the other(s) may do, violate the Sherman Act even though there is no other evidence of an agreement to follow such a course. To some observers, the Supreme Court had done nothing less than to outlaw rational oligopoly behavior, for parallel action in some markets reflects only a taking account of the mutual dependence that confronts firms.

Whether or not the courts had intended to formulate such a policy, there has been some backing away during the past four decades. In the late 1940s and

---

[9]306 U.S. 208 (1939).

[10]328 U.S. 781 (1946).

[11]See *Paramount Pictures, Inc. v. U.S.,* 334 U.S. 131 (1948) and *U.S. v. Griffith,* 334 U.S. 100 (1948).

early 1950s, a number of lower courts began to rule that parallel behavior did not necessarily imply a breach of Section 1. Companies might, for example, charge the same prices merely because they faced identical cost and demand conditions, not because of conspiracy or collusion in any meaningful sense.[12] The question became, in cases of detailed parallelism, whether such behavior was consistent with independent decision making, and thus with innocence under the law.[13]

The Supreme Court spoke to this issue in *Theatre Enterprises, Inc. v. Paramount Film Distributing Corp.*[14] A suburban Baltimore theater owner sued Paramount and other film distributors, charging that their failure to supply him with first-run films constituted, in effect, a conspiracy to boycott him. The theater, the Crest, was located in a shopping center 6 miles from downtown Baltimore. All distributors had refused to provide it with the desired movies on similar grounds: they had an established policy of restricting these films to eight downtown theaters. The Crest would have been competing with the eight, none of whom would waive their existing clearance rights to allow a simultaneous showing. In short, the distributors contended that they had followed a legitimate business strategy: restricting first-run showings to downtown houses with greater drawing power, for the purpose of expanding profits.

The critical issue as the Court defined it, was whether this behavior reflected an "independent decison or . . . an agreement." Said Justice Clark:

> To be sure, business behavior is admissible circumstantial evidence from which the fact finder may infer agreement. . . . But this Court has never held that proof of parallel business behavior conclusively establishes agreement or, phrased differently, that such behavior itself constitutes a Sherman Act offense.

Strong conscious parallelism, then, was not the order of the day. Parallel behavior is pertinent. It might support a *prima facie* case of conspiracy. But taken alone it is insufficient. Collusion may thus be proved in two ways: either by direct evidence (testimony of a conspirator, records of telephone calls, meetings, and the like); or by parallel behavior plus something more. Precisely what that something more might be, however, has never been spelled out by the courts and is likely to vary with the circumstances surrounding each case.

Corporate Agreements Not Specifying Price   The Supreme Court has made clear that where corporate agreement does exist, it runs afoul of the per se rule even though price-fixing is not a direct part of the agreement. In *United States v. Container Corp.*, a group of corrugated container manufacturers exchanged highly detailed information with one another, including the prices charged on

---

[12]See especially *Peveley Dairy Co. v. U.S.*, 178 F.2d 363 (8th Cir. 1949) and *Milgram v. Loew's, Inc.*, 192 F.2d 579 (3rd Cir. 1951), certiorari denied, 343 U.S. 929.

[13]For a useful discussion, see A. Phillips, *Market Structure, Organization and Performance* (Cambridge, Mass.: Harvard University Press, 1962), Chapter 3.

[14]346 U.S. 537 (1954).

specific sales to identified customers.[15] There was clearly an agreement to exchange the information, but no overt understanding about what prices would be charged—that is, no fixing of price.

Justice Douglas wrote for the Court that the effect of the information exchange "was to stabilize prices" since "knowledge of a competitor's price usually meant matching that price." Moreover, such a "limitation or reduction of price competition" brings the agreement within Section 1 prohibitions, because "interference with the setting of price by free market forces is unlawful per se."

It may be further observed that agreements violate Section 1 even where price itself is not directly affected. Collusive action to allocate customers, to boycott customers or suppliers, or to fix product characteristics—all of which may well have indirect effects on price—have been successfully challenged by the government.

Assessment of the Law on Collusion Sherman Act Section 1 policies are, in short, a mixture of surface clarity and underlying fuzziness. Nothing could be plainer than a per se prohibition on agreements by independent companies to limit competition. If the agreement exists, the law is breached. Vagueness enters, however, when we ask how the existence of an agreement is to be proved. Where the collusion is obvious or admitted, no problem exists. In nonobvious cases, the courts have been willing to infer collusion from surrounding circumstances, including parallel behavior. But the point at which such circumstances in themselves amount to collusion is not precisely defined.

The Economics of the Policy

Economists commonly distinguish between overt and tacit agreement. The Sherman Act, as interpreted legally, takes direct aim at the former, with strong effects. Formal cartels simply do not exist as an important force in the American economy, a policy result that Posner calls "the major achievement of . . . antitrust law."[16] This characterization seems fair, but (as Posner himself is quick to point out) some difficulties remain.

The legal restriction of formal collusion leaves open the possibility that tacit collusion will flourish. Even if the courts wished to stop such informal activities, one fact would remain clear: tacit agreement is, by its very nature, difficult to detect. The government cannot prosecute conspiracies, much less win convictions, unless those conspiracies become visible.

The immediate questions thus concern the importance of tacit or informal collusion. How widespread is it? How well does it work? Have we legally closed one form of monopolistic behavior while permitting firms to follow a somewhat different route to the same end?

[15]393 U.S. 333 (1969).
[16]R. A. Posner, *Antitrust Law* (Chicago: University of Chicago Press, 1976), 39.

There are, unfortunately, few satisfactory *a priori* answers to such questions. It is possible to speculate about the conditions under which tacit agreement seems likely to arise. We may even be able to define the circumstances under which we would expect such agreements to be easy or difficult to maintain. What we would really like to know, however, is the effectiveness with which companies can coordinate their policies in the absence of direct communication. This is not a question to which economic analysis supplies a clear or general answer.[17]

If we cannot assess the quantitative importance of tacit collusion theoretically, and if such behavior is, as a rule, unobservable, what can be said about the effects of public policy under Section 1? The obvious answer is: not too much. But there are some bits of pertinent evidence available. There is no question, for example, that conspiracies of the type that are prosecuted—those that tend to be overt and even flagrant—often yield higher market prices, sometimes dramatically so.[18]

At the same time, it has been observed that firms convicted of collusion are, *ceteris paribus*, less profitable than (a random sample of) clean firms.[19] This result is surprising, since the purpose of collusion surely is not to reduce profits. Two explanations seem plausible. First, causation may run from profitability to collusion, that is, unsatisfactory profits may stimulate firms to take desperate measures, including illegal conspiracy with rivals. While such conspiracy may indeed raise price and profit levels, the profit rates of these firms remain relatively low.

A second possible explanation is that the low profit rates of colluders reflect a legal rather than an economic event: a tendency of Sherman Act prosecution to center on unsuccessful conspirators. The law, as we have seen, focuses on overt agreement. But since this conduct is illegal, it may be that overtness itself is a symptom of failure in collusive efforts. The truly successful conspiracies probably remain invisible.

Unfortunately, there is no ready way to distinguish among alternative interpretations of such phenomena. Statistical analysis is notoriously impotent when it comes to defining cause and effect, and it may be that several explanations contain elements of truth.

To the extent that the Sherman Act is used to prosecute unsuccessful attempts to collude while the more successful escape notice, its real economic impact is diminished. To the extent that it deters prospective colluders, how-

---

[17]For some pertinent discussion of the issues, see D. F. Turner, "The Definition of Agreement under the Sherman Act." *Harvard Law Review* 75 (February 1962): 655-706; and R. A. Posner, "Oligopoly and the Antitrust Laws: A Suggested Approach," *Stanford Law Review* 21 (June 1969). Posner suggests that tacit collusion can be identified, and appropriate action taken by the courts. Plainly, however, this would require a significant reorientation of judicial attitudes.

[18]See, for example, W. B. Erickson, "Price-Fixing Conspiracies: Their Long-Term Impact," *Journal of Industrial Economics* 42 (Winter 1968/1969).

[19]P. Asch and J. J. Seneca, "Is Collusion Profitable?" *Review of Economics and Statistics* 58 (February 1976): 1–13; and "Characteristics of Collusive Firms," *Journal of Industrial Economics* 23 (March 1975): 223–237.

ever, its impact is enlarged. Since the relevant magnitudes are unknown, claims made for the effectiveness of anticollusion policy are best viewed with some measure of skepticism.

PRICE DISCRIMINATION

Discriminatory pricing is another mode of behavior that involves some definitional and ideological controversy. We shall examine the legal policy and then the economic argument about that policy, but brief attention to analytics and definitions is needed first.

The usual analysis of full or partial monopoly assumes that firms charge all customers the same price (refer to Chapters 3 and 4). In many circumstances, however, profit-seeking companies may prefer a different course of action. Under first-degree (or perfect) price discrimination, for example, the firm would charge each customer the maximum price that that customer is willing to pay. (There would be no consumer surplus.) One might regard such a procedure as unfair—why should I pay more than you for the same item?—but the welfare implications are ambiguous. Perfect price discrimination will increase the output levels of monopolistic firms, perhaps to the competitive level, a result that may be regarded as beneficial. Whereas this type of discrimination would, as a rule, be profitable, it obviously requires that the seller have an enormous amount of information about the willingness-to-pay of customers, plus the ability to exploit it. Every sale would have to be individually negotiated. Although theoretically interesting, such discrimination does not pose a practical issue for antitrust law.

Antitrust problems usually arise in connection with third-degree price discrimination.[20] This occurs when a firm with some market power can divide its market into two or more segments. Arbitrage between the segments cannot occur—that is, customers in one cannot resell the product to customers in the other. The diagrammatics are shown in Figure 11.2.

D_1 and D_2 are the demand curves for two market segments. The associated marginal revenue curves are MR_1 and MR_2, respectively. MC is the marginal cost curve, which we assume to be applicable to both submarkets. The profit-maximizing output for the firm is found by horizontally summing the marginal revenue curves—the result is curve ABC—and equating the summed MR with MC, at output Q.[21] This output is distributed between the two market segments in such a way that the marginal revenues in each segment are equal, that is, $MR_1 = MR_2 (= MC)$.[22] Price in each submarket is simply the maximum that customers' demands will support for the quantity supplied:

[20]Second-degree discrimination is an intermediate case that may be thought of as an imperfect approximation of the first degree.

[21]This summed MR curve (ABC) is the same as the marginal revenue curve for the summed demand curves.

[22]Were the marginal revenues unequal, the firm could increase total revenue (for a given level of cost) by shipping more items to the high-MR segment.

Figure 11.2 Third-Degree Price Discrimination

The firm sells its products in market segments 1 and 2. The demand curves are D_1 and D_2 and the marginal revenue curves are MR_1 and MR_2, respectively. To maximize profits overall, the firm will produce $Q = Q_1 + Q_2$, where marginal cost (MC) equals the summed MR curve (ABC). It will sell Q_1 at price P_1 in market segment 1 and Q_2 at price P_2 in segment 2.

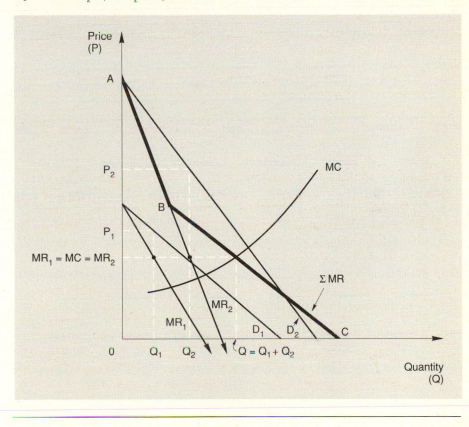

output Q_1 will be sold at price P_1 in segment 1; Q_2 will sell at P_2 in segment 2. Customers in segment 1 thus wind up paying a lower price.

Will profit-seeking firms wish to price discriminate in this fashion? The answer is usually yes (although they will not always be able to do so). As long as there exist identifiable and segmentable groups of customers with *differing demand elasticities* for the product in question, it will pay the firm to take advantage of these differences by charging the more inelastic group a higher price.

Let us turn now to a definitional problem. The familiar meaning of price discrimination is the charging of different prices to different customers for the same good or service. The surgeon who charges poor (or uninsured) patients less than the well-to-do for an appendectomy price discriminates. So does the new-car dealer who gives a price break to a friend or a hard-bargaining

Figure 11.3 Discriminatory Pricing

The firm divides its market into segments A and B. The demand curves are D_a and D_b, respectively. MC_a and MC_b show the marginal cost of supplying customers in the A and B segments, respectively. The firm charges customers prices P_a and P_b in the two segments. Plainly, the customers in A pay more for the product, but which segment is discriminated against?

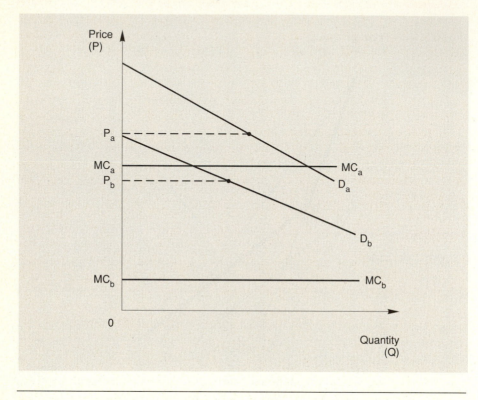

customer. This way of defining price discrimination is both reasonable and widely accepted under simple market conditions.

Consider, however, a rather common complication: that the costs of supplying the good or service vary significantly among customers. (Notice that we avoided this complication in Figure 11.2 by assuming that a single MC curve applied to both submarkets.) This may be the case, for example, if customers are at different locations, if they purchase very different quantities (or volumes over time), or if some pay for their orders more promptly than others. It is in such circumstances that the definition of a discriminatory price becomes somewhat more complicated.

Economists argue that charging different prices to different customers is no longer a sufficient description of discrimination. Indeed, it is not even a necessary component. The question is not "do prices vary?" but "do price variations or similarities reflect cost variations or similarities?" Discrimination does not consist of different prices as such, but rather of differences in the price-cost relationship among customers.

In Fig. 11.3, for example, the firm has (conceptually) divided its market into segments A and B, each with its own demand curve, D_a and D_b, respectively. Costs of supplying the two segments are represented by MC_a and MC_b. Customers in segment A pay the higher price for the product ($P_a > P_b$). Yet in economic terms, it is customers in segment B who are discriminated against. Although they pay a somewhat lower price, they are far less costly to serve. The price they pay plainly exceeds the costs they impose on the firm by more than is true of customers in segment A. The firm extracts at the margin a greater profit from B than from A.

Price discrimination, to state the point a bit differently, takes advantage of differences in customer demands. While prices may also vary for supply-side (cost) reasons, these variations are economically nondiscriminatory. It follows, incidentally, that if all customers pay the same price but impose varying costs on the firm, discrimination (against low-cost customers) exists. Price differences are thus neither a necessary nor a sufficient condition for the existence of price discrimination.

Legal Status

The main price discrimination law is the Robinson-Patman Act of 1936, amending Section 2 of the Clayton Act. Under Robinson-Patman, it is illegal:

> ... to discriminate in price between different purchasers of commodities of like grade and quality . . . where the effect of such discrimination may be substantially to lessen competition or tend to create a monopoly in any line of commerce.

The law was stimulated by the growth of large retail chains, especially in foods and drugs during the 1920s and 1930s, and by fears that such firms could and would use price concessions from suppliers to drive smaller rivals from the market. The amendment was, in Bork's phrase, "a child of the Depression."[23]

Under the Robinson-Patman Act, a company accused of price discrimination has at least two possible defenses: (1) Its price differentials made "only due allowance" for differences in cost. (2) A lower price to some customers "was made in good faith to meet the equally low price of a competitor." These two arguments—known as the cost and good faith defenses, respectively—have been held by the courts to be absolute. A firm that successfully argues either position will win acquittal even if it has been proved to have discriminated in ways harmful to competition.[24]

Demonstrating Harm to Competition The first question that confronts the courts in Robinson-Patman cases is how a demonstration of substantially lessened

---

[23]Robert H. Bork, *The Antitrust Paradox* (New York: Basic Books, 1978), 382.

[24]See, for example, *Standard Oil Co. (Indiana) v. FTC*, 340 U.S. 231 (1951).

competition is to be made. This is precisely the same question that we see in the merger law (Clayton Act, Section 7) and under most other provisions of the Clayton Act. An answer was provided by the Supreme Court in *FTC v. Morton Salt Co.*[25] Morton had offered its retail grocery customers discounts on large quantity purchases and on high cumulative volumes over time. Only five customers, large supermarket chains, had ever bought enough to qualify for the top discounts.[26] After finding that the discount schedule was in fact discriminatory, the Court turned to the issue of competitive effects.[27]

The type of discrimination practiced by Morton implies a possibility of what is known as secondary-line injury, that is, whatever competitive damage occurs is present in the buyers market. (Primary-line injury in contrast implies competitive harm in the market of the discriminating seller.) The company contended that since salt was just one among many items sold in even the smallest groceries, differences in the price paid by these stores carried little or no competitive impact. The Supreme Court disagreed, noting that since every item sold by grocery stores may be small taken alone, the only means of protecting such stores from discrimination is to apply the law "to each individual article . . . ."

More significant was the Court's interpretation of congressional intent in passing an antidiscrimination statute. "Congress," said Justice Black, "intended to protect a merchant from competitive injury attributable to discriminatory prices" and "was especially concerned with protecting small business(es) which were unable to buy in quantities." Thus, the evidence of lessened competition was probable injury to a competitor.

Two further points of significance emerged from *Morton Salt*. First, if a cost defense of discrimination is to be advanced, it is the defendant who bears the burden of proof. Morton would have had to show that its discounts matched its own actual cost savings in sales to large buyers. It was not sufficient to contend, as the company did, that the FTC had failed to prove the absence of a cost justification. Second, the Court declared that it may not be necessary to prove an actual lessening of competition under Robinson-Patman. The FTC is authorized to move against discriminatory prices on the reasonable possibility that an anticompetitive effect may occur.

Products of Like Grade and Quality An issue of some recent importance is whether the same product—the statute refers to goods "of like grade and quality"—is in fact being sold to different customers. Price differentials among different products are clearly not subject to legal restriction. This issue arises when a physically standardized product is packaged differently or sold under different brand names.

---

[25]334 U.S. 37 (1948).

[26]A buyer of 50,000 cases of salt in 12 consecutive months received the best price, $1.35 per case; others paid $1.40 to $1.60, with price rising as order size declined.

[27]The Court rejected as theoretical Morton's lame argument that since discounts were available to all, no discrimination was present. It is clear that discounts were in fact available only to large buyers.

The Borden Company, for example, had sold Borden evaporated milk during the 1960s to a number of supermarkets. At the same time it supplied the supermarkets with "physically and chemically identical" milk at lower prices to be sold under their own "private" labels. The FTC sued, charging price discrimination. Borden's response was that the products, although physically the same, were commercially distinct and thus not of like grade and quality under Robinson-Patman. Consumers, it was noted, were willing to pay higher prices for Borden evaporated milk than for private-label milks. Presumably, therefore, the market did not consider the products to be the same.

In 1966, however, the Supreme Court upheld the commission's view that "labels do not differentiate products for purposes of determining grade or quality even though . . . one label may have more customer appeal and command a higher price . . . from a substantial segment of the public."[28]

Competitive Discrimination   The competitive impact of discriminatory pricing was considered at length by the Court in a significant 1967 decision.[29] The Utah Pie Company filed a treble damage action charging three large food manufacturers (Continental Baking Company, Carnation Company, and Pet Milk Company) with conspiracy and discrimination in the Salt Lake City market for frozen pies. Utah Pie, a relatively small firm, held a major (45 to 65 percent) share of this market, but faced an aggressive invasion by the larger companies. The primary charges of discriminatory pricing were that: (1) Pet Milk had supplied Safeway supermarkets in Salt Lake City with low-priced pies to be sold under Safeway's Bel-Air label at the same time it supplied its own higher-priced Pet-Ritz pies; and (2) all three firms had sold certain pies in Salt Lake City at prices substantially below those they were charging in other western markets—this despite the fact that each incurred additional transportation costs in shipping into the Utah area. A jury found that Continental, Carnation, and Pet Milk had discriminated in violation of Section 2(a) of the Robinson-Patman Act, but the defendants won reversal in an appeals court.

In restoring the lower court finding, the Supreme Court found specifically that price differences between Pet Milk's Pet-Ritz and Bel-Air pies could reasonably be interpreted as not "cost justified in their entirety."[30] More broadly, the Court concluded, the three defendants' pie prices in Salt Lake city were not only substantially lower than elsewhere, but were at certain times "below cost," reflecting "predatory tactics."

The appeals court had found no evidence of competitive damage resulting from the price variations. Utah Pie had reacted to low prices by cutting its own prices, a stratagem that succeeded in boosting its sales and market share significantly. The Supreme Court, however, refused to conclude that the

---

[28]*FTC v. Borden Co.*, 383 U.S. 637 (1966); reconsidered, 391 F.2d 175 (5th Cir. 1967).

[29]*Utah Pie v. Continental Baking Co.*, 386 U.S. 685 (1967).

[30]Note the implication here: it would not be sufficient for Pet Milk to prove that Bel-Air pies were less costly to supply than Pet-Ritz, as they may well have been. The company needed to show that the price difference precisely matched (that is, was justified "in . . . entirety" by) the cost difference between the two.

company had suffered no competitive damage, stating: "[W]e disagree with . . . [the Court of Appeals] view that there is no reasonably possible injury to competition as long as the volume of sales in a particular market is expanding and at least some competitors continue to operate at a profit." Citing a "drastically declining price structure," the Court declared that a likelihood of substantially lessened competition in the future could be inferred from "proven conduct in the past."

The *Utah Pie* decision capsulizes one of the most controversial questions in price discrimination law: whether price differentials may not be a sign of competition rather than of (presumptively undesirable) discrimination. Ward Bowman, for example, accused the Court of using Robinson-Patman "to strike directly at price competition itself."[31] Robert Bork has cited *Utah Pie* as the clearest demonstration that "the statute . . . is essentially anticompetitive and anticonsumer."[32]

While the conclusions remain arguable, the Court's opinion contains two important omissions: (1) There is—once again—no recognition that harm to a competitor and harm to competition are not invariably the same thing. (2) The fact that consumers of pies in Salt Lake City likely benefited from lower prices is completely ignored.

Receiving a Discriminatory Price   A 1979 Supreme Court decision, *A&P v. FTC*, created an important precedent under Section 2(f) of the Robinson-Patman Act.[33] This provision prohibits the knowing inducement or receipt by purchasers of a discriminatory price. Borden had supplied A&P's private-label milk in Chicago area stores and submitted a bid to renew its contract. A&P's response was that Borden's offer to renew was too costly ("not even in the ballpark"), the implication being that better offers were available and Borden had best come down substantially in price to retain A&P's business. Borden did return with a better offer, which A&P accepted.

The Federal Trade Commission found that A&P had knowingly induced a discriminatory price in extracting a better deal than Borden offered other customers. (Interestingly, Borden itself was not charged with discrimination.) The Supreme Court overturned the commission ruling. Section 2(f) of Robinson-Patman, the Court observed, bars the inducement of a price prohibited by the act. A buyer (here A&P) cannot therefore violate Section 2(f) unless the seller (here Borden) has violated Section 2(a). But Borden (had it been charged) had a valid good faith defense: its price cut to A&P was plainly made to meet the lower prices of competitors. Since Borden had not in fact promulgated an illegal discrimination, A&P could not have induced one. The Court pointed out, however, that A&P might have been liable had it misrepresented the facts to Borden in order to obtain the price concession, despite the fact that Borden would have retained a valid defense.

---

[31]W. S. Bowman, "Restraint of Trade by the Supreme Court," *Yale Law Journal* 77 (1968).
[32]Bork, *Antitrust Paradox*, 387.
[33]440 U.S. 69 (1979).

Economic Content of the Law

The cases above illustrate some important legal principles in treating price discrimination:

1. The test of lessened competition is (actual or probable) harm to competitors.

2. It is physical similarity and not consumer perceptions that determine whether goods are of like grade and quality.

3. A cost defense, to be successful, must demonstrate that price differentials precisely match cost differentials among customers.

4. The good faith defense, in contrast, is interpreted rather liberally: if a customer threatens to take his business elsewhere without a price concession, that concession is likely to be permissible.

It should not be surprising to find that economists have been highly critical of Robinson-Patman Act interpretations. The failure of the courts to distinguish between harm to competition and harm to competitors—and to recognize that the rationale of competition is precisely that it penalizes (and thus harms) inefficient competitors—has been noted at several points. This is essentially the same criticism that is raised with regard to some merger decisions under Section 7 of the Clayton Act.

When Are Price Differences Discriminatory? A second difficulty with Robinson-Patman interpretation is the effective legal definition of price discrimination as any difference in price. It might be thought that the cost defense would deal with this problem. A cost-justified price difference, while legally discriminatory, is nevertheless permissible. The cost defense, however, has proved exceptionally difficult to use. As Morris Adelman has observed:

> The burden of proof of a cost differential is on the seller. Any cost differential is presumed to be "unjustified" unless and until the Commission finds to the contrary. The procedural requirements are such that a cost differential must be disregarded unless it is certain and precise. But, since cost differentials are inherently uncertain and imprecise, most of them cannot exist in the contemplation of law.[34]

This statement, which remains accurate today, implies that the Robinson-Patman Act may, under rather common circumstances, require firms to price discriminate.[35]

The likelihood of advancing a successful cost defense may be even further diminished by the difficulty of identifying the costs that are relevant to

---

[34]M. A. Adelman, A&P: *A Study in Price-Cost Behavior and Public Policy* (Cambridge, Mass.: Harvard University Press, 1959), 164–165.

[35]Suppose that certain of a firm's customers are cheaper to serve than others, but that the cost differences cannot be precisely demonstrated. The law will as a rule require that all customers pay the same price, but if they do so in the presence of cost variations, discrimination against lower-cost customers exists.

a particular price differential. Is it marginal cost variations that must be shown? These are unlikely to be demonstrable. Cost variations that firms can demonstrate ordinarily reflect accounting practices that have little to do with measurement of true economic (opportunity) costs. Indeed, the Supreme Court has itself observed that "too often no one can ascertain whether a price is cost-justified."[36]

Is Price Discrimination Always Bad?   A final economic objection to Robinson-Patman is the law's presumption that price discrimination is socially undesirable. Although the word discrimination has some evil connotations—amply justified where based, for example, on race or sex—price discrimination is quite a different phenomenon. On efficiency grounds, it is far from clear that such discrimination is consistently bad. It may result in reduced or increased output levels vis-a-vis nondiscriminatory pricing, and in certain cases, there is a strong argument that discrimination will improve allocative welfare.[37]

One may, of course, object that even where price discrimination is efficient, it is unfair. The end result may be seen as an unjustifiable transfer of income—from poor consumers to rich sellers or from small weak firms to large strong ones. This sort of judgment may underlie Robinson-Patman decisions, but the courts have never explicitly stated such a rationale. Moreover, the effects of price discrimination on the distribution of income or wealth are likely to be very difficult to define in any given instance.

What Is the Purpose of the Law?   What then are we to make of the law? Public treatment of price discrimination is perhaps viewed appropriately as another battleground of the equity-versus-efficiency conflict. The Robinson-Patman Act, as enforced, is almost certainly anticompetitive in some circumstances. Yet society may, as a matter of (noneconomic?) values, wish to protect smaller companies even at some sacrifice of competitive efficiency. At this point, the objective analyst may be left with only two legitimate complaints:

1.   If we are going to promote policies that may be anticompetitive, we ought to call them by their proper name and stop claiming to protect competition.

2.   If we are determined to aid small businesses, the price discrimination law is itself likely to be an ineffective and inefficient way to do so. Direct subsidies to the businesses we want to assist would probably work better and cost a good deal less.[38]

---

[36]*Automatic Canteen Co. v. FTC*, 346 U.S. 61 (1953).

[37]As noted above, perfect price discrimination by a monopolist may well yield the competitive-market level of output.

[38]The Utah Pie Company, for example, was forced out of the market in the early 1970s despite its Robinson–Patman protection. For a useful discussion, see K. G. Elzinga and T. F. Hogarty, "Utah Pie and the Consequences of Robinson–Patman," *Journal of Law and Economics* 21 (October 1978): 427–434.

VERTICAL RESTRAINTS

Vertical restraints usually involve a supplier's imposition of conditions on customers' behavior. A *tying* (or *tie-in*) arrangement requires customers to buy one product (the tied good) in order to obtain another (the tying good). *Exclusive dealing* is precisely what it sounds like: the supplier tells customers "if you wish to deal with me, you must deal only with me." These practices have two points in common: (1) they are widely practiced and thus presumably regarded by many firms as profitable, although the sources of profits are varied and, occasionally, not obvious; and (2) they are potentially illegal under both the Clayton and Sherman Acts. *Resale price maintenance,* although a related type of practice, is legally a distinctive event. Efforts by manufacturers to influence or control the prices at which their products are resold by wholesalers and retailers have a varied history which we shall examine briefly.

Tying

Trivial examples of tie-in sales are familiar to all: a restaurant meal in effect ties meat to vegetables; to read the Sunday sports and comics you must buy other sections of the newspaper. Indeed, the sale of any product with separable components could be viewed as a tie-in sale of those components (shoes and laces; cars and tires; a watch and watchband). In none of these instances, however, does the tie-in carry plausible implications for competition.

Legal Status More serious cases arise when a supplier occupies a strong—that is, monopolistic—position in one market. The classic case is that of the true monopolist whose product is protected by patents. Such a firm can conceivably force customers to buy a second product, sold in more competitive circumstances, in order to purchase the first. This was the situation, for example, in *International Business Machines, Inc. v. United States*.[39] IBM required its customers to use IBM tabulating cards in its machines. The Supreme Court rejected IBM's contention that it was merely trying to protect its good will, stating: "The Clayton Act names no exception to its prohibition of monopolistic tying clauses. . . ."

The* Per Se *Rule Similar circumstances appeared with the same result in *International Salt Co. v. United States*.[40] International Salt required lessees to use its own salt tablets in its patented industrial salt dispensing machines. The Supreme Court disallowed the practice, observing that "it is unreasonable, *per se*, to foreclose competitors from any substantial market." Here competing salt manufacturers were foreclosed from selling to International's leasing custom-

[39]298 U.S. 131 (1936).
[40]332 U.S. 392 (1947).

ers.[41] The Court conceded a company's right to impose reasonable restrictions on the use of its equipment and hinted that had International shown its machines to be "allergic" to the salt of rival manufacturers, the decision might have been different. No such argument had been advanced, and the Court saw the tie-in purely as an attempt to exclude competing manufacturers from a segment of the market.

In *Northern Pacific Railway Co. v. United States*, the railway sold and leased its large landholdings on condition that customers "ship over its lines all commodities produced or manufactured on the land . . . ."[42] Such preferential routing clauses, said the Supreme Court, amount to a tie-in, and tie-ins "serve hardly any purpose beyond the suppression of competition."[43] The *per se* illegality of tying was reemphasized, although the Court noted that without "control or dominance over the tying product," these kinds of arrangements would be "insignificant at most."

The Court took a consistent position in *United States v. Loew's Inc.*, finding the practice of "block booking" motion pictures illegal under Section 1 of the Sherman Act.[44] Loew's and other movie distributors offered films to television stations only in packages (blocks). The purpose seemed apparent: in order to obtain desirable films (such as *Casablanca*), stations were forced to purchase others that they might well have chosen not to buy had they been offered for sale individually (such as *Gorilla Man*). Terming the practice an "injurious" restraint of trade, the Supreme Court reiterated its belief that tie-ins serve no positive social purpose. The Court noted that the seller must have "sufficient economic power with respect to the tying product to appreciably restrain free competition in the market for the tied product." Such power, Justice Goldberg stated, "is presumed when the tying product is patented or copyrighted," as the affected motion pictures were.

In two more recent decisions, the Court ruled on a private damages suit by Fortner Enterprises against United States Steel.[45] Fortner charged that in order to obtain land development loans from Credit Corporation (a subsidiary of U.S. Steel), it was required to buy from the company a prefabricated house for each lot purchased with the loan proceeds. A district court dismissed the initial case on the grounds that (1) U.S. Steel did not have sufficient economic power in the tying market (the credit market), and (2) the amount of commerce involved was insubstantial.

---

[41]J. L. Peterman has argued plausibly that foreclosure of rival salt suppliers was not the purpose of the tie-in. The likely purpose, rather, may have been price discrimination. See J. L. Peterman, "The International Salt Case," *Journal of Law and Economics* 22 (October 1979): 351–364.

[42]356 U.S. 1 (1958).

[43]The Court was quoting itself. See *Standard Oil Co. of California and Standard Stations Inc. v. United States*, 337 U.S. 293 (1949).

[44]371 U.S. 45 (1962).

[45]*Fortner Enterprises, Inc. v. United States Steel Corp.*, 394 U.S. 495 (1969); and *United States Steel Corp. v. Fortner Enterprises, Inc.*, 429 U.S. 610 (1977). These cases are commonly referred to as *Fortner I* and *Fortner II*.

In remanding the case—that is, sending it back for retrial—the Supreme Court held that the district court had misunderstood the two controlling standards. A not insubstantial amount of commerce need not involve a large share of the affected market, but only a sufficient "dollar volume so as not to be merely de minimis . . . ." Furthermore, the requirement of sufficient market power does not mean that the defendant must have "a monopoly or even a dominant position" in the market for the tying good.

Upon retrial, the district court found that U.S. Steel held sufficient economic power in the tying (credit) market to render the arrangement unlawful, a finding upheld by the appellate court. The Supreme Court once again reversed, however, holding that "the record does not support the conclusion . . . [of] appreciable economic power." Credit Corporation had indeed provided Fortner with unique credit terms, but only because it was willing to accept lower profits or incur greater risks than its competitors. There was no evidence, said Justice Stevens, that Credit Corporation held significant competitive advantages over rivals. While monopoly or dominance need not be shown to prove the illegality of a tie-in, it is necessary to ask whether the seller can "require purchasers to accept burdensome terms." The mere fact that Credit Corporation gave Fortner a good bargain hardly did so.

It is interesting to observe that although the courts have repeatedly referred to tying as a *per se* offense, the standard of illegality is quite different from that applied in areas such as price-fixing. The seller's power in the tying market and the volume of commerce affected are both examined in tie-in cases, something that would not occur under a strict *per se* rule. The distinction between *per se* and rule of reason approaches is in fact less clear-cut than is commonly thought.

Economic Perspective   Many economists regard the courts' analysis of tying as deficient. Although *leverage*—the extension of monopoly power from the tying to the tied market—is a conceivable result of tie-ins in some circumstances, it does not appear to deserve the prominence that judicial discussion accords it. As Posner has pointed out, legal treatment of tying is frequently deficient in two respects.[46] First, the courts assume that extension of monopoly is the motivating factor, but fail to ask whether such extension is a plausible result in specific instances. The answer is usually (and obviously) no. Second, the courts fail to ask whether extension of monopoly is desirable from the firm's standpoint. The answer, perhaps surprisingly, is not always obvious. Where the tied goods are complements—the typical, although not universal, case— they may be viewed as components of a single service. For example, IBM sold computing services that consisted of both computers and tabulating cards. To monopolize the second component (cards) will enable the firm to raise its price in that market. But the price increase necessarily raises the cost to customers of the service as a whole, thereby discouraging demand for the service (as well as

---

[46]See R. A. Posner, *Antitrust Law*, 171 ff.

for the computers component). On balance, the profitability of the practice is thus not as clear as one might suspect.

The objectives and consequences of tying in fact vary. In some instances, it serves primarily as a metering device. IBM was able to force heavy users of its machines to pay more by requiring them to buy cards. Xerox was in a similar position with respect to copying machines and copying paper. (Judicial restriction of Xerox induced the company to install meters on its copiers, a device that achieved the goal of the tie-in, perhaps at somewhat greater cost.)

There is, in fact, a somewhat more general argument that tie-in sales serve as a price-discriminating mechanism. Consider the rather odd example of a firm that has monopoly in computers but also sells radios in a competitive market, as shown in Figures 11.4(a) and 11.4(b). This firm could conceivably tell its computer customers: "If you wish to continue using our computer services, you must also purchase any radios you want from us at a price (P_m) above the competitive market level (P_c)." Why should any customers agree to such a condition? The answer is that some would have been willing to pay a higher price than P for computers (those located on the upper part of demand curve D in Figure 11.4(a)). The company can in effect sell radios at a premium to those who feel that their computer terms are a bargain. This is price discrimination pure and simple, and it is very likely profitable. It is extremely difficult to believe, however, that monopolization of the radio market would result.

Yet another purpose of tying, which has been recognized by the courts despite their strong per se language, is to protect the condition or performance of the tying product. Jerrold Electronics argued successfully in 1960 that it had a legitimate need temporarily to tie maintenance and repair services to its community antenna television systems.[47] The equipment was "sensitive and unstable," and might have been damaged if serviced by persons unfamiliar with it. This tie-in could be viewed as a response to *transactions costs*, which are usually defined as costs of using the market.[48] In this instance, Jerrold would have faced considerable risk to the integrity of its trade name had it allowed others to service its equipment. It therefore insisted on performing its own maintenance and repairs, in effect internalizing the activity and avoiding the costly use of the market.

Finally, tying may on occasion serve as a method of competition that is perhaps less provocative than direct price cutting. The offer of a "free" frozen pizza with the purchase of $7.50 worth of groceries, recently made by a market chain, was a type of tie-in sale. The purpose and result of the offer was surely not to monopolize either the frozen pizza market or the market in retail groceries generally.

---

[47]*United States v. Jerrold Electronics*, F.Supp. 545 (E.D. Pa. 1960), affirmed *per curiam*, 365 U.S. (1961).

[48]See R. H. Coase, "The Nature of the Firm," *Economica* 4 (November 1937): 386–405; and O. E. Williamson, *Markets and Hierarchies: Analysis and Antitrust Implications* (New York: Free Press, 1975).

Figure 11.4   A Tie-in as Price Discrimination

(a.) A monopolist sells computers at price P.
(b.) The same firm sells radios in a competitive market at price P_c. But it forces its computer customers to pay P_m for any radios they purchase. This tie-in is a form of price discrimination.

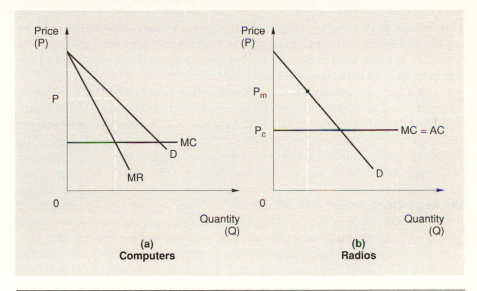

(a)
Computers

(b)
Radios

Exclusive Dealing

Exclusive dealing arrangements ("in order to buy from me you must buy only from me") seldom affect final consumers, but are observed in various markets at the manufacturer–distributor levels.

Legal Status   A 1922 legal decision, *Standard Fashion Co. v. Magrane-Houston Co.*, established that this sort of practice falls within Section 3 of the Clayton Act.[49] Magrane-Houston had been required by Standard to carry its dress patterns exclusively in order to obtain the patterns at discount under a series of 2-year contracts.   The Supreme Court agreed with lower courts that such arrangements, which characterized about 40 percent of the market in dress patterns, would substantially lessen competition.

The *Standard Stations* case of 1949 tested the practice of exclusive dealing in gasoline service stations, where it has been commonplace. Standard Stations held 23 percent of western-area gasoline sales in 1946; 6.7 percent of sales were accounted for by retail stations under exclusive contract to Standard. The primary issue, as defined by the Supreme Court, was how the Section 3 requirement of substantially lessened competition was to be addressed. Jus-

[49]258 U.S. 346 (1922).

tice Frankfurter held for the majority that direct evidence of what would have occurred in the market absent the exclusivity agreements was neither obtainable nor necessary. Instead, he concluded, the requisite anticompetitive impact is established "by proof that competition has been foreclosed in a substantial share of the line of commerce affected" (here the 6.7 percent of the market subject to Standard's exclusivity). The Court, however, did not apply a *per se* prohibition. In its view, exclusive dealing serves some positive purposes for buyers and sellers. Long-term planning is facilitated and risk of supply (or demand) interruptions reduced. The practice was thus not relegated to the same category of socially useless activities as tying.

This position was advanced further by the Court in *Tampa Electric Co. v. Nashville Coal Co.*[50] The companies had signed a contract under which Nashville would fill all of Tampa's coal requirements for 20 years. Nashville sought to renege and Tampa sued, asking for a finding that the contract was legal. The Supreme Court complied, noting that the proportion of the market affected was small. While the dollar volume of commerce involved was not negligible, this "by itself is not the test." The absence of a dominant market position by either company, and the possible benefits of exclusive contracts, proved decisive. (Notice that in both *Standard Stations* and *Tampa Electric*, the exclusive dealing provisions could be viewed as a response to transactions costs.)

Despite such apparent leniency, the Supreme Court has permitted the Federal Trade Commission to act against rather modest exclusivity arrangements under the easier test of the FTC Act (Section 5). In *FTC v. Brown Shoe Co.*, the commission had attacked as an unfair practice, Brown Shoe's provision of valuable benefits to retailers agreeing to its exclusive supply arrangements.[51] Ruling on narrow grounds, the Court held that "the Commission has broad powers to declare trade practices unfair," and that it "acted well within its authority" in this instance.

Exclusive dealing contracts may be appealing from a supplier's standpoint for two reasons. First, it is possible that there are significant efficiencies in distributing through a relatively small number of (relatively large) outlets. Second, it is likely that one's exclusive distributors will market a supplier's products more aggressively than will a seller who carries competing lines. (Of course this works both ways. If exclusive dealing is the rule in the market, rivals' outlets will push their suppliers' products more strongly as well!)

Manufacturers frequently offer benefits, in the form of *franchise* agreements, to induce distributors to sell exclusively. The most common inducement is a grant of territorial exclusivity, that is, an assurance to the dealer that the manufacturer will establish no competing franchises within a defined geographic area.

The ability of a manufacturer to limit outlets in this way is not seriously hindered by law. The Supreme Court did hold in 1967 that a bicycle manufac-

---

[50]365 U. S. 320 (1961).
[51]384 U.S. 316 (1966).

turer who told dealers where and to whom they could sell had committed *per se* violations of the Sherman Act.[52] But the Court explicitly overruled itself 10 years later, declaring that restrictions imposed on dealers by a television manufacturer had not been shown to have "a pernicious effect on competition" or to "lack ... any redeeming virtue."[53] Where dealer restraints might abridge the law, the Court held that they are to be judged by a rule of reason. In addition, there does not appear to be a strong presumption of illegality, even though the restrictions are designed to limit competition.

Economic Perspective   Have the courts treated exclusive dealing sensibly? Conditions may be envisioned under which exclusivity, especially in conjunction with territorial restraints, will create the "clog on competition" that the Supreme Court looks for. A tight-knit system of franchised dealerships might, for example, make it difficult for new suppliers to enter the market, both because preferred outlets are preempted and because the prospective entrant must establish an extensive system of dealers to come in with a good chance of success. Short of this situation, however—and especially where the market shares held by exclusive dealers are low—the practice appears unlikely to pose a serious threat to competition. The Supreme Court has proceeded with reasonable caution and flexibility and may recognize implicitly that exclusive dealing is at times an efficient response to high market transactions costs. It may nevertheless tend to see somewhat greater dangers in the practice than objective analysis ordinarily suggests.

Resale Price Maintenance

Resale price maintenance (frequently known as fair trade) refers to the establishment by suppliers of minimum resale prices. Why suppliers would want to set such prices has been a topic of discussion for some time.[54] It has been suggested that manufacturers fear that their products may be used as *loss leaders* (sold by distributors below cost as a gimmick to attract customers to their stores). According to this argument, substantial numbers of consumers, judging quality by price, will conclude that the products in question are inferior. At least this is what suppliers worry about when they attempt to impose a price floor.

A more persuasive argument notes simply that minimum resale prices protect distributors from competition. Whereas a product manufacturer might not object to such competition among its distributors, such protection provides

---

[52]*United States v. Arnold, Schwinn and Co.*, 388 U.S. 365 (1967). For sharp criticism of the government's position and the Supreme Court's decision, see O. E. Williamson, *The Economic Institutions of Capitalism: Firms, Markets, Relational Contracting* (New York: Free Press, 1985), 183 ff.

[53]*Continental TV v. GTE Sylvania Inc.*, 433 U.S. 36 (1977).

[54]The classic discussion is Lester Telser, "Why Should Manufacturers Want Fair Trade?" *Journal of Law and Economics*, 3 (October 1960). For a good recent discussion of the effects of this practice, see H. P. Marvel and S. McCafferty, "The Welfare Effects of Resale Price Maintenance," *Journal of Law and Economics*, 28 (May 1985).

distributors with an inducement to carry and perhaps to promote enthusiastically the products of the manufacturer. It may additionally persuade distributors to offer higher quality maintenance and repair services to customers in some markets.

There is also a possible free-rider problem associated with product information in some markets. Consider the following example: I wish to buy a video cassette recorder (VCR), but know nothing about the product. I go to my local video store, where the owner or salesperson spends considerable time demonstrating various brands and advising me about the advantages and disadvantages of each. With this information in hand, I go to a discount store (that does not offer product demonstrations) and buy one of the recommended VCRs for $100 less than my local video store charges. I am merely acting as a rational consumer, while the discount store enjoys a free ride. My behavior, however, penalizes the seller who provides valuable product information. Such sellers surely will feel that their efforts should be rewarded. VCR manufacturers may agree, fearing in part that retailers will become reluctant to supply information without some protection from free riders.

How could such protection be provided? Minimum resale prices are one obvious possibility. Alternatively, VCR manufacturers might refuse to deal with discounters and forbid their customers to do so as well. (Such vertical restrictions are similar to those seen in *Schwinn* above.) Or, in the extreme, manufacturers could integrate forward, taking over the retailing function themselves. We are, once again, looking at an example of market transactions costs that business managers will (quite rationally) seek to minimize or avoid.

Legal Status The legal history of resale price maintenance is a strange episode in American antitrust. In two early decisions, the Supreme Court placed severe restrictions on the ability of manufacturers to control the terms under which their products were sold further down the distribution chain.[55] A supplier could announce the conditions under which it would supply wholesale or retail dealers, perhaps including minimum resale prices, and refuse to trade with noncomplying sellers. But the supplier could go no further to enforce or encourage the acceptance of those terms and, most particularly, could do nothing that would suggest an agreement or conspiracy with sellers to maintain resale prices.

During the period 1937 to 1976, federal legislation permitted resale price maintenance agreements in those states which also had enacted enabling statutes. In effect, these fair trade laws exempted from Sherman Act prosecution agreements that otherwise might have been challenged as a form of vertical price fixing.

Economic Perspective Resale price maintenace has had a perceptible effect on prices in some product and geographic markets. Legal protections, however,

---

[55]*Dr. Miles Medical Co. v. John D. Park and Sons*, 220 U.S. 373 (1911); and *United States v. Colgate and Co.*, 250 U.S. 300 (1919).

eroded over a period of decades, in part because some state courts were finding their own statutes to be unconstitutional. By 1976, when federal protection was repealed, resale price maintenance had ceased to be a widespread force in American business. Retailers, however, retain a certain interest in dampening the vigor of price competition (an interest, incidentally, that is shared by virtually all business managers). In light of this interest, fair trade, although presently a dead issue, may reappear on the political agenda before many years elapse.

PREDATORY PRICING

So-called predatory pricing poses a thorny issue for antitrust decision makers. Low prices and price cutting are the essential elements of competition, the means by which rivals vie for business. Under some circumstances, however, a low price charged by one firm may drive rivals out of the market, leading to monopoly power and higher prices later on.

We have seen in two legal cases—*Standard Oil* (1911) and *Utah Pie* (1967)—clear judicial hostility to what were considered predatory tactics. But the problem of definition is stubborn. Every active competitor seeks to outdo its rivals—to inconvenience them, to reduce their business, and even to force them from the marketplace. Without such efforts, the market does not function properly. Firms are not driven to their best efforts. At what point, then, does healthy competition become unfair predation?

Economists and lawyers have paid much recent attention to this question.[56] Phillip Areeda and Donald Turner observed in 1975 that meaningful predatory pricing involves "a temporary sacrifice of net revenues in the expectation of greater future gains." That is, the firm gives up short-run profits in order to expand long-run profits. Some analysts question whether such tactics are ever rational. Not only is this sort of pricing a costly and uncertain strategy, but it may not be the most effective route to monopoly. John S. McGee, in an important article some years ago, suggested that predatory pricing would not pay, if only because it is cheaper to buy out a competitor than to drive him from the market in this fashion.[57]

It seems clear, however, that there are circumstances under which predatory behavior will pay. Even if it turns out to be an extremely expensive activity

[56]See, for example, P. Areeda and D. F. Turner, "Predatory Pricing and Related Practices under Section 2 of the Sherman Act," *Harvard Law Review* 88 (1975); F. M. Scherer, "Predatory Pricing and the Sherman Act: A Comment," *Harvard Law Review* 89 (March 1976); O. E. Williamson, "Predatory Pricing: A Strategic and Welfare Analysis," *Yale Law Journal* 87 (December 1977); P. Areeda and D. F. Turner, "Williamson on Predatory Pricing," *Yale Law Journal*, 87 (June 1978); W. J. Baumol, "Quasi-Permanence of Price Reductions: A Policy for Prevention of Predatory Pricing," *Yale Law Journal* 89 (November 1979); P. Joskow and A. K. Klevorick, "A Framework for Analyzing Predatory Pricing Policy," *Yale Law Journal* 89 (December 1979). For a useful earlier discussion that has been neglected of late, see B. S. Yamey, "Predatory Price Cutting: Notes and Comments," *Journal of Law and Economics* 15 (April 1972).

[57]J. S. McGee, "Predatory Price Cutting: The Standard Oil (N.J.) Case," *Journal of Law and Economics* 1 (October 1958). Most observers would not go as far as McGee, but most agree that predatory behavior is less than a routine mode of business conduct.

in the short run, the predator may succeed in sending a message to actual and prospective rivals: "If you disturb me, you will suffer retaliation." This may prove a valuable communication, especially over the long term.

At this point, we confront a more practical problem. How is a truly predatory price to be defined and measured? Areeda and Turner propose to identify the phenomenon by examining the relationship between price and cost. Specifically, a price below short-run marginal cost is to be considered predatory. Since marginal costs are frequently immeasurable, it is suggested that reasonably anticipated average variable costs be used as a proxy.

The reasoning behind this proposal is clear. Rational firms (short-run profit maximizers) may at times price below average total cost. The profit-maximizing price may simply fail to cover full costs in the short run, even though as a persistent long-run condition this implies failure for the firm. In what might be considered the normal course of events, however, a best-profit price would not lie below marginal cost. Any such price is marginally unprofitable—a sale at that price increases the firm's losses. Accordingly, such a price is interpreted as predatory.[58]

The courts have attempted to apply the Areeda-Turner test in a number of recent decisions. An appeals court in *Hanson v. Shell Oil*, for example, held that a failure to demonstrate that the defendant's prices were below marginal cost or average variable cost was, in effect, a failure to present a prima facie case of predatory pricing.[59] Similarly, prices above average (total) costs have been viewed as presumptively legal. In the *Calcomp* decision, charges of predatory behavior against IBM were dismissed by a trial judge.[60] The dismissal was upheld by an appellate court, primarily on the ground that there was no clear evidence of below-cost pricing.

A difficulty with price-cost comparisons has been pointed out by Williamson and recognized, at least implicitly, by certain courts.[61] A predatory strategy, designed to eliminate a particular rival(s) is likely to involve numerous price changes, with costs also shifting over time. (Indeed, one of Williamson's objections to predatory pricing cost rules is that they could induce firms to adopt production techniques that, while not optimally efficient, would conform to the legal tests.)

The momentary price-cost snapshot may reveal little about the significance of longer-term patterns. Is competition actually impaired? Is the firm in question truly sacrificing short-run profits in order to enlarge long-run gains? If, for example, we accept Posner's definition of a predatory price as one "at a

---

[58]A good student of economics should be able to construct a few counter examples, situations in which a price below marginal cost would maximize short-run profits. These would be rather special cases, however.

[59]541 F.2d 1352 (9th Cir. 1976); see also *Janich Bros., Inc. v. American Distilling Co.*, 570 F.2d 848 (9th Cir. 1977); and *Transamerica Computer Co. v. International Business Machines Corp.*, U.S. District Court (N.D. Calif. 1979), Trade Regulation Reporter, 62, 989.

[60]*California Computer Products v. IBM*, 613 F.2d 727 (1979).

[61]O. E. Williamson, "Predatory Price Cutting."

level calculated to exclude from the market an equally or more efficient competitor," it is apparent that prices above marginal cost (and conceivably above some average cost measures) may fill the bill.[62]

Williamson has proposed some alternative rules to identify predatory tactics. For example, if a firm responds to new entry by increasing its output, this might be regarded as predation whether or not price falls below average or marginal cost.[63] Baumol approaches the same problem with a different suggestion: permit any firm to cut price to any level in response to entry. But if the response is successful in eliminating the entrant, do not permit the firm to raise its price for some specified period of time.[64]

SUMMARY

Antitrust treatment of market behavior covers a wide area and cannot be easily capsulized. Conspiracy occupies a special place. Where firms seek to coordinate their policies, they violate the law. Indeed, it is the very attempt to do so that runs afoul of the Sherman Act—results, if any, are irrelevant. The clarity of this *per se* prohibition is marred only by difficulties in proving the existence of conspiracy.

The treatment of most other forms of market behavior contains some common strands. In dealing with price discrimination, tying, and exclusive dealing, the courts have not applied strict *per se* tests. The demonstration of these practices is followed by further legal examination of the market position and power of defendant firms, and of possible or actual injury to competitors.[65] Where harm can be shown, findings of illegality often follow directly.

CONCLUSION

Do these standards serve society well? The answer, yet again, is likely to depend upon one's view of the marketplace. If the market is regarded as an effective economic decision maker, much antitrust activity will appear wasteful and intrusive. After all, if firms continually seek the most efficient means of using resources, policies that get in the way of their arrangements must, to some degree, squander those resources.

If, on the other hand, the market is viewed as a place in which economic decisions are distorted by the powerful, the assessment of public policies may well be more favorable. Forces of market competition appear ineffective, and checks on the abuse of power are therefore appropriate.

---

[62]See Posner, *Antitrust Law* 188; and Yamey, "Predatory Price Cutting," for an argument that price cuts may convey predatory messages even though price remains above average cost.

[63]Williamson, "Predatory Pricing."

[64]Baumol, "Quasi-Permanence of Price Reductions."

[65]The status of predatory pricing is a bit harder to characterize. The courts' hostility is sufficiently strong to suggest a *"per se"* state of mind, yet the courts may not find violations unless the alleged predator is sufficiently powerful to inflict meaningful injury.

Many observers, regardless of viewpoint, will agree that behavioral antitrust doctrines raise some basic—and by now familiar—dilemmas. Perhaps the most fundamental of these arises from the courts' focus on injury to competitors. We have noted at several points that to be effective, competition must injure certain competitors. One may not wish to go as far as Arthur Jerome Eddy, whose motto was "Competition is war and war is hell."[66] But if the market is to use society's resources efficiently, there is no way around the need to penalize the inefficient.

Few judges have appeared to recognize this need, or expressly to concede it. It is for this reason that certain legal decisions, taken in the name of protecting competition, are likely to prove anticompetitive. This does not mean that such decisions are indefensible. We may not wish to have all matters decided on the basis of competition, and social values very likely suggest the protection of some inefficient concerns. One would hope, however, that actions based on such judgments would pay some attention to potential costs as well as benefits and would not be mislabeled or misinterpreted as procompetitive.

Discussion Questions

1. The courts have long prohibited overt conspiracy to fix prices or other terms of supply, but have been relatively lenient toward tacit and informal agreements. Some observers believe that the prohibition of overt conspiracies is itself a major achievement and that it has prevented the development of tight-knit, effective cartels in the United States. Others contend that the courts have merely blocked one form of collusion, while leaving others open, and that the effectiveness of policy is therefore quite limited. Which position do you find more persuasive?

2. A few people argue that collusion may be socially beneficial and that the courts have erred in defining such behavior as *per se* illegal. What social benefits might collusion yield?

3. "The Robinson-Patman Act probably requires as much price discrimination as it prohibits." Is this a plausible statement?

4. Some observers argue that the main effect of judicial restrictions on price discrimination, tying, exclusive dealing, and resale price maintenance is to prevent businesses from adopting efficient practices that would in most cases do little harm to competition. Do you agree? In all cases?

5. Company Alpha is a leading producer of ceramic tiles. Company Beta enters this market and offers ceramic tiles at prices that are not only lower than Alpha's prices but also lower than its own average total costs of producing and distributing these tiles. Alpha sues Beta, charging that

---

[66]A. J. Eddy, *The New Competition* (Chicago: A. C. McClurg and Company, 1916).

Beta is engaged in a predatory pricing strategy. Do you believe that Beta's pricing behavior should be presumptively illegal? What additional information might you want before reaching a final judgment?

Selected Readings

Asch. P. and J. J. Seneca. "Is Collusion Profitable?" *Review of Economics and Statistics* 58 (February 1976): 1-12. *Evidence on the profit rates of colluding and noncolluding firms.*

Dewey, D. "Information, Entry, and Welfare: The Case for Collusion." *American Economic Review* 69 (September 1979): 587–594. *An argument that, from a social standpoint, collusion is not all bad.*

McGee, J. S. "Predatory Price Cutting: The Standard Oil (N.J.) Case." *Journal of Law and Economics.* 1 (October 1958). *A classic article which argues that predatory pricing may be an irrational form of business behavior.*

Posner, R. A. *Antitrust Law.* Chicago: University of Chicago Press, 1976, especially Chapters 4 and 7. *Economically useful discussions of a variety of behavioral issues in antitrust law.*

Turner, D. F. "The Definition of Agreement under the Sherman Act." *Harvard Law Review* 75 (February 1962). *A still-pertinent discussion of how collusion is defined legally.*

CHAPTER 12

· · · · · · · · · · · · · · · · ·

THE EFFECTS OF ANTITRUST: DOES IT ACCOMPLISH ANYTHING?

Antitrust activity consumes substantial resources. Although federal enforcement budgets are comparatively small, other costs are significant. Trials tend to be complex and prolonged, placing burdens on the court system. Private expenditures, both by defendant companies and by those who bring suit, are large and growing. Finally, of course, antitrust decisons—including numerous out-of-court settlements—affect corporate behavior in a variety of ways.

An important question concerns the economic impact of all this activity. Does it provide us with a more competitive market system? Does it permit markets to function in closer accord with our ideals, and thus to serve the purposes that are the underlying justification of that system? Or is it instead a wasteful intrusion by government into the private marketplace?

MEASUREMENT

Perhaps unsurprisingly, there exist no precise and direct estimates of the economic impact of antitrust policy on the American economy. The difficulties of measurement and the nature of the limited evidence that has been gathered, however, deserve attention.

Problems

Defining the effect of a particular policy on an economy is often a difficult task. The fundamental problem, common to all social sciences, is our inability to run well-controlled experiments. We may ask, for example, whether one variable (say the money supply) affects another (the price level). We may even be able to gather and examine tolerably good data for both. But the variable whose behavior we seek to explain (prices) is influenced by so many factors that isolating the effect of a single determinant (money)—and determining whether it has causal significance—frequently proves quite difficult.

This is, in significant part, the measurement problem that handicaps the assessment of antitrust. We would like to know whether the policies have made the economy more competitive than it otherwise would have been. But we cannot define with great precision or confidence what would have happened in the absence of antitrust policy as enforced historically. The problem is further compounded by the fact that there exists no single, well-defined, agreed-upon measure of competitiveness. As we have noted earlier, many people extol the virtues of a competitive market system but have quite different conceptions of the term. To determine whether a policy has increased competition, will plainly be no simple task if we lack a consensus index of the phenomenon!

Such difficulties are bound to limit our ability to draw strong conclusions about policy effects. They have not, however, deterred some economists and lawyers from addressing the issue.

Evidence

Attempts to say something about antitrust effectiveness have proceeded in a number of distinctive ways.

International Comparisons   The United States has a strong antitrust policy compared with most other industrialized nations. Conceivably, then, one might be able to identify differences in the structure or behavior of economies that are attributable to differences in antitrust activity. There are, however, some serious limitations to this approach. First is the fact that comparisons among nations will inevitably reflect important differences that have nothing whatever to do with antitrust policies.

A second difficulty with international comparisons is more mundane, but also important. Data in different countries may not correspond very well. It might be, for example, that concentration ratios are reported on a four-firm basis in one place and three-firm basis in the other or that the reporting of company data such as profits and assets is based on different accounting procedures. Valid comparisons may require that the data rest on a common base. To the extent that the bases in fact differ, investigators will be hindered, perhaps confined to rather small samples of comparable firms or industries.

George J. Stigler confronted these problems in a 1966 study of the United States and Great Britain.[1] As one would expect, Stigler was unable to draw very strong conclusions. Indeed, his clearest finding was based on U.S. evidence alone: the 1950 Celler-Kefauver amendment to Section 7 of the Clayton Act apparently produced a sharp drop in horizontal mergers (and a corresponding increase in verticals and conglomerates). Stigler also concluded that by impeding the "most efficient methods" of conspiracy, the Sherman Act has "reduced the amount and effects of collusion." But this conclusion was more a plausible

---

[1]G. J. Stigler, "The Economic Effects of the Antitrust Laws," *Journal of Law and Economics* 9 (October 1966).

expectation based on the nature of the law than a finding derived from quantitative evidence.[2]

While there is now quite an extensive literature comparing the public competition policies of various nations, the limitations evident in Stigler's effort remain endemic to the subject.[3] Policy differences are easy enough to describe, but it is not generally possible to construct precise conceptual experiments that would tell us how or to what degree those differences produce distinctions in the structure and behavior of the affected economies.

Examination of Firms and Markets   An approach more fruitful than making international comparisons may be to examine whether and how particular firms and industries respond to antitrust enforcement. For example, when the Department of Justice successfully prosecutes an antitrust violation, does this have a perceptible impact on the behavior and/or market position of the convicted violator(s)? If such effects are discernible, do they spill over to other companies within the same industry, and even perhaps to other industries? The evidence on these questions is limited but intriguing.

Two recent studies suggest that antitrust prosecution of price fixers has significant effects on the behavior of the defendant companies.[4]   Feinberg observes that Sherman Act indictments result in a reduced deviation of price from cost in the indicted firms, and further, that there is a "weak demonstration effect" against other firms within the industry. Block, Nold, and Sidak report reduced mark-ups (that is, price closer to marginal and average cost) not only by defendant manufacturers in the bread industry, but by other bread producers as well. Although the authors of both studies confronted measurement difficulties and were forced to adopt some arguable assumptions, their results are striking and theoretically plausible. One might, in fact, argue on *a priori* grounds that it would be surprising if challenged firms did not alter their behavior in some way.

Some earlier examinations of specific antitrust cases also suggest a potentially important impact on affected firms and markets. William Lee Baldwin has demonstrated that in several major government prosecutions, conduct-oriented remedies appeared to exert significant feedback effects on market

---

[2]Stigler further observed "only a very modest" effect of U.S. antitrust, via the Sherman Act, on industry concentration. The effect was, in fact, so modest and was inferred from so few observations that one cannot be confident of its existence.

[3]The Organization for Economic Cooperation and Development (OECD) publishes the *Guide to Legislation on Restrictive Business Practices*, which contains comprehensive, up-dated descriptions of antitrust-type laws in several nations. For useful but somewhat dated summaries of West German and British policies, respectively, see K. E. Market, "The New German Antitrust Reform Law," *Antitrust Bulletin* 19 (Spring 1974); and W. G. Shepherd, "Changing Contrasts in British and American Antitrust Policies," in W. Sichel, ed., *Antitrust Policy and Economic Welfare* (Ann Arbor, Mich.: University of Michigan, Bureau of Business Research, Graduate School of Business Administration, 1970), 119-144.

[4]R. M. Feinberg, "Antitrust Enforcement and Subsequent Price Behavior," *Review of Economics and Statistics* 62 (November 1980): 609–612; and M. K. Block, F. C. Nold, and J. G. Sidak, "The Deterrent Effects of Antitrust Enforcement," *Journal of Political Economy* 89 (June 1981): 429-445.

structures.[5]   Limiting the permissible behavior of companies may have an impact (a downward impact, according to Baldwin's observations) on the concentration of their markets. Don E. Waldman has also concluded, on the basis of case studies, that antitrust action may affect both the structure and performance of affected markets.[6]

The findings of Baldwin, Waldman, and Feinberg are especially noteworthy, because they suggest that the impact of an antitrust case may go well beyond what one might predict on the basis of the legal remedy imposed. Indeed, the evidence of Feinberg and Waldman raises the possibility that in certain instances, it may be the act of investigation and prosecution more than the outcome of a case that yields a significant market result.

Such findings are interesting and also encouraging to those who would like to believe that our public competition policies matter to the economy. The kind of evidence amassed, however, permits us to state only a limited general conclusion: antitrust action does have perceptible and potentially important effects on its targets—prosecuted firms and their markets. The frequency with which significant results occur, however, is undefined, as is the overall magnitude of policy benefits vis-a-vis policy costs. About all that we can state with full confidence is that some policy impact—which we hope is beneficial—can be observed.

Enforcement Patterns A third empirical approach considers patterns of antitrust enforcement as an indirect clue to policy effectiveness. Richard A. Posner concluded a detailed statistical examination in 1970 by stating that the Department of Justice and Federal Trade Commission "are ignoring the prerequisites . . . of serious planning," and further that "antitrust enforcement is inefficient."[7] If Posner is correct, one would necessarily believe that policy effects, whether large or small absolutely, fall far short of their potential. The issue, however, is an elusive one.

Three recent studies have attempted to shed light on the policy process by analyzing case-bringing patterns in the major enforcement agencies.[8] Perhaps the most significant finding is negative. Long, Schramm, and Tollison report that welfare losses (estimates of the deadweight loss welfare triangle discussed in Chapters 4 and 9) do not appear to be a significant determinant of enforcement. That is, industries whose characteristics suggest a large welfare loss are not prosecuted with greater frequency than other industries. When industry

[5]W. L. Baldwin, "The Feedback Effect of Business Conduct on Industry Structure," *Journal of Law and Economics* 12 (April 1969): 123–153.

[6]D. E. Waldman, *Antitrust Action and Market Structure* (Lexington, Mass.: Lexington Books, 1978).

[7]R. A. Posner, "A Statistical Study of Antitrust Enforcement," *Journal of Law and Economics* 13 (October 1970): 365–419.

[8]W. F. Long, R. Schramm, and R. Tollison, "The Economic Determinants of Antitrust Activity," *Journal of Law and Economics* 16 (1973): 351–364; J. J. Siegfried, "The Determinants of Antitrust Activity," *Journal of Law and Economics* 18 (October 1975): 559–574; and P. Asch, "The Determinants and Effects of Antitrust Activity," *Journal of Law and Economics* 18 (October 1975): 575–581.

size is broken into its component parts—average firm size and number of firms—all appear to play a role in the pattern of prosecutions.

Siegfried comes to the conclusion that economic variables have little influence on Antitrust Division policies. The implications of the evidence, however, are debatable. In one sense, the observed patterns of enforcement appear consistent with one of the most frequent criticisms of antitrust: that enforcement activities are, from an economic standpoint, haphazard. There is some suspicion, for example, that the agencies pursue easy targets and cases that can be won without regard to the economic impact of these efforts. The likely result would be a large number of easily proven but perhaps trivial violations.[9]

Yet, this is only a suspicion—not an established fact. Masson and Reynolds point out a number of important pitfalls in broad-gauged empirical studies of enforcement.[10] Most troublesome, perhaps, is that certain benefits of successful prosecution defy precise quantification. The value of a legal decision as precedent for future cases is one example. The *Philadelphia National Bank* (PNB) merger decision, discussed in Chapter 10, is a classic example.[11] The Supreme Court's prohibition of PNB's acquisition of Girard Trust undoubtedly had an important effect on the Philadelphia commercial banking market. Its major impact, however, may have come in future cases decided on the basis of the rules set forth in PNB but extending to many other sectors of the economy.

In a similar vein, antitrust decisions may carry important deterrent effects. The conviction of three upstate New York diaper service companies for price-fixing, for example, will have a very limited direct impact on the economy. In fact, the prosecution might appear, on observable cost–benefit grounds, to be a waste of resources. Conceivably, however, 100 other conspiracies—some of them important—will never see the light of day because of this conviction. As John R. Allison has put the point in correspondence with the authors, "the most important procompetitive effects of antitrust probably occur in lawyers' offices, where they say 'no' to clients . . . ."

The problem is, of course, that neither the precedent nor the deterrent effects of antitrust cases can be measured precisely. Among policymakers it is an article of faith that such effects are significant, and they well may be. It is quite possible that deterrence alone produces greater social benefits than any other antitrust result, but there is no reliable way to determine whether this is so. Lacking such knowledge, any assertion about the quantitative economic impact of policies contains an inevitable element of uncertainty.

---

[9]Although such a pattern is far from ideal, notice that it is not socially irrational to prosecute according to the probability of winning a case. Policies that consistently produced important but unsuccessful prosecutions might yield little social benefit.

[10]R. T. Masson and R. J. Reynolds, "Statistical Studies of Antitrust Enforcement: A Critique," *Proceedings of the American Statistical Association* (1977): 22–28.

[11]374 U.S. 321 (1963).

CRITICISMS OF POLICY

Substantive criticisms of antitrust policy are almost as old as the laws themselves. The issue here is not only the magnitude of policy effects, but also the
question of whether certain effects should be counted as costs or benefits.
Some critics believe that although antitrust yields economic and social gains, it
proceeds timidly and does not go far enough. Others contend that at least some
alleged policy benefits are, in fact, costs that prevent firms from operating
efficiently. If one holds the latter view, then antitrust in a sense goes too far,
interfering too much with free market processes. The debate deserves some
attention, although it is not readily resolvable.

Proposed Reforms

Should We Deconcentrate? Recall two conclusions from our earlier discussions.
First, there exists a substantial degree of economic concentration in the United
States, both within individual markets and at an aggregate (national) level.
Second, the antitrust laws have not had a strong, general, direct effect on either
concentration levels or trends.[12]

If one believes that concentration of size—and perhaps of power as
well—is a bad thing, an obvious antitrust reform suggests itself: deconcentrate. That is, change the laws and/or enforcement patterns so as to reduce the
size of our most dominant firms. Suggestions to do precisely this have been
commonplace for decades. In 1959, for example, Carl Kaysen and Donald F.
Turner stated:

> We propose statutory authorization for the reduction of undue market
> power, whether individual or jointly possessed ... by dissolution, divorce-
> ment, or divestiture ... a program [aimed at] ... undue concentration of
> market power.[13]

The Kaysen-Turner proposal has since served as the model for a series of
deconcentration programs, some of which have been introduced to Congress.
A typical example, the Industrial Reorganization Act, was proposed by the late
Senator Philip A. Hart in 1973.[14] It contained the following provisions:

1.   The possession of monopoly power by one or more corporations would
    be illegal. A rebuttable presumption that monopoly power exists would
    be created by any of the following conditions:
    a. An average rate of return to net worth of 15 percent (after taxes) is
    earned by a corporation during five consecutive years;

---

[12]Effects in some specific markets have been important, however. Moreover, the possibility of
indirect effects cannot be ruled out. See Baldwin, "The Feedback Effect."

[13]C. Kaysen and D. F. Turner, *Antitrust Policy* (Cambridge, Mass.: Harvard University Press,
1959), 46. It is interesting to note that when Turner served as Assistant Attorney General in charge
of antitrust, his division undertook no broad effort to reduce industry concentration. To do so,
however, probably would have required significant changes in existing law.

[14]S. 1167 (1973).

b. "No substantial price competition" between two or more corporations occurs for three consecutive years in a defined market; or

c. Four or fewer corporations account for 50 percent or more of sales in a defined market.

2.   A finding of monopoly power would ordinarily be remedied by requiring offending firms to divest themselves of it. Divestiture, however, would not occur if the corporations could show either:

a. That monopoly power is due solely to the ownership of valid patents; or

b. That such a divestiture would result in a loss of "substantial economies."

3.   An Industrial Reorganization Commission would be established to enforce the provisions of the act, including plans for the restructuring of several designated groups of industries.

4.   A special Industrial Reorganization Court would be established to conduct trials of matters arising under the act. This court would, in effect, serve as a district court specializing in issues of industrial reorganization.

Whereas the legislative prospects of such bills are extremely dim, debate about their merits is ongoing. Reformers—here the deconcentrators—argue that high concentration is akin to monopoly, and monopoly (as we all know) is a bad thing. It forces consumers to pay a price in excess of marginal cost, thereby distorting society's allocation of resources. Further, there is now some evidence that monopoly power is associated with increased inequality in the distribution of wealth, a phenomenon that many, although not all, regard as undesirable (refer to Chapter 3).[15] It is even possible—although we must emphasize that the evidence to date is fragmentary and inconclusive—that concentrated power contributes to such social ills as labor market discrimination and worker alienation.[16] Finally, as we have noted before, economic concentration may affect political processes in ways that at least some would regard as undemocratic.

This menu of monopoly miseries is imposing. Is deconcentration, then, the way to go? Although it is always a bit risky to generalize, it seems likely that the large majority in the economics profession would oppose any broad effort to reduce American industry concentration. The primary reason, as our earlier discussions have pointed out, is that high concentration by itself is not conclusive proof of undesirable monopoly. (Nor, by the same token, does low concen-

---

[15]W. S. Comanor and R. H. Smiley, "Monopoly and the Distribution of Wealth," *Quarterly Journal of Economics* 89 (May 1975): 177–194.

[16]For some relevant discussion and evidence, see W. S. Comanor, "Racial Discrimination in American Industry," *Economica* 4 (November 1973): 363–378; W. G. Shepherd and S. G. Levin, "Managerial Discrimination in Large Firms," *Review of Economics and Statistics* 55 (November 1973): 412–422; and F. M. Scherer, "Industrial Structure, Scale Economies, and Worker Alienation," in R. T. Masson and P. D. Qualls, eds., *Essays on Industrial Organization in Honor of Joe S. Bain* (Cambridge, Mass.: Ballinger, 1976), 105–121.

tration necessarily indicate active competition.) The situation is more complicated.

Part of the complexity traces back to problems of market definition and
measurement (recall Chapter 9). If we observe, for example, that Alpha
Corporation has 80 percent of the market in canned minestrone soup, should
we believe that this company is a near monopolist? Clearly, the canned
minestrone market is highly concentrated. But minestrone manufacturers
surely face competition from other firms who supply such soups as vegetable,
beef, chicken, and mushroom. If this competition is strong enough, Alpha
Corporation may have little leeway in its behavior regarding price and other
supply terms. And, if this is true, the company is no monopolist. The high
market share and concentration that we observe are a kind of statistical fairy
tale. Alpha's apparent market dominance has been created by an overly
narrow definition of that market.[17]

Let us abstract, however, from problems of market definition. Suppose
that Beta Company has 80 percent of the market in baking chocolate, a product
for which no very close substitutes exist. Should we presume that Beta is a
monopolist or something close to it? The answer remains "not necessarily."
Beta's market share may be attributable to its own efficiency. The company
may simply have produced a better product than rivals—a phenomenon that
many observers would term competitive superiority rather than monopoly.

Alternatively, it may be that there are numerous other firms ready to
jump into the baking chocolate market if Beta's performance falters in any way.
Existing manufacturers (those who account for the remaining 20 percent of the
market) similarly may be prepared to expand their outputs and shares at any
sign of Beta's weakness. The company's market position, apparently powerful
in a momentary snapshot, is vulnerable to competition over time. The applicability of the term monopoly power to Beta in this situation is thus dubious.

High market shares and concentration, then, cannot be viewed as sure
indicators of monopoly. A more accurate picture can be gained by examining
the ability of leading firms in concentrated markets to set high prices (relative
to costs) without losing substantial sales to rivals, current or potential. As we
have noted, many investigators have explored the relationships between market
share, concentration, and profits, frequently finding positive and statistically
significant—though not necessarily strong—links.[18]

---

[17]An analogous case in point is the U.S. automobile manufacturing market during the late 1970s
and early 1980s. According to conventional concentration measurement, as pursued by the
Census Bureau, the domestic market was dominated by three firms: General Motors, Ford, and
Chrysler accounted jointly for over 90 percent of output. The companies, however, faced serious
competition from foreign manufacturers whose output was not counted in the national concentration statistics. The calculated concentration figure was thus a somewhat misleading indicator
of the market power of these manufacturers.

[18]Recall Chapter 9. The market share of a firm appears to exert a stronger influence on its profit
rates than do broader indexes of market concentration. See W. G. Shepherd, "The Elements of
Market Structure," *Review of Economics and Statistics* 54 (February 1972): 25-37; and J. W. Kwoka,
Jr., "The Effect of Market Share Distribution on Industry Performance," *Review of Economics and
Statistics* 59 (February 1979): 101–109.

Some recommendations for deconcentration have relied on such observations of "monopoly profits" in concentrated industries. Yet even here, the proper interpretation of the evidence is ambiguous. Are high profits the result of monopoly power gained by simple misallocation and exploitation? Or do they reflect socially useful activities, such as innovation, production efficiency, and managerial excellence? Despite an enormous amount of investigation, no one has succeeded in ruling out either alternative. Indeed, it may prove impossible to do so. The unhappy fact is that statistical associations, such as those between industry concentration ratios and profit rates, do not tell us much about underlying cause and effect.

This is not to say that high concentration is no cause for concern. It may be a symptom of monopoly with all its attendant evils. It calls for suspicion. But it may be wise to proceed cautiously. To deconcentrate on the assumption that high concentration is invariably a sign of bad things would imply far-reaching action on the basis of scanty information.[19]

Should We Worry about Mere Size?   Is overall firm size (regardless of whether the company in question holds power within any given market) something with which public policy should be concerned? The context of this question must be specified. No one seriously suggests that we can or should limit the internal growth of firms in most instances. The company that performs well will tend to prosper and to grow. To restrict such growth is simply to reject the natural implication of worthwhile performance. But size limits have been proposed with respect to conglomerate mergers.[20] As we have noted, merger is a method of firm growth that, in a sense, circumvents market tests.

A recent example of such proposals is the Small and Independent Business Protection Act, introduced to Congress in 1979.[21] This bill specified an absolute prohibition on mergers between companies, if the sales or assets of either exceeds $2 billion. It would also prohibit mergers if: (1) both firms have sales or assets over $350 million; or (2) the sales or assets of one firm exceeds $350 million and the other firm has a 20 percent or higher share of a $100 million market. Companies violating these provisions would nevertheless escape the prohibitions if they prove that the merger would enhance competition substantially or would result in substantial efficiencies, or if they divest themselves of a going concern with sales and assets comparable to those of the smaller merging partner.

---

[19]We are in effect stating: "When in doubt (about the dangers of high concentration) do not act." Such a viewpoint places a heavy burden of proof on those who would argue for deconcentration. The implied risk is that we may at times permit the persistence of high concentration where it does imply serious costs. Whereas one may regard this approach as sensible to some point, then, we may not wish to push it to the extreme.

[20]Large horizontal and vertical mergers are likely to be prohibited under established legal standards (see Chapter 10). Legislative proposals are accordingly directed towards conglomerates, an area in which legal rules are less well defined.

[21]S. 600 (1979), proposed by Senator Kennedy, and HR 3169 (1979), proposed by Representative Seiberling.

The economic rational behind such proposals argues that large conglomerates are likely to possess several undesirable characteristics, most notably:[22]

1. *Subsidization.* The conglomerate firm can choose to behave in a predatory fashion in one market, subsidizing its predation from profits earned elsewhere. For example, the company producing both power tools and soups might price its soups at artificially low levels (perhaps even below cost), financing this activity out of its power tool profits.

2. *Reciprocity.* The large conglomerate may have numerous opportunities for reciprocal buying arrangements. (For example, Firm A will buy steel from Firm B only if B agrees to fulfill its power tool requirements by buying from A.)

3. *Mutual forbearance.* More generally (it is sometimes claimed) large firms treat each other with deference, avoiding competitive confrontation whenever possible.

4. *Absence of efficiencies.* Conglomerate growth is often portrayed as inefficient. It possesses little of the potential for resource saving that may occur in horizontal or vertical expansion (scale economies and vertical economies respectively). Furthermore, in the pure conglomerate case, the firm moves into unfamiliar areas in which its management likely lacks expertise. The probability of efficient operation may thus be relatively low.

How compelling are these points? The usual rejoinder is that whereas the undesirable effects of large-firm conglomeration are frequently asserted, they cannot be demonstrated to be either common or important.[23] Subsidization is a problem only if it becomes a basis for predatory behavior. But predatory behavior is itself illegal (under Section 2 of the Sherman Act) and may therefore not require this oblique sort of attack.

Reciprocity? This is more likely to occur among large multi-market firms, but it does not appear to be a particularly efficient way to do business. Therefore, its impact on competition may well be minor. The efficiency arguments against conglomerates are plausible but speculative. One may, in fact, reverse the speculation: perhaps the conglomerate firm—a diversified entity—will be freer than specialized companies to pursue inventive efforts and risky activities. Since its eggs are in many baskets, the cost of failure in any one is supportable. It may thus be well suited to socially useful tasks that more traditional, safety-conscious organizations tend to avoid.

Supporters of conglomerate size limitations frequently respond to such claims with a noneconomic argument. William S. Comanor puts the case

---

[22]The best single description of potential conglomerate evils remains C. D. Edwards, "Conglomerate Bigness as a Source of Power," in *Business Concentration and Price Policy* (Princeton: National Bureau of Economic Research and Princeton University Press, 1955), 331–352.

[23]Whether the undesirable effects flow from conglomeration *per se*, or are rather a function of size, is often unclear in discussions of the large conglomerate. One may suspect that size is a key, since few attacks are directed toward small conglomerates.

succinctly, stating that the relevant issue for policy rests not in the "actual harms, however defined" that conglomerates create, but rather in "a fundamental ideological concern with giant aggregations of privately held assets"[24] American society has had a traditional distrust of concentrated political power, preferring instead the Jeffersonian ideal under which decisions, because they are made by all, are controlled by no one.

Economic aggregations of assets may imply concentrated political power. (Theories linking one to the other are not yet very precise.) If this is so, then aggregations are a source of public concern. The view presented by Comanor and others suggests a policy presumption against large conglomerate mergers: we should permit them only where positive benefits can be shown. (Comanor would probably concede the possibility but not the probability.) This would precisely reverse the policy position favored by some other writers: prohibition of large conglomerate acquisitions only where actual harm can be shown (a possibility they regard as remote).[25]

Where does the truth lie? It is clear that generalizations about the goodness or badness of large conglomerate firms will be difficult to defend objectively. The problem is not an absence of arguments, but a plethora of contentions on both sides of the issue, mostly logical, some more plausible than others, but all finally speculative. Some observers candidly concede that there is little useful evidence. We are arguing largely about effects that we cannot see. The ultimate policy question—what is the proper treatment of conglomerates?—is therefore unanswerable, at least for the moment. Rather, the pertinent question may be: given substantial ignorance about conglomerate effects, what kinds of policy errors would we risk? One's answer to this question is likely to be a function of one's ideology.

Should We Place Stricter Limits on Firm Behavior? We have seen a sharp dichotomy in antitrust views. At one side is the structuralist position, which states roughly:

1.   Power itself presents the central policy problem;

2.   Power inheres in concentrated market structure; thus

3.   Antitrust policies ought to act against undesirably concentrated structures.

In contrast, consider what may be termed the behaviorist view:

1.   Power itself is not a key problem;

---

[24]W. S. Comanor, "Conglomerate Mergers: Considerations for Public Policy," in R. D. Blair and R. F. Lanzillotti, eds., *The Conglomerate Corporation: A Public Problem?* (Cambridge, Mass.: Oelgeschager, Gunn and Hain, 1981), 15.

[25]R. H. Bork, for example, states simply: "Conglomerate mergers should not be prohibited by judicial interpretation of Section 7 of the Clayton Act." Bork does concede the possibility that mergers classified as conglomerates may harm competition, but in his view the conglomerate element is by itself innocuous. See Bork, *The Antitrust Paradox* (New York: Basic Books, 1978), 262.

2.   In any event, power cannot be inferred reliably from structure;

3.   Antitrust policies ought to be addressed exclusively to instances of anti-competitive behavior, sometimes referred to as the "abuse of power."

One might expect to find a comparable dichotomy in policy prescriptions: one side arguing for structural limitations while deemphasizing attacks on specific forms of conduct; the other expounding conduct restrictions while rejecting policies that would impose structural constraints. In fact, however, this distinction does not characterize the policy debate. What we find instead is a different division of opinion. Structuralists support structural reform, but also believe in stricter conduct regulation. Behaviorists oppose structural policy limitations, but believe also that attacks on conduct should be narrowly confined.

This difference of opinion harks back to a disagreement we have stressed throughout: faith in, versus distrust of, the marketplace. The structuralist view is distrustful. The market can easily generate undesirable, monopolistic, concentration of power, and the stratagems employed by companies as normal business practice will frequently damage competition.

The behaviorist view, in contrast, accepts a very broad range of market outcomes as desirable. The market structures that emerge and persist are, as a rule, the most efficient for society.[26] Companies may act abusively or anticompetitively, but such behavior is an aberration, not part of the market routine. Moreover, behavior that is anticompetitive in intent often lacks significant market impact.[27] Where this is the case, it is not worth the attention of the public enforcement agencies.

The idea of enforcing more stringent limits on corporate behavior is one that attracts few strong adherents. Behaviorists regard such restrictions as unnecessary, and perhaps as damaging to efficiency. Structuralists may favor them, but only as an inferior, second-best policy that avoids the fundamental issue of structural reform.

Enforcement Problems

Problems of antitrust enforcement have been touched on earlier. It is possible to paint a rather pessimistic, yet plausible, picture of public enforcement efforts.[28] The major federal agencies—the Department of Justice (Antitrust Division) and the Federal Trade Commission—operate with limited resources

---

[26]As John S. McGee puts it: "In the absence of artificial strictures, there is a strong presumption that the existing structure of industry is the efficient structure." See McGee, "Efficiency and Economics of Size," in H. J. Goldschmid, H. M. Mann, and J. F. Weston, eds., *Industrial Concentration: The New Learning* (Boston: Little, Brown, 1974), 93.

[27]For example, a price-fixing conspiracy that, because of squabbling and cheating, fails to affect market price or output in a substantial way.

[28]For a realistic, and not entirely pessimistic description, see W. G. Shepherd, *Public Policies toward Business,* 7th ed. (Homewood, Ill.: Richard D. Irwin, 1985), Chapter 11.

and appear frequently to be outmanned by affluent corporate defendants.[29] The typical length of a litigated case indicates that defendant firms can delay outcomes for a substantial period. (Posner reported in 1970 that about 30 percent run over six years.)[30] It also suggests the complexity of the cases themselves, a problem that is now widely recognized. Not only juries but judges as well may lack the background to extract a clear picture from enormous volumes of economic evidence, often statistical in nature.

Turnover of agency personnel is a further problem in protracted cases. The Antitrust Division lawyer who initiates a suit, for example, may not be there by the time an outcome is determined. In fact, one prominent attorney has counseled private defendants to delay as long as possible. Sufficient turnover may leave the prosecution's case in the hands of lawyers who do not fully grasp the issues because they have not been involved in the full proceedings.[31]

Finally, it must be noted that antitrust enforcement efforts are subject to political pressure. Agency heads are appointed by the President and may well be sensitive to the executive branch's view of an appropriate attitude toward the business community. Even if an agency is nominally independent, Congress and the executive branch have the power to "clip its wings." Thus, the political environment may not be conducive to innovative and aggressive policy-making.

There is, however, some basis for a more optimistic view. As we have seen, some evidence suggests that investigation and prosecution have a real impact on the market and that remedies limited to market conduct will, at times, have an impact on market structure. Government antitrust activity may have important effects that are, by their very nature, difficult to isolate and measure.

A further qualification to one's view of public antitrust policy is the recent growth of private enforcement. For every case filed by a government agency, there are a thousand or more initiated by private parties, usually companies claiming that they have been injured by violations on the part of other firms. These suits are often conduct cases in which the plaintiffs claim that particular actions and strategies harmed their businesses. Far-reaching remedies are seldom sought. Indeed, plaintiffs are often lured by the prospects of treble-damage awards, sums that are potentially important to the compa-

---

[29]Corporate affluence further suggests that defendants may be more successful than government in attracting well-qualified attorneys. A good number of able government employees eventually move to the private sector.

[30]R. A. Posner, "A Statistical Study of Antitrust Enforcement." More recently, Salop and White report that the average length of all antitrust cases is about 25 months. The large majority (at least 70 percent) of all cases are settled out of court, usually on terms favorable to defendants. S. C. Salop and L. J. White, "Economic Analysis of Private Antitrust Litigation," *Georgetown Law Journal* 74 (April 1986): 1001–1064.

[31]James T. Halverson, formerly Chief of the FTC Bureau of Competition, later a member of a New York law firm, "advised corporate attorneys to make certain that the Government gets enough documents and data so that personnel on the Government team will turn over several times during the law suit." *Antitrust and Trade Regulation Reporter*, No. 792, December 12, 1976, A-2.

nies involved.[32] Whether private antitrust enforcement can truly compensate for deficiencies in public policy is questionable. But even treble-damage suits can, at times, result in significant legal precedent.[33] There is no doubt that the threat of private action exerts an important policing effect on the behavior of American corporations.

CONCLUSION

As we have seen, antitrust policies are commonly pursued in the name of promoting and protecting competition. But what different individuals mean by that term (and what they see as the proper means of implementing a competitive system) varies a good deal.[34] It is therefore not surprising that views of what antitrust actually accomplishes also are highly divergent.

Kenneth G. Elzinga observes, for example:

> Antitrust enforcement generally serves to help those at the low end of the income distribution range without decreasing efficiency .... The congenial thing about antitrust is that the equity objectives that bear on its enforcement do not seriously conflict, and at times harmonize, with the pursuit of economic efficiency.[35]

Robert H. Bork's view is far less sanguine:

> There is no prospect that equality of condition will be achieved, but antitrust demonstrates some of the costs of moving toward it. The first and most obvious cost is the destruction of wealth through the inhibition of efficiency. The second is the accumulation of power in government .... The third is the replacement of free markets with government-regulated markets .... The fourth is the shift of lawmaking from elected representatives to courts and bureaucracies.[36]

The gap between these views is so broad as to raise the question whether there exists any agreement about the effects of antitrust policy in the United States. The answer is yes, but not much. Most observers probably agree that the equity result of policy is to move us in the direction of greater equality. This follows from the tendency of the law to protect smaller business units from being overrun by larger ones and, at times, to protect both consumers and businesses from exploitation by collusive groups. How large this effect may

---

[32]For an interesting analytical criticism of the current system of private antitrust litigation, see Warren F. Schwartz, *Private Enforcement of the Antitrust Laws: A Critique* (Washington, D.C.: American Enterprise Institute, 1981). Discussion of a range of issues based on the most recent evidence about private enforcement is presented by Lawrence J. White, ed., *Private Antitrust Litigation: New Evidence, New Learning* (Cambridge, Mass.: M.I.T. Press, 1988).

[33]K. G. Elzinga and W. Breit argue that the availability of treble damages creates perverse incentives, one of which is a propensity to sue where actual damages are trivial or nonexistent. See Elzinga and Breit, *The Antitrust Penalties* (New Haven, Conn.: Yale University Press, 1976).

[34]See for example, *Berkey Photo, Inc. v. Eastman Kodak Co.*, 603 F.2d 263 (2d Cir. 1979).

[35]K. G. Elzinga, "The Goals of Antitrust: Other Than Competition and Efficiency, What Else Counts?" *University of Pennsylvania Law Review* 125 (1977): 1191–1213.

[36]R. H. Bork, *The Antitrust Paradox*, 423.

be—that is, whether it has had a meaningful impact on the distribution of society's income and wealth—is far from clear.

Agreement about the efficiency effects of antitrust is severely limited. Whereas any sensible observer of policy will conclude that it creates both costs and benefits, the relative importance of the two is subject to wildly varying interpretation. Some believe with Elzinga that the policies are, as a rule, efficient or neutral. The occasional obvious instances of inefficiency may be viewed as a small price to pay for beneficial equity effects. In the view of Bork and others, however, inefficiencies dominate policy effects, sapping the basic incentives of the market system.

The nation's views of antitrust appear to have changed markedly in the past two decades. During the 1960s and 1970s, public debate was dominated by structuralists whose main concern was the concentration of economic power that they frequently saw in the market system. During the latter 1970s and 1980s, much greater attention has been paid to the productive efficiency of American firms, perhaps as the result of increased international competition and balance-of-trade problems.

Market power remains a legitimate concern, but it is now argued with some frequency that traditional indexes of such power—most notably the concentration ratio—are irrelevant and potentially misleading.[37] Antitrust policies based on concentration measures are, accordingly, viewed with some skepticism. A very few writers have gone so far as to suggest that existing antitrust laws serve no useful purpose and ought to be repealed.[38]

The structuralists, however, are still with us, alive and well despite the waning of their influence in government during the Reagan years. Indeed, some go farther than simple structuralism, attacking what they see as overreliance on abstract (presumably irrelevant) economic analysis, and heavy emphasis on economic efficiency in antitrust cases. Is the pendulum of debate likely to swing back soon, favoring once again a strongly structural approach to antitrust policy? Our best guess is that a major change of opinion will not occur quickly among economists, many of whom now believe that the earlier structuralism was an error. We are reluctant to hazard predictions about legal or political trends, but note that the federal courts are now heavily staffed by conservative judges who may not be enthusiastic about rapid reversals of current policy criteria.

[37]Industrial organization economists often place more credence on the condition of entry than on any concentration measure. At the extreme, some contend that entry is virtually the only factor that determines market power. This is one implication of the contestability theories, discussed in Chapter 13. See William J. Baumol, John C. Panzar, and Robert D. Willig, *Contestable Markets and the Theory of Industry Structure* (New York: Harcourt Brace Jovanovich, 1982).

[38]For example, D. T. Armentano, *Antitrust Policy: The Case for Repeal* (Washington, D.C.: Cato Institute, 1986).

Discussion Questions

1. Some industrialized nations with much weaker antitrust laws than the United States appear to have substantially higher levels of market concentration. Discuss two or three possible cause-and-effect explanations.

2. "The best antitrust policy would be: (a) no policy at all; (b) a policy limited to prosecution of horizontal conspiracy and some occasional flagrant instances of predatory pricing; (c) roughly the policy that we now have." Explain which alternative you regard as most reasonable.

3. Economists occasionally complain that the main difficulty with antitrust policy is that it is determined largely by lawyers who may not fully understand the economic implications of what they are doing. Do you consider this a fair criticism? If economists rather than lawyers had been deciding policy issues during the past century, what important differences in current procedures would we see?

4. During 1980 to 1984, the federal government initiated about 500 antitrust cases. During the same period, over 5,800 cases were initiated by private parties. The overwhelming majority of cases were settled by mutual consent before going through the full litigation process, and most of the settlements appeared favorable to defendants. Do these facts tell us anything about the probable effectiveness of antitrust policy during this period? If so, what? If not, why not?

Selected Readings

Baldwin, W. L. "The Feedback Effects of Business Conduct on Industry Structure." *Journal of Law & Economics* 12 (April 1969): 123–153. *An examination of conduct remedies in antitrust cases, and their apparent effects on structure.*

Elzinga, K. G. and W. Breit. *The Antitrust Penalties.* New Haven, Conn.: Yale University Press, 1976. *A broad discussion of the importance and role of various antitrust remedies.*

Long, W. B., R. Schramm, and R. Tollison. "The Economic Determinants of Antitrust Activity." *Journal of Law and Economics* 16 (October 1973): 351–364. *Statistical analysis of government case-bringing patterns.*

Posner, R. A. "A Statistical Study of Antitrust Enforcement." *Journal of Law and Economics* 13 (October 1970): 365–419. *Detailed analysis of antitrust enforcement patterns.*

Stigler, G. J. "The Economic Effects of the Antitrust Law." *Journal of Law and Economics* 9 (October 1966): 225–258. *An early effort to assess the economic impact of antitrust enforcement.*

PART THREE

. . . .

Old-Style Regulation:
Public Utilities

. . . .

CHAPTER 13

· · · · · · · · · · · · · · · · · ·

REGULATION: RATIONALE AND BASIC PRINCIPLES

We have seen in Part I many of the reasons for advocating a government role in a free enterprise system. These are associated with market failure of several types: monopoly, public goods, externalities, and information problems. We examined the implications of failure in terms of two normative criteria, efficiency and equity. Of course, explanations for government intervention are also found in the historical development of specific industries and in social and political pressures which led to the passage of particular regulatory laws.

In the first part of this chapter we reexamine the main economic reason for the creation of a public utility (that is, for the direct regulation of an industry by government): natural monopoly. We look in more detail at the specific supply and demand conditions in an industry which might lead to a prescription for direct government regulation and consider an empirical approach for assessing the importance of these conditions. In the second half of this chapter, we develop a framework to analyze the basic pricing problem that natural monopoly presents. (Chapter 14 considers the various regulatory mechanisms which may be adopted in response to the basic problem. In the following chapters we assess these responses in a number of industries.)

ECONOMIC RATIONALE FOR GOVERNMENT REGULATION

The Natural Monopoly Argument

Recall the definition of natural monopoly in our earlier discussion of scale economy barriers to entry (Chapter 3). A natural monopoly exists when the competitive process of an industry leads to the dominance and survival of only one firm. Recall also that there are, in fact, two pertinent questions:

1. Under what conditions does natural monopoly exist?

2. Under what conditions is natural monopoly sustainable?

Both these questions can be accurately answered using the concept of the *subadditivity of costs*. This concept is related to scale economies, but is broader because it can apply both to single product and multi-product firms. Industries such as transportation and communications are typically comprised of multi-product rather than single-product firms. If we want to ask whether, for example, the telecommunications industry is a natural monopoly, we must include in our definition the idea that the firm(s) in that industry may produce a variety of products and services ranging from consumer equipment (telephones and answering machines) to the short- and long-distance phone calls themselves.

Sharkey's definition of the subadditivity of costs is as follows:[1]

If $q^1, \ldots q^k$ are output vectors that sum to q, then a single firm is more efficient than a multifirm market if

$$C(q) < C(q^1) + \ldots + C(q^k) \tag{1.1}$$

assuming, of course, that all firms in the market have the cost function C. If inequality (1.1) holds for any possible disaggregation of an output vector q, then C is said to be subadditive at q and the market is said to be a natural monopoly at q.

To understand this definition, first consider single-product firms. In this case, the quantities $q^1 \ldots q^k$ represent the amounts of a product produced by firms 1 through k respectively, where the total quantity produced by all k firms sums to q units: $q^1 + q^2 \ldots + q^k = q$. The inequality (1.1) means that it is cheaper for one firm to produce all q units than for several firms to split the production up among themselves.

Figures 13.1(a) and 13.1(b) show two examples of cost functions for a single product firm which are subadditive. In Figure 13.1(a) we see economies of scale—the average cost of production (AC) declines as output increases.[2] The average cost of producing q units of output if one firm produces the entire output (AC_q) is clearly less than the average cost if output is divided between

[1]W. H. Sharkey, *The Theory of Natural Monopoly* (Cambridge: Cambridge University Press, 1982), 2. For a complete exposition of the theory, see W. J. Baumol, J. C. Panzar, and R. D. Willig, *Contestable Markets and the Theory of Industry Structure* (New York: Harcourt Brace Jovanovich, 1982), 17. For an accessible discussion of these issues, see also D. S. Evans and J. T. Heckman, "Natural Monopoly," in D. S. Evans, ed., *Breaking Up Bell* (New York: North Holland, 1983), 127–156.

[2]In mathematical terms "given a cost function C, scale economies are said to exist at an output q if

$$C(\lambda q) < \lambda C(q)$$

for all λ such that $1 < \lambda < 1 + \delta$, where δ is a small positive number." (Sharkey, *Theory of Natural Monopoly*, 4). Dividing through by λq we have:

$$\frac{C(\lambda q)}{\lambda q} < \frac{C(q)}{q}$$

which means that the average cost of output declines as output increases. Economies of scale are therefore a term that can be used interchangeably with declining average costs.

Figure 13.1 The Subadditivity of Costs

a. The firm's average cost curve decreases throughout its range.

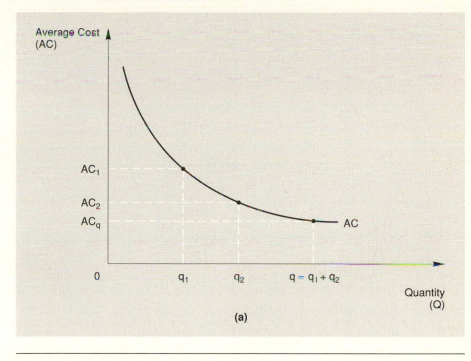

(a)

Source: Sharkey, *The Theory of Natural Monopoly.*

two firms with the same cost function, where one firm produces q_1 units (at average cost AC_1) and a second firm produces q_2 units (at average cost AC_2), and $q_1 + q_2 = q$.[3]

In Figure 13.1(b), average cost curve AC_1 is U-shaped. (For output levels greater than q_0, average costs of production increase.) When there are two firms (or one firm with two plants) the total cost of producing different quantities of output is minimized when output is divided between the two firms such that their marginal costs are equal. When the two firms have identical cost curves (the same cost function) total cost is minimized with equal outputs per firm.[4] In Figure 13.1(b) curve AC_2 represents the costs of producing twice as

[3]Note that the average cost of producing the entire q units of output, when it is divided between two firms, is equal to:

$$\frac{AC_1 \cdot q_1 + AC_2 \cdot q_2}{q} > ACq$$

[4]This assumes that both MC curves are rising with output. However, if total output is less than twice the firm output at minimum marginal cost, the equal marginal cost rule for minimizing costs does not necessarily hold.

Figure 13.1

b. The firm's average cost curves are U-shaped. Costs are subadditive at output levels below q_1.

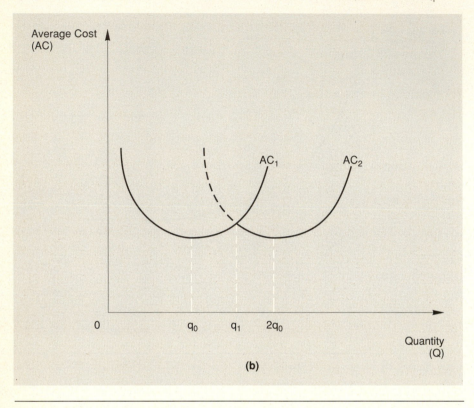

(b)

Source: Sharkey, *The Theory of Natural Monopoly.*

much output as for curve AC_1. That is, $AC(q)_1 = AC(2_q)_2$ for all values of q. However, as Figure 13.1(b) shows, for output levels less than q_1 it would be cheaper for one firm to produce the entire output than for two firms to divide the output between them. That is, for any $0 < q^* < q_1$, $AC(q^*)_1 < AC(2[0.5q^*])_2$, and costs are subadditive.[5] Subadditivity, then, means that it is cheaper for one firm to produce the entire output than for several firms to divide the output between them.

    When we use the concept of subadditivity to identify natural monopoly in multi-product firms, the theoretical issues become more complicated. We confine ourselves here to noting that:

---

[5]If $q < q_1$ there is subadditivity so that $C(q) < C(x) + C(q - x)$ for any x such that $0 < x < q$.

1.   Economies of scope occur when it is cheaper for one firm to produce a number of different products than for several firms to produce each product separately.

2.   It is possible that economies of scale exist in the production of each individual product, while at the same time there are diseconomies of scope, so natural monopoly only exists for each product when it is produced separately.

3.   Natural monopoly for multi-product firms requires both economies of scale and economies of scope.

We turn now to the issue of the sustainability of natural monopoly. Recall from Chapter 3 that when a single-product monopolist produces under economies of scale (declining average costs), it is possible for the monopolist to prevent the entry of competitors by setting a price below the price at which a competing firm facing the same declining cost curve can profitably enter. In this case, the natural monopoly is sustainable. It is cheaper for one firm to produce all the output, and the competitive process will also lead to that outcome—the survival of only one firm.[6] However, in other cases, while it may be cheaper for one firm to produce the output or array of outputs (natural monopoly exists because costs are subadditive), it may nevertheless be profitable for an entrant to serve only a subset of customers at an average cost that is lower than that which would be incurred by the firm which served all the customers. In these cases entry may occur even though it is not efficient. Natural monopoly then exists, but is not sustainable.

In Figure 13.2, AC is the average cost curve facing each potential producer and D is the industry demand curve. If there is a single incumbent firm (a monopoly), the lowest market-clearing price which the firm could charge and still break even is P_S at output Q_S. A potential entrant facing the same cost curve could offer output Q_E at price P_E which is clearly lower than P_S.[7] This would mean that of the original output Q_S, $Q_S - Q_E$ (equal to Q_M in Figure 13.2) would remain to be supplied by the original firm. But the average cost of supplying Q_M is AC_M, which is much higher than $AC_S = P_S$. Thus the second firm's entry would raise the total cost of producing Q_S (($AC_M \cdot Q_M + AC_E \cdot Q_E$) is greater than ($AC_S \cdot Q_S$)) and entry would be socially inefficient.[8] However,

---

[6]Whether or not resources are allocated efficiently under natural monopoly depends on the price set by the monopoly firm. In the absence of price regulation, one would *not* expect a profit-maximizing monopolist to set the efficient price (recall Chapter 3, p. 52).

[7]This model does not assume the Sylos postulate—that the established firm maintains output at Q_S. Indeed, the behavioral interactions between the established and entering firm are not spelled out. All we offer here is one scenario which shows that inefficient entry is possible. Whether or not it would actually occur would depend on particular industrial circumstances.

[8]For this to be true, the shaded area P_M times Q_M must be greater than the inverted L-shaped cross-hatched area. This example does not spell out how the established firm could sell even the reduced output Q_M at a price (equal to AC_M) much higher than the entering firm's price, P_E. In other words, for the described sequence of events to occur, the markets of the established and entering firms must be separable.

Figure 13.2 An Unsustainable Natural Monopoly

A monopoly that produces Q_S and charges price P_S may find itself undercut by an entrant that sells Q_E at the lower price P_E. The remaining output Q_M must then be sold at the much higher price P_M. Thus the entrant who achieves entry by undercutting the established firm causes the average cost of total output to rise.

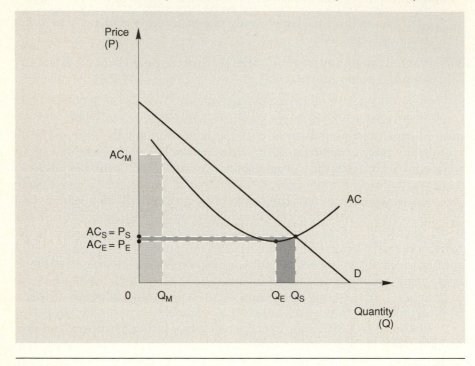

under certain conditions such entry may occur leading to a breakdown of the natural monopoly.[9] Therefore, if government wants to sustain a natural monopoly when the socially efficient price pattern also permits inefficient entry at the fringe, it will have to make entry illegal.

[9]G. R. Faulhaber offers a numerical example of this phenomenon. Faulhaber posited a situation in which three towns desire water supplies in given quantities. The cost of supplying any one of them via one facility is $300, of supplying any two of them, via one facility is $400, and of all three towns jointly is $660. He pointed out that, from the point of view of society, it was cheaper for only one company to supply all three towns because $660 is less than the cost of supply by three separate plants (3 X $300 = $900), or of supply of any two towns by one plant, with the other town supplied by a second plant ($400 + $300 = $700). However, there are then no fixed prices at which a single firm can keep the market entirely for itself. For example, at a price per town of $660/3 = $220, it is cheaper for some two of the towns to split off and supply themselves (at a cost of $400/ 2 = $200 a piece) than for them to join the third town as customers of the single supplier. Note that Faulhaber is assuming three separable markets in each of which different prices may be charged. G. R. Faulhaber, "Cross-Subsidization: Pricing in Public Enterprises," *American Economic Review* 65 (December 1975): 966–977, from Baumol, Panzar, and Willig, *Contestable Markets*, reprinted by permission of the publisher.

A real-world example of this problem is the antitrust verdict for MCI Communications Corporation against the American Telephone and Telegraph Company.[10] AT&T had been charged among other things with impeding MCI's efforts to do business and to expand by making it difficult for MCI to obtain the intercity connections needed to complete the long-distance calls on MCI's national microwave network. AT&T argued that MCI's entry constituted cream-skimming, that is, supplying the most profitable market only, without sharing the obligation borne by AT&T to supply other less profitable markets. Its natural monopoly status was being infringed by inefficient entry and should be protected. In other words, AT&T argued that it was an unsustainable natural monopoly and required both price and entry regulation. As we shall see in Chapter 18, the question of whether AT&T is a sustainable natural monopoly is still not completely resolved even after the 1982 restructuring of the telecommunications industry that substantially increased competition.

We now look in more detail at specific types of supply and demand conditions that might support a prescription for direct government regulation. It should be noted that while many of the points below have often been raised in connection with the natural monopoly argument, particularly important are the explanations of why the long-run average cost curve for public enterprises may be decreasing. These explanations are neither necessary nor sufficient for the failure of competition. However, by identifying and explaining these points in some detail we can evaluate their importance in providing a rationale for government policy.

Supply Conditions

At the outset, it is important to define and distinguish among five concepts: *fixed costs, common costs, external costs, economies of scale, and pecuniary costs.*

Fixed Costs A formal distinction is made in economic theory between the short and the long run. The short run is defined as a length of time short enough for at least one factor to be fixed; in the long run all factors can be varied.

In some industries, however, technology is such that production can only take place after large sums have been invested in fixed capital that is not divisible. This fixed capital may have a life span of 30 years or more. Before electricity can be supplied to any consumer, a generating plant must be built, wires run from the plant to each consumption point, and meters put in at the point of consumption. Railroads must have roadbeds, bridges, tunnels, and track, before trains can run. Telephone services cannot be provided without a complete system of connecting and coordinating centers. Water cannot be

---

[10]In the matter of Microwave Communications, Inc., 18 FCC 953 (1969). Note that this verdict was reached some time before the January 1982 antitrust settlement allowing the complete reorganization of AT&T. In Chapter 18 we discuss the break-up of AT&T and the related issues of cream-skimming and cross-subsidization more fully.

supplied to households without wells or reservoirs, pumps, treatment plants, and pipes. When fixed costs are large, the average fixed cost (AFC) of providing additional units of output will fall rapidly as output expands. If variable costs (AVC) are relatively small, the curve of average total costs (ATC) will decline as output expands over a large range (see Figure 13.3). Note that this cost curve is strictly a short-run cost curve because capital is fixed. However, the short run will be quite a long time if necessary capital has a long life span. The important point to remember is that the decline in average costs is the result of a significant indivisibility.

Common Costs When a single firm produces more than one product or service, it often becomes difficult to determine the cost characteristics of each product. Railroads carry freight, passengers, and mail using the same infrastructure: roadway, track, switches, and stations. Salaries of managers, maintenance workers, and other employees, may also be independent of the number and quality of services provided (or if not strictly independent, very difficult to allocate among different outputs). Common costs are, therefore, the fixed costs of providing the *product set* (as opposed to a single product) of a multi-product firm. Morover, while it may be possible to impute the variable costs of adding an additional train, or one extra car to a train for each individual product, it is not necessarily possible for all production processes. When products are joint (for example, petroleum and its by-products, or mutton and wool), the marginal as well as the total costs of one product depend on the level of output of the other products, which in turn depend on the interaction of supply and demand.[11] Therefore, the average total cost curve can be constructed only if some allocation of the fixed costs of the operation as a whole is made to each product. This allocation procedure is inevitably arbitrary and lacking in true economic significance.[12]

External Costs External costs have been discussed in some detail in Chapter 5. When a firm's production of a product imposes costs on society for which it does not have to pay, these costs are external to the firm. If a gas company digs up city streets in order to lay its gas lines, the inconvenience, noise, and danger to pedestrians are costs, albeit temporary, that the firm imposes on the members of society. The electrical power company may impose external costs when it pollutes the air with emissions from its generating plant. Alternatively, a firm that builds a road to move its own trucks creates an external benefit if others can use the road without having to pay. If prices were charged for the inconvenience of street digging, the damage from air pollution, or the benefit to

---

[11]For a detailed discussion of the derivation of marginal cost curves in the presence of joint products, see A. E. Kahn, *The Economics of Regulation: Principles and Institutions*, vol. 1 (New York: John Wiley and Sons, 1970), 77–83.

[12]Note, however, that "stand alone" costs are sometimes offered as a solution. These refer to the estimated total costs of producing each product in the product set alone. This involves estimating the cost of different amounts of fixed capital as well as the variable costs of each product. In the case of joint products, however, stand alone costs cannot be sensibly estimated.

Figure 13.3 Decreasing Average Total Costs

The ATC curve is the vertical sum of the declining AFC curve and the U-shaped AVC curve. The more significant fixed costs are as a proportion of total costs, the greater the range of output over which average total costs are declining.

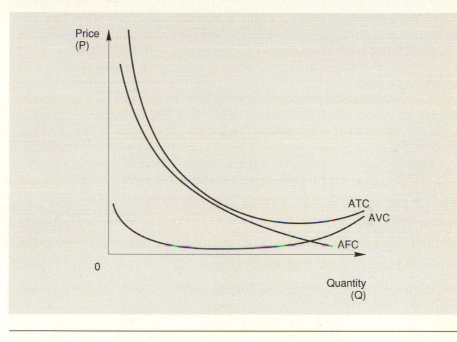

others from the private road, then the cost or benefit would be internalized. Externalities frequently remain external, however, and distort the allocation of resources.

Externalities are closely related to the phenomenon of common costs. For example, when different services share their costs (as when the same roadbed is used to transport both food and lumber), the original provision of one service facilitates provision of the other service at zero or low marginal cost. Thus, building a roadbed to transport food carries the external benefit of being able to transport lumber without incurring the cost of a second roadbed.

Economies of Scale   The strict definition of economies of scale in economic theory is: a given proportional increase of all factors of production leads to a more-than-proportional increase in output.[13] One example is the two-thirds rule used by engineers: "Since the area of a sphere or cylinder of constant proportions varies as the two-thirds power of volume, the cost of constructing process industry plant units can be expected to rise as the two-thirds power of

[13]See Footnote 2.

their output capacity."[14] In this case technological considerations determine the minimum efficient plant size. At the firm level many situations in which average costs diminish as output expands are linked to an indivisibility, that is, to an unmeasured fixed factor. In other words, the ubiquitous phenomena of fixed and common costs can account for many of what are called economies of scale. For example, if a large output makes it possible for a firm to realize economies of organization and administration, then management can be viewed as a fixed factor whose unit cost is reduced at higher output levels.

Dynamic economies are cost savings that accrue to a firm that has been producing a product over a period of time and has incorporated new ideas as a result of its historical production experience. In other words, the firm has learned by doing. Such economies can be related to the common cost phenomenon and related once again to fixed costs. Just as a multi-product firm requires a given fixed outlay to produce a set of different products at any time, so a single-product firm requires a given current outlay to produce a series of outputs, say Q_{t_1}, Q_{t_2}, Q_{t_3} at periods in the future. If learning by doing occurs, then the cost of producing output Q_{t_2} depends on the experience gained in producing Q_{t_1}. Savings experienced when Q_{t_2} is produced depend on the cost incurred to produce Q_{t_1}. Put another way, outlays incurred at time t_1 may reduce the cost of producing a larger output, Q_{t_2}, at a later time, t_2. These outlays are the common costs of producing different output levels Q_{t_1} and Q_{t_2} at different time periods.[15]

Pecuniary Costs   A firm that buys inputs in large quantities relative to the market may be able to get them at a lower price per unit. (This could result from a policy of price discrimination by the seller.) In such a situation, the firm's LAC curve will diminish, not because it needs fewer inputs per unit of output, but because of the pecuniary phenomenon that input prices are lower at higher outputs. These pecuniary cost savings are not considered true cost reductions since they do not save resources. They simply involve a redistribution of monopoly rent from the seller of the input to the buyer.

In fact, it is difficult to distinguish pecuniary costs from *technological economies* since technological (that is, resource-saving) changes may create a chain of effects throughout the economy which are difficult to trace to the original change. However, at the micro level, large firm size saves resources only if lower costs are of the technological variety.

We have noted that the term economies of scale is often used interchangeably with decreasing average costs. In view of the distinctions above, a more general term is simply economies of size. Recall, however, that the

---

[14]F. M. Scherer, *Industrial Market Structure and Economic Performance*, 2d ed. (Chicago: Rand McNally, 1980), 82–83.

[15]Strictly speaking, the learning curve argument suggests that average costs cannot be defined in terms of *current* output levels. Since the LAC curves represented in this chapter do not include time, they cannot properly be used to represent dynamic economies.

presence of such economies does not by itself imply natural monopoly or signal the need for government intervention.

Demand Conditions

Let us turn to the demand side of the market and identify the characteristics of an industry that may provide a rationale for government regulation.

Inelastic Demand   The profit-maximizing price of a monopolist is inversely related to the elasticity of demand of the commodity produced.[16] Therefore, the lower the elasticity of demand, the higher the price an unregulated monopolist could charge.[17] For this reason it sometimes is argued that the monopolization of an industry will be more harmful to consumers if it produces a low-elasticity commodity than a high-elasticity commodity.

Consider two industries, each consisting of one firm with identical and constant costs, AC = MC in Figures 13.4(a) and 13.4(b). The demand and marginal revenue curves for Monopolists 1 and 2 are D_1 and MR_1 in Figure 13.4(a), and D_2 and MR_2 in Figure 13.4(b). Assume that, if each industry were organized competitively, output and price would be the same (Q_c, P_c) in both figures. Under monopoly, each monopolist will determine a price and output to maximize profits where MR = MC. This occurs for both monopolists at the same output level $(Q_1$ in Figure 13.4(a), and Q_2 in Figure 13.4(b)). But Monopolist 1 can charge a price (P_1) higher than Monopolist 2's price (P_2) because the elasticity along D_1 between points C and A in Figure 13.4(a) is lower than the elasticity along D_2 between points C and E in Figure 13.4(b). The profits and revenues of Monopolist 1 will be higher than those of Monopolist 2. Compared with the competitive price–quantity combination, the deadweight efficiency loss for Industry 1 is the area of consumer's surplus, triangle ABC. For Industry 2, it is the much smaller triangle EBC. In Industry 1, area P_cP_1AB would be part of consumer's surplus if the industry were competitive. But it is now captured by the monopolist and is a partial measure of the redistributional effect. In Industry 2, this area is smaller: P_cP_2EB.[18] Therefore, it is argued on both

---

[16]Recall that if the firm's demand curve is p = f(q) and the elasticity of demand is

$$e = -\frac{dq}{dp} \cdot \frac{P}{q}, \quad \text{then MR} = P\left(1 - \frac{1}{e}\right).$$

In equilibrium MR   = MC, therefore

$$p\left(1 - \frac{1}{e}\right) = MC \quad \text{and} \quad P = \frac{MC}{1 - \frac{1}{e}}$$

Therefore p and e are inversely related.

[17]Note that the *point elasticity* of demand is different at every point along the demand curve in all but a few cases. Therefore, referring loosely to the elasticity of demand for electricity is a short cut that omits the necessary qualifying statement "over the current output range."

[18]For a detailed exposition of the use and validity of areas under the demand and cost curves to measure changes in welfare, see E. J. Mishan, *Cost–Benefit Analysis* (New York: Praeger Publishers, 1976).

Figure 13.4 Inelastic and Elastic Demands Compared

Monopoly 1 produces Q_1 units of output and charges price P_1. Monopoly 2 produces Q_2 units of output and charges price P_2. The competitive price and output combination is P_c Q_c for both industries. The net welfare loss from monopoly compared with competition is area ABC for Industry 1, larger than area EBC for Industry 2.

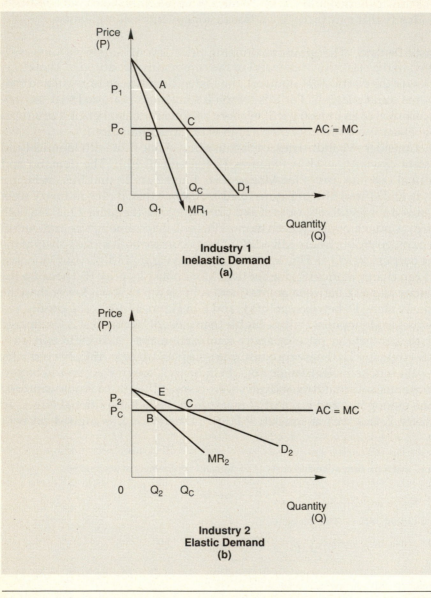

Industry 1
Inelastic Demand
(a)

Industry 2
Elastic Demand
(b)

efficiency and distributional grounds that the distorting effect of monopoly pricing is less when the elasticity of demand is higher. Consequently, the benefits obtained by enforcing a regulated price P_c is higher for the lower elasticity industry.[19]

On closer examination, however, the elasticity argument for regulation is weak. First, the magnitude of welfare loss will depend more directly on the size of the monopolized industry than on its elasticity of demand. Thus the total welfare losses generated by prices slightly above marginal cost in a large industry may be substantially higher than losses generated by prices much higher than marginal cost in a small industry. (Furthermore, some items—salt or toothpicks—have low elasticities precisely because they are trivial in individuals' budgets.)

Second, an industry's elasticity of demand is a creature of market definition—a high elasticity may simply mean that the industry has been incorrectly defined. To suggest, therefore, that low-elasticity industries should be likelier candidates for regulation than high-elasticity ones is an argument which contains only a very small kernel of theoretical truth.

The Peak-Load Problem If capacity and output could always be altered immediately in response to demand shifts, there would be no peak load problem. But in some industries, the presence of large fixed capital equipment is combined with demands that fluctuate widely over periods of time as short as an hour or 30 minutes. During one day, the demand for electricity may be high around noon and dinnertime and low in the early morning. This means that if customers are to be provided with electricity on demand, producers must install sufficient capacity to supply the peak demand, even though that capacity is seriously underutilized at off-peak times. Demand fluctuations can provide an additional reason for the existence of a natural monopoly. A firm that can use the same plant and equipment to supply a product (electricity) to different customers at different times and in different places may be able to produce at lower total cost than a firm that produces for a more uniform customer group. This is because the peak demand by different customers may occur at different times, and the overall capacity utilization rate can therefore be kept fairly steady with no costly bottlenecks or revenue-losing troughs. For both firms, appropriate pricing policy can mitigate the peak-load problem (discussed further in Chapter 14).

An Empirical Approach

We have identified and discussed a variety of cost and demand conditions that in combination may imply natural monopoly, that is, an industry in which output can be supplied at lowest total cost by only one firm. None of these characteristics alone necessarily provides a sufficient rationale for government

---

[19]Note that this conclusion assumes, among other things, that both industries' demand and cost curves remain the same regardless of whether the industry is organized competitively or as a monopoly.

regulation, but it is clear that a variety of combinations of these characteristics *could* do so.

It is useful to observe industries that are subject to government regulation and see to what extent they possess the characteristics identified above. A revealing study by Frederic Pryor provides an example.[20] Pryor compares the level of public ownership (extent of nationalization) in industry across countries. Public ownership is not an index of government regulation (in the United States, many public utilities are privately owned and government ownership is the exception rather than the rule). However, in many countries public ownership is the standard method for treating the natural monopoly problem. Pryor's comparisons thus provide at least a starting point for an analysis of the extent of government regulation across countries. He shows that the share of public ownership in industry differs markedly among countries, ranging from 9 percent in West Germany to 71 percent in East Germany. The U.S. figure was 15 percent in 1960.[21] But if, in each country, industries are grouped by type and ranked by share of public ownership, the rank orders are quite similar. Transport and utilities are usually near the top of the list, with commerce and finance, and agriculture, forestry and fishing at the bottom.[22] Pryor then offers an empirical explanation for the average degree of public ownership in each industry, using such explanatory variables as economies of scale, the prevalence of externalities, and the amount of earned monopoly rent. He concludes that economic factors cannot be rejected as determinants of the degree of public ownership. However, the fact that the extent of government ownership in all industries differs so much between countries indicates that a country's historical experience, its social and political system, and the legal basis for government intervention in the economy are also important explanatory factors.

REGULATION: THE FUNDAMENTAL DILEMMA

Earlier in this chapter we discussed the industry supply and demand characteristics that often provide a rationale for government regulation and pointed out that in several cases these arguments are weak. We have emphasized the complexity of the natural monopoly argument, suggesting that particular cost, demand, and behavioral conditions *in combination* lead to the breakdown of competition.

Once the decision has been made to regulate an industry, the regulatory activity itself raises a host of new problems. When the government recognizes a natural monopoly and decides to protect the monopolist from competition, it subjects the firm to a variety of regulations designed to prevent the undesir-

---

[20]F. L. Pryor, *Property and Industrial Organization in Communist and Capitalist Nations* (Bloomington, Ind.: Indiana University Press, 1973). See also the condensed discussion by Pryor in W. G. Shepherd, *Public Enterprise: Economic Analysis of Theory and Practice* (Lexington, Mass.: Lexington Books, D.C. Heath and Company, 1976), 3.

[21]Pryor, *Property and Industrial Organization*, Tables 1-2, 6.

[22]Pryor, *Property and Industrial Organization*, Tables 1-6, 11.

able consequences of uncontrolled profit maximization. The regulation of prices, profits, and services will also affect the firm's investment decisions and hence the direction of the industry's growth and other performance characteristics. But because of the number and complexity of a firm's decisions, the effects of government regulation can vary enormously depending on the precise way in which the rules are formulated and enforced. Indeed, the effect of government regulation of an industry may turn out to be very different from its original intention.[23]

We look next at the basic theoretical issues involved in the regulation of prices. (In Chapter 14, we will outline the possible governmental responses in dealing with the basic problem. In following chapters, we shall see how these have been applied to specific industries.) As we shall see, it is the existence of decreasing costs and the indivisibility of supply that form the basis for most of the pricing problems facing regulated industries. Complications on the demand side—in particular, rapidly fluctuating demand—exacerbate the pricing difficulties. Throughout this section, the assumption is that the natural monopoly test has been met and entry is therefore ruled out. The problem of regulating industries that are subject to increasing competitive pressure, and the resulting move towards the deregulation of these industries, are discussed more fully in Chapters 17 and 18.

The Basic Problem

We now examine a model that shows the fundamental dilemma inherent in regulating prices in a decreasing cost industry.

We must first ask: What are the *objectives* that government hopes to achieve through regulation? The answer is complex and lies in the link between economic theory and economic policy. Theorists may begin by identifying allocative efficiency and equity as the goals of regulation and viewing regulated monopoly as a replacement for the perfect market. If so, the prices and outputs that result from regulation should be quite similar or identical to those that would result from a competitive market structure. Even if the cost and demand structures of the two types of industrial organization were somehow comparable, the twin goals of efficiency and equity remain static concepts. The theorist must also face the dynamic problem of choosing an optimal investment strategy to determine rates of output growth, product innovation, and technological change.

---

[23]In his assessment of the effects of regulation, Paul W. MacAvoy documents the relative decline in growth rates and deterioration in the services of regulated industries compared with the nonregulated sector during the 1970s. He attributes this to commission procedures for regulating prices and profits and to the existence of regulatory lag. See P. W. MacAvoy, *The Regulated Industries and the Economy* (New York: W. W. Norton and Company, 1979).

The Model

We begin by examining some of the theoretical problems encountered in a simple static case. Assume:

1.   A monopolist produces a single commodity, X, for which there is a certain and unfluctuating demand, DD' in Figure 13.5.

2.   The firm's average cost curve, AC, diminishes over the relevant output range.

3.   Marginal costs, MC, are constant at level OP_1.

4.   The government's objective is to enforce a price and output combination that maximizes the net benefit to society from the production of commodity X.

Let us now return to the same normative framework, developed in Chapter 3, used to evaluate the effect of monopoly power on the economy.[24] As before, we denote net social benefit (welfare) by the expression $W = TR + S - (TC - R)$, where W is net social welfare, TR is total revenue equal to the price of the product (P) multiplied by the quantity (Q), S is consumer's surplus, TC is total cost, and R is intramarginal rent.[25] If factors of production are available in perfectly elastic supply, the intramarginal rents are zero, and the net welfare expression becomes, as before, $TR + S - TC$.

The objective is to find that level of output which maximizes W. This occurs where price equals marginal cost.[26] In Figure 13.5, the output level at which $P = MC$ is Q_1. At Q_1 net welfare is equal to:

$$OP_1CQ_1 + P_1DC - OLJQ_1 = LDK - KJC$$
$$\quad\text{(TR)}\qquad\text{(S)}\qquad\text{(TC)}$$

No other price would yield as large a welfare area. P_1 is not, of course, the price that maximizes the firm's profits. That is P_3 where marginal cost (MC) and marginal revenue (MR) are equal. At P_3, net welfare is equal to:

$$OP_3MQ_3 + P_3DM - OUNQ_3 = UDMN$$
$$\quad\text{(TR)}\qquad\text{(S)}\qquad\text{(TC)}$$

This is clearly less than LDK - KJC.

---

[24]As noted in Chapter 3, this partial equilibrium welfare approach and some of the following analysis—in particular of the capacity and peak-load problems—is based on the classic article by O. E. Williamson, "Peak-load Pricing and Optimal Capacity under Indivisibility Constraints," *American Economic Review* 56 (1966): 810–827.

[25]Refer to Chapter 3 for a detailed description of each term in the net welfare expression and the shortcomings of this approach.

[26]$W = TR + S - TC$. Differentiating with respect to output, Q, we have:

$$\frac{dW}{dQ} = \frac{d(TR + S)}{dQ} - \frac{dTC}{dQ} = 0$$

which gives $P - MC = 0$, or $P = MC$ (recall that $TR + S = \int P \cdot dQ$).

Figure 13.5 Price Regulation in Public Enterprise—The Basic Problem

With industry demand at level DD', constant marginal costs, MC, and declining average costs, AC, the efficient (welfare-maximizing) output Q_1 (where DD' intersects MC) is sold at price P_1. Since that price lies below the average cost of output (OL = Q_1J), the firm makes a loss equal to P_1LJC.

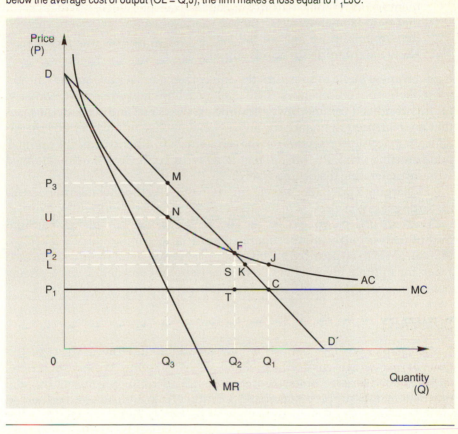

The important point is that at price P_3 profits are maximized (UP$_3$MN), whereas at the welfare-maximizing price P_1 the firm takes a loss (= P_1LJC). This is the fundamental dilemma of public enterprise, which generates a multitude of problems, both theoretical and practical. When a good can be provided at a marginal cost that is less than the average cost of its provision (that is, when average costs are decreasing), setting the welfare-maximizing price (P = MC) will not allow the enterprise to break even. Government has some options to deal with this situation:

1.   It could take over the ownership of the firm and subsidize the provision of the optimal output at P = MC.

2.   It could allow the enterprise to remain under private ownership, but subsidize the provision of the optimal output and price.

3.   It could allow the privately-owned enterprise to charge a price equal to or higher than average cost, for example, P_2 (Point F) in Figure 13.5. This permits the firm to break even or make profits, but prevents the price from being raised to the profit-maximizing level. In this case, government and the regulated firm could develop an alternative pricing scheme that would somehow weigh the loss in allocative efficiency from a higher-than-optimal price against the firm's gain in profits, and that would allow the enterprise to be self-supporting.

If government elects to subsidize the enterprise, it must raise subsidy funds, most likely from tax revenues. Two main problems now arise: first, nonusers of the subsidized commodity will subsidize the users; and second, the taxes that are increased to finance the subsidy (say, excise or income) will distort allocation decisions elsewhere in the economy.[27] In other words, the optimal, nondistorting price, $P = MC$, in regulated industry X cannot be maintained without generating distortions elsewhere.

Charging a price above average cost in the X sector obviates the need for distorting taxation elsewhere but allocates X resources inefficiently. Thus, in the presence of decreasing costs, the allocative efficiency problem (determining optimal output) cannot be separated from the distributional problem (how that output is to be financed.) This dilemma becomes still more complicated when the optimal investment (a dynamic issue) is considered, since pricing policy today affects future demands and the profitability of investments.

SUMMARY

In this chapter we have defined natural monopoly in terms of the subadditivity of costs and discussed the problem of sustainability. We have described and evaluated some common theoretical justifications for government regulation that relate to supply and demand conditions in an industry and presented an empirical approach to identify those industry conditions that are likely to result in government regulation. Finally, we presented the basic model which shows the fundamental dilemma of public utility pricing: When a good can be provided at a marginal cost that is less than average cost, setting the welfare-maximizing price ($P = MC$) will not allow the enterprise to break even.

CONCLUSION

Notice that what we have called the fundamental dilemma of public enterprise is really the public goods problem in a different guise. In Chapter 5, we identified one of the characteristics of a public good as joint supply—once the

[27]Only lump-sum taxes might avoid the distortions. A "lump sum transfer (or tax) is one in which neither the loser nor the gainer can affect the size of the transfer by modifying his behavior." P. R. G. Layard and A. A. Walters, *Microeconomic Theory* (New York: McGraw-Hill, 1978), 36. In other words, a lump-sum tax is one which does not induce substitution effects and therefore appears nondistorting.

good has been provided to one user in a given amount, it can be provided simultaneously to others at low or zero marginal cost. This means that pricing the good is not simply a matter of efficiency. The pricing scheme—say, charging all users the same price—also determines the distribution of benefits from producing the good. In effect, efficiency and equity are inseparable elements in the pricing of a public good.

We also noted in Chapter 5 that one may view the joint supply characteristic in marginal cost terms. Once the good has been provided to one user in a given amount, the marginal cost of supplying all other users with the same amount is zero. If the fixed cost of supplying the good is high (this can be viewed as the marginal cost of supplying the first user), the average cost of expanding supply to a large number of users must be initially high, declining as output increases. This is precisely the cost configuration shown in Figure 13.5, the only difference being that marginal cost in the figure is constant and positive rather than zero. If, in Figure 13.5, marginal cost were zero, the optimal price would also be zero, and the firm's losses at that price would be equal to the total cost of supply.[28]

The underlying phenomenon that links the concept of a public good to the phenomenon of decreasing average costs (implying natural monopoly) is the indivisibility or "lumpiness" of supply.[29] As we noted in the first part of this chapter, if the provision of a bridge, railroad, or electricity service requires a large initial expenditure on land and capital equipment, the average cost curve will decline over a large output range and will reach its minimum point at a very high output level. Depending on the relative level of demand, it may, therefore, be most efficient for a single firm (a natural monopolist) to provide the output in order to achieve lowest average cost.

A public good may also be viewed as a good for which provision in incremental (that is, small) amounts is not efficient. A bridge is not a bridge if it has only one pier and crosses one-quarter of a river. A railroad must link two communities to be useful—it cannot go one mile and stop in the middle of a field. In other words, the technological characteristics of the good are such that its minimum efficient size may be rather large, but, having been provided, it can then be made available at zero marginal cost to a large number of users. Thus, the difficulty of adjusting the quantities supplied of such goods to changes in demand—the indivisibility of supply—results in the failure of competitive markets to ensure that the good is provided in appropriate quantities and provides a rationale for government intervention.

[28]Only if we could identify each user's true willingness to pay for the product and enforce those individual prices—the Lindahl solution—could we find a pricing scheme that is both Pareto optimal *and* enables total costs to be fully covered by total revenues. In the absence of such complicated, and plainly unrealistic, pricing devices, the fundamental dilemma reemerges. A price equal to marginal cost (which may be close to zero) will not generate enough revenues to cover the supplier's total cost.

[29]See J. G. Head, *Public Goods and Public Welfare* (Durham, N.C.: Duke University Press, 1974), 176 ff.

In the next chapter, we discuss various ways in which the government can attempt to solve the fundamental dilemma of public utilities. In the following chapters, we evaluate their use in a number of specific industries.

Discussion Questions

1.   Explain how natural monopoly can occur when average costs do not decrease over the entire output range. In which industries is this cost structure likely to occur?

2.   What is the relationship between fixed costs, common costs, and economies of scale? Is the distinction between these cost categories significant for the definition of natural monopoly?

3.   Evaluate the argument that industries with an inelastic demand are more likely candidates for regulation than those with an elastic demand. What kind of empirical evidence might be useful for your evaluation?

4.   Many industries experience regular demand fluctuations. How should one decide which of these industries should be regulated and subject to peak-load pricing and which left alone?

5.   "The existence of the fundamental dilemma of public utility pricing calls into question the viability of the free enterprise system; planning would be better." Discuss.

Selected Readings

Baumol, W. J., J. C. Panzar, and R. D. Willig. *Contestable Markets and the Theory of Industry Structure.* New York: Harcourt, Brace, Jovanovich, 1982. *A controversial new contribution to the theory of market structure—advanced.*

Faulhaber, G. R. "Cross-Subsidization: Pricing in Public Enterprises," *American Economic Review* 65 (December 1975): 966–977. *A seminal article that develops the concept of sustainability—advanced but accessible.*

Pryor, F. L. *Property and Industrial Organization in Communist and Capitalist Nations.* Bloomington, Ind.: Indiana University Press, 1973. *An interesting cross-country comparison of industrial organization.*

Sharkey, W. H. *The Theory of Natural Monopoly.* Cambridge: Cambridge University Press, 1982. *A clear, comprehensive review of the natural monopoly concept from its origins to the most recent developments.*

CHAPTER 14

• • • • • • • • • • • • • • • • • • • •

REGULATORY RESPONSES TO THE BASIC PROBLEM

We have seen that, in perfectly competitive markets, both cost and demand conditions are important in the determination of price—prices are set by supply and demand. In markets where there is oligopoly or monopoly, profit-maximizing firms are also bound by cost and demand when they choose to produce where marginal revenue equals marginal cost. For a regulated firm, however, competitors are absent and profit maximization is not necessarily the objective. Thus the entire range of price-quantity combinations that lie along the industry demand curve are potential choices. The role of cost in determining the choice then depends on the firm's (or regulator's) objective. In this chapter we identify a variety of pricing rules that government regulators could adopt in an effort to solve the fundamental dilemma of pricing in decreasing-cost industries. In every case, cost and demand both play a role, but the labels attached to the various pricing schemes often emphasize the role of only one determinant (for example, marginal cost pricing refers only to cost, value of service pricing refers only to demand).

As we shall see, the determination of prices depends also on the time horizon under consideration. Thus, whereas we may assume that capacity is fixed in the short run, in the long run the investment decision must be explicitly introduced and the question of what constitutes optimal capacity directly addressed. As always, it is impossible ultimately to separate pricing decisions from investment decisions. For example, if financial self-sufficiency is required, a low short-run price that generates too little revenue now will jeopardize investment in future capacity and necessitate higher prices later. Possibly, inadequate time-of-day pricing may lead to a greater need for capacity to meet peak demand. Thus, the optimal decision-making process should, at some point, include simultaneous consideration of price and investment.

Public utilities recognize this twin problem—pricing and investment—by distinguishing between the *rate schedule* and the *rate level*. State commissions allow privately owned utilities to set rates sufficiently high to reap a fair rate of return on their invested capital. This allows the companies to attract and retain private capital so that they remain viable private concerns.[1] Of course, the definition and measurement of the fair rate of return and of the value of the investment (the rate base) on which the return is allowed are fraught with difficulty.

Once the rate level that generates a fair rate of return has been set, the structure of rates can be determined. While some gas and water utilities charge a flat rate per unit of volume taken (which simply means a uniform price), most companies use more complicated schemes that involve setting different prices for different classes of consumers and/or for different quantities bought or for different times, locations, or other circumstances. A rise (or fall) in the overall rate level need not involve a change in the rate structure if all the rates for different categories move up (or down) in the same proportion. While the rate structure could (in theory) be changed without significantly affecting revenue (in other words, different rate structures may yield the same revenue), most changes in structure do indeed affect revenue and are advocated or opposed precisely because they do.

In this chapter we consider a variety of possible rate structures. We identify the extent to which they meet the objectives of efficiency and equity, and whether or not they raise sufficient revenue to cover costs. We also indicate their importance in the real world of regulated industries. First, we discuss the general policy of marginal cost pricing, which is particularly important for promoting an efficient allocation of resources. We then introduce average, or full-cost pricing and follow with a discussion of pricing schemes that explicitly take into account a break-even constraint—called value of service pricing. Next, we discuss peak-load pricing. Finally, we return to price discrimination as another method of generating sufficient revenue to cover costs.

Chapter 15 provides a more detailed discussion of the break-even constraint—namely, what we mean by normal profit and its counterpart in the practice of price regulation, the fair rate of return. We also discuss some incentives problems arising from the imposition of a profit constraint.

Chapters 16, 17, and 18 contain extensive examples of how these rate structures have been employed. We consider the electricity industry in Chapter 16 and the transportation and communications industries in Chapters 17 and 18.

MARGINAL COST PRICING

In Chapter 2 we saw that in a perfectly competitive industry, the price that equates supply and demand also equals the marginal cost of producing the last unit of output. (Recall that the supply curve for a perfectly competitive firm is

---

[1]Government-owned utilities are also allowed a fair rate of return. A number of studies have investigated whether public and private utilities respond in similar or different fashion to such profit regulation. See, for example, S. Peltzman, "Pricing in Public and Private Enterprise: Electric Utilities in the United States," *Journal of Law and Economics* 14 (April 1971); and L. deAlessi, "Some Effects of Ownership on the Wholesale Prices of Electric Power," *Economic Inquiry* 13 (December 1975).

identical to its marginal cost curve.) We showed that if all industries were perfectly competitive, an efficient (Pareto optimal) allocation of resources would result. Furthermore, if there are constant or increasing average costs (as for firms operating on the upward sloping part of their average cost curves), then the entry (exit) of firms into (out of) the industry in response to changes in demand ensures that all firms are earning at least a normal profit. An extension of the argument to regulated industries might suggest that setting prices equal to marginal cost in these industries (imitating the market result) would preserve efficiency. As we have seen, however, the existence of decreasing costs in a publicly regulated industry creates difficulties even if private sector prices equal marginal costs. An efficient price structure in the regulated industry would yield revenues less than total costs, thus creating the need for a subsidy (probably financed by distorting taxation).

It is apparent that many theoretical problems are associated with marginal cost pricing, and government regulators are unlikely to be cognizant of all the issues. Objections to marginal cost pricing as a general policy frequently include claims that, as a practical matter, it is very difficult to operate. It turns out that these practical difficulties often have a theoretical basis. We shall use the well-known bridge example as a way of introducing some of these issues.[2]

Suppose there exists a bridge of given size that can allow a maximum of $\bar{Q}_1$ cars per day to cross without congestion (see Figure 14.1). What is the meaning of marginal cost in this situation? Suppose the bridge is empty—crossings per day are zero. What is the marginal cost of the first car and of all additional cars up to $\bar{Q}_1$? If there is no wear and tear and no maintenance, then marginal cost is zero. In other words, each car up to $\bar{Q}_1$ imposes no additional cost on society as it crosses the bridge. Now suppose that the demand curve for bridge crossings is D_1. At a zero price $Q_2 < \bar{Q}_1$ crossings are demanded. What toll should be charged?

Assume now that government regulators wish to maximize the net welfare of providing bridge crossings to the general public rather than maximizing the profits generated from bridge tolls. Suppose further that they are not now concerned about whether the costs of the bridge are fully covered. As before, net welfare is defined as TR + S - TC, and is maximized where P = MC = 0. The area of maximum welfare is OAQ_2 in Figure 14.1. (TR, total revenue, and TVC, total variable cost, are both zero, and OAQ_2 consists entirely of consumer's surplus.) This is the welfare condition that a pure public good should be priced at zero.

Suppose now that demand for the use of the bridge rises to D_2. Assume that the first car beyond $\bar{Q}_1$ results in complete congestion and the stopping of traffic so that the marginal cost of providing one additional trip *in the absence of new investment* is effectively infinite. The short-run marginal cost curve SMC_1

[2]See J. R. Minasian, "Indivisibility, Decreasing Cost, and Excess Capacity: The Bridge," *Journal of Law and Economics* 22 (October 1979): 385–397.

Figure 14.1   The Bridge Problem

The bridge has a capacity of $\overline{Q}_1$ cars per day. With demands at D_1, the welfare-maximizing price is equal to SMC_1 at zero; with demand at D_2, the optimal price, equal to SMC_1 at point M, is P_2.

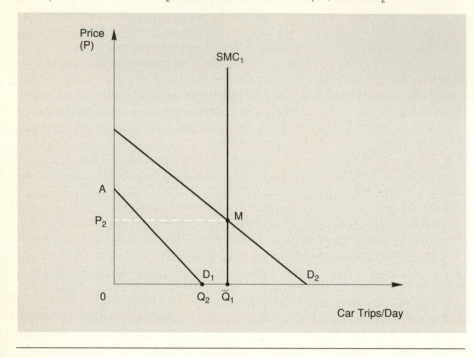

has a reverse L-shape (zero up to $\overline{Q}_1$ and then vertical).[3] Now welfare maximization requires that $\overline{Q}_1$ units be sold. Therefore, price should be set at the level that induces just that quantity to be demanded. This occurs at P_2, where the demand curve intersects the vertical portion of SMC_1 (point M). A higher price will result in a lower welfare area; a lower price will result in queuing or congestion delays.[4] At P_2 total revenue is positive, but there is no particular reason to expect that revenue will be either more or less than the amount needed to defray the original cost of constructing the bridge.

There is, then, a further problem. One could surely argue that the price of a bridge crossing to the consumer should include a portion of capital construction

---

[3]The assumption that the SMC curve has a reverse L-shape is rather unrealistic. In fact, as the number of cars per day increases, the crossing time will increase. In other words, $\overline{Q}_1$ is defined as the capacity limit in the sense of crossings per time unit *at a given speed*. Congestion would then mean that speed falls and the time to cross rises for any given number of car trips across the bridge. We have ignored the speed element here and simply assumed constant speed up to $\overline{Q}_1$ and zero speed (complete congestion) beyond $\overline{Q}_1$. We are also ignoring the variation in the demand curve with time of day and day of the week.

[4]With a low price P, the time delays of queuing and congestion are implicitly equal in value to the difference between P_2 and P; i.e., the money price plus the imputed price is still equal to P_2.

costs, since resources used to build the bridge are not available to be used elsewhere. In other words, while the marginal cost of one additional car crossing may be zero, the cost of the bridge itself is not zero and may be very high.

Does the existence of high capital costs affect the short-run marginal cost pricing rule, and if so, how? What we are talking about here is the investment decision: how large a bridge (or how many bridges) should we build? Clearly, we must know the capital costs of different sized bridges to answer this question. If bridge capacity could be divided into infinitely small parts—in other words, if different sized bridges could be built to accommodate a maximum of 1, 2, 3, or n cars—then all costs would vary with output and one could estimate the additional cost, including the capital cost, associated with each car. This cost curve is the long-run marginal cost curve LMC in Figure 14.2(a), which we have assumed to be constant.[5] We also assume constant returns to scale. The optimal bridge size is then determined by finding the output and price at which net social welfare is maximized. With demand at D_1, this occurs where P = LMC at Q_1^*. Net welfare is P_1AN. If the demand curve now shifts, optimal bridge size changes. But if a bridge of capacity Q_1^* was built to accommodate demand D_1, then in the short run more than Q_1^* trips cannot be provided, and we must operate once again with short-run cost curves. If demand rises to D_2 and capacity is fixed at Q_1^*, price would have to rise to ration the available output. Of course, with demand at D_2, the optimal bridge size is now larger—Q_3^*. But in the short run we are stuck with size Q_1^*; price rather than output must be the market-clearing device. Williamson has shown that if capacity can be added only in lumps (for example, if the choice of bridge size is constrained to either Q_1^* or Q_2^*), it is efficient to move to the larger size only if demand shifts so far to the right that area IJN > area JKL.[6] At the new capacity level Q_2^*, the long-run marginal cost of the last output unit exceeds consumers' marginal willingness to pay for it. Nevertheless, Q_2^* generates greater social welfare than Q_1^*, even though at price P_1 there would now be excess capacity of JK. To use up the excess (which must be done for efficiency) thus requires that price be cut to $P_3 = SMC_2$ at L.

In other words, the optimal bridge size is determined by the intersection of the demand curve with the LMC curve. If demand were stable, the optimal price would remain at LMC. But if demand varies while capacity is fixed, then price must vary so as to equal SMC at each time period. (Price may or may not be above LMC, depending on the relative positions of the demand and cost curves.) Thus, complicated though it may be for public policy, the appropriate price cannot be determined by reference simply to marginal cost. The circumstances of time—short or long run—and the expected level of demand

---

[5]The assumption of constant long-run marginal cost substantially simplifies the argument and makes graphical representation of the model much easier. It does not fundamentally alter the conclusions we will reach.

[6]O. E. Williamson, "Peak-load Pricing and Optimal Capacity under Indivisibility Constraints," *American Economic Review* 56 (September 1966): 810–827.

Figure 14.2   The Bridge Problem with Changing Demand and Capacity

a. With demand at D_1, optimal capacity is Q^*_1. If demand increases to D_2, with capacity at Q^*_1, price should be P_2. If capacity can only be installed in lumps, it should only be increased to Q^*_2 when demand shifts out such that area IJN > area JKL.

b. With capacity at Q^*_2 and demand at D_3, the enterprise makes a loss at the optimal price P_4.

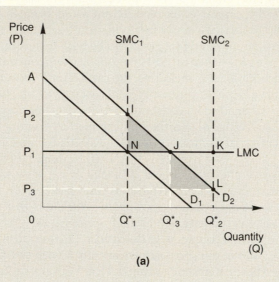

(a)

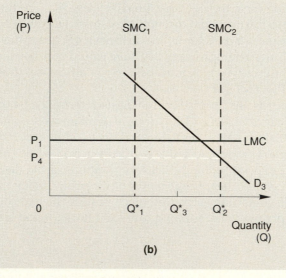

(b)

must be taken into account. Note that if, as we have assumed, the objective of the regulator is to set prices that maximize net welfare, then in the short run there is nothing to guarantee that the enterprise breaks even. If, for example, demand is at D_3 in Figure 14.2(b) and is expected to remain at that level, and if technological considerations restrict maximum bridge size to Q^*_2, then Q^*_2 is the welfare-maximizing choice assuming that price is set permanently at P_4. Notice that at P_4 the enterprise would not break even. In other words, the short-run welfare-maximizing pricing rule does not tell us whether society is in fact willing to bear the cost of the investment in question. It only identifies the best use of the capacity once the investment has been made.

If demand is steady, then choosing capacity so that P = LMC will ensure that resources are invested up to the point where marginal social benefit equals marginal social cost. With constant returns to scale, revenues will just cover costs. However, if technology is inflexible, the capacity to be installed should be based on a comparison between the incremental benefit and the incremental cost. Increments should be added as long as benefit exceeds cost. If that level involves capacity in excess of demand (at a price equal to LMC), the short-run welfare-maximizing price strategy will generate losses for the enterprise, and the problem of subsidy or alternative pricing strategy emerges once again.[7] Indeed, there may be no price at which total cost will be covered.

The two important points to remember are: (1) the criterion for choice in this model is assumed to be the maximization of net welfare, and (2) prices are set in the short run in accordance with this criterion. If some other pricing rule is adopted, then the rules for choosing the optimal capacity levels would have to be adjusted accordingly.

The problem of defining and measuring marginal cost is also complicated by the joint or common cost problem (discussed in Chapter 13). What is the marginal cost of carrying an additional set of coal shipments by rail? Is it the cost of putting the coal into half-empty cars, of adding additional cars, additional trains, or of laying additional track which can support hundreds of trains? As we emphasized above, the question cannot be answered unless we know all the surrounding circumstances of cost interdependencies and (this point is frequently overlooked) *demand*. Moreover, most actual pricing decisions are made on a piecemeal basis. Once again we meet the second best maxim: pricing at marginal cost in one sector is not necessarily efficient if prices in other sectors do not equal marginal cost.

We can already see that the welfare-maximizing approach to pricing in decreasing cost industries raises enormous problems for government regulators. The optimal capacity rule ensures that no investment is made for which the cost is greater than society's evaluation of the benefit. This benefit will itself depend on the way the product is expected to be priced. But once the invest-

---

[7]In this model the bridge possesses alternately the characteristics of a public and a private good, according to the level of demand. When demand exceeds capacity at P = LMC, the short-run price must rise to ration demand (as for a private good). When capacity exceeds demand at P = LMC, then additional output units can be sold at zero short-run marginal cost and the good has "publicness" characteristics.

ment is in place, if actual demand differs from forecast demand, or if demand changes over time, the welfare-maximizing price rules are not only complicated but may often involve financial losses to regulated firms.[8] The public utility commission may be much more concerned about these losses than it is about preserving an efficient pricing scheme and may therefore find it easy to ignore the advice of economists to pay attention to resource allocation. Subsidies for privately owned, publicly regulated firms may be difficult to secure because of political opposition to tapping the general tax pool in order to subsidize users of a specific commodity.[9] Moreover, one cannot readily identify a resource allocation lobby in the political system. In contrast, consumers, stockholders, managers, Congress, and the regulators themselves can all attempt to steer the regulation process in their favor.

Let us look now at pricing schemes that allow a decreasing cost industry to break even, and hence obviate the need for tax financed government subsidies.

AVERAGE COST OR FULL COST PRICING

In the last chapter, we showed that setting a price equal to average cost is one way to solve the break-even problem of decreasing cost industries. In Figure 14.3, DD′ is the regulated monopolist's demand curve; AC and MC are the average and marginal cost curves, respectively. As we saw in Chapter 13, the welfare-maximizing price and output are P_1 and Q_1, where the marginal cost of producing the last unit is just equal to consumers' willingness to pay for that unit (that is, where the marginal cost curve intersects the demand curve at point C). However, at point C the firm makes losses equal to JC per unit of output. One way to avoid these losses is to raise price to P_2 and cut output to Q_2, that is, to choose point F, where DD′ intersects AC. Now the price at which the product is sold is just equal to the average cost of production ($OP_2 = FQ_2$), and total revenue and total cost are equal—the firm is breaking even.

Since welfare is maximized when price equals marginal cost (at point C), it is clear that setting any other price, including a price equal to average cost, will lower welfare. In Figure 14.3 the deadweight welfare loss attributable to average cost pricing is the shaded area FTC.[10] For a single-product monopoly

---

[8]If there are economies of scale, optimal pricing will usually involve financial losses. This is true even if the forecast is precisely realized and there is technological inflexibility.

[9]The use of tax funds to subsidize regulated firms has both efficiency and equity implications. A thorough review of this issue would require an analysis of different tax schemes, in conjunction with the pricing schemes discussed in this chapter. For discussion of the literature on taxation, see Joseph E. Stiglitz, *Economics of the Public Sector* (New York: W. W. Norton, 1986), Part Four.

[10]When price rises from P_1 to P_2, and output falls from Q_1 to Q_2, consumers surplus falls by area P_1P_2FC. But this area is not all lost welfare since area P_1P_2FT represents an increase in total revenue. The *net* loss in revenue plus surplus equals area FTC. (Note that with the fall in output from Q_1 to Q_2, resources equal in value to the area under the marginal cost curve (area $Q_2TCQ_1 = OP_2FQ_2 - OLSQ_2$) flow out of this industry into other productive uses.)

Interested readers can prove that the net welfare loss associated with average cost pricing as compared with marginal cost pricing is also equal to $LP_2FK-KJC$ (=FTC).

Figure 14.3 Average Cost Pricing

With demand at DD', price is equal to average cost at P_2. The marginal cost price is P_1. The deadweight loss of pricing at P_2 rather than P_1 is area FTC.

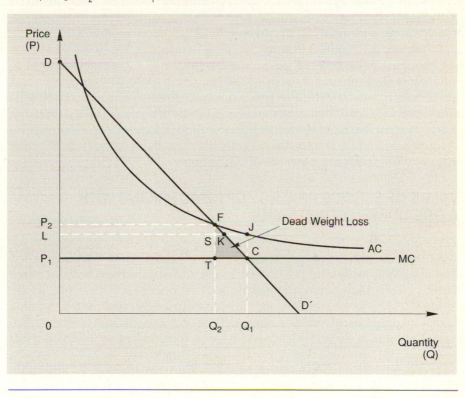

with no close substitutes (thus a low elasticity of demand), the inefficiency caused by pricing at average cost may be fairly small and politically preferable to marginal cost pricing with a subsidy.

But the issue of average cost versus marginal cost pricing becomes particularly important in a regulated industry that contains *competing* firms. Transportation is the major example. This industry does not fit the pattern of other regulated industries. It originally consisted of one dominant mode—the railroads. Railroads often had a near monopoly of shipments to or from small communities. Between major centers, however, many shippers had a choice of two or more competing railroads. Under these circumstances, government regulation was initiated in part to protect the railroads from competition among themselves (see Chapter 17). Over time competition grew, first from water carriers and later from airlines and trucks. These diverse modes became part of the transportation industry and government regulation was extended to include them.

Increasing competition between these modes led to a demand for even-handed regulation of all. As a result, instead of regulating one monopolist, the government found itself responsible for managing a competitive industry. This resulted, paradoxically, in a set of regulated prices different from those that would have obtained under competition. For example, government successfully enforced average cost pricing and prevented the railroads from reducing their prices to marginal costs. Regulation thereby distorted the allocation of traffic between the different transportation modes.

We saw in Chapter 3 that the changing structure of industries and hence the changing boundaries of government regulation of specific industries is inherent in the problems of defining a natural monopoly. The conditions and likelihood of entry and the interaction between dominant firms and potential entrants are all factors that determine the structure of the unregulated industry. A government that regulates the industry without taking entry conditions into account may find the results dramatically different than anticipated. We shall discuss these issues in greater detail in Chapter 17.

VALUE OF SERVICE PRICING: OPTIMAL PRICING WITH A BREAK-EVEN CONSTRAINT

Value of service pricing refers generally to a policy of setting prices for regulated industries based on the elasticity of product demands. We have noted that regulators must (and do) take both cost and demand into account when setting prices. Thus, for example, marginal cost prices are determined where the demand curve intersects the marginal cost curve. By the same token, value of service prices also depend on costs. In this section we discuss the theoretical basis for value of service pricing and refer to some instances in which it has been used. It turns out that recent theoretical contributions have come as a response to existing price-setting practices (in particular by the Interstate Commerce Commission). Theory has largely followed policy, rather than the reverse. But we begin with the theory for the sake of clarity.

We have seen that when prices are set equal to marginal cost, net social welfare is maximized; but if average costs are decreasing, the enterprise sustains losses. Suppose now that, in order to avoid losses, regulators seek a price-output combination that will maximize welfare subject to the constraint that the total revenue of the enterprise must exceed its total costs by some fixed amount M, that is, $TR - TC = M$.[11]

The necessary condition for a maximum is

$$\frac{P - MC}{P} = \frac{\lambda}{1 + \lambda} \cdot \frac{1}{e}$$

[11]Much of the following discussion is based on W. J. Baumol and D. F. Bradford, "Optimal Departures from Marginal Cost Pricing," *American Economic Review* 60 (June 1970): 265-283. Note that optimal pricing with a break-even constraint is sometimes referred to as Ramsey pricing from the seminal article on optimal taxation by F. P. Ramsey, "A Contribution to the Theory of Taxation," *Economic Journal* 37 (March 1927): 47–61. A full discussion of how M is determined appears in Chapter 15.

where: $e = -\dfrac{P}{Q} \cdot \dfrac{dQ}{dP}$ (the elasticity of demand for the commodity).[12]

λ is a multiplier reflecting the cost of the reduction in welfare resulting from the break-even constraint. This condition shows that when a profit constraint is present, the optimal price will exceed marginal cost by an amount proportional to the (inverse of) the price elasticity of demand. When demand elasticity for a commodity is high, the optimal price will exceed marginal cost by *less* than when it is low.

Figure 14.4 clarifies this point. Consider the demand curves D_a and D_b for commodities a and b, which intersect at K. Both commodities have identical and constant marginal costs MC. Suppose the price of each is P_0. What is the loss in net social welfare for each commodity as each one's price rises from P_0 to P_1? Demand is less elastic between P_0 and P_1 for commodity b than for commodity a. The net welfare change is equal to the change in consumers surplus plus the change in net revenue. Since $W = TR + S - TC$, then $\Delta W = \Delta S + \Delta(TR - TC)$. For commodity b, $\Delta S = -P_0 P_1 BK$, and, since initial $TR - TC = OP_0 KH - O(MC)GH = P_0 KG(MC)$, then $\Delta(TR - TC) = P_0 P_1 BD - DKGF$. Therefore,

---

[12]The mathematical derivation of the formula is as follows:

Maximize $W = TR + S - TC$, subject to: $TR - TC = M$. Setting up the equation, using the method of Lagrange multipliers, we have: $L = TR + S - TC + \lambda(TR - TC - M)$. Differentiating with respect to Q, we have:

$$P = \frac{dTC}{dQ} + \lambda\left(\frac{dTR}{dQ} - \frac{dTC}{dQ}\right) = 0$$

that is, $P - MC = \lambda(MC - MR)$.

$$\text{Now } MR = P + Q \cdot \frac{dP}{dQ}, \text{ and } e = -\frac{dQ}{dP} \cdot \frac{P}{Q}$$

Therefore, we can manipulate the first-order condition and, by substitution, derive the required expressions thus:

$$P - MC = \lambda MC - \lambda\left(P + Q\frac{dP}{dQ}\right)$$

$$P + \lambda P = MC + \lambda MC + \lambda Q\frac{dP}{dQ}$$

Dividing through by P we have:

$$\frac{P(1 + \lambda)}{P} = \frac{MC(1 + \lambda)}{P} - \frac{\lambda Q}{P} \cdot \frac{dP}{dQ}$$

Dividing through by $(1 + \lambda)$ and rearranging terms we have:

$$1 - \frac{MC}{P} = \frac{\lambda}{1 + \lambda} \cdot \frac{1}{e}$$

which gives:

$$\frac{P - MC}{P} = \frac{\lambda}{1 + \lambda} \cdot \frac{1}{e}$$

Figure 14.4   Value of Service Pricing

Commodity a has a more elastic demand than commodity b. The welfare loss sustained when price is raised from P_0 to P_1 is equal to area BKGF for commodity a, less than area AKGE for commodity b.

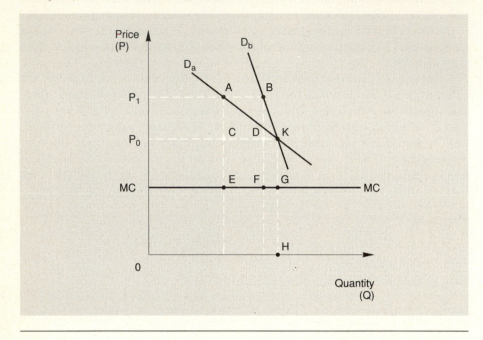

$$\Delta W = -P_0 P_1 BK + P_0 P_1 BD - DKGF = -BKGF.$$

In other words, the price rise for commodity b has resulted in a loss of welfare equal to BKGF. Using the same argument for commodity a, the welfare loss from the price rise is AKGE > BKGF. Therefore, as Baumol and Bradford note:

> In general then (with marginal costs constant), a given price rise will exact a larger social cost in consumers surplus not offset by increased revenues the more elastic the demand curve. That is essentially the reason for the theorem that calls for a relatively small deviation between the price and marginal cost of any commodity whose demand is comparatively elastic.[13]

This rule is interesting, not just from the theoretical point of view, but also because it provides a justification for value of services pricing, which has been common practice in transportation and other industries.

For many years the Interstate Commerce Commission used a complex method to set rates for railroads and trucks.[14] It involved determination of a

---

[13]Baumol and Bradford, "Optimal Departures," 272.

[14]For a detailed description of this system, see Stephen Breyer, *Regulation and Its Reform* (Cambridge, Mass.: Harvard University Press, 1982), 231–234.

large number of commodity classifications. Rates for each class were then set according to formulas that took into account cost factors (tonnage, mileage, weight density, likelihood of damage, and so on) and demand factors (value per pound in comparison with other articles, trade conditions, and competition with other commodities transported). The practical result of this system was to allow higher rates for commodities with low elasticities of demand than for commodities with higher elasticities.[15] Agricultural and bulk commodities with relatively high elasticities, produced primarily in the West, could thus compete successfully in eastern markets. Meanwhile, the high rates on manufactured goods, coming mainly from the East, maximized the burdensome cost of transportation on eastern manufacturers and assisted the development of the infant manufacturing plants of the West. The system could thus be interpreted as an attempt to redistribute sales and income from the eastern to western states.

Another explanation is simply that it was a profit-maximizing strategy for the railroads. The demand for transportation by producers of manufactured goods was relatively less elastic because transportation held a less important share of their cost. Thus the railroads could increase their profits by charging higher prices to shippers whose elasticities were low.[16]

Whatever the reasons for the adoption of value of service pricing, it may be a welfare-improving policy.[17] If government decides against the subsidy route and instead manipulates prices to allow a regulated enterprise to break even, then a set of prices in which the price–marginal cost ratio is low for commodities with high demand elasticities and high for low demand-elasticity commodities, distorts the allocation of resources less than would a uniform price.

PEAK-LOAD PRICING

The peak-load problem arises in industries that combine large fixed capital equipment with demand structures that fluctuate widely over time. Look again at the case of the bridge in Figure 14.1. Assume that the bridge has a maximum capacity of $\overline{Q}_1$ car trips/day and that demand is D_1 for 50 percent of the day in period 1 and D_2 for the other 50 percent in period 2. Now the net welfare-maximizing fee will change from zero in period 1, to P_2 in period 2. In

---

[15]The elasticity of demand by shippers for transportation may be lower, the fewer the available alternatives and the lower the proportion of transportation cost in total cost. Thus, the shipper of a commodity that sells for a very high price, of which transportation expenses are a very small proportion, is less likely to cut demand for transportation when the price goes up, because the effect on the final product price will be small. However, this relationship between high value and low elasticity of demand for transportation does not invariably hold.

[16]This explanation has also been offered for the trucking industry. See Breyer, *Regulation and Its Reform.*

[17]Note, however, that in the case of trucking, for example, where decreasing costs were not present and competition was viable, the effect of regulation was to keep prices higher than would have been the case under competition.

other words, at peak traffic times price should rise to ration excess demand; at off-peak times (when short-run marginal costs are zero) the welfare-maximizing price is zero.[18]

As in all marginal cost pricing schemes, the complication of peak-load pricing arises both in choosing a set of prices that rations the available capacity between the peak and off-peak times and in the choice of optimal capacity—in this case the choice of bridge size. How should the peak and off-peak demands be weighted? Should a bridge be built to accommodate the peak traffic at zero price as well as the off-peak? If not, should capacity be chosen such that the off-peak traffic always goes free? Once again the general problem of interdependence emerges: for a given pricing rule, the choice of capacity implies the appropriate set of prices. Yet selection of the pricing rule must influence demand quantities, thereby affecting optimal capacity.

In the uniform-load case (Figure 14.2(a)) we saw that optimal capacity was determined where the demand curve intersects the long-run marginal cost curve. In the fluctuating-demand case (Figures 14.2(a) and (b)), account must be taken of the fact that in the course of one day various levels of demand, two in our bridge case, obtain at different times.

Williamson develops an ingenious way of aggregating these periodic demand curves into one *effective demand for capacity curve*.[19] In Figure 14.5, D_1 is the off-peak demand curve. Note that the units of the quantity axis are car trips per day and that D_1 measures the number of car trips per day that would be demanded at each price if D_1 held over the whole day. (In fact, we assume it holds only over half the day.) D_2 is the peak demand curve and measures the number of car trips per day that would be demanded if D_2 held over the whole day. (In fact, D_2 holds only over half the day.) To aggregate D_1 and D_2 into D_E, the effective demand for capacity curve, deflate the portion of D_1 which lies above marginal cost vertically by 50 percent as shown by the dotted line D_1(50 percent) in the figure and deflate the portion of D_2 which lies above marginal cost vertically by 50 percent, the dotted line D_2(50 percent).[20] Add D_1(50 percent) to D_2(50 percent) vertically and derive the kinked D_E curve. (A numerical example is provided in the appendix.)

The effective demand for capacity curve can be explained intuitively as follows: Our definition of the net social welfare that results from the production of a good takes into account both the costs and the benefits of the good.

---

[18]Note that while the use of the price system to avoid congestion and excess capacity problems for public goods in the presence of fluctuating demand is the central issue here, such a policy is often *not* chosen in practice. For example, we shall see in Chapter 16 that among the various possible pricing schemes adopted by the utilities and their regulating state commissions, those based on marginal cost have *not* been the choice for many states. We devote space to marginal cost–based schemes because of their efficiency properties and because they provide a useful benchmark for comparison with other schemes.

[19]19 O. E. Williamson, "Peak-Load Pricing," 817.

[20]Recall that the SMC curve has a reverse L-shape. For output levels below $\bar{Q}$, marginal cost is zero. So in this case we simply deflate by 50 percent the entire D_1 curve and the entire D_2 curve.

Figure 14.5   Peak-Load Pricing

The effective demand for capacity curve, D_E, is the vertical sum of the deflated off-peak and peak demand curves. Optimal capacity is at $\bar{Q}$, where D_E intersects LMC. The peak price is P_2, and the off-peak price is zero.

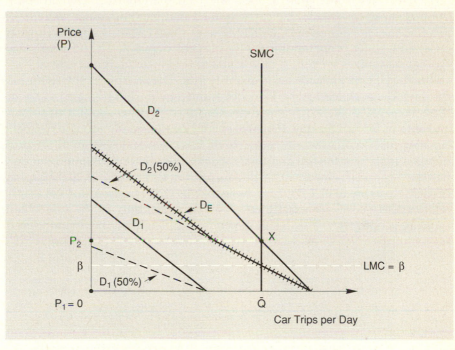

Under this definition, it is clearly inefficient to produce goods for which the marginal costs exceed the marginal benefits. Marginal benefits are measured by people's willingness to pay for the good—in other words, by the demand curve. Since we should produce only those output levels for which marginal benefits exceed marginal costs, we should also invest only in capacity for those output levels for which marginal benefits exceed marginal costs. The relevant part of any demand curve is thus the segment for which demand exceeds marginal cost. When marginal costs are zero, the entire demand curve is included. When marginal costs are positive, the relevant demand for determining capacity construction is that part of the demand curve for which $P - MC > 0$.

Now suppose that there are several independent demands to be considered, for which we must construct an aggregate demand for capacity curve. We will include in the aggregate curve only the relevant parts of each demand curve, the parts for which $P - MC > 0$, and omit those parts for which $P - MC < 0$. The aggregate demand for capacity curve will, therefore, be the vertical summation of the relevant parts of such demand curves, each weighted by the proportion of the day for which they obtain.[21]

Now express the bridge capacity costs on a cost per car trip per day basis—assume they are constant at β. This is the long-run marginal cost curve, LMC. We have assumed that off-peak, short-run marginal costs are zero. Now optimal capacity—that is, the capacity load that maximizes net welfare—is given by the intersection of D_E with LMC at $\bar{Q}$. Once installed, $\bar{Q}$ is the capacity constraint, which is not binding for the off-peak demand. The off-peak price, P_1, that maximizes welfare is now equal to short-run marginal cost at zero, where the D_1 curve intersects the quantity axis. The zero price obtains for half the day. The peak-load price, P_2, is determined by the intersection of D_2 with the vertical part of the SMC curve (reflecting the capacity constraint) at point X, and obtains for half the day. P_2 in this special case is exactly equal to twice the capacity cost. In other words, since the off-peak demand is so small, the peak demand must bear the full marginal capacity cost. Since P_2 obtains over only half the day, and β is measured in dollars per day, P_2 must equal 2β if marginal capacity costs are to be covered.[22] Note that, as in the uniform-load example, total capacity costs are exactly covered (TR = TC) only in the case where capacity is optimal.[23] This result depends completely on the assumption of

[21]To see this another way, consider two demand curves, $P_1(Q_1)$ and $P_2(Q_2)$. Let the weights be W_1 and W_2, respectively, where $W_1 + W_2 = 1$. If $W_1 = 1$ and $W_2 = 0$, the relevant demand for capacity curve is $P_1(Q_1)$ above MC. If $W_1 = 0$ and $W_2 = 1$, the relevant demand for capacity curve is $P_2(Q_2)$ above MC. And if both W_1, $W_2 > 0$, a curve located between the two will be the relevant demand for capacity curve.

[22]Off-peak users share in paying for capacity costs when the LMC curve intersects the D_E curve above the kink. Conversely, when the LMC intersects the D_E curve below the kink (as shown in Figure 14.5), only the peak users pay for the capacity costs.

[23]The pricing and capacity problem can be formulated and solved algebraically as follows: Let Net Welfare = $(TR + S)_1 \cdot 50$ percent + $(TR + S)_2 \cdot 50$ percent - TC. $(TR + S)_1$ is total revenue plus surplus generated in period 1 by the demand curve D_1. Since it is generated over only half the day, the daily $(TR + S)_1$ must be multiplied by 50 percent. Similarly $(TR + S)_2$ is total revenue plus surplus in peak period 2, which is generated over only half the day. TC is total capacity costs at the optimal capacity level (to be determined) and is equal to $\beta\bar{Q}$ where $\bar{Q}$ is optimal capacity. Below capacity, short-run marginal costs are zero by assumption. Thus

$$W = (TR + S)_1 \cdot 50\% + (TR + S)_2 \cdot 50\% - \beta\bar{Q}.$$

Maximizing first with respect to Q_1, we have:

$$\frac{\delta W}{\delta Q_1} = P_1 \cdot 50\% - \frac{\Delta TC}{\Delta Q_1} = 0. \text{ That is,}$$

$P_1 = 0$ for 50 percent of the time; capacity is not binding for the off-peak demand for the case we have chosen.

Maximizing with respect to Q_2, we have

$$\frac{\delta W}{\delta Q_2} = P_2 \cdot 50\% - \frac{\delta TC}{\delta Q_2} = P_2 \cdot 50\% - \beta = 0$$

This gives $P_2 \cdot 50\% = \beta$. That is, $P_2 = \dfrac{\beta}{50\%} = 2\beta$

Capacity is binding for peak demand, and peak price equals twice the capacity costs β.

constant returns to scale. If marginal capacity cost is not constant over all levels of output, revenues generated under peak-load pricing schemes may exceed or fall short of total costs.

If D_1 or D_2 (or both) were to shift, then off-peak and peak prices would be set equal to SMC, but total revenues would not necessarily equal total costs. This is because, given these cost curves, net welfare is maximized and no break-even constraint has been imposed. In general, for a given amount of investment, efficient pricing is not necessarily money making. The imposition of a break-even constraint in the peak-load case complicates considerably the static welfare-maximizing pricing rules. Furthermore, the pressure of such a constraint may give both an unregulated profit-maximizing firm, and a firm subject to rate-of-return regulation an incentive to set prices *lower* at the peak than at the off-peak.[24] In other words, the presence of the breakeven constraint not only complicates the efficiency rules, but may give the regulated firm incentives for inefficient behavior.

In general the rules for dealing with periodic demands are as follows:[25]

1.   Optimal plant size (assuming fully divisible plant) is given by the intersection of the LMC curve and the effective demand for capacity curve.

2.   Optimal price in every subperiod is given by the intersection of the SMC curve and the subperiod demand curve.

3.   In a fully adjusted, continuously utilized system with only two periodic loads:

    a.   Peak-load price always exceeds LMC.
    b.   Off-peak-load price is always below LMC.
    c.   Only when the off-peak load fails to use plant to capacity when priced at SMC does the peak load bear the entire burden of the capacity costs.

The bridge case falls into the 3(c) category above.

The model we have used here employs some important assumptions. When these are relaxed, the peak-load pricing problem becomes a great deal more complicated. On the demand side, we have assumed that the peak and off-peak demand curves are independent of each other. In other words, a change in the peak price will not shift the off-peak demand and vice-versa. This implies that peak and off-peak uses of the bridge are not substitutes (or complements). A change in the price of one will not affect the quantity demanded of the other; the cross-elasticity of demand is zero. But if the demand curves are interrelated, then the solution to the welfare-maximization problem must take this into account. Each demand curve must now be defined

[24]See E. E. Bailey and L. J. White, "Reversals in Peak and Off-Peak Prices," *Bell Journal of Economics* 5 (Spring 1974): 75–92, for a detailed and complete discussion of the problem of peak-load pricing when a profit or break-even constraint is present.

[25]Williamson, "Peak-Load Pricing," 821.

for every price charged in the alternative period. In other words, the position of the off-peak demand, D_1, will depend, among other things, on the level of peak price. If D_1 in Figure 14.5 is drawn under the assumption that the peak price is equal to β and P_2 is set as the peak price, the D_1 curve will shift out in response to the rise in the substitute's price from β to P_2. Similarly, if the peak demand P_2 is drawn under the assumption that the off-peak price is equal to b and the off-peak price is reduced to zero, then D_2 will shift backwards as a result of the fall in the substitute's price. Thus a shift from a uniform pricing scheme (all prices equal to β) to a peak-load pricing scheme could conceivably shift the peak and off-peak demand curves so far that they actually cross over. Then D_2 would become the off-peak and D_1 the peak curve.

Of course, this problem of shifting peaks arises only when insufficient account is taken of the interdependence between the demand curves in setting prices in the first place. It is essentially a result of moving from one price structure to another when demands are interdependent.

On the supply side, we have assumed constant short-run marginal costs (equal to zero in our model) up to the capacity point—the short-run marginal cost curve has a reverse L-shape. This assumption does not necessarily imply that at the optimal capacity level peak users bear the full capacity costs, although this is the case we have shown. If peak and off-peak demands are not very different, it is quite likely that the optimal solution will involve requiring off-peak demand to bear some of the costs. Nevertheless, if the assumption of constant short-run marginal costs up to capacity is relaxed and short-run marginal costs are assumed to be an increasing function of output, then the choice of optimal capacity will depend not only on demand and long-run marginal cost, but also on a comparison of short- and long-run marginal cost.[26]

PRICE DISCRIMINATION

In Chapters 3 and 11, we discussed price discrimination as a strategy open to a monopolist under some circumstances—and one that is illegal in some cases. Through price discrimination, a monopolist can increase profits by tapping the area of consumer's surplus which accrues to consumers under the usual uniform pricing scheme. We have noted that the welfare implications of price discrimination are uncertain. We will not repeat all the arguments here but rather draw attention to two points which are important for public utility pricing.

First, despite its potential illegality in unregulated markets, some forms of price discrimination are employed by public utilities to raise revenue. The two-part tariff (or, more generally, the declining block rate) under which consumers pay a high price for the first units of the commodity bought and lower prices for high quantities is one example (see Chapter 16).

---

[26]Thus Williamson notes that in the nonlinear case, "Price in every period is set equal to short-run marginal cost, and capacity is extended until the weighted average marginal change in operating costs is equal to the marginal capacity cost β." O. E. Williamson, "Peak-Load Pricing," 826.

Figure 14.6 Price Discrimination with Low Demand

Demand curve AD lies everywhere below the average cost curve. With first-degree price discrimination, Q_s would be produced and welfare would be area ABD - DCE>0. Uniform price, P_s, would yield a loss equal to area P_sBCE.

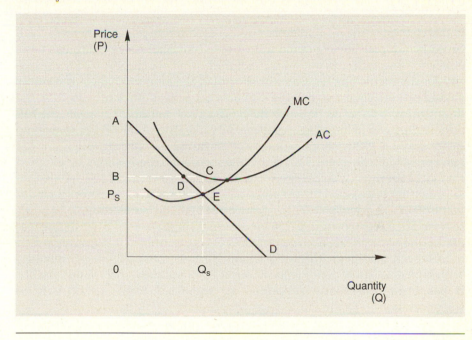

Second, price discrimination may be the only pricing scheme that allows a monopolist (or public utility) to provide a good for which demand is low and still break even (or make a profit). In Figure 14.6, the demand curve AD for a commodity lies everywhere below the average cost curve AC. The socially efficient output occurs at Q_s where the marginal cost curve intersects the demand curve. Net social welfare is maximized at this output level and is given by Total Benefit-Total Cost = $OAEQ_s$ - $OBCQ_s$ = ABD - DCE > 0. Since, by definition, net welfare is positive, the good should be provided. However, if the good is sold at a price P_s, equal to marginal cost, the firm will take a loss (=P_sBCE) and require a subsidy if it is to stay in business. Moreover, there is not other uniform price that will allow it to break even. However, if first-degree price discrimination is adopted, the firm's total revenue will be equal to the entire area under the demand curve. There are now several output levels for which total revenue exceeds total cost. Profit will be maximized at Q_s, which is also the welfare-maximizing output. Of course, one could argue that it is not desirable to have the good provided under such circumstances because consumers are only marginally better off (all their consumer's surplus has been removed) and the benefit from the provision of the commodity goes to the monopolist. This is, as we have noted elsewhere, a question of equity. In practical policy terms, first-degree price discrimination is an unlikely choice, first because detailed knowledge of the demand curve is seldom available, and second because charging different consumers different prices for the same commodity or service is not likely to be acceptable politically.[27]

SUMMARY

In this chapter we have identified a number of different pricing schemes which could be adopted for regulated industries. Marginal cost pricing has basic efficiency properties. In our example of the bridge, we emphasized the necessity for distinguishing between the short and the long run. Short-run prices should ration demand so that the available capacity is efficiently used. In the long run, prices should be set so that consumers pay, at the margin, the full opportunity cost of the good, including the capacity cost. However, there is no guarantee that either short- or long-run marginal cost pricing will allow the enterprise to break even. Therefore, other pricing schemes may be adopted that yield revenues greater than costs.

Setting price equal to average cost is one alternative. Another scheme—value of service pricing—uses the elasticity of demand to determine how much to raise price above marginal cost for different commodities. The welfare loss associated with pricing above marginal cost is minimized if prices are raised more for commodities with low elasticities of demand, and less for commodities with high elasticities. Since value of service pricing also yields higher profits, it has been consistently supported by regulated firms, particularly in transportation.

Peak-load pricing is essentially a more complicated version of marginal cost pricing. The complication arises in the determination of optimal capacity, when different demands are in effect for only part of each day. Once optimal capacity has been determined, peak and off-peak prices are set according to short-run cost and demand.

Finally, we added to our discussion of price discrimination.

CONCLUSION

The pricing rules presented in this chapter are not simple. They all require that the demand and cost functions of the regulated firm be fully known. Moreover, as these functions change over time, optimal prices also change. Given these complexities, one could argue that government policymakers and regulators cannot possibly hope to pursue systematically a policy of marginal cost or peak-load pricing. This is an extreme position. As long as an optimal pricing structure can be identified, it can be used as a benchmark against which to compare existing prices. The fact that marginal cost and peak-load pricing schemes have been successfully employed in other countries should encour-

---

[27]It is interesting that arguments in favor of the declining block rate for electricity were often based on the structure of costs and arguments against it based (among other things) on its inequities (see Chapter 16). In other words, although price discrimination is occasionally used by public utilities, it is a policy vulnerable to attack on equity grounds.

age policymakers in the United States to pursue pricing schemes with a sound theoretical base.

Discussion Questions

1.   "The wrong choice of short-run pricing policy will distort the allocation of resources in both the short and the long run." Discuss.

2.   Value of service pricing is an old policy with a modern theoretical justification. Evaluate the pros and cons of value of service pricing.

3.   Solve the following peak-load pricing problem. Off-peak demand is $P = 20 - 1/3\ Q$; it obtains over one-quarter of the day. Peak demand is $P = 30 - 1/10\ Q$; it obtains over three-quarters of the day. Short run MC is constant and equal to zero. Long run MC is constant and equal to 15.

    a.   Determine the optimal level of capacity.
    b.   Determine the optimal peak and off-peak prices.

4.   "The fact that price discrimination may not be an inefficient policy is irrelevant since it is always an unfair policy." Evaluate this statement.

5.   Is it unrealistic to expect policymakers to put into operation the pricing rules presented in this chapter? In what specific industries might the application of one of these rules improve industry performance?

Selected Readings

Baumol, W. J., and D. F. Bradford. "Optimal Departures from Marginal Cost Pricing." *American Economic Review* 60 (June 1970): 265–283. *This article restates and draws together the preceding literature on optimal pricing when a break-even constraint is present. It is the basis of much subsequent work.*

Kahn, A. E. *The Economics of Regulation: Principles and Institutions*, Vol. 1. New York: John Wiley and Sons, 1970. *Part II of this volume contains a comprehensive treatment of pricing schemes for regulated industries.*

Minasian, J. R. "Indivisibility, Decreasing Cost, and Excess Capacity: The Bridge." *The Journal of Law and Economics*, 22 (October 1979): 385–397. *A complete analysis of the bridge problem.*

Ruggles, N. "Recent Developments in the Theory of Marginal Cost Pricing." *Review of Economics Studies* 17 (1945–1950): 107–126. *The classic and much quoted article that discusses the fundamental dilemma of public utility pricing and its place in the welfare economics literature.*

Williamson, O. E. "Peak-Load Pricing and Optimal Capacity under Indivisibility Constraints." *American Economic Review* 56 (September 1966): 810-827. *The most lucid and complete presentation of the peak-load problem in the literature.*

APPENDIX 14A
Peak-Load Pricing:
A Numerical Example

- Off-peak demand, D_1, is $P = 10 - \frac{1}{5} Q$; it obtains over one-third of the day.
- Peak demand, D_2, is $P = 15 - \frac{1}{10} Q$; it obtains over two-thirds of the day.
- Short-run MC is constant and equal to zero.
- Long-run MC is constant and equal to 10.

Problem: A. Determine the optimal level of capacity.
B. Determine the optimal peak and off-peak prices.

A.   We construct the effective demand for capacity curve, D_E, following these steps (refer to Figure 14A.1):

   1.   Draw the off-peak demand curve, D_1.

   2.   Deflate D_1 by one-third, so we have: $P = \frac{10}{3} - \frac{Q}{15}$. Draw the deflated D_1 curve on the diagram as a dotted line. (Note that since SMC equals zero, it can be ignored in the construction of D_E.)

   3.   Draw the peak demand curve, D_2.

   4.   Deflate D_2 by two-thirds, so we have: $P = 10 - \frac{Q}{15}$. Draw the deflated D_2 curve on the diagram as a dotted line.

   5.   Add the two deflated demand curves vertically, noting that for output levels above $Q = 50$, D_E coincides with the deflated D_2 curve. So D_E is given by:

$$P = (\frac{10}{3} - \frac{Q}{15}) + (10 - \frac{Q}{15}) = \frac{40}{3} - \frac{2}{15} Q, \text{ for all } 0 < Q < 50;$$

$$P = 10 - \frac{Q}{15}, \text{ for } Q > 50$$

Draw D_E on the diagram.

   6.   To find the optimal level of capacity, find the output level at which D_E intersects LMC, that is, for which $P = LMC = 10$. D_E is given by

$$P = \frac{40}{3} - \frac{2}{15} Q, \text{ for } 0 < Q < 50 \text{ Setting } P = 10, \text{ we have}$$

$$10 = \frac{40}{3} - \frac{2}{15} Q; \text{ which yields } Q = 25.$$

The optimal level of capacity is 25.

Figure 14A.1 Peak-Load Pricing—A Numerical Example

Peak demand is D_2, off-peak demand is D_1, and LMC = 10. Optimal capacity is 25, where the effective demand for capacity curve, D_E, intersects LMC. With a capacity of 25 units, the peak price is 12.5 and the off-peak price 5.0.

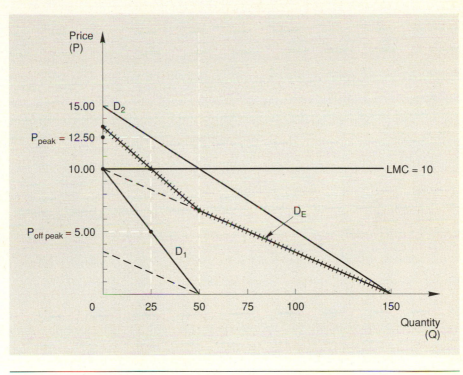

B.   Now find the peak and off-peak prices that obtain when Q = 25.

   1.   Referring to D_1 ($P = 10 - \frac{1}{5} Q$), when Q = 25, P = 5. The off-peak price is 5.

   2.   Referring to D_2 ($P = 15 - \frac{1}{10} Q$), when Q = 25, P = 12.5. The peak price is 12.5.

CHAPTER 15

. . . .

DYNAMIC EFFICIENCY, OPTIMAL INVESTMENT, AND REGULATORY INCENTIVES

In the last two chapters, we considered the problem of optimal pricing for a public utility company with a large amount of fixed capital and an average cost curve decreasing over the relevant output range. We observed that since current pricing policies affect future (as well as current) demands, costs, and profits, they ultimately affect future investment opportunities. The distinction between the rate level and the rate structure made by utilities and their regulating commissions is a recognition of this link between pricing and investment decisions. In Chapter 14, we considered various price structures by which the fundamental dilemma of public utilities could be solved, including a model of optimal pricing subject to a break-even constraint that allows the firm to earn (only) a normal profit.

In the first part of this chapter we look at the meaning of normal profits in economic theory and discuss both what regulators mean by a fair rate of return and how they estimate it. The assumption of fixed capital is relaxed in the second section; some of the factors involved in the firm's choice of an optimal investment level are discussed. Finally, we see how regulation of prices and profits may at times create incentives for regulated firms to act inefficiently— by departing from optimal investment choices. Since investment theory and policy are extremely complicated topics, we will attempt only to raise important issues and indicate some fruitful lines of thought.

THE BREAK-EVEN CONSTRAINT

Normal Profits

In economic theory, profit is defined simply as the difference between total revenue, TR, and total cost, TC. When this difference is zero, the firm is said to be breaking even. Total revenue is the value of sales. Total cost is the value of all inputs used in production and is determined by estimating the opportunity cost (value in the next best alternative use) of the inputs. If we include as inputs management, use of owners' capital, and risk taking, and value these activities at their opportunity costs, then a firm that is breaking even is one that is earning revenue just sufficient to pay all its factors to prevent them from moving to their next best alternative. Risk-taking investors receive a return high enough to prevent them from moving their funds elsewhere. Managers and workers are earning salaries and wages sufficient to prevent them from taking other jobs. Suppliers of materials are just prevented from turning to higher bidders.

The term breaking even, then, does not mean that the firm is failing to make a profit and cannot continue in business. Rather it means that the firm is earning just sufficient revenue to provide the necessary return to its factor inputs, thus allowing it to remain in business. In this situation, the firm is said to be earning normal profits. Normal profits are those returns that the firm must earn to retain all factors of production. In this sense, such profits are an economic cost in that the firm cannot survive without them. Some portion of them, however, is likely to appear as profits in the firm's income statement.

Pure or economic profits are sometimes called excess profits—they exceed the norm. In a perfectly competitive world, resources will always move to those industries in which excess profits are being earned. The resulting expansion of supply will drive industry price down until excess profits in that industry have disappeared. If perfect competition breaks down (for example, because of decreasing costs) and one or several firms become dominant in the industry, then the expectation about the profits the surviving firm(s) will earn is less clear. Should the industry have high barriers to entry, a monopoly price and excess profits may exist. Or if an unstable monopoly structure results, price wars may cause firm profits to become negative. Moreover, if, in the presence of decreasing average costs, the government regulates a firm's price so that it is equal to marginal cost, then losses must result.

One of the characteristics of American public regulation is that in most cases the enterprise itself is privately owned. The regulation of prices and profits is carried out by federal and state commissions that implement laws passed by Congress and state legislature, and whose actions are subject to review by the courts (see Chapter 1 for a more detailed account). Sensible private investors will not keep their funds in an unprofitable business. Government must therefore hold forth the prospect that regulated firms will be allowed to set a price structure that yields all factors a return equal to or greater than their opportunity costs, permitting investors at least a normal rate of return on their funds. For a single-product firm, the price which yields zero excess profits is a price equal to average cost (and greater than marginal cost if average cost is decreasing). In Figure 13.5 (Chapter 13) for example, this price is P_2 where the demand curve intersects the average cost curve.

For a multi-product firm the same level of profit could be achieved by a variety of price sets. The set that maximizes net welfare subject to the break-even constraint follows the inverse elasticity rule explained in Chapter 14.

Two fundamental questions are raised by the requirement that a privately owned, government-regulated enterprise be allowed to set a rate level that permits it to break even. First, does the concept of normal profits have any normative significance in an economy that is not organized in a perfectly competitive way? Second, even if we decide that normal profits are a desirable goal, how can we measure them in an imperfectly competitive economy?

As we have seen, the static case against monopoly as compared with perfect competition contends that monopoly is undesirable for both efficiency and equity reasons. The efficiency case is that the allocation of resources is distorted by monopoly. The equity case is that under monopoly, excess profits persist in the long run and are not reduced by competitive entry. These profits are likely to accrue to those members of society who are already relatively better off than the consumers of the product produced by the monopolist, although this is not inevitably so. In other words, the redistribution from consumers to owners of the firm is likely to be regressive. Therefore, if all industries but one were competitive and constant returns to scale prevailed, the government choice of a price level that generated just normal profits for the single remaining regulated industry would certainly be efficient and most likely equitable. In the absence of perfect competition elsewhere or in the presence of economics of scale, efficient pricing rules become complicated and the distributional consequences of pursuing normal profits become less clear (although limiting a monopolist to a normal return is still likely to be progressive).

There is, however, a dynamic issue involved. Consider the dual function of profits. They are both income to the owners of the firm and an incentive for investors to provide funds for investment in capital equipment (possibly including technical innovation). A firm that wishes to invest in new capacity in order to provide for current and expected future growth in demand may raise the necessary funds in a variety of ways. It may simply retain its current earnings and use them for investment rather than paying them out as dividends to its shareholders. It may borrow from the bank at a fixed rate of interest. It may issue bonds that pay a fixed amount to bond holders. Or it may issue new stock for which the dividend payment to stockholders will vary according to the firm's future earning capacity. The firm's cost of funds in each of these categories will be different and will reflect the different risks and returns associated with each financial instrument. The cost to the firm of raising investment funds—the firm's cost of capital—will therefore depend on the firm's sources of funds and will be a weighted average of the costs of those sources. The cost of capital will vary with the weights chosen (according to the firm's choice of capital structure), with changes in the structure of market interest rates, and with changes in the current market price of the firm's shares.[1] In the absence of regulation, a profit-maximizing firm will assess the cost of raising funds from different sources by looking at market rates of interest and

---

[1]There is much literature concerning the definition and measurement of the cost of capital, including a famous article proposing that the average cost of capital to a firm is constant, irrespective of its capital structure, F. Modigliani and M. H. Miller, "The Cost of Capital, Corporation Finance and the Theory of Investment," *American Economic Review* 48 (June 1958): 261–297. See also W. G. Shepherd, *The Economics of Industrial Organization* (Englewood Cliffs, N.J.: Prentice-Hall, 1979), Chapters 5, 6, and 7, for a good discussion of the basic principles of the financial structure of firms.

share prices.[2] There may be disagreements within the firm about the appropriate choice. For example, some shareholders may prefer a higher dividend payout policy while others prefer to sacrifice current dividends in order to allow for financing investment through retained earnings. A management that systematically pursues policies contrary to the perceived interests of the shareholders may be voted out of office or find its firm the target of a takeover bid. However, in the normal course of events, a competent management will undertake investment if the returns are greater than the cost of capital and where the market has provided an accurate measure of that cost. Investment funds can therefore be expected to flow into profitable opportunities (and away from less profitable ones), insuring an appropriate allocation of resources over time (in the absence of economies of scale).[3]

Consider now the case of the regulated firm. As noted, the regulating commission must allow a privately owned firm to set a rate level that yields at least normal profits or investors will remove their funds. The rate structure that will yield the necessary revenues will then be determined by the kinds of efficiency and equity considerations discussed in Chapter 14. Two difficulties now arise. First, how are the true opportunity costs of funds to be assessed? In other words what rate of return must be promised to investors to prevent them from removing their funds?[4] Second, in the event that demand is expected to grow in the future, what rate of investment is appropriate and what return must therefore be offered to investors to attract new funds? We postpone a detailed discussion of the optimal rate of investment to the second part of this chapter and confine ourselves here to a discussion of the opportunity cost of capital. Note, however, that government regulators may find considerable conflict between the interests of those groups affected by its determination of an appropriate profit constraint. They are thus subject to substantial pressure from all sides to lean one way or the other, quite apart from the overall issues of efficiency involved.[5]

---

[2]Note that when the definition of profits is expanded to include expected future profits, the notion of profit maximization is no longer unambiguous. Since any given current price and investment policy may be associated with a number of different expected outcomes, all with different probabilities of occurrence, management's attitude toward risk and its time horizon for decision making will also determine how it makes its current policy decisions.

[3]We may expect profits to be high in the future if the firm has and maintains a monopoly position in the market. Whether investment is likely to be high or low in industries with monopolistic market structures compared with more competitively organized industries is an open question (see Chapter 3).

[4]Note that where equity investment is concerned the removal of funds from the firm is not strictly possible. That is, shareholders cannot remove their common equity investment since the company will not usually buy the shares back. Rather, they must sell their shares to other buyers.

[5]For example, the interests of the consumers of the firm's product will be served initially by low prices and profits. But if low profits jeopardize future investment and technological change, then future prices may be high as a result. The interests of the shareholders will initially be served by high prices and profits. (Indeed, since regulated industries are in many cases natural monopolies,

Fair Rate of Return

The legal history of the issues surrounding determination of the profit constraint for regulated industries is complex. It is closely bound up with the question of how we should measure the profit rate. So far, we have defined profit simply as TR - TC, a dollar flow per unit of time. For the purpose of comparison between firms of different sizes, the dollar flow is usually expressed as a rate of return on the owners' capital stock:

$$\text{Rate of Return} \ = \ \frac{\text{Profit (TR - TC)}}{\text{Capital Stock (K)}} \tag{15.1}$$

that is,

$$r_x \ = \ \frac{TR - TC}{K}$$

Knowing the value of total revenue (TR), total cost (TC), and the capital stock (K), we can determine the rate of return r_x. Or, rewriting the equation as:

$$TR \ = \ TC + r_x K \tag{15.2}$$

and given the values of TC, r_x, and K, we could determine TR.

In practice, the equation used by government regulators to determine the set of prices that would yield a fair rate of return is different from equation 15.2:

$$RR \ = \ OC + T + D + r_a K \tag{15.3}$$

where

RR = the revenue requirement
OC = operating costs
T   = taxes
D   = depreciation allowance
r_a = the allowed or regulated rate of return
K   = the value of the firm's capital assets.

---

the regulated price is almost certainly below the short-run profit-maximizing price and the shareholders and management of the regulated firm will almost invariably push for higher prices.) But if the high current price reduces future demand, then profits may eventually fall. Government regulators may have a clear idea about how the choice of profit constraint will affect distribution in the short run. Lower prices and profits, for example, favor consumers and harm stockholders. The long-run effects on distribution are much less clear and may be unexpectedly undesirable. Paul MacAvoy argues, for example, that regulation during the 1970s forced industries such as electricity, airlines, and railroads into decline, with profit constraints curtailing investment to such an extent that the quantity and quality of service seriously deteriorated. P. MacAvoy, *The Regulated Industries and the Economy* (New York: W. W. Norton and Company, Inc., 1979), 73. It would be difficult to argue that such an eventuality represents either a boon to the customers of these industries or a goal of government regulators. Rather it appears to be the unfortunate outcome of a clash of perceived interests in determining the level of the profit constraint.

The regulating commissions then determine prices as follows: the allowed (or "fair and reasonable") rate of return is determined first using information from the regulated firms, consumers, and other interested parties. After estimating values for K, OC, T, and D, the commissions then allow the regulated firms to set prices so that the revenue raised from the sale of output equals the revenue requirement RR. That is, RR is determined, *given* the values of OC, T, D, K, and r_a. These values cannot then be determined by RR, but are its determinants. RR is then the value of total revenue (TR) which just equals OC + T + D + r_aK.

Let us consider how equations 15.2 (derived from theory) and 15.3 (used in practice) can be reconciled. We begin by looking at total cost (TC). As we have seen, in economic theory this term should include the opportunity costs of all factors used by the firm in producing its product, including the opportunity cost of capital. Indeed, the opportunity cost of capital must be included in TC if r_x is to be a measure of the *excess* profit rate. (For a firm earning normal profits r_x would then be zero.) Let us call the opportunity cost of capital r_o and write TC as the sum of operating costs OC (variable costs) and fixed costs, written as r_oK. Thus TC = (OC + r_oK). Now

$$r_x = \frac{TR - (OC + r_oK)}{K} \qquad (15.4)$$

that gives TR = $K(r_x + r_o)$ + OC. Thus, if TC is used in its theoretically correct form, the rate of return, r_x, is an excess profit rate. However, in practice, as we have noted, the allowed rate of return, r_a, is not an excess profit rate. Moreover, two other cost categories (taxes and depreciation) are explicitly introduced. Rewriting equation 15.3 we have:

$$r_a = \frac{RR - (OC + T + D)}{K} \qquad (15.5)$$

For simplicity, let T = D = O, and define RR as equal to TR. Now from equations 15.4 and 15.5 we have:

$$r_a = r_x + r_o. \qquad (15.6)$$

where

r_o = opportunity cost of capital
r_a = allowed rate of return
r_x = $r_a - r_o$ = excess rate of return.

Let us now consider some of the issues that arise when we attempt to measure the variables in these equations.

Total Cost (TC)   The total cost curve, in economic theory, is drawn under the assumption that factors are combined in such a way as to minimize the costs per unit of output. This implies the absence of nonessential expenses and complete efficiency in firm organization. Under competitive pressure, this assumption may be approximately realized. Under government regulation, however, the firm may allow its costs to increase wastefully. Such an increase must reduce measured profits. But if the allowed rate of return is fixed, the cost increase will justify a request for a price increase. Now prices, revenues, and costs are higher than before and the rate of return is the same.[6] But included in costs are, for example, higher wages or perks for management and an easier, though less efficient, management system. In other words, the higher costs include an element of economic waste that would not be allowed if it had to be explicitly reported as profit. This is precisely the difficulty that characterizes all *cost-plus* contracts. If one agrees to pay a supplier a given amount above costs of supply, there is no strong incentive to minimize those costs.

To prevent this situation from occurring, a system of accounts for public utilities has been designed to help identify what can legitimately be included as expense. In general, the managers of regulated firms are allowed a great deal of discretion in determining the appropriate level of costs, but in 1936 the Supreme Court upheld the right of regulatory commissions to disallow improper expenses.[7] However, even if costs are monitored, the regulated manager may not seek out cost savings as vigorously as the manager under competitive pressure. We discuss the problem of regulatory incentives further below.

Capital Stock (K)   The rate base is the value net of depreciation of the assets used by the regulated firm in the production and distribution of its commodities or services. It comprises the company's plant and equipment as well as an allowance for working capital. How to value the firm's plant and equipment has generated years of economic and legal controversy. The question of the value of capital lies at the heart of all economic theories of value.[8] It is, therefore, important to remember that the inability of public utility regulators to solve the problem for regulation purposes, and the extraordinarily muddled statements made by the courts, spring from the extremely complicated theoretical issues involved. We saw in Chapter 1 that the *Munn v. Illinois* (1877) decision legalized government regulation of prices for private property "affected with a public interest." No guidance was given, however, as to the appropriate level of prices and profits for such firms. But in 1898 in the famous case of *Smyth v. Ames,* the Supreme Court established (on the basis of the Fourteenth Amendment) that the owners of regulated property were entitled to just compensation based on the fair value of the property. Thus:

---

[6]This assumes implicitly that the elasticity of demand is less than one, so that raising prices will raise revenue. If the elasticity were greater than one, the appropriate revenue-raising policy would be to lower prices (providing that the marginal revenue from the additional output units were greater than their marginal cost). A good example of regulated firms pushing government regulators for lower prices is the railroads, who often argued with the ICC that they should be allowed to reduce prices to marginal cost so as to increase revenue. In this case the elasticity of demand was very high because of the presence of close substitutes (see Chapter 17). For many public utilities, however, raising revenue is treated almost synonymously with raising rates.

[7]*Acker v. U.S.,* 298 U.S. 426.

[8]We cannot begin to discuss this problem here, but see P. Deane, *The Evolution of Economic Ideas* (Cambridge: Cambridge University Press, 1978), for an excellent approach.

The corporation may not be required to use its property for the benefit of the public without receiving just compensation for the services rendered by it . . . . The basis of all calculations as to the reasonableness of rates to be charged by a corporation . . . must be the fair value of the property being used by it for the convenience of the public.[9]

Underlying this language is the idea that the owners of private property should not be unfairly deprived of the income from that property. The government has a right to regulate the private sector in some circumstances but it may not upset the preregulation distribution of income in such a way as to be unfair to the owners of the regulated property.

In the first of his essays on capital theory and the rate of return, Robert Solow suggests that the important issues are those relating to the causes and consequences of saving and investment—the dynamic counterpart of the static idea of the efficient allocation of resources.[10] The distribution of the income from capital, Solow argues, is an entirely different and perhaps less important issue.

The dynamic issues are, however, essentially planning questions. Consideration of these issues, he suggests, does not require an evaluation of the existing capital stock, but rather estimation of the rate of return on additions to the capital stock or new investment. The future profitability of investment is more important than the value of the existing capital stock.

Without a satisfactory account of behavior under uncertainty we cannot have a complete theory of capital . . . . It does not really matter whether "capital" is a primary factor of production, nor is it especially important to ask how "capital" is to be measured. For there is no reason to suppose that any single object called "capital" can be defined to sum up in one number a whole range of facts about time lags, gestation periods, inventories of materials, goods in process, and finished commodities, new machines and buildings of various desirability and more or less permanent improvements to land.[11]

As we have seen, any decision about the appropriate level of profit for a regulated firm affects both current income distribution and future investment. Both questions are the legitimate concern of policymakers and they are so intertwined that decisions about one alone must directly affect the other. In 1898, the focus of *Smyth v. Ames* was clearly on the relative income of capitalists, the legitimacy of government activity in the private sector, and its effect on the value of private property. The dynamic effects of regulation on the investment policies of regulated firms were ignored. Thus, the problem of how precisely to sum up the values of the different types of assets owned by a regulated firm became one of the major issues in the history of government regulation.

In *Smyth v. Ames* the Court did in fact list a number of factors to be taken into account in determing the fair value of assets:

The original cost of construction, the amount expended in permanent improvements, the amount and market value of its bonds and stock, the

[9]*Smyth v. Ames*, 169 U.S. 466 (1898).

[10]R. Solow, *Capital Theory and the Rate of Return* (Chicago: Rand McNally, 1964).

[11]Solow, *Capital Theory*, 13–14.

present as compared with the original cost of construction, the probable earning capacity of the property under particular rates prescribed by statute, and the sum required to meet operating expenses, are all matters for consideration, and are to be given such weight as may be just and right in each case. We do not say that there may not be other matters to be regarded in estimating the value of the property.

Charles Phillips notes that of the measures specifically mentioned by the Court, four were subsequently rejected as being improper measures of value and only two remained: (1) original cost, including expenditures on permanent improvement; and (2) present, current, or reproduction cost.[12] Two items mentioned by the Court, earning capacity and the market value of stocks and bonds, were rejected because they involve circular reasoning. The rate base, K, is used to determine rates and hence total revenue, TR. But company earnings, TR - TC, and the market value of stocks and bonds both depend on TR and therefore cannot simultaneously be used as a determinant of K.

A debate raged for decades over whether original cost or reproduction cost of assets was the correct measure. Not surprisingly, issues of equity seem to be at the heart of the controversy. Phillips observes:

> Before World War I, regulated companies based their valuation estimates on original cost, while commissions based theirs on reproduction cost. But during the war, construction costs soared, and reproduction cost became higher than original cost. Consequently the two parties changed sides. The companies now began to demand consideration of reproduction cost; the commissions started to urge original cost. This switch led one observer to comment: "The position of the various contestants has been largely opportunistic."[13]

These remarks raise obliquely the question of the objectives of the regulatory commissions in the setting of rates. Whose interests are the commissions pursuing when they enter into the rate-setting process? By 1944 the confusion of arguments had become so great that the Supreme Court made an important change in the rules. In the *Hope Natural Gas* case, the Court introduced what became known as the end result doctrine, stating that a commission (here the Federal Power Commission):

> Was not bound to the use of any single formula or combination of formulae in determining rates . . . . [U]nder the statutory standard of "just and reasonable" it is the result reached not the method employed, which is controlling. It is not theory but the impact of the rate order which counts. If the total effect of the rate order cannot be said to be unjust and unreasonable, judicial inquiry under the Act is at an end. The fact that the method employed to reach that result may contain infirmities is not then important . . . .[14]

It was widely noted that determining whether final rates are reasonable is problematic if we cannot determine whether the method used to determine them is reasonable. This decision did, however, relieve the regulated firms and the commissions from ploughing through the quagmire resulting from *Smyth*

[12]C. F. Phillips, Jr., *The Economics of Regulation* (Homewood, Ill.: Richard D. Irwin, 1969), 220.

[13]Phillips, *Economics of Regulation*, 221.

[14]*Federal Power Commission v. Hope Natural Gas Co.*, 320 U.S. 591 (1944).

v. Ames and gave them more leeway in deciding upon the method of rate determination.

Most modern assessments of the rate base are now based on original cost less (plus) economic depreciation (appreciation). The reason for this choice is that attempting to assess replacement cost (which may indeed be a closer measure of the opportunity cost of the firm's assets) is simply too difficult a task for regulators to achieve.[15]

Let us now turn to the measurement of the rate of return and evaluate more carefully the premises on which the rate-making procedure is based.

The Rate of Return   Recall Equation 15.6 that identifies the relationship among three different definitions of the rate of return:

$$r_a = r_x + r_o$$

Where

r_a = allowed rate of return
r_o = opportunity cost of capital
r_x = $r_a - r_o$ = excess rate of return.

Much of the discussion of the appropriate rate of return for regulated industries focuses on the measure of r_o, the opportunity cost of capital, and is therefore really an argument about cost rather than profit. Once r_o is determined, the r_x part of r_a is then added on. But as we shall see, procedures for the determination of r_x are nowhere clearly set out. Thus in regulatory commission proceedings and court statements, rate of return refers to r_a, not r_x. Of course, if the regulating commission is trying to duplicate the competitive result when it sets prices, then excess profits, r_x, will be zero and the allowed rate of return, r_a, will be exactly equal to the opportunity cost of capital, r_o. This does not solve the problem of how to attract new investment funds when demand is rising.

Judicial statements about the factors that should enter into the determination of the rate of return are typically vague. For example, in 1923, in the *Bluefield* decision, the Supreme Court stated:

> A public utility is entitled to such rates as will permit it to earn a return on the value of the property which it employs for the convenience of the public equal to that generally being made at the same time and in the same general part of the country on investments in other business undertakings which are attended by corresponding risks and uncertainties; but it has

[15]Stephen Breyer gives the following example: "How should a regulator determine the replacement value of an airplane that costs $10 million when new? Its value (if the regulator's objective is to replicate competitive prices) is the cost of new equipment that would do a similar job—say, carry 150 passengers from Boston to Atlanta. But this cost is not necessarily the $10 million price for a new plane, for, if replacement were at issue, the company might change its route or fleet configuration or simply shrink its fleet size. Indeed, if fewer planes could do the same job as effectively (by increasing the load of each plane), the replacement value of any individual plane is arguably zero." S. Breyer, *Regulation and its Reform* (Cambridge, Mass.: Harvard University Press, 1982), 39.

no constitutional right to profits such as are realized or anticipated in highly profitable enterprises or speculative ventures. The return should be reasonably sufficient to assure confidence in the financial soundness of the utility and should be adequate, under efficient and economical management, to maintain and support its credit and to enable it to raise the money necessary for the proper discharge of its public duties. A rate of return may be reasonable at one time, and become too high or too low by changes affecting opportunities for investment, the money market and business conditions generally.[16]

Elsewhere, the Court has argued that government regulation of the rate of return should not protect a company's profits against mismanagement or adverse economic conditions.[17] In other words, regulation should permit but not guarantee a fair rate of return. In recent years rules for determining the cost of capital as a major element of the rate of return have been emphasized and conflicts have arisen far more at the commission level than in the courts. This, of course, is the result of the *Hope Natural Gas* decision giving the commissions much more flexibility in developing their own rules of rate-making.

Recall that the cost of capital is defined as a weighted average of the cost of raising money in various ways. We can write this in simplified form as:

$$r_o = r_D \cdot \frac{D}{K} + r_E \cdot \frac{E}{K} \qquad (15.4)$$

where

r_o = opportunity cost of capital
r_D = after-tax cost of debt
r_E = cost of common equity
D = market value of debt
E = market value of equity
K = $D + E$.

The cost of debt may be fairly easy to determine because interest rates on these relatively less risky assets have not (until recently) been very volatile. The cost of raising funds from equity is much harder to determine. The first problem which arises is that if new investment is to be undertaken, new shares may be sold to raise the required funds. Even if the dividend expected by new shareholders is less than the dividend currently earned by existing shareholders, the firm may still be able to raise the required capital by selling new shares. However, more new shares will have to be sold at a reduced price and the price of all shares will come down. The result will be a loss for the old shareholders. Their shares are now worth less and they hold a lower percentage of the total shares.[18] Even if such dilution of equity is avoided, the problem of measuring the cost of new investment funds remains. There are three main approaches:[19]

---

[16]*Bluefield Water Works and Imp. Co. v. Public Service Comm. of West Virginia*, 262 U.S. 679, 692–693 (1923).

[17]*Public Service Commission of Montana v. Great Northern Utilities Co.*, 289 U.S. 130, 135 (1935).

[18]See Breyer, *Regulation and Its Reform*, for a numerical example of this phenomenon.

[19]Breyer, *Regulation and its Reform*, 43.

(1) In the comparable earnings method, attempts are made to assess the earnings in comparable industries with similar risk. (2) In the discounted cash flow method, an attempt is made to evaluate the internal rate of return on a given investment by estimating the implied rate of return, given the stock price and the stream of future profits.[20] (3) The capital asset pricing model states that the rate of return on equity in utilities is a function of the rate of return on a risk-free asset, the stock-market risk premium, and the extent to which utility stocks have historically varied compared with the market in general.[21] All of these methods involve quite complicated analysis and calculations. The effect, in rate hearings, is to provide considerable flexibility for advocates of different interests to argue for a different final number.

As we pointed out at the beginning of this chapter, once the decision is made to set prices at or above average cost, the rate level chosen is essentially an equity decision. Insofar as the courts have been concerned with the protection of the value of private property, this decision has been made in favor of the existing distribution of income. It is interesting that, in spite of frequent references to the need to give investors a fair and adequate return on their invested funds, there is little systematic discussion of the problem of the optimal rate of investment of new capital for regulated firms. This problem seems to be viewed as an internal firm management decision rather than a direct concern of the regulators.

The dynamic investment question should be high on the agenda of public regulation. As important as it is to be fair today, decisions about the expansion of vital industries will affect our economic well-being for generations to come. Defining the socially correct investment or expansion rate, moreover, is a formidable task under the best of circumstances. In a regulated industry setting, the job is even more intractable.[22] In the following section, we introduce some of the basic principles involved.

OPTIMAL INVESTMENT

In Chapter 2, we examined the virtues of the market system and saw that perfect competition would result in an efficient allocation of resources. This is a state of affairs in which resources are combined in production of goods and services and distributed among consumers in a way that could not be changed so as to make one person better off without making another person worse off.

This idea, Pareto efficiency, has to do with the appropriate use of existing scarce resources. It provides a criterion for evaluating economic performance

---

[20]See the section on optimal investment in this chapter for an explanation of this concept.

[21]Breyer, *Regulation and Its Reform*, 46. See also D. R. Hesington, *Portfolio Theory and the Capital Asset Pricing Model* (Englewood Cliffs, N.J.: Prentice-Hall, 1983).

[22]There is, however, much regulatory and public interest in rationing demand (for example, by more efficient pricing schemes) so that expansions in capacity will not be so essential.

in a static context and allows us to compare the economic outcomes of different market structures—say, perfect competition versus monopoly—using allocative efficiency as the benchmark.

However, all economies change over time. New natural resources may be discovered, capital investment takes place, population grows, and the output of goods and services expands as a result. The problem now becomes one of identifying the optimal growth rate for society; in other words, developing a criterion for evaluating economic performance over time.

The importance of this question for economic policy in general, and for government regulation of industry in particular, lies in the fact that societies have some control over their growth rates via investment. Investment is defined as additions to the capital stock. Capital is a productive resource itself produced from existing resources. The decision to produce capital today will involve some sacrifice of other goods if the economy is close to full employment, but it will expand the resource base so that more of all goods can be produced in the future. Societies must make choices about how much current consumption to give up in order to increase future consumption through capital investment. The choices depend on the cost and productivity of capital (how much current consumption must be sacrificed for each additional capital unit), on the potential gains from each unit of capital, and on society's preferences for future versus current consumption.

A full discussion of the relationship between capital investment and growth, the choice of an optimal growth rate, and the kind of economic organization that would generate that growth rate would take at least another book.[23] In this section, we confine ourselves to a few of the problems faced by an individual firm when it decides on its investment policy. In the next section, we shall examine the effect of government regulation of prices and profits on the firm's investment choices. Bear in mind throughout that normative questions concerning the best use of resources are quite fuzzy in a dynamic context. Some of the reasons for this are explained next.

The Optimal Choice of Inputs

We can start by considering the most efficient combination of inputs used by a firm when one of the inputs is capital. By efficient we mean the least costly way of producing a given output level. (Given output puts us squarely in a static framework.) Suppose the firm's production function is given by:

$$Q = f(K,L),$$

where

---

[23]Recall Chapter 3, in which we present an argument to show that while monopoly may be inefficient compared with perfect competition in the static sense, it may generate faster growth rates and therefore be more desirable in a dynamic context.

Q = output
K = capital, measured in machine hours
L = labor, measured in labor hours.

The optimal combination of capital and labor then satisfies the equation:

$$\frac{MP_K}{MP_L} = \frac{P_K}{P_L}$$

where

MP_K = marginal product of capital
MP_L = marginal product of labor
P_K = price of capital
P_L = price of labor.

In other words, the cost of producing a given quantity of output is minimized when the amounts used of capital and labor are such that the ratio of the marginal product of capital to the marginal product of labor is equal to the ratio of their respective prices. For example, suppose the last machine hour is three times as productive as the last labor hour, MPK/MPL = 3/1. If the price of one machine hour is equal to the price of one labor hour (if P_K/P_L = 1/1), then it would clearly reduce the cost of producing a given number of output units if more capital were used and less labor, since one dollar's worth of capital produces three times as much as one dollar's worth of labor. The firm should continue to shift from labor to capital as long as the ratio MP_K/MP_L exceeds the price ratio P_K/P_L. As the shift is made, the relative productivity of capital compared with labor falls. When the ratios MP_K/MP_L and P_K/P_L are equal, costs are minimized. (See Appendix 15A.1 for a diagrammatic explanation.)

Consider another approach. Assume that labor is held constant and the firm is a profit maximizer. Recall that the marginal product of any input is defined as the addition to output associated with the use of one additional unit of input when all other inputs are held constant. The marginal revenue product (MRP) of an input is the addition to total revenue resulting from the use of one additional unit of the input. Under perfect competition, an input's marginal revenue product equals its marginal product multiplied by the price at which one unit of output is sold. It is referred to as the value of the marginal product (MRP = VMP = MP· price of output.) The optimal amount of capital to be used, given fixed labor, will occur when the value of the marginal product of capital (VMP_K) equals the price of capital (the price of a machine paid to machine suppliers). VMP = $MP_K · P_O$= P_K where P_O equals the price of output and P_K equals the supply price of a machine. As long as VMP_K exceeds the price of capital, the firm can increase its profits by employing more capital. But if VMP_K is less than the price or cost of capital to the firm, employing less capital would increase profits. The equilibrium or profit-maximizing amount of

Figure 15.1   The Choice of Optimal Capital Stock

The value of the marginal product of capital (VMP_K) diminishes as more capital is employed. When the price of capital is P_K, the efficient amount of capital is K^*.

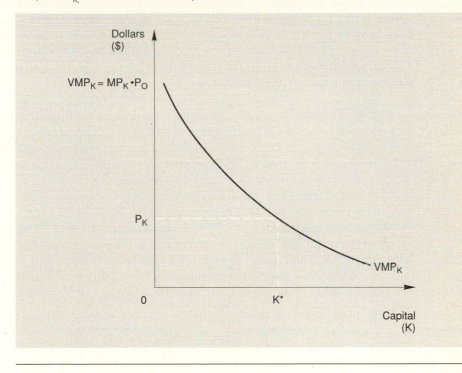

capital, therefore, occurs where VMP_K and P_K are equal.[24] For an imperfectly competitive or monopoly firm, the marginal revenue product of an input equals its marginal product multiplied by the marginal revenue derived from the output produced by the additional input unit ($MRP = MP \cdot MR$). In Figure 15.1 the curve VMP_K represents the value of the marginal product of capital as different quantities are combined with the given amount of labor to produce different output levels. The curve declines as K increases, reflecting the law of diminishing returns. If the price of capital is P_K, then K^* is the optimal amount of capital, where $VMP_K = P_K$.

---

[24]This is the condition under perfect competition. For an imperfectly competitive firm, the condition is that $MP_K \cdot MR_o = P_K$ where MR_o equals the marginal revenue for the last unit of output. Note that, as more capital is added to fixed labor, output increases. Therefore the condition $VMP_K = P_K$ is based on the premise of fixed labor and varying output and capital. By contrast, the condition $\frac{MP_K}{MP_L} = \frac{P_K}{P_L}$ defines the optimal combination of capital and labor to produce a given or fixed output. That is, capital and labor vary, output is fixed.

Some Complications　This is a very simplified picture of the process by which a firm's most efficient input combination can be identified.[25] It also masks some complicated problems that arise when we attempt to fit capital into an essentially static framework. Consider first what is meant by the marginal product of capital. For capital, the increase in output or revenue from one additional machine hour may be measured in a time-free context. But the increase in output or revenue associated with one new *machine* is spread out over future years. The total additional output or revenue from the machine therefore involves adding up the stream of future outputs or revenues.

Discounting Future Returns　Two basic problems now arise. First is the fact that a dollar to be received in the future is worth less than one dollar received now. Thus 50 units of output or $50 of revenue produced or received next year is worth less than 50 units or $50 now. If $50 of revenue earned next year is to be added to $50 earned now, next year's $50 must be reduced or discounted in value before it is added into the sum. The proximate reason for this is the interest rate. If, by putting $1 in a savings account at the bank, I can earn 5 percent per year in interest, that dollar will be worth $1.05 at the end of the year. Let R_o equal the original principal—one dollar—and i equal the rate of interest, 5 percent; then R_1, the value of R_o at the end of the year, is equal to $R_o + iR_o = R_o(1 + i) = R_1$. After two years, R_o will be augmented by two years' worth of interest. Thus, the value of the principal at the end of two years, R_2, equals

$$R_o + iR_o + i(R_o + iR_o) = R_o + 2iR_o + i^2R_o$$

$$= R_o(1 + 2i + i^2) = R_o(1 + i)^2 = R_2.$$

After n years R_o will be equal to $R_o(1 + i)^n = R_n$. If R_o is worth $R_o(1 + i) = R_1$ at the end of the year, then the present value of R_1 (the value of R_1 dollars were they to be received now) equals $\dfrac{R_1}{(1 + i)}$. The present value of R_2 dollars received two years hence equals $\dfrac{R_2}{(1 + i)^2}$. The present value of R_n dollars received n years hence is $\dfrac{R_n}{(1 + i)^n}$.

Suppose a firm acquires a new machine that is expected to produce a stream of output over n future years and calculates the revenue that it expects to receive in the future from the sale of this output. (This also involves forecasting future output prices.) The present value (PV) of the marginal

---

[25]Profit-maximizing firms in a perfectly competitive world will be driven to minimize costs of production by using the most efficient input combination. If they did not, their costs would rise and their more efficient competitors would put them out of business. In a less competitive environment, a firm would not always seek to minimize costs if profit-maximization were not the single objective of the firm. Thus, for example, if finding the cost-minimizing combination of inputs took time and effort on the part of management, managers who loved a quiet life might sacrifice profits and produce inefficiently. However, only a firm with some market power and protection from entry would have such leeway.

revenue product of a new machine which will yield returns R_o in year zero (now), R_1 next year, R_2 in year 2, . . . , R_n in year n, will therefore be:

$$PV = R_o + \frac{R_1}{(1 + i)} + \frac{R_2}{(1 + i)^2} + \cdots \frac{R_n}{(1 + i)^n}$$

where i is the market rate of interest. In other words, the marginal revenue product of the machine is the discounted sum of the stream of future returns.[26]

Uncertainty   The fact that some of the earnings from the machine will be received in the future raises a second major problem—uncertainty. A firm that purchases a machine may estimate the likely future productivity and length of life of the machine and the prices at which output from the machine will be sold, but it can never be certain about what will in fact occur. The act of capital investment is thus a risky undertaking. It occurs anyway because capital is highly productive. Investment in capital can raise output and revenues far beyond what could be achieved without it. The promise of high future returns will often outweigh the investment's current cost and future uncertainty and insure that it is undertaken.

Optimal Investment

Present Value Approach   Consider the determination of optimal capital in another way. Suppose the firm faces the choice whether to add one new machine to its existing stock of machines. Using the present value formula for estimating the value of the marginal product of one new machine, the firm should buy the machine if its present value (PV) exceeds its current cost (P_K); that is, where

$$PV = R_o + \frac{R_1}{(1 + i)} + \frac{R_2}{(1 + i)^2} + \cdots \frac{R_n}{(1 + i)^n} > P_K.$$

Indeed, the firm should continue to add machines as long as $PV > P_K$. As the firm's capital stock is increased, the law of diminishing returns comes into play and reduces the present value of additional machines. The firm will cease to add machines when the present value of the last machine is just equal to its cost.

Internal Rate of Return   This rule can be reformulated in terms of rates of return. Note that the value of PV diminishes as the value of i increases. Suppose we ask what is the value of i that will bring the present value of the project into equality

[26]In most cases, the purchase of a machine now will also commit the firm to future outlays as well as generating future revenues. Future costs such as maintenance and insurance should be deducted from future revenues, so that the stream of future returns, the R's, is really the stream of net returns. However, new investment in capital may also require greater expenditure on labor and raw materials. In other words, the firm's production function may be characterized by fixed proportions. In this case the marginal revenue product of capital cannot in theory be defined as the partial derivative of revenue with respect to the capital input without reference to the cost of complementary inputs.

Figure 15.2   The Internal Rate of Return

The internal rate of return diminishes as capital increases—curve i^*. When the market rate of interest is i, the efficient amount of capital is K^*.

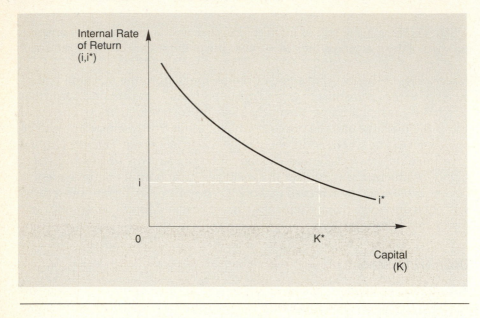

with its current cost. This value of i (called the internal rate of return of the investment) is found by solving the equation:

$$C = PV = R_0 + \frac{R_1}{(1+i^*)} + \frac{R_2}{(1+i^*)^2} + \cdots \frac{R_n}{(1+i^*)^n}$$

where i^* = internal rate of return.[27] We may now reformulate the rule for finding the optimal amount of capital: the firm should undertake all investment projects for which the internal rate of return, i^*, exceeds the market interest rate, i. In Figure 15.2, the amount of capital, K, is measured on the horizontal axis and the internal rate of return on the vertical axis. The internal rate of return, i^*, diminishes as capital increases, as shown by the curve i^*. This reflects diminishing returns to capital. If the market rate of interest is i, then the optimal capital stock is given by K^* where i and i^* are equal.[28] This K^* is identical

---

[27]In many cases there may be multiple solutions to this equation. This, and other complications of the use of the internal rate of return, will not be pursued here.

[28]All the diagrams shown in this section identify the optimal capital stock for a firm. However, investment (additions to the capital stock) is a flow variable and should be defined per unit of time. For example, if the value of current capital stock is $10,000 and the value of the optimal capital stock is $15,000, then the difference between the actual and desired stock can be made up at different rates—$5,000 all in one year, or $1,000 per year for 5 years, or $500 per year for 10 years, and so on. The additions to capital stock per period of time constitute the flow of investment. The

to the K^* achieved by equating the present value of the machine discounted at the market rate to the current cost. The market rate of interest is what the firm could earn on its money without investing in capital and is also referred to as the cost of capital. (Earlier, the cost of capital, which also included the cost of equity, was called r_o.) The firm must receive a return on its investment at least as great as what it could earn elsewhere—the market rate. Therefore, the market rate represents the opportunity cost of funds invested in capital equipment. (This cost should be carefully distinguished from P_K, the current cost or price of the machine.) The measurement of the cost of capital is therefore important, since it helps determine the amount of investment a firm will undertake. At the beginning of this chapter, we saw that measuring the cost of capital is a complicated procedure. Shortly, we will show how regulation further affects the amount of investment a firm chooses.

Profit Maximization versus Welfare Maximization

Note, finally, that the present-value and internal-rate-of-return rules are based on the assumption that the firm is a profit maximizer. Recall the difference between profit maximization and welfare maximization in the static model described in Chapters 13 and 14. We have seen that a monopolist maximizes profits by selecting that output and price for which the marginal revenue and marginal cost of output are equal (for example, point M in Figure 13.5). However, welfare, defined as TR + S - TC, is maximized at the higher output level where marginal cost equals price (point C in Figure 13.5).

A welfare-maximizing firm is one that is constrained by government regulation to produce output levels which maximize welfare rather than profits. Not surprisingly, the long-run investment decision will differ for the profit maximizer compared with the welfare maximizer. The profit maximizer will invest in all projects for which the discounted sum of future profits exceeds their current cost. The welfare maximizer will select projects for which the discounted sum of future benefits exceeds their current cost, where benefits include both future revenues and consumer's surplus.[29]

The discount rate used in calculating present values also may be different for the two types of firms. The profit maximizer will use a cost of capital based on market rates. A welfare-maximizing firm may use a different estimate of the opportunity cost of funds, the so-called social rate of discount.[30] For example, suppose a bridge is built that will yield future benefits in excess of current building costs. Suppose further that use of the bridge will be free once

---

speed at which the capital stock is increased will be a function of the cost of doing so as well as of the expected rates of change in future output.

[29] A full-fledged cost–benefit analysis will also include estimates of the external benefits and costs of the project.

[30] For a good introduction to the literature on the social discount rate, see R. E. Just, D. L. Heuth, and A. Schmitz, *Applied Welfare Economics and Public Policy* (Englewood Cliffs, N.J.: Prentice Hall, 1982), 296–336.

the bridge is built.[31] The original cost of the bridge must then be financed entirely out of the general tax pool. The opportunity cost of these funds must be measured by what they could earn elsewhere, in other government investment projects or in the private sector. If the government and private sectors are treated separately, the social rate of discount used for government projects may differ from the market rates used for private investment.

We now turn to a discussion of the effect of government regulation on a firm's choice of investment.

REGULATORY INCENTIVES

Recent moves toward deregulation in the United States are in part a response to concern about the kinds of economic incentives that government controls may create.

Incentive problems fall into the category of economic and organization theory called the theory of agency.[32] When one person, the principal, hires another person, the agent, to perform a task, the principal must find a way of giving the agent an incentive to perform the task in the best possible manner. To accomplish this, the principal must tie the reward offered to the agent to a measure of best possible performance. If the measure of performance to which the agent's reward is tied does not exactly correspond to the performance in which the principal is interested, and if the principal has less information than the agent, the agent may have an incentive to deceive the principal or take other actions that maximize the agent's utility, but which are not in the interests of the principal.

An example of the principal–agent relationship and its concomitant problems is the relationship between a regulating agency, such as a state public utility commission (the principal) and a regulated firm such as an electricity utility (the agent). Joskow and Schmalensee identify three basic assumptions that are usually made about this relationship:

1. The commission is assumed to have a single, well-defined objective, usually to maximize aggregate consumer welfare.

2. The commission is constrained to maintain the viability of the utility. In other words, it cannot enforce a set of prices that does not allow the utility a just and reasonable rate of return.

---

[31]To charge a zero price is not necessarily efficient. In Chapter 14 we showed that the optimal bridge size is determined where price equals long-run marginal cost. If demand shifts, the optimal short-run price might be above or below this.

[32]For an excellent introduction to these issues, on which we also draw, and a full bibliography, see Paul L. Joskow and Richard Schmalensee, "Incentive Regulation for Electric Utilities," *Yale Journal on Regulation* 4 (Fall 1986): 1–49.

3.   The commission is assumed to have less information than the utility. For example, commissioners may not know the cost structure of the utility and may therefore find it difficult to monitor the utility's true costs.[33]

Given these assumptions, the task of the regulating agency is to construct a set of regulatory rules that result in the optimal performance of the regulated firm, that is, that result in the maximization of consumer welfare and do not offer incentives to the regulated firm to bend or break the rules.

One further layer of principal–agent relations is found in the relationship between the public (Congress or consumers in general) and the regulating agency. The public as principal delegates authority to the regulating commission as agent to carry out the task of regulating a utility. Now the public must construct incentives to ensure that the regulating agency carries out its task in the best possible manner.[34]

In this section we examine some incentive problems which arise in regulation, and consider some solutions.

The Averch-Johnson Effect

A familiar incentives difficulty in public utilities management is the Averch-Johnson (or A-J) effect.[35] This refers to the tendency of the regulatory system to promote overinvestment in capital assets. Intuitively, the A-J effect is quite straightforward. A regulated public utility company, like any other firm, buys a variety of inputs—labor, fuel, and capital machinery. When the firm buys such things as labor and fuel, it pays whatever prices have been established in the markets for such commodities. The same is true when the company buys capital—say, a new piece of machinery—but there is now a further consideration.

The capital that is purchased becomes part of the company's rate base, and the firm is permitted to earn its approved rate of return (ROR) on that asset. That ROR is frequently thought to be above the cost of capital, though below the monopoly return that an unregulated company could earn. Where this is the case, the firm's purchase of capital is subsidized by the regulatory apparatus to a greater degree than are purchases of other inputs.

Consider a specific example. An electric utility company buys new generation equipment for $100,000 and is permitted a rate of return to capital of 12 percent. The result of this purchase, then, is that the firm's allowable profits increase by $12,000 per year over the life of the new equipment. No such

[33]Joskow and Schmalensee, "Incentive Regulation," 17–18.

[34]See J. M. Cox and R. M. Isaac, "Mechanisms for Incentive Regulation: Theory and Experiment," *The Rand Journal of Economics* 18 (Autumn 1987): 348–359; and J. S. Demski and D. E. M. Sappington, "Hierarchical Regulatory Control," *The Rand Journal of Economics* 18 (Autumn 1987): 369–383.

[35]H. Averch and L. L. Johnson, "Behavior of the Firm under Regulatory Constraint," *American Economic Review* 52 (December 1962): 1053–1069.

phenomenon occurs when the firm buys labor or fuel, however. A $100,000 increase in the company's cost of fuel, for example, will have no net effect on profits.[36] The company may be permitted to pass on the additional cost to its customers, thereby maintaining its ROR at the approved level.

This kind of discrepancy—the A-J effect—is potentially important because, in a sense, it lowers the relative price of capital in relation to the prices of other inputs, thereby inducing the regulated firm to use more capital (and perhaps less labor and fuel).[37] (See Appendix 15B for a graphical exposition of the A-J effect.)

The tendency is thus clear in simple directional terms. Regulated utilities will use too much capital, a phenomenon sometimes called gold plating. The quantitative importance of the A-J effect in recent years, however, is doubtful.[38] This distortion depends upon a rate of return in excess of the cost of capital. Many utility companies have recently failed to earn such returns.

More General Efficiency Incentives

The A-J effect is highly specific. Consider now a somewhat more general incentives problem in public utilities that arises in the context of the principal–agent relationship between the regulating commission and the regulated firm: the possibility that wasteful behavior will not be strongly penalized or, in more extreme cases, will not be penalized at all or actually encouraged. These rather unpleasant contingencies follow from the broad incentive structure of the regulatory apparatus.

Consider the following example. A regulated utility is permitted to earn a 12 percent rate of return on its capital asset base, a rate that is above the cost of capital but below the monopoly level. The managers of the company, however, squander resources in a variety of ways so that the firm, although charging its maximum permitted rates (prices), earns only a 10 percent rate of return.[39] Now it is possible that in this circumstance the company will appeal for rate increases on the ground that it has failed to earn the rate of return to which it is entitled. Recall now the second and third assumptions about the principal-agent relationship: the commission (principal) is constrained to allow the utility a just and reasonable return, and is assumed to have less information than the utility (agent). Given these assumptions, it is conceivable

---

[36]Of course the other inputs also have value for the firm, but using them does not directly affect the dollar profits that the firm is permitted to earn.

[37]Suppose an actual capital subsidy to a regulated utility were combined with a profit regulation that permits only a normal profit on the rate base. This subsidized cost of money capital to the regulated firm is lower than to an unregulated firm, and the regulated firm will use relatively more capital input.

[38]For a suggestion that its quantitative importance may not be overwhelming, see W. J. Baumol and A. K. Klevorick, "Input Choices and Rate-of-Return Regulation: An Overview of the Discussion," *Bell Journal of Economics and Management Science* 1 (Autumn 1970): 162–190.

[39]For example, by failing systematically to buy from the lowest-cost suppliers, failing to monitor production costs on an ongoing basis, buying managerial perks, installing plush offices, setting up long golf games, conferences abroad, and so on.

that, following a rate hearing, the commission may be persuaded to allow the rate increase.

Notice what has happened if such a scenario comes to pass. Company management has acted inefficiently, but the public utilities commission has bailed them out. Resources have been wasted and company profits have suffered temporarily, but ultimately it is consumers who will foot the bill via higher utility rates. The system thus has tolerated the inefficiency rather than acting to correct it. It is important to observe, however, that the regulatory commission need not (and should not) act as posited in this example. Notice, also, that the longer it takes the commission to grant rate requests, the longer the company's profits stay down. Ironically then, such bureaucratic inefficiency (regulatory lag) may provide a better incentive structure by penalizing the inefficiency of regulated firms. Joskow and Schmalensee note that the improvement in incentives as a result of regulatory lag comes about because costs are decoupled from prices.[40] If prices can be raised any time costs go up, then there can be no incentive for cost minimization. This observation gives a clue towards finding a better incentive structure.

Capital Prices

Still another variant of the regulatory incentives problem emerges when we consider the prices that regulated firms pay for their capital. It turns out that in at least one case, regulated company profits will actually increase if the firm's capital suppliers raise their prices. This remarkable conclusion may be seen with the help of Figure 15.3. The curve Π_{P_K} shows the relationship between profits and physical capital for a company, assuming some price of capital, P_K.[41] If unregulated, we might expect the firm to use capital level K_{max}, thereby maximizing its profits. The regulated firm, however, is constrained by ROR (P_K) showing the dollar profits that the regulatory commission permits at each level of capital use.[42] The firm does as well as possible at point E: profit Π_{P_K} and capital K_{reg}.[43]

Suppose now that the price of capital rises from P_K to P'_K. The profit curve falls to $\Pi_{P'_K}$. The unregulated firm, doing its best, would find profits reduced from Π_{max} to Π'_{max} (and would decrease its capital use from K_{max} to K'_{max}).

---

[40]Joskow and Schmalensee, "Incentive Regulation," 14.

[41]This curve reflects the idea that since an unregulated firm has a profit-maximizing level of output and capital, any departure from it must, by definition, reduce profits.

[42]ROR is a ray, reflecting the assumptions that (1) all capital units are assigned the same price for regulatory purposes, and (2) the permitted profit rate is itself constant at all capital levels. The allowed rate of return thus equals

$$\frac{\$ \text{ Profits}}{\text{Value of Assets}} = \frac{\Pi}{K \cdot P_K}$$

[43]Observe that $K_{reg} > K_{max}$. This is the A-J effect once again.

Figure 15.3   Regulatory Distortions

Curve Π shows the level of profits for each amount of capital. With K_{max} capital profits are maximized. The ROR (P_K) ray shows the level of profits for each amount of capital when the rate of return is held constant below the maximum. A firm subject to rate-of-return regulation will locate at E and employ K_{reg} capital, earning $Π_{max}$ profits. A rise in capital prices will cause the profit hill to fall and the ROR ray to rotate upwards. Now the regulated firm will locate at E′, employing less capital at K_{reg} but earning higher profits at $Π_{P'_K}$.

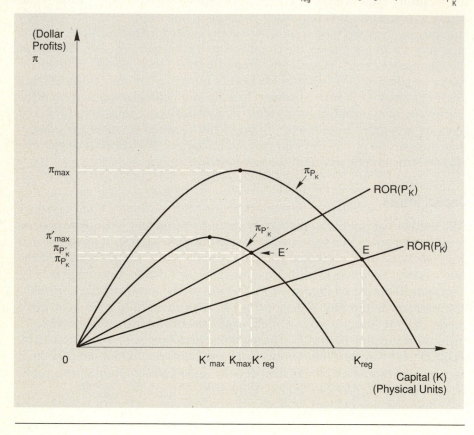

Observe, however, what happens to the regulated firm. The regulatory constraint pivots up to ROR (P'_K). Since the firm is permitted a fixed percentage return to capital, its dollar return to each capital unit will increase if its assets are revalued at the higher price P'_K (that is, if the rate base is valued at replacement cost).[44] Most striking is the new outcome E′ confronting the regulated firm. In response to a capital price increase, the company has

---

[44]If the allowed rate of return $\dfrac{Π}{K \cdot P_K}$ is to remain constant when P_K increases, then Π must rise

for every given level of K. That is, the ROR ray pivots upwards. However, as noted earlier in this chapter, it may not be the case that the rate base is valued at replacement cost.

reduced its use of capital (K_{reg} to K'_{reg}), but its dollar profits have increased (from Π_{P_K} to $\Pi_{P'_K}$). This is an extreme case.[45] But, as usual, the general lesson reaches farther than the specific example. When capital suppliers raise prices, the profit possibilities for unregulated companies deteriorate—the expected result. But because an increase in capital prices may swell the regulated company's rate base substantially, there is a range within which such firms actually do better when forced to pay the higher price. This phenomenon may destroy the incentive of the managers of the regulated company to seek out diligently low cost suppliers.

Capture Theories of Regulation

Still further possibilities for weakened regulatory incentives are suggested by a number of so-called capture theories.[46] These theories, which are seldom very specific, propose that regulated firms and industries frequently control (or capture) the regulatory agencies and run the system for their own ends. There are at least three reasons why such an event might occur with some frequency.

1.   Efforts are usually (and properly) made to staff regulatory commissions with experts on the industries whose performance is to be regulated. Such experts, however, are most often found within the relevant industry and may therefore be sympathetic to the interests of constituent firms.

2.   By somewhat similar token, top staff people in the agencies may hope to return to positions in the regulated industry when their government service ends. This may again predispose the regulators to view industry interests with considerable sympathy.

3.   The resources available to regulators are typically limited. The regulated firms, on the other hand, are well financed and can treat their regulatory expenses as costs for which they can seek reimbursement from the commissioners in the form of higher rates.

These points suggest that regulation may be soft rather than tough. It is also apparent that public regulation has at times been sought by affected industries. Such efforts surely do not mean that civic-minded managers want government to hold down their prices or profits. Rather, the company managers likely see regulation as a means of limiting the degree of competition that they face.

---

[45]See for pertinent analysis, F. M. Westfield, "Regulation and Conspiracy," *American Economic Review* 55 (June 1965): 424–443.

[46]See M. Friedman and R. Friedman, *Free to Choose* (New York: Harcourt Brace Jovanovich, 1979); and G. J. Stigler, "The Theory of Economic Regulation," *Bell Journal of Economics and Management Science* 2 (Spring 1971): 3–21.

Incentive Problems: Aspects of a Solution

The examples above reveal that perverse incentives can arise in the context of a regulatory framework (such as rate-of-return regulation) that is designed to constrain a regulated monopoly to behave more in the interests of consumers than it would otherwise do. It turns out that the design of regulations which do not also set up perverse incentives is extremely complicated.[47]   We confine ourselves here to identifying aspects of an appropriate incentive structure. In subsequent chapters we will indicate to what extent these aspects have been put into practice.

As we noted above, a regulatory system that allows prices to rise every time the regulated company's costs rise (cost-plus pricing rules) destroys incentives to minimize costs. Paradoxically, regulatory lag, which delays price rises following increases in costs, penalizes a regulated firm whose costs are rising for the length of the lag (until rate hearings permit prices to rise as well). The difficulty for regulators is to be able to identify those costs rising because the utility is inefficient and those rising for reasons beyond the utility's control, such as higher fuel prices. Consumers should presumably share the burden of higher fuel prices with the utility by paying higher prices, but should not be burdened with paying for management's inefficiency. To address this problem some incentive schemes modify the straightforward cost-plus scheme by introducing a sharing factor that is applied to the difference between the utility's actual costs and estimated (minimum) costs (determined in a rate hearing). Thus prices rise by a smaller proportion than the rise in costs, maintaining the efficiency incentive while not penalizing the utility altogether for uncontrollable cost increases. The difficulty with this scheme lies, of course, in the necessity for the regulators to estimate accurately minimum costs that can then be compared with the utility's actual costs. One method is to estimate costs using statistical cost functions based on a sample of data from other utilities. A utility's costs would be a function of various explanatory variables including fuel prices, the efficiency of generating capacity, and so forth. Unfortunately, the estimated cost functions may be of doubtful reliability.[48] Another method (the yardstick approach) is to construct an index of the costs of utilities in comparable circumstances and use the index as a measure of the regulated utility's minimum cost. But here the limitations of accounting costs as estimates of true economic cost may render the yardstick inappropriate. Finally, regulators may attempt to control individual elements of a utility's cost, by instituting fuel adjustment clauses that allow rates to rise concomitantly with fuel prices, or by attaching incentives to increase generating unit heat rates.

---

[47]Joskow and Schmalensee, "Incentive Regulation," 21–49.

[48]Joskow and Schmalensee, "Incentive Regulation," 31.

Assessment

It is apparent that government regulation, especially of the rate of return, may give rise to some noneconomic incentives for regulated firms, and further that these incentives are potentially quite important. The actual quantitative importance of noneconomic behavior in regulated industries is typically difficult to pin down with precision. Surely many managers of affected firms want to operate efficiently and succeed in doing so. Many regulators are no doubt vigilant and determined to pursue vigorously what they see as the public interest. The fact remains, however, that no sensible government program should invite inefficient behavior—even if many public officials and private managers are able to resist the temptations. For this reason, the existence of dubious incentives has provided strong economic arguments for modification, if not abandonment, of some regulatory programs.

SUMMARY

In this chapter we have addressed the issue of investment and efficiency in regulated industries. We discussed the meaning of normal profit and its relationship to the fair rate of return. We noted that the history and development of regulatory rules have emphasized problems of defining the fair rate of return, sometimes to the detriment of the pursuit of an efficient investment policy. We discussed the methods by which appropriate levels of capital investment could be estimated. We then identified some situations in which perverse incentives inherent in rate-of-return regulation might distort actual investment from its efficient level. Finally we indicated some routes to follow for solutions to these incentive problems.

CONCLUSION

Given the complexity of the economic issues involved in regulating prices and profits and the intractability of the practical measurement problems, it can be argued that the case for regulating an industry rather than allowing the market to perform its allocative function should not be accepted unless it is very strong. In other words, since the costs of regulation are high, the benefits should be shown to be correspondingly high. In the next three chapters, we consider the working of the regulatory process in two types of industry—electricity, typically produced by public utilities, and transportation and communications, both characterized by a competitive structure yet with a long history of regulation.

Discussion Questions

1. Defining the following terms is complicated. Explain why.

    a. Normal profits.
    b. Cost of capital.
    c. Fair rate of return.

2.   Explain the significance of the *Hope Natural Gas* decision for public utility pricing.

3.   Explain the difference between the choice of the optimal capital stock and the choice of the optimal rate of investment. What additional factors would you have to take into account for a full explanation of the choice of the optimal investment rate?

4.   An electric power company must replace an expensive piece of power-generating equipment. If the company were an unregulated profit-oriented enterprise, it would have an incentive to seek out the lowest-cost supplier of this equipment (assuming constant quality of the machinery). Explain how and why this incentive might be weakened if the company is subject to regulation of its rate of return.

5.   Give three reasons why regulatory and judicial attempts to determine the appropriate rate level and structure for public utilities have resulted in a muddle.

Selected Readings

Averch, H. and L. L. Johnson, "Behavior of the Firm under Regulatory Constraint," *American Economic Review* 52 (December 1962): 1053–1069. *A seminal article identifying the distorting effect of rate-of-return regulation.*

Hesington, D. R. *Portfolio Theory and the Capital Asset Pricing Model.* Englewood Cliffs, N.J.: Prentice-Hall, 1983. *An up-to-date monograph.*

Hirschleifer, J. *Investment, Interest and Capital.* Englewood Cliffs, N.J.: Prentice-Hall, 1970. *An advanced treatment of the optimal investment decision, also containing an excellent section on investment under uncertainty.*

Joskow, P. R. and R. Schmalensee. "Incentive Regulation for Electric Utilities." *Yale Journal on Regulation* 4 (Fall 1986): 1–49. *An accessible summary of incentive regulation and its application in the electricity industry.*

Just, R. E., D. L. Hueth, and A. Schmitz. *Applied Welfare Economics and Public Policy.* Englewood Cliffs, N.J.: Prentice-Hall, 1982, Chapter 13. *A good introduction to the literature on the social discount rate.*

Modigliani, F. and M. H. Miller. "The Cost of Capital, Corporation Finance, and the Theory of Investment." *American Economic Review* 48 (June 1958): 261–297. *This famous article was the starting point for a large literature investigating the determinants of a firm's cost of capital.*

Phillips, C. F., Jr. *The Economics of Regulation.* Homewood, Ill.: Richard D. Irwin, 1969. *Part II of this book contains a comprehensive and detailed account of the practice of rate-of-return regulation.*

Appendix 15A
The Optimal Choice of Inputs

The firm's production function is given by:

$$Q = f(K, L)$$

where
Q = output
K = capital, measured in machine hours
L = labor, measured in labor hours.

In Figure 15A.1, the vertical and horizontal axes represent quantities of labor, L, and capital, K, respectively.

The curves labelled Q_1, Q_2, and Q_3 are isoquants. Curve Q_1 traces out all the different combinations of capital and labor that can produce Q_1 units of output. Curve Q_2 traces out the combinations of capital and labor that can produce a higher level of output, Q_2, and so on. The slope of an isoquant for any particular combination of capital and labor measures the ratio $\frac{MP_K}{MP_L}$ at that point. Isoquants are convex to the origin, reflecting the fact that the ratio $\frac{MP_K}{MP_L}$ diminishes as more capital and less labor is used. (This phenomenon is known as the diminishing marginal rate of technical substitution.) The curves C_1, C_2, and C_3 are called isocost curves. C_1 measures all the different combinations of capital and labor that can be bought for a given outlay (or total cost, TC_1), given prevailing market prices P_K and P_L. Total cost equals the sum of the total expenditure on capital plus total expenditure on labor, that is, $TC_1 = P_K K + P_L L$. Thus the slope of the isocost curve is constant for all capital-labor ratios and equal to $\frac{P_K}{P_L}$ as shown in Figure 15A.1. Cost curve C_1 represents a lower total cost than C_2 and so on.

The optimal, or cost-minimizing, combination of capital and labor for a given output is found by selecting the lowest isocost curve for that output level. For example, if output Q_2 is to be produced, the lowest-cost combination of capital and labor is found at point E_2 (using K_2 capital and L_2 labor). Point M_1 on isocost curve C_3 is feasible in that it represents a combination of capital and labor that will produce Q_2 output units. C_3 is not desirable, however, because it represents a higher cost than C_2. Cost curve C_1 is not feasible—it includes no combination of capital and labor that will result in Q_2 output units. The condition for achieving the minimum cost for a given output is that the slope of the isoquant and isocost curves be the same. This occurs where the two curves are tangent to each other. Points E_1, E_2, and E_3 mark three such tangency

Figure 15A.1   The Optimal Capital–Labor Choice

The isoquants Q_1, Q_2, and Q_3 show the combinations of capital and labor that can be combined to produce given output levels. The isocost curves C_1, C_2 and C_3 measure the combinations of capital and labor that can be bought with a given outlay of dollars. Cost-minimizing factor combinations are found at the points of tangency between the isoquants and isocost curves at E_1, E_2, and E_3.

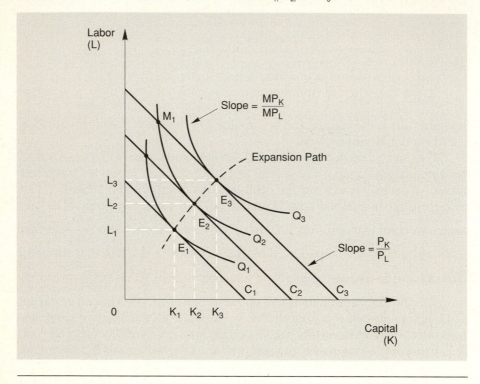

points. Thus for output Q_1, the combination of capital and labor (K_1, L_1) that minimizes cost (C_1) is such that $\dfrac{MP_K}{MP_L} = \dfrac{P_K}{P_L}$. The locus of optimal points E_1, E_2, and E_3 is called the firm's expansion path.

Appendix 15B
The Averch-Johnson Effect

Figure 15B.1 shows a firm that uses both labor and capital. Line PP is the firm's isocost curve or budget constraint. Its slope reflects the relative prices of the two inputs. Curve I is a production isoquant. As we have seen, the unregulated, cost-minimizing company will locate at point E, using capital K_p. The effect of regulation allowing a given rate of return to capital (but not to labor) is to pivot the company's isocost curve to PP'. Unsurprisingly, the response is a move to E', an expansion of capital to $K_{p'}$.[a] Recall that the original equilibrium, E, is production-efficient. Indeed the unregulated profit seeker will move along the efficient expansion path. Point E' is therefore a departure from efficient production arrangements. The firm has expanded its use of capital not because it is inherently useful to do so, but because there is a regulatory payoff—the A-J effect.

Figure 15B.1 The Averch-Johnson Effect

Rate-of-return regulation allows the firm to earn more dollar profits when the amount of capital employed increases. Therefore, the price of capital to the firm is effectively reduced. This price reduction rotates isocost curve PP outwards to PP' and increases the amount of capital employed from K_p to $K_{p'}$.

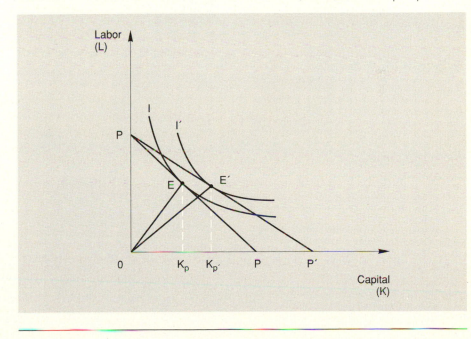

---

[a]Whether we should expect this response to produce an increase or decrease in the firm's employment of labor is unclear. As drawn in Figure 15B.1, there is little effect.

CHAPTER 16

· ·

REGULATORY DILEMMAS: THE CASE OF ELECTRICITY

INTRODUCTION

The electricity industry has undergone enormous changes since its beginning in the 1870s with the invention of the first generators.[1] Its structure and development have been affected not only by major technological changes, but also by the history of government regulation. The dramatic shift in the economic environment in the early 1970s from a world of oil abundance to a situation of supply reductions and rapidly rising oil prices also radically affected the condition of the industry. All these influences have been, and remain, so strong that it is virtually impossible to disentangle them.

We begin with a brief history of the development of the industry. We then consider whether the industry's cost and demand characteristics correspond to those of a natural monopoly. Next we consider the pricing policy that has been pursued by government regulators. We examine some recent policy changes and discuss the basis for these changes—in particular the issues of incentive regulation and the viability of competition at the generating and other stages of production. Finally we consider the impact of environmental regulation and focus particularly on nuclear power generation.

HISTORICAL ORIGINS

In its incipiency, the industry consisted of a large number of small producers (some of which were direct competitors) each generating electricity that was

---

[1]For good descriptions of the electricity industry, its history and development, see C. Wilcox and W. G. Shepherd, *Public Policies toward Business*, 5th ed. (Homewood, Ill.: Richard D. Irwin, 1975), Chapter 15; C. F. Phillips, Jr., *The Economics of Regulation* (Homewood, Ill.: Richard D. Irwin, 1969), Chapter 15; and A. E. Kahn *The Economics of Regulation*, Vol. 2 (New York: John Wiley and Sons, 1971), 70–77.

distributed to a relatively small surrounding area. By the 1900s, some of these producers had achieved local monopoly status by obtaining a municipal franchise. Others had been taken over by the municipalities themselves and were now publicly owned firms. The regulation of all electricity-producing utilities by individual state commissions followed apace, many times with the support of the utilities themselves.[2]

Over the next several decades, technological developments made it possible to exploit economies of scale in the generation and transmission of power. As a result, an enormous amount of consolidation took place, spurred on not only by the technological economies from producing large amounts of output, but also by the opportunities for enormous financial gain that certain kinds of merger afforded. In particular, the growth of holding companies accelerated.

As Charles F. Phillips describes it:

> A holding company is an enterprise that owns sufficient stock in another company or number of companies so that it may influence the management of the company whose stock it holds. Sometimes the holding company is a stockholding firm entirely and operates no properties directly—pure holding company. Other holding companies both hold securities and operate some properties in their own names—operating holding companies. By the early 1930s many electric utility holding companies had assets of $1 billion or more. Further, by 1932, 16 holding companies accounted for 76.4 percent of the electricity generated, with three systems (United Corporation, Electric Bond and Share Company, and the Insull interests) accounting for 44.5 percent of the total electricity produced.[3]

The pyramiding of holding companies, in which one company held a controlling interest in a number of other holding companies that in turn controlled others, and so on, enabled the owners of the company at the top to control a large quantity of capital with a relatively small initial investment and to earn extremely high rates of profit (or loss).[4] It has also been suggested that dishonest financial practices on the part of holding company owners led to the inflation of the rate base and ultimately to higher prices.[5] That the state regulating commissions failed to control such practices may be as much a reflection of the fact that utility regulation was still in its infancy and of the commissions' lack of expertise and resources, as of the economic power of the holding companies.

The collapse of the stock market in 1929 converted many of the holding companies' inflated profits into huge losses. The Public Utility Holding Company Act of 1935, designed to prevent the recurrence of financial abuse,

[2]See D. D. Anderson, *Regulatory Politics and Electric Utilities* (Boston: Auburn House Publishing Company, 1981), 33–35, for a detailed description of the origin of state utility regulation and the role played by Samuel Insull.

[3]Phillips, *Economics of Regulation*, 554.

[4]For good numerical examples, see Wilcox and Shepherd, *Public Policies*, 399; and Phillips, *Economics of Regulation*, 556-558.

[5]Kahn, *Economics of Regulation*, 71; and Phillips, *Economics of Regulation*, 561.

was the result. The Federal Power Act was passed the same year. These two acts were important, not only for the immediate reforms achieved, but also because they created roles for two federal agencies—the Securities and Exchange Commission (SEC) and the Federal Power Commission (FPC)—in the regulation of the industry.

Note that before the passage of the Public Utility Holding Company Act, the major function of the SEC (organized in 1934) was to regulate the stock exchanges and the conditions of sale of new securities. The 1935 Public Utility Holding Company Act extended the SEC's power to encompass regulation of the financial affairs of utilities. In particular, the act brought under the control of the SEC the issuing of new securities by interstate holding companies, the purchase and sale of assets, and the accounting methods of the companies. The SEC was given power to require registration and to limit the number of holding companies. Furthermore, the act required that all holding companies more than twice removed from their operating subsidiaries be abolished. Thus the law gave the SEC substantial power to influence the structure of the electricity industry, although its prime objective was the prevention of further financial abuses.

The Federal Power Act led to an expanded role for the Federal Power Commission, whose authority was extended to include control over the interstate sale of electric power. The modern version of this commission is the Federal Energy Regulatory Commission, created in 1977. Note that the state commissions have an important (even predominant) role in the regulation of rates and services.

In addition to bringing the federal government into utilities regulation, the holding company episode engendered a certain reluctance on the part of the SEC and state commissions to allow further systematic merger or consolidation in the industry. Whether this policy has had the effect of hindering the efficient integration of the industry, or whether it has been successful in its attempts to preserve vital competitive elements in the industry's structure, is a question that is in some dispute.

Recently, there has been renewed interest in the idea that competition in the electric power industry is both viable and desirable, particularly at the generation stage.[6] The Public Utilities Regulatory Policies Act of 1978 required utilities, among other things, to purchase unused cogeneration power (power produced as a by-product of another industrial process) and introduced certain price reforms. This act provided an economic and political environment in which competitive tendencies in the industry could be encouraged.

To evaluate this view and its opposite—that the electricity industry is a natural monopoly—we must consider in more detail the relevant economic characteristics of the industry—economies of scale, demand elasticities and so forth—that help determine whether or not it is a good candidate for regulation.

---

[6]See for example V. L. Smith, "Currents of Competition in Electricity Markets," *Regulation* (1987): 23–29.

COST CONDITIONS

On the supply side the industry has three stages of production—the generation of power, the transmission of power (from generators to distribution centers), and the distribution of power (to final users— residential and commercial customers). Vertical integration of firms, especially in the first two stages of production, is common.[7]

In the first two stages of production, economies of scale have historically been large. While electricity is generated in plants of varied sizes using quite different methods (steam, hydroelectric, and internal combustion) and different fuels (coal, oil, gas, and nuclear power), the size of generating plants has been increasing over time. In a study of economies of scale in the electric power industry, William R. Hughes suggests that a steady stream of technological developments in the two decades following World War II facilitated the building of increasingly large generators.[8] Figure 16.1 shows a set of hypothetical cost curves for electricity generation. Notice that the capacity of a generator is measured in megawatts. However, the amount of electricity used is calculated as the product of power (in kilowatts or megawatts) and the length of time that power is used. Thus the cost of electricity use is most sensibly measured per kilowatt-hour. Cost curves C_1 and C_2 measure the average cost of electricity generation for two steam generators of different capacities (200 megawatts and 500 megawatts, respectively). Curve C_3 represents the cost curve of a modern nuclear power plant with substantially larger capacity. Note that minimum average cost decreases with increases in plant size, reflecting economies of scale. It is now apparent that in the last two decades, the rapid exploitation of new scale economies has slowed. In a detailed study of construction costs for coal-burning generating units, P. L. Joskow and N. L. Rose note that there are significant economies of scale in the construction of coal-burning generating units, tending to increase the size of plants and reduce the average cost of the electricity produced by such large plants.[9] However, maintenance costs and unreliability of performance increase as the plant size increases. These cost increases, together with increases in fuel and labor costs and the costs of complying with environmental regulations, have tended to offset the contin-

---

[7]See L. W. Weiss, "Antitrust in the Electric Power Industry," in A. Phillips, ed., *Promoting Competition in Regulated Markets* (Washington, D.C.: Brookings Institution, 1975). Weiss estimates that in 1968 "about 92 percent of all sales to ultimate customers are on a privately owned, vertically integrated basis" (p. 139). More recently there has been an increase in the number of firms that produce at the generating stage only and sell their entire output either to vertically integrated companies (who also generate their own power) or to firms that operate only at the transmission and distribution stages. See below (page 374) for a further discussion of the causes and consequences of these structural changes.

[8]W. R. Hughes, "Scale Frontiers in Electric Power," in W. M. Capron, ed., *Technological Change in Regulated Industries* (Washington, D.C.: Brookings Institution, 1971). This is a good example of the dynamic economies discussed in Chapter 13.

[9]P. L. Joskow and N. L. Rose, "The Effects of Technological Change, Experience and Environmental Regulation on the Construction Cost of Coal-Burning Generating Units," *The Rand Journal of Economics* 16 (Spring 1985): 1–27.

Figure 16.1   Economies of Scale in Electricity Generation

Cost curves C_1 and C_2 measure the average cost of electricity generation for two steam generators with capacities of 200 megawatts and 500 megawatts, respectively. Curve C_3 is the cost curve of a modern nuclear power plant with 1,500 megawatts of capacity.

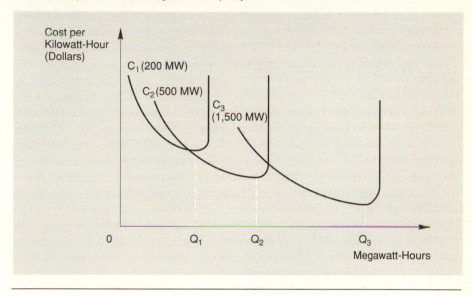

ued exploitation of new economies of scale at the construction stage. High maintenance and environmental costs and low reliability of performance are also typical of nuclear power plants.[10]

At the transmission level, scale economies occur when increasing amounts of electricity can be carried over longer distances with smaller loss of energy so that the cost per mile of transmitting each kilowatt-hour of electricity decreases as the distance and voltage of the transmission lines increase.[11]

The interconnection of transmission lines from different generating sources and the possibilities for allowing power to be shared (pooled) from different sources before it is distributed allows the generating firms more flexibility in dealing with the problem of peak loads and improves the reliability of the system.

---

[10]We discuss below the environmental problems associated with the production of electricity using different methods and also focus specifically on the issue of nuclear power.

[11]Phillips suggests the following rule of thumb: "The power that a transmission line can carry increases by the square of its voltage. If the voltage is tripled, therefore, a line can carry nine times more power and do so more efficiently. Thus, even though a 345,000–volt line costs four or five times as much as a 115,000–volt line, the cost per kilowatt hour is approximately half as great due to the greater quantity carried. Further, it is estimated that for every 1,000 volts added to a line's capacity, the distance over which electricity can be economically transmitted is increased by one mile, thereby contributing to more effective interconnections and power pools." Phillips, *Economics of Regulation*, 547.

The existence of significant scale economies at both the generation and transmission stages of production and the fact that such a high proportion of firms in the industry have in fact integrated these two stages give weight to the argument that electricity may be a natural monopoly at the wholesale level. Leonard Weiss disputes this with respect to generation. He suggests that "most regions could support enough generating plants to permit extensive competition if the plants were under separate ownership and had equal access to transmission and distribution."[12] Equal access may involve what is called wheeling. A firm whose electricity production exceeds the local demand may be able to sell its excess power to a more distant market if it can use the transmission lines of an appropriately located firm. The ability of firms owning intermediate transmission facilities to refuse to wheel the power of other firms would indicate that natural monopoly in transmission still exists.

V. L. Smith observes that there has been a recent significant increase in the number of firms that sell all the electricity they produce to other firms (that is, they produce all their electricity for the wholesale power market) and also in the number of vertically integrated firms that buy and sell excess power in the wholesale market.[13] The development of competition in the wholesale market has been encouraged by the willingness of firms to enter into long-term contracts to buy and sell power from each other, the growth in the number of firms prepared to wheel power, and changes in the regulatory environment that make vertical integration more costly.

At the distribution level, scale economies are also significant. In addition, the prevalence of common and external costs has provided a rationale for government regulation. The provision of electricity to each individual building requires labor and resources (stringing wires, installing meters, and so forth). Nevertheless, if reception points are clustered together (in densely populated and industrialized areas), then the costs of bringing electricity close by are common to a large number of reception units. Furthermore, the process of installing the necessary infrastructure (wires and poles) imposes external costs on the surrounding area, providing a second reason for avoiding the duplication of electricity service facilities by competing companies.

It should be noted that some firms install their own electricity generators to provide an independent back-up source of power and therefore compete with the utilities at the point of consumption. The feasibility of the self-generation option depends, of course, on relative costs. In general, if economies of scale are sufficiently large, an electric utility should be able to compete successfully with self-generated power. But in many cases, risk factors such as the possibility of power black-outs at times of peak demand are the real incentive for the installation of private generators. Used as back-up sources of supply, most are not in operation on a regular basis. Indeed, if it were not

[12]Weiss, "Antitrust in the Electric Power Industry," 136.
[13]Smith, "Currents of Competition."

cheaper for electricity to be provided by large-scale generators and transmitted through a vast network of power lines, then presumably each individual
building would have its own generator.[14]

DEMAND CONDITIONS

Some characteristics of the electricity industry cited in the rationale for regulation include inelastic demand and the peak-load problem. However, as we
emphasized in Chapter 13, neither of these characteristics implies that government regulation is always necessary.

   Electricity is a well-defined commodity that can be considered heteroge-
neous if time and place of consumption are taken into account. It is also very
expensive to store.[15] Individual and business use of electricity is monitored by
meters, making it a particularly good candidate for peak-load pricing and
price discrimination. It is subject to rapidly fluctuating demand, exhibiting
regular daily, weekly, and seasonal cycles. Its value lies partly in its uninter-
rupted availability. When I switch on a light or the air conditioner I expect the
electricity to flow, and my enthusiasm (demand) for it as a regular source of
energy depends partly on this characteristic. If the light worked only 50
percent of the time, I might well consider changing to a more reliable source of
power.[16]   As with all other commodities, of course, prices and income also
determine the shape of the demand curve for electricity. However, the routine
of daily living—length of the work day, hours when most people eat dinner—
and seasonal variations in the weather generate substantial demand fluctuations. The nonstorable nature of the commodity and the importance of reliability as one of its marketable characteristics mean that the supplier must install
sufficient capacity to meet peak demands. These are partly, though not entirely, predictable. Thus, it is well known that power usage in New York City
in August is high, when hot summer days result in the heavy use of air
conditioners. Although some days are hotter than others and the exact peak
demand is not known in advance, its general magnitude can be estimated. To
prevent August power failures, utilities must have sufficient capacity to meet
the unexpected demand peaks—although this may mean substantial under-

---

[14]Self-generation is not widely used. One alternative to the mass production of electricity—solar
energy—cannot under current technology challenge conventional fuels.

[15]Consider the cost of a battery for a car and you will have some idea of the relative cost of storing
electricity. However, there are some clever storage systems that exploit the price differences of
time-of-day pricing. Thus for example, water can be pumped up to a great height using low-
priced off-peak electricity and then released to generate high-priced electricity at the peak.

[16]But note the growing demand for interruptible service by business establishments who may
find it desirable to take advantage of a lower electricity rate in return for agreeing to a specified
reduction of service during peak periods. Interruptible service becomes more attractive as self-
generation increases.

utilization at other times.[17] We will discuss the way in which electricity producers and their state regulatory commissions have approached the pricing and investment problems raised by fluctuating and uncertain demand.

Another demand characteristic often cited as a justification for the direct regulation of an industry is inelasticity of demand for the product. Recall the argument that since the profit-maximizing price of a monopolistic producer is relatively greater than marginal cost for a product with an inelastic demand than for a product with a higher elasticity, the efficiency and equity losses are more serious. Thus the potential social benefit to be reaped from a government-regulated price set below the profit-maximizing price is greater for low-elasticity products. Apart from the many theoretical problems associated with measures of efficiency and equity on which this argument rests, the actual measure of elasticity may simply reflect the way in which industry boundaries are drawn. Thus, a high price elasticity may result from a product definition that excludes many close substitutes.

There are many empirical studies of the shape of the demand curve for electricity.[18] Most of these recognize that electricity is an energy input for other durable goods used by consumers. Thus, home heating devices, lamps, stoves, and so on, as well as industrial machines, are all capital goods that use the factor of production, electricity, as their source of power. The demand for electricity is therefore a derived demand. In the short run, the stock of capital is fixed and the possibilities for substituting other energy sources (if the price of electricity should rise) are very limited. On the other hand, people may use their appliances less, producing less heat, light, and so on; they may substitute conservation for electricity. In the absence of this kind of conservation effect, one might expect that the short-run price elasticity of demand for electricity would be low. In the long-run, one might expect more consumer substitution of other energy sources. If the price of electricity rises and is expected to remain high relative to other sources consumers can eventually replace their electricity-using durable equipment with other types using alternatives such as gas or oil. Moreover, higher prices may lead to more self-generation and the development of more efficient appliances. The long-run elasticity of demand should therefore be higher than the short-run elasticity, as is the case for most goods.

In surveys of demand studies, both Taylor and Bohi found a very wide range of estimated price and income elasticities. Taylor suggests that the long-run price elasticity of demand is indeed larger than the short-run, that this is

---

[17]Note that electricity is unique in that every demander can claim a share any time by switching on; there is no queuing mechanism. Therefore, if capacity is not sufficient to meet peak demand, power failures will result. By contrast, if high demands are placed on the highway system congestion and delays occur, but journeys are still completed even though they take longer—the whole system does not break down.

[18]See L. D. Taylor, "The Demand for Electricity: A Survey," *Bell Journal of Economics* (Spring 1975): 74–110; and D. R. Bohi, *Analyzing Demand Behavior: A Study of Energy Elasticities, Resources for the Future* (Baltimore: Johns Hopkins University Press, 1981).

also true of the income elasticities, and that while the long-run price elasticity of demand appears quite elastic, the evidence on the long-run income elasticity is more mixed.[19]

Bohi is less willing to draw conclusions from the available studies:

> There is unanimous agreement that the price of electricity is important and that price has an inverse relationship with consumption. Beyond this there is considerable disagreement about the responsiveness of consumption behavior .... [W]e conclude that a great deal of the information contained in studies of residential electricity demand is mutually inconsistent and potentially misleading ....[20]

In the presence of barriers to entry, the low short-run elasticity of demand for electricity might imply high short-run prices for an unregulated monopoly. However, the higher long-run elasticity would mitigate this effect.[21]

The estimation techniques employed in the studies surveyed by Taylor and Bohi were complicated by the complexity of the price structure facing consumers.[22]

We now turn to issues of pricing, bearing in mind that knowledge of the demand curve is necessary for choosing an appropriate price structure.

PRICING POLICY

The decade of the 1970s saw substantial changes in the pricing policies adopted by state commissions regulating public utilities. In particular, time-of-day (peak-load) pricing was introduced in some states following the example of earlier adoption abroad, especially in France. These changes were in some cases sought and approved by the electric utilities themselves. To understand such developments, it is necessary to review briefly the changes in the economy that radically affected the position of the electricity producers and fos-

---

[19]Specifically, Taylor states:

1. The price elasticity of demand for electricity, for all classes of customers, is much larger in the long-run than in the short-run (short-run price elasticity estimates ranged from - 0.14 to -.90, long-run price elasticity estimates ranged from -1.02 to - 2.00).

2. This is also the case for the income elasticity of demand (short-run income elasticity estimates ranged from .02 to 1.16, and long-run income elasticities ranged from 0 to 1.94).

3. The long-run price elasticity of demand is indicated to be elastic. All of the studies considered support this for industrial demand, and all but one for residential demand.

4. The evidence on the magnitude of the long-run income elasticity is mixed. Estimates range from 0 to 2, and clearly depend on the type of model employed. See L. D. Taylor, "The Demand for Electricity," 101.

[20]D. R. Bohi, *Analyzing Demand Behavior*, 77, 79.

[21]Note that most demand studies are based on current price and output ranges. Elasticities can be very different at different points on the demand curve, and for different curves.

[22]The usual assumption is that the consumer faces a single product price and chooses to consume at this price a quantity that maximizes her total utility. When she is faced with, for example, a declining block rate scheme, this alters the shape of the budget constraint line, changes the solution of the utility-maximization calculation (often there are multiple equilibrium points), and hence alters the characteristics of the resulting demand curve.

Table 16.1 Electricity Prices

Average charge per kilowatt-hour (kwh) for residential service using between 250 kwh and 500 kwh (in cents).

1935	1940	1945	1950	1955	1960	1965	1970	1975	1980	1982
2.77	2.11	2.04	2.02	2.06	2.12	2.08	2.10	3.59	5.56	7.45

Average charge per kilowatt-hour for industrial service using between 30,000 kwh and 60,000 kwh.

1935	1940	1945	1950	1955	1960	1965	1970	1975	1980	1982
1.81	1.66	1.67	1.74	1.82	1.89	1.93	1.97	3.67	5.71	7.81

Source: Typical Electric Bills, January 1, 1982, U.S. Department of Energy, pp. 278, 10.

tered an economic and political climate in which major changes in pricing policy could occur.[23]

As we have seen, in the two decade following World War II, technological advances in the electricity industry allowed for the exploitation of substantial economies of scale at the generation and transmission stages of production. The resulting factor productivity increases and the continuation of stable fuel prices meant that unit costs of electricity production declined relative to the general price level. Demand growth kept pace with post-war expansion.[24] (It also slowed during the recessions of the late 1950s and 1960s.) Demand was further encouraged by a pricing policy that made it cheaper to buy electricity in large rather than small quantities (this is the declining-block rate discussed later). In line with falling average costs, the relative price of electricity fell during this period. Table 16.1 shows the average charge per kilowatt-hour of electricity for selected categories of residential and industrial users from 1935 to 1982. Note that for both kinds of users, the price in cents per kilowatt-hour changed very little from 1945 to 1970, rising from 2.04 cents in 1945 to 2.10 cents in 1970 for residential users and from 1.67 cents to 1.97 cents for industrial users. Several studies have shown that these relatively low rates were not so much the result of effective price regulation by the state commissions, but rather a reflection of underlying technological improvements and exploitation of scale economies.[25] Thus, for the first 20 years following World War II, the electricity industry was in fact a highly stable and profitable industry in which regulation fostered a secure environment for innovation and growth.

---

[23]Much of the information in the following section is based on P. W. MacAvoy, *The Regulated Industries and the Economy* (New York: W. W. Norton and Company, 1979); and D. D. Anderson, *Regulatory Politics and Electric Utilities.*

[24]Recall that the average of the estimates of income elasticity reviewed by Taylor is a little less than one.

[25]See MacAvoy, *The Regulated Industries,* 35–37.

At the end of the 1960s, the situation changed. Productivity gains slowed and relative costs began to rise. The utilities more frequently asked state commissions for cost-justified rate increases. They found that the regulatory procedures followed by the commissions did not rapidly dispose of the rising number of requests. Electricity prices thus lagged behind the rise in costs, with consequent reductions in profits. This situation was aggravated in the 1970s by several new factors. The formation of the OPEC oil cartel and the Arab oil embargo of 1973 led to an enormous increase in the cost of fuel oil. At the same time, the resulting shift to cheaper substitute fuels—coal, gas, and nuclear power—was hampered by new federal regulations. These had two goals: to encourage energy conservation, and to establish standards for the protection of the environment. The ill effects of burning dirty fuels such as coal and the potential radiation hazards of nuclear power plants had become widely publicized.[26]

As a result of these measures, the utilities found themselves unable to generate adequate internal funds to expand capacity.[27] Difficulty in achieving rate increases sufficient to keep pace with rising costs continued. They were also faced with longer lead times before new capacity could become operational even when sufficient funding was available because of stricter government regulations. Fears of serious capacity shortages in the future therefore surfaced.[28]

Since a shortage is a function of the relative levels of supply and demand, and since capacity additions became increasingly costly, emphasis shifted to the possibility of using the price structure to ration demand more effectively. In some states this resulted in time-of-day pricing closely related to peak-load, and hence to marginal cost pricing. Other states moved to an entirely different rate structure, called life-line rates. We shall evaluate three rate structures (declining-block rates, time-of-day rates, and life-line rates) in turn and determine to what extent they fulfill the objectives of the regulators and meet the social welfare criteria of efficiency and equity.

Declining Block Rates[29]

It is useful at the outset to note that accountants for the electric utilities have traditionally divided costs into three categories:

---

[26]See *Energy Programs/Energy Markets, Overview,* U.S. Department of Energy, Energy Information Administration, Washington, D.C. (July 1980). Chapter 2 of this study analyzes the effects of several major energy bills enacted by Congress in the 6 years following the 1973 embargo.

[27]To overcome this problem some states passed Fuel Adjustment Clauses that allowed utilities to pass along increased fuel costs to their customers without the usual lengthy rate hearings. See M. Taschjian and J. Hewlett, *State Regulation of Electric and Gas Utilities* (Washington, D.C., January 1980), 41–44, for a fuller discussion of the pros and cons of such automatic adjustment clauses. See also our discussion of incentive regulation below.

[28]See *The Adequacy of Future Electric Supply: Problems and Policies,* Advisory Committee report to the Federal Power Commission, as part of the National Power Survey, March 1976. The Chairman of the Advisory Committee was Irwin M. Stelzer.

[29]The following discussion draws on examples given by Taschjian and Hewlett, *State Regulation of Electric and Gas Utilities.*

- Output costs are those that vary with the energy (kilowatt-hours) produced—the associated costs of labor, fuel, materials and supplies, and
  wear and tear of plant. They vary with the volume of production.
- Customer costs are those incurred in reading meters, sending and collect-
  ing bills, keeping accounts, and the like. They vary with the number of
  customers.
- Demand costs are also known as readiness-to-serve costs. They are the
  overhead costs of capital and management involved in providing and
  maintaining a plant that is large enough to meet the peak demand that
  may be made on it at any day and hour. They are thus a function of capacity.[30]

Most rate structures are based, in some way, on these cost categories.

The declining-block rate structure consists of a fixed user charge per
month and a per kilowatt-hour charge that falls in blocks as consumption
increases. For example, assume the following rate structure for residential
service. The fixed charge is $3.50 per month. This is also called the customer
charge and its level is determined by the level of customer costs—meter
reading, billing, and so on—that are approximately equal for each customer
and do not vary with the amount of electricity consumed. The energy charge
is divided into two parts—$.10 per kilowatt-hour for the first 500 hours, $.05
per kilowatt-hour for all additional hours (see Figure 16.2).[31] The energy
charge curve is equivalent to a supply curve as seen by an individual customer.
Note that whatever quantity a single customer consumes, the price paid for the
marginal kilowatt-hour consumed will differ from the average price (equal to
total amount paid by the consumer/number of kilowatt-hours consumed).

Now the combination of the fixed charge and the two-part energy charge
can be viewed as an approximation to price discrimination (review Chapters
3, 11, and 14).

In Figure 16.3, D is the demand curve facing a monopolist. AC and MC
are the average and marginal cost curves, respectively. If the producer can
charge the maximum amount for each unit sold (P_1 for the first unit, P_2 for the
second, P_3 for the third, and so on), then she will expand output until the
marginal revenue from the last unit produced just equals the marginal cost at
Q_B with a marginal price OC. Total revenue is equal to the entire area under the
demand curve $OABQ_B$. Had the producer charged a uniform price equal to
marginal cost, she would have produced OQ_B at price OC for each unit, and
total revenue would be $OCBQ_B$. First-degree price discrimination has enabled
the monopolist to capture the full area of consumer's surplus, ABC, that would
otherwise (at uniform price OC) accrue to the consumer.

---

[30]Wilcox and Shepherd, *Public Policies toward Business*, 408.

[31]In practice, these charges vary a good deal among electric utility companies. In New Jersey, for
example, the Public Service Electric and Gas Co. has a fixed charge of $2.75 per month, and the
first 600 kilowatt-hours are billed at $.125/kwh. Usage beyond 600 kilowatt-hours costs $.14/
kwh from June to September, and $.11/kwh the rest of the year. (The higher charge during the
summer represents an effort to discourage peak-period demand.)

Figure 16.2 Pricing for Residential Service

The declining-block rate structure consists of a fixed charge of $3.50 per month, and a declining energy charge: $.10 per kilowatt-hour for the first 500 hours, $.05 per kilowatt-hour for all additional hours.

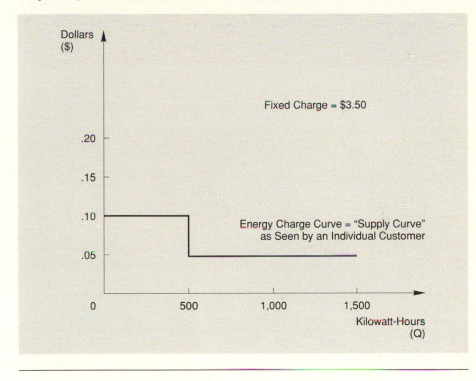

Now consider the declining block scheme. The monopolist charges OG for less than Q_E units and OC for Q_E units or more. She produces OQ_B, the maximum amount that can be sold at the marginal price, OC. Total revenue equals $OGEQ_E + Q_EFBQ_B$. This equals $OCBQ_B + CGEF$. In other words, a declining-block rate yields revenue above what would be earned at the uniform price (by amount CGEF). However, there is still an untapped area of surplus, namely AGE and EFB. If the monopolist knew the exact shape of the demand curve, she could impose a fixed charge per customer equal to

$$\frac{AGE + EFB}{\text{number of customers}}$$ in addition to the declining-block rate, and so capture the total area of surplus, ABC.[32]

---

[32]CGEF is the surplus captured on the first OE units; zero surplus is captured on Q_B - Q_E units. AGE + EFB would be the surplus captured from the fixed charge. Thus AGE + CGEF + EFB = ABC would be the total consumer's surplus converted into revenue.

Figure 16.3 Two-Part Tariff

The monopolist charges OG for less than Q_E units and OC for Q_E units or more. It produces Q_B. Total revenue equals $OGEQ_E + Q_E FBQ_B$. The untapped area of surplus is AGE + EFB.

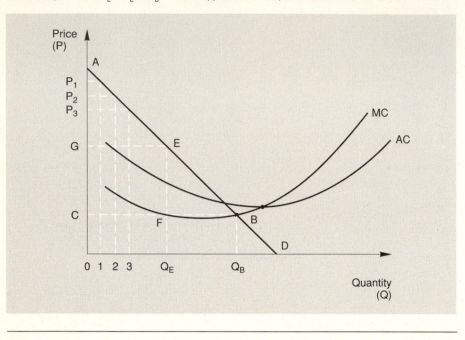

The combination of a fixed charge and a declining-block rate could therefore yield a result close to perfect price discrimination.[33] In fact, however, it is most unlikely that the declining-block method will yield the optimal output (at Q_B in Figure 16.3).[34]

For industrial users (commercial service) the declining-block structure is complicated not only by a larger number of blocks (see Figure 16.4(a)) but also

---

[33]Note that we assume that the fixed charge will not itself affect the quantity consumed at the margin, that is, there are negligible income effects. In fact, increases in the level of fixed charge may well knock marginal customers out of the market. Thus we should really use an income-compensated demand curve—one that measures only substitution effects.

[34]This is both because the firm's knowledge of the shape of the demand curve is imperfect and because the firm does not know the reservation price of individual customers. In other words, it does not know how specific customers are ordered along the demand curve. Also, the fixed charge is determined, as noted, not by demand but by the level of customer costs. These determine how much of the surplus is actually captured. J. H. Crockett has pointed out that even if the market demand curve were known, the declining block structure designed to capture the appropriate area under the market demand curve, will not in fact achieve its objective because individual demand curves differ and not all consumers make their consumption decisions on the basis of the final block price (equal to marginal cost). Some make their decisions based on an inframarginal price. This is a complicated point that we will not pursue. J. H. Crockett,

Figure 16.4   Pricing for Commercial Service

The declining-block rate has a larger number of blocks for commercial service than for residential service and a fixed charge of $3.50. There is a demand charge of $2.00 when more than 50 kilowatts are consumed at the time of customer's peak usage.

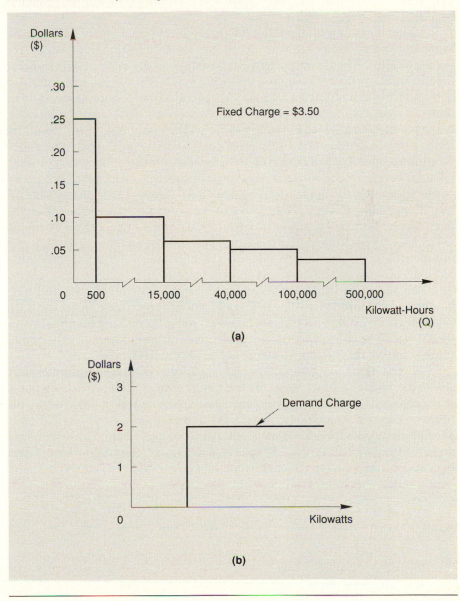

"Differential Pricing and InterConsumer Efficiency in the Electric Power Industry," *Bell Journal of Economics* 7 (Spring 1979): 293–298.

by the addition of a demand charge to the fixed charge. "Essentially, this demand charge is measured in kilowatts and is based on the maximum expected amount of electricity used in a very short time period, usually 1–15 or 30 minutes."[35] This involves monitoring the customer over some long period to determine both when and how great the customer's maximum demand becomes.

Thus, for example, the demand charge might be zero for less than 50 kilowatts and $2.00 per kilowatt per month for all additional kilowatts (see Figure 16.4(b)). The demand charge is based on an estimate of demand cost that the utilities employ to suggest the extent to which users impose peak-load demands on them requiring additional capacity to meet those demands. The demand charge is a function of kilowatts, the measure of demand for capacity, not kilowatt-hours, which measure use. To set the charge, therefore, the utility must meter the average consumption of a customer during the maximum 10 to 30 minute interval over a period of 3 to 6 months. Or the utility can "compute the total horsepower rating of a customer's connected equipment."[36] Because of metering costs, the demand charge is usually imposed only on large industrial or commercial users. Note also that the demand charge is based on the individual customer's heaviest use, which may or may not coincide with the overall market peak demand. Therefore, while the demand charge may smooth out the customer's use pattern, whether this will have the effect of smoothing out market demand sufficiently is entirely unclear.

We have noted that if rates are set at appropriate levels, the declining block structure could yield an efficient allocation of resources. However, if the cost categories used to set the rate levels do not reflect actual marginal costs, then it would be entirely fortuitous for efficient output to result.[37] The equity implications of this pricing structure are not immediately clear.

Furthermore, to the extent that it is cheaper to buy large quantities than small, the declining-block structure encourages rather than restricts demand. In the changed economic environment of the late 1960s and 1970s, in which the future expansion of electricity capacity became uncertain, emphasis shifted to possibilities for the effective management (restraint) of demand growth. Many economists advocated time-of-day and seasonal rates—the practical equivalent of peak-load pricing—in which the cost categories employed for setting rates would reflect true long- and short-run marginal costs.

[35]Taschjian and Hewlett, *State Regulation of Electric and Gas Utilities*, 50.

[36]Phillips, *The Economics of Regulation*, 350.

[37]However, in testimony in a rate hearing before one of the state commissions, one economist justified the declining-block rate in efficiency terms. The argument was that until the late 1960s long-run marginal cost was below long-run average cost, and that low prices for the tailblock (marginal) users ensured marginal prices close to long-run marginal cost and below average cost, with the shortfall in revenue recouped from higher intramarginal prices.

Time-of-Day Rates

Perhaps the most effective advocate of marginal cost pricing for utilities and its peak-load pricing variation is Alfred Kahn.[38] In his study of state pricing regulation in New York and California, Douglas D. Anderson documents Kahn's successful campaign in New York.[39] Kahn convinced various interest groups—state regulation commissions, utilities, consumers' lobbies, and environmentalists—that a shift from declining-block rates to time-of-day and seasonal rates based on good estimates of marginal cost could simultaneously slow the profit decline of the utilities and restrict demand growth (a specific goal of the environmentalists). Such a shift might even allow a reduction in the overall level of rates through a more rational use of existing capacity and smaller demand for additions to capacity. In short, Kahn suggested, a shift to peak-load pricing would yield an unequivocal improvement in social welfare.

We saw earlier (Chapter 14) that peak- and off-peak prices are determined by the position of both the long- and short-run marginal cost curves and the level of demand. Specifically, the optimal capacity level is determined at the intersection of the effective demand for capacity curve and the long-run marginal cost curve. The welfare-maximizing peak- and off-peak prices are then determined at the intersection of the peak- and off-peak demand curve and the short-run marginal cost curves. Recall that if capacity and prices are chosen so as to maximize social welfare, there is no guarantee that the utility will break even. (Only in the case of constant cost with optimal capacity is total revenue equal to total cost.) Even in the constant cost case, there may be a failure to break even with peak-load pricing if capacity levels are set too high so that pricing at peak marginal cost is insufficient to cover the high capacity costs. In other words, the larger is capacity compared with demand (both peak- and off-peak), the easier it is to supply additional units at low marginal cost and the more likely it is that prices at marginal cost will fail to yield revenue greater than total cost. We thus encounter again the fundamental dilemma of public utility pricing.

In the United States, time-of-day pricing is a two-part price system and consists of a kilowatt charge and a kilowatt-hour charge where both charges may vary over the day and/or season. For example, consider the following rate structure for high tension service (HTS) set by the Public Service Electric and Gas Company in Newark, New Jersey, in February 1982.[40]

---

[38]He was not, however, the first. The father of marginal cost pricing in the United States is William Vickrey. See, for example, his article, "Some Implications of Marginal Cost Pricing for Public Utilities," *American Economic Review Supplement* 45 (1955): 605–620.

[39]D. D. Anderson, *Regulatory Policies and Electric Utilities.*

[40]*Tariff for Electric Service, Public Service Electric and Gas Go.,* (P.U.C.N.J. No. 9 Electric) Newark, New Jersey 07101 (February 14, 1982).

Rate Schedule HTS High Tension Service

Applicable to Use of Service for
General purposes at subtransmission and transmission voltages

Character of Service
Continuous

Rate
Fixed Charge:
$1,970.00 in each month
Kilowatt Charge—in the months of June through October:
    $8.60   per kilowatt of monthly maximum demand, on-peak
    0.00   per kilowatt of monthly maximum demand, intermediate
    0.00   per kilowatt of monthly maximum demand, off-peak
Kilowatt Charge—in the months of November through May:
    $7.70   per kilowatt of monthly maximum demand, on-peak
    0.00   per kilowatt of monthly maximum demand, intermediate
    0.00   per kilowatt of monthly maximum demand, off-peak
Kilowatt-hour Charge:
    $5.88   per kilowatt-hour, on-peak
    5.66   per kilowatt-hour, intermediate
    4.40   per kilowatt-hour, off-peak

Time Periods
On-peak time period shall be considered as the hours from 8 A.M. to 10 P.M. Monday through Friday, or as otherwise designated by Public Service. Intermediate time period shall be considered as the hours from 8 A.M. to 10 P.M. Saturday, or as otherwise designated by Public Service. All other hours shall be considered the off-peak time period.

Note that this schedule prescribes higher prices in summer than in winter, which suggests that in New Jersey summer air-conditioning demand is higher than winter heating demand. In more northern states, demand will be higher in the winter. Many states have some time-of-day pricing schemes in operation for some types of service, and many are conducting experiments for residential service. There is not yet widespread use of time-of-day pricing for residential service, however, although differentiation of rates by season is now very common.

The introduction of some peak-load pricing into New York and other states has been viewed as a prime example of the successful application of the lessons of economic theory to a real-world pricing problem. However, in some other states, notably California, an entirely different pricing scheme was adopted in response to the pressures of rising fuel and electricity prices generated by the changing economic environment. This is the life-line, or inverted rate scheme. It has much less justification in theoretical terms and was pushed through in California by a powerful coalition of citizen, environmental, and political groups.

Life-Line Rates

Like the declining-block and peak-load pricing schemes the life-line scheme also has two parts. Each household pays a fixed charge per period, then a low price as long as the quantity demanded does not exceed a given number of

Figure 16.5 Life-Line Rates

Each household pays a fixed charge of $2.00, a low price for less than 500 kilowatt-hours consumed per month, and a higher price for all subsequent units.

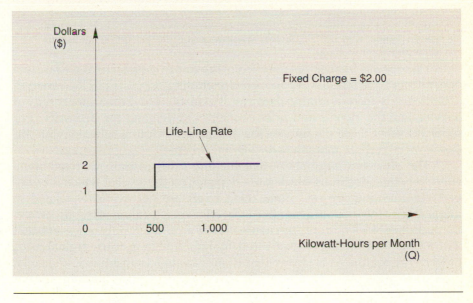

units (say 500 kilowatt-hours) and a high price per unit for all units in excess of this number (see Figure 16.5). The rationale for such a scheme sprang from the argument that poor people should be provided with a minimum amount of electricity at a cheap rate because electricity is essential for reasonable living conditions.[41] It was further argued that, since the rate was higher for larger unit purchases, life-line pricing would restrain demand more effectively than the declining block scheme, which encouraged the consumption of large quantities. Thus, the argument was that life-line pricing is efficient as well as equitable, especially when compared with the declining block rate.

On closer examination, both arguments are weak. Were life-line pricing to be restricted to a particular group of needy people, then the argument for reducing the price of a necessary commodity consumed by this group as a way of raising their real income is essentially the same as advocating rent control and subsidized school lunches—a merit good argument (see Chapter 5). However, the proponents of life-line pricing also claimed that were such a scheme to be generally enforced, the same redistributive effect towards lower

---

[41]See D. D. Anderson, *Regulatory Politics*, 144-183. See also D. Dimopoulos, "Pricing Schemes for Regulated Enterprises and Their Welfare Implications in the Case of Electricity," *Bell Journal of Economics* 12 (Spring 1981): 185–200.

income groups would occur. In a comprehensive study of life-line pricing schemes compared with, among others, the declining-block rate, Dionissios Dimopoulos concludes that:

> Even if there is a very high correlation between consumption of electricity and households' income, and even if we weigh more highly the benefits that low income households derive than the ones derived by high income households, it is not at all clear whether a life-line pricing scheme will increase total welfare.[42]

He suggests further that the effect of life-line pricing on total welfare will depend on a large number of parameters, including, for example, the variation of households' income around the mean, the elasticity of the marginal utility of income, and the income and price elasticities of demand for electricity. For some values of these parameters the declining-block rate scheme might increase social welfare more than the life-line scheme.

The efficiency argument—that life-line rates restrain demand more effectively than declining-block rate—depends on the level at which the two-part life-line rates are set. Since these levels are not explicitly related to marginal cost they would generate a more efficient allocation of resources than the declining-block rate only by chance.[43] They would certainly be less efficient than a peak-load pricing scheme based on short- and long-run marginal costs. Indeed, the argument is strong that if one wants to subsidize low-income people, there are more direct and sure ways to do it. If one wants an efficient electricity industry, income distribution considerations ought to be kept out altogether.

In spite of these weaknesses in its economic rationale, a life-line scheme was adopted in California and some other states as a political response to consumer frustration with rising utility bills and, in California at least, as part of a more general political thrust by citizens' groups, unions, and environmentalists who were seeking an issue around which to coalesce.

PRACTICAL POLICYMAKING: THE COMMISSION'S ROLE

Economists often disagree, and the history and ramifications of theoretical and ideological discussions among economists have often been blamed for the failure of economic policy. Policymakers have not been given clear-cut guidelines, runs the complaint. If economists would only agree, how easy it would be to make good policy!

The history of marginal cost pricing in this country tends to refute this complaint, which usually comes from noneconomists and is at least sometimes misinformed. Most economists agree that prices related to marginal costs, with all the necessary provisos about reasonable rates of return, will usually

---

[42]D. Dimopoulos, "Pricing Schemes for Regulated Enterprises," 199.

[43]See D. D. Anderson, *Regulatory Politics*, 148–149, for two examples of the revenue effects of different life-line schemes.

yield a more efficient allocation of resources than other pricing schemes and will not necessarily result in reductions in equity. Of course, the discussions of this chapter and Chapters 13 to 15 reveal that, in even the simplest case, the problem of optimal pricing for utilities raises complex questions. Furthermore, when the complications of fluctuating demand and investment in an uncertain world are added, the solution to any given pricing problem is a complex function of cost and demand. Problems of measurement, in particular of identifying and measuring marginal cost, compound the difficulties.

Regulation of the electricity industry occurs at two levels of government—federal and state. In 1977, the Federal Energy Regulatory Commission (FERC) was created as an independent commission within the Department of Energy. Its five members are appointed by the President subject to Senate approval and serve staggered terms of 4 years. The FERC inherited many of the powers of the Federal Power Commission, which it replaced. Its jurisdiction covers:

1.   The establishment and adjustment of rates for the sale of natural gas and wholesale purchases of electricity.

2.   The regulation of mergers and securities acquisitions under the Federal Power and Natural Gas Acts.

3.   The establishment of rates for pipeline transportation of oil.

4.   Proposals by the Energy Secretary to alter oil price regulations. However, this power can be nullified by a Presidential declaration of the existence of an emergency.

Commission decisions on matters under its jurisdiction become the final decisions of the Energy Department. In addition, the Federal Energy Regulatory Commission has the power of judicial review of the Energy Department's decisions regarding the Emergency Petroleum Allocation Act of 1973, passed in response to the OPEC oil embargo. The Department of Energy and the FERC thus have regulatory authority in all energy industries and some rate-setting authority in the areas of electricity and natural gas.

In the 1970s, two laws were passed in response to the energy crisis precipitated by the OPEC oil embargo. They extended federal government authority to regulate the use of fuel for power plants producing electricity. The Energy Supply and Environmental Coordination Act of 1974 and the Power Plant and Industrial Fuel Use Act of 1978 had as their chief objective to encourage the use of indigenous energy resources (the most outstanding example being coal) in electrical power plants, instead of petroleum and natural gas. The Fuel Use Act imposed restrictions on both new and existing plants. For example, new electric power plants were prohibited from using oil or natural gas as their primary energy source except under special circumstances. Existing plants were encouraged to switch from natural gas to coal. As we noted above, these new regulations contributed to the increase in costs experienced by utilities in the 1970s, particularly for capacity expansion.

At the state level of regulation, the state commissions (which are often blamed for anomalies in their rate-making approach) are charged with the basic task of regulating rates and quality of service.[44] The interconnections between federal and state regulatory authorities increase the complexity of political interests in the industry, which interferes with rational policymaking.

The state commission's first task is to establish the overall rate level that permits a utility to earn a fair rate of return. Then the rate structure that will yield this overall fair rate of return is determined. However, the rules for determining the rate structure often contain inconsistencies. For example, the Public Utility Regulatory Policies Act of 1978 establishes federal standards for rate setting. It specifies that electricity rates shall "be designed, to the maximum extent practicable, to reflect the costs of providing electric service," that time-of-day rates and seasonal rates should be followed where possible, and that declining-block rates are not permissible except where the declining-block pattern is a true reflection of costs. While the term marginal cost is not specifically mentioned in the preamble to the act, the regulations for compliance specify that utilities must report information about marginal cost to the state commissions, presumably for use in the setting of rates. A paragraph on life-line rates, however, states:

> No provision of this title prohibits a state regulatory authority (with respect to an electric utility for which it has rate-making authority) or a nonregulated electric utility from fixing, approving or allowing to go into effect a rate for essential needs . . . of residential electric consumers which is lower than a rate under the standard referred to above.

Thus Congress is essentially saying to the state commissions: you are to use cost in setting prices, but you may also use life-line pricing if you wish. Since marginal cost and life-line pricing are two entirely different schemes, Congress has given completely contradictory instructions to the state commissions.

Note that although the President had wanted to require state agencies to follow the federal guidelines in rate-making, the bill as passed did not so mandate. Essentially, Congress argued that the states should continue to oversee the utilities without excessive federal interference.

The method by which these instructions are translated into actual price decisions by the commissions further muddies the waters. When a regulated utility wishes to raise prices in response, for example, to increases in fuel costs, it must file its request with the state regulatory commission, which then calls for a rate hearing.[45] In addition to state commissioners, their staffs, and representatives of the company, representatives of other groups, other firms, and U.S. government departments (the Army, for example) may participate in the hearing. Phillips notes that the role of the regulators is complex:

> Regulatory commissions have been characterized as quasi-judicial and quasi-legislative. Contrary to the basic pattern of American government,

---

[44]For a detailed description of the structure and procedures of the regulatory commissions see Phillips, *The Economics of Regulation*, Chapters 4 and 5.

[45]Fuel adjustment clauses allow utilities to avoid seeking commission approval for new rates based on fuel cost increases in some circumstances.

which is based upon the doctrine of separation of powers, a commission assumes the task of administrator, judge and legislator. When investigating rates or service and safety standards, a commission is performing an administrative function. When holding hearings, examining evidence and making decisions, a commission is acting as judge of a company's conduct. Moreover, a commission can even determine the rules it wants to administer, and it can decide to prosecute a company and to gather evidence as well as the evidence presented by the company, and makes a decision. When prescribing certain rules of conduct for a company, such as fixing rates, a commission is acting in a legislative capacity.[46]

Given the number and diversity of interests expressed at regulatory hearings, it is not surprising that, in its choice of price level and structure, a commission's final decision may be influenced as much or more by the distributional arguments between the company and the intervenors as by the basic problem of how to generate an efficient price structure.

Incentive Regulation

We saw in Chapter 15 that the relationship between government regulators and the utilities they regulate falls into the principal–agent category. A state utilities commission (the principal) gives price setting rules to a utility (the agent). The question immediately arises about what circumstances are likely to encourage the agent to comply with the rules. In other words, what is the structure of incentives offered by the regulatory framework that will ensure that the principal's goals are met by the actions of the agent. We showed that cost-plus pricing rules destroy the incentive for regulated utilities to minimize costs. Fortuitously, however, the delays that are typical of many rate hearings usually ensure that price rises are granted by the regulators some time after the increase in costs that prompted the rate hearing. Knowing about the likelihood of delay (the regulatory lag), utilities then have an incentive to minimize costs during the lag so as to offset a fall in profits.

In their comprehensive review of regulatory incentives, P. R. Joskow and R. Schmalensee identify a number of alternatives to rate-of-return rate regulation, discussed in Chapter 15.[47] They note further that "as of January 1, 1986, thirty-one incentive programs in operation in twenty states, as well as FERC, incorporated at least some of the incentive payment concepts discussed above." They offer a number of specific examples, including the following:

> In 1983 the New York Public Service Commission initiated an incentive payment designed to encourage utilities to minimize fuel and purchase power costs. The program currently applies to two utilities in New York, but it may be extended to others. The utilities are required to make forecasts of their expected fuel cost for a year into the future. These predicted costs are included in the rates. Differences between actual fuel costs and forecast fuel costs are shared between the utility and its customers; electricity rates are changed to recover 80% of the difference, and the utility bears the

---

[46]Phillips, *The Economics of Regulation*, 113–114.

[47]Joskow and Schmalensee, "Incentive Regulation for Electric Utilities," *Yale Journal on Regulation* 4 (Fall 1986): 1–49.

remaining 20%. The program includes a cap on the amount of the utility's penalty or reward. Once the year-to-date deviation between forecast fuel costs and actual fuel costs reaches $50 million, the share of additional deviations passes through as increases or decreases in rates increases to 90%—in other words, the utility's share falls to 10%. When the year-to-date deviation reaches $100 million, the adjustment mechanism reverts to a full fuel cost pass through. This provision effectively places an annual $15 million cap on rewards and penalties that the firm can bear.[48]

Joskow and Schmalensee note that the percentage of the difference between actual and forecast costs borne by the utility is reduced when this difference becomes large. The rationale is that a large difference is more likely to reflect unforseen changes in costs or revenues that are not in the utility's power to control, and for which the utility should therefore not have to pay.

The Revival of Competition

The Argument for Competition Another approach towards mitigating the inadequacies of rate-of-return regulation is to encourage competition. This strategy, of course, is only sensible if indeed the industry is not a natural monopoly. As we have observed many times, the conditions for the existence of natural monopoly are complicated and depend not only on the cost structure of firms, but also on the extent to which dominant firms conduct a stay-out pricing policy that deters or completely excludes entrants. In electricity, as in transportation and telephones (Chapters 17 and 18), the existing price structure is the combined result of costs, demand, and regulated price decisions. Under rate-of-return regulation, prices are likely to be held at or above average cost so as to allow the utility a fair rate of return. When average cost is declining over quantity produced and over time, as was the case for several decades in electricity, prices that also decline over quantity produced and time will still allow for normal or above normal profits.

While demand for electricity was growing and technological change was raising the efficient plant size, government regulators were in a position to set prices that remained relatively low and still returned a reasonable profit to utilities. Investment in ever larger plants was not discouraged. The perception of both investors and regulators was that the growth in demand would take up the excess capacity. Furthermore, if the rate of return exceeded the cost of capital, the Averch-Johnson effect would tend to encourage investment.

As we noted above, rising costs in the early 1970s led the utilities to ask the regulating commissions more frequently for rate increases. The commissions, however, were reluctant to grant them. More construction expenses than before were disallowed in the calculation of the rate base, regulatory delays increased, and utilities' profits suffered. In this economic environment there was excess capacity in large plants; smaller plant sizes were now more profitable. Moreover, the *Otter Tail* case, which held a refusal to wheel illegal,

---

[48]Joskow and Schmalensee, "Incentive Regulation," 41.

made it possible for some producers at the generating stage to buy and sell excess power.[49]   The willingness of buyers to enter into long-term contracts with producers for the supply of power made vertical integration comparatively less attractive. Relatively small generating firms could now sell power for transmission and distribution to a larger market by buying wheeling rights. New entry occurred at the fringe of the industry, putting downward pressure on the wholesale prices in this market.

Because regulators sometimes failed to grant rate increases that allowed the utilities to recover fully the capacity costs of new investment, and because of the generally depressed state of the market, some utilities have attempted to divest themselves of their generating capacity, leaving them operable only in the transmission and distribution markets. The success of this strategy depends on persuading state regulators to release the spun-off generating firm from state regulation as soon as all current supply contracts are fulfilled.[50]   The generating firm would then be free to sell to any buyer, and buyers would be free to look elsewhere if necessary for cheaper wholesale power. However, the spun-off firm would still be subject to federal regulation.

While the deregulation hearings may be long and drawn out, the hoped-for outcome is that the generating firm must no longer bear the time and money costs of further rate hearings. Thus, the argument goes, competition is viable in wholesale markets, prices will be set by supply and demand, and normal profits will be earned by competing firms.

The Argument against Competition   One difficulty in assessing the potential competitiveness of a regulated industry is that observable regulated prices are unlikely to reflect the prices that competition would yield. If the industry were deregulated, however, dominant firms could undercut the new entrants and drive them out. In other words, if the industry is a natural monopoly, then deregulation will ultimately result in the survival of only one or a few firms. The ability of new firms to price compete successfully with regulated established firms cannot be discovered by looking at current prices. Rather an attempt must be made to compare true economic costs, a task that is prone to inaccuracy. As we shall see in Chapters 17 and 18, the deregulation of the airlines and of telecommunications have not ultimately resulted in the very competitive market structures that were forecast, but rather in the continued dominance of the previously regulated firms.

We now consider the issue of pollution, and raise the question whether more competition at the generation stage would increase or decrease pollution from the generation of electric power.

---

[49]*U.S. v. Otter Tail Power Company*, 410 U.S. 366 (1973).

[50]V. L. Smith, "Currents of Competition," 27.

Electricity and Pollution

First, we note that the different types of fuel currently used in the generation of power have different effects on the environment.[51] The worst polluters are coal and nuclear power, oil and natural gas come next, and hydroelectric power and solar energy are the cleanest. Unfortunately, the cleanest types of fuel are very scarce compared with others and are also location specific. With the rise in the relative price of oil and gas at the beginning of the 1970s, many utilities switched to coal-fired plants. The likelihood of many new nuclear plants being built is now very small, especially following the disastrous accident at the Soviet nuclear power plant in Chernobyl in 1986. However, the choice of power for the generation of electricity for the immediate and middle-range future (the next 30 to 50 years) is likely to be mainly between coal and nuclear power, the worst polluters.

In Chapter 5 we defined pollution as a production externality, a by-product from a productive process that imposes costs on the society at large for which the producing firm does not directly pay. Furthermore, there is no incentive for an individual firm to incur costs to reduce its own pollution. One firm acting alone might have a very small effect on reducing the total amount of pollution from all firms and would put itself at a distinct competitive disadvantage. In Chapter 22 we shall examine in some detail the various policy options available for controlling pollution and evaluate current policies. Here we confine ourselves to noting some basic differences in the social costs of coal and nuclear fuel.[52] We will also consider the issue of competition and pollution.

Coal-fired plants discharge pollutants into the air, such as sulphur dioxide, that cause lung disease resulting in fatalities. In addition fatalities from black lung disease and accidents result from the working conditions in coal mines. Acid rain from airborne pollutants destroys crops and pollutes water supplies. Strip mining destroys the landscape. And it is possible that destructive climatic changes may result from a surfeit of carbon dioxide in the atmosphere. By contrast nuclear power is relatively clean. Its social costs, however, may be as large or larger than coal if the possibility of disastrous accidents in which large quantities of radiation are leaked is taken into account. This was precisely the case at the plant in Chernobyl. The large quantities of radiation emitted in the plant failure caused several immediate deaths and more cases of radiation sickness and sent a huge radioactive cloud across Europe, whose ill effects on the health of many will be felt long into the future. In addition, nuclear power plants generate radioactive waste that must be disposed of if it is not to cause long-range pollution. If no accidents happen, then nuclear power may be considered relatively clean compared with coal, but the "if" does not have any reliable probabilities attached to it. It turns out that people are particularly afraid of large disasters, even if the estimated probabilities of occurrence are

---

[51]See W. Ramsay, "Unpaid Costs of Electrical Energy," (Baltimore: National Energy Strategies Project, Resources for the Future, John Hopkins University Press, 1979).

[52]We draw on William Ramsay, "Unpaid Costs of Electrical Energy," for much of the material in this section.

very small. A stable number of deaths from mining accidents and black lung disease may be more socially acceptable than virtually any probability of a nuclear accident.[53] Moreover the disposal of hazardous nuclear waste is fraught with difficulty and very costly.

The question now becomes whether competition at the generating stage would make matters better or worse. Certainly the antipollution laws would apply as well to competitive as to regulated firms. The issue is really whether enforcement is likely to be more or less successful with competition. A regulated firm is subject to at least two regulating authorities—the state commission and the Environmental Protection Agency. There is no formal link between the two except insofar as investment in pollution control equipment affects the size of the rate base. It is possible that state commissions could more formally adopt plans for pollution control in coordination with the EPA. With competition, the state commissions no longer play a role, and all enforcement would be left to the EPA. However, under either market structure, the larger social choice would remain, namely to assess the relative social costs and risks now and in the future for different types of fuel and to establish pollution-control laws that push the electricity industry in the appropriate direction.

SUMMARY

In this chapter we have discussed the structure of the electricity industry and the development of regulation. In particular we described how rising fuel prices and slower technical change in the early 1970s halted the long decline in the relative price of electricity. The new environment of rising costs reduced utilities' profits and strained the system of rate-of-return regulation. We discussed the cost and demand conditions in the industry and the extent to which it could be called a natural monopoly. We examined the efficiency and equity effects of various pricing schemes. We discussed incentive regulation as a route towards solving some of the problems of regulating the industry in the current environment of rising costs. We then discussed the extent to which competition has been introduced in the generation stage of production and to what extent it will be viable in the future. Finally we addressed the pollution effects of different fuels and the uncertainties involved in planning for the future.

CONCLUSION

Government policy for efficiency in the electricity industry need not lack for direction from economic theory. Marginal cost and peak–load pricing are sound policies with a long history of support from economists and have been successfully practiced elsewhere (France is the prime example). However, there is in this country no lobby for efficiency. Nevertheless, although the political pressures are strong, and the rules from Congress inconsistent, the

---

[53]Ramsay, "Unpaid Costs of Electrical Energy," 158.

Public Utility Regulatory Policies Act of 1978 explicitly recognizes the importance of marginal cost as a basis for rate setting. In some states, (for example,
New York) this has resulted in a move towards a more rational price structure;
in others (such as California) it has not. However, in the absence of a clear
statement from Congress enforcing marginal cost-based prices, or a complete
reform of the commission system, a nationwide move towards marginal cost
pricing in electricity is not likely to occur soon. Since the viability of competition in the generation stage is still uncertain, the various proposals for incentive regulation become an important route towards greater efficiency in the
industry.

Discussion Questions

1.   In the first 20 years following World War II, the electricity industry was
      stable and profitable, experiencing demand growth and real price stability.
      What economic and political factors changed this picture? How have
      these affected pricing policy in the industry?

2.   What is a demand charge for electricity? Is there any theoretical rationale
      for it?

3.   Compare and contrast the efficiency and equity properties of declining-
      block rates and life-line rates. Why have these schemes been chosen in
      some states rather than time-of-day pricing? Which scheme would you
      advocate?

4.   What characteristics of the electricity industry have made it a candidate
      for regulation? Are there any arguments for deregulating this industry?

5.   Is rate-of-return regulation (cost-plus) pricing a good incentive scheme?
      Is there another incentive scheme that might be an improvement? Explain
      fully.

Selected Readings

Anderson, D. D. *Regulatory Politics and Electric Utilities.* Boston: Auburn House Publishing
Company, 1981. *An original discussion of the interaction between political and economic forces in
determining the rate-setting policies of state regulatory commissions for public utilities.*

Crew, Michael A., ed. *Regulating Utilities in an Era of Deregulation* (London: Macmillan, 1987).
Articles covering a variety of recent analytical issues in public utility regulation.

Gordon, R. *Reforming the Regulation of Electric Utilities.* Lexington, Mass.: Lexington Books, D. C.
Heath and Company, 1982. *An advanced analysis of the electric-power industry and the impact of
government regulation.*

Hines, L. G. *The Market, Energy, and the Environment.* Boston: Allyn and Bacon, Inc., 1988. *A clear,
up-to-date, accessible text.*

Phillips, A., ed. *Promoting Competition in Regulated Markets.* Washington, D.C.: Brookings
Institution, 1975. *Two chapters in this book contain interesting assessments of the electricity industry:
Chapter 5, "Antitrust in the Electric Power Industry" by L. W. Weiss; and Chapter 6, "A Reexamination
of the Monopoly Market Structure for Electric Utilities" by W. J. Primeaux, Jr.*

Weiss, L. W. *Case Studies in American Industry,* 3d ed. New York: John Wiley and Sons, 1980,
Chapter 3. *A lucid introduction to the electricity industry.*

CHAPTER 17

· ·

REGULATION AND PUBLIC POLICY PARADOXES: TRANSPORTATION

INTRODUCTION

At the beginning of this book, we noted that government activity in the marketplace falls into three main areas: policies that encourage competition and rely on the market (antitrust); policies by which the government overrides the competitive process and substitutes its own decisions to some degree (for example, price and profit regulation of public utilities); and new types of regulation (for example, consumer protection).

The transportation and communications industries were subject to government regulation of the second type almost from their inception.[1] A close look at the structure and performance of these industries, now and in the past, reveals that while they possess some characteristics making them good candidates for regulation, other aspects suggest that the competitive process is viable and antitrust enforcement rather than direct regulation may be the most appropriate government policy.

Recent events include decisions to deregulate the airlines and reduce regulation in railroads and trucking, and the settlement between the Justice Department and the American Telephone and Telegraph Company (AT&T) to break up the largest regulated company in the world. Such events reflect arguments that these industries have sufficient potential for competition to yield acceptable performance.

There is still some controversy, however. One argument explains the establishment and growth of federal regulation in these industries in terms of historical and political pressures and points to deregulation as the triumph of good economic analysis over political interests. In this argument, the perform-

---

[1] For good introductions to the transportation industry and transportation economics, see W. K. Talley, *Transportation* (Cincinnati, Ohio: Southwestern Publishing Co., 1983); and C. F. Phillips, Jr., *The Economics of Regulation* (Homewood, Ill.: Richard D. Irwin, Inc. 1969), Chapters 13 and 14.

ance of these industries since deregulation shows unequivocally that competition is viable. Another view recognizes that the clear-cut economic rationale for regulation is harder to identify in transportation and communications, but suggests that arguments for unregulated competition are simplistic. This view assesses postderegulation performance in these industries as mixed and points to some further questions. For example, does it make sense to regulate only one part of an industry? Is it sensible to regulate railroads, but not competing transport modes (trucks and airlines)? Or to regulate local telephone service, but not long-distance communications? Does the consideration of transactions costs in transportation, particularly in the airline industry, alter the viability of competition and point to the need for continued regulation of a different variety?

Many common theoretical and regulatory issues arise in the transportation and communications industries. In this chapter these are discussed and the record examined with reference to transportation. In Chapter 18 we continue the discussion with reference to communications. In both chapters we identify similarities and differences between the two industries. We will look carefully at the changes that have occurred as a result of deregulation.

Since the analysis is complicated and adequate descriptions sometimes lengthy, it is easy to lose sight of the woods for the trees. We will begin our discussion with an explanation of the industry's characteristics—cost conditions, demand conditions, and market structure. We will then present the theoretical problem of price determination and regulation. The last portion of the chapter presents a history of government regulation and discusses recent policy changes (such as deregulation) and their effect on the industry. Into the forest we now step gingerly.

OVERVIEW OF THE INDUSTRY

Table 17.1 identifies the various modes that make up the U.S. intercity transportation network and the associated regulatory agencies.[2] In Chapter 9 (Table 9.1) we saw that the share of national income originating in transportation declined from 4.1 percent in 1965 to 3.4 percent in 1985. This decline results partly from the decline in the price of transportation services relative to the overall price level, reflecting declining relative costs and the effect of regulation in the industry.[3] Within the transportation industry there have been dramatic changes in the division of services between modes. Table 17.2 shows changes in freight transportation and passenger travel by mode during the last three decades. Note the declining fortunes of the railroads for both freight and passengers between 1950 and 1985. This decline has been checked by deregulation and we see a small upturn between 1980 and 1981. The proportion of

---

[2]We omit urban transportation from our discussion. These networks are generally subject to regulation by local rather than federal authorities.

[3]See *Transportation in America*, 4th ed. (Washington, D.C.: Transportation Association of America, March, 1986); and Paul W. MacAvoy, *The Regulated Industries and the Economy* (New York: W. W. Norton and Co., 1979), 42–52.

Table 17.1 The Transportation Industry and Its Regulating Bodies

ICC — Interstate Commerce Commission
FAA — Federal Aviation Administration
CAB — Civil Aeronautics Board (now defunct)

	Rail	Motor Carriers	Water Carriers	Pipelines	Air
Freight	ICC	ICC (Trucks)	ICC	ICC	FAA (CAB)
Passenger	ICC	ICC (Buses)	ICC	—	FAA (CAB)

freight carried by water on the Great Lakes has declined, as has the proportion of passenger miles travelled by bus. In freight transport, the predominant place held by the railroads and Great Lakes water carriers has been taken by trucks and oil pipelines. For passengers, the great competitors for the railroads have been automobiles and airplanes.

These changes reflect a combination of forces.[4] Public investments in transportation infrastructure (roadbed, railroad track, bridges, and tunnels) favored railroad development in the nineteenth century. In the middle of the twentieth century, equivalent investments in the interstate highway network dramatically shifted the pattern of relative costs, making truck transportation relatively cheaper. Technological changes in trucking and air transportation, particularly those that improved their quality of service, made these newer modes into effective competitors. The shift to trucks was aided by strong railroad unions that prevented railroad labor costs and prices from falling. Had rail freight rates declined relative to trucking, the decline in demand for railroad services might have been stemmed. The working of the Interstate Commerce Commission (ICC) and its effect on the relative rate structure for all transportation modes may also have contributed to the relative decline in the railroad industry. As noted above, however, this decline has recently been checked by deregulation.

Cost Conditions

Transportation is a service with complicated characteristics. Supplying firms fall into modes (railroads, barges, trucks, airlines) with very different technologies and diverse cost structures. In freight transportation, the buying firms (called shippers) buy transportation as an intermediate product. Their demand is derived from the demand for the product to be shipped, and their

[4]See G. W. Wilson, "The Relative Importance of Economic Regulation of Transportation vis-à-vis Everything Else," in K. D. Boyer and W. G. Shepherd, eds., *Economic Regulation: Essays in Honor of James R. Nelson,* (East Lansing, Mich.: Michigan State University, 1981).

Table 17.2   Intercity Transportation Volume by Modes Intercity Freight by Modes* (billions of ton-miles)

Year	Rail Amount	Rail %	Truck Amount	Truck %	Oil Pipeline Amount	Oil Pipeline %	Great Lakes Amount	Great Lakes %	Rivers and Canals Amount	Rivers and Canals %	Air Amount	Air %
1950	597	56.2	173	16.3	129	12.1	112	10.5	52	4.9	.30	.03
1960	579	44.1	285	21.8	229	17.4	99	7.5	121	9.2	.89	.07
1970	771	39.7	412	21.3	431	22.3	114	5.9	205	10.6	3.30	.17
1980	932	37.4	555	22.3	588	23.6	96	3.9	311	12.5	4.84	.20
1981	924	38.1	527	21.7	564	23.2	98	4.0	312	12.8	5.09	.21
1982	810	36.0	520	23.1	566	25.1	63	2.8	288	12.8	5.14	.23
1983	841	36.0	575	24.6	556	23.8	68	2.9	291	12.5	5.87	.25
1984	935	37.5	605	24.2	568	22.7	76	3.0	306	12.3	6.60	.26
1985	898	37.2	600	24.9	562	23.3	67	2.8	281	11.6	6.39	.26

Intercity Passenger Travel by Modes
(billions of passenger-miles)

	Private Carrier						Public Carrier							
	Auto		Air		Total		Air		Bus		Rail		Total	
Year	Amt	%	Amt	%	Amt	%	Amt	%	Amt	%	Amt	%	Amt	%
1950	438.3	87.0	0.8	0.2	439.1	87.2	9.3	1.8	22.7	4.5	32.5	6.5	64.5	12.8
1960	706.1	90.4	2.3	0.3	708.4	90.7	31.7	4.1	19.3	2.5	21.6	2.8	72.6	9.3
1970	1026.0	86.9	9.1	0.8	1035.1	87.7	109.5	9.3	25.3	2.1	10.9	0.9	145.7	12.3
1980	1300.4	83.5	14.7	0.9	1315.1	84.4	204.4	13.1	27.4	1.8	11.0	0.7	242.8	15.6
1981	1319.3	83.6	14.6	0.9	1333.9	84.8	201.4	12.8	27.1	1.7	11.4	0.7	239.6	15.2
1982	1344.9	83.6	13.1	0.8	1358.0	84.4	213.6	13.2	26.9	1.7	10.9	0.7	251.4	15.6
1983	1364.1	82.8	12.7	0.8	1376.8	83.6	232.2	14.1	26.5	1.6	11.1	0.7	270.5	16.4
1984	1436.8	82.6	12.5	0.7	1449.3	83.4	250.7	14.4	27.1	1.5	11.5	0.7	289.3	16.6
1985	1484.2	81.9	12.7	0.7	1496.9	82.6	277.2	15.3	25.5	1.4	12.0	0.7	314.7	17.4

*Includes both for-hire and private carriers and also mail and express.

p = preliminary
e = estimated

Source: *Transportation in America*, 4th ed., pp. 6, 8.

transportation requirements depend on the quantity and nature of the product, its location of production and use, and the necessary distance and speed of shipment. Price is, of course, another key determinant of demand, and we discuss this below. For passengers, transportation is both a consumption and production activity, with quality, frequency, and speed important determinants of demand. For some, however, transportation may be the final consumption good, in which slowness rather than speed is desired![5]

[5]This is perhaps more likely to be true of trains or boats than other modes. A nice long slow ride in a car or airplane may not have so much appeal.

The Measurement of Output Before we can identify the shape of the cost function of each mode, an appropriate unit of output must be specified. The most common definition of transportation output is ton-miles and passenger-miles: number of tons (or passengers) multiplied by the number of miles traveled. Thus 1 ton carried 1,000 miles, or 1,000 tons carried 1 mile both amount to 1,000 ton-miles.[6] Ton-mile measures do not reflect the density of traffic over a fixed distance. Density is measured as ton-miles per week per mile of road or track. These output distinctions are important because the shape of the firm's cost curve may change dramatically depending on how output is measured. For example, it may be true that average costs per ton-mile are higher for firms producing more ton-miles per year, but average costs per ton-mile may fall as output increases over a given route system, that is, average costs may fall as density increases.[7]

Kinds of Costs In comparisons between the cost structures of different modes, note first that the full social cost of transportation includes the value of resources used in producing the necessary infrastructure (railroad track, bridges, tunnels, roads, runways, canals), terminal and switching facilities (railroad stations and junctions, truck terminals, barge ports, airports), as well as the vehicles that actually accomplish the movement of freight or passengers (engines, cars, trucks, barges, airplanes), labor (including managers, administrators, and workers), and fuel. To the extent that public funds have financed investment in infrastructure (particularly airports, highways, and canals), the private costs for firms using these facilities do not reflect full social costs. In effect, a large element of fixed cost (for example, the highway and canal systems) is omitted from the cost calculations of trucking and barge companies. Both public and private investment in railroad infrastructure is large, and private costs also do not fully reflect social costs.

---

[6]There are three ton-mile measures—gross, net, and revenue. Gross ton-miles includes only the weight of the vehicle and the shipment. Net ton-miles includes only the weight of the shipment. Revenue ton-miles excludes the transportation of empty vehicles. Thus, if a load of 50 tons is carried 100 miles by train from point A to point B, and the train then returns empty to point A, the round trip will be measured as 5,000 revenue ton-miles (50 tons X 100 miles) with the backhaul omitted.

[7]This point is explained by Robert G. Harris: "There has been a serious confusion between economies of scale and economies of density, and a concomitant failure to specify clearly which is being measured . . . . Economies of scale refer to a long-run average cost curve which declines as the size of the firm increases, i.e., the larger the firm, the lower the cost per unit of output. While this issue is of considerable importance (e.g. with respect to merger policy in the industry), the critical determinant in pricing and (dis)investment policies is whether or not there are economies of density. Specifically, we want to know what happens to average cost as output increases holding the route system, or miles of rail line constant. A small firm with high traffic density may very well have lower average costs than a large firm with low density." R. G. Harris, "Economies of Traffic Density in the Rail Freight Industry," *Bell Journal of Economics* 8 (Autumn 1977): 557.

For the airlines, the understatement of social costs is not so severe because, while the cost of airports and traffic control systems may be financed publicly, the use of the air remains effectively free.[8]

Common costs are also frequently encountered in transportation (recall the distinctions made in Chapter 13 between fixed and common costs).[9] These arise when different services share their costs. For example, suppose the same roadbed is employed to transport both food and lumber. It may be impossible to divide the cost of maintaining the common running tracks and other structures between these two services. Other costs, such as insurance and property taxes, also may not be attributable in any meaningful sense to either service and are truly fixed costs for the firm as a whole.

Transactions costs are the costs incurred by both parties to a transaction in drawing up a contract or agreement. In transportation the necessary contracts are many and complicated. A transportation firm typically deals not only with suppliers of inputs into the production of the service (workers, fuel suppliers, railroad car and airplane manufacturers) and the shippers who use the service, but also with other transportation firms. A shipment of manufactured goods from New Jersey to California must be transferred from one firm to another at various switching and loading locations. The firms must also agree to the division of revenues from the shipment. As we shall see, transactions costs play a significant role in determining the organization of different sectors of the industry, particularly in airlines.

While problems of output definition and the presence of social, common, and transactions costs make accurate measurement of cost curves in transportation a difficult task, it is still possible to make some meaningful statements about cost differences between modes and to assess their impact on the structure of the transportation industry.

Railroad Costs   For the railroads, fixed costs comprise a large proportion of total expenses.[10] Moreover, the fact that investment costs are sunk for long periods of time, often longer than the relevant time span for most managerial and regulatory decisions, suggests that the average cost curve decreases also in the long run.[11] The marginal cost of each service (which is very difficult to measure accurately because of the existence of common costs) will almost certainly lie

[8]There may be substantial external effects associated with each mode that are also not included in private cost calculations (recall Chapter 5). Thus, for example, cars generate pollution, air traffic lanes may become congested so that accident rates increase, and so on.

[9]See W. J. Baumol, et al., "The Role of Cost in the Minimum Pricing of Railroad Services," *Journal of Business* 35 (October 1962): 1–10; A. F. Friedlaender, *The Dilemma of Freight Transport Regulation* (Washington, D.C.: Brookings Institution, 1969): 28; and Phillips, *The Economics of Regulation*, 303.

[10]Outlays that must be made regardless of the volume of traffic carried are interest, payments on investment, and some maintenance of track and equipment. Other expenses that do not vary with the volume of traffic include property taxes and the wages of salaried staff.

[11]See M. J. Roberts, "Transport Costs, Pricing and Regulation," in *Transportation Economics* (New York: Conference of the National Bureau for Economic Research, 1965), 4.

below the average cost curve and may also be decreasing as output rises.[12] The presence of long-run decreasing average costs—that is, economies of scale—combined with the railroads' long history of building infrastructure well ahead of demand has resulted in what is often referred to as an excess capacity problem.[13] As noted above, there may also exist economies of density: average costs fall as output increases over a given route system. Moreover, large common costs may indicate the presence of economies of scope. Given the large and varied nature of the outlays needed to carry freight and passengers over a complex railroad network, it may frequently be cheaper for one firm to provide a variety of different transportation services than for several firms each to specialize in the provision of only one type.[14]

Transactions costs in railroad transportation are of varying importance. Until recently the railroads have not had much flexibility in drawing up contracts. The ICC regulated prices according to specific rules and determined how jointly earned revenues were to be shared between firms. Thus, some important terms of contracts were mandated. Deregulation has enabled firms to make individual contracts with shippers, lowering both transactions and ultimately production costs.

Water and Motor Carrier Costs   The cost characteristics of water and motor carriers differ from those of the railroads in that neither requires such large initial capital investment (although the water carriers require more than the motor carriers). These carriers use publicly provided facilities (highways and waterways), the payment for which would comprise a large part of their fixed costs.[15] Therefore, most of the costs incurred by these carriers vary with the volume of traffic. Services provided by these modes are to some extent indivisible. Provision of the carriage of 1 ton per period of daily carload of freight, for example, may enable extra carloads to be carried at low marginal cost. Their services also are to some extent complementary, as when the cost of the empty backhaul to the original destination would be incurred whether or not a load is carried. The water and motor carriers therefore tend not to suffer from the scale economies or the excess capacity problem of the railroads. Costs are closely associated with the quantity of barges or trucks used, which can be adjusted to varying traffic levels. For these modes, average costs are constant

[12]While there is substantial literature on the slope of the average cost curve for the railroads (see Harris, "Economies of Traffic Density"), there is very little on the slope of the marginal cost curve, mostly because marginal costs are so difficult to measure. But see A. Friedlaender, *The Dilemma of Freight Transport Regulation*, 32–34, for criticism of the ICC's cost estimation measures that yield a decreasing marginal cost curve for rail transportation.

[13]In basic microtheory, excess capacity exists whenever the firm produces a level of output less than the output at which average costs are minimized.

[14]See Robert D. Willig and William J. Baumol, "Using Competition as a Guide," *Regulation* 11 (1987): 28–35.

[15]See A. Friedlaender, *The Dilemma of Freight Transport Regulation*, 45, for an estimate of these costs.

or increasing and marginal costs are constant or increase with the volume of traffic.[16]

Air Transportation Costs In air transportation, the largest elements of fixed cost—airports and the air traffic control system—are financed by federal and local governments. While airlines pay the operating costs of these facilities through landing fees and rents for space, they do not contribute to capital costs. Their main expenses, therefore, consist of airplanes, fuel, and personnel. An airplane may be considered a fixed expense in the sense that different quantities of output (measured in passenger-miles) can be provided by the plane—that is, its cost does not vary significantly with the quantity of output.[17] However, unlike railroad track, bridges, or tunnels, an airplane can be shifted from one route to another in response to shifts in demand. Moreover, if demand falls so much that any individual airline becomes unprofitable, its planes can be sold and used by other firms. Therefore, while an airplane is a fixed cost within certain output ranges, it is not a sunk cost because its owner can recoup at least part of its value by selling it for another use.[18] Since deregulation, airlines that serve a large number of different routes have been able to exploit economies of scope and keep their costs below those of less diversified competitors.[19] Moreover, the provision of computer reservation systems to travel agents by some large airline companies reflects an effort to reduce transactions costs below those of smaller competitors.[20]

In general, therefore, production economies of scale are not significant for the airlines, particularly on high density routes.[21] However, economies of scope and transactions costs savings work to the advantage of large diversified firms even in the absence of significant production economies.

On the cost side, then, the transportation industry consists of modes with very different cost structures. Sometimes costs are decreasing (some railroads, some airlines), sometimes constant or increasing (barges, trucks, and some airlines). However, the effects of these costs on the structure of the industry and the viability of competition cannot be determined without looking at the demand side—in particular, the extent of substitutability between the transportation services produced by different modes.

---

[16]For a comprehensive discussion of costs in trucking see R. Klein, "Market Structure and Conduct," in P. W. MacAvoy and J. W. Snow, eds. *Regulation of Entry and Pricing in Truck Transportation* (Washington, D.C.: American Enterprise Institute, 1977), 119–138. See also G. Chow, "The Status of Economies of Scale in Regulated Trucking: A Review of the Evidence and Future Directions," *Transportation Research* 19 (1978): 365.

[17]This is also true of trucks, engines, railroad cars, and barges, the only distinction being that airplanes are generally more expensive.

[18]This distinction between fixed and sunk costs is crucial for the new theory of the sustainability of natural monopoly discussed in Chapter 13.

[19]See Michael E. Levine, "Airline Competition in Deregulated Markets: Theory, Firm Strategy, and Public Policy," *Yale Journal on Regulation* 4 (Spring 1987): 393–494.

[20]M. E. Levine, "Airline Competition," 415 ff.

[21]The advantages of more frequent service and the economies of using larger planes make for economies of scale on low density routes, especially if quality of service is taken into account.

Demand Conditions

Recall that the demand for freight transportation comes from shippers for whom transportation is an input into the production or distribution process. Their demand for transportation will therefore depend on the demand for their final products, their location, the location of their customers, their production function, and the price of transportation. The market demand for transportation as a whole (the horizontal sum of all shippers' demands) may be relatively inelastic in the short run—there are few, if any, substitutes. One long-run substitute (in principle) is to change the shipper's plant location, but this would occur only in response to expectations that transportation prices would remain so high in the future as to make such a costly move efficient.

With a low demand elasticity, if there is only one supplier of transportation between two points (that is, the supplier is a monopolist), there is a high potential for raising price substantially above marginal cost. This was characteristic of the railroads in the nineteenth century, when shipper protests against railroad monopolies resulted in the Granger laws. These laws introduced maximum rates for railroads and marked the beginning of regulation in transportation.

The demand curve facing a single supplier of transportation in the presence of competition, however, may be very elastic. Its elasticity will depend on the extent of substitutability between the services offered by competitors. This depends in turn upon the precise characteristics of the transportation service required by each shipper. Both the degree of substitutability and demand elasticity are therefore likely to vary substantially for different suppliers.

Market Structure

In Chapter 9, we discussed some of the problems involved in measuring the competitiveness of industries. In particular, we identified the advantages and drawbacks of concentration as a measure of competitiveness. For transportation, the appropriate market definition is crucial. Concentration within the railroad sector or the trucking sector, for example, tells us nothing about the number and size distribution of transportation suppliers between any two cities, and it is the latter measure that is relevant to competitiveness. Indeed, it may be that monopoly exists for some routes and competition for others. It is partly this variation in competitiveness within the industry that has resulted in the existing anomalies in government regulation of the industry.

Railroads Examining the railroad sector as a whole, Phillips notes that within the class of railroads with annual operating revenues of $5 million or more, "eighteen railroads controlled nearly 84 percent of the mileage operated and collected over 60 percent of the freight revenues" (in 1963).[22] However, many routes are served by only one railroad, with two or more railroads competing

---

[22]*The Economics of Regulation*, 484.

over only a few major routes. Where two railroads are in direct competition, both providing very similar service and with similar and probably decreasing costs, price wars are likely. (Recall the duopoly and oligopoly models of Chapter 4.) Frequent episodes of cutthroat competition in the early days of railroad history led to the establishment of rate bureaus (trade associations) to prevent destructive price wars between railroad firms. The opposite problem— that of railroad monopolies—led to the establishment of the ICC and the beginning of government rate regulation. These conflicting forces, and how they affected and were affected by government regulations, will be discussed below.

Two developments in the railroad industry may influence its competitive viability. The first is the interlinking of lines. This involves transferring a long-distance shipment from the equipment of one railroad to that of another (thus increasing the need for cooperation between railroads, which may increase transactions costs). The second is the advent of piggy-backing or trailer-on-flat-car (TOFC) service, a system by which truck trailers can be loaded directly onto railroad flatcars, thereby cutting out the stage of unloading the shipment from the truck and reloading it onto the freight car. This innovation reduces production costs, but increases transactions costs as more coordination is required between railroads and trucks. However, the effect of these changes on competition is hard to disentangle from the effect of recent regulatory policy changes in the industry. The Staggers Rail Act of 1980 allowed the railroads (among other things) to negotiate contracts with individual shippers.[23] This act, together with deregulation in trucking, has resulted in a changing price structure that simultaneously reflects changing costs and different government policies.

Truck Transport   Trucking is much less concentrated than railroads, and as we have seen economies of scale are not significant.[24] The number of competing carriers is great, especially over densely traveled routes. Note, however, the division of the trucking sector into three parts and the difference in regulation between them. Forty percent of intercity truck ton-miles are moved by private carriage, that is, firms that carry only their own goods. Twenty percent are accounted for by for-hire carriers that are exempt from ICC regulation (for example, carriers of agricultural commodities and other intrastate traffic). The remaining 40 percent consists of ICC-regulated carriers. The latter are divided into contact carriers, which sign contracts with shippers for specialized services, and common carriers, which carry mainly less-than-truck-load (LTL) shipments.[25]

[23]The act will be discussed at greater length.

[24]Breyer states that the four largest firms account for 12 percent of all revenues and the largest ten for 20 percent. See S. Breyer, *Regulation and Its Reform* (Cambridge, Mass.: Harvard University Press, 1982), 224.

[25]S. Breyer, *Regulation and Its Reform*, 223. Thus common carriers sell truck space to anyone and are bound by ICC regulations to provide, for example, reasonable efficient service and not to discriminate.

There are substantial possibilities for substitution between these different types of service in addition to the presence of substitutes in rail and air transportation. The recent effective removal of entry restrictions by the ICC means that trucking can be classified as a competitive sector of the transportation industry.

Water Carriers   The water carriers are also a relatively unconcentrated sector, with a large amount of freight being shipped by unregulated private carriers over toll-free waterways. As a result, entry and rate restrictions have not had as significant an impact on the structure of this sector as they have on trucks and railroads.

Airlines   The structure of the airline sector has changed as a result of the Airline Deregulation Act of 1978. This law abolished the regulating body, the Civil Aeronautics Board (CAB), in 1984 and removed most price and entry restrictions. Before deregulation, the sector was dominated by ten major trunk airlines that in the late 1970s provided about 90 percent of scheduled airline service in the United States. However, if we look at major city pairs, only a few were served by one airline alone. Most had two or more competitors.[26] The relaxation of entry restrictions began in 1977, when the CAB took a less restrictive line towards applications for new route authorities. It continued until the abolition of the CAB effectively removed government enforced entry barriers. New entry reduced industry concentration so that, by 1984, the share of the ten major trunk airlines had fallen to 74 percent and the share of new entrants had expanded to 12 percent from 2.4 percent in 1978.[27] Recently, however, mergers and consolidations between companies have halted this trend. There is evidence that economic barriers to entry are being successfully exploited by large firms and have to some extent replaced the old government-enforced entry restrictions.[28]

Another change in the structure of the industry as a result of deregulation is the growth of hub-and-spoke networks.[29] Under this system, an airline develops a hub centered in a particular city, from which most of its flights originate. A passenger wishing to fly from one spoke city to another, where both are served by this airline, will be flown into the hub and connected with another flight out to the destination spoke city. Nonstop flights will consist

---

[26]See G. C. Eads, "Competition in the Domestic Trunk Airline Industry: Too Much or Too Little?" in A. Phillips, ed., *Promoting Competition in Regulated Markets* (Washington, D.C.: Brookings Institution, 1975), 14.

[27]Daniel P. Kaplan, "The Changing Airline Industry," in Leonard W. Weiss and Michael W. Klass, eds., *Regulatory Reform: What Actually Happened* (Boston: Little, Brown and Co., 1986), 50. Kaplan also notes the adverse effect that new entry had on the smaller trunk airlines whose share of traffic declined.

[28]See Michael E. Levine, "Airline Competition in Deregulated Markets," 425. We discuss the effects of deregulation in airlines in greater detail below.

[29]See Kaplan, "The Changing Airline Industry," 51.

only of those between spokes and the hub. Most other flights will entail a change at the hub airport. This system allows a single airline to provide more frequent service from spoke cities, where demand for any particular flight may be low, by combining passengers from different spoke flights into one flight at the hub for service out to another spoke. The hub-and-spoke system is not only efficient, but can be exploited by established carriers to prevent further entry of new firms.

PRICE DETERMINATION AND REGULATION: THE THEORETICAL PROBLEM

An appropriate starting point to discuss price determination in transportation is to ask the normative question first: how *should* prices be set in this industry? The answer(s) to this question then gives us a benchmark for evaluating the actual price-setting mechanism and the regulatory policy that governs it. As we have frequently observed, the task of evaluating industry performance must begin with the definition of social goals. We have emphasized efficiency and equity as being most important to economists. If we begin by defining efficiency in transportation, we shall probably find ourselves looking for an allocation of resources between modes within the industry and between the industry as a whole and other industries to maximize the net social benefit (total benefit minus total cost) that society derives from consumption of transportation services.

In competitive industries, where prices are set by supply and demand, the market price coincides with the efficient price (in the absence of external effects). In industries where there is natural monopoly, the efficient price equals marginal cost but fails to generate sufficient revenues to cover total cost. This leads to the need for a subsidy or a different price structure. In transportation, the efficient price structure is harder to define because the industry consists of competing modes with very different costs. The railroads and some airlines have decreasing costs, while their competitors—trucks, barges, and other airlines—have increasing costs. Under these circumstances one might immediately suggest that since the decreasing cost mode can always undercut its competitors, whose costs increase as output increases, the industry is a natural monopoly. However, this is not necessarily the case. As we saw in Chapter 13, there may be circumstances in which a natural monopoly is successfully challenged by relatively inefficient entrants; that is, the monopoly is not always sustainable. Moreover, it turns out that a comparison of marginal costs between a decreasing-cost mode and an increasing-cost mode will not always yield an allocation of traffic between modes that minimizes total cost.[30]

Disentangling the general theoretical issues is a complicated task. We proceed instead with an example applicable to both the transportation and

---

[30]See R. S. Seneca, "Inherent Advantage, Costs and Resource Allocation in the Transportation Industry," *American Economic Review* 63 (December 1973): 945–956.

communications industries, to show that the usual economic rules do not always hold.

Example

Consider the case of a regulated, decreasing-cost firm (for example, a bridge or AT&T) for which the regulators have set price so as to maximize welfare, subject to a break-even constraint (recall Chapter 14).[31] A price has not been set equal to marginal cost because of the need for revenues sufficient to cover the (substantial) fixed cost of the bridge. Now, suppose a competing firm, a ferry boat, enters and offers a price to the bridge travelers that is lower than the price they are currently paying. The bridge would lose revenue and might possibly go out of business. The price of a bridge crossing can be reduced to marginal cost only at the risk of incurring losses. Its decreasing cost structure means that marginal costs are less than average costs. The regulator has the choice of banning the new entrant or permitting it (that is, allowing the two firms to compete), with the possibility that the bridge may find itself incurring continuing losses (very much like the railroads) by being forced to price below average cost. To decide which policy is preferable, regulators must have some idea about relative costs and demand levels, but this information may simply not be available. In particular, while the agency may have some information about the costs of the regulated firm (the bridge), it may have very little idea about the costs of potential entrants such as the ferry.[32] It may therefore be very difficult for regulators to evaluate the merits or the magnitude of the threat posed by potential entry.

Bridge regulators may decide to reduce price only for those travelers who would otherwise shift to the ferry. In other words, they may impose price discrimination in order to allow the bridge to break even and to prevent entry, simultaneously. But this means they might have to raise the bridge price to its remaining users, an action to which this group would strongly object.[33]

In this example we see that the efficiency issues are complicated both theoretically and in practice, due to the uncertainties of assessing costs and demand. We also see that the distributional issues are complicated. Each possible pricing scheme will yield not only a different allocation of resources, but also a different distribution of net benefits. If we are to make sensible statements about the appropriate weights that should be attached to the net benefits received by different groups in order to rank different pricing schemes

[31]This example is based on an example in Breyer, *Regulation and Its Reform*, 289; and W. A. Brock and D. S. Evans, "Creamskimming," in D. Evans, ed., *Breaking Up Bell* (New York: North-Holland, 1983), 69.

[32]Until recently, AT&T followed procedures for estimating costs for the purpose of determining rates set down by the FCC. These procedures do not allow for the accurate estimation of marginal costs, but rather involve rules for allocating fixed costs to the various different services produced.

[33]But see A. E. Kahn, *The Economics of Regulation*, vol. 1 (New York: Wiley, 1971), 138–139, for an argument showing that the bridge price need not rise when the ferry price is reduced.

in terms of equity, we need, strictly speaking, a full-fledged theory of justice. In practice, various groups (producers, consumers, shippers, employees, and so forth) have used the political system to push for their particular interests. Given these complexities, it is not surprising that regulators have experienced enormous difficulties in developing coherent rules for price setting and entry in both transportation and communications. To see what has been done, we will review the history of government regulation of transportation and then assess recent policy changes.

HISTORY OF GOVERNMENT REGULATION AND RECENT POLICY CHANGES

The early history of the transportation industry in the United States is dominated by the building of the railroads, which transformed and unified the country. The first important regulatory legislation—the Granger laws—came in the 1870s, at the end of a half century of rapid expansion in the size of the railroad track network. (Between 1830 and 1880, over 90,000 miles of track were laid; by 1916 there were over 254,000 miles of track in the United States.)[34] Both freight and passenger transportation (which had previously consisted only of horse-drawn vehicles and water transportation along rivers and early canals) were revolutionized by the railroads, which remained dominant until they were subjected to competition from motor carriers and airlines in the 1930s.

Early Regulation

While most railroads were owned by private companies, their rapid expansion of capacity was facilitated by considerable financial support by local governments, the states, and also the federal government (in the form of land grants). This process was sometimes accompanied by speculation, financial abuse, and corruption on the part of the railroad builders and their government supporters. Since the expansion of supply often outran the slower-growing demand for railroad services, many railroads faced excess capacity and severe competition. Rate wars broke out, which led to attempts by competing companies to form cartels or pools. These had the dual purpose of preventing destructive price wars and of pushing cartel prices toward monopoly levels. It was in these circumstances—a rapidly developing industry with somewhat chaotic pricing—that regulation was initiated.

The Granger Laws   The first regulatory laws were the Granger laws (recall the *Munn v. Illinois* decision discussed in Chapter 1). These were passed by some midwestern state governments in response to political pressure by the shippers of agricultural commodities in depressed farming areas. The laws introduced

---

[34]Phillips, *The Economics of Regulation*, 443.

maximum rates to counteract widespread price discrimination by the railroads. The railroads made a practice of charging monopoly prices on routes where competition was absent, but lower rates where there were competing railroads. This was viewed as a particularly inequitable contributing factor to the depressed economic condition of the farming states (whose shippers were often served by monopoly lines).

From our present perspective, however, it may not have been any more inefficient than uniform rates would have been, given the break-even constraint. The lower the elasticity of demand, the more a monopolist can raise price above marginal cost without causing welfare losses. In this context, a pricing policy that essentially uses revenues earned from monopoly routes (where the elasticity of demand is low) to subsidize operations on competitive routes (whose elasticity is high) may improve efficiency. The redistributive effects, however, may be (and clearly were in this case) substantial.[35]

The Act to Regulate Commerce, 1887   The Granger laws were not successful, however, in preventing price discrimination or curbing financial abuses. Moreover, the growing railroad network was transporting more and more traffic across state lines. An 1886 decision by the Supreme court drew a sharp distinction between interstate and intrastate commerce.[36] Rates on intrastate commerce were within the control of each state. But rates on interstate commerce were declared to be exclusively under the control of the federal government. There was, therefore, a need for federal legislation to regulate interstate commerce. The Act to Regulate Commerce, in 1887, was the result.[37] This act applied to all railroad common carriers engaged in interstate or foreign commerce and therefore included almost all railroads. The act did not apply to common carriers wholly by water, although it did include common carriers partly by railroad and partly by water.

Among other provisions, the act established that carrier rates must be "just and reasonable," and prohibited personal discrimination between shippers

---

[35] A model concluding that raising price above marginal cost may not be a bad thing, particularly if the elasticity of demand is low, is a model of optimal pricing subject to a break-even constraint in the presence of decreasing costs. Here, the idea is to raise the price only until sufficient revenues are generated to cover costs and no further. Thus, if, in the extreme case, the demand elasticity were zero, a rise in price would cause no fall-off in output and hence no efficiency loss at all. Of course, if a profit-maximizing monopolist faced a zero-elasticity demand curve, it would keep raising the price in order to generate more revenues far above what was necessary to break even. This kind of circumstance might well justify government regulation to set maximum prices. This was precisely the thrust of the Granger laws.

[36] *Wabash, St. Louis & Pacific Railway Co. v. Illinois*, 118 U.S. 557 (1886).

[37] J. C. Nelson reviews in some detail the motivations and interests of different groups that promoted federal regulation of transportation. He suggests, among other things, that early regulation "was at times supported by some or all railroads . . . because of the railroads' realization that regulation was inevitable because of public demands and that some aspects of regulation might be useful to the railroads in their attempts to stabilize competitive areas of rail pricing to increase profitability."   J. C. Nelson, "The Changing Economic Case for Surface Transport Regulation," in *Perspectives on Federal Transportation Policy* J. C. Miller, ed. (Washington, D.C.: American Enterprise Institute for Public Policy Research, 1975), 7–25.

or "undue preference or prejudice" towards shippers in the setting of rates. The act also forbade the pooling of traffic and revenues, although cartels (rate-fixing) remained legal.

The Interstate Commerce Commission   The Interstate Commerce Commission (ICC), consisting at first of five members, was established to enforce the act. Originally, the commission had powers only to hear complaints of alleged violations of the act and to investigate matters in dispute. But as weaknesses in the act became apparent, more legislation was passed to fill the gaps. In 1906, Congress passed the Hepburn Act, which enlarged the commission to seven members and gave it the power to prescribe maximum limits for rates. Rates could be prescribed if existing rates were found to be unreasonable or otherwise unlawful, in which case, only maximum rate levels could be set. Neither the actual rate to be charged nor the minimum rate could be fixed by the commission. An enforcement provision made commission orders binding on the carrier.

By the beginning of World War I, the ICC had become a genuinely effective regulating body. The ICC was effective in preventing monopoly pricing over routes that lacked competing transportation suppliers. However, it did not allow profit pooling that would have enabled cartels to be even more effective, and there was some antitrust action against price-fixing.[38]

Therefore, it can be argued that during this early period, the commission viewed the transportation industry as one in which the preservation of competition was not only desirable but also feasible over many routes, with the role of regulation being to curb the abuse of monopoly in the remaining instances.

The Rule of Rate-Making, 1920   In 1917, during World War I, the government took over the operation of the railroads and the powers of the ICC were somewhat restricted. The war generated enormous concern for national security and explicit recognition was given to the importance of the transportation industry in preserving it. The Transportation Act of 1920, which restored the railroads to private ownership, was passed to implement a policy of building an adequate national transportation system and a regulatory system that would adequately monitor the system. An important part of this act was the rule of rate-making, Section 15a of the Interstate Commerce Act. The rule was that rates in transportation should be "just and reasonable," as before, and should also yield a fair return, which the commission was authorized to define. Further, the commission was enlarged to 11 members and given power to prescribe both minimum and actual rates.

This rule represents a far more interventionist approach to regulation. First, the rule that prices should be set to yield a fair return introduced the idea of government responsibility for the financial viability of individual transportation suppliers, even though it did not guarantee it. Second, the fact

---

[38]Nelson, "The Changing Economic Case," 9.

that the ICC was given the power to prescribe minimum rates implied government willingness to supersede the process of price competition.

It is also significant that this new approach to regulation occurred at the beginning of a 20-year period that saw both the Great Depression and the rise of new forms of competition in the transportation industry. Both these changes combined to put downward pressure on transportation prices just at a time when the regulating procedures were establishing support for higher price levels.

New Members of the Industry During the 1920s, new forms of transportation—motor carriers, pipelines, airlines, and especially the revival of inland water transportation (diesel engines to propel tugboats were introduced at this time)—greatly increased the competition that the railroads faced. At the end of the decade came the Great Depression, which devastated the railroads as their revenues and profits plummeted. The airlines were also very hard hit.

The Establishment of Comprehensive Regulation

The Emergency Transportation Act of 1933, the Motor Carrier Act of 1935, and the Transportation Act of 1940 were all enacted in response to the drastic changes that had occurred since 1920. Their effect on the development of the industry was substantial. Indeed, the present movement toward deregulation is essentially an attempt (sometimes successful) to dismantle regulatory frameworks that were established in those extremely abnormal times.

The Emergency Transportation Act of 1933 changed the rule of rate-making by removing the fair return requirement and substituting a rather longer admonition to the ICC to consider such issues as efficiency, the effect of rates on the movement of traffic, and the need for carriers to earn sufficient revenues. The act also introduced measures for the financial support of the railroads.

The Motor Carrier Act of 1935 brought motor carriers under the regulatory umbrella of the ICC. This act established different categories of carriers (common, contract, and private) and allowed for some controversial exemptions (for example, carriers of agricultural commodities). Two points are worth noting. First, the act initiated the regulation of entry into trucking by requiring that common and contract carriers obtain licenses from the ICC to operate. Second, it gave the ICC the power to fix minimum and maximum rate levels and to set actual rates for common carriers. For contract carriers, the ICC could set minimum but not maximum rates.

The Civil Aeronautics Act of 1938 established the Civil Aeronautics Board (CAB), granting it responsibility not only to regulate rates and entry in the airline sector, but also to promote air transportation by administering subsidies. These subsidies were initially administered by the Postal Service with the two-fold objective of promoting the growth of an infant industry and improving the mail-carrying network. When the CAB took over regulation of the airlines, the administration of subsidies remained an important task. Rate regulation was relatively less important.[39] Safety matters and the administration of airports were assigned to the Civil Aeronautic Authority. In 1957, these tasks were transferred to the Federal Aviation Administration. The CAB was abolished in 1985.

The Transportation Act of 1940 completed the new regulatory movement by bringing the domestic interstate water carriers under the control of the ICC (albeit with many exceptions). Furthermore, in the Declaration of National Transportation Policy, which was part of the act, Congress provided a statement of its intent to regulate effectively the transportation industry. A new rule of rate-making was also attached to the act. The statement of intent and the rule of rate-making laid out explicitly the goals considered desirable for the transportation industry. These included safe, adequate, economical and efficient service, fair wages and equitable working conditions, and the preservation of the inherent advantage of each mode. Destructive competition was condemned. However, these terms were not precisely defined, and the act did not specify exactly how the ICC was to achieve the goals.

In the four decades following the end of World War II, regulatory policy was made by the ICC according to its interpretation of the 1940 act in a host of specific rate decisions. It was also influenced by precedents set in court decisions on challenges to the ICC's interpretation of the regulatory laws.

Problems since World War II Two major controversies characterized this period. The first concerned the question of whether prices should be set equal to fully distributed costs or out-of-pocket costs. Neither of these cost categories employed by the ICC accurately reflects economic cost concepts. According to the ICC, out-of-pocket rail costs "reflect the costs which, over the long-run period and at the average post-war density of traffic, have been found to be variable with traffic changes."[40] They are similar to average variable costs but are sometimes used to represent marginal costs. Fully distributed cost is determined by adding an allocated portion of constant expenses to the out-of-pocket cost of service, where constant expenses include fixed and common costs. Since constant expenses are not traceable to any particular service, the determination of fully distributed cost requires an arbitrary assignment of costs to particular traffic.[41]

The railroads had high fixed costs but relatively low marginal costs. Since it was profitable to carry additional traffic as long as the marginal

---

[39]Breyer, *Regulation and Its Reform*, 200.

[40]ICC, Bureau of Accounts, *Rail Carload Cost Scales by Territories for the Year 1962*, Statement 264 (March 1, 1964): 3. See A. Friedlaender, *The Dilemma of Freight Transport Regulation*, 32–34 for a detailed critique of the ICC's cost estimation methods.

[41]Fully distributed cost as defined by the ICC cannot really be identified with the economist's concept of average cost. The average total cost per unit of transportation is simply the total cost of all the units provided divided by the number of units, and it equals the average variable cost per unit plus the average fixed cost per unit. Fully distributed cost is calculated by adding some proportion of fixed cost, not necessarily the average per unit, to out-of-pocket cost, which is similar to, but not always the same as average variable cost.

revenue from the new traffic covered marginal cost, the railroads pushed for prices set close to marginal cost, that is, out-of-pocket cost pricing. By contrast, the water and motor carriers had relatively low fixed costs, but their marginal costs were higher. They urged the ICC to maintain a price floor at average or fully distributed cost and argued that to allow the railroads to undercut them by pricing at the railroads' marginal cost was to permit destructive competition, forbidden by law. During the post-war decades the ICC and the courts essentially held to the fully distributed cost floor, a policy that denied traffic to the railroads and kept prices high in trucking.[42] As we shall see, this pricing policy came under severe attack by the proponents of deregulation and was successfully overturned. Nevertheless, it is worth recalling our theoretical example that shows the difficult underlying issues. Where the railroads have no competition, they will be in a position to charge high (monopoly) prices, and it is a legitimate goal for regulators to prevent this. Where competition exists, there is no guarantee that marginal cost pricing will be efficient or remunerative. Indeed, there is no systematic rule that regulators can follow. The choice is very much a case of the lesser of two evils.

Licensing Entry   The second major controversy in the ICC's performance since World War II concerns the regulation of entry into trucking. The Motor Carrier Act of 1935 had established the requirement of licenses to operate, with some exemptions. Before 1980, if a new firm wished to enter the industry, it had to prove that the service provided by existing shippers was inadequate. Since this was extremely difficult to do, the majority of entry applications were rejected.[43] The result of these entry restrictions was to keep rates much higher than would most likely have been the case under competition. This was facilitated by the fact that rates in trucking were set initially by rate bureaus, which achieved exemption from the antitrust laws under the Reed-Bulwinkle Act of 1948.

Rates were filed with the ICC, which considered protests from competitors, most of which were unsuccessful. This procedure destroyed the incentive for individual shippers to challenge established rates at the same time that entry restrictions removed the challenge of potential rivals. Moreover, as Breyer notes, "The filing system gives competing firms notice of the rate cut, making it impossible for a maverick to capture business through secret price cutting."[44]

Specified routes were attached to each license. This made it impossible for a firm to alter its routes as cost or demand conditions changed and often required that trucks remain empty on the backhaul.

---

[42]There were some exceptions. Moreover, the direct attempts of the motor and water carriers to make a full-cost price floor an official rule for the ICC failed. The Transportation Act of 1958 included a sentence that reads "rates of a carrier shall not be held up to a particular level to protect the traffic of any other mode of transportation, giving due consideration to the objectives of the national transportation policy declared in this Act."

[43]Breyer, *Regulation and Its Reform*, 226.

[44]Breyer notes that up to 80 percent of protested rates were withdrawn. Breyer, *Regulation and Its Reform*, 225.

It is important to remember that the inefficiencies that resulted from ICC activities derived ultimately from the laws passed by Congress, which the ICC is pledged to carry out. Nevertheless, that the ICC was a consistent supporter of rate and entry regulation, and had not been the initiator of reasonable change, attracted increasingly harsh criticism. Its role in the regulation process, its relationship within the industries it regulated and with Congress and the courts, and its main objectives were all questioned. For example, Robert Fellmeth states:

> The ICC was set up by Congress as an agency of experts to protect and represent the public interest in matters of transportation in interstate commerce. In fact the agency is predominantly a forum at which transportation interests divide up the national transportation market.[45]

To assess this statement, we consider now the work and policy formation procedure of the ICC. Then we look at some important changes that have been made by recent legislation.

The ICC is among a number of regulatory agencies that have unusual status under the federal government. They are independent agencies and as such, they often seek to assert their independence of congressional and presidential control. The rationale for this independence is the principle of the separation of powers, which requires that legislative and judicial functions be separated from presidential control. Since many of the activities of the regulatory agencies have traditionally been regarded as legislative functions, the agencies are often viewed as arms of Congress rather than as instruments of the executive branch.

The Interstate Commerce Commission

Following, we discuss the responsibilities of the commission, its composition, its structure, its methods of operation, and its political role.

Responsibilities   The major responsibilities of the ICC include settling controversies over rates; ruling on applications for mergers, consolidations, and acquisitions; approving the sale of carriers and the issuance of securities; acting to prevent unlawful discrimination, destructive competition, and rebating; granting operating rights to carriers; approving applications to construct and to abandon railroad lines; and enforcing decisions, if necessary.

Membership   The ICC has been composed of seven members, instead of the authorized eleven members, since the mid–1970s. In 1982, Congress enacted legislation that cut the commission to five members (on a phased basis) and decreased the members' terms from 7 to 5 years. The commission consists of two divisions. Some of its work is assigned to boards of employees, but the commission itself usually addresses matters that deal with general

---

[45]R. Fellmeth, *The Interstate Commerce Omission* (New York: Grossman Publishers, 1970), 1.

transportation policies and has the final responsibility for the decisions that are made.

The rules regarding appointments are designed to insulate the agencies from the executive branch. Members are appointed by the President and confirmed by the Senate. No more than a simple majority of the members may be from the same political party, and appointments are for staggered terms. The independence of the agency, however, is to some extent limited by the President's right to fill vacancies resulting from resignations and deaths and to appoint a chairman for the commission (from among its membership) without the confirmation of the Senate.

Methods of Operation   When a formal decision of the ICC is disputed, the chief administrative law judge assigns it to be heard, either in a formal docket or a modified procedure.

Cases in the formal docket require a hearing. Oral arguments are heard before the ICC's administrative law judges. Following the hearing, the judge may decide to issue an initial report, which, if no objections are made, becomes the final order of the commission. If no initial report is made, or if objections are filed, one of the commission bureaus reports the decision. (The bureaus handle specific operational areas, for example, accounting, operations, etc.)   The decisions may then be appealed to the full commission.

Cases with little or no opposition usually go through the modified procedure. An attorney makes a recommendation, which is then referred to one of the two divisions of commissioners. They review the recommendation and issue an initial decision that may be appealed.

The Motor Carrier Act of 1980 ordered the ICC to streamline its appellate process and, as a result, new rules were adopted in April 1981. The ICC appellate procedure involves a two-step process consisting of one mandatory initial review and one administrative appeal for each case. An appeal must be filed within 20 days of the initial decision. The commission will accept certain appeals for which there is no automatic right if the matter involves general transportation policy.

The decision of the ICC may be appealed through the court system, starting with the court of appeals.

The ICC may ask for a court order to force a carrier to comply with a ruling and may request the U.S. Attorney General to start proceedings in federal district courts to enjoin carriers from illegal actions.

Since 1966, the ICC has been able to enter settlement agreements in which disputing parties can reach a compromise, thus saving the expense of litigation proceedings. This change is one explicit recognition of the problems associated with the judicial character of ICC policymaking procedures. The fact that ICC cases are argued and then appealed by parties employing lawyers highly skilled in regulatory law often means that a case will stand or fall on small legal issues and that wider economic implications may be ignored. Moreover, the presentation of a case to the ICC (say, the application for a rate reduction or increase, or for a license to operate, which may be challenged) has become extremely expensive. For small businesses and private individuals the expense precludes access to the ICC. Only large interests can afford to collect evidence and employ lawyers for the period of time that it takes to get even a rate change approved. Rates are set and licenses granted mostly in response to those large companies and seldom for the benefit of small businesses. Finally, since the ICC spends most of its time adjudicating cases presented to it by private interests, very little time is left for what are called *ex parte* cases, cases initiated by the ICC for the purposes of formulating policy changes that directly concern the public interest.

Political Role and Controversies   There is some disagreement about what are and what should be the goals of the ICC. Some argue that the public interest should be paramount but is not.[46] Some argue that the ICC responds (or should respond) also to the direct interests of the firms that it regulates.[47] Some argue that the ICC performs a redistributive function.[48] More recently, many economists have advocated deregulation, particularly in trucking.[49] Such a policy would relieve the ICC of many of its regulatory tasks and allow competition in the market to perform the allocation function. Antitrust laws could then be enforced to prevent monopolistic practices.

In 1980 two laws were passed that dramatically changed regulatory policy in railroads and trucking. We now consider these acts, identify the forces that led to their passage into law, and examine their effects on these two sectors of the transportation industry. In the last section of this chapter we consider deregulation in airlines and the demise of the CAB.

Deregulation of Railroads and Trucks

Two critical victories for President Carter's transportation policy occurred in 1980 with the passage of the Motor Carrier Act and the Staggers Rail Act. The deregulation of the railroad and trucking industries was initiated with the intentions of promoting competition by giving carriers greater flexibility in setting rates and providing services, encouraging entry, and restricting collective rate setting.

The major provisions of the Motor Carrier Act served to loosen (but not abolish) entry requirements by directing the ICC to issue permits to qualified applicants and by shifting the burden of proof from the applicant to the person

---

[46]Fellmeth, *The Interstate Commerce Omission*; M. Bernstein, *Regulating Business by Independent Commission* (Princeton, N.J.: Princeton University Press, 1955).

[47]G. Stigler, "The Theory of Economic Regulation," *The Bell Journal of Economics* 2 (Spring 1971): 3; and R. Ash, *A New Regulatory Framework: Report on Selected Independent Regulatory Agencies*, The President's Advisory Council on Executive Organization, January 1972, U.S. Government, Washington, D.C. This report suggests that while the public interest should be a major objective of ICC policy, Congress has also instructed the ICC to promote the transportation industry (for example, for reasons of national defense) and this objective is likely to clash with the first.

[48]R. A. Posner, "Taxation by Regulation," *The Bell Journal of Economics* 2 (Spring 1971): 22.

[49]See, for example, Breyer, *Regulation and Its Reform*; and B. M. Mitnick, *The Political Economy of Regulation* (New York: Columbia University Press, 1980).

objecting to the permit. The entry test of public necessity (for proposed service to points not served by an existing carrier) was eliminated and other route restrictions were removed. Additional flexibility was granted to trucking companies in setting rates, for example, by permitting carriers to raise or lower their rates by as much as 10 percent of existing levels without ICC interference.

The Staggers Rail Act of 1980 advocates a national policy designed to minimize regulation and allow competition a greater role in the determination of rates. It allows the ICC to determine whether a rate is reasonable only if the firm in question has market dominance and if the rate is greater than a specified percentage of variable or out-of-pocket costs. If a rate is below the given percentage, the ICC is not allowed to review it. A zone of flexibility permits some rate hikes without review to allow for inflation. These provisions are directed at preventing the railroads from raising prices to monopoly levels in the absence of competition, but also allow the railroads flexibility to raise rates sufficiently to generate adequate revenues.[50] The bill also made it easier for carriers to build more rail lines, abandon service, or sell a line if the service were to be discontinued.

The Politics of Deregulation   In their book, *The Politics of Deregulation,* Martha Derthick and Paul J. Quirk ask why it was possible for the supporters of deregulation in trucking to succeed in 1980 after many years of unsuccessful attempts.[51] They also consider why the deregulators were less successful in railroads (the Staggers Rail Act is a less far-reaching reform). They suggest first that pressures for reform came from economists, who presented a convincing case that competition in trucking would be viable if government-enforced barriers to entry (operating license requirements) were removed.   The economists' case was buttressed by a number of empirical studies showing that rates would come down and service would be maintained, if not improved, following deregulation.[52] Second, they note that Presidents Ford and Carter advocated some movement toward deregulation. Mainly, however, they draw attention to the fact that forces for change came from the staff and commissioners within the ICC (and particularly, as we see later, the CAB). By the time the deregulation acts were passed, there had already been a substantial increase in the flexibility shown by the ICC toward rate reductions for the railroads and eased license requirements in trucking. This made it easier for Congress to act. Nevertheless there was controversy. The regulated trucking firms and the

---

[50]We have not had space to deal in detail with the whole history of the financial vicissitudes of the railroads, but have concentrated rather on the question of intramodal competition. In fact, throughout the whole post-World War II period, the railroads had claimed that the regulation process hindered them from raising rates sufficiently high on non-competitive traffic to meet rising costs. The provisions of the Staggers Rail Act, which allow more flexibility on the up-side, are designed to meet their complaint.

[51]M. Derthick and P. J. Quirk, *The Politics of Deregulation* (Washington, D.C.: Brookings Institution, 1985).

[52]See for example Paul W. MacAvoy and John W. Snow, eds., *Regulation of Entry and Pricing in Truck Transportation* (Washington, D.C.: American Enterprise Institute, 1977).

International Brotherhood of Teamsters opposed deregulation, fearing it would lead to lower profits and wages. Consumer and farm groups and many shippers and independent truckers supported it. In the case of railroad deregulation, the groups reversed positions: industry and labor supported the bill, while consumer groups, utility companies, and shippers opposed it. The latter feared that if government regulation were removed, railroads would raise rates on bulk goods over which they have a near monopoly.

There has been no significant change in the rules since the 1980 acts. Now a century old, the ICC is a venerable political institution, that seems to be successfully resisting its own abolition. There have been significant changes in the industry, however. To these we now turn.

The Effects of Deregulation

The Railroads   There is a disagreement about the effect of the Staggers Rail Act on the railroad sector and to what extent the predictions of advocates of deregulation have been borne out.[53] Thomas Gale Moore estimates that "from the pre-deregulation year of 1978, profits more than doubled by 1981 and nearly tripled by 1983."[54] He argues that this increase was caused mainly by a fall in costs, which in turn resulted from the more competitive environment in which the railroads found themselves. Since they could now negotiate individual contracts with shippers and had a great deal more flexibility in setting prices, it paid both railroads and shippers to ship traffic by the cheapest, most efficient method. Moore notes that revenue per ton-mile (a measure of price) has declined, although he adds that some shippers complain about higher prices on routes where competition is absent. Baumol and Willig argue that further deregulation of prices is warranted, except where there is evidence of monopolistic behavior.[55] They also argue that allowing shippers to determine for themselves the division of revenues from joint shipments would increase efficiency. This rosy picture of the beneficial effects of deregulation is disputed by K. D. Boyer.[56] He notes first that the longevity of capital in the railroad industry means that changes in market forces and government policy do not have an immediate effect on the structure of the industry. Changes in prices, profits, costs, and so forth that are observed 1, 2, or even 5 years after deregulation can almost certainly not be attributed to the change in government

[53]The Staggers Rail Act had been preceded in 1976 by the so-called 4-R Act (Railroad Revitalization and Regulatory Reform Act). This act mainly addressed the poor financial condition of the railroads, but also included some regulatory reform clauses giving the ICC more flexibility in setting rates. This flexibility was expanded in the Staggers Rail Act.

[54]T. Gale Moore, "Rail and Trucking Deregulation" in Leonard W. Weiss and Michael W. Klass, eds., *Regulatory Reform: What Actually Happened* (Boston: Little Brown and Co., 1986), 14-36. See also Christopher C. Barnekov, "The Track Record," and Robert D. Willig and William J. Baumol, "Using Competition as a Guide," both in *Regulation* 11 (1987): 19–35.

[55]Baumol and Willig, "Using Competition as a Guide," 56.

[56]K. D. Boyer, "The Costs of Price Regulation: Lessons from Railroad Deregulation," *Rand Journal of Economics* 18 (Autumn 1987): 408–415.

Table 17.3   Average Real (1985) Rates and Modal Shares, All Commodities, 1970–1985[*]

| | Average Real (1985) Revenue per Ton-Mile | | | Share of Intercity Tonnage | | | |
Year	Rail	Motor Carrier	Rail	ICC Regulated Truck	Unregulated Truck	Total Intercity Tonnage (miles)
1970	3.82	22.73	31.1	13.1	23.0	5060
1975	3.68	20.93	29.6	14.4	20.7	4962
1978	3.53	20.11	25.9	16.2	23.4	5710
1980	3.38	21.43	28.9	14.8	21.7	5502
1981	3.47	21.78	28.9	14.9	21.8	5359
1982	3.35	21.72	27.4	14.6	21.8	4921
1983	3.20	22.70	27.1	14.9	22.9	5077
1984	3.11	22.40	27.8	15.2	23.1	5470
1985	3.05	22.90	26.8	15.4	23.8	5251

*Taken from K. D. Boyer, "The Costs of Price Regulation: Lessons from Deregulation," *Rand Journal of Economics* 18, No. 3, (Autumn 1987), Table 1, p. 410. Boyer quotes the following sources: "Transportation Policy Associates, *Transportation in America*, 4th ed., March 1986, various tables. Rate figures for 1985 are from the 1987 edition. Real rates were computed by deflating by the 1985 Producer Price Index."

policy, but rather to industrial conditions many years before. Boyer notes from the data in Table 17.3 that rail rates in manufacturing have indeed been falling (as Moore also notes) but that the falling trend goes back as far as 1970; it does not begin in 1980. He also notes that the market share of the railroads has been systematically falling since 1970. Using regression analysis, he concludes that more than 90 percent of the variation in rail rates since 1970 can be explained by an increase in the average weight of freight trains. This in turn was caused by "larger lot size and less frequent service associated with heavier trains, and increased railroad specialization in bulk commodities."[57] He suggests that the effect of deregulation on rail rates was minimal, but, if present, raised rather than lowered rates. The complaints of shippers about higher rates, referred to by Moore, would fit into this picture. Boyer concludes that the effect of regulation by the ICC was not to hold average rail prices above costs, but rather to alter the structure of prices in inefficient ways.[58] Derthick and Quirk are also somewhat skeptical about the effectiveness of the Staggers Rail Act.[59] They argue that political compromises to secure its passage effectively weakened the act and prevented a significant change in the structure of prices.

[57]Boyer, "The Costs of Price Regulation," 411.

[58]See also Ann F. Friedlaender, "Equity, Efficiency, and Regulation in the Rail and Trucking Industries," in L. W. Weiss and M. W. Klass, eds., *Case Studies in Regulation: Revolution and Reform* (Boston: Little Brown and Co., 1981), 102–141. She also emphasizes that the inefficiencies of regulation were associated more with the structure than the level of rates.

[59]M. Derthick and P. J. Quirk, *The Politics of Deregulation*.

Trucking   The benefits from deregulation in trucking have been substantial, although the costs to some groups have also been high.   One immediate measure of the impact of deregulation is the fall in the value of operating licenses.   When entry regulation was in force, the ICC granted a new operating license to a potential entrant only if the firm could show that the established carriers were not providing adequate service—a virtual impossibility in most cases.   The only remaining way to enter the industry was to purchase an operating license from an established firm.   Thomas Gale Moore estimates that the average value of a common carrier's operating license in 1975 was $398,000 (in 1982 dollars), reflecting the value of discounted excess profits earned as a result of the barrier to entry.[60]   Deregulation effectively removed the entry restriction by shifting the burden of proof to established firms to show why entry should not occur.   Many new licenses were granted and their average value fell to $15,000 in 1982.   The number of carriers rose between 1975 and 1982.   According to Moore, real freight rates paid by shippers declined over the period, as did the average compensation earned in the industry.[61]   K. D. Boyer paints a different picture of trucking rates before and after deregulation (see Table 17.3).   He notes that average real revenue per ton-mile in trucking fell between 1970 and 1978, and then rose between 1978 and 1985 to just above the 1970 level.   The share of the market held by ICC-regulated trucks rose between 1970 and 1978, fell from 1978 to 1980, and then rose slightly until 1985.   The market share of unregulated trucks fell between 1978 and 1981 and rose slightly thereafter.   The difference between these two interpretations of events is to be found in the fact that average revenue per ton-mile is precisely that— an average figure.   If prices are broken down by type of commodity shipped and location of route, a more varied picture emerges with some routes showing substantial price reductions and others showing no change or increased prices.[62]   Also, Boyer uses a different base price year from Moore.[63]

The financial condition of many firms was damaged both by deregulation and by the economic recession in 1981, so that the number of bankruptcies rose.   By contast, as we have seen, the financial condition of the railroads improved dramatically, the recession notwithstanding.

It therefore appears that the removal of regulatory constraints benefited shippers using trucks and railroads over competitive routes.   The financial condition of the railroads improved, benefiting the owners, although employees faced lay-offs and lower wages.   Shippers using less competitive railroads faced price rises.   Many trucking firms went bankrupt, and in others wages fell.   These redistributive effects of deregulation also point up the extent to which

[60]T. Gale Moore, "Rail and Trucking Deregulation," 30.

[61]Moore, "Rail and Trucking Deregulation," 32, Table 5.

[62]See Moore, "Rail and Trucking Deregulation," 32, Table 5.

[63]Boyer's disagreement with Moore's interpretation of the effects of deregulation in railroads and trucking reflects the perennial problem encountered in measuring the effects of economic policy: it is hard to disentangle those changes in economic performance that are the result of the new policy and those resulting from other changes in the economic environment unrelated to the policy change.

regulation had distorted the distribution of income, as well as the allocation of resources, in these sectors of the transportation industry.

We now consider the airline sector. We look briefly at the circumstances surrounding the abolition of the CAB, and then discuss the effect of deregulation.

The Civil Aeronautics Board and Airline Deregulation[64]   By the time the Airline Deregulation Act was passed in 1978, the undesirable effects of the CAB's regulation of the industry were well recognized.[65] Two major problems were identified. First, the effect of price regulation was to keep prices too high and to generate overcapacity in the form of too many flights carrying few passengers. Second, the effect of entry regulation was to stabilize market shares of existing carriers, foster inefficiency, and reinforce the unnecessarily high prices. The definition and measurement of such terms as too high prices, overcapacity, and inefficiency is a particularly difficult task for the airline industry. Following the models in Chapter 13, we may state simply that prices above marginal and average cost are too high.[66] But the measurement of costs in the airline industry is complicated. The large number of routes served, the variety of possible schedules involving different distances, equipment, and fuel use mean that while the marginal cost of any additional flight by a given plane, given the existing schedule, may be relatively easily calculated, the average (or fully allocated) cost per flight may be much harder to assess.[67]

The term overcapacity reflects the fact that the airlines adopted schedules that offered very frequent flights between city pairs as a form of nonprice competition. This type of schedule was not optimal because many passengers might have preferred a combination of fewer (more crowded) flights and lower fares. The charge that regulation of entry generated inefficiency implied that the costs of established firms were higher than would be the case if new, more efficient firms were permitted to enter and bid down prices.

Breyer suggests that these effects resulted from the way in which the CAB approached its regulatory task. Its mandate for regulating prices, embodied in the 1938 act, contained instructions for rate-making that were very similar to those in the rule of rate-making used by the ICC. Among other things these

---

[64]Much of this section is based on the account of the effects of regulation on the airline industry in Breyer, *Regulation and Its Reform,* Chapter 11. Breyer was staff director of an investigation by the U.S. Senate Subcommittee on Administrative Practice and Procedure in the Airline Industry, chaired by Edward Kennedy in 1975. The committee's findings are contained in U.S. Senate Committee on the Judiciary, Subcommittee on Administrative Practice and Procedure, *Civil Aeronautics Board Practices and Procedures,* 94th Cong. 1st Sess. (1975).

[65]Deregulation did not, of course, go undisputed. Among the groups that opposed it were most airline companies, small communities who feared the loss of service, and airline labor unions, who feared the loss of jobs.

[66]In the presence of decreasing costs, marginal cost prices will generate losses. Average cost prices—prices that maximize welfare subject to the constraint that the firm make normal profits— may then be preferred. Marginal and average costs may not diverge much if economies of scale are not large (the case for airlines over major routes).

[67]See G. W. Douglas and J. C. Miller, III, *Economic Regulation of Domestic Air Transport: Theory and Policy* (Washington, D.C.: Brookings Institution, 1974) for a detailed analysis of optimal price and service levels in the airline industry.

rules provided that prices be set so as to preserve the inherent advantages of carriers, to insure that service be provided at lowest cost and be adequate, economical, efficient, and so forth. Since the CAB could not possibly have collected sufficient information to enable it to prescribe appropriate rates for each individual route, it attempted to use the regulatory process as a means for negotiating rates with the regulated firms. This informal procedure allowed the CAB to respond rapidly to changing economic conditions as represented by the regulated firms. When this practice was declared unlawful, the CAB adopted a set of rules that could be applied automatically.[68] These rules allowed fares to be based on industry, rather than firm, costs and revenues which could be more readily calculated. It now became very difficult for individual firms to justify lower prices in the attempt to win passengers from competitors. The new rules effectively established an industry cartel, freezing market shares and ending price competition.

Entry restrictions imposed by the CAB reinforced the cartel. These restrictions also resulted from the nature of the regulatory task faced by the CAB in awarding routes to different firms. First, the facts associated with licensing each route were very complicated, and second, the many criteria for choosing the appropriate firm failed to yield any clear-cut priorities.[69] The result was that the burden of proof was very much on new entrants to show that they should be awarded a route, and the decison of the CAB was invariably to preserve the status quo.

Among its other provisions, the Airline Deregulation Act of 1978 allowed virtually free entry into the airline industry and allowed firms to increase or decrease fares within a zone of reasonableness without CAB approval. This has since been expanded to include unlimited downward flexibility. The act also provided for the abolition of the CAB by January 1985, with its remaining tasks being transferred to the Transportation Department and the U.S. Postal Service. Issues of safety remain with the Federal Aviation Administration.

The Effects of Deregulation   An empirical study of developments in the airline industry, completed relatively soon after deregulation, concluded that deregulation had indeed brought prices closer to the cost of service, reduced excess capacity, and increased efficiency.[70] It had also resulted in lower wages and some bankruptcies. These changes would seem to support the view that competition in airlines was viable, that is, that airline markets were contestable.

---

[68]*Moss v. CAB.*, 30 F.2d 891 (D.C. Cir., 1970). These rules resulted from the Domestic Passenger Fare Investigation launched by the CAB in the late 1960s. See Breyer, *Regulation and Its Reform*, 211; and Douglas and Miller, *Economic Regulation of Domestic Air Transport*, 150–169.

[69]Breyer lists ability to render effective services, responsiveness to the needs of the traveling public, route integration, and historic participation in traffic as just some of the criteria used. Breyer, *Regulation and Its Reform*, 214.

[70]D. R. Graham, D. P. Kaplan, and D. S. Sibley, "Efficiency and Competition in the Airline Industry," *Bell Journal of Economics* 14 (Spring 1983): 120. These authors also conclude that "there appears to be some price-setting power exercised by airlines in relatively concentrated markets. But if the Herfindahl index is .5 or higher, further increases in concentration have little effect on fare."

The argument stated that since airplanes could be shifted from route to route and bought and sold relatively easily, they represented fixed rather than sunk costs. Entry and exit from the industry was therefore not impeded. No established firm could set a price too far above average cost without attracting entry. It was thus foreseen that deregulation would bring more firms into the industry, reducing market concentration and keeping prices low. In the first years following deregulation, this picture seemed to be coming true.

Michael E. Levine has recently disputed the view that the airline market is contestable.[71] The following discussion is based on his arguments. Levine notes that, since the initial flurry of entry following deregulation, there have been a number of mergers, consolidations, and bankruptcies. Remaining in the market are largely the same firms that had been dominant before deregulation (for example, American, United, TWA, Eastern). These firms maintain their dominance by exploiting various unforeseen cost advantages, making it possible for them to adopt entry-deterring strategies.

Information costs for airlines are large (although lower for established firms). Before a consumer buys a plane ticket, information is needed about the availability, scheduled times, and prices for flights from origin to destination, as well as some idea of safety and service. If consumers call individual airlines to get this information, they will only find out about that airline's flights. They may also want to investigate other airlines. It is costly for consumers to search for all this information and for airlines to advertise their services. In many cases, passengers rely on travel agents to direct them to flights. As incentives to consumers, the airlines offer frequent flyer bonuses; as incentives to travel agents, they offer commissions. Both these plans create transactions cost economies of scope. Consumers and travel agents are much more likely to qualify for bonuses if they consistently book flights on one airline. This will be possible only if the airline has a large route network. Moreover, computer reservation systems are owned by the major carriers and programmed so that the owner's flights come up first on the screen, thus biasing the choice in their favor.[72]

Levine suggests that these transactions cost economies are significant enough to deter entry. Computer reservation systems also make it possible for the major carriers to track ticket sales as they are made and strategically reduce

[71]Michael E. Levine, "Airline Competition in Deregulated Markets."

[72]The issues discussed here can also be seen in terms of the principal–agent relationship. A passenger can be viewed as principal, the travel agent (clearly) the agent. The passenger wants to find the most convenient flight at the lowest cost; the travel agent has a different goal—to maximize profits. Now certainly the maximization of profits by the travel agent can be compatible with booking the passenger on the appropriate flight. However, when an airline offers a bonus to the travel agent for booking a certain number of passengers on that airline, a larger wedge is driven between the goals of the passenger and the agent, and the passenger no longer has so much control over the actions of the agent. If in addition the passenger (now the agent) is booking a flight in order to carry out business for an employer (the principal), for which the employer pays, the passenger is less likely to object to an expensive flight if the cost can be passed back to the employer. Once again, the employer as principal has reduced control over the actions of the agent (passenger). See M. E. Levine, "Airline Competition in Deregulated Markets."

prices on flights that are being competitively challenged. If profits are lost by this strategy, they can be made up by raising prices on other flights where there is high demand and less competition.

As we noted above, the hub-and-spoke system was developed after deregulation in order to overcome the production indivisibilities associated with nonstop flights. In order to compete with established airline service between two cities, a new entrant must be able to provide frequent enough service to attract passengers. This may mean that many flights are not full and hence not remunerative. By contrast, an airline that controls a hub can fly passengers into the hub from spoke cities and combine them into one flight to another spoke. The established firms can therefore offer many more flights and cluster them around an entrant's schedule so that every single flight of the entrant has competition from the established firm. By such means entry is prevented, and the airline market begins to look much as it looked before deregulation, albeit with a substantially different route network and somewhat lower prices.

Levine argues that whether or not a case can be made for reregulating the airline sector depends not so much on a comparison between the emerging oligopoly structure and perfect competition, but rather between the situation now and what existed under regulation. He suggests that such procompetitive policies as mandating divestment of computer reservation systems by established firms may be more sensible than attempting a full-scale reregulation with its concomitant inefficiencies.

SUMMARY

In this chapter we have examined the characteristics of the different sectors of the transportation industry and noted that they are sometimes competitive and sometimes monopolistic. We introduced an example to explain the theoretical difficulty of identifying optimal prices in industries of this type. We discussed the history of regulation, from its beginning as an attempt to curb the monopoly power of the railroads, to its extension during the Depression to all other modes of transportation. As competition within and between railroads, trucking, and airlines grew, the rationale for regulation changed. However, it was not until the late 1970s that the now competitive structure of the industry was recognized by a change in government policy. The deregulation acts abolished the CAB and changed the rules under which the ICC functioned. Entry restrictions into trucking were essentially abolished and rate-setting for both trucks and railroads became much more flexible. Finally, we discussed the effects of these significant policy changes on the industry.

CONCLUSION

It is clear that the regulatory decisions made many years ago have had a surprisingly long-term effect on the development of the regulated industries and that regulation institutions are robust and not particularly adaptable. One reason for such staying power is that regulation creates benefits for some groups who then resist changes in the rules. Uncertainty about how an industry will work following a policy change increases their resistance. Entry restrictions that benefited truckers and price policies beneficial to airlines were the result of regulations that were originally put in place to improve industry performance as a whole. We have seen that the theoretical difficulties associated with finding optimal prices and constructing a policy to enforce them were formidable. Regulators had no clear working guidelines. The regulating mechanism therefore tended to reflect a compromise between different groups pushing to increase their share of the regulatory benefits.

In the next chapter we discuss the communications industry and the effect of the break-up of AT&T, drawing some comparisons with the transportation industry as we go along.

Discussion Questions

1.   Compare and contrast the cost characteristics of the surface freight transportation industry and the airline industry. Do these characteristics make these industries good candidates for regulation? How have these characteristics changed during the twentieth century?

2.   What would be the appropriate response of regulators of a bridge to attempts by a new ferry service to compete for traffic?

3.   The CAB has been effectively abolished. By contrast, the ICC remains a strong regulatory force. What explains the difference in the strength of these two agencies? Distinguish carefully between the economic and political factors involved.

4.   Under what circumstances might a policy of deregulating the trucking industry while leaving the railroads subject to rate regulation be a sensible one? What regulatory problems might result?

Selected Readings

Breyer, S. *Regulation and Its Reform*. Cambridge, Mass.: Harvard University Press, 1982. *One of the best assessments of regulation to date. Absolutely required reading.*

Douglas, G. W. and J. C. Miller III. *Economic Regulation of Domestic Air Transport: Theory and Policy*. Washington, D.C.: Brookings Institution, 1974. *This study predates deregulation by some years. It provides an excellent analysis of the structure and performance of the airline industry.*

Fellmeth, R. *The Interstate Commerce Omission*. New York: Grossman Publishers, 1970. *A readable and interesting, if not altogether objective, assessment of the working of one of the oldest regulatory institutions in the country, the ICC.*

Friedlaender, A. F. *The Dilemma of Freight Transport Regulation*. Washington, D.C.: Brookings Institution, 1969. *A classic treatment of the problems of regulating freight transportation.*

Griliches, Z. "Cost Allocation in Railroad Rate Regulation." *The Bell Journal of Economics* 3 (Spring 1972): 26–41. *A review and critique of ICC and other railroad cost studies. A valuable and important article.*

Levin, R. C. "Allocation in Surface Freight Transportation: Does Rate Regulation Matter?" *The Bell Journal of Economics* 9 (Spring 1978): 18–45. *An up-to-date assessment of the evidence concerning the effect of rate regulation on resource allocation in surface freight transportation.*

Levine, Michael E. "Airline Competition in Deregulated Markets: Theory, Firm Strategy and Public Policy." *Yale Journal on Regulation* 4 (Spring 1987): 393–494. *A comprehensive and convincing analysis of the airline industry after deregulation.*

MacAvoy, P. W. and J. W. Snow. *Regulation of Entry and Pricing in Truck Transportation.* Washington, D.C.: American Enterprise Institute, 1977. *A complete analysis of the trucking industry, containing many interesting papers. The thrust of the book is that deregulation is the appropriate policy route.*

Phillips, A. ed. *Promoting Competition in Regulated Markets.* Washington, D.C.: Brookings Institution, 1975. *There are two articles in this excellent collection that address the problems of regulation in transportation: G. Eads, "Competition in the Domestic Trunk Airline Industry," 13–54; and T. Gale Moore, "Deregulating Surface Freight Transportation," 55–98.*

CHAPTER 18

· · · · · · · · · · · · · · · · · ·

REGULATION AND PUBLIC POLICY PARADOXES: TELECOMMUNICATIONS

INTRODUCTION[1]

Until recently, if an economist was asked for an example of an industry that met all the conditions for a natural monopoly and was typically treated as such in most countries, the example offered might well have been telephones. In the United States, before January 1982, the telephone industry consisted of one enormous firm, the American Telephone and Telegraph Company (AT&T), that owned and operated almost all the plants necessary to provide local and long-distance telephone service to the entire country. AT&T also jointly owned and operated an equipment-producing subsidiary (Western Electric) and supported a highly productive research and development laboratory (Bell Labs). As shown in Figure 18.1, AT&T was a vertically integrated firm, producing both the equipment and technical expertise necessary for the provision of two major final products—local and long-distance telephone service. There were other producers in the industry at both stages. Some independent local companies provided competition for the local operating subsidiaries of AT&T. Some larger, vertically integrated companies (for example, General Telephone and Electronics (GTE) and United Telecommunications) produced equipment and provided some service in less populated areas. Nevertheless, AT&T maintained a high market share of equipment and intercity service and

---

[1]For introductions to the telecommunications industry see C. Wilcox and W. G. Shepherd, *Public Policies towards Business*, 5th ed. (Homewood, Ill.: Richard D. Irwin, Inc. 1975), 429–460; D. F. Greer, *Business, Government and Society* (New York: Macmillan, 1983), Chapters 16 and 17, 323–361; D. S. Evans, ed. *Breaking Up Bell* (New York: North-Holland, 1983); and S. Breyer, *Regulation and Its Reform* (Cambridge, Mass.: Harvard University Press, 1982), 285–314.

Figure 18.1   The Breakup of AT&T

The breakup of AT&T in 1982 gave independent status to the local Bell operating companies. AT&T now consists of an equipment-producing division (Western Electric), a research division (Bell Labs), and the Long-Lines division, which produces long-distance service.

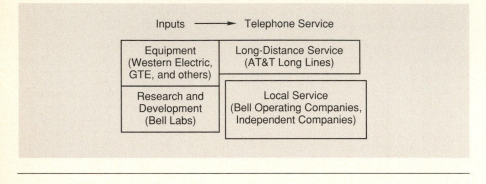

held a pure monopoly in some local markets.[2] This large company was regulated by two levels of government. The Federal Communications Commission (FCC) regulated prices and entry in long distance telephone service and exercised authority (for example, to specify product characteristics) in the equipment market. State public utility commissions regulated the prices of local calls within each state. The telephone industry clearly fit the description of a regulated natural monopoly.[3]

In January 1982 everything changed. AT&T reached an agreement with the U.S. Department of Justice in an antitrust suit that the department had filed in 1974. AT&T agreed to divest itself of its local operating companies and in return was permitted to enter new (unregulated) markets for computers and information services. This extraordinary agreement was implemented in the absence of any formal public discussion or congressional decision and totally transformed the industry.

To understand these events requires that we look not only at the technological and economic forces that changed the underlying cost structures in the industry and fostered the growth of competition, but also at the working of the regulatory and political system that ultimately failed to produce a

---

[2]MacAvoy and Robinson suggest some market share figures ranging from 77 percent to over 90 percent. They also note the increase in competition in telecommunications at both equipment and service stages of production during the 1950s, 1960s, and 1970s. Paul W. MacAvoy and Kenneth Robinson, "Winning by Losing: The AT&T Settlement and Its Impact on Telecommunications," *Yale Journal on Regulation* 1 (1983): 9. See also Albert L. Danielson and David R. Kammerschen, "A Methodological Study of Market Power and Market Shares in Intrastate Inter-LATA Telecommunications," in A. L. Danielson and D. R. Kamerschen, eds., *Telecommunications in the Post-Divestiture Era* (Lexington, Mass.: D.C. Heath, 1986), 135–180.

[3]Not everyone agrees and we discuss this point further below. See Greer, *Business, Government and Society*, 335.

coherent and sensible response to changing economic conditions and led to the restructuring of the industry on the order of a single judge.

In this chapter we begin with a brief history of the industry. We then discuss how the cost and demand structure of the industry and the policies of the regulatory bodies before divestiture jointly determined prices and investment strategies. We describe the circumstances of the 1982 consent decree and finally consider the effect of the agreement on the structure and performance of the industry. As we proceed we will see that the events in telecommunications point up weaknesses in the present system of government regulation of industry. In particular we note the lack of logic in government economic policy that allows a regulated monopoly to be sued by the Justice Department under the antitrust laws for acting like a monopoly!

THE HISTORY OF THE INDUSTRY

The history of government intervention i\n telecommunications before 1982 can be viewed either as a rational response of government to the cost and demand conditions in a natural monopoly industry (it established AT&T as a regulated monopoly and protected it from entry) or as a successful attempt by AT&T to achieve domination of an inherently competitive industry by using the regulatory power of the government. The truth may include elements of both.

Initially the industry was made up of many small companies that did not (except in a few cases) compete in overlapping areas. The American Telephone and Telegraph Company was incorporated in 1885 as a subsidiary of American Bell, which had inherited the original telephone patent awarded to Alexander Graham Bell in 1876. AT&T established a long-distance network connected to the local exchanges of subsidiary operating companies. American Bell already owned an equipment supplier, Western Electric. Thus, even before the turn of the century (which saw a huge increase in independent telephone companies), AT&T held all the ingredients for successful domination of the industry.

The FCC and Regulation

During the first 30 years of this century, government regulation was carried out by state-level commissions. These commissions tried, but failed, to regulate telephone rates. Their failure was due partly to the fact that they had very little information about costs on which to base appropriate prices. Also, since the same capital equipment was frequently used to produce both local and long-distance service, it was difficult, if not impossible, to attribute costs to each service individually. Moreover, AT&T, operating both local and long-distance lines, refused to reveal its method for allocating costs between the two services. When federal regulation of the industry (under the FCC) was established by the Communications Act of 1934, the problem of how to allocate joint costs between local and long-distance service, where the same equipment could be used to provide both, was at issue. The local operating companies, through their state commissions, succeeded in achieving a cost allocation that assigned a relatively small proportion to the local base, thereby making it possible for state regulators to keep these rates low. By comparison, long-distance rates were based on an assessment of cost that was too high.[4] In other words, higher long-distance rates were used to subsidize local rates. This system applied until the agreement of 1982, which of necessity, shifted some of the costs back to the now independent operating companies. As we shall see, however, long-distance rates are still subsidizing local rates, and precisely the same controversy that occurred in 1934 persists today.

The FCC and Growth of Competition

The cost-of-service approach used by state commissions for determining local rates was also applied by the FCC to long-distance rates. A comprehensive investigation by the FCC in 1939 resulted in new rules for estimating costs and in the separation of costs between local and long-distance services.[5] Douglas Greer suggests that the lackadaisical approach of the FCC to regulation in the subsequent 30 years helped to maintain long-distance rates that were too high.[6] He suggests that there was a close working relationship between the FCC and AT&T such that rates were negotiated in hearings, in much the same way as airlines negotiated rates with the CAB before the adoption of industry-wide rules. It is, as always, hard to assess these assertions without a detailed analysis of cost and demand conditions. Moreover, the FCC rules for estimating costs, and in particular for allocating fixed costs among the various services, did not conform closely to the economic concepts of marginal and average costs.

Recall the example of the bridge and the ferry discussed in Chapter 17. We noted there that while the bridge had decreasing average costs, the competing ferry had increasing costs. In these circumstances, it was not clear whether efficiency would be served by preventing entry by the ferry or by allowing entry and permitting the bridge to lower prices—at least to those groups that were more likely to switch to the ferry. The decision became more difficult if the regulators lacked the necessary accurate cost data to compare the profitability of different services. This describes the dilemma of the FTC in responding to pressures from firms seeking to enter the telecommunications industry.

In Chapter 17 we saw that the CAB's prevention of new entry into the airline industry was effective in maintaining high prices and stable market shares for many years. The FCC's approach toward new entry into telecommunications was somewhat more flexible. Before 1959, the use of the spectrum above 890 megacycles was reserved by the FCC for AT&T. In the *Above 890* decision the FCC relaxed this rule, enabling other firms to build their

---

[4]Technological development in the long-distance sector was already putting downward pressure on the price of long-distance calls. This offset the upward bias resulting from the cost allocation, which made it easier for federal regulators to agree to it in the first place. S. Breyer, *Regulation and Its Reform* (Cambridge, Mass.: Harvard University Press, 1982), 297.

[5]C. F. Phillips, Jr., *The Economics of Regulation* (Homewood, Ill.: Richard D. Irwin, Inc., 1969), 667.

[6]Greer, *Business, Government and Society*, 335.

own private microwave systems using these frequencies.[7] Originally, these firms were not significant competitors.   However, in 1965, Microwave Communications Inc. (MCI) was granted authority to build equipment for long-distance microwave service to paying subscribers and thus to compete in a limited way with AT&T's long-distance services. The FCC's decision to allow the entry of MCI was then expanded to include many firms that promptly applied for authority to offer what were called specialized common carrier services. Furthermore, AT&T was instructed to provide interconnection with local service. AT&T's response was two-fold: it was dilatory in providing interconnection, and it attempted to reduce some prices to meet the competition.[8] Since the cost-based pricing rules were not designed to assess the desirability of lower prices in the presence of competition, the FCC now found itself embroiled in a dispute over marginal cost versus fully distributed cost very similar to the one that characterized the controversies over ICC rate-making in the 1950s and 1960s. Like the railroads, AT&T argued that prices should be set equal to long-run marginal cost (which would put the company in a better competitive position). The FCC resisted and upheld its own methods of cost determination, none of which relied on marginal cost and which forced AT&T's prices above marginal cost. As our example in Chapter 17 (page 391) suggests, even if the FCC had known AT&T's costs, it could not have known the entrant's costs so that an accurate assessment of the welfare effects of allowing AT&T to reduce prices to marginal costs could not in practice have been discovered.

The legitimacy of AT&T's monopoly in terminal telephone equipment was formally challenged as early as 1949 when the Justice Department brought suit against AT&T and Western Electric for monopolizing the equipment markets (handsets and terminal equipment at that time).[9] The department's case was that since the AT&T operating companies bought all their equipment from Western Electric, AT&T had a captive monopoly in phone equipment and should divest itself of Western Electric.[10] This suit was finally settled in 1956 by a consent decree in which AT&T was allowed to keep Western Electric but agreed not to enter the new and growing markets for computer equipment as a producer.[11] The rapid growth of the computer equipment market during

---

[7]*Allocation of Microwave Frequencies above 890* Mc., 27 FCC 359 (1959).

[8]MCI won the legal battle over interconnection in 1976. See Greer, *Business, Government and Society,* 340.

[9]Robert W. Crandall, "Has the AT&T Break-up Raised Telephone Rates?" *The Brookings Review* 5 (Winter 1987): 41.

[10]See Steve Coll, *The Deal of the Century* (New York: Atheneum, 1987), 58.

[11]Coll and Crandall have different interpretations of this agreement. Coll suggests that the 1956 consent decree was a victory for AT&T over the Justice Department, which then held the defeat in its institutional memory. The department then seized on the next opportunity to renew the battle in 1974. By contrast, Crandall states, "This consent decree was perceived to be a major burden to AT&T . . . . AT&T's decision to sacrifice its operating companies in the 1982 settlement was the price it had to pay to have this 1956 decree vacated." Crandall, "Has the AT&T Break-up Raised Telephone Rates?" 41; and Coll, *The Deal of the Century.*

the 1950s and 1960s, as well as the continued attempts by new firms to enter the market for handsets and other telephone attachments, generated pressure on the FCC to deregulate equipment and anticipated the pressure to deregulate the telecommunications market.

To clarify the significance of the 1982 consent decree, it is useful to describe the cost, demand, and market structure of the telecommunications industry before divestiture and to analyze the effects of the FCC's price-determination policy before divestiture on the growth of competition.

THE TELECOMMUNICATIONS INDUSTRY BEFORE DIVESTITURE

Figure 18.2 is a simplified picture of the telecommunications industry before the breakup of AT&T, showing the telephone service stage of the industry (but not the market for equipment). The diagram shows the AT&T Long-Lines division and two of its local operating subsidiaries. The company as a whole operates under the regulatory umbrella of the FCC. The local subsidiaries operate under the regulatory umbrellas of their respective state commissions. One small local independent company is shown (at the left), and the shadow of a potential competitor (for example, MCI) is seen hovering in the wings.

Cost Conditions

The cost structure of the telephone industry is complex, and there is continuing debate about the validity of different estimation procedures.[12] The key question is whether the telephone industry is a natural monopoly. Recall the definition of a multi-product natural monopoly (Chapter 13) and particularly the distinction between economies of scale (average cost declines as the output of any one specific product increases) and economies of scope (average cost declines as the number of different products produced by one firm increases). AT&T and many economists have consistently argued that both types of economies are sufficiently important in telecommunications to maintain AT&T as a regulated monopoly and to prevent entry at the fringe.[13] Recall that fringe entry is referred to as creamskimming, reflecting the idea that new entrants would enter only the most profitable markets, leaving the regulated monopolist to provide service in less profitable (and even unprofitable) areas. Others

---

[12]See D. S. Evans and J. J. Heckman, "Natural Monopoly," in D. S. Evans, ed. *Breaking Up Bell*, 127–156. See also P. W. MacAvoy and Kenneth Robinson, "Winning by Losing," 31, for a full bibliography of cost studies in telecommunications.

[13]See for example, A. Phillips, "Theory and Practice in Public Utility Regulation: The Case of Telecommunications," in K. D. Boyer and W. G. Shepherd, eds., *Economic Regulation: Essays in Honor of James R. Nelson* (East Lansing, Mich.: Michigan State University, Public Utilities Papers, 1981), 181–196. In a more recent paper, Phillips continues to argue in favor of the existence of significant economies of scale and scope in telecommunications: "The Reintegration of Telecommunications: An Interim View," in M. A. Crew, ed., *Analyzing the Impact of Regulatory Change in Public Utilities* (Lexington, Mass.: D. C. Heath and Company, 1985), 5–16. B. L. Copeland, Jr., and A. Severn also present cogent arguments that telecommunications is a natural monopoly, especially at the local level: "Price Theory and Telecommunications Regulation: A Dissenting View," *Yale Journal on Regulation* 3 (Fall 1985): 53–85.

Figure 18.2 The Market for Telephone Services before Divestiture

AT&T is shown under the regulatory umbrella of the FCC. Its local subsidiaries are regulated by state commissions. One of a few local independent companies is shown connected with the long-distance network. The shadow of a potential competitor, MCI, is shown waiting in the wings.

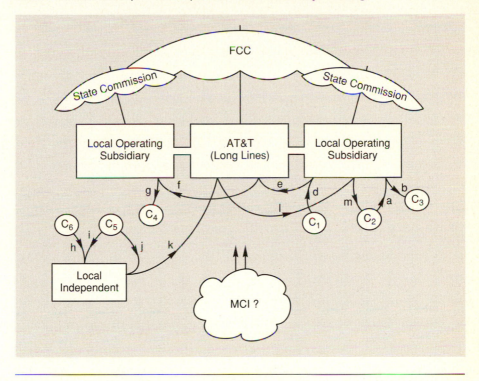

have disagreed, arguing that all significant economies of scale and scope have been fully exploited at existing demand levels, and competitive entry is therefore desirable.[14]

Measurement of Output and Cost—Local Service In Figure 18.2, a local call between customers C_2 and C_3 is shown. For C_2's call to C_3 to be completed both customers must have access to the local telephone network. C_2's call is made using a telephone (probably produced by AT&T before 1982) and received by C_3 on another AT&T produced phone. The message is carried through copper wires from C_2's house connected to the local switching center (connection a in Figure 18.2), which switches the call to wires leading to C_3's house (connection b). For local calls made by customers C_6 and C_7 (connections h and i), the local switching center is not owned by AT&T but rather by a small independent

[14]See, for example, Evans and Heckman, "Natural Monopoly." Robert W. Crandall states, "There are no convincing studies that demonstrate joint economies in the provision of local and long-distance service." Crandall, "Has the AT&T Break-up Raised Telephone Rates?" 44.

company. The costs of making a local call can be broken into two parts. The cost of access to the telephone network includes the costs of the infrastructure (poles, wires, ducts and so forth) necessary to attach each residence or business to the network.[15] The marginal cost of access is therefore the cost of connecting an additional customer to the network. The cost of switching and transmitting the call includes the construction of a centralized switching plant and the energy necessary to carry the signal.

In measuring costs, the problem of choosing the appropriate unit of output arises, as in the case of transportation. Leonard Waverman describes it thus:

> The product of the communications industry is communications services— providing the ability to send a message to a particular place at a particular time . . . . A proper measure of the product flow must include some notion of the origin and destination of the message (two calls between equidistant points are not substitutes), the distance transmitted, the duration (one 10-minute call does not equal ten 1-minute calls), and a measure of quality (static, interference and, for data, the error rate).[16]

It is sometimes useful to consider costs in relationship to the number of subscribers. For example, in local telephone service there are increasing returns to scale if we measure costs as a function of subscribers. These arise mainly from economies in the distribution network. There may be some increasing costs—for example, those associated with providing directories— but these are not significant. In the early years of the telephone industry, independent companies had provided some competition for AT&T and some localities were initially served by more than one telephone company.[17] Since then, technological improvements (particularly in switching) have significantly altered the cost structure and economies of scale at the local level have been realized.

There are two additional reasons why local service is a good candidate for regulation. First, infrastructure (poles, wires, and so forth) would be duplicated if more than one company served an area.[18] Second, the addition of new subscribers confers external benefits on existing subscribers by increasing the size of the network and hence the calling options of all subscribers.[19]

---

[15]See A. E. Kahn and W. B. Shew, "Current Issues in Telecommunications Regulation: Pricing," *Yale Journal on Regulation* 4 (Spring 1987): 200. They argue that access should be treated as a separate service from the call itself. Copeland and Severn argue precisely the opposite. Copeland and Severn, "Price Theory and Telecommunications Regulation."

[16]L. Waverman, "The Regulation of Intercity Telecommuncations," in A. Phillips, ed., *Promoting Competition in Regulated Markets* (Washington, D. C.: Brookings Institution, 1975), 209.

[17]See R. Bornholz and D. S. Evans, "The Early History of Competition in the Telephone Industry," in D. S. Evans, ed., *Breaking Up Bell*, 7–40.

[18]A. Kahn, *The Economics of Regulation: Principles and Institutions*, vol. 2 (New York: Wiley, 1971), 123.

[19]Kahn and Shew, "Current Issues in Telecommunications," 241. Of course there is no practical reason why two separate firms should not agree to interlink. This certainly occurs in long-distance service. See D. S. Evans and S. J. Grossman, "Integration," in D. S. Evans, *Breaking Up Bell*, 25–126.

Long-Distance Service   In Figure 18.2 a long-distance call between customers C_1 and C_4 is represented by connections d, e, f, and g. Clearly C_1's call to C_4 requires that both customers already have access to the local network (connections d and g) and that this network is in turn connected to AT&T's long-distance network (connections e and f). The long-distance call may be transmitted by a variety of technologies—coaxial cable, microwave radio, satellite, or fiber optics. If a customer who is served by a local independent company (C_5) wishes to make a long-distance call to a customer served by an AT&T local subsidiary (C_2), the call must be switched from the originating local company into the AT&T long-distance network to be completed (connections j, k, l, m). This obviously requires an agreement between the local independent and AT&T to link their respective networks.

Economies of Scale and Scope in Long-Distance Service   For intercity or long-distance service, Waverman suggests that potential economies of scale can occur at four levels:[20]

1.   At the plant level, "production economies of scale will be defined as the internal scale economies presented in joining two points by a communicating plant providing a simple output."   All methods of transmission—coaxial cable, microwave radio, and satellites—involve (sometimes substantial) fixed costs. These insure that there are economies of scale up to capacity levels, which are substantially greater than demand levels over many routes.[21] Technological innovations in fiber optics in the future may also increase relative economies of scale for bulk line-haul facilities, while possibly decreasing these economies relative to total costs inclusive of switching costs.[22]

2.   At the firm level, increasing returns to scale exist in management, finance, research and development, and emergency devices. AT&T argued that such economies are substantial. Opponents suggested that methods of instituting different systems were readily available. They were already used, for example when international calls were made, and also in many other industries where firms agreed to maintain common standards.

3.   Multi-product economies of scope occur when a single firm can produce a wide variety of services more cheaply than many single-product firms. Waverman suggests that these are not important at capacity levels above

[20]Waverman, "The Regulation of Intercity Telecommunications," 205–207.

[21]Waverman, "The Regulation of Intercity Telecommunications," 209–221.

[22]Before 1982, AT&T argued that the demand levels necessary to exploit these new economies would be larger than those that could be sustained by a number of competing firms. This was difficult to test at the time because the argument involved estimating future costs and future demand levels that were subject to great uncertainty. Breyer, *Regulation and Its Reform*, 292. A. Phillips argues that the record since 1982 in fact bears out AT&T's contention that economies of scale are still significant. A. Phillips, "The Reintegration of Telecommunications," 6–8. See also Copeland and Severn, "Price Theory and Telecommunications Regulation," for arguments that there are decreasing costs in local service.

those determined by plant and firm economies. Phillips suggests that economies of scope are of continuing and possibly increasing importance as new equipment is designed to produce a variety of different services.[23]

4.   Contract economies of scale may exist. Imagine a telephone industry in which each locality is served by a different local monopoly and each city is linked by different intercity monopoly firms. The establishment of long-distance connections for subscribers would involve bilateral bargaining between pairs of monopolists. Even if the city-pair links were competitively supplied, problems might still arise in making contracts to establish the terms for linking the networks. These problems might disappear if a single firm owned the entire network.[24]

Demand Conditions

Demand for telephone calls is a function of the usual factors: income, the price of calling, the prices of substitutes (such as letters or telegrams), time of day or week, and special conditions such as Mother's Day.[25] For firms, demand also depends on the characteristics of the final product. For example, the demand for telephone service of a brokerage house is likely to have different characteristics than the demand of a manufacturing firm. One study suggests that the short-run price and income elasticities of demand for both households and business are very low (perhaps reflecting the fact that demand for telephone services is characterized by habit formation), but that long-run elasticities are much higher.[26]

Types of Services   There is now a wide range of local and long-distance services for which both cost and demand may vary. Plain Old Telephone Service (POTS) consists of offering a customer access to the national network, and the option of making either a local or long-distance call. Other long-distance services include Wide Area Telephone Service (WATS), which allows a subscriber for a fixed charge to dial anywhere within a given area without paying an additional charge per call. (This may include contiguous states or even the whole country, and some queuing may be necessary for an open line.) Private-

---

[23]A. Phillips,"The Reintegration of Telecommunications: An Interim View," in M. A. Crew, ed., *Analyzing the Impact of Regulatory Change in Public Utilities* (Lexington, Mass.: D. C. Heath and Co., 1985), 8.

[24]See O. E. Williamson, *Markets and Hierarchies* (New York: The Free Press, 1975), for a comprehensive theory of transactions costs and contracts. See D. S. Evans and S. J. Grossman, "Integration," for a critique of the transactions cost argument.

[25]Mother's Day has the largest number of calls of any day of the year.

[26]A. R. Dobell, et al., "Telephone Communications in Canada: Demand Production and Investment Decisions," *Bell Journal of Economics* 3 (Spring 1972): 175–219. See also L. Taylor's estimates quoted in Kahn and Shew, "Current Issues in Telecommunications Regulation," 210. Taylor's estimates also suggest low elasticities for local calls and higher elasticities for long-distance calls.

line service is a single subscriber's exclusive right to use an open line between two fixed points. The WATS and private-line services are directed at high volume users. Under the fixed-charge payment method, the user's marginal price of additional calls is zero; the average price per call therefore falls as volume increases. Other types of services, which may require special equipment, include Custom Calling (for example, call-forwarding, call-waiting, and teleconferencing) and high-speed transmission of data.

Pricing before Divestment   The Communications Act of 1934 and subsequent decisions by the FCC and state regulatory commissions identified a major public objective to be the provision of universal telephone service at affordable prices. This commitment to universal service led to a system of price setting whereby the price of local calls was kept so low that almost everyone could afford a telephone. As a result the costs of access (basic service) and local calling (for which a toll was charged according to usage) were not covered by the revenues earned from these services. The shortfall was made up by charging prices much higher than costs on long-distance services. Thus, long-distance users systematically subsidized local users.[27]

Another source of revenue to cover local costs was found by charging business customers a different rate than residential customers. This added a value of service element to the cost-based pricing system. Since the elasticity of demand for business calls was less elastic than for residential calls, relatively more revenue could be earned by charging businesses a higher price.

Over time the costs of providing local service rose faster than long-distance costs, which tended to decrease relatively as new technologies were exploited. Local prices, however, failed to rise with costs, and the relative fall in local prices was very small compared with the substantial relative fall in long-distance costs. The subsidy of local users out of long-distance revenues increased over time.[28] In 1970, the Ozark Plan further increased the share of costs allocated to long-distance service, and drove a bigger wedge between long-distance rates and economic costs.[29]

It is therefore not surprising that high excess profits earned from AT&T's long-distance operation attracted competitors into this part of the industry. Since AT&T's regulated prices were so far above economic costs, a new entrant would not need to be as efficient as AT&T. It could operate quite profitably by

[27]This definition of subsidization implies that it is possible to separate the costs of local service from those of long-distance service. Whether this can be achieved is a matter continual controversy, as will be seen in more detail below.

[28]MacAvoy and Robinson, "Winning by Losing," 2–6.

[29]See P. W. MacAvoy and K. Robinson, "Winning by Losing," 5, for a detailed description of the series of FCC decisions that resulted in the new separations procedure called the Ozark Plan. The initiating pressures were an attempt by AT&T to reduce its long-distance rates to take advantage of new economies at the same time that state regulators were being asked for increased local rates to cover rising local costs.

pricing somewhat below current price levels.[30] New firms, such as MCI, began to seek entry into the industry and to petition the FCC to be permitted to provide not simply specialized, private-line service but universal long-distance service in direct competition with AT&T. AT&T's response was to request reductions in long-distance rates to meet the competition and to argue vociferously against allowing new entry on the grounds that its universal service obligation forced it to provide costly service in rural areas. New entry only in profitable routes would be creamskimming.

AT&T also resisted new entry into the terminal equipment market, although the justification here was much weaker. Economies of scale were not so evident. It was not at all clear that equipment markets were not viable competitively. In the 1956 Consent Decree AT&T had been banned from entering the computer market. It was the sole producer in markets for handsets, answering machines, and so forth. Now, however, the pace of technological change in the production and development of new types of telephone equipment increased, as did consumer demand. Potential producers saw profitable opportunities and petitioned the FCC to allow them to enter the market. During the 1960s the FCC slowly began to permit entry.[31]

THE DEAL OF THE CENTURY [32]

In spite of the FCC's willingness to permit limited entry into the equipment and interstate telephone service sectors of the telecommunications industry during the 1960s and early 1970s, it was not prepared to allow new long-distance entrants to compete directly for common carrier status with AT&T. It was less reluctant to allow entry into the private-lines market, but clearly the bulk of potential profits lay in the long-distance common carrier market. Microwave Communications Inc. (MCI) was a relatively new corporation that had already invested substantial resources in preparing to enter the telecommunications industry with long-distance service using microwave technology. MCI was not satisfied with the FCC's response to its attempts to enter and objected to AT&T's reluctance to provide interconnection with its local networks. Interconnection was essential if MCI was to compete for common carrier status with AT&T. MCI took another tack—it approached the U.S. Department of Justice and in 1974 filed an antitrust suit against AT&T seeking

---

[30]MCI Corporation was so confident that it could produce with substantially lower costs than AT&T's current prices that it invested $10 million and spent seven years in legal battling in order to win entry into the long-distance telecommunications industry. Greer, *Business, Government, and Society*, 339. Copeland and Severn argue that this situation accurately identifies AT&T as an unsustainable natural monopoly and suggest that government-enforced entry barriers are the appropriate remedy, rather than more competition. Copeland and Severn, "Price Theory and Telecommunications Regulation," 74.

[31]See Copeland and Severn, "Price Theory and Telecommunications Regulation," 55, for a description of the sequence of FCC decisions that resulted in easier entry into equipment markets.

[32]*The Deal of the Century* is the title of a very interesting, well-researched, if somewhat overly dramatic account by Steve Coll of the events leading up to the 1982 consent decree. We draw on Coll's discussion in this section and the next.

huge damages. Later that year the Justice Department itself filed an antitrust suit against AT&T under Section 2 of the Sherman Act, alleging,

> ... in essence, that AT&T had illegally manipulated its dominant position in three sets of telecommunications markets—equipment, local exchange, and long-distance—in order to monopolize the entire domestic telecommunications industry. The Department accused AT&T of illegally refusing to provide competitors with local interconnection service and of setting entry-inhibiting prices in potentially competitive parts of its business.[33]

This suit finally came to trial in 1981 and was settled in 1982 with a consent decree between Charles Brown (the board chairman of AT&T) and William Baxter (Assistant Attorney General).[34] The consent decree, which was approved by Judge Harold Greene, required that AT&T divest itself of its local operating companies, reducing the company to one third of its current size, in return for permission to enter the market for computers. In the years between 1974 and 1982, AT&T had been unsuccessful in persuading Congress to reaffirm its status as a regulated monopoly and to legislate against new entry into telecommunications.

Steve Coll traces in detail the events leading up to the trial and ultimate settlement. He identifies various individuals, groups, and institutions whose differing motives and attempts to move government policy in their direction clashed, resulting in the 1982 settlement. For example:

- The chairman of MCI was determined to enter what he perceived as the lucrative long-distance telephone market and to out-maneuver AT&T in the legal battle for entry.
- AT&T systematically attempted to work through Congress to shore up its natural monopoly status, emphasizing the universal service objective.
- The FCC was unclear in its rulings about entry and this lack of clarity increased the likelihood that entrants would seek an alternative route through the Justice Department.
- Within the Justice Department there were various groups with slightly different objectives, but all committed to the enforcement of antitrust policy and to proving the department's effectiveness.
- Judge Greene was determined to show that the courts could successfully enforce antitrust policy and did not wish to see Congress shelter AT&T from antitrust action.

Coll offers the following conclusion:

> [T]he crucial decisions made in the telecommunications industry during the 1970s and early 1980s were driven by opportunism, short-term politics, ego, desperation, miscalculation, happenstance, greed, conflicting ideologies and personalities, and finally, when Charlie Brown thought there was nothing left, a perceived necessity. The point is, if anyone had emerged

---

[33]MacAvoy and Robinson, "Winning by Losing," 14.

[34]*United States v. AT&T Co.*, 552 F.Supp. 131 (D.D.C. 1982). See Copeland and Severn, "Price Theory and Telecommunications Regulation," 57, for a complete list of the rulings that comprised the consent decree.

triumphant from that embarrassing history in how not to make public policy, it would have been a phenomenal accident. And no one did. Not telephone consumers, not AT&T, not MCI.[35]

Coll also suggests that, in the end, the Justice Department's decision to prosecute AT&T was based not so much on economic arguments about the the competitive viablity of telecommunications as on the perception that AT&T was so large and powerful that it actually threatened the power of the government. Only by breaking it up could the government reassert its ability to control the industry.

Whatever the truth about the causes of the AT&T breakup, the fact remains that the telecommunications industry is now very different than before 1982. (We now examine its new structure and discuss the problems of pricing and investment that have arisen since 1982.)

TELECOMMUNICATIONS AFTER DIVESTITURE

Figure 18.3 shows the present organization of the industry. AT&T now consists only of the Long-Lines division, Western Electric, and Bell Labs. It is still subject to regulation by the FCC, and the agreement reached with the Justice Department is still monitored by Judge Greene (the Judiciary in Figure 18.3). AT&T therefore finds itself with two regulatory umbrellas that overlap. The Bell operating companies are independent corporations subject to regulation by state commissions. They are permitted to provide telephone service within a LATA (Local Access and Transport Area).[36] A local call is now an intra-LATA call (for example, from customer C_2 to C_3 over connections a and b). There are other common carriers (OCCs) such as MCI and Sprint. These firms buy access to the LATAs from the Bell operating companies and then offer long-distance service to consumers in competition with AT&T. The OCCs are not subject to price regulation by the FCC. A long-distance call may either be carried on AT&T's network, as between customers C_1 and C_4 (connections d, e, f, g in the figure), or by an OCC, as between customers C_2 and C_5 (connections h, i, j, k). There also exists the possibility for a customer to bypass the LATA completely by buying a private line from either AT&T or an OCC, as between customers C_3 and C_6 (connections l and m).

In 1983 four changes in the settlement were ordered by Judge Green:[37]

1.   The operating companies were permitted to enter markets for marketing and installing telephone equipment.

2.   AT&T was ordered to give the yellow-pages operation to the operating companies.

---

[35]Coll, *The Deal of the Century*, 369.

[36]Some of the LATAs are so large that some intra-LATA calls are effectively long-distance.

[37]P. W. MacAvoy and K. Robinson, "Losing by Judicial Policymaking: The First Year of the AT&T Divestiture," *Yale Journal on Regulation* 2 (Spring 1985): 233–234.

Figure 18.3 The Market for Telephone Services after Divestiture

The local operating companies are now independent and produce local service within a LATA. They are regulated by state commissions. AT&T now produces only long-distance service and falls under two regulatory umbrellas—the FCC and the Judiciary. Other common carriers (OCCs) such as MCI are now permitted to produce long-distance service and to connect with the national network through the local operating companies.

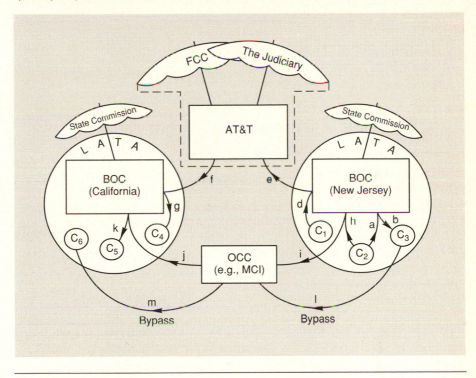

3.   More long-distance traffic was transferred to the operating companies than in the original agreement.

4.   AT&T was banned from entering the electronic publishing business for 7 years, and the operating companies were completely excluded from this market.

Pricing and Investment

We turn first to the identification of optimal prices for local and long-distance service. We then consider the system of prices actually charged by telephone service producers to consumers.

The Theoretical Picture   The analytical problems involved in identifying optimal prices for local and long-distance service are legion—we address only a few. Note first that much of the capacity that produces local calls can also produce long-distance calls. Indeed, it was originally designed to produce both. While one can envision a system that results from investment in capacity designed only for local calls, or a system designed only for long-distance calls, the capacity that is in place is designed for both. Moreover, it is not clear that separate systems for local and long-distance calls would necessarily be cheaper than the joint system.[38] The portion of capacity that is joint to both local and long-distance calls is also nontraffic sensitive (NTS)—that is, these costs do not vary with the volume of traffic, but are largely fixed. The variable—traffic sensitive (TS)—costs of local calls are those that increase when the volume of local traffic increases. The variable costs of long-distance traffic also increase with the number of long-distance calls. Therefore, given existing capacity, the marginal cost of a single additional local or long-distance call can be identified as the addition to variable cost of making that type of call.

The marginal cost curves of long-distance and local calls are MC_D and MC_L in Figures 18.4(a) and 18.4(b). For simplicity we have assumed constant marginal costs equal to average variable costs in both cases. Given demand curve D_D for long-distance calls in Figure 18.4(a), the efficient price is P_{D_1}, with quantity Q_{D_1}, where the consumer of the last call is just willing to pay the marginal cost of supplying it. The net welfare from selling Q_{D_1} units at price P_{D_1} is the area of consumer surplus $P_{D_1}LM$. For local calls, given demand curve D_L in Figure 18.4(b), the efficient price–quantity combination is P_{L_1}, Q_{L_1} with net welfare equal to area $P_{L_1}WS$. Now assume that the profits earned from these efficient price–quantity combinations fail to cover variable and NTS costs. Indeed, our assumption of constant marginal and average variable costs ensures that total revenue from long-distance and local calls (areas $OP_{D_1}MQ_{D_1}$ and $OP_{L_1}SQ_{L_1}$ in Figures 18.4(a) and 18.4(b), respectively) just covers total variable costs (also equal to areas $OP_{D_1}MQ_{D_1}$ and $OP_{L_1}SQ_{L_1}$). There is nothing remaining to put towards the joint NTS costs. Assume, further, that consumers and regulators think that the price of local calls, P_{L_1}, is too high for fairness reasons (some consumers cannot afford to buy calls at that price).[39] The solution adopted is to increase the profits earned from long-distance calls and use these to defray the NTS costs and subsidize local service. This is achieved by raising the price of long-distance calls to P_{D_2} and lowering the local call price to P_{L_2}. Now the total revenues earned from long-distance calls exceed total variable

[38]The costs of providing each service alone are called stand alone costs. In this context, economies of scope exist if one firm can provide both services using joint capacity more cheaply than two firms providing each separately. However, such a natural monopoly may not be sustainable. In other words, one firm may still be able to provide one service more cheaply than the joint service—the creamskimming example (see Chapter 13). See also Kahn and Shew, "Current Issues in Telecommunications Regulation," 228.

[39]It is not intuitively clear that the priority for low-income families is to make only local calls, but this has always been the policy-driving assumption.

Figure 18.4 Long-distance Service Subsidizes Local Service

a. D_D is the demand for long-distance calls. MC_D is the constant marginal cost curve, equal to the average variable cost of long-distance service. The welfare-maximizing price and output combination is P_{D_1}, Q_{D_1}. If the FCC rules that long-distance calls must be priced at P_{D_2} quantity falls to Q_{D_2}. Profits to subsidize local service are $P_{D_1}P_{D_2}NK$. The deadweight welfare loss is NKM.

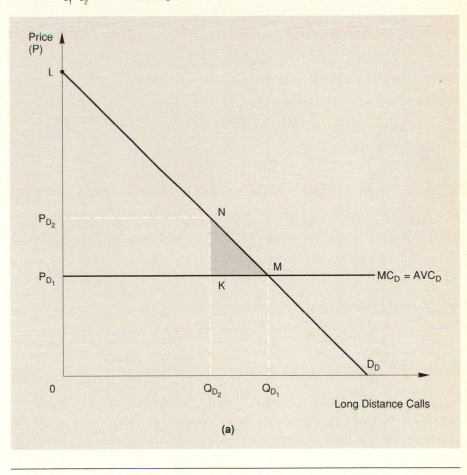

(a)

costs by area $P_{D_1}P_{D_2}NK$. These excess long-distance revenues can be used partly to offset the losses sustained by reducing the price of local calls to P_{L_2}— area $P_{L_2}P_{L_1}RT$—and partly to defray NTS costs. Thus a redistribution of income is achieved whereby users of long-distance service subsidize the local service users. Although it was widely understood that long-distance rates were being kept up in order to subsidize local rates, this fact was not explicitly identified as a distributional policy decision. Instead, the system of cost separations, initiated in 1934, was perpetuated precisely because it delivered the desired subsidy. In this system, a proportion of average NTS costs were added to the

b. D_L is the relatively inelastic demand curve for local calls. MC_L is the marginal cost curve. The welfare-maximizing price and output combination is P_{L_1}, Q_{L_1}. If the FCC mandates a price reduction to P_{L_2}, the firm sustains losses equal to $P_{L_2} P_{L_1} RT$. The deadweight welfare loss is SRT.

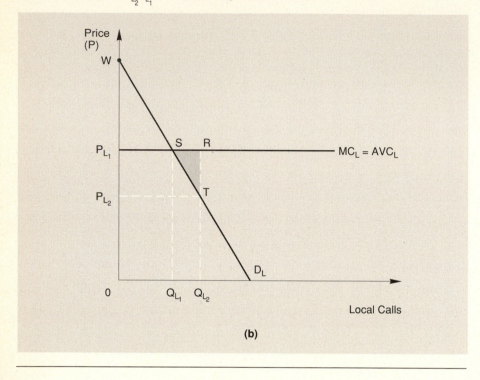

(b)

variable costs of long-distance service so that a price based on the sum of the two costs would equal P_{D_2}. In other words, if the FCC wanted the long-distance price to rise by the amount NK per call, it would allocate average NTS costs equal to NK per call to long-distance service. The resulting price P_{D_2} could therefore be said to be cost-based. By similar token, the variable costs for local calls were actually reduced below their true level, but still identified as cost-based.

There is an efficiency cost to this policy. When long-distance rates increase, net social welfare (TR + S - TC) falls by the deadweight loss triangle KMN. For local calls, there is also a deadweight loss triangle SRT.[40] The welfare loss from pricing long-distance calls in excess of marginal cost will be greater the higher the elasticity of demand and the larger the number of calls bought at the too

---

[40]This deadweight loss occurs because the cost of producing Q_{L_2} minus Q_{L_1} additional local calls exceeds consumers' willingness to pay for those additional calls by area SRT.

high price. For local calls the welfare loss also increases with the elasticity of demand and the number of local calls.[41]

The Performance of the Industry after 1982

The division of assets between AT&T and the now independent Bell operating companies led, as predicted, to some rise in local rates (see Table 18.1). This occurred because, following divestiture, new cost allocation rules were put in place (using new depreciation rates) and also because the assets transferred from AT&T to the independent local companies were added to variable costs in determining the price of local calls, which rose as a result.[42] However, both the FCC and the state commissions were reluctant to see an even larger rise in local rates after divestiture for two reasons. First, higher local prices jeopardizes the concept of universal service and is politically undesirable. Second, high local prices encourage consumers to bypass the local network entirely and to buy relatively cheaper private lines from AT&T or the OCCs. This further reduces the revenues of the Bell operating companies.

In Figure 18.5 the demand for local service is D_L; the price is P_{L_1} and quantity is Q_{L_1}. Assume that the elasticity of demand for local calls is less than one for prices below P_B. Thus, if price rises from P_{L_1} to P_B, the percentage fall in the quantity demanded (to Q_B) will be less than the percentage rise in price, and total revenue will rise. At price P_B however, bypass technologies become profitable. Now a rise in the local price above P_B, say to P_{L_2}, will make a call produced with the bypass technology relatively cheap at P_B. Large volume users will therefore switch to the service using the bypass technology. Demand for local service will fall by a relatively large amount, from Q_B to Q_{L_2}. The demand curve has become more elastic (between points B and F). When price rises from P_B to P_{L_2}, revenue falls.[43]

At first the FCC proposed to increase local revenue by raising the access charge to consumers by 1 dollar (per month) each year for up to 7 years, rather than increasing rates for local calls. The rationale was that the demand for

[41]Copeland and Severn, "Price Theory and Telecommunications Regulation," draw attention to the fact that deadweight loss measures of allocative inefficiency are based on distributional assumptions to which many may object. In the presence of significant joint and fixed costs, prices set equal to marginal costs will not generate sufficient revenue to cover total costs. Some other pricing scheme must be chosen. The distribution of welfare among consumers will be different for different schemes, and there is no systematic way to distinguish between them. Recall Chapter 2, in which we discuss the application of various concepts of justice to economic policy.

[42]Note that splitting off the operating subsidiaries does not by itself remove the problem of the optimal allocation of common costs between local and long-distance service. But the division of assets did point up the insufficiency of local revenues.

[43]With quantity Q_B and price P_B, total revenue is area OP_BBQ_B. With quantity Q_{L_2} and price P_{L_2}, total revenue is area $OP_{L_2}FQ_{L_2} < OP_BBQ_B$(compare areas $Q_{L_2}GBQ_B$and $P_BP_{L_2}FG$).

Table 18.1   Real Producer Price Indexes for Telephone Services, 1972–1985

Year	Interstate Toll	Intrastate Toll	Local Residential	Local Business
1972	100.0	100.0	100.0	100.0
1973	96.9	97.2	96.9	97.9
1974	87.4	91.4	92.3	94.3
1975	86.8	88.5	88.1	91.0
1976	87.4	92.3	87.4	91.1
1977	83.3	91.1	82.4	84.5
1978	78.2	84.6	78.3	80.8
1979	69.6	75.8	71.1	74.1
1980	63.3	67.2	65.0	67.5
1981	63.2	63.2	66.3	68.4
1982	65.9	63.1	69.6	70.5
1983	64.4	63.9	70.8	72.5
1984	59.9	64.0	73.2	74.5
1985	55.7	63.0	74.9	75.6

Note: All indexes deflated by Consumer Price Index-Urban.

Source: R. W. Crandall, "Has the AT&T Break-up Raised Telephone Rates?" 40, Table 2. Crandall quotes his source as the Bureau of Labor Statistics.

access was less price elastic than the demand for calls, so that the revenue increase would be relatively larger from a rise in access charges. However, the jeopardy to the universal service concept was sufficiently threatening to consumer groups that they successfully opposed the FCC's policy. In response the FCC fixed the subscriber access fee at not more than 2 dollars per month for residential service, and up to 6 dollars per month per line for multi-line business service.[44]

In theory, any customer willing to pay more than the marginal cost of access should optimally be provided with a connection, whether or not any calls are actually made. But if the average cost of connecting the last customer exceeds the marginal cost, (that is, if there are economies of scale in providing access), then pricing access at marginal cost will lead to losses (the fundamental dilemma of public utility pricing). One possible solution is to recognize that the elasticity of demand for access to the telephone network may be very low and that raising price above marginal cost so as to generate sufficient revenues to cover the high fixed costs may not cut volume or welfare very much. (Recall Chapter 14, in which we discussed optimal pricing subject to a break-even constraint.) This is precisely the solution that was proposed but not fully implemented by the FCC.

Following the consent decree, it was expected that long-distance rates would fall significantly. Indeed, competition from the OCCs would virtually ensure this result. Table 18.1 shows that both interstate and intrastate real rates have fallen. However, the real price declines in long-distance service did not

---

[44]Kahn and Shew, 'Current Issues in Telecommunications Regulation," 197.

Figure 18.5 The Effect of Bypass on the Demand for Local Calls

When the price of local calls rises from P_{L_1} to P_B, total revenue rises. When the price of local calls rises above P_B it pays large-volume users to switch to bypass technology and total revenue falls.

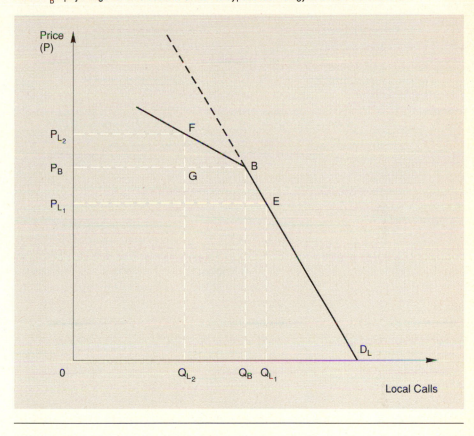

begin in 1982, but have been falling since 1970. The real cost of long-distance telephone service in 1985 was just over half its level 15 years earlier. This pattern of price declines indicates that there has been systematic technical change in the industry resulting in increased productivity.[45] Although prices did in fact decline after 1982, AT&T continued to ask the FCC to allow them to reduce long-distance rates even further. The FCC was reluctant for several reasons. First, the FCC resisted large price cuts for fear of immediately

[45]Copeland and Severn state that "From 1973 through 1981, gross product per person employed in communications increased 5.1 percent per year, whereas for private industry as a whole, the annual rate of increase in gross product per person employed was only 0.4 percent." They note that the structure of regulated prices before 1982 cannot be considered inefficient if indeed it generated such enormous productivity gains. Copeland and Severn, "Price Theory and Telecommunications Regulation," 82.

threatening the financial viablity of AT&T's competitors. The logic here is circular. If an independent AT&T is able to sustain lower prices in a freely functioning market and to capture a larger market share from its competitors, then this indicates that AT&T's costs are lower at higher output levels. In other words, AT&T can take advantage of economies of scale and scope to set a stay-out (limit) price that makes entry unprofitable for competitors with higher costs. Theory tells us that if one firm is able to become and remain dominant in an industry, it is a natural monopoly and a good candidate for regulation. The FCC implicitly recognizes the force of this argument by preventing AT&T from lowering its prices.[46] In theory, efficient prices would be set equal to the marginal cost of long-distance calls; but with economies of scale, losses would result. Kahn and Shew make a case for a two-part tariff, whereby a fixed charge would be made for access to long-distance service sufficient to cover the shortfall of revenue by pricing toll calls at marginal cost. Alternatively the price could be raised for some initial block of usage.[47] Another reason why long-distance calls are still priced at several times their marginal cost is because the access fee that AT&T must pay to the independent local companies remains, by FCC ruling, substantially higher than the fees paid by competing OCCs. (Note, however, that the quality of the OCCs' connection to the local network is lower.) Higher access fees raise long-distance costs and prices. Thus, in effect, AT&T is still subsidizing local service with its long-distance revenues.

The fact that AT&T's long-distance prices have remained substantially above costs has allowed competitors to make investments in long-distance service that could not have been made with lower prices. Moreover, it has been suggested that AT&T's drive to find new markets for sophisticated communications services has resulted in overinvestment in new equipment that is not necessary to produce the majority of calls (POTS). Taken together with new investment in facilities to bypass the local network, it may be the case that deregulation has resulted in an inefficient level of new investment that would not be sustained if the markets were truly deregulated. Certainly, as long as telephone prices are unrelated to costs, the inefficiency (deadweight) losses will be large.[48]

To the extent that deregulation has brought prices more in line with costs, some net social gains have occurred. Whether or not the industry is competi-

[46]See A. Phillips, "The Reintegration of Telecommunications," 7.

[47]Kahn and Shew, "Current Issues in Telecommunications Regulation," 250. See also Copeland and Severn, "Price Theory and Telecommunications Regulation," who argue that the old system of flat rates was just as efficient as these suggested alternatives.

[48]In a 1982 study, James M. Griffin estimated welfare losses for interstate long-distance service at $1.8 billion a year. J. M. Griffin, "The Welfare Implications of Externalities and Price Elasticities for Telecommunications Services," *Review of Economics and Statistics* 64 (February 1982): 65. John T. Wenders and Bruce L. Egan estimated the welfare loss to be $15 billion to $20 billion when intrastate toll markets were included. J. T. Wenders and B. L. Egan, "Improving Economic Efficiency in State Telecommunications Markets," paper presented at Rutgers University Advanced Workshop on Regulation and Public Utility Economics, August 1984, 4. For further discussion, see James A. Leggette, "Separations and Telecommunications Pricing Issues," in Danielson and Kamerschen, eds., *Telecommunications in the Post-Divestiture Era*, 105–118.

tively viable is still an open question. The Bell operating companies are trying to diversify so that they are not totally dependent on revenue from local calls. They have been permitted some flexibility here—how much varies with the policy of particular state commissions. As long as the FCC keeps AT&T's rates well above costs, competitors will appear viable. Reregulation of long-distance markets is not likely in the near future. The Bell operating companies are still treated as natural monopolies subject to price and entry regulation. However, there is pressure from the operating companies and potential entrants to open the local as well as the long-distance market to competition. Whether this pressure will be successful is hard to predict.

SUMMARY

In this chapter we have described the cost and demand characteristics of the telecommunications industry and considered whether the industry is a natural monopoly. We described the history of the regulation of the industry by the FCC and the state commissions and the events that precipitated the breakup of AT&T. We discussed the settlement between AT&T and the Justice Department and described the resulting changes in the markets for local and long-distance service. Finally, we discussed the new regulatory environment.

CONCLUSION

There are several important lessons to be learned from the extraordinary events surrounding the breakup of AT&T. First, the U.S. Constitution is both flexible and vague with respect to government economic policy. It appears that the power of the FCC, Justice Department, and the state commissions can wax and wane depending on the various political pressures exerted on them. The effectiveness of such pressure, however, is not certain. No one correctly predicted the outcome of the 1982 settlement decree. Second, the lack of clarity in policy-making procedure has completely changed the industrial structure of a technologically complex industry, a change that very few now regard as good. In fact, it may have been an economic policy that generated many more losers than winners. If indeed it turns out that economies of scale and scope continue to be realized in the production of telephone service, and if the FCC eventually allows AT&T or any OCC to reduce prices sufficiently to exploit these economies, we may expect to see the structure of the industry revert back to its previous shape—the dominance by only one firm.

The view that the breakup was a response to the overwhelming absolute size of AT&T and the threat it posed to the government regulating institutions may help identify other large firms, regulated or not, as potential targets for breakup. This may give policymakers a new task: to develop ways of solving the natural monopoly problem other than by allowing one firm to grow to enormous size.

Finally, since competition in the long-distance market now has a chance to work, it seems sensible not to constrain it. This would suggest less rather than more price regulation by the FCC so that actual prices more accurately reflect costs. However, if the result of the competitive process is the emergence of a dominant firm, then reregulation in some form may ultimately be inevitable.

Discussion Questions

1. The breakup of AT&T led to a rise in rates for local calls. What is the reason for this? Is the rise in local rates a good thing?

2. Make a case for reregulating the telephone service sector of the telecommunications industry. Can you also make a case for reregulating equipment?

3. The Justice Department suit against AT&T accused the company (among other things) of predatory pricing. How would a lawyer for the Justice Department make the case? For the defense?

4. "The 1982 settlement between AT&T and the Justice Department shows that, when all is said and done, economic analysis has nothing to do with how economic policy is actually made." Evaluate this statement.

Selected Readings

Coll, S. *The Deal of the Century: The Break-up of AT&T.* New York: Atheneum, 1987. *An interesting, well-researched account.*

Copeland, B. L., Jr. and Alan Severn. "Price Theory and Telecommunications Regulation: A Dissenting View." *Yale Journal on Regulation* 3 (Fall 1985): 53–85. *A cogent argument that telecommunications is a natural monopoly and that the regulatory solutions arrived at before 1982 were appropriate.*

Danielson, A. L. and D. R. Kamerschen, eds. *Telecommunications in the Post-Divestiture Era.* Lexington, Mass.: D. C. Heath and Co., 1986. *A varied collection of accessible papers on different aspects of the industry.*

Evans, D. S., ed. *Breaking Up Bell* New York: North Holland, 1983. *A collection of many interesting papers on theories of natural monopoly and their implications for the reorganization of the telecommunications industry.*

Kahn, A. E. and W. B. Shew. "Current Issues in Telecommunications Regulation: Pricing." *Yale Journal on Regulation* 4 (Spring 1987): 191–256. *A comprehensive and clear review of pricing issues, including a useful list of common pricing fallacies.*

MacAvoy, P. W. and K. Robinson. "Winning by Losing: The AT&T Settlement and Its Impact on Telecommunications." *Yale Journal on Regulation* 1 (1983): 1-42; and "Losing by Judicial Policymaking: The First Year of the AT&T Divestiture." *Yale Journal on Regulation* 2 (1985): 225-262. *Two clear and detailed articles offering a changing assessment of the divestiture.*

CHAPTER 19

· ·

GENERAL ASSESSMENTS

Like antitrust policy, direct regulation of industry uses up substantial resources. One estimate suggests that the total direct cost of government regulation by federal agencies came to more than $8.5 billion in 1986.[1] The indirect cost borne by firms and other government agencies in reponding to regulatory requirements was many times that amount.[2] This does not take into account the costs of complying with state and local government regulation, which are substantial in such industries as electricity and telecommunications. These costs are spread by higher taxes and higher prices. Moreover, to the extent that the regulatory proceedings of federal and state commissions (for rate-setting, granting licenses, etc.) involve the participation of consumer groups, the costs of regulatory activity are spread very widely indeed.

Are these costs warranted? Is the right amount of government regulation undertaken? An economic efficiency test applied to government regulatory activity suggests, in principle, that regulation should be expanded until its net social benefit is maximized, that is, until the marginal benefit of regulation equals its marginal cost. The level of activity should be reduced when marginal benefits are less than marginal costs. Deregulation in transportation and telecommunications indicates that lawmakers do not believe that the benefits of regulating such industries justify the costs, at least at the margin. Indeed, arguments are sometimes made that regulation, while costly, generates no benefits at all.

Recently, the thrust of government policy to solve the problems of regulating industry has been threefold:

---

[1] P. N. Tramontozzi and K. W. Chilton, *U.S. Regulatory Agencies under Reagan*, 1980–1988 (St. Louis, Mo.: Center for the Study of American Business, Washington University, Op. 64, May 1987), 24.

[2] M. L. Weidenbaum estimated that indirect costs were more than 40 times the direct costs of federal regulation in 1976. M. L. Weidenbaum, *Business, Government and the Public*, 2d ed. (Englewood Cliffs, N.J.: Prentice Hall, 1981): 343, Table 18.1.

1.   Deregulate the industry completely and allow competition to work (airlines and trucking).

2.   Reduce the extent of regulation and allow firms more freedom to determine price (railroads, long distance telecommunications, wholesale power).

3.   Introduce incentive regulation in industries where competition is not considered viable (electricity).

To understand the forces behind these policy changes and evaluate them, we must determine three things: First, why has deregulation occurred in some industries and not others? More generally, which industries *should* be regulated? Second, how should regulation best be carried out? Third, can we learn any lessons from recent experience to help us decide how reform proposals can best be implemented? In sum, we ask how the political system can be made to work in an economically sensible way. In this chapter we look at each of these questions in turn.

WHICH INDUSTRIES SHOULD BE REGULATED?

The idea of natural monopoly has a long history and is very much alive. The problem is to determine which industries are natural monopolies. As we saw in Chapter 13, this can be a complicated task. Whether competition or natural monopoly characterizes a specific industry depends on the cost structure, the pattern of demand, and the behavioral interactions (for example, pricing strategies) between established firms and potential entrants. Econometric techniques make it possible to estimate cost and demand functions for specific industries. However, the accuracy of estimates can always be challenged on the basis of inaccurate or insufficient data or inadequacy of estimation techniques, which may not take into account all appropriate parameters or interdependencies.[3] Past behavioral interactions between firms may be assessed on the basis of historical performance, but future behavior cannot be predicted with certainty.

The performance of recently deregulated industries reveals that the confident predictions of many economists about the viability of competition have not been fully borne out. There is ongoing dispute about the relationship between deregulation and the current performance of trucking, airlines, long-distance telecommunications, and wholesale power. After deregulation in trucking, new entry increased and the value of operating licenses fell as predicted. However, the number of bankruptcies rose. There is disagreement about whether trucking rates have fallen or risen since the Motor Carrier Act of

---

[3]For one good example, see the study of cost function estimates and critique of previous estimation techniques in telecommunications by D. S. Evans and J. J. Heckman, "Natural Monopoly," in D. S. Evans, ed., *Breaking Up* Bell (New York: North-Holland, 1983), 127–156.

1980, and indeed whether the act affected the overall rate level at all. As we have seen Chapter 17, K. D. Boyer argues that while regulation in trucking altered the structure of rates within the industry, the overall level was more likely determined by larger economic forces (national income, employment, inflation and so forth).[4] Boyer also argues that deregulation in railroads may have had some downward effect on rates, but that rates had been declining since 1970, a decade before the Staggers Act. He argues that, as for trucking, regulation affected the structure rather than the level of railroad rates.[5]

In the airlines industry, prices have come down and the hub-and-spoke system has increased load factors. However, after an initial flurry of new entry, followed by some bankruptcies, the industry is still dominated by precisely the same companies that dominated under CAB regulation.[6] Moreover, these companies have learned to use a variety of entry-limiting techniques that have blocked further entry and expansion of new competitors.

In telecommunications, the MCI company, whose determination to enter the industry helped to bring about the breakup of AT&T, failed to earn the huge profits it expected and in 1985 sold 30 percent of its shares to IBM.[7] By contrast, after some inital setbacks, AT&T has succeeded in defending its market share by strategic price reductions. Whether or not the industry is a natural monopoly is still in dispute, partly because industry performance since deregulation has been ambiguous and is subject to varied interpretations. In all these cases we encounter the familiar problem of isolating the effects of policy changes on industry performance when other economic conditions are also changing.

Even if the results of deregulation were clearer, there are other reasons offered for deregulating an industry, such as inelasticity of demand, external effects, and merit goods. These, combined with broader political views about the general desirability of government intervention in the marketplace, may well determine how lawmakers interpret the natural monopoly evidence and how much weight is given to other arguments.

HOW SHOULD REGULATION BE CARRIED OUT?

The historical answer to this question is through independent commissions set up by Congress. From the discussions in the preceding chapters, we can see some difficulties with the system that can be related to the principal–agent

---

[4]K. D. Boyer, "The Costs of Price Regulation: Lessons from Railroad Deregulation," *Rand Journal of Economics* 18 (Autumn 1987): 408–416.

[5]See also A. F. Friedlaender for a detailed discussion of the structure of rates in railroads and trucking. A. F. Friedlaender, "Equity, Efficiency, and Regulation in the Rail and Trucking Industries," in L. W. Weiss and M. W. Klass, eds., *Case Studies in Regulation* (Boston: Little, Brown and Company, 1981).

[6]Recall our discussion in Chapter 17, and see Michael E. Levine, "Airline Competition in Deregulated Markets: Theory, Firm Strategy, and Public Policy," *Yale Journal on Regulation* 4 (Spring 1987): 393–494.

[7]See Steve Coll, *The Deal of the Century* (New York: Atheneum, 1987), 371.

problem. When voters elect members of Congress, the voters are principals who are trying to ensure that their agents (senators and representatives) carry out their wishes. When Congress establishes and instructs a regulatory commission, Congress becomes the principal trying to control its agents—the commissions. Finally, the commissions, as principals, carry out their tasks of regulating firms, their agents. Thus, there are three layers of instructions between the voters and the regulated firms, and problems may arise at each level.

We begin with the second level of instruction and note that the goals of regulation as expressed in laws passed by Congress are often fuzzy. Such terms as "reasonable rate of return," "safe, adequate, economical, and efficient service," "destructive competition," and "inherent advantage" appear in congressional instructions to commissions, but are seldom defined. No priorities are offered to determine which goals are to take precedence. Frequently the result has been that commissions have been left to their own best judgment and their decisions have lacked clarity and consistency. Moreover, there has been significant variation among industries in the approach of the regulating commissions, which has led, as we have seen, to a wide variety of different policies being pursued simultaneously.

While the goals of Congress in instructing commissions have been unclear, the goals of the commissions have varied over time and across industries. An extensive literature has addressed this topic over many years. A well-known study by Marver Bernstein in 1955, for example, suggests that regulatory commissions go through a lifecycle.[8] At first, the initial public-interest focus of the commission that prompted its establishment (railroad monopoly in the case of the ICC, frequency assignments in the case of the FCC, support of the infant airline industry in the case of the CAB) enables the commission to carry through effective policy changes. As it matures, it faces challenges from the industry it regulates and rapidly develops vested political interests of its own. Eventually, its public support evaporates and the commission surrenders to the interests of the regulated industry, serving merely as a forum to which controversies are brought for resolution. This gloomy picture was reinforced by subsequent studies, among which the capture theory of George Stigler received much attention and pointed the way to the more general analysis of rent-seeking behavior. Stigler's thesis is that, "as a rule, regulation is acquired by the industry and is designed and operated primarily for its benefit."[9] The idea that commissions pursue the public interest is rejected.

However, recent events have shown that the regulatory commissions have not always behaved as anticipated in the capture theory. Diverse economic and political pressures have affected commission decisions. In particular, the move to deregulate transportation and telecommunications was partly due to

---

[8]M. Bernstein, *Regulating Business by Independent Commission* (Princeton, N.J.: Princeton University Press, 1955).

[9]G. J. Stigler, "The Theory of Economic Regulation," *Bell Journal of Economics* 2 (April 1971): 3-21.

changes in commission behavior before the acts deregulating these industries were passed by Congress.

In Chapter 16 we referred to Douglas Anderson's explanation of time-of-day pricing for electricity by the regulatory commission and public utilities in New York, while California adopted a life-line pricing structure.[10] Anderson's analysis of the complex interactions of various pressures suggests that general theories of commission behavior may not be possible. More recently, Derthick and Quirk have analyzed the economic and political events that completely changed the policies of some commissions and had a smaller but significant effect on others.[11] For example, at one extreme is the story of airline deregulation, in which the CAB participated in its own demise under the leadership of Alfred Kahn (who also played a key role in changing electricity pricing). Deregulation of trucks was spurred on by the relaxation of entry barriers by the ICC before the Motor Carrier Act of 1980 made deregulation official. This occurred in spite of opposition from trucking companies who stood to lose monopoly rents. By contrast, deregulation in railroads (also regulated by the ICC) was less far-reaching. In telecommunications, deregulation of the equipment market was encouraged in FCC decisions (recall Chapter 18). The attitude of the FCC towards current pricing in long-distance markets has been to allow AT&T to reduce its price closer to marginal cost in order to be able to compete with other common carriers.

Derthick and Quirk attribute part of the change in commission goals to the presence of well-trained economists on the commissions who were agreed that competition could be successful and whose views were backed by economic studies revealing the high costs of regulation. One may not completely subscribe to the theory that the commissions have now become captives of successful economists in a political environment that fosters a reduction of the role of government in the marketplace. However, it is important to recognize that economic analysis can play an important part in policy-making.[12]

Thomas McCraw argues that, in some circumstances, individual personalities have determined the course of regulatory change. In *Prophets of Regulation*, he offers biographies of four men—Charles Adams, Louis Brandeis, James Landis, and Alfred Kahn—as examples of regulatory innovators without whom the ICC, FTC, SEC, and CAB would not have taken their current institutional shape.[13] While arguments can be offered that their influence was not as great as McCraw suggests, there is no doubt that turning points in policy can be influenced by individuals.[14] This is borne out in Steve Coll's description

---

[10]D. Anderson, *Regulatory Policies and Electric Utilities* (Boston: Auburn House Publishing Company, 1980).

[11]Derthick and Quirk, *The Politics of Deregulation* (Washington, D.C.: The Brookings Institution, 1985).

[12]But recall that the predictions of economists about how deregulation should work have not always been borne out.

[13]Thomas McCraw, *Prophets of Regulation* (Cambridge, Mass.: Harvard University Press, 1984).

[14]See for example the review of McCraw's book, George L. Priest, "The Personality Theory of Agency Regulation," *Yale Journal on Regulation* 3 (Spring 1986): 391–399.

of the breakup of AT&T and his identification of the players both inside and outside the FCC who played important roles at various crucial stages.[15]

These examples show that the route to regulatory change is circuitous and varied. Moreover the desirability of its effects are also in dispute. Robert Leone draws attention to what he calls an Iron Law of Public Policy, namely that any regulatory policy creates winners and losers.[16] This means that regulatory policy never results in a Pareto improvement by which all benefit; rather, some lose, some gain, and the distribution of welfare must change. But now we are no longer in the world in which we evaluate the relative efficiency of resources as they are deployed in various uses. Instead, issues of fairness predominate. This means that the pressures for changes in policy are as likely to come from groups with a stake in the outcome as from groups claiming to represent a broader public interest.

HOW CAN DESIRABLE REFORM BE IMPLEMENTED?

We look first at some recent changes in the policy process that have attempted to address the problems outlined above.

During the 1970s policymakers and economists began to tally the costs of government regulation on a more detailed basis. As we have seen, total direct and indirect costs were found to be very large. No systematic attempt was made to measure the total national benefits from regulation, so that no direct comparison could be made with costs. Nonetheless it was recognized that there were serious inefficiencies in the existing method of regulation by commission, and attempts were made to improve it.[17] In 1981, President Reagan issued an Executive Order that gave the task of regulatory oversight to the Office of Management and Budget (OMB) and required that regulatory impact statements be made part of the regulatory process.[18]

Impact Statements

Another term for impact statement is cost–benefit analysis. Periodically, every regulatory agency should be required to perform a cost–benefit analysis for each major policy activity to justify continuing the activity. The new executive order established such a review procedure for pending legislation. The objective of the rule is to force agencies to consider directly the full social costs as well

---

[15]Steve Coll, *The Deal of the Century*. Recall also the discussion of Coll's book in Chapter 18.

[16]Robert A. Leone, *Who Profits: Winners, Losers and Government Regulation* (New York: Basic Books, 1986). See also the review by Rebert Crandall, "Who Wins the Regulatory Game?," *Yale Journal on Regulation* 4 (Spring 1987): 495–502.

[17]For example, the Ford administration argued that deregulation was a tool to fight inflation, thus suggesting that regulation was contributing to higher prices. President Carter created a Regulatory Analysis Review Group to oversee regulatory agencies and a Regulatory Council to suggest reforms. See M. Fix and G. C. Eads, "The Prospects for Regulatory Reform: The Legacy of Reagan's First Term," *Yale Journal on Regulation* 2 (1985): 293–318.

[18]See M. Weidenbaum, *Business, Government and the Public*, 204.

as the benefits of their activities. Thus, for example, had entry restrictions in trucking been subjected to such a test, the costs might have been seen to exceed benefits and the restrictions curtailed accordingly. The drawback is that cost–benefit analysis, if conducted properly, is a complicated procedure that requires a large amount of information and considerable technical expertise. It also involves weighting and adding up various social costs and benefits, which in turn involves value judgments concerning equity. It is doubtful whether regulatory commissions have the time or resources available to perform the task adequately. Moreover, there may be a tendency for commissions to overstate the benefits of regulation that (for whatever reason, perhaps political) they want to see continued. Attempts to cut down the task by directing commissions to consider the impact of their regulations on specific economic variables—for example, inflation and the competitiveness of the industry— may result in answers that reflect the political pressures of the day rather than the economic facts of the situation.[19] However, the complexity of the task and the possibility that there will be incentives for regulators to circumvent its objectives do not vitiate its importance. Cost-benefit analysis, realized in compact statements, may at the least force regulators to think about the consequences of their activities.

In 1985, at the beginning of President Reagan's second term, a further executive order was issued whose ultimate objective was to establish a regulatory budget listing the costs and benefits of all proposed regulations.[20] Agencies would then be allotted a certain amount of money to spend on introducing new regulations, just as they are currently given a fixed budget for salaries, operating expenses. and the like. This would force them to economize on new regulations.[21] Fix and Eads note that the 1985 executive order places the authority for developing the idea of a regulatory budget within OMB, that is, within the executive rather than the legislative branch. This shifts the balance of power to influence the regulatory change from Congress to the President.

An alternative proposal for controlling the total amount of economic regulation is for agencies to be subject to *sunset laws*. Sunset laws require that regulatory agencies disband at a given date unless Congress passes legislation to the contrary. The intention is to force examination of each agency—its justification and procedures. The laws reflect awareness that reform of regulatory agencies may always have rather low priority on the legislative agenda, especially if there is political pressure resisting reform. For any given agency, a sunset law would ensure that (as the deadline for the agency's demise

---

[19]Fix and Eads point out that the new executive order was criticized immediately for providing an avenue through which regulatory policies could be changed without the sanction of Congress. While federal legislation is passed by Congress, decisions of the OMB about rule changes based on impact statements are not subject to congressional scrutiny and are therefore more likely to be unfairly manipulated. Fix and Eads, "The Prospects for Regulatory Reform," 299.

[20]Fix and Eads, "The Prospects for Regulatory Reform," 312.

[21]If the agency's objective was to maximize the net benefits from new regulations subject to a budget constraint, it would attempt to equate the relative marginal benefits from different rules with their relative marginal costs.

approached) Congress would be forced to consider the merits of suggested reforms. If the agency's mandate is reconfirmed, the revised policy is likely to reflect proposals for reform. Alternatively, deadlines created by sunset laws provide the opportunity to discontinue the regulation altogether by abolishing the regulatory agency. Once again, there is no guarantee that such laws would in fact result in the appropriate regulatory reform or that Congress would not routinely reconstitute regulatory agencies as they came up for review. However, such laws would shift the burden of proof for continuing regulation onto the regulatory agencies, which would have to convince a majority of Congress and the President that their existence is necessary. This new presumption favors competition and treats government regulation as a policy of last resort rather than of first choice. This change in emphasis would reestablish the rationale that direct government regulation of industry should be a reluctant response to market failure, rather than an equally desirable alternative to free competition.

Whether the executive or congressional route to regulatory change is ultimately chosen, the public policy dilemmas of natural monopoly and public goods remain stubbornly in the foreground, to be solved in different ways by each new generation of policymakers.

PART FOUR

. . . .

New-Wave Regulation

CHAPTER 20

· · · · · · · · · · · · · · · · · · ·

WHY NEW-WAVE?

What we term new-wave regulation—policies to protect consumers, workers, and the environment—is not entirely new. It is, however, an area in which government regulation has expanded greatly in recent years, often to the accompaniment of strong controversy.

WHAT IS NEW ABOUT THE NEW WAVE?

Recent regulatory initiatives have been qualitatively distinct from both anti-trust and old-style public utility regulation in a number of fundamental ways. For example:

- Unlike both antitrust and utility regulation, recent public efforts do not respond to concerns about the state of competition or monopoly within industries. A primary motivation is rather the protection of health and safety.
- Unlike utility regulation, the newer type is not industry specific. Instead, it tends to cut a broad swath across numerous industries that may have little in common, and its economic impact is similarly wide-ranging.
- Unlike many older forms of regulation, the newer type does not impinge directly on the price and output decisions of private companies. The focus of new-wave regulation is more on qualitative decisions such as the types of production processes and the characteristics of products that firms offer to the market.

New-wave regulation has generated heated criticism from a number of economists. Milton and Rose Friedman, for example, note disapprovingly that this "veritable explosion in regulatory activity" has taken a new tack:

> Instead of being concerned with specific industries, [the new policies] covered the waterfront . . . . In addition to concern with the consumer's pocketbook, with protecting him from exploitation by sellers, recent

agencies are primarily concerned with the consumer's safety and well-being, with protecting him not only from sellers, but also from himself.[1]

Others argue, somewhat along the same lines, that much of the new wave is an effort by government to impose its own values on society and, correspondingly, to restrict the play of the private market.[2] As Lilley and Miller put it:

> With the new-style regulation, government often becomes involved with very detailed facets of the production process. As a result, the business manager has fewer "degrees of freedom."[3]

In their view, such usurpation of the management role may carry two particular dangers: an increase in the power of government, especially the presidency; and "an undermining of the public's 'faith in government'—a backlash against all government because of an eventual negative reaction to the perceived regulatory excesses."[4]

Such objections deserve a serious hearing, but their force should not be overemphasized at this point. Bear in mind that environmental and consumer and worker protection programs seem to be highly popular among Americans. Presumably, then, many see important benefits in these activities.

The controversial nature of new-wave regulation is not at all surprising. In the first place, the costs of these programs are substantial and are obvious—especially to the directly affected manufacturers and distributors. Second, this regulation seems to many observers to represent a genuine expansion of government's role in the economy. In effect, intervention in choices that we once regarded as the proper domain of private business managers and their customers and employees.

This is a delicate point in the minds of many. Both antitrust and public utility regulation have been closely tied to well-established and widely understood arguments about market failure. The newer regulation is also tied to some market failure considerations, but the arguments are themselves newer and perhaps less clear-cut. It is hardly astounding, then, that some citizens regard these arguments as unpersuasive and undemonstrated—perhaps even frivolous.

RATIONALES FOR THE NEW WAVE

Why should we regulate such things as the truthfulness of toothpaste advertising, the safety of automobiles and lawnmowers, the chemicals touched or inhaled by a factory worker, or the air pollution created by a steel manufacturer? This is a natural question, since only a few decades ago we seemed content to leave these matters largely to the marketplace. We shall explore the

---

[1]M. Friedman and R. Friedman, *Free to Choose* (New York: Harcourt, Brace, Jovanovich, 1979), 190.

[2]What is meant by government's own values, however, is seldom spelled out in detail. In a democracy, one would hope and expect that government's values are simply those of the citizenry that elects the government.

[3]W. Lilley, III, and J. C. Miller, III, "The New 'Social Regulation,'" *The Public Interest* 47 (Spring 1977): 49–61.

[4]Lilley and Miller, "The New 'Social Regulation,'" 55.

rationales for newer forms of regulation in detail in the chapters to follow, but initially it may be useful to note some possible—and very general—answers.

1.   *Big government.* Perhaps recent regulatory expansion does reflect a new attitude toward the proper role of government in economic affairs, in effect a decision that we should not rely as extensively on the market as we have in previous decades (and centuries). This is the conclusion of the Friedmans as they view with alarm a trend in which the judgment of government agencies is increasingly substituted for that of individuals. But it is also the conclusion of some who do not foresee social and economic disaster as the likely result.

2.   *A response to new problems.* Alternatively, one might interpret new-wave regulation as an effort to deal collectively with problems that did not exist, or were less severe, in times past. Consumer protection policies, for example, have surely expanded in response to the belief that consumers are subject to substantial and unforeseeable dangers in the goods they buy and use. (Whether this belief is correct, is a separate question.) Our pollution-control policies are associated with a perceived crisis in environmental quality—an issue that simply did not attract much attention 30 years ago. One might thus argue that the world has changed in ways that require novel uses of government authority.

3.   *A middle view.* It may well be that both of the positions above have some merit. Certains kinds of problems may well be more severe—and are surely more visible—today than they were, say, at the turn of the century. The world in some respects *has*, no doubt, changed.

     In addition, an industrially advanced and relatively affluent society is likely to develop new priorities and may decide that it is no longer desirable to leave the disposition of certain problems entirely (or mainly) to private markets. Not only the world, but our view of the world and of our responsibility to each other, have surely undergone meaningful changes in the past 50 years. It should not, therefore, be surprising that we use government in somewhat different ways today.

ANALYTICAL DEVELOPMENTS

Although the role of economic analysis in the formulation of American public policy should not be overemphasized, new-wave regulation has coincided with some important analytical advances.

We have already discussed two of these (in Chapter 5): the theory of externalities, which has served as an important motivation for environmental protection policies; and analysis of failure in information markets, which provides one justification for programs of consumer and worker protection.

To this we may add the development and wide acceptance of benefit–cost analysis. Speaking generally, this type of analysis defines and compares the favorable and unfavorable consequences of public programs. The basic efficiency condition should be quite familiar by now: as long as the marginal benefits of a public project exceed its marginal costs, expansion of the activity in question will yield net gains; should costs exceed benefits at the margin, a reduction of the activity will provide net gains. Equality at the margin implies maximum efficiency.

As we shall see, the use of benefit-cost analysis has provoked disagreement. Some argue strongly that it is prerequisite to sensible policy determination (although not the only prerequisite). Others counter by claiming that benefit–cost comparisons attempt to assign dollar values to precious things (a pretty sunset, clean air, even human life) that cannot have meaningful prices. Wherever one may come down in this debate, benefit–cost analysis has become a central arena for arguments over the wisdom of new-wave regulation.

SUMMARY

New-wave regulation differs from older forms in some very basic respects and is thus a source of controversy. In general terms, it has come about either because the problems we confront have changed or because our view of government's role has changed. Or, quite possibly, for both reasons.

Is new-wave regulation warranted in principle? Has it in practice been worthwhile—that is, has it improved our welfare at reasonable cost? We consider these questions in the next two chapters. The wise reader, however, will not expect simple answers.

CHAPTER 21

· · · · · · · · · · · · · · · · · · · ·

CONSUMER AND WORKER PROTECTION

INTRODUCTION

Public policies to protect consumers have a long history; laws to protect workers are somewhat newer.[1] Yet both raise the same basic questions. Why is government intervention needed? (Won't free markets naturally provide adequate protections?) Do our current laws and rules provide important benefits? Would different policies yield better results? These are the main questions we address in this chapter.

The public policies that we discuss fall into three broad categories:

1. *Informational.* For example, product labeling requirements designed to tell consumers more about the qualities of the items they buy.

2. *Regulatory.* Usually the formulation and implementation of safety standards, with noncomplying products or working conditions prohibited.

3. *Liability.* The area of tort law that establishes responsibility when consumers suffer product-related injuries or workers suffer job-related injuries.

In practice, the distinctions between these policy categories are sometimes blurred. An information disclosure requirement might, for example, cause a manufacturer to change the nature of its product. A legal liability rule may affect the care that employers take to safeguard their production workers.

---

[1]Both church and state laws assisting consumers trace back hundreds of years. Federal legislation in the United States dates to the Food and Drug Act of 1906, which prohibited the sale of adulterated or misbranded items.

CONSUMER PROTECTION

Theoretical Considerations: Why Not Trust the Market?

As we have observed, markets tend to do an efficient job of allocating resources. Why then do we not simply depend on the private sector to produce and disseminate appropriate amounts of such things as information and safety, holding government intervention to a minimum?

We may begin by noting that there is basic disagreement about the power consumers hold. (Somewhat similar arguments could be made with respect to workers.) The standard market-oriented view is stated concisely by David B. Hamilton:

> The producer, in order to remain in business, must respond to the dictates of the consumer in the marketplace. If he should produce shoddy, he will find few buyers. If he should cheat the consumer by fraud and deception, the consumer will pass him by on the next round of purchases .... Failure by the producer to obey the dictates of the sovereign consumer is tantamount to signing his own economic death warrant.[2]

A very different picture is presented by Richard J. Barber:

> [T]he individual buyer besieged by advertising, deceived by packages, confronted with an expanding range of highly complex goods, limited in time . . . is simply not qualified to buy discriminately and wisely.[3]

These statements obviously imply very different positions on the need for government intervention to protect consumer interests.

Market Failure   Traditional economic analysis in the United States is sometimes associated with the pro-market view expressed by Hamilton, yet economists have long recognized that markets may at times fail to provide appropriate (or even tolerable) outcomes. The immediate question is whether we should expect such failure to be widespread. Will markets, for example, tend frequently to produce too little information or safety from society's point of view? If so, there is a clear case for government to act.

The most important economic analysis concerns the production and distribution of information. It is axiomatic that information is necessary to the proper functioning of any market. Consumers cannot make satisfactory choices unless they know what is available on what terms, and unless they can form reasonably accurate expectations about the qualities of alternative offerings.

Information is therefore valuable, but it also may be costly to obtain.[4] The costs can range from trivial to prohibitive. It is easy enough to discover which candy bar or brand of soup yields the most enjoyment, but more difficult to locate the best automobile, washing machine, or physician. Simple, frequently purchased items generally present the fewest informational problems.

---

[2]D. B. Hamilton, *The Consumer in Our Economy* (Boston: Houghton Mifflin, 1962), 329–330.

[3]R. J. Barber, "Government and the Consumer," *Michigan Law Review* 64 (May 1966): 1204.

[4]The classic discussion is presented in G. J. Stigler, "The Economics of Information," *Journal of Political Economy* 69 (June 1961).

Consider how buyers learn about the qualities of products or services. In simple cases, inspection of the item or a little experience with it may suffice.[5] Is a shirt worth buying? Look at it and see.[6] Is the local barber any good? Try one of his haircuts. One may make a mistake, but the cost of doing so is limited.

Frequently the learning process is more difficult and costly. Few buyers can tell from inspection whether a television set or an air conditioner will perform well over time. Experience may still be a good teacher, but if the product is not up to expectations, the lesson will be expensive. Many consumers will therefore look to alternative information sources before buying—the experience of friends, the manufacturer's or distributor's reputation for standing behind the product, or perhaps the opinion of an independent testing organization such as Consumers Union.

Will consumers as a rule obtain adequate product information? It is difficult to generalize, but there is reason to suspect that in at least some instances, market provision of information will be inadequate. The fundamental difficulty is that information has some of the characteristics of a public good (refer to Chapter 5).

Consider an earlier example concerning the production of information about the risks of a new drug. Virtually every advanced society regulates such information, but why? The usual popular answers are: first, that the consequences of unsafe drugs are unusually severe; and second, that consumers have essentially no ability to inform themselves about drug safety. (Few of us have laboratories in our homes!)

Although both points have some validity, public goods analysis provides a more complete and persuasive argument for government intervention. The result or output of drug testing is purely informational—it consists of data about how animals and people respond to the drug in carefully observed situations. The salient features of this information are:

1.   It is subject to nonrivalrous consumption (joint supply).

2.   It is very likely to encounter problems of nonexcludability.

The fact that I consume a bit of information about the risks posed by drug X in no way diminishes the ability of any other person to consume that same bit. Quite possibly the information is very costly to produce (it may involve years of large-scale laboratory work). But once produced, the marginal cost of supplying the information to additional consumers is very low—perhaps not much greater than zero.

---

[5]Phillip Nelson distinguishes between search qualities of products, which may be checked before purchase, and experience qualities, which require use of the good. See Phillip Nelson, "Advertising as Information," *Journal of Political Economy* 82 (July-August 1974). Michael R. Darby and Edi Karni refer to credence qualities, attributes of a product that are difficult or impossible to evaluate even with experience. See M. R. Darby and E. Karni, "Free Competition and the Optimal Amount of Fraud," *Journal of Law and Economics* 16 (April 1973).

[6]Of course the durability of the shirt may be difficult to judge from simple inspection.

By similar token, it would be extremely difficult to confine the use of the drug safety information to those who are willing and able to pay for it. Purchasers of the information may well tell others about it.[7] Enterprising journalists are likely to convey the findings to a wide audience. Moreover, we would suspect (and hope) that once safety information has been produced, society would not on ethical grounds condone withholding the data from those unable to pay for it—especially since dissemination is close to costless.

These are the familiar reasons why markets in information may not arise, or may not be as widespread as is socially desirable. If this is the case, however, consumers may be forced to rely more heavily on information provided by sellers, who are hardly objective, disinterested parties. The data they provide is likely to be both incomplete (they may not tell you as much as you wish to know) and biased (you will hear mainly about the positive qualities). At times, the information may even be misleading, deceptive, or demonstrably false.

It should be emphasized that perfect or complete information is usually not a reasonable objective because of its cost. Some degree of buyer uncertainty and disappointment is, although not desirable, simply too expensive to eradicate. The reasons above, however, suggest that whatever we define as the correct level of information, one should be a bit skeptical about whether the market will do a satisfactory job of supplying it.

The issue should not be prejudged.   Unquestionably, consumer information is adequate for many, perhaps the vast majority of buying decisions. Yet in some instances, the costs of ignorance are large while the market's provision of information is uncertain. It is here that government plays a clearly legitimate role.

Human Failure   In recent years economists have begun to examine a somewhat different problem that may impinge on consumer protection issues: the limited ability of consumers to process or interpret available information. The seminal work in this area is that of Herbert A. Simon. In 1957, Simon described the concept of *bounded rationality*, by which he meant:

> The capacity of the human mind for formulating and solving complex problems is very small compared with the size of the problems whose solution is required for rational behavior in the real world.[8]

People respond to this difficulty, Simon argues, by building and acting upon simplified models of reality. But whereas this is a sensible procedure it may produce behavior that is "not even approximately optimal with respect to the real world."

Do consumers act nonoptimally or even irrationally? Direct evidence is meager, but some experimental findings developed mainly by psychologists

---

[7]See K. Greenawalt and E. Noam, "Confidentiality Claims of Business Organizations," in H. J. Goldschmid, ed., *Business Disclosure: Government's Need to Know* (New York: McGraw-Hill, 1979).

[8]H. A. Simon, *Models of Man: Social and Rational* (New York: Wiley, 1957), 198.

suggest that this may be the case. It appears specifically that people confronted with risky choices may be poor decision makers in two distinct ways.

First, they may choose inconsistently. Subjects state, for example, that they *prefer* a gamble or lottery ticket A to another lottery, B, but that they will *pay more* for B than for A.[9] This kind of pattern, which has been observed in different experimental settings, raises some question about the assumptions of rational choice that underlie conclusions of market efficiency.

Second, it appears that people who confront uncertain choices have little ability to estimate the probability of alternative outcomes. Tversky and Kahneman, for example, have shown that probability judgments frequently follow a few simplification processes of the type broadly suggested by Simon.[10] But whereas the adoption of such simplifications, which Tversky and Kahneman call heuristics, may be sensible in one way, it also may lead to wildly unrealistic probability estimates. (For example, many people seem to regard the likelihood of death from tornadoes or grizzly bear attacks in national parks as quite high despite the fact that both are exceptionally rare events.)

Any general inability to formulate reasonable probability estimates would have serious implications for consumer protection. Virtually all consumer choices are subject to risk, although the degree and importance of risk are frequently small. The product that one buys may or may not perform as expected, and in some instances, product failure implies some probability of injury. If the purchasers of products have little ability to judge the relevant probabilities—of product failure and of injury, given that failure occurs— it is difficult to believe that they will consistently make sensible choices.

At this stage, the evidence of such human failure in decision making is suggestive rather than conclusive. We cannot be sure to what extent failure in experimental situations implies failure in a market setting. Nor is it easy to specify the appropriate governmental intervention if consumers do in fact act unreasonably or even irrationally.

The difficulty is as follows. A problem of inadequate information points to a clear public policy solution: encourage or require the production of more information. But where the difficulty is that consumers do not know what to do with information, the correct policy response is unclear. To require more, or even better information may prove futile. Yet to take stronger steps—say, to ban from the market products that present an unreasonable risk to consumers— may lead to questionable and unpredictable welfare consequences.

The suggestion we are left with at this point is an uncomfortable one. Even if markets function with tolerable efficiency, consumers subject to bounded rationality may be in need of some outside help. But what forms that

---

[9] See S. Lichtenstein and P. Slovic, "Reversals of Preference between Bids and Choices in Gambling Decisions," *Journal of Experimental Psychology* 89 (July 1971); and D. M. Grether and C. R. Plott, "Economic Theory of Choice and the Preference Reversal Phenomenon," *American Economic Review* 69 (September 1979).

[10] A. Tversky and D. Kahneman, "Judgment under Uncertainty: Heuristics and Biases," *Science*, September 27, 1974.

help should take, and who is wise enough to make this sort of decision, are questions that are not easily answered.

POLICY RESPONSES

The discussion above points to some reasons why consumers may need governmental protection. In this section, we examine ways in which the government has responded to such need.

Informational Policies

As we have noted, market provision of information is subject to potentially significant problems. Accordingly, government has made substantial efforts to assure that consumers receive adequate and accurate data about the goods and services they buy.

Advertising   Sales promotion, especially advertising, has long been a controversial market activity. Some writers—notably Nelson and Brozen—argue vigorously that advertising as a source of information both reduces consumer ignorance and stimulates competition.[11] Others contend that advertising, especially where it is heavy, may create or enhance monopoly power, in part because it is not consistently informative.[12]

Whether advertising is good or bad, however, is neither a vital question nor an objectively answerable one. Like virtually all activities, it generates both benefits and costs. In principle there exists a socially optimal or efficient amount of advertising, but despite some complaints about overcommercialization in American life, identification of that optimum is difficult. Very few people, moreover, would suggest that government ought seriously to restrict the right of sellers to convey honest advertising messages or of consumers to receive them.[13]

Historically, government's involvement with advertising has concentrated on eliminating deception and outright falsehood. Legislative authority rests in the Federal Trade Commission Act of 1914, which established the Commission to act against unfair methods of competition in interstate commerce. Although Congress apparently intended that that the commission devote itself largely to anticompetitive practices, the FTC quickly focused on deceptive activities.[14] In

---

[11]See P. Nelson, "Advertising as Information," and Y. Brozen, "Entry Barriers: Advertising and Product Differentiation," in H. J. Goldschmid, H. M. Mann, and J. F. Weston, eds., *Industrial Concentration: The New Learning* (Boston: Little, Brown, 1974).

[12]For balanced discussions, see J. S. Bain, *Barriers to New Competition* (Cambridge, Mass.: Harvard University Press, 1956); W. G. Shepherd, *The Economics of Industrial Organization* (Englewood Cliffs, N.J.: Prentice Hall, 1979); and F. M. Scherer, *Industrial Market Structure and Economic Performance*, 2d ed. (Chicago: Rand-McNally, 1980).

[13]Advertising ceilings have occasionally been proposed as a possible antitrust remedy in markets in which abnormally heavy promotional spending seems to create serious barriers to entry.

[14]There was no mention of advertising in congressional debate preceding passage of the act. See "Developments in the Law—Deceptive Advertising," *Harvard Law Review* 80 (March 1967).

1938, the law was amended by the Wheeler-Lea Act, prohibiting unfair or deceptive acts or practices, a somewhat more direct acknowledgment of the commission's role as a consumer protection agency.

Why would a seller advertise falsely? The obvious answer is that it may be profitable to do so.[15] A supplier benefits from product sales, but providing complete and accurate information may not always encourage consumers to buy! Incomplete, and perhaps distorted, information may spur sales, for example, when the product in question is not superior to others on the market. (Can you imagine the Campbell Soup Company telling customers, "Buy our soup—it's no worse than Heinz"?)

There are, however, some real incentives against false advertising. A flagrantly untrue claim may be spotted quickly by consumers—especially the more knowledgeable and skeptical—and the reputation for dishonesty that follows is hardly likely to enhance company profits over the long term. Should deception cause serious harm, moreover, consumers may undertake (and win) legal actions.

Plainly deceptive or false advertising, while it certainly exists, is not epidemic—a fact that may be taken as a tribute to government regulation. It is most likely to occur where buyers cannot easily check the claims that are made—that is, where information is costly. This could be the case if verification of product or service quality requires lengthy experience (for example, an automobile), or if verification is ordinarily impossible (was that "vitamin enriched" bread really vitamin enriched?). Deceptive advertising also may occur more frequently when the seller is not heavily dependent on repeat purchases. (Once you discover that the washing machine I have sold you is inferior, you will not buy another one from me—but I have already turned a nice profit on the sale.)

Fraudulent advertising also is facilitated when the harm done to any individual consumer is small. This is really the free-rider problem in yet another guise. It might be worthwhile for consumers as a group to eliminate a false claim, but absurd for a single consumer to undertake the legal costs of doing so. A possible solution to this problem is the *class action suit*, in which an individual brings an action on behalf of all persons harmed by a particular practice. The Supreme Court, however, has in recent years created some substantial barriers to class actions.[16] With this avenue of relief thus limited,

---

[15]In fact, this *must* be the proximate answer if one believes that firms are rational, as that term has traditionally been defined.

[16]In *Eisen v. Carlisle and Jacquelin*, 417 U.S. 156 (1974), the plaintiff (Eisen) sued on behalf of the customers of two brokerage houses alleged to have conspired to fix their fees. The Supreme Court held that Eisen was required to notify individually and at his own expense the two million members of the class who could be identified with reasonable ease. This would have cost Eisen, who stood to recover only $70 on his own behalf, $225,000! Such a requirement obviously provides strong discouragement of similar suits where the class is large. In *Oppenheimer Fund v. Sanders*, 437 U.S. 340 (1977), the Court ruled that plaintiffs must ordinarily bear the costs of compiling the names and addresses of members of the affected class, thus adding further to the expense of such action.

government regulation may be the most effective available response to the free-rider problem.

The Federal Trade Commission monitors advertising in the broadcast and print media and investigates complaints. Perusal of any year's dockets quickly conveys a sense of what the commission does in this area.

One prominent type of case, although it has become less common recently, concerns false price claims. A price might be advertised as "50 cents off" or "20 percent off" or "lowest ever!"—claims that are often difficult for a buyer to verify. The FTC has moved actively against advertisers of reductions of prices that were seldom or never charged.

One of the most notorious cases involved an advertisement by the Mary Carter Paint Company. With every purchase of a $6.98 can of paint, the buyer would receive one can "free." Since Mary Carter had never sold the advertised paint in single cans, the commission regarded the promise of a free can to be deceptive. Its objection was upheld by the Supreme Court in 1965.[17]

Primary commission attention is devoted to false or misleading product claims. Some examples:

- It objected when SCM advertised that use of its typewriters by students would produce "top grades" and "academic improvement."
- A manufacturer of locks was required to cease using the words "pick proof" in its advertising after two witnesses succeeded in picking the locks during a commission hearing.
- A seller of electric hair clippers was forbidden to claim that they produce "no vibrations" when vibrations could be felt during use.
- Procter & Gamble Company agreed to stop claiming that foods fried in *Crisco* will be less greasy or lower in calories than foods fried in other cooking oils.

The mere definition of a false or deceptive claim can be surprisingly difficult to formulate. Upon occasion, the fact that a statement is literally correct may not protect it from a charge of deception. P. Lorillard, for example, accurately claimed that its cigarettes had been found to be "lowest in nicotine and tars" in an independent laboratory test. The FTC held, however, that the test results, which showed no important differences in tar or nicotine content among brands, had been used to mislead consumers.[18] Conversely, a literally false demonstration—for example, the use of potatoes in an ice cream commercial on television—is permissible where no deceptive purpose exists.[19]

The FTC has very limited tools with which to act against a false advertiser. Indeed, until recently, an order to cease and desist was virtually its only weapon. An offending firm might comply with such an order and discontinue

---

[17]*FTC v. Mary Carter Paint Co.*, 382 U.S. 46 (1965). In similar circumstances in 1973, Berkey Photo, Inc. agreed to cease advertising "FREE Kodak film" with its film processing service. The commission had determined that Berkey's processing charges included the cost of film replacement.

[18]*P. Lorillard Co. v. FTC*, 186 F.2d 52 (1950).

[19]Potatoes are used because ice cream would melt under hot television lights.

the offending message, or it might contest the order through the commission and ultimately appeal to the courts. In either event there are no real sanctions. The company's only penalty is that it would likely incur extra legal fees if it chose to fight the commission order, and it might incur some negative publicity.[20]

Such limitation to FTC action has at least three undesirable implications:

1.   Because there is effectively no regulatory penalty, advertisers have little added incentive to be truthful.

2.   Because the incentive for consumers to complain is often weak, the commission receives little private help in its enforcement efforts.

3.   The effects of misleading advertising may persist for some time after the material is withdrawn.

In response to such deficiencies (especially the last), the FTC has experimented with corrective advertising in a number of cases. In 1971, for example, ITT Continental Baking Company agreed to devote 25 percent of its advertising expenditures for one year to correct prior claims for Profile bread. Profile had been advertised as a low-calorie food; in fact, it contained just seven fewer calories per slice than other breads and only because it was sliced thinner. Similarly, in 1975, Warner-Lambert Company, the manufacturer of Listerine mouthwash, was required to make clear in future advertising that Listerine does *not* prevent colds or ameliorate cold symptoms, as its past advertising had suggested.

This sort of requirement imposes some additional costs on false advertisers and may eliminate some residual effects of the offending message. It is not obvious, however, that corrective advertising is an effective remedy for deception. Corrective orders are a controversial tool, used only sparingly. While hardly a panacea, however, they may provide the Commission with somewhat greater powers in certain circumstances.[21]

Disclosure Requirements   Positive disclosure requirements comprise a significant portion of information-related consumer protection arrangements. Disclosure is especially important where verification of product or service qualities is costly or impossible.

One may wish to take vitamins with extra iron, but most consumers have absolutely no way to determine, either before or after taking the vitamins, whether the extra iron was there.[22] One might have a severe allergy to sesame oil; the presence of the oil can be verified by the allergic consumer, but only by a costly and unpleasant trip to the local hospital. In both instances, there is an argument for government to require truthful disclosure of product contents: it is likely to be less costly than placing the burden of verification on consumers.

---

[20]Violation of a valid cease and desist order, however, may subject a company to substantial fines.

[21]For an assessment, see "Corrective Advertising Orders of the Federal Trade Commission," *Harvard Law Review* 85 (December 1971).

[22]This is another example of a credence quality.

Laws requiring accurate labeling of food and drug products have, accordingly, been part of the American regulatory system for many years.[23]

Truth in lending legislation (the Consumer Credit Protection Act of 1968) was motivated by a similar argument: that most buyers could not accurately assess borrowing costs. The law mandates disclosure of all finance charges, both in dollars and as a true annual rate of interest, and further restricts garnishment of wages by lenders. The Fair Credit Reporting Act of 1970 gives consumers access to their credit rating files and provides the opportunity to correct inaccurate, misleading, or obsolete information.

Truth in packaging (the Fair Packaging and Labeling Act of 1966) requires informative packaging and disclosure of content quantities on package labels. It is an addition to a long line of labeling and packaging requirements that began with the Food and Drug Act of 1906. In many cases, consumers can easily determine for themselves whether package shapes and sizes are misleading, and one might argue that this sort of regulation is excessive. It is rather difficult, however, to criticize a law that simply assures buyers that what they get is reasonably close to what they see, especially when the costs of such assurances are quite modest.

Evaluation of Information Requirements   Taken as a group, laws promoting accurate consumer information are widely accepted as reflecting a legitimate public concern. Buyers no doubt enjoy knowing that sellers are held to certain standards of truthful advertising and disclosure. No one wants to find a can labeled spaghetti to be filled with broccoli, or a cereal box to contain 50 percent air. The laws prohibiting such surprises do not as a rule impose heavy costs on product suppliers.

Whereas disclosure requirements have stimulated relatively few complaints, some economists and lawyers have lodged serious objections to advertising regulation. One frequent argument is that enforcement of the law has focused on trivialities, instances in which the benefits won for consumers are likely to be outweighed by the expenditure of administrative resources.[24] Liebeler, for example, has called the FTC's record of advertising regulation "dismal beyond ready belief."[25]

---

[23]Expansion of such regulations, for example, to the contents of items served by fast-food stores, is now a subject of some controversy.

[24]Examples are unfortunately not hard to find. One oft-cited case involved a television commercial that showed sandpaper being shaved after the application of Rapid Shave, a cream manufactured by Colgate-Palmolive. The FTC objected, not merely because the commercial involved a phony mock up—it was not sandpaper but plexiglass covered with sand that was shown being shaved—but because sandpaper of the type depicted could not be shaved using Rapid Shave unless it was first soaked for 80 minutes! This case was appealed by the company, went through the appellate courts twice, and finally resulted in a Supreme Court decision upholding the commission (*FTC v. Colgate-Palmolive,* 380 U.S. 374 (1965)). The substantial public and private resources consumed by this case do not seem compensated by any readily imagined consumer benefits.

[25]W. J. Liebeler, "Commentary," in D. G. Tuerck, ed., *Issues in Advertising* (Washington, D.C.: American Enterprise Institute, 1978), 53. Liebeler cites a case in which the FTC investigated the

A somewhat different criticism is that, apart from the wisdom of specific enforcement choices, the role of government has been overextended, occupying areas in which public agencies try to perform tasks that consumers could easily do for themselves. R. K. Winter goes still further, arguing that consumer advocates often attempt to provide more information than consumers themselves desire to have.[26]

The objective truth of the matter is, as usual, hard to define, depending as it does upon whether one believes that the unregulated market consistently compels sellers to provide enough data about their offerings. Advocates such as Ralph Nader plainly do not, rather envisioning consumers as helpless, frequently gullible beings in need of collective protection. Market-oriented persons, on the other hand, are inclined to see shrewd and skeptical buyers roaming the aisles of our stores—people who do not have much need for a public policeman and who ought not to be forced to pay for one.

Product Quality and Safety

There is now a wide range of product and service quality legislation oriented toward consumer safety, much of it enacted since the middle 1960s. The laws pertain both to such broad categories as consumer goods and to narrower product lines, for example, foods, drugs, cosmetics, and motor vehicles. The general issue raised by safety regulation is the same as that arising under information laws: what is the proper role of government?

Some important subsidiary questions, however, are quite different. Should government prevent well-informed persons from taking risks that they wish to assume? Or, if it is agreed that some public reduction of risk is desirable, how should this be done? (The options range from education programs to outright prohibition of products.) Such questions point to controversial policy choices that have not yet been fully resolved.

Why should government play any role in providing product safety? Or, to turn the question around, why not leave decisions about safety to consumers and producers interacting in the marketplace? Familiar market arguments suggest that it will be profitable for suppliers to produce those product qualities, safety included, that consumers desire; and that, if the market functions properly, the amount of safety provided will be socially correct in the sense that we will get what we want.[27] There are, however, several reasons (which should by now be familiar) why the market solution might not prove satisfactory:

---

claim by Bristol-Myers Co. that its deodorant, Dry Ban, was dry. He states: "The consumer loss from advertisements of this type cannot conceivably be large enough to justify the extensive attentions of a federal agency."

[26]R. K. Winter, Jr., *The Consumer Advocate versus the Consumer* (Washington, D.C.: American Enterprise Institute, 1972).

[27]More precisely, we will get what we are willing to pay for. This in turn suggests that as long as a high value is attached to product safety, it will pay producers to supply safer products. Where the associated value is low, reflecting an unwillingness to pay much for safety features, suppliers will not provide them.

1.   The argument for the market, as always, presupposes some effective level of competition. Where competitive pressures are weak, there is no presumption that the socially desired level of resources will be devoted to safety (or to other product attributes).

2.   Some product hazards have external effects. (If my car has no horn or lights, you may suffer!) Similarly, many safety activities, such as highway speed control, are of a public goods nature.

3.   Some product hazards may be invisible (the appliance capable of generating a severe shock), or the risk, though known to exist, may be hard for people to estimate.[28]

Any of these circumstances creates a case for public intervention. Where none is present, government safety regulation is likely to provoke debate.

To shift the point slightly, one might argue on efficiency grounds that government should require or supply additional safety when consumers desire it but the market will not respond adequately. Unfortunately, these conditions are harder to identify than one might suspect. Different consumers of a product are of course likely to desire different levels of safety. Some people, for example, will be pleased when the Consumer Product Safety Commission requires more protective devices on power lawn mowers, but others will not. (It is not that the latter necessarily dislike safety, but simply that they do not value it at a level as high as its supply cost.)[29]

How, then, are we to decide whether consumers as a group want more safety devices? The market makes this sort of decision on the basis of willingness to pay. (Will safety sell?) But once we concede that the market solution may be wrong, it can prove difficult to define what alternative is better, let alone best. We turn our attention now to the way in which the policy issue has been addressed in a number of important areas.

Food and Drugs   Federal regulation of food and drugs dates to the Food and Drug Act of 1906. This modest law consisted primarily of labeling requirements: products could not be "adulterated" or "misbranded," and medicine ingredients were to be listed on package labels. In 1938 Congress enacted the Food, Drug, and Cosmetic Act, still the fundamental regulatory law in this area.[30]

---

[28]When risks are invisible, government may simply act to make the appropriate information available. What ought to be done when the existence of risk, but not its magnitude, is known, is less clear-cut.

[29]Interested readers should see J. M. Buchanan, "In Defense of *Caveat Emptor*," *University of Chicago Law Review* 38 (Fall 1970): 64-73. Buchanan argues that if consumers desire varying levels of safety, laws that require safer products will tend to reduce product variety; and that it is low-income people, who might choose risky but low-priced products, who are likely to bear the burden of this reduction. This argument suggests an obvious equity—as well as an efficiency—issue.

[30]The act was passed partly in response to a tragedy involving the drug sulfanilamide. The drug was distributed in liquid suspension form; the suspending solvent turned out to be highly toxic, killing over 100 persons, most of them children. Under the 1906 law, the manufacturer (Massengill Co.) was guilty only of mislabeling the product.

The act greatly expanded the powers of the Food and Drug Administration to deal with unsafe products.

Foods, drugs, and cosmetics were now defined as adulterated if they contained any substance unsafe for human use. The introduction of a new drug to the market required a New Drug Application (NDA) supported by safety data from animal and clinical tests. Although an NDA was automatically approved if the FDA failed to reject it within 180 days, the law provided government with its most potent weapon by far for keeping questionable products off the market.

Several important amendments to the 1938 law have since been enacted. The Pesticides Chemical Amendment of 1954 required the FDA to define and enforce safe levels of pesticide residues in foods. (This responsibility has since been transferred to the Environmental Protection Agency.) The Food Additives Amendment of 1958 requires manufacturers to demonstrate the safety of many intentionally added substances in order to obtain marketing approval. A series of 1962 amendments significantly tightens the rules governing new drug introductions. Manufacturers are required to prove to the satisfaction of the FDA that substances are not only safe, but effective in serving the claims that are made for them.

The Impact of Drug Regulation   There can be no doubt that federal regulation has increased the safety of the nation's food and drug supply during the past 50 years. This fact was dramatically illustrated by our avoidance of the thalidomide tragedy in the early 1960s.

Thalidomide was a nonbarbiturate sedative widely prescribed in Britain and Western Europe during the late 1950s and early 1960s. It failed to receive FDA approval and was therefore not sold in the United States, although some physicians received samples for experimental use. Among those using the drug were large numbers of pregnant women.

Whether the drug would eventually have won approval for American distribution is uncertain.[31] By 1961, a virtual epidemic of deformed babies being born was occurring in every country where thalidomide was being taken by pregnant women. The deformities "covered a wide spectrum of limb deficiencies ranging from virtual limblessness to relatively minor defects . . . as well as defective sight and hearing."[32] Once the connection to thalidomide was established, of course, use of the drug stopped everywhere.

Despite this sort of success, drug regulation is—like most activities—a double-edged sword, providing benefits but imposing costs as well. It goes without saying that it is desirable to prevent dangerous drugs from reaching the market. But to achieve this goal requires testing and administrative review

---

[31]Dr. Frances Kelsey, an FDA physician, withheld approval of thalidomide despite intense pressure from its manufacturer, Richardson-Merrell, Inc. In 1962 she received the Distinguished Federal Civilian Service Award for her resolute efforts.

[32]H. Teff and C. R. Munro, *Thalidomide: The Legal Aftermath* (Westmead, Farnborough: Saxon House, 1976), 4.

procedures that slow the introduction of all drugs, safe and risky alike. In principle, therefore, the benefits of avoiding unsafe drugs are accompanied by the costs of discouraging safe ones. Patients whose lives might be saved or suffering eased by newly developed substances must wait while these products run the gamut of regulatory approval procedures.

Although few have argued for substantial relaxation of drug safety requirements, criticism has been aimed at the 1962 proof-of-efficacy requirements.[33] Sam Peltzman in a well-known study concluded that the main result of this requirement has been to reduce the flow of new drugs, and that while some ineffective substances have been kept off the market, such gains have been outweighed by the lost benefits of safe and effective drugs that fail to reach the market.[34]

Whether or not one accepts Peltzman's conclusions, two points are clear:

1.   An efficacy requirement such as that prescribed by the 1962 amendments raises the costs of introducing new drugs and must therefore result in some discouragement of innovation.

2.   The actual flow of new drugs in the United States has declined very substantially since 1962.[35]

The first point is hardly controversial. The most elementary principles of economics tell us that if an activity becomes more expensive, less of it will occur. The only open question is empirical: Will the magnitude of the reduction be large or small?

With regard to the second point, it may well be that factors other than public regulation contributed to the slowing of new drug introductions. Some observers believe that a kind of technological plateau had been reached during the 1950s and that the slowdown in scientific development was bound to result in a reduced flow of new drugs regardless of government policy. The FDA has further argued that the bulk of reduction in new drugs has involved substances of little or no therapeutic value.[36]

---

[33]An exception has been created by the AIDS epidemic. It is now commonly argued that potentially useful drugs for treating AIDS should be approved even though they may carry significant risks.

[34]S. Peltzman, *Regulation of Pharmaceutical Innovation: The 1962 Amendments* (Washington, D.C.: American Enterprise Institute, 1974). It has also been claimed that the proportion of ineffective drugs on the market did not fall after 1962. If so, this would mean that although the efficacy requirement kept some ineffective drugs out, its main impact was to reduce the introduction of *effective* substances.

[35]Total development and clearance time for a new drug has been estimated at 2.5 years in 1962 and 7.5 to 10 years in 1972. L. H. Sarett, "FDA Regulations and Their Influence on Future R&D," *Research Management* (March 1974). Further, the annual number of FDA approvals of new chemical entities in the 12 years following 1962 was less than half that of the previous 12 years. For compilations, see H. G. Grabowski, *Drug Regulation and Innovation* (Washington, D.C.: American Enterprise Institute, 1976).

[36]Testimony by Alexander Schmidt, FDA Commissioner, *Hearings on Legislation Amending the Public Health Service Act and the Food, Drug and Cosmetic Act*, Senate Committee on Labor and Public Welfare (1974).

It does appear, however, that the rate of drug innovation in the United States has fallen *relative* to that in countries such as Britain, which have less stringent premarket regulation. It is difficult to avoid the conclusion that the 1962 amendments played a significant, if not an exclusive, role in that decline. By itself, this observation does not condemn the amendments, but it does point out once again that social costs are invariably attached to desirable policy moves.

Does strict federal regulation of drug markets serve the public interest? The answer is almost surely yes—to some point. But the question then becomes: have we gone beyond that point, into the realm of regulation that costs more than it is worth? Consider the two types of risk inherent in pharmaceutical market activity:

1.   The failure to develop, approve, and introduce safe, useful drugs.

2.   Development, approval, and introduction of unsafe drugs.

J. E. S. Parker, among others, has argued with some force that American regulation is aimed exclusively at the second type of risk, with the probable result that we incur relatively high risk of the first type. As he puts it, "the patient is protected from drug hazard and not from disease and discomfort."[37]

It is interesting to consider the reasons for this sort of regulatory bias.[38] Why, in other words, are we more concerned about the danger of bad drugs than the danger of failing to develop good ones? Part of the explanation may lie in the relative visibility of the two hazards. Introduction of a toxic substance produces dramatically observable results. We know, for example, who were the victims of thalidomide and what they suffered. In contrast, to delay or preclude introduction of a useful (even a lifesaving) drug may produce no correspondingly visible drama. We are unlikely to see newspaper or television coverage of those who might have been helped, or even to know who they are.

Another possible explanation, noted by Parker, is widespread mistrust of U.S. pharmaceutical manufacturers. To the extent that these companies are viewed as exploiters of vulnerable consumers—and highly profitable ones at that—it is not surprising that our regulatory arrangements have evolved to their present form.

The Impact of Food Regulation   Regulation of food products is designed to prevent the introduction of unsafe substances to the market. Public enforcement focuses largely on added substances and on the sanitary conditions surrounding food production and processing. It is widely recognized that complete safety in the nation's food supply is an unattainable goal. There may in fact be few individual foods that are completely safe when consumed in very large

---

[37]J.E.S. Parker, "Regulating Pharmaceutical Innovation: An Economist's View," *Food Drug Cosmetic Law Journal* (April 1977): 165.

[38]That such bias exists is not really debatable. Note, however, that some may well regard the bias as a strength rather than a weakness of the regulatory system.

quantities. The central policy question is therefore: what degree of safety should government attempt to assure?

That government should play some role is seldom disputed. Consumers simply are not equipped to evaluate food safety, and the consequences of ignorance are potentially severe. Even if the market were to function efficiently by punishing suppliers of harmful foods, consumption of these substances implies costs that most would regard as unacceptable. Despite such agreement, however, the ways in which government seeks to assure food safety is a topic that arouses debate.

Primary responsibility for the safety of the nation's food supply belongs to the Food and Drug Administration (FDA), which operates under a complex legislative mandate. Natural or unavoidable ingredients are treated with relative leniency. For these, the agency establishes "tolerances" or permissible levels, consistent with the public health. Intentionally added substances are treated more strictly. In fact, the most controversial single law governing product safety in the United States is very likely the Delaney anticancer clause of the Food, Drug and Cosmetic Act, which states:

> No additive shall be deemed to be safe if it is found to induce cancer when ingested by man or animal, or if it is found, after tests which are appropriate . . . to induce cancer in man or animal.[39]

Two narrow objections to the Delaney clause may be noted:

1. Because it is totally unqualified, the clause could be read to prohibit substances for which the weight of scientific evidence suggests safety.

2. The technology for detecting minute quantities of substances (including carcinogens) in food has advanced so far since 1958 that the clause has become far stricter than originally envisioned. Read literally, it could be used to prohibit substances whose cancer-causing potential is close to zero.

The more general objection to the Delaney provision relates to its implicit criterion for public safety decisions. The clause states that a food additive is not safe—and must therefore be banned under existing law—if it carries *any* risk of causing cancer. This criterion is easily reduced to an absurdity. Suppose one were to develop a cheap, delectable, nutritious food that could greatly reduce hunger around the world, but that the food required use of a preservative that gives each person consuming it a one-in-ten-million chance of developing cancer. Under the Delaney standard, such a food could not be approved. Millions might perish in order to avoid the risk of a small number of cancer cases—a risk that the famished might gladly have borne.

The essential problem with the Delaney clause, and with other similar provisions of food safety law, is that they permit no balancing of costs (risks) and benefits. Rather, they state: if any cost is identifiable, the substance must go. This sort of standard, if applied broadly, would eliminate much of the American diet. Health risks may be posed, for example, by heavy consump-

---

[39]This clause is part of the 1958 Food Additives Amendment.

tion of salt, sugar, coffee, tea, beef, eggs, milk, and butter. Yet it is inconceivable that people would, or should, agree to the prohibition of these foods under a zero-risk approach of the type exemplified by the Delaney provision.

Some consumer advocates believe that the Delaney clause bolsters FDA authority, giving the safety enforcement program teeth that it would otherwise lack. Yet the futility of attempting to achieve complete safety is evident. The saving grace of such provisions is that the FDA has not enforced them strictly. They have therefore had less impact on food regulation than one would expect from reading the relevant statutes. This is, however, a weak defense of poorly drawn law.

Saccharin and Sodium Nitrite   Recent controversies over saccharin and nitrites illustrate some of the most basic issues in public safety regulation.

Saccharin was until recently the only noncaloric sugar substitute available in the United States. Although aspartame is now an alternative in some uses, saccharin was and is still widely consumed. In 1977, a Canadian study showed that rats fed large quantities of saccharin (the equivalent of 800 cans of diet soda per day) developed significantly more bladder tumors than a control group. Other studies have confirmed a relatively weak cancer-causing effect in rats, although the implications for human consumption are not entirely clear.

Shortly after the Canadian study appeared, the FDA announced a ban on saccharin and all saccharin-sweetened products. The public response was rapid. Congress received complaints not only from the diet food industry but from large numbers of consumers—dieters, diabetics, and others who wished to restrict their sugar consumption but still satisfy a sweet tooth. The Senate responded with a moratorium on the ban that has been renewed three times. It is unlikely that saccharin will disappear from the market until a completely acceptable substitute is introduced. Products containing saccharin, however, carry a warning: "Use of this product may be hazardous to your health. This product contains saccharin which has been determined to cause cancer in laboratory animals."

There is considerable irony in the saccharin episode. Several years earlier, the FDA had banned cyclamates, an artificial sweetener suspected of causing cancer. Yet the evidence marshaled against cyclamates was weaker than the later evidence against saccharin. The cyclamate ban, which stimulated saccharin consumption, may therefore have had a cancer-causing effect!

Sodium nitrite is a preservative used in cured meats to prevent the growth of potentially lethal botulism. Without it, the sale of such delicacies as ham, hot dogs, salami, kielbasa, and corned beef, could end—there is now no available substitute. There exists some evidence, however, linking nitrite consumption to cancer.[40]

While fully cognizant of the problem, the FDA has not moved to ban nitrites. (It has reduced the permissible limits, however.) It may have learned

---

[40]Nitrites react with acids in the digestive system to form nitrosamines, an extremely potent carcinogen.

from its experience with saccharin that attempting to protect consumers who do not want protection, is at best difficult and at worst futile.[41]

Both cases present difficult policy issues. It may well be that prolonged consumption of both saccharin and sodium nitrites poses relatively small health risks. What is abundantly clear, however, is that many Americans in the wake of widely publicized cancer findings, are willing to take these risks. In economic terms, they appear to regard the benefits of consumption as greater than the costs implied by possible adverse health effects.

Motor Vehicles   Motor vehicles, especially automobiles, have been one of the most extensively regulated product categories in the American economy in recent years. Following passage of the National Traffic and Motor Vehicle Safety Act of 1966, numerous safety features have been required. These include safety belts, front seat head restraints, energy-absorbing steering columns, dual braking systems, padded dashboards, and penetration-resistant windshields. Under the act, the National Highway Traffic Safety Administration (NHTSA) promulgates safety requirements and monitors the need for recall of existing vehicles.

As noted earlier, government intervention is supported by the externalities that accompany some driving hazards. A failure to equip one's car with headlights, for example, could injure others. The issue is less clear-cut, however, with respect to devices that protect only the driver or occupants of the car equipped with them. One might argue, for example, that drivers without safety belts can hurt only themselves, and that government therefore has no business forcing them to buy or use such devices.

An element of externality does operate, however, via the automobile insurance system. Liability insurance is mandatory in many states. The costs of such insurance are tied to claims that follow accidental injury and death. To the extent that equipment such as seat belts reduces these costs, all drivers benefit through lower insurance premiums. By precisely the same token, my failure to buy and use the belts may impose higher insurance costs on you.

To note that there is a rationale for government intervention, however, is not to imply that the type of regulation we have is socially appropriate. Safety devices are costly. Crandall et al., for example, place the costs in the range of $470 to $690 per vehicle.[42] Do the benefits justify this substantial expenditure of resources? There is some disagreement here. Government engineering studies suggest that mandated safety devices save perhaps 10,000 lives per year. Crandall et al. provide similar estimates, and Graham and Garber have also found substantial lifesaving effects.[43] Peltzman, on the other hand, has

---

[41]A strict reading of the Delaney clause seems to imply prohibition of both saccharin and nitrites. The agency has maintained, however, that even without the Delaney restriction, saccharin would properly be banned as unsafe under the more general safety requirements of the law.

[42]Robert W. Crandall, Howard K. Gruenspecht, Theodore E. Keeler, and Lester B. Lave, *Regulating the Automobile* (Washington, D.C.: Brookings Institution, 1986).

[43]J. D. Graham and S. Garber, "Evaluating the Effects of Automobile Safety Regulation," *Journal of Policy Analysis and Management* 3 (1984).

concluded that the impact of safety regulation has been overstated (a) because many drivers would have made adaptations in the absence of regulation—that is, driving would have become somewhat safer for other reasons; and (b) because at least some drivers may adapt to safer vehicles by driving less carefully.[44]

Conclusions about the effect of auto safety requirements on society's well-being are thus a matter of debate. The costs of the program are large. The benefits may be enormous but are, as is typical, more difficult to define. The highway death rate has declined significantly since 1966, the year in which the safety law was passed. Did the law cause this decline? The current consensus is yes, at least in part. But we cannot be certain about what would have happened during this period in the absence of the law.[45] In the case of auto safety requirements, the potential gains are so large that most people probably consider the effort worthwhile. An element of subjective judgment, however, is unavoidable.

A final pertinent question is whether our current auto safety program is the best way to reduce injury and death. The issue is important because numerous alternative uses of funds are available—for example, improvement of highway lighting and markings, expanded driver education, and stricter enforcement of drunk driving laws. Conceivably some other program mix could provide greater safety gains for the same expenditure. No definitive assessment of this possibility has yet been made.

Cigarettes   Consider two facts:

1.   The effects of cigarette smoking on human health are beyond serious debate. Smoking over the long term leads to illness and death.

2.   Millions of Americans continue to smoke knowing the risks. It is in fact unclear precisely what effect public policy with respect to cigarettes since 1964 has had on the nation's habits, although a significant decline in smoking has occurred.[46]

These facts pose the most fundamental public policy questions in dramatic terms. What risks should individuals be permitted to assume? What obligations does government have when the risks are very high?

Most people no doubt agree that government does have certain obligations with regard to cigarette smoking. First, to assure that health information is widely disseminated. The right of consumers to take risks surely presup-

---

[44]S. Peltzman, "The Effects of Automobile Safety Regulation," *Journal of Political Economy* 83 (July-August 1975): 677-725.

[45]This is a problem common to most evaluations of safety programs. Since safety measurements—such as highway fatality rates—are affected by so many variables, defining the influence of a single event such as enactment of a law often proves difficult.

[46]For some evidence that public policies have had an especially noteworthy impact on tobacco consumption, see L. Schneider, B. Klein, and K. M. Murphy, "Governmental Regulation of Cigarette Health Information," *Journal of Law and Economics* 24 (December 1981): 575–612.

poses that the risks are known. Second, to prevent risk-taking by those who may not be capable of rational evaluation (for example, young children). Governmental responses to these obligations are familiar. Cigarette sale to minors is illegal. The dangers of smoking are well-publicized and, presumably, understood (the publicity includes required health warnings on cigarette packages and printed advertisments). Broadcast advertising of cigarettes is prohibited.[47]

Should government go still further and restrict the ability of presumably rational and informed consumers to take the risks associated with smoking?[48] No serious effort has been made to do so, and any such effort in the future would be surprising. It is interesting to note, however, that under the standards applied to both food additives and drugs, cigarettes could not be approved as safe.   Does their continued sale reflect our commitment to free consumer choice? Perhaps, but we do not find similar commitment in other product areas. Cigarette sales may also reflect the economic importance and political power of the tobacco industry.

Consumer Products   The Consumer Product Safety Act of 1972 is potentially one of the most important pieces of consumer safety legislation to date. The law established the Consumer Product Safety Commission (CPSC) to act against "unreasonable risks of injury" associated with a wide variety of products that were not previously covered by specific statute.

What is an unreasonable risk?   The words of the commission that recommended the 1972 law are noteworthy:

> Risks of bodily harm are not unreasonable when consumers understand that risks exist, can appraise their probability and severity, know how to cope with them, and voluntarily accept them to get benefits that could not be obtained in less risky ways. When there is a risk of this character, consumers have reasonable opportunity to protect themselves; and public authorities should hesitate to substitute their value judgments about the desirability of the risk for those of the consumers who choose to incur it.
>
> But preventable risk is not reasonable (a) when consumers do not know that it exists or (b) when, though aware of it, consumers are unable to

---

[47]The ban on television advertising represents a curious effort in safety regulation. Intended originally to reduce the appeal of cigarettes, especially to the young, it is now suspected that the prohibition may have had the opposite effect. Cigarette advertising probably had some impact on the market shares of rival manufacturers while doing little to affect the overall level of smoking. Anti-smoking messages, broadcast on television under the so-called fairness doctrine, may well have worked in the other direction: little effect on firms' market shares but some discouragement of smoking generally. The effect of the advertising ban was to remove both the pro- and anti-smoking commercials from the air, with the possible result that cigarette consumption increased. See for some evidence, J. L. Hamilton, "The Demand for Cigarettes: Advertising, the Health Scare, and the Cigarette Advertising Ban," *Review of Economics and Statistics* 54 (November 1972).

[48]Whether the decision to smoke cigarettes is in fact rational, has been a question of interest to some psychologists and economists. The answer may depend upon how rationality is defined. As Thomas C. Schelling points out, for example, most cigarette smokers make efforts to quit, and many would pay a considerable price to do so. These are hardly the patterns that one ordinarily associates with a rational and informed choice. T. C. Schelling, "The Intimate Contest for Self Command," *The Public Interest* 60 (Summer 1980).

estimate its frequency and severity; or (c) when consumers do not know how to cope with it . . . ; or (d) when risk is unnecessary in . . . that it could be reduced or eliminated at a cost . . . that consumers would willingly incur if they knew the facts and were given the choice.[49]

The CPSC was granted extensive powers to deal with unreasonable risks in ways ranging from public warnings and labeling requirements to product seizure. Recently, Congress has trimmed the commission's powers somewhat, requiring it to give preference to voluntary over mandatory safety standards in many circumstances.

The effect of CPSC policies to date is rather difficult to gauge. The commission's analyses of some safety requirements have been severely criticized.[50] It has, for example, proposed rules for such products as matchbooks, swimming pool slides, and pacifiers that provide little persuasive reason to expect that the rules would be worthwhile. Furthermore, its record in having its standards overturned by the courts has been an unhappy one. The agency has, however, been handicapped by serious cuts in its real budget (since its inception it has been a small, sparsely supported organization), and some of its recent analyses appear to be of higher quality. Whether the CPSC will become a substantial force in U.S. safety regulation remains an open question.

Product Liability

Despite our best efforts, some consumers will inevitably be injured by the products they use. Who should bear the financial responsibility for the losses suffered in such instances? This is the basic question addressed by the area of tort law known as products liability.[51]

Caveat emptor ("let the buyer beware") is frequently cited as the traditional standard of liability. An unqualified *caveat emptor* rule would make consumer-victims financially responsible for their injuries regardless of circumstances— in effect a *per se* approach. Typically, however, such doctrines have been qualified: a consumer bears liability, for example, unless the supplier of the injuring product was negligent—that is, failed to take due or reasonable care in design or construction.

For many years, manufacturers liability in the United States was limited by the doctrine of privity of contract. Under this rule, the manufacturer was

---

[49]*Final Report of the National Commission on Product Safety* (Washington, D.C.: 1970). The definition of "not unreasonable" risk is attributed to Corwin D. Edwards.

[50]The bulk of the criticism has not come from sources hostile to consumer protection laws. See S. Kelman, "Regulation by the Numbers: A Report on the Consumer Product Safety Commission," *Public Interest* 37 (Summer 1974); N. W. Cornell, R. G. Noll, and B. Weingast, "Safety Regulation," in H. Owen and C. L. Schultze, eds., *Setting National Priorities: The Next Ten Years* (Washington, D.C.: Brookings Institution, 1976); and W. K. Viscusi, *Regulating Consumer Product Safety* (Washington, D.C.: American Enterprise Institute, 1984).

[51]A tort is usually a civil (as opposed to a criminal) wrong, frequently an unintentional or incidental failure to discharge an obligation to someone, which failure causes harm to that person. For fuller discussion, see W. Z. Hirsch, *Law and Economics: An Introductory Analysis* (New York: Academic Press, 1979), 127ff.

potentially liable only to direct purchasers of its goods, who were usually distributors rather than final consumers. (Privity in the law refers to an immediate or direct relationship between parties.) An injured consumer would thus have to demonstrate not only manufacturer negligence but an immediate relationship with that manufacturer in order to recover damages.

An important change in the law occurred in a famous 1916 court decision, *MacPherson v. Buick Motor Co.*[52] MacPherson, who bought his Buick automobile from a dealer, was injured when a wheel on the car collapsed. The court held not only that the car had been negligently constructed, but that Buick owed the consumer a "duty of vigilance" despite the absence of privity.

In recent years, American courts have moved away from *caveat emptor* toward its mirror image, strict liability for manufacturers and distributors. Injured consumers may sometimes recover damages without demonstrating a supplier's negligence, although certain legal tests must be met. The accident victim must prove that injury was suffered as the result of a defective product. Manufacturers have at times argued successfully that they should not be liable if a consumer's use of their product was unreasonable, negligent, or impossible to foresee. The law has tilted significantly, but not totally, in the consumer's favor. Given an injury traceable to a defect in a product that was used correctly, that product's manufacturer is likely to have difficulty escaping legal liability.[53]

Although we shall not pursue the case law in detail, it is important to ask about the consequences of a rule that places greater responsibility for safety on product suppliers. Specifically, we ask:

- Will such a rule lead to more safety in a meaningful sense?
- Will it promote a fairer distribution of the burden that accompanies the inevitable accidents of an uncertain world?

It turns out that neither question has an entirely simple answer. When the courts permit consumers injured by products to recover damages, they are in effect providing a type of accident insurance policy. The economic consequences of this policy may be far-reaching and quite indirect. Consider, for example:

1. The costs of this insurance are in the first instance borne mainly by liable manufacturers and distributors. Some costs fall also on the court system, which is financed by taxpayers.

2. The costs may well cause manufacturers to devote more resources to product safety.[54]

---

[52]111 N.E. 1050 (1916).

[53]Consider the case of a drug that was thought to be safe at the time it was introduced, but which is found many years later to have damaging side effects. Under current legal standards, the manufacturer might well be held liable even though all required testing procedures were followed and the risk was not foreseeable at the time of testing.

[54]Some observers suspect, however, that the main effect of strict liability may be to induce manufacturers to buy liability insurance rather than to make safer products.

3.   It is highly probable that the costs of additional product safety will be at least partially passed on to consumers. The visible results will be higher product prices, smaller outputs, and possibly some reduction in variety as riskier items are forced off the market.

4.   The existence of insurance and/or safer products may cause consumers to take less care in the use of products. We would not of course expect that cautious souls will be transformed into daredevils, but even marginal changes may be significant.

What, then, are the net effects of a move toward strict liability likely to be? The total quantity of safety that is produced by manufacturers *and* consumers may well increase, although this is not logically inevitable.[55] Whether the change will be large or significant or worthwhile, cannot be predicted. This will depend upon the reactions of both manufacturers and consumers to increased manufacturer responsibility for safety, and in a sense to the relative efficiency of both groups as safety producers.[56]

Whether strict(er) liability results in a fairer distribution of injury costs remains ultimately a question of values. It may tend to spread the costs more widely, among all buyers of the products in question. Notice that there is no way to shift the full burden to product manufacturers. Strict liability may yield more safety, but safety is costly and the costs will enter manufacturers' pricing and production decisions. The buyers of safer products are thus likely to see smaller quantities of these goods and to pay more for them.

WORKER PROTECTION

Theory

No one will question that accidental injuries and damage to the health of workers are a bad thing, but the same question that we have posed with regard to consumer protection is relevant here: why should government intervene? Why, in other words, should we not allow the market to make appropriate adjustments for occupational hazards?

Such adjustments could occur in at least two ways. Workers might refuse to work in unsafe conditions, thereby forcing employers to provide greater safety. Or they might agree to hazardous work only in return for a wage

---

[55]For the assignment of legal liability to affect the amount of safety seems to contradict the well-known Coase theorem (see Chapter 5). This theorem states roughly that in a freely functioning market with no transactions costs, divisions of liability do not affect resource allocation. James Buchanan contends that the Coase theorem may not apply "where varying qualities of product" are sold. J. Buchanan, "In Defense of *Caveat Emptor*," 68.

[56]It is sometimes assumed that manufacturers are better producers of safety than consumers, yet this is not always so. Many lawn mower injuries, for example, occur when people reach into the blade housing with the mower running, usually to remove wet grass. Manufacturers can build mowers that make this impossible, but the same degree of safety could plainly be produced by consumers at lower cost—simply by deciding not to reach into a live blade housing.

premium. Such a premium, by raising labor costs, would encourage (though not compel) employers to provide greater protection for their workers.[57]

The arguments for public protection of employees are roughly parallel to those for consumers:

1.   Information may be inadequate. Workers can hardly demand appropriate protection or compensation if they are ignorant of occupational hazards.

2.   Although the existence of risk is known, workers may be poor judges of its magnitude—even though information is, in a sense, adequate. People may, for example, believe that bad things always happen to the other guy and thus disregard risks to their own health and safety.

Policy

The Occupational Safety and Health Act of 1970 provided the first concerted federal effort to protect worker health and safety.[58]   This law, creating the Occupational Safety and Health Administration (OSHA) as the governing agency, has as its major purpose:

> to assure so far as possible every working man and woman in the Nation
> safe and healthful working conditions.

The law also provides that "to the extent feasible," no worker "will suffer material impairment of health."   These are plainly noble objectives, but they are stated in the most general terms.   Precisely what the law requires is a question that has, with some frequency, ended up in the courts.

Under the 1970 act, OSHA has several weapons to deal with threats to worker health and safety.

1.   *Rule-making procedures.* The agency may propose standards and wait 30 days for public responses to its proposal.   Hearings will be held if there are objections and a hearing request is filed.   The agency may then enter a final standard, which is subject to challenge in the courts.

2.   *Emergency temporary standards (ETS).* OSHA may issue an immediately effective ETS if it finds that workers are exposed to grave danger. The ETS must be superseded by a permanent standard within 6 months. It is, like other standards, subject to court challenge.   In practice, very few ETSs have been issued by OSHA.

3.   *Inspection and fines.* Once a standard is in effect, OSHA may inspect for compliance and issue fines for violations.   Until recently, such fines have been trivial (more on this shortly).

---

[57]If prospective employees demand a higher wage to work in my hazardous plant, it may pay me to reduce the hazard rather than to pay that wage.

[58]Under tort law, injured workers could sue their employers.   However, the usual legal standard —negligence—presented very difficult legal tests.

Legal Interpretation

The major substantive question in OSHA regulation has been one of legal interpretation: what criteria is the agency required to use in setting health and safety standards? The broad wording of the law provides little guidance.

Arguments have clustered around two polar positions. (1) The law mandates a technology only standard—that is, a requirement that workers receive all protections that existing technology permits, without regard to cost or efficacy. (2) The law's reference to feasible protections implies that protections are required only if their benefits exceed their costs. It is these sharply opposed arguments that the courts have had to consider. To date, they have responded with somewhat mixed signals.

The Benzene Standard   Benzene is an industrial chemical used in a variety of products including motor fuels, solvents, detergents, and pesticides. At high dosage levels, it is associated with the development of leukemia. In 1978 OSHA issued a final standard limiting workplace benzene exposure to 1 part per million (ppm).

In its standard, OSHA conceded that the leukemia risk posed by actual workplace exposure to benzene—which is relatively low level—could not be reliably estimated. The agency's position was that no safe level of exposure to a carcinogen can be established. The only truly safe exposure would be zero, but since this was not feasible under existing technology, the permissible limit was set at 1 ppm.

The American Petroluem Institute sued to have the standard set aside. In its decision, a circuit court of appeals held that OSHA had in fact exceeded its authority.[59] The agency had done so by setting the benzene standard without attempting to estimate its costs and benefits. It had therefore failed to show that the standard was "reasonably necessary or appropriate" to provide safe or healthful employment, as required by the law.

The Supreme Court upheld this decision, but on somewhat narrower grounds.[60] The benzene standard, according to the Court, was invalid because OSHA had never established that actual workplace exposure poses a significant health risk. It had therefore failed to meet the threshold requirement of the law. The Court did *not* hold that OSHA was required to compare costs and benefits—it was silent on this issue. Rather, its decision stated, a valid standard could not be issued without first determining that there exists a risk to which the standard responds.

The Cotton Dust Standard   Exposure to cotton dust is known to induce byssinosis, a serious respiratory disease commonly called brown lung. OSHA issued a rather complex standard designed to reduce cotton dust exposure among

---

[59]*American Petroleum Institute v. OSHA*, 581 F.Rep 493 (5th Cir. 1978).

[60]*Industrial Union Department, AFL-CIO v. American Petroleum Institute*, 448 U.S. 607 (1980).

textile workers. The American Textile Manufacturers Institute sued to set aside the standard, arguing that the agency had failed to demonstrate a reasonable relationship between the cost and benefits that it would generate. In response, the Secretary of Labor and two labor organizations contended that OSHA was required by law to issue "the most protective standard possible to eliminate a significant risk of . . . health impairment."[61]

Some observers had anticipated, in light of the benzene decision, that the Supreme Court would strike down the cotton dust standard. It did not do so. Rather, the Court held, the agency is not required to conduct benefit–cost comparisons of its standards. Indeed, the Court's position appears even stronger: OSHA is, it seems, *not permitted* to conduct such comparisons. Said Justice Brennan:

> Congress itself defined the basic relationship between costs and benefits by placing the "benefit" of worker health above all other considerations save those making attainment of this "benefit" unachievable.

Where do the benzene and cotton dust decisions leave occupational health and safety regulation? It is clear that OSHA is not to base its standards on cost–benefit comparisons. This leaves feasibility as the test—that is, standards that reduce significant risks are to be issued as long as they are feasible. But precisely what does that mean? Justice Rehnquist, dissenting in the cotton dust case, states: "The 'feasibility standard' is no standard at all." That is something of an exaggeration, yet the Court's decision provided little specific guidance for future standard setting.

The Effects of Regulation

Has OSHA done an effective job of protecting workers' health and safety? Several empirical studies have recently tried to provide an answer to this question.[62] Remarkably, the common finding has been that, at least through the middle 1970s, OSHA activities had no perceptible effects.[63] How could this be? There are at least two possibilities:

1.   The agency may simply have lacked the resources to force companies to comply with its standards.[64]

[61]*American Textile Manufacturers Institute, Inc. v. Donovan*, 452 U.S. 490 (1980).

[62]See R. Smith, *The Occupational Health and Safety Act: Its Goals and Achievements* (Washington, D.C.: American Enterprise Institute, 1976); W. K. Viscusi, "The Impact of Occupational Safety and Health Regulation," *Bell Journal of Economics* 10 (1979): 117-140; J. Mendeloff, *Regulating Safety: An Economic and Political Analysis of Occupational Safety and Health Policy* (Cambridge, Mass.: MIT Press, 1979); A. Bartel and L. Thomas, "Direct and Indirect Effects of OSHA Regulation," *Journal of Law and Economics* 28 (1985): 1-26; and W. K. Viscusi, "The Impact of Occupational Safety and Health Regulation, 1973-1983, "*Rand Journal of Economics* 17 (Winter 1986): 567-580.

[63]Most studies have focused on worker injury rates. Health effects tend to be longer term and more difficult to evaluate.

[64]Bartel and Thomas, "Direct and Indirect Effects of OSHA Regulation," point out that in 1975 the average OSHA fine per violation was $26 and the average number of inspections per firm was 0.02. This implies an expected fine per violation of 52 cents, not a very strong incentive to comply with a costly safety standard!

2.   The agency's standards may have been misdirected—that is, so inherently ineffective that even reasonable compliance would not have prevented many injuries.[65]

Recently, however, Viscusi has reported evidence showing that OSHA activities may be producing some safety gains.[66] He finds, for example, that industries subject to more frequent OSHA inspections during one year experience somewhat fewer injuries and lost workdays in the following year. These effects are not dramatic: agency activities appear to reduce lost workdays by 1.5 to 3.6 percent and to prevent 1 to 2 injuries involving at least one lost workday per 1,000 workers annually. Furthermore, the results are not robust with respect to risk measures.[67] Viscusi's results nevertheless comprise the first serious evidence that OSHA regulation may have some discernible impact on worker safety.[68]

A Brief Perspective

Everyone will surely agree that safer workplace environments are a good thing. It does not necessarily follow, however, that any and all regulation of worker safety is desirable. Regulatory activity is costly, and the costs may outweigh the gains. This is of course a probable result whenever regulation is ineffective, because it then produces few benefits.

A generous view of the net effects of OSHA regulation to date would be that "the jury is still out." Attempts to improve worker safety have imposed costs unevenly across industries without producing generally impressive benefits. Policy efforts may be improving, however, and OSHA may yet fulfill at least some hopes of its early supporters.

However one may evaluate OSHA's experience thus far, it is clear that regulation of worker safety has a place where the market fails. The best known, and probably most tragic, example concerns asbestos workers.

Long-term exposure to asbestos is exceptionally dangerous. Few workers were aware of the risks prior to the time at which thousands were already suffering the effects of asbestos-caused lung disease. Court cases have suggested that employers' knowledge of the risks varied.[69] In at least some instances, companies did little to warn their employees and may actually have misled them by acting as though inhalation of asbestos dust was no more than

---

[65]This could be the case, for example, if most injuries do not result from poorly designed equipment, which is what many OSHA regulations seek to change.

[66]W. K. Viscusi, "The Impact of Occupational Safety and Health Regulation."

[67]That is, no safety effect is observed for some measures of risk.

[68]OSHA is also levying much heftier fines than in the past. In 1987 it fined Chrysler Corporation $1.57 million for violations, including exposure of workers to toxic chemicals, and has sought a $2.59 million fine against IBP Inc., the nation's largest meatpacking concern. IBP was charged with failure to report more than 1,000 job-related injuries and illnesses over two years.

[69]Both legally and ethically, the issue is not simply whether an employing company knew about asbestos risk, but whether it should have known, given the current state of scientific information.

a nuisance. It is apparent that the market provided asbestos workers with little or no protection from a critical health hazard—a clear-cut case of information-market failure that government regulation might have been able to remedy.

SUMMARY

In this chapter we have surveyed the arguments for government protection of consumers and workers, and looked at some protective programs and their effects. The justification for this type of public activity rests with the market failures discussed in Part I—most notably, information deficiencies that make sensible or rational choices difficult.

We have seen that although the argument for *some* public action may seem clear-cut, defining the most appropriate policies is no simple task. In the cases of consumer and worker protection, a good deal of controversy persists. This controversy traces to a situation that is, once again, typical of many areas of government intervention. The costs of protective policies are frequently substantial, and are highly visible, especially when they are concentrated in particular firms and industries. The benefits may also be substantial, yet at times less visible, either because they are more widely dispersed or because those who are protected from injury or illness may not be aware they are protected. When we add to this the observation that public protection programs may restrict choice (especially for consumers) and are sometimes viewed as an infringement on personal freedom, we should not be surprised at the vigor and persistence of controversy in this area.

CONCLUSION

Protection of consumers and workers is a well-established facet of public regulation in the United States. As we have seen, there are legitimate economic arguments for these types of intervention, but the nature of correct or optimal policies is often difficult to define.

Advocates of protective programs tend to focus on the failure of markets. Consumers and workers are seen as powerless actors, perhaps misinformed or uninformed about the risks they face. Critics of public protection, on the other hand, place greater faith in the market. They are more inclined to see consumers and workers as competent judges of their own interests and, correspondingly, to see less need for government intervention.

As the debate continues, we should not lose sight of the real achievements of consumer protection programs in the United States. Our state of information, health, and safety are unquestionably better today than they would have been had government stayed out of the arena. The costs of intervention are high, but net gains are almost certainly substantial.

The record of worker protection policies is less clear. In principle, it is easy to envision situations in which public protection is necessary and important. In practice, it is not obvious that actual protections have had much effect. The policies, however, are relatively new, and final judgments are at this point premature.

Discussion Questions

1. "If all markets were perfectly competitive, there would be no need for public protection of consumers or workers." Do you agree? Do you think most economists would agree? What about psychologists?

2. Consumer protection policies are sometimes divided into two categories: (1) provision of information, and (2) provision of safety. Are the economic rationales for these two types of policies similar or distinct?

3. It has been observed that wages tend to be relatively higher, *ceteris paribus*, in riskier occupations. Does this observation have any implication for public protection of workers?

4. Automobile fatality rates have declined markedly since passage of the National Traffic and Motor Vehicle Safety Act of 1966. Some investigators argue, however, that the act did not cause this reduction in fatalities. Is this a plausible argument? If the law was not (fully) responsible for the decline, what other factors might explain it?

5. Several senators and congressmen observed in the late 1970s that the largest and loudest protest they had seen against any government policy came in response to the FDA's proposed ban on saccharin. Surely, government rules about saccharin consumption are far from the most important item of public policy in the United States. Why was the public response to this issue so strong?

Selected Readings

Asch, Peter. *Consumer Safety Regulation: Putting a Price on Life and Limb.* New York: Oxford University Press, 1988. *A critical assessment of safety regulation issues.*

Nelson, P. "Advertising as Information," *Journal of Political Economy* 82 (July-August 1974). *An interesting discussion of how apparently uninformative advertising may send useful signals to consumers.*

Peltzman, S. "The Effects of Automobile Safety Regulation," *Journal of Political Economy* 83 (July-August 1975). *A controversial empirical study that concludes that auto safety requirements have been highly inefficient.*

Rosner, D. and G. Markowitz, eds. *Dying for Work: Workers' Safety in Twentieth Century America.* Bloomington, Ind.: Indiana University Press, 1987. *A collection of articles about worker health and safety in the United States.*

Simon, H. A. *Models of Man: Social and Rational.* New York: Wiley, 1957). *A classic discussion of rational and irrational behavior by a Nobel–Prize winning economist.*

Stigler, G. J. "The Economics of Information." *Journal of Political Economy* 69 (June 1961). *An important analysis of information as a commodity.*

Swann, D. *Competition and Consumer Protection.* Harmondsworth, England: Penguin, 1979. *A basic text that discusses market power and consumer welfare.*

Winter, R. K., Jr. *The Consumer Advocate versus the Consumer.* Washington, D.C.: American Enterprise Institute, 1972. *An argument that consumer advocates do not improve the well-being of most consumers.*

Viscusi, W. K. *Risk by Choice.* Cambridge, Mass.: Harvard University Press, 1983. *Analysis of the role of public policy in regulating health and safety risks.*

CHAPTER 22

· · · · · · · · · · · · · · · · ·

THE ENVIRONMENT

POLLUTION AND THE CASE FOR INTERVENTION

The broad case for government intervention to protect the environment was presented in Chapter 5 and bears only brief review at this point. Recall first that pollution—the accumulation of damaging substances in the environment—frequently implies an external cost. That is, the costs of harming the environment, while they are quite real, fall at least partially on individuals who have nothing directly to do with the pollution-creating activity. Parties to the activity may therefore lack strong incentives to consider these costs, which are external to them, and if so, will almost certainly act in socially inefficient ways.[1]

Our original example of such externalities concerned a chemical manufacturer that discharged sulfur dioxide (SO_2) into the air while producing chemicals. The SO_2 created various costs, such as aesthetic deterioration, the need to clean and repaint outdoor surfaces more frequently, and human health problems. The particular difficulty implied by this situation is not the existence of these costs *per se*, for virtually every activity is costly. Rather, the problem is that the pollution costs can be expected to fall partly, perhaps largely, on third parties—in this case, nearby residents who are not directly involved in the transactions of the chemical manufacturer.

Since these costs are external, both chemicals and the attendant SO_2 will tend to be overproduced as shown in Figure 22.1. Market demand is D, and supply is MPC, the marginal private cost of chemical production. When pollution costs are considered, however, the full marginal social costs of production are represented by MSC. More chemicals (and pollution)—at

---

[1]Individuals might decide to limit their polluting activities out of a sense of social responsibility, but there are few (if any) other incentives to do so. Unless we are willing to place great faith in social conscience, we cannot expect reasonable resolutions of the pollution problem in the absence of collective intervention. As we argued in Chapter 6, even if people wish to act responsibly, appropriate decisions may not be forthcoming.

Figure 22.1 Manufacture of Chemicals and Sulfur Dioxide:
The External Costs of Pollution

Market demand is D and MPC (marginal private costs) represents the market supply curve. A competitive market will therefore tend toward equilibrium price P_m and output Q_m. When external pollution costs created by sulfur dioxide are counted, the marginal social cost curve is MSC. Optimal or efficient output is thus Q^* (at price P^*), and it is clear that the competitive market overproduces both chemicals and pollution.

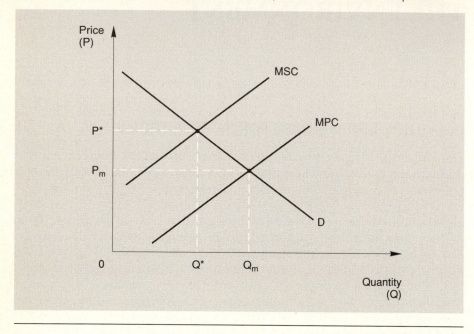

output Q_m—will be created than would have been the case if the full costs of the activity were taken into account, at output Q^*.

    This, in microcosm, is the pollution problem in economic terms: because some costs of polluting activities are not borne by those who engage in the activities, the unconstrained market tends to produce excessive pollution. Thus there exists, in principle, a clear-cut case for collective intervention to correct the inefficiency of overproduction.

    There is, furthermore, no real doubt about the quantitative importance of pollution problems. Pollution is inevitable, and its magnitude is linked closely to economic growth. The major air pollutants, discharged primarily by automobiles, industrial plants, and electric power generating plants that burn fossil fuels, are known to be associated with a wide variety of damage to environment, property, and human health.[2] Water pollutants, consisting mainly of organic wastes and chemicals discharged into lakes and streams, carry

---

[2]For a comprehensive evaluation of health effects, see L. B. Lave and E. P. Seskin, *Air Pollution and Human Health* (Baltimore: Johns Hopkins University Press, 1977).

broadly similar implications. Precise estimates of pollution costs are difficult to make, but those that have been attempted, usually under quite conservative procedures, are impressive.[3]

In addition, there is some suspicion that our estimates of pollution damage are seriously understated. Some potentially important costs—most notably human health damage and aesthetic deterioration—are extremely difficult to quantify. For this reason, investigators who take a cautious approach may ignore much of the true cost simply because it cannot be documented in a fully convincing way. By somewhat similar token, certain pollution effects involving health and the earth's climate may be very long term, thus not yet (fully) visible. These magnitudes are subject to precise estimation and may thus be understated.

Note that pollution is a problem that arises in severest form in the context of sustained economic growth. In a classic article, Robert U. Ayres and Allen V. Kneese traced the relationship between production and consumption activities and the generation of waste matter.[4] They pointed out that since "nature does not permit the destruction of matter, except by annihilation with antimatter," both production and consumption activities involve the transformation of matter from one form to another and its disposal into an environment whose assimilative capacity is ultimately fixed. As more and more is produced and consumed each year, the mass of waste products grows, mitigated only by efforts to recycle them back into the production system.

From their materials balance approach, Ayres and Kneese conclude that pollution is an economy-wide problem that cannot adequately be dealt with on a piecemeal basis.[5]

Policy Approaches

As we have frequently noted above, it is far easier to identify a need for collective—usually governmental—intervention in many areas than to specify what it is that should be done once the decision to intervene has been made.[6]

---

[3]In a report prepared for the Council on Environmental Quality (CEQ), A. Myrick Freeman, III estimates that the annual benefits of actual pollution abatement to date amount to $21.4 billion. See A. M. Freeman, "The Benefits of Air and Water Pollution Control: A Review and Synthesis of Recent Estimates," (Washington, D.C.: Council on Environmental Quality, December 1979).

[4]R. V. Ayres and A. V. Kneese, "Production, Consumption and Externalities," *American Economic Review* 59 (June 1969): 282–297.

[5]A second conclusion is that the cost of economic growth will always rise concomitantly with its benefits in the absence of substantial technological change to increase the amount of recycling. This is similar to the "limits to growth" argument of D. H. Meadows, et al., who predict that production and consumption at currently high rates will lead to the exhaustion of the earth's natural resources before the year 2100. The Meadows's argument is fundamentally flawed, however, for it ignores price responses to increasing resource scarcity. This failure is common to so-called doomsday models. See D. H. Meadows, et al., *The Limits to Growth* (New York: Universe Books, 1972).

[6]For a detailed discussion of policy instruments, see W. J. Baumol and W. E. Oates, *Economics, Environmental Policy, and the Quality of Life* (Englewood Cliffs, N.J.: Prentice-Hall, 1979), Chapter 15.

The case of environmental protection is no exception. The argument for some public regulation is very strong, and even the appropriate direction of the regulation is apparent. (Since pollution is overproduced, the correct policy will yield some reduction.) At this point, however, the pertinent questions become more difficult. By how much should various polluting activities be decreased? How should the costs of limiting pollution be distributed among the members of society?[7] What policy tools are most likely to achieve the desired results?

"Jawboning" or Moral Suasion   One way to reduce pollution is to convince those engaged in polluting activities to behave responsibly. So-called jawboning or moral suasion refers broadly to public efforts at such persuasion, attempts to elicit some (more or less voluntary) form of self-regulation.

Jawboning may go beyond simple appeals to social conscience. Government officials can create unfavorable publicity for polluting businesses. Environmental groups may similarly generate bad press, and might even suggest that consumers avoid the products of irresponsible polluters. An implicit threat often lurks behind such efforts: cut pollution yourself or we—that is, society—may take the decision out of your hands via more direct and stringent measures.

Moral suasion probably has beneficial effects at some times and in some places. It may prove particularly useful in short-term emergencies (for example, industrial plants will respond to a plea to curtail operations during a temperature inversion that creates dangerous air pollution levels). As a general approach, however, it is unlikely to provide an adequate solution to environmental problems. In the first place, the effect of appeals to social conscience or statesmanship—with or without veiled threats—is not readily predictable. Will people listen? How seriously will those listening take the message? The overall result cannot be known.

A second difficulty with jawboning is that it seldom can provide much specific guidance. The manager of the chemical plant may ardently desire to be a good citizen, but what does this mean? By how much should emissions be curtailed, and which ones? How heavy a cost must the company bear in order to transform itself from an irresponsible polluter to a corporate statesman? Jawboning is likely to leave the manager without a very clear idea.

Still further problems with this approach to environmental protection might be cited, but the point should already be clear. The main arguments for regulation through jawboning—emergencies aside—involve the speed and inexpensiveness of the policy. (It does not cost much for a public official to speak out against pollution.) Any results that it achieves may thus be close to a pure gain.

---

[7]This question raises an important point: protecting the environment will impose significant burdens on many people. The objective may be worthwhile, even noble, but its achievement is far from free.

Direct Regulation   Direct public control of pollution clearly has more teeth than moral suasion and is likely to imply more definite results.   This type of regulation takes two forms, both of which are employed in most industrialized nations.

1.   *Specification of Technology.*   The government agency responsible for environmental protection determines the acceptable equipment (and perhaps other inputs) to be used in potentially polluting activites. Individuals and organizations engaged in those activities are then required to employ the appropriate items, with provision for enforcement against violators.

2.   *Specification of Emission Levels and/or Ambient Standards.* The responsible agency mandates the maximum permissible amounts of pollution in various activities, but leaves open the means of compliance.   Again, provision for enforcement is necessary.

Despite the popularity of direct controls, they are characterized by significant, and to some extent unavoidable, shortcomings.   Specification either of technology or of emission levels presupposes that the specifying agency has a defined objective in mind, often an ambient quality standard.   The ultimate goal of environmental policies is not merely to employ particular kinds of technology, nor even to control the quantities of various pollutants that will be released into the environment.   Viewed broadly and in a classic economic context, the objective is to balance various costs and gains.

Figure 22.2 portrays the marginal social costs, MSC, and marginal social benefits, MSB, of a pollution abatement program.   Notice that MSB declines as the quantity of abatement rises.   The negative slope has a clear intuitive interpretation. Where the level of abatement is low—in other words, where we do not have much of a pollution-control program—pollution itself is likely to be relatively severe.   Reducing pollution may therefore be a matter of some urgency, which is simply to say that the marginal benefits of abatement are high.   Where there is already a large abatement program, however, pollution will be relatively mild, all else being equal.   Further reductions in pollution, although useful, are not likely to be so urgent; that is, the marginal benefits of abatement are still positive, but are now relatively low.   The declining MSB curve thus reflects a simple chain of reasoning: the more pollution abatement, the cleaner is the environment; but the cleaner the environment, the less pressing is the need to reduce pollution still further—that is, the smaller are the benefits of additional abatement.

Observe also that in Figure 22.2, MSC increases as the quantity of pollution abatement rises (much as the marginal costs of many activities increase with size).   The interpretation is again straightforward.   Where the level of abatement is low, there may be various, relatively easy ways to reduce pollution a bit.   For example, install some simple filtering equipment or extend the height of some existing smokestacks. If so, the marginal costs of abatement will be low. As abatement efforts expand, however, further reductions in pollution become more difficult to achieve.   The easy steps have already been taken, and

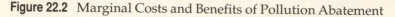

Figure 22.2 Marginal Costs and Benefits of Pollution Abatement

The marginal social benefits (MSB) of pollution abatement and the marginal social costs (MSC) of abatement define the optimal (efficient) quantity of abatement at Q*. More abatement would be too costly; less would sacrifice net benefits.

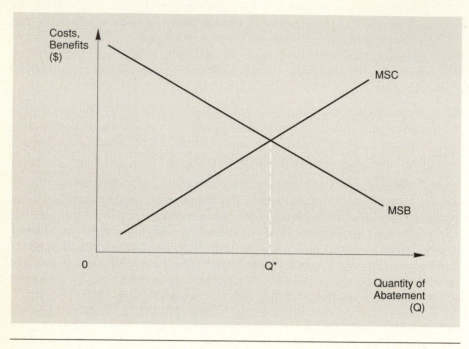

we may now be forced to turn to increasingly complex and costly methods of abatement. Marginal abatement costs have thus risen. Indeed, it may be that, beyond some point, it will become exceptionally difficult (or practically impossible) to achieve additional abatement. Many industrial activities cannot be run at a zero or near-zero pollution level without incurring enormous costs. If so, MSC will turn sharply upward and go off the map.

Applying the usual marginal criterion, the socially optimal size of a pollution abatement program is Q*. Beyond this level, additional gains fail to justify the extra costs of the effort. In a sense, then, the appropriate objective of pollution regulation is to reach Q*, that is, to secure that amount of abatement that equates society's costs and benefits at the margin.

We are simply observing that pollution abatement is a good that should be provided in allocatively efficient quantities. There is a complication, however. Virtually all pollution control programs are public goods; clean up the air or water for one individual and everyone enjoys the benefits. But, as we have seen in Chapter 5, the decision to supply any amount of a public good has such far-reaching equity implications that the notion of an optimally efficient quantity may not have a completely clear meaning.

Whether a regulatory agency setting technological or emissions standards can come close to the efficient point is doubtful, because it faces severe information problems. The agency must know, at least roughly, the costs of implementing alternative standards, the direct effects of the alternatives upon emissions, and the values that should be placed on the possible emissions reductions (these are the program benefits). The last type of information is typically very difficult to obtain. Reductions in SO_2 or carbon monoxide (CO)—unlike loaves of bread or lawn mowers—are not traded in markets and do not have observable prices. Without a tolerably accurate idea of what these program effects are worth, however, the regulatory body will have little basis upon which to formulate reasonable standards.

Information problems may, of course, hamper other policy approaches to pollution. Direct regulation, however, has further characteristics that may limit its usefulness. Technology or emissions standards are administratively appealing because they are relatively simple. Yet as Stephen Breyer puts it, the complex conditions surrounding environmental problems "spell disaster for simple, uniform" responses.[8] At the heart of the difficulty is the fact that the relationships between a given emission and resulting pollution (environmental damage) are both complicated and variable. A release of carbon monoxide, for example, has different implications in midtown Manhattan than in Neshanic Station, New Jersey. Its implications in either location are likely to depend upon such factors as weather and time of day. When we consider that there are vast numbers of pollutants and of pollution sources, each operating under different and variable conditions, it is necessary to ask whether any system of simple and uniform emissions standards can possibly prove adequate.

The opposite side of simplicity is rigidity. If a system of standards is made flexible, thus capable of responding to varied circumstances, its main administrative attraction—simplicity—is compromised. We can thus see quite clearly how some disagreements over pollution controls are likely to arise. On one side we may find administrators arguing for simple, uniform, enforceable rules.[9] On the other we see those (including many economists) concerned with end results, arguing that simple rules are unlikely to cope well with what is in effect a large family of complex problems.

Use of Incentives: Taxes, Subsidies, and Licenses to Pollute

What might be termed the economic approach to environmental regulation emerges in straightforward fashion from the analysis of external costs. Consider the example of a polluting chemical industry, as shown in Figure 22.3.

Manufacturers confront demand curve, D, and marginal private costs, MPC; market output is thus Q. We may be satisfied that market demand is a true measure of the marginal social benefits, MSB, of the chemicals produced,

---

[8]S. Breyer, *Regulation and Its Reform* (Cambridge, Mass.: Harvard University Press, 1982), 264.

[9]Even simple standards may prove difficult and expensive to enforce. Regulation of emissions, for example, requires effective monitoring (or at least a credible threat of monitoring) of a vast number of pollution sources, and legal action against violators.

Figure 22.3 A Pollution Tax to Resolve External Costs

D (=MSB) is market demand, MPC is the marginal private costs of producers, and MSC is marginal social costs (that is, private costs plus external pollution costs). The market produces output Q, which is greater than optimal (efficient) output Q*. (Notice that this is the same as Figure 22.1.) If tax T, equal to external cost EC, is imposed on manufacturers, their costs will now coincide with MSC, and they will respond by producing Q*. The tax thus resolves the pollution externality.

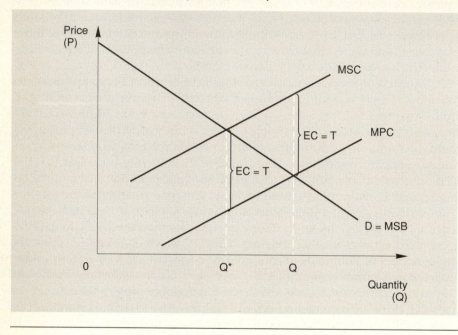

but because pollution is produced in conjunction with chemicals, MPC understates the social costs of supplying these products. True marginal social cost is shown by MSC and is assumed to exceed MPC by a constant amount, EC, at all output levels. The socially optimal output Q* would occur if the market could balance the full costs and benefits of its activities. The actual market result, however, shows us a now familiar picture: because costs are understated (by amount EC), chemicals are overproduced (by Q - Q*).[10]

The appropriate public policy is, in principle, quite obvious. If a tax, T, equal to external cost, EC, is levied on chemical production, the socially appropriate correction will automatically occur.[11] Producers must now add tax

[10]Observe that Figure 22.3 implicitly assumes a competitive market in chemicals. Were the market monopolistic, output would be restricted. The monopoly result in this case may be socially preferable to the competitive result, a point that we discuss in more detail below.

[11]In a similar vein, a tax might be levied on the pollution itself rather than the companies' chemical products. Such taxes, called effluent charges, should be based again on the external cost of the pollution. Effluent charges have the virtue of stimulating technological change to reduce pollution. Taxes directly on output, in contrast, may serve mainly to reduce the levels of affected outputs.

T to the other costs they incur in manufacturing each unit of their output. But because T is set equal to EC, the result is precisely as if the manufacturers were counting external costs in their production decisions. Market incentives, now modified by taxation, will lead us to the desired result, Q*.

This description raises an important point, the notion of an optimal level of pollution (or of any other costly spillover). Economists are sometimes regarded as a bit odd, if not downright silly, for thinking that there can be an optimal or efficient amount of pollution. After all, one might say, "Pollution is a bad thing—the 'optimal' amount of it is obviously none at all!" In a utopian world this might be so, but the analytical view is in this case more realistic. The pollution level implied by Q* in Figure 22.3 is optimal in the sense that any change would be too costly. Reducing pollution further would require sacrificing benefits (of chemical products) that are greater than the attendant cost savings implied by the lower pollution level. Allowing pollution to rise would mean increasing costs by a greater amount than the associated benefits of higher chemical output. When we speak of optimal pollution levels, then, we are not declaring our love for smoke or noxious odors. Rather, we are recognizing that to reduce pollution is itself a costly undertaking. Unfortunately, there is usually some point beyond which these costs become excessive.[12]

Recall from our discussion in Chapter 5 that externalities are two-sided, involving both a creator and a victim. If either party would merely leave the scene, the problem would disappear, yet this is unlikely to occur. The reason is obvious: to leave—that is, to move away—is costly. The problem is resolvable, but the solution is not free. Bear in mind also that externalities result from productive activities that the market would not support unless those activities had positive value. In our example, pollution is simply one component of the costs we incur in producing useful chemical products. The cost cannot be made to vanish by waving a wand or even by assigning blame to polluters (or victims). Rather, the task is to find appropriate ways to take this type of cost into account in our production and pricing decisions.

Policies of the pollution tax variety are in principle highly efficient. Measurement difficulties, however, may present important obstacles to the use of such tools. In Figure 22.3 we have effectively assumed that the external cost of producing chemicals is known (and is also constant at all output levels). Where we do not have full knowledge—because it is difficult to monitor emissions, because the effects of pollution are uncertain, or because known effects are difficult to translate into dollar costs—it may prove exceedingly difficult to devise the appropriate tax.

Consider, for example, the task of formulating an appropriate tax on the hydrocarbons emitted by automobiles. Ideally, we should charge each driver

---

[12]An obvious case in point is the air pollution created by running motor vehicles. Given our technology, today and in the foreseeable future, the only way to eliminate this pollution entirely is to stop all driving. Such a move would have benefits in the form of cleaner air, but the cost would be so enormous that not even the most dedicated environmentalist would suggest such a step.

and car its marginal external pollution cost, but the practical obstacles are likely to be insurmountable. Any given individual is likely to do some high cost driving (in center city during rush hours) and some low-cost driving (on empty roads late at night) during the course of, say, a one-month period. How can we possibly monitor this activity and send each driver the correct monthly bill—one reflecting the true cost of his polluting activity?[13] Realistically, we are likely to compromise by levying similar taxes on all drivers, perhaps with some variation according to engine size and amount of driving. (A gasoline tax, for example, will effectively penalize those who do a great deal of driving and those who drive large cars.)

Whereas such practical difficulties cannot be ignored, the virtues of a tax (or subsidy) approach to pollution control are quite evident. Such a system responds to the creation of external costs by assuring that the costs will be considered and balanced against accompanying gains. If the tax can be designed to reflect social costs, even approximately, an enormous network of emissions can be dealt with in relatively simple fashion, via the pricing system.[14] Polluting activity is permissible, but only where its previously neglected costs are borne by parties to the activity—in our examples, drivers and chemical manufacturers and their customers. The attractiveness of this scenario should be clear. By bringing home external pollution costs, the virtues of the marketplace—which we have examined in detail earlier—can be largely restored.

An alternative market-type approach to environmental protection that has received some attention and use involves the exchange of rights or licenses to pollute.[15] The idea is a simple one. The pollution regulatory agency determines maximum permissible emission/discharge levels for a defined geographic region and issues the corresponding volume of rights to emit. These licenses or permits may then be sold to the highest bidders. There may also be a secondary market in which the original purchasers can resell their licenses to others.

Such a system could produce somewhat different results than a tax/subsidy arrangement, but would retain basic efficiency virtues.[16] Those who could eliminate their polution easily—that is, cheaply—would do so in order to avoid the necessity of purchasing a license. The licenses would be bought

---

[13]This is merely a practical monitoring problem. We are ignoring for the moment the very formidable task of placing an accurate price tag on the pollution generated by each hour of driving.

[14]Taxation, like direct regulation, requires monitoring. It would not, however, depend upon the legal system to discover, prosecute, convict, and penalize violators.

[15]See T. H. Tietenberg, "The Design of Property Rights for Air Pollution Control," *Public Policy* 22 (Summer 1974): 275–292.

[16]Under taxation, one does not know precisely how much pollution we will wind up with, although the (maximum) cost to polluters is known. With licenses, the (maximum) pollution level is known, but not the cost to polluters (which depends upon license prices).

and held by those for whom pollution reductions are most difficult (costly).[17] Notice, however, that licensing requires the regulatory agency to set emission targets on a geographic basis (the relevant regions might be either large or small). Whereas this is a far more flexible procedure than setting standards for individual polluters, the possibility that poor targets will be chosen, with correspondingly poor results, cannot be ruled out.

WHAT IS DONE

Despite the economic arguments for retaining market incentives, public environmental policies in the United States rely largely on direct controls administered by the Environmental Protection Agency, an approach typical of many industrialized nations. As Seneca and Taussig describe the situation:

> Congress sets broad environmental objectives, often phrased in ambiguous language, and then instructs the EPA to develop and enforce any policies necessary to achieve the goals of the law.[18]

As recently as the 1960s, pollution was viewed in the United States as an essentially local problem. Today, however, the major controlling legislation operates via a federal agency (the EPA) that is required to consider differences in state and regional conditions in setting and implementing standards.

Air and Water Pollution

The Clean Air Act (CAA) amendments of 1970 establish national ambient air quality standards (NAAQSs) for six pollutants: suspended particulates (TSP), sulfur dioxide (SO_2), carbon monoxide (CO), hydrocarbons (HC), nitrogen oxides (NO_x), and photochemical oxidents (O_3). The standards exist at two levels: primary, defined as sufficient "to protect the public health" with "an adequate margin of safety," and secondary, defined as sufficient "to protect the public welfare from any known or anticipated adverse effects" of ambient air pollution.

The law required each state to submit an implementation plan (SIP) that would at least meet the primary national standards by July 1975 and the

---

[17]Underlying the virtue of such an outcome is an important principle of equalizing marginal costs among pollution-abating firms. Suppose that our policy objective is a specified reduction in total emissions within some geographic region, but that the emitting companies in that area encounter widely varying abatement costs. The most efficient way to achieve the desired reduction is to have it undertaken by those who can do it most cheaply, a procedure that will tend to equalize the abatement costs of the companies at the margin. This is an essential principle of cost minimization that we observe in a variety of economic problems. Thus, for the marginal license buyer, the cost of the license would be just less than the cost of eliminating pollution, and these costs would be equated across all buyers. The licenses might also be bought by conservation groups who would simply hold them, simultaneously preventing other firms from buying them (and subsequently polluting) and bidding up the price (thus raising the cost to other firms of polluting activity). Some margin for growth in productive activity would also have to be allowed for, implying an increase in the number of available licenses over time.

[18]J. J. Seneca and M. K. Taussig, *Environmental Economics*, 3d ed. (Englewood Cliffs, N.J.: Prentice-Hall, 1984): 195.

secondary standards by July 1977. These plans were to be submitted to the EPA for approval, or for promulgation of new plans where the state proposals were unacceptable. (Later amendments to the CAA in 1977 extended the earlier legislation and adopted new measures, including some relaxation and postponement of standards, in order to deal with noncompliance.) The 1970 amendments further authorized the EPA to set emissions standards for moving pollution sources (primarily motor vehicles), new stationary sources, and specified hazardous pollutants such as asbestos and vinyl chloride.

The amendments also introduced requirements, called offsets, under which any firm generating new emissions (or the state in which the firm produces) must reduce emissions from other sources in the area by an equivalent amount, so that the total emission level of the pollutant remains the same. The Clean Air Act is subject to periodic re-authorization by Congress; continuing changes are therefore likely.

The Federal Water Pollution Control Act (FWPCA) of 1972 states a remarkable objective: the elimination of all discharges of pollutants into navigable waters by the year 1985.[19] The primary mechanism of the act is technologically based standards. The best practicable control technology (BPT) was required to be in use by 1977, and the best available technology (BAT) by 1983. The 1983 standards were to achieve, where possible, the interim objective of "water quality which provides for the protection and propagation of fish, shellfish, and wildlife and provides for recreation in and on the water . . . ." The FWPCA gives the EPA initial authority to regulate the activities of dischargers (by permit), with states taking over this responsibility as the dischargers comply with water quality standards. Unsurprisingly, in view of these ambitious goals, widespread noncompliance was observed by 1977 and resulted in further amendments to the law that modify and extend some of the 1983 requirements.[20]

Whether our approach to pollution control has been successful is a difficult question to answer. Trends in nationwide emissions showed some strong improvements in the 1970s and 1980s, as seen in Table 22.1 (notice especially particulates and carbon monoxide). The Council on Environmental Quality has further reported that national ambient standards for SO_2, TSP (suspended particulates) and NO_2 have been met "almost everywhere in the nation." Surveys of standard metropolitan statistical areas (SMSAs) show declines in the frequency of high-pollution days in many (although not all) areas.[21]

---

[19]As A. M. Freeman, III observes, however, "none of the major implementation provisions of the act is designed specifically to achieve this goal." A. M. Freeman III, "Air and Water Pollution Policy," in P. R. Portney, ed., *Current Issues in U.S. Environmental Policy* (Baltimore: Johns Hopkins University Press for Resources for the Future, Inc., 1978), 16.

[20]Numerous reasons for noncompliance with both air and water quality standards may be cited. Most refer to what Freeman terms the complexities and sheer enormity of the tasks enumerated by the laws.

[21]*Environmental Quality 1984*, Fifteenth Annual Report of the CEQ, (1984).

Table 22.1 National Emissions Estimates, 1970–1983
(millions of metric tons per year)

Year	Particulates	Sulfur Oxides	Nitrogen Oxides	Carbon Monoxide
1970	18.0	28.2	18.1	98.3
1971	16.7	26.8	18.5	96.3
1972	15.0	27.4	19.7	93.8
1973	13.9	28.7	20.2	89.5
1974	12.2	27.0	19.6	84.6
1975	10.3	25.6	19.1	80.5
1976	9.6	26.2	20.3	85.3
1977	9.0	26.3	20.9	81.1
1978	8.9	24.5	21.0	80.6
1979	8.8	24.5	21.1	77.4
1980	8.3	23.2	20.3	75.0
1981	7.7	22.3	20.5	72.3
1982	6.8	21.3	19.6	66.1
1983	6.9	20.8	19.4	67.6
1983 level as percentage of 1970 level:	38.3%	73.8%	107.2%	68.8%

Source: *Environmental Quality 1984*, Fifteenth Annual Report (Washington, D.C.: Council on Environmental Quality, 1984), p. 586.

The picture, however, is not entirely favorable. Certain kinds of atmospheric pollution appear to be worsening. Although water pollution control legislation has had an impact, recent examinations suggest that the severity and pervasiveness of groundwater contamination is a more serious problem than was previously believed. There is also suspicion that even some environmental gains that we have enjoyed to date may have more to do with reversible economic trends than with regulatory policies.[22]

Vinyl Chloride Standards: A Brief Case Study

Our experience with air pollution standards for vinyl chloride illustrates some of the most fundamental dilemmas facing public officials. Vinyl chloride is a chemical gas used primarily to produce a wide range of plastics products—everything from flooring to wire insulation. It is regarded as a carcinogen (or cancer-causing substance). In 1976, the EPA promulgated standards for vinyl chloride that user industries were required to meet. The agency took account of compliance costs in formulating these standards.

Some environmental groups challenged the standards as too weak, and in June 1977 the EPA (under the Carter administration) issued tighter proposed rules. The tighter standards never took effect, however, and in 1985 (now

---

[22]The decline in sulfur dioxide, for example, may well be due to the substitution of oil and natural gas for coal during the 1960s and 1970s, a trend that is now likely to reverse because of changing energy price structures.

under the Reagan administration), the EPA withdrew them and returned to the more lenient 1976 provisions. The Natural Resources Defense Council sued, arguing that the Clean Air Act requires the EPA to consider *only* the health effects of its actions. The agency's consideration of compliance costs was, according to the council, illegal.

In 1986 a panel of the Washington, D.C. federal appeals court held that the EPA had the discretion to choose the more lenient standards. The relevant provision of the Clean Air Act, said the panel, was ambiguous. Under the circumstances, the agency's consideration of the costs of its standards was reasonable. Eight months later, the full appeals court reversed its panel, stating: "The determination [of an air pollution standard] must be based solely upon the risk to health." The issue was remanded to the agency for reconsideration.

Regardless of its ultimate resolution, the issue posed by the vinyl chloride standards is as basic as one can imagine. Should pollution (or other policy) choices reflect some weighing of costs and benefits, as the EPA had attempted initially? Or should the agency pursue safety regardless of cost—in effect aiming for zero risk?[23] (Virtually identical issues arising in areas such as consumer and worker protection have been discussed in Chapter 21.)

Hazardous Substances

The environmental significance of hazardous and toxic substances has received wide attention only during the last few years. Certain chemicals, heavy metals, and minerals are now released into the environment in rapidly increasing quantities—largely as the waste products of industrial activities. They may pose extremely serious health risks, yet confident estimation of those risks is often difficult or impossible. The pertinent policy issues are distinctive from those posed by air and water pollution, although there is some overlap.[24]

Superfund I and II The hazardous substances problem relates in significant part to waste disposal. In 1980 Congress responded to a perceived crisis by creating the so-called Superfund.[25] This was a trust fund providing up to $1.6 billion over 5 years for emergency and long-term cleanup of chemical spills and abandoned waste dump sites. Motivated by a desire to resolve a major part of the hazardous substances problem, Superfund has been marked by a discouraging array of difficulties.

Courts have criticized the law (CERCLA) as a hastily drawn and vague statute that forces the judiciary to guess at what Congress may have intended.[26]

---

[23]Scientists are generally agreed that there is no completely safe level of exposure to carcinogens— or at least that such levels cannot be defined. If so, then the search for safety can be satisfied only by an environment in which the carcinogen is completely absent, posing zero exposure risk.

[24]For example, a poorly designed toxic waste dump may result in groundwater contamination.

[25]The Comprehensive Environmental Response, Compensation and Liability Act of 1980, commonly referred to as CERCLA.

[26]*U.S. v. Northeastern Pharmaceutical and Chemical Co.*, WDMo., January 31, 1984, No. 80–5066–CV.

Scientific uncertainty about the risks posed by waste sites is, as noted, an important problem. The EPA, which was responsible for administering Superfund, estimated that between 1,200 and 2,000 (of some 30,000 to 50,000) hazardous waste sites in the United States posed significant risks to health. But the agency, under the Reagan administration, apparently had little enthusiasm for cleanup efforts.[27] By mid-1987 only 13 official cleanups had been completed. Recently, the Conservation Foundation has observed:

> After eight years and $1.5 billion, the Superfund program . . . has yielded disappointing results. Distressingly little is known about how many toxic waste sites there are and how serious a risk each poses. No one has yet satisfactorily determined the standards to which sites should be cleaned . . . . Too few scientifically and legally defensible standards exist for troublesome chemicals.[28]

In 1986 Congress enacted Superfund II, providing a huge increase in funds ($8.5 billion over 5 years) for the EPA and other agencies to expand cleanup activities.[29] The effects of this program will not be visible for some time. In light of recent history, however, there is a question whether the EPA has the capacity to administer an effort of the size.

A Policy Perspective

Have we done enough to protect the environment? The long-term effects of many types of pollution remain mostly unknown. Whether we have come anywhere near an optimal result—such as Q^* in Figure 22.1—is thus uncertain and debate persists. Optimists may contend that we have indeed done enough, perhaps even too much.

By 1980, the nation was spending close to $40 billion to comply with federal environmental regulations. (Real expenditures, however, declined under the Reagan administrations.) Substantial indirect costs may also exist. It has been suggested, for example, that pollution-control efforts have contributed to a decline in national productivity during the past decade.[30] If, in fact, increased environmental quality would yield sharply diminishing marginal gains, we may already have reached or surpassed an optimal level of abatement. There is, however, a very significant qualification to the argument that environmental policies hamper productivity. Conventional productivity measures at the national level, most notably gross national product (GNP), are not truly comprehensive. While counting marketed goods and services, they tend to ignore precisely those quality-of-life elements that comprise the outputs of environmental protection programs. Clean air, for example, is not traded in

---

[27]The EPA administrator, Anne M. Burford, and some of her associates were forced to leave office in part because of their perceived failures in this program.

[28]*Conservation Foundation Letter*, 5 (1987): 3.

[29]Superfund Amendments and Reauthorization Act of 1986.

[30]See for example R. W. Crandall, "Pollution Controls and Productivity Growth in Basic Industries," in T. Cowing and R. Stevenson, eds., *Productivity Measurement in Regulated Industries* (New York: Academic Press, 1981): 347–368.

explicit markets. Governmental efforts that yield more clean air thus tend to be seriously undervalued in our usual productivity estimates.

Pessimists frequently point out that the uncertainties of pollution effects, especially over very long periods, embrace some potentially horrifying possibilities. Should any of the worst-case scenarios come to pass, the kinds of improvements that we have achieved to date—essentially incremental in nature—will prove wholly inadequate. A distinction is now made between conventional pollutants such as sulfur dioxide or particulate and organic waste, and hazardous wastes such as PCB's, hydrocarbon pesticides, heavy metals, and radioactive waste. It has been discovered that hazardous wastes have often been improperly disposed of over a number of years, and the resulting effects on human health and life expectancy may prove to be far more severe than previously recognized. Indeed, our entire approach to environmental protection could be viewed at some future time as misguided. Whatever their virtues, our laws and administrative arrangements have stimulated few major breakthroughs in the technology of pollution control.

The Fairness of Policy

Environmental protection policies consume substantial resources. Both the burden of program costs (which are borne privately as well as publicly) and the enjoyment of attendant gains are distributed in a nonobvious fashion. Whether the policies are equitable is therefore a question that requires at least some examination of these distributions.

Distribution of Program Costs   The real cost of environmental protection is a sacrifice of resources. To reduce the polluting propensity of an activity, we must employ productive inputs that could be doing other valuable jobs. Whereas we wish to minimize these costs, we cannot escape them. The relevant question is: Who will pay?

Public Costs   To the extent that the costs of pollution control are paid publicly—for example, through the budgets of federal and state regulatory agencies, and municipal waste treatment programs—they fall ultimately upon taxpayers. The distribution of this portion of the cost burden can thus be inferred from the distribution of the tax burden, assuming that the financing of pollution control expenditures does not alter previously existing tax structures in a substantial way.

The distribution of the tax burden (or tax incidence), however, is not known with certainty or precision. Pechman and Okner, for example, have concluded that "the tax system is virtually proportional for the vast majority of families in the United States."[31] This would mean that families in various income classes in most instances pay about the same proportion of their

---

[31]J. A. Pechman and B. A. Okner, *Who Bears the Tax Burden?* (Washington, D.C.: Brookings Institution, 1974): 64.

income in taxes. Browning and Johnson, however, disagree, finding that the tax system is strongly progressive—that is, that higher income families tend to pay a larger proportion of their incomes in taxes.[32]

Private Costs   The private costs of pollution control may be conveniently divided into two categories: those related to automobiles and those related to all other industrial compliance activities. (Only minor private costs to date have been borne by individuals outside the business sector of the economy.) The estimation problems within both categories are subtle and cannot be resolved with certainty.

The initial effect of compliance is to increase production costs. To meet the requirements, either a plant must operate differently than it otherwise would (for example, by treating its wastes before discharging them into a river), or (as in the case of automobiles) the product itself must be altered before it is sold.

In both instances, we would expect the profits of affected companies to decline, but the pattern (or incidence) of the final burden is far from obvious. Certain companies and industries will be far more heavily affected than others. Chemical manufacturers feel more serious effects from environmental laws than do barbers. Companies that bear heavy compliance costs will inevitably differ in their ability to pass on such burdens to their customers (and perhaps to their employees). The customer (and employee) populations themselves will likely have widely varying economic characteristics across industries.

All these considerations complicate efforts to define the distribution of privately paid pollution-control costs. In attempting to characterize the distributions, we are likely to be forced into a number of assumptions that will in turn bear heavily upon the conclusions we reach.

The most carefully developed conclusion to date, drawn from still-fragmentary evidence by Dorfman and Snow, is that pollution-control costs are distributed regressively—so as to take a larger percentage of income from low-income families.[33] Such findings must be regarded as tentative, however. In addition, there is very likely a large random element in the distribution that is not visible in the gross relationship between average family income and average pollution cost. For example, families with an annual income of $12,000 may on average pay a larger proportion of their incomes for pollution control than do families at the $30,000 level. Yet among families earning $12,000 and

---

[32]E. K. Browning and W. R. Johnson, *The Distribution of the Tax Burden* (Washington, D.C.: American Enterprise Institute, 1979). Although this study is more recent than that of Pechman and Okner, the difference in conclusions does not hinge mainly on changes in the tax structure. Rather, the discrepancy appears to lie in a difference in assumptions, especially with regard to the burden of indirect business taxes. It is not clear that the tax reductions of the early and middle 1980s will have a well-defined impact on tax burden patterns. Moreover, the tax reforms of 1986 will certainly change the previous distributions.

[33]N. S. Dorfman, assisted by A. Snow, "Who Will Pay for Pollution Control? The Distribution by Income of the Burden of the National Environmental Protection Program, 1972–1980," *National Tax Journal* 28 (March 1975): 101–115.

among those earning $30,000, there is likely to be a great deal of variation in this cost, depending upon factors such as where each family lives. Neither regressivity nor randomness argues strongly for an equitable distribution of program costs.

Distribution of Program Benefits   Estimating the distribution of program benefits poses even more severe problems than those encountered on the cost side. The benefits of pollution control consist of reductions in pollution damages that would not have occurred in the absence of an abatement program. Estimation therefore requires some knowledge of (a) the magnitude of damage associated with various kinds of pollution, and (b) who would have suffered the various ill effects. Quite obviously, we are again dealing with some highly uncertain values, and the available evidence is thus scanty.

The most ambitious studies to date are those of Gianessi, Peskin, and Wolff, who have found that the per capita monetary costs of pollution increase with income—and therefore that pollution reductions will confer larger benefits (on average) upon higher income families.[34] These investigators have examined a wide variety of standard metropolitan statistical areas (SMSAs), and their results thus have relevance at a national level. They have also observed large geographic variations in pollution damage. This suggests that how much a particular family suffers from pollution—or benefits from its reduction—may depend largely upon where it lives once its income level is taken into account.

Some other, more narrowly drawn, studies suggest a rather different picture than that presented by Gianessi, Peskin, and Wolff. There is some evidence, for example, that within urban areas, poor families tend to be concentrated in neighborhoods with the worst air quality.[35] This suggests that pollution abatement programs in these areas will have progressive effects in the sense that low-income groups will receive the major benefits. Findings with respect to water pollution are thus far fragmentary and rather equivocal.[36]

Assessment of Fairness   Whether our environmental protection programs operate fairly, is not a readily answerable question. One may suspect on the basis of available evidence that low-income families bear the major burden of program costs, but also enjoy a disproportionate share of the benefits. The evidence, however, is only suggestive. The true incidence picture could turn out to be very different from what we have seen to date. It must also be noted—yet

---

[34]L. P. Gianessi, H. M. Peskin, and E. Wolff, "The Distributional Implications of National Air Pollution Damage Estimates," in F. T. Juster, ed., *The Distribution of Economic Well-Being* (Cambridge, Mass.: Ballinger Publishing Company for the National Bureau of Economic Research, 1977).

[35]J. M. Zupan, *The Distribution of Air Quality in the New York Region* (Washington, D.C.: Resources for the Future, 1973). P. Asch and J. J. Seneca, "Some Evidence on the Distribution of Air Quality," *Land Economics* 54 (August 1978): 278–297.

[36]See P. Asch and J. J. Seneca, "The Incidence of Water Quality: A County Level Analysis," *Water Resources Research* 16 (April 1980): 319–324.

again—that fairness is a subjective notion. Even if we knew without doubt the distributions of benefit and cost, there might be no consensus (and surely would be no unanimity) about the desirability of the result.

THE POLLUTING MONOPOLIST: A SECOND-BEST QUIRK

There is a peculiar relationship between monopoly and external costs such as pollution that bears attention at this point, if only to illustrate the complexity of formulating optimal economic policies. Recall from earlier discussion (especially Chapter 3) that the allocative distortion of monopoly occurs via output restriction. The monopolist produces too little in that additional output would be more highly valued than its resource (or supply) cost.

As we have just seen, however, the welfare problem posed by external costs is one of overproduction. A competitive market, which ordinarily would produce the socially correct or efficient quantity of a product, will tend to produce too much in the presence of an externality such as pollution.

Consider the intuitive implication for an industry that is monopolistic and also creates an external cost. The monopoly tendency is to hold output beneath the optimal level, while the tendency generated by the external cost is to push output above the optimal level. Conceivably, then, these effects might cancel out, and the monopolist might behave in a socially optimal fashion! Although this result is improbable, the issue raised by the simultaneous presence of monopoly and an external cost is an important one.

Figure 22.4 illustrates the situation. The monopolist confronts demand curve, D, and marginal revenue, MR. MPC is the marginal private cost of supplying the product in this industry, and MSC is the marginal social cost. The difference between MPC and MSC is (by assumption) the cost of pollution. Optimal output is q^*, occurring at the intersection of D and MSC. (This is the old rule once again: producing to the point at which social costs and benefits are equated at the margin maximizes social welfare in an allocative sense.)

The unconstrained monopolist, producing to the point at which MPC = MR, will provide output q_m, too little from a social standpoint. This is the usual monopoly result.

Consider now a public policy to correct the external cost, specifically a tax of T on each unit of the monopolist's output. With tax T added onto his other costs of production, the monopolist's effective marginal cost becomes MSC—that is, MSC = MPC + T. Recall that this is precisely the purpose of a pollution tax: to force the monopolist to take account of the externality in his production and pricing decisions. The monopolist, still seeking the highest possible profit, will now produce where MSC = MR, output level q'_m. The effect is graphically clear: q'_m is not only a suboptimal output, but represents a worse result than the monopolist's original output, q_m! The corrective public policy has caused a deterioration in allocative welfare.

By similar token, consider what will happen if a different corrective policy is pursued: removal of the monopoly and substitution of a competitive industry. Output will now rise to q_c which, because of the external pollution costs, is too large (that is, above q^*). Not only is q_c too large, it is an allocatively

Figure 22.4 A Polluting Monopolist

Market demand is D (the associated marginal revenue is MR), MPC is marginal private costs and MSC is marginal social costs. Optimal or efficient output is q*. An unregulated monopolist will produce q_m, slightly below the efficient level. If antitrust policy is used to make the market competitive, output will rise to q_c, a worse result than q_m. Similarly, if the monopolist is taxed by amount T (equal to the external cost of its pollution), output will fall to q'_m—again worse than q_m. Only if *both* policies—antitrust and a pollution tax—are invoked will the efficient result occur.

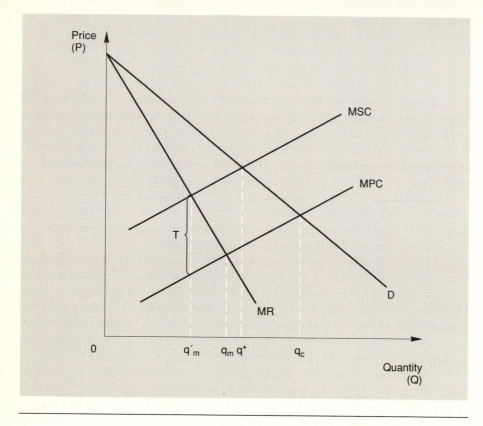

worse result than the one produced previously by the monopolist (q_c lies further from q* than does q_m). Once again, a corrective public policy reduces welfare.

What is happening in this case is not really very complicated. The effects of monopoly and external cost, working in opposite directions, do tend to cancel each other out, albeit imperfectly. In our example of Figure 22.4 the unregulated monopolist produces too little, although its output does not look very far from the optimum. When we impose a pollution tax on the monopolist, it responds precisely as we should expect, by producing less. Thus an existing condition of underproduction is worsened by the tax. Conversely, if we make the market competitive, output increases too far because of the external pollution cost. This policy moves in the right direction but overshoots the mark. In a sense, the monopolist had solved part of the pollution problem for us by holding output down.[37]

Complications created by the simultaneous presence of monopoly power and external cost are of practical importance. These conditions coexist in a number of important manufacturing industries, for example, some chemical products and some of the basic metals. The policy implications are fundamental and can be generalized from our very specific example.

1. Where two efficiency-distorting elements coexist (here monopoly and an external cost), correction of both elements will restore optimal efficiency. (If, in Figure 22.4, tax T is levied and the market is made competitive, q^* will result.)

2. If, on the other hand, both corrective policies are not undertaken, it is no longer clear that either policy alone will improve welfare. In our example, either a corrective environmental policy or a corrective antitrust-type policy, taken alone, will reduce welfare. (In different scenarios, of course, this might not be the case.)

3. The equity implications of the policy alternatives (do nothing, correct the externality only, correct the monopoly only, correct both) are likely to differ profoundly.

The broad lesson is quite obvious, although it may not be especially appealing to officials of the EPA or the Antitrust Division. The desirability of a policy pursued by one agency may well depend upon what is being done by the other. This is a classic problem in the theory of second best (discussed in Chapter 3) and suggests that the two agencies must coordinate their actions if they hope to achieve a socially efficient result.

SUMMARY

In this chapter we have reviewed the theory and practice of public environmental policies. Various approaches to policy—from informal jawboning to elaborate incentives schemes—are possible. Economists often favor the latter, but our actual policies follow mainly a direct regulation approach. To date, efforts to improve the environment have resulted in some notable pollution reductions. Whether these are an adequate response to current environmental hazards—and whether the effort has been made in a fair way—are questions to which clear answers cannot yet be formulated.

The central observation of this chapter is both apparent and important: economic analysis in the area of environmental protection suggests clearly the

---

[37]Figure 22.4 illustrates only one of many possible cases involving monopoly and external cost. For an exploration of some alternatives, see P. Asch and J. J. Seneca, "Monopoly and External Costs: An Application of Second-Best Theory to the Automobile Industry," *Journal of Environmental Economics and Management* 3 (1976): 69–79.

general direction in which we should move, but practical policy choices must be made under the handicap of enormous uncertainty.

CONCLUSION

The case for government intervention to protect against excessive pollution is, as we have seen repeatedly, quite clear. Precisely what, or how much, should be done is as usual less obvious. Whether our environmental policies to date have been successful is a question subject to debate.

One important point should be borne in mind when assessments of our pollution-control efforts are made. These programs are indeed costly. They not only consume public resources and place compliance burdens on affected industries, but they result ultimately in price increases and output decreases for a rather broad range of goods. Yet this apparently unhappy result is precisely what one should expect and desire from environmental protection programs. That we pay more for our automobiles and home heating as the result of pollution rules may not be cause for rejoicing, but it is not the rules that created these additional costs. The costs are inherent in polluting activities. The higher prices represent only an attempt to take account of such costs in a rational way.

Discussion Questions

1.   "It is all very well for economists to argue in favor of policy tools such as taxes and effluent charges in environmental protection programs. The practical difficulty, however, is that marginal benefit curves cannot be precisely estimated in the vast majority of cases. When this is so, the notion of an appropriate tax on pollution or emissions is a nice-sounding but practically useless one." Explain your agreement or disagreement.

2.   "We should treat pollution just as we treat most other socially obnoxious activities: prohibit it." Do you agree? Do we as a rule prohibit socially obnoxious activities?

3.   "Environmental pollution is a regrettable but unavoidable aspect of modern industrialization. Fortunately, however, a good deal of polluting activity occurs in industries characterized by some monopoly power." Is this statement logical? Is it factually accurate?

4.   It has been observed that political support for environmental protection programs is strongest among high-income families. Is this surprising? What do you believe to be the most plausible explanation of such a relationship?

Selected Readings

Baumol, W. J. and W. E. Oates. *Economics, Environmental Policy, and the Quality of Life.* Englewood Cliffs, N.J.: Prentice-Hall, 1979. *Lucid analysis and assessment of environmental protection policies.*

Burrows, P. *The Economic Theory of Pollution Control.* London: Martin Robinson, 1979. *Useful analysis of the case for collective action; some discussion of British policies.*

Dorfman, R. and N. S. Dorfman, eds. *Economics of the Environment.* New York: W. W. Norton, 1977. *Broad-gauged readings covering theory, policy, and policy impact.*

Lave, L. B. and E. Seskin. *Air Pollution and Human Health.* Baltimore: Johns Hopkins University Press, 1977. *Detailed study of how air pollution affects human health; an instructive guide to measurement technique.*

Peskin, H. M., P. R. Portney, and A. V. Kneese, eds. *Environmental Regulation and the U.S. Economy.* Baltimore: Johns Hopkins University Press for Resources for the Future, 1981. *A collection of papers examining U. S. environmental regulations and their effects.*

Seneca, J. J. and M. K. Taussig. *Environmental Economics,* 3d ed. Englewood Cliffs, N.J.: Prentice-Hall, 1984. *Wide-ranging discussion of environmental problems and economic approaches to policy.*

CHAPTER 23

. . . .

WHERE WE STAND

Has government intervention in the marketplace worked well? Some final, if not totally confident, assessments are now in order.

THE THEORY AND PRACTICE OF GOVERNMENT INTERVENTION

One possibility, noted early in our discussions, is that the theory of government intervention does not correspond closely to our actual practices. Is this frequently the case?

Theory: Intervene When the Market Fails

As we have pointed out, the virtues of the unregulated marketplace are both real and important. The market permits individual preferences about economic choices to be expressed, albeit imperfectly in most instances. By so doing, it performs a task of staggering complexity: deciding the kinds and amounts of resources that are devoted to literally millions of activities. To have this job done in an alternative way—say by government agencies—will at the very least prove cumbersome and expensive, even if the agencies make tolerably good decisions.

For this reason alone, it is sensible to require a rationale for government intervention in private market choices. And as we have seen repeatedly, economic arguments for intervention are related to a variety of market failures—instances in which the expected virtues of market choice are lacking. Monopoly, the existence of public goods and serious externalities, and inadequacies of information are the most prominent of these failures.

503

Practice: Intervention beyond Market Failure?

A frequent complaint in the United States is that government gets into the act where it has no business doing so; or, in our terms, that collective intervention occurs where no clear market failure has been demonstrated. Is this complaint on target?

Our answer, based on the extensive discussions above, is: not very often. Reasonable people may disagree, and government intervention is not always successful. But in most cases there exists some plausible rationale for the regulatory effort. In the case of antitrust policy, the rationale is monopoly power. Old-style public utility regulation rests in significant part on natural monopoly arguments, although as we have seen, the existence of natural monopoly often turns out to be quite difficult to establish. What we term new-wave regulation is in substantial part related to public goods, externalities, and information market failure.

This is not to say that the arguments advanced to support specific government programs are always convincing. In some instances, they are not. Generally, however, the arguments for intervention deserve serious attention.

Equity versus Efficiency

If serious arguments for most government intervention exist, it does not necessarily follow that the *type* of intervention that takes place is sensible. It appears that there is often a discrepancy between the market failure that stimulates government action and the type of action that is taken. This discrepancy commonly harks back to the equity–efficiency distinction that we have touched on at many points throughout.

Market failures as a rule imply inefficiencies, circumstances under which the expected efficient properties of the market do not surface. We see quite frequently, however, that policies adopted in response to such difficulties attempt not so much to improve efficiency as to enhance equity or fairness. Some do not appear to improve either efficiency or fairness.

1. We adopt antitrust laws ostensibly in order to improve the competitive functioning of markets. Among these laws is the Robinson-Patman Act, a price discrimination statute that, as interpreted, seeks to protect small business even where it may be inefficient (and anticompetitive) to do so.

2. We have introduced product safety laws that allow relatively safe products such as saccharin to be banned (at least temporarily), while permitting the sale of riskier products such as cyclamates and cigarettes.

3. We *deregulate* markets such as airlines and long-distance telephone communication on the ground that old efficiency arguments for regulation are now obsolete. There follow widespread complaints that deregulation—that is, the private market itself—will impose unfair burdens on such groups as airline employees and people who enjoy low-priced

telephone service. (Many of the latter group were subsidized under the previous regulatory scheme.)

4.   Regulation reform in the pricing of electricity has often been directed at keeping prices low for low-income groups rather than establishing an efficient allocation of resources in the industry.

There is of course nothing wrong with a desire to treat people, especially the disadvantaged, fairly (although we may have some trouble agreeing on a definition of the term or about how much we are willing to sacrifice in the name of fairness). But efforts to improve equity tend *not* to be sensible responses to problems of market inefficiency. Indeed, economists argue quite logically—though often not too successfully—that the two issues ought to be separated wherever possible. Do we wish to help the poor? Of course! (At least we do, and we hope you do.) But it is neither necessary nor useful to dismantle market pricing mechanisms in order to do so.

HAS REGULATION WORKED?

This is what used to be called the $64 (and later the $64,000) question. After decades of inflation, it probably should be called the million-dollar question. There is no simple answer.

Antitrust

The stated purpose of antitrust policies is to protect and enhance a competitive market system. As we have seen, the effects of this effort on the economy are exceptionally difficult to quantify. We cannot know precisely what the competitive state of our markets would have been had we followed a different policy course.

There is some real basis for the optimism that is frequently expressed by public officials. The antitrust laws as enforced by the Department of Justice and the Federal Trade Commission, and as interpreted by the courts, have placed serious obstacles in the path of overt collusion. Further, they have barred some corporate mergers that could well have reduced the competitive vigor of certain industries. These results alone may have produced important competitive gains for the economy.

As we have been at pains to suggest, however, the picture is not one of unalloyed victory for the forces of competition. Antitrust policies have been used in some instances to prohibit business policies that, in all likelihood, would have done little or no competitive harm. Upon occasion—price discrimination remains the prime case in point—policies have been pursued perversely, striking down activities that were the very evidence of healthy competition.

On balance, we suspect that policy gains outweigh losses, perhaps by a wide margin. The proposition, however, is not readily demonstrable in a precise or objective way.

Old-Style Regulation

Of all the economic activities pursued by government, regulation of public utilities is at first sight one of the least controversial. After all, such regulation dates back to preindustrial times in Europe and was instituted in the early stages of such important industries as transportation, electricity, and communications in the United States. Moreover, while the natural monopoly rationale for government regulation has been theoretically refined, it has never been seriously questioned.

However, it has become harder to identify natural monopolies since new technologies have broadened the scope of many industries. The question of which industries should be subject to utility-type regulation has become increasingly a matter of political controversy. Decisions to regulate trucking in the 1930s and then to deregulate it in the 1970s and 1980s, to deregulate the airlines, and to dismantle the monopoly position of AT&T, all indicate that changing economic conditions stimulate (largely political) efforts to redefine the regulatory status of industries. Some will argue that government regulatory institutions, such as the ICC, once in place, tend to endure for decades beyond the end of their useful lives. The question of public versus private ownership of public utilities (the nationalization argument) is more often raised by economists than others but is not a serious item on the nation's political agenda.

Quite apart from the knotty problem of which industries should be regulated, the regulatory *process* has long been a subject of continuing political struggle. There are two strands to the debate. First, equity issues have historically superseded efficiency considerations. The system of commission regulation was designed to reconcile the conflicting interests of regulated firms and their customers; efficiency was never a primary objective. Nevertheless, when the costs of regulatory policy appeared too high—that is, when inefficiency ran rampant—demands for deregulation arose and were eventually successful in some industries.

The second strand in the debate is a renewed interest in establishing incentive structures that will reward efficient behavior within the regulatory framework. Recall, for example, the various schemes for incentive regulation that have replaced rate-of-return regulation in electricity and the increased flexibility of the pertinent commissions in allowing price reductions by the (still regulated) railroads and the (less regulated) telecommunications industries. Whereas some are disappointed with the results of deregulation (for example, the continued domination of air travel by a few firms), the emphasis on efficiency goals has strengthened considerably. This represents an important change in the political treatment of regulatory issues.

New-Wave Regulation

Recent regulatory innovations, particularly in the area of consumer and worker protection, continue to generate controversy. The jury is still out on new–wave regulation, however, in part precisely because it is new. Although our experience with the policies is accumulating rapidly, it may not yet be adequate to support fully confident judgments.

Environmental protection programs have provided some salutory results. Widespread improvements in air quality have indeed occurred. Water quality enhancement, although less well measured, is also a likely result. These are clear steps in the right direction, compensating for an important market failure—external pollution costs. Whether the magnitude of the correction has been appropriate is less obvious. Our environmental policy institutions have not employed market-type incentives to the extent that many economists would like. Whether our efforts will ultimately prove successful is not yet clear.

Consumer protection policies create intense disagreement, largely because they often touch on freedom of individual choice—most notably the right of informed consumers to take risks on their own behalf. Some programs to assure the safety of foods and drugs have unquestionably produced major social benefits. These efforts have no doubt been pushed too far in some instances, yet few would question the legitimacy of government's role.[1]

As in other areas, however, the public debate about new-wave regulation has shifted in an important way. The attempt to be fair in our policies remains a matter of fundamental concern. Yet the efficiency of our efforts is increasingly questioned and debated. Clean air, safe products, and healthful work environments are of course desirable. They can, however, be costly to achieve, and the idea that both costs and benefits should be considered has made important inroads in our national dialogue.

MARKET FAILURE AND GOVERNMENT FAILURE

Anyone who reads large volumes of congressional hearings and popular discussions of government regulation is likely to come away with a mixed view of the way in which policy choices are approached. Much of the discourse represents advocacy rather than analysis—not so much an objective or open-minded search for the best policies as a rationalization of preconceptions and an unwillingness to consider evidence that conflicts with one's views.

We often find on one side of regulatory debates those who, explicitly or implicitly, believe that the market is a vehicle for the exploitation of a helpless and hapless citizenry. Such people hold out government intervention as the best hope that an ordinary person has to receive fair or reasonable treatment in the marketplace—for example, decent prices and qualities of the things we all consume. The market is seen as the problem, government as the solution.

On the other side are those with precisely the reverse view. The market is a wonderful mechanism that will solve many problems if only we will leave

---

[1]The Food and Drug Administration's effort to ban saccharin is a case in point. More generally, many observers now accept the argument that attempts to prevent unsafe drugs from reaching the market have been carried to the point at which the introduction of useful (and safe) drugs has been hindered.

it alone. Much of our woe—spiritual and ethical as well as economic—comes from our misguided efforts to tamper with free markets.

It is easy to slide into one extreme or the other on specific issues, but the temptation should be resisted. Markets do both splendid and cruel things. Government agencies can provide important protections that would not be supplied by markets, but they can also—even with the best intentions—make good or bad situations worse. To maintain that the market is always the problem (or the solution) and government always the solution (or the problem) is to eliminate any basis for sensible policy choice.

Most basic economic problems originate in scarcity and uncertainty. Where scarcity is the difficulty, it is important to realize that government cannot, as a rule, move us to a condition of abundance. We cannot legislate more of everything, and government intervention seldom provides painless solutions. At best, it facilitates more acceptable ways to deal with costs that will not disappear.

Where uncertainty is the difficulty, government action offers promise but not the assurance of improvement. People in their role as consumers, for example, have limited information about some choices. (Few of us are experts about market competition, drug safety, or the environmental impact of nuclear power plants.) Where market incentives to supply the appropriate information are faulty, public agencies can improve on their performance. Whether the agencies will in fact do so, however, is problematic. Public officials, like consumers and corporation managers, bring biases, misconceptions, and imperfect intelligence to their jobs.

SUMMARY

The role of government in the U.S. economy is, in a sense, surprising. This is, after all, a system grounded in the free market. Our private enterprise tradition is both old and respected. One does, of course, hear some complaints about big business and big labor, both private market institutions. But complaints about big government seem frequently louder. Candidates for public office at times find that an anti-government posture makes for successful campaigns, and even recent presidents have found it useful to run against Washington and politicians.

Yet with all the bad feeling that government engenders, an inescapable fact remains. We have placed a very substantial portion of our economic decisions in the public sector, and we have kept them there despite our own complaints. Have we gone too far? Is there too much government?

Although there is no fully objective answer, we have tried to suggest nonideological ways of approaching the question. In principle, we can often identify and measure those situations in which markets fail to carry out economizing tasks with reasonable efficiency and fairness. This should enable us to invoke useful public policy, at least in cases where the market failure is significant and the prospects for improvement are clear. As our discussions above suggest, however, little of our public intervention reflects broad social consensus. Much of what we do collectively is controversial from start to finish.

The reasons are partly ideological. If I were a true believer in the efficacy of the market, I might argue strongly against most government intervention, which I regard as interference. In part, however, policy disagreements also arise from imperfect information and measurement. Fortunately, we suspect, there are relatively few true believers—ideologues whose beliefs cannot be modified by evidence. But the evidence itself is often imprecise. The market failures that we can define precisely in principle may prove in practice to be fuzzy and difficult to assess.

Do we speak about government and the marketplace in one way while acting in another—praising the market while relying heavily on government to protect us from market results? In our view, this sort of gap between words and actions does exist. Words are important, but in the realm of policy, action constitutes the bottom line. Analysis of our public efforts cannot be fully objective. It can, however, be rational, balanced, and helpful in clarifying the kind of economic system we wish to achieve.

Name Index

Subject Index

Case Index